KARL MARX'S PHILOSOPHY OF MAN

KARL MARX'S PHILOSOPHY OF MAN

by

John Plamenatz

CLARENDON PRESS · OXFORD
1975

Oxford University Press, Ely House, London W.1

GLASGOW NEW YORK TORONTO MELBOURNE WELLINGTON
CAPE TOWN IBADAN NAIROBI DAR ES SALAAM LUSAKA ADDIS ABABA
DELHI BOMBAY CALCUTTA MADRAS KARACHI LAHORE DACCA
KUALA LUMPUR SINGAPORE HONG KONG TOKYO

ISBN 0 19 824551 3

Printed in Great Britain by
Richard Clay (The Chaucer Press) Ltd
Bungay, Suffolk

JOHN PLAMENATZ 1912–1975

JOHN PLAMENATZ, Chichele Professor of Social and Political Theory in the University of Oxford and Fellow of All Souls College until his death on 19 February 1975, was born in Montenegro—then an independent kingdom and before its incorporation, in 1918, into modern Yugoslavia. Montenegro, although it paid taxes haphazardly and intermittently to the Turks, was, uniquely in that part of the world, never physically subjugated by them. It remained a fiercely proud and independent, semi-tribal society, ruled, formerly, by the Prince or Prince Bishop, with Ministers, advisers and Generals drawn from influential members of village clans: such influential persons were John Plamenatz's forbears.

His parents, fleeing from Montenegro during the First World War, settled first in France, and then in Austria, whence they returned to Montenegro in the mid-thirties. He himself was sent, speaking only French, to England in 1919 to begin his formal education, first at school, later at Oxford, returning from time to time to visit his parents and to be stimulated, increasingly, by continental—particularly French—literature and thought.

He never forgot, was firmly proud of, his Montenegrin ancestry: at the same time, he thought of himself as 'an Oxford man', a member of that University and of that place he so much admired.

The cosmopolitan nature of his background explained, in part, his independent spirit, his ability to sympathize with the 'outsider', and to observe, fondly but critically, the English setting into which he had been plunged at so tender an age: its customs, its literature, its philosophical and political traditions. Early, he developed an interest in, a concern for, the problems, not only of Englishmen, but of man in general, man as a social being. Rousseau's analyses of the human condition fascinated and attracted him, and set him more firmly on his academic path; his literary taste and style were influenced, deeply, by the elegance and lucidity of writers like Racine and Pascal, and his critical faculties nourished by the latter and by other French writers.

Over the years, he produced a number of profound and penetrating studies of the effects of society on the human spirit, excavating the classical political texts with a clear head but a passionate trowel, seeking to uncover and to expose to view, from beneath a tangle of undergrowth, the tumuli of verbiage and unassimilated ideas, the true and the false.

This book is the latest of his books to be published. It was finished not long before his death; it shows the same fastidious concern for the truth, the same strengths, the same lucidity and independence of mind, the same desire to establish the validity of other men's concepts, the fantasy and the realism in them. But it does more. It reveals Plamenatz's own analysis of the human condition, and, perhaps, also himself, in more sustained and greater depth than anything previously published.

PREFACE

IN this book I deal with aspects of Marxism much discussed lately, and I ought perhaps to explain why I venture to add to the discussion. First, let me say that the book is not only about these aspects of Marxism, for it does more than merely interpret and assess some of Marx's doctrines. It seeks also to clarify ideas about man as a self-conscious and progressive being who develops his powers in social intercourse with other beings of his own kind, and in that sense is 'self-creative'. These ideas are not peculiar to Marx or original with him, though today they are most widely familiar in the forms he gave to them. Though their first beginnings go back a long way, their fast-growing popularity at the end of the eighteenth century and the beginning of the nineteenth was an intellectual revolution, a transformation of men's ways of thinking about both society and human nature.

Not all of these ideas are specifically radical, though radical critics of the established order, from Rousseau onwards, have made a large use of them. Many of them are prominent in the social and political philosophy of Hegel, which on the whole is conservative, and Marx took them over in their Hegelian forms. To use these ideas is, of course, to recognize that men and their institutions, as also their beliefs about themselves and the world, are always changing. But this a conservative may do as well as a radical. A conservative is not someone who denies the fact of social and cultural change, or even who seeks to slow it down; he is either someone who wants to preserve the advantages of privileged social groups or someone who, on broader and more philosophical grounds, believes that the ability to make large social changes according to plan is severely limited, and that the attempt to make them ordinarily does more harm than good.

Even in the first two parts of the book in which I discuss some of Marx's ideas and arguments in considerable detail, I am as much concerned with types of reasoning, of which his arguments are examples, as with the arguments themselves. Which is not to say that I have not looked closely—and some readers may think too closely—at what he said. But the last thing I have wanted to do is to engage in controversy with other critics of Marx about what exactly he meant. In the third part of the book, except for the concluding chapter, I have little to say about Marx; I there consider in a wider context ideas he shared with other thinkers, or ideas akin to his and still widely canvassed.

I have tried hard to explain Marx's ideas without distortion in an idiom

different from his own. It seems to me that many critics of Marx, not to
speak of defenders, do not look closely at what they interpret, and are too
ready to use his words and phrases as if their meaning were clear. This is
especially true when they interpret the aspects of his thought that I discuss
in this book: not his account of the capitalist economy but his conception
of man as a self-creative being liable to alienation and his ideas about false
consciousness and the forms of alienated life. These are perhaps the most
difficult and obscure of Marx's ideas, not only because he expresses them
in a vocabulary taken largely from Hegel, the most pretentious and
cryptic of the great German philosophers, but also because they are elusive
in themselves—as so many of the ideas are that we use to express our
beliefs about ourselves and the human condition. Some of these ideas are
familiar enough, when taken out of their Hegelian or Marxist dress, and
yet are not the less difficult to elucidate for being familiar. I have tried in
the first two parts of the book to throw light on them, and this has
required, not only my translating what Marx says (or what I take him to be
saying) into a more familiar idiom, but also my pointing to the ambiguities
and obscurities of that idiom. Marx—and Hegel too—is often nearer to
the common sense of the matter than his long sentences and odd language
may lead one to suppose, but then this common sense, looked at more
closely, turns out to be equivocal or confused.

Already in Marx's day there existed something that deserved to be called
a science of economics. The ideas economists used were already precise
enough to enable them to construct fairly clear and comprehensive explanations, and Marx had studied many of their theories. Though he
disagreed strongly with the economists about some things, he could use
their ideas (or adaptations of them) to explain how his position differed
from theirs. Marx may not be the most lucid of economists but his account
of the capitalist economy is the clearer and the more coherent for his close
study of the writings of Adam Smith and Ricardo. But, in his day as in
ours, the vocabularies of the sociologist and psychologist were less
precise than that of the economist. No doubt, the sociologist and psychologist have in the last hundred years gone a long way towards clarifying
their ideas, and the sociologist has done it, at least to some extent, by
subjecting certain aspects of Marxism to close analysis. Yet this work of
analysis has involved taking over or adopting only some of Marx's ideas,
while rejecting or ignoring others. Its purpose has been largely academic.
The sociologist has looked into Marx's store of ideas to see what he could
find there to help him put the sort of questions he wanted to put. But Marx
used these ideas to quite different purpose, so that the student of Marxism
who wants to explain the issues that Marx raised, why he thought them
important, and how they are related to anxieties, resentments, and hopes
still widely shared, can get only limited help from the academic sociologist.

Take, for example, an idea of Marx's discussed at length in this book
and in others recently published, the idea of alienation. It has attracted,
not only students of Marxism, but also sociologists, of whom two or three
have given it a more definite meaning than Marx ever did, and have used
it to good purpose. They would not deny a debt to Marx, and yet what
they have taken from him is less an idea than a word to which they have
given a sense different from any he gave it, though one perhaps suggested
to them by reading him. Sociologists, no doubt, owe a considerable debt
to Marx, which they are ready enough to acknowledge, but this, unfortunately, does not mean that we can go far in clarifying Marx's ideas by
interpreting them in the light of theirs.

The ideas discussed in this book are, in their Marxist forms, radical
ideas. Though they do not apply only to industrial societies, it was mainly
to them that Marx applied them. So, in discussing them, we discuss ideas
widely used to assess and condemn industrial society as it has developed
in the West, and to justify its wholesale transformation, if necessary by
force. While Marx lived, industrialism was everywhere capitalist. Today
this is no longer true, for in some parts of the world it claims to be
socialist. Whether it is so, as Marx understood socialism, is very much to
be doubted; but what cannot be doubted is that there are now in the world
industrial societies that are not capitalist, whatever else they may be. Many
of Marx's reasons for condemning capitalism would seem to apply also to
them. Marx, of course, accepted large-scale industry as an agent of progress, and condemned it only in its capitalist form. How far did he
mistake his target? How far had he good reasons for believing that the
evils of industrial society would disappear when it ceased to be capitalist?

Certainly, radicals today can, and already to some extent do, use Marx's
ideas, or ideas akin to his, to condemn more than mere capitalism. They
can and do use them to condemn features of industrial society which are
not necessarily capitalist. How far they recognize this is not clear: sometimes they seem to do so, and at other times not. They are so much
dominated by Marxist ideas that they are still too much inclined to see
traces of capitalism wherever they notice these obnoxious features, even
to the extent of speaking of 'state capitalism' in the Soviet Union. Instead
of revising Marx's ideas the better to use them to describe adequately
developments he could not foresee, they are moved by piety to stick to the
ideas unchanged and to misdescribe the developments.

The radical who uses ideas akin to Marx's to condemn more than
capitalism need not, any more than Marx did, condemn industrialism
wholesale. He too can see in it a potentially liberating force which, while
it brings new dangers into the world (new forms of oppression and confusions of purpose and belief), also brings new opportunities. But, if he is
to do this coherently and realistically, he must sharpen his ideas, making

distinctions that Marx failed to make, and must look critically at whatever he borrows from Marx. If he wants to explain how industrialism could be liberating without also being oppressive, he must put himself to the trouble of doing what Marx never seriously attempted: he must explain, at least in general outline, how an industrial society might be organized to provide the opportunities and avoid the dangers of industrialism.

To convinced Marxists this book will probably seem disrespectful. Again and again, Marx is accused of equivocation or obscurity, of failing to make quite simple distinctions, of reckless generalization, and even at times of superficiality. But, for all that, the book is not disrespectful; it takes a great thinker seriously. Marx was perceptive and shrewd; he was bold and imaginative. He was not only a harsh critic of our type of society and culture; he also produced a host of ideas that can be used (or adapted for use) to explain how industrial society differs from earlier social forms, how it has emerged and developed, and how it affects its members. He is, along with Rousseau and Hegel, one of the three great social thinkers of the modern age. Even today, when the social studies flourish as never before in hundreds of universities, the ideas we use to explain social behaviour and social change are among the most elusive, the most difficult to define. To treat Marx as if he were a systematic and clear thinker, all of whose ideas and doctrines fit together into a consistent whole, or even come close to doing so, is—so it seems to me—quite to mistake the character of his achievement. And he was never more obscure and less systematic than in putting forward the ideas discussed in this book. Yet no ideas of his are more important, for it is above all to them that men have turned to express widely shared attitudes to the fast-changing industrial societies which have generated such strong hopes and such deep misgivings.

JOHN PLAMENATZ

CONTENTS

MAN AS A SOCIAL AND AN ALIENATED BEING

CHAPTER I

THE MARX OF RECENT CRITICISM

I

IN recent years there has been in the West a change of direction in the study of the Marxism of Marx. Students of his thought have been less interested in his analysis of the capitalist economy and his predictions about the course of social and political change and more interested in his idea of man as a self-creative being: that is to say, a being who develops the capacities peculiar to his species as he lives and works with his fellows, and who in this process acquires his ideas of the world and of himself. They have been interested, too, in the closely related idea of alienation.

This shift of interest has been due in part to the publication of hitherto unpublished early writings of Marx or, outside Germany, to their being translated for the first time. But this has not been the whole cause, for these early writings might have passed largely unnoticed in the West, as indeed they have done outside the West, especially in countries ruled by parties that pride themselves on being Marxist. These early writings—or rather the ideas contained in them as interpreted by commentators and translators—have attracted notice because they express, or seem to express, anxieties and attitudes widely shared, at least in intellectual circles. The condition of man in industrial society, how he sees himself and how society appears to him, and the root causes in human nature and the structure of society of these appearances: these are the themes in Marx's early writings which, despite the obscurity of his style and argument, and perhaps even because of it, have been found exciting.

Why, then, has interest in them been confined largely to the West? For these themes, clearly, do not apply only to the West. Industrial society is not confined to that part of the world, and in any case Marx's ideas about the human condition apply, or could plausibly be held to apply, to man not only in industrial society but in other types of society as well. Man is 'self-creative' in all societies, and he is liable to alienation wherever the social causes of alienation operate. As we shall see later, it follows from Marx's account of these causes that they can operate (though less strongly) in pre-industrial as well as industrial societies.

Perhaps two reasons explain the indifference outside the West to aspects of Marxism which have aroused so much interest inside it. Marxist parties outside the West are either intent on transforming, economically and socially and at an unprecedented speed, 'backward' regions of the world, or else are manoeuvring for power in the hope of being able to carry through such transformations. In their efforts to do this they are inspired even more by the ideas of Lenin, Stalin, and other non-Western Marxists than by those of Marx and Engels. Their Marxism is only to some extent the Marxism of Marx; it is a mixture of his ideas and of later accretions. They look to Marx and to his later disciples, especially to those active in countries like their own, for ideas they can use to justify their ambitions for their peoples and their parties; and so they see in Marxism, not a theory which has failed to predict the course of social and economic change in the West, but an armoury of doctrines which Lenin and others have adapted to their needs.

Another reason for this indifference is that the early writings of Marx, in which these themes are prominent, are obscure and difficult. They are so partly because they are fragmentary and loosely constructed, because they are unfinished products; but they are so also because the ideas they contain are difficult in themselves. These ideas are taken from Hegel or from other philosophers and are then adapted and used by Marx to reach conclusions often quite different from those reached by the philosophers. It is by no means easy to state these ideas clearly, let alone explain how Marx used them to reach his conclusions. It is not surprising, then, that these ideas, derived from philosophies alien to them, should be less interesting to Marxists and students of Marxism outside the West. Even if they have similar ideas in their native philosophies, they are ideas differently expressed, and so such similarities as there may be go unrecognized.

These two reasons are perhaps sufficient to explain the indifference. But, even if there were not this indifference, there might be suspicion or hostility, at least in countries ruled by 'Marxists'. To the extent that Marx's account of alienation makes sense, it would seem to apply as readily to these countries as to the capitalist West. To be sure, Marx believed that alienation was worse under capitalism than in any economically less advanced society known to him, and he also believed that it would not disappear unless capitalism did so too. But then, in his day, the less advanced countries were not being rapidly industrialized by political parties with a virtual monopoly of power. If we look at the symptoms and causes of alienation, as Marx describes them, they would appear to be just as much present in the countries now making rapid industrial progress, whose rulers claim to be Marxists, as in the West; just as evident in the Soviet Union as in the United States. It would seem to be against the interest of any Communist government in the world today to encourage a close study of Marx's early writings.

Even in the West, and for obvious reasons, these writings have been attractive mostly to intellectuals. Not only because they are difficult but also because there are no obvious practical conclusions to be drawn from them. They offer little or no guidance to a socialist or proletarian party as to what it should do to transform society in the interest of justice or of the class it claims to speak for. In general, left-wing groups and parties in the West no longer look to Marx or Engels for practical advice, and if they did, would do better to look for it in their later writings, where there is much more said in detail about class conflicts and the fight for power. Politically the West is now very different from what it was when Marx and Engels were alive, and their predictions about it, to which such practical advice as they had to give was related, have mostly either proved false or have come to seem so ambiguous as to be incapable of being put to the test of experience. The Marxism of Marx, to scholars and intellectuals in the West, now seems valuable, not for the insight it gives into the future, but as a rich source of ideas that can be used to explain the many respects in which industrial society differs, not only economically and socially but culturally and ideologically, from earlier types of society. They look to it too for ideas and arguments which they can adapt to changing circumstances and can use to condemn 'bourgeois society' in its various forms. They see in the Marxism of Marx a store of useful and exciting hypotheses rather than a philosophy to be swallowed whole.

Marx's early writings have provoked some unprofitable controversy and inspired some extravagant claims. Some writers have argued that the ideas prominent in them are not 'central' to his thought, and that he soon discarded them as he turned his mind to other things. Why, they ask, if these writings, which everyone admits are obscure and ambiguous, contain ideas which continued to seem important to Marx, did he not publish them? If he was dissatisfied with them, why did he not put himself to the trouble of improving them? Why did he move on to other things, to which he devoted incomparably more time and thought? Though he has much to say about man as a self-creative and an alienated being in the short, chaotic, and opaque pieces that he wrote when he was young, he barely touches on these themes in the later, better-constructed, and more lucid books and articles which he saw through the press. Is it not a mistake to look long and closely at what he himself seemed not very keen to remember?

Others have argued that these ideas, so much more prominent in the early than in the later writings of Marx, nevertheless do persist into the later writings, though more often implicit in them than express. Unless we take account of them, we fail to do justice to the subtleties of Marx's idea of progress, to his reasons for assigning a special role in history to the proletariat, to his conception of ideology as a form of false consciousness. We fail to understand fully why he believed that the human condition can grow worse as society becomes more affluent, why he denounced bourgeois morality, and why he thought it a condition of human emancipation that the state, as we now know it, should disappear. We can perhaps, knowing nothing of these ideas, understand his account of the capitalist system, considered merely as a form of the production and distribution of wealth, and of the division of society into classes, but we cannot see why he believed that this system and this division have the cultural, moral, and psychological effects which he ascribed to them, not merely in his youth but throughout his life.

In my opinion, those who argue in this second way are right. There are ideas about man and his social condition that Marx expressed, even though obscurely and inadequately, in his early writings and in the *Grundrisse*, to which he held all his life. Part of my purpose in this book is to try to explain these ideas and their lasting importance for him. It seems to me that, just as we fail to understand his later writings fully if we neglect these ideas, so too we fail to understand these ideas unless we notice how they are involved in a wide variety of his doctrines and arguments, late and early.

Even if this were a mistaken interpretation of Marx, it would not follow that these ideas were unimportant. They might still be important to us even though, as he grew older, they ceased to be important to him. The aspects of a man's thought in which he loses interest as he grows older are not for that reason alone the less worthy of interest. He may have had in his youth good ideas which he later neglected because he failed to see what could be done with them. Nor need we suppose him to have grown less imaginative with the years for this to have happened to him. Every maker of theories has, in the course of his life, more ideas then he knows how to make good use of; and this applies even more to the great thinkers than to the lesser ones. The more fertile their imaginations, the more abundant the ideas they have not time enough to elucidate and refine and to fit into carefully made theories.

Some enthusiasts for Marx's early writings make excessive claims for them and for him. For example, J.-Y. Calvez, a French Jesuit, in a book which attracted much praise in France some years ago (and was not quite unnoticed, even in England) argued that interest in Marxism in the West had not only changed direction since the publication of the 'Economic and Philosophical Manuscripts' in 1931 but had gained immensely in depth and relevance. Actually, as Calvez himself noticed, it was some time before students of Marxism came to realize the importance of these manuscripts. The war put a stop to many intellectual activities, and it was not until after the war against Hitler that the close study of these manuscripts began, and with this study a reappraisal of Marxism.

Calvez was not content to point to this reappraisal and to its causes, and to welcome it because it drew attention to aspects of Marxism hitherto neglected and which he found exciting and worth close study. He went further and said that critics of Marxism, who wrote before this reappraisal began, had not really touched the essence of the theory. I take it that he meant by this, not that the essence of Marxism is to be found only in his fragmentary and opaque early writings and not also in his more extensive and more carefully prepared later writings, but that, if we are to get at what is really profound and illuminating in his theory, we need to interpret it in the light of ideas which were not understood—or not fully understood—until his early writings were closely studied. These early writings, difficult though they are, provide us with the clues we need to enable us to identify the ideas about man as a social being which inspired Marx at all stages of his working life. Therefore, the critic who misses these clues criticizes what he has failed fully to understand, and his criticism is largely irrelevant. Calvez does not stop at saying that there is an early Marxism, more exciting and more profound than the later doctrines, which is untouched by the attacks made on these doctrines; he also says—or at least implies—that the attacks made on these later doctrines are often misconceived, and that students of Marxism can now see this more clearly for having studied the early writings.

This seems to me a mistake. Not only are the later writings just as much 'essential' Marxism as the earlier ones, but many of the doctrines they contain, even when they have been reconsidered in the light of ideas culled from the early writings, are just as vulnerable as ever they were to the attacks made upon them by critics who never read the 'Economic and Philosophical Manuscripts' and took little notice of *The German Ideology*. The interest of these early writings is not, to my mind, that they oblige us to reinterpret long-familiar—or, perhaps I should say, often-discussed—Marxist doctrines in such a way as to put them out of reach of criticisms which used to pass muster in a less enlightened period of Marxist scholarship; it is rather that these writings introduce us to aspects of Marxism which used to be neglected and are worth close study. It is a mistake to suggest that older criticisms of the Marxism of Marx—and it is of it that I speak and not of what passed for Marxist orthodoxy in Germany after Marx's death and before Moscow set itself up as the custodian of this orthodoxy—were misdirected. They were aimed at important parts of the theory, and many of them were well grounded and well conducted, and therefore really damaging. To be sure, they were aimed only at parts of the theory; but they were parts to which Marx himself, and not merely his interpreters, attached great importance.

The first interpreters of Marx saw him as primarily an economist, a sociologist, and a social and economic historian; they saw him as concerned above all to explain capitalist and bourgeois society, its origins and course of development, the conflict of classes inside it, and what that conflict was likely to lead to. They paid only passing attention to aspects of his thought which today are sometimes called his 'philosophical anthropology': his conception of what is characteristically human about man, of what makes him uniquely a social being involved in a course of cultural change in which both he and his social environment, as they are in themselves and as they seem to him, are changed continually as a result of his own activities. This Hegelian aspect of Marx's thought meant much less to them than it means today to many students of Marxism in the West. Such expressions as 'self-creation' or 'estrangement' or 'alienation' or 'false consciousness' hardly occur in their books and articles. They were not unaware that Marx had spoken of man as if he were somehow 'dehumanized' in the society of his day, as if he were 'estranged' from it and also from himself, as if he were the victim of an environment, a social world, which was both a product of human activities and consisted in them, and yet was frustrating to peculiarly human and social needs. They were not unaware of this, because Marx did not speak of man in these ways only in his early writings; but they did neglect these ways of speaking. They passed them over as elements in his thought which were both difficult to understand and difficult to relate to the rest of his teaching.

These earlier interpreters were no more selective or partial in their treatment of Marx's thought than later ones have been who have pored over his early writings or have sought a deeper understanding of his doctrines in the *Grundrisse*; they merely gave the best of their attention to other problems. To my knowledge, nobody who has made a close study of texts unpublished or neglected some fifty years ago has used what he has found there to produce a new interpretation of Marx's thought, taken as a whole, which shows it to be more coherent than it appeared to be to its earlier critics or else explains more satisfactorily the respects in which it is incoherent. It is not enough to point to aspects of his thought neglected by these critics and to assert that this neglect has led them to misinterpret certain of his doctrines, imputing beliefs to him which he never held; it is necessary to offer alternative explanations of these doctrines in the light of these neglected ideas and to show how they make better sense of what Marx actually said in the context in which he said it.

For example, it used to be said more often than it is now that Marx was an 'economic determinist'. Some critics held this against him, while others reckoned it a point in his favour. They did not all understand the same thing by 'economic determinism', and some of the bolder of them ventured to explain what they meant by it. One of the bold was Professor Bober who in his book, *Karl Marx's Interpretation of History*, imputed the doctrine to Marx and also rejected it as ambiguous and badly argued. Even in the years immediately following the publication of this book in 1927, at a time when some of the texts now so much studied were not yet published or not translated into English, Bober was accused of misinterpreting

Marx. He may perhaps have done so; but it is worth noticing that his accusers did little more to sustain their charge than point to passages in Marx inconsistent with economic determinism, as Bober understood it. It seems not to have occurred to them that this was no refutation of Bober, who never claimed that Marx was *consistently* an economic determinist. To have refuted Bober, or at least to have shown that his interpretation of Marx was doubtful at this point, they would have needed to offer an alternative to it which made better (or as good) sense of the passages from Marx on which Bober relied.

This way of 'disposing' of Marx's critics is not new; it has not become the fashion since his long-unpublished early writings and the *Grundrisse* began to be studied. It was always the fashion among his admirers who felt the need to reject criticisms of him which they disliked without putting themselves to the trouble of meeting them, perhaps because they failed to see the point of them. It was never more the fashion than it is today, especially among admirers eager to make as much as they can of the new 'insights' into Marxism which they find exciting but are incapable of putting into words of their own. The phrases of Marx are so familiar to them, and they get so much pleasure from using them, that they honestly believe they have understood them, and are impatient of critics who find them obscure or who even at times suspect them of being empty. They are intoxicated with Marxism and have the illusion of profundity, and are grateful to the master who has taught them, so they believe, to think deeply about society and man's condition in it. Gratitude is a respectable emotion; and if in this case it is misplaced, it is so, not because there is little of value to be learned from Marx, but because the attitude to him of these admirers is not propitious to learning. Unfortunately, nobody can learn anything from a great thinker, especially one as obscure and difficult as Marx, unless he makes the painful effort of trying to put the master's thoughts into words of his own. The effort may, of course, be unsuccessful. But, surely, it is better to risk being a shallow critic of Marx than to be seduced by his phrases into the illusion that you understand him; better to remain critically awake while you read him than to be his sleeping partner in profundity. On at least one occasion Marx protested angrily that he was no Marxist; and this protest was aimed, presumably, not at his critics but at his admirers. Criticism, especially when it is unjust, provokes anger, but then so too does undiscriminating praise. Marx was not easy to please. In his lifetime he got less recognition, probably, than he felt was his due; but this most irritable of men was at least spared much the greater part of the admiration that his writings have inspired.

The ideas that I shall be discussing were not original with Marx. Some of the best of them he got from Hegel, and others he took from other writers. My interest is not only in Marx's use of these ideas; it is as much in the uses that can be made of them, in possibilities and limitations. Yet they are ideas which, for many people, are more closely associated with Marx than with any other writer; and so I have thought it best to look first at what Marx did with them before considering what can be done with them. I want both to assess the importance of certain ideas, inadequately presented by Marx in his early writings, to his thought taken as a whole, inquiring how far they enter into doctrines of his, whose enduring hold on him nobody denies, and to look critically at these ideas and doctrines from a more general point of view.

Some of these ideas are Hegelian as much as Marxist; or rather, in the forms in which I shall be discussing them, they are Marxist adaptations of Hegelian ideas—Marx's contribution being chiefly to detach them from their metaphysical setting and so bring out more clearly, or at least more forcefully, their social implications. Hegel, as is now more widely recognized than it used to be, was a social theorist of the first rank, but his ideas about society, and above all of man as essentially a social being, are part of a grand philosophical system from which it is difficult to disentangle them. It has been claimed for Marx that he brought Hegel down to earth. I should prefer to say that, by dissipating some of the clouds in which Hegel loved to move, he revealed him moving on the earth and not in some region high above it. He did not just translate Hegelian metaphysics into Marxist sociology; rather, he helped to uncover Hegel's sociology in his metaphysics. Not that he took over Hegel's ideas about man in society without adding to them, any more than he did full justice to what he borrowed. As we shall see, he sometimes misunderstood Hegel, the social theorist, and learned less from him than he might have done. In some respects Hegel's ideas about society and ideology are more perceptive and discriminating than are Marx's.

I want first to look critically at Marx's conception of man, at the ideas he uses to explain what, in his opinion, is distinctively human about man, what is peculiar to his condition when he lives (as he always does) with his fellows, what makes him social in ways in which other animals are not so, and what is involved in his being alienated. I shall try to put these ideas in words different from Marx's, and I hope more easily understood, so as to bring out the advantages and disadvantages of speaking about man and his social condition in these ways. This is by no means easily done, and my attempt to do it may well seem tedious. I can plead only that I have found it indispensable to make distinctions whose importance is not perhaps immediately obvious but which, in my opinion, have to be made if the strong and the weak points of Marx's conception of man are to be clearly seen. I shall also inquire how far these ideas make up a coherent account of man as a uniquely social being.

These will be two of my main purposes. But I want also to consider several of Marx's doctrines to which these ideas are essential: his account of the proletariat as the most alienated class in capitalist society and the only one that is essentially revolutionary, his conception of ideology as a form of false consciousness, his ideas about religion, bourgeois morality, and the state, and his reasons for believing that alienation is at its worst under capitalism. These doctrines are not confined to Marx's early writings, and cannot be discussed adequately without taking large notice of his later writings. Indeed, they are not confined even to Marxists: to Marx and his collaborator, Engels, and to their disciples. To discuss them is to turn to themes that recur again and again in the radical social and political theories of this century and the last.

When I put my questions about Marx, I shall not produce one answer to each question. Marx is too difficult, too obscure a writer, especially in the texts that I shall be studying (sometimes in considerable detail) to enable me to do that. Sometimes I shall offer several answers to one question on the ground that each of them is a reasonable interpretation of some of the things Marx said about the subject in question. For example, Marx made many assertions about man as a social being, and many also about alienation. These assertions are not all consistent with each other. It would be a mistake, I think, to try at all costs to reconcile them with one another, or to insist that some of them come closer than others to saying what Marx really meant. Quite often, where two or more interpretations of what he said seem to me equally plausible, I shall not pretend to know what he meant, nor even venture a guess. Many of his ideas and doctrines, even the most familiar (because the most often debated), are important in spite of being ambiguous, because they are suggestive and ingenious. Marx discusses some of the most complicated and elusive forms of social behaviour or social relations, and his discussion of them, especially in his early writings, is often brief, disjointed, and oracular.

Everyone agrees that Marx is a difficult writer, and never more difficult than when he speaks of *alienation*. Everyone agrees that by alienation he meant, not one thing but several, which he believed to be closely connected. There is wide disagreement about what things he had in mind, and how he thought they were connected. Yet, in spite of this disagreement, there have been few attempts made to look carefully at what Marx says about alienation, and to distinguish the senses in which he uses the term. Indeed, there have been few attempts to explain in detail what he meant, or may reasonably be supposed to have meant, when he said that man is essentially a social being. For only a creature who is social in the sense that man alone is so can be alienated.

To do justice to Marx, to reveal both the richness and the limitations of his thought, it is, of course, not enough to offer a variety of interpretations and to refrain from choosing between them. The importance of a man's ideas consists in more than what he has succeeded in doing with them; it consists also in what can be done with them. That is why, as I consider Marx's ideas, I shall not confine myself to pointing to different interpretations which seem to me equally plausible, but shall venture from time to time to point to the advantages of one version over another, not as being closer to his meaning, but as better suited to explaining the facts or to justifying certain ideals.

I shall not confine myself to interpreting and criticizing Marx. I shall also consider answers to questions that he put different from the ones he gave; and sometimes even answers to questions which, though he never put them, are closely allied to others he did put. Thus, for example, apart from the question, *What did Marx understand by alienation?*—to which, as I have suggested, there are several answers, each as plausible an interpretation of his actual words as the others—there is the different but related question, *Given what he wanted to explain, what should he have meant by it?* Or, in other words, there is the question, *How are the social relations or forms of behaviour or attitudes that Marx had in mind when he spoke of alienation best described?*

So, too, to the question, *What did Marx point to as the causes of alienation?* there are several plausible answers, of which some are incompatible with others. But there is also the question, *What are the likely causes of it?* Of alienation as Marx understood it, or else—if his account of it has to be rejected—of something closely analogous to it? When it is said that Marx is a rich and imaginative thinker rather than a rigorous and lucid one, a man of ideas rather than a constructor of a coherent theory, part of what is meant is that his ambiguities repay close scrutiny, that he raises more questions than he answers, and even that he inspires more questions than he raises.

I make no attempt to revise the Marxism of Marx, to produce a version of it that meets the more obvious objections to it, any more than to produce a different theory not open to those objections. I do no more, when I move from exposition and criticism to speculation, than consider possibilities. I do not criticize Marx for not putting questions which he might have put, though I do from time to time suggest alternative answers to the questions he did put which seem to me better than his own. I also put questions of my own which would not have occurred to me had I not attempted a critical examination of his ideas, especially about the forms and consequences of alienation.

For example, Marx speaks of religion as both a symptom and an effect of alienation, and therefore implies that where men cease to be alienated, they cease to need religion. Thus, according to him, if ever religion disappears, it will do so, not because science will have exposed the illusions of which it consists, but because these illusions will have ceased to be necessary to men. Religion will have lost its functions, social and psychological. I want, of course, to consider what these functions, as Marx describes them, are, but I want also to consider what other functions it might have besides those discussed by Marx. For, if it does have other functions, then men might still feel the need for it—even though perhaps in a different form—in conditions which Marx believed would make it obsolete.

To take another example, Marx says that the proletarian is the most alienated of men, and that the proletarians are, or will eventually become, the most whole-heartedly revolutionary class. Apart from his reasons for holding these particular beliefs, I want to consider more generally what connections there are, or might be, between alienation and revolution. The alienated worker, so Marx says, is a mere 'fragment of a human being' but he never says as much of the peasant or the bourgeois. Are we then to conclude that the most revolutionary of classes, destined (as he puts it) to redeem mankind in redeeming itself, consists of men who are the least adequately human?

Marx, when he speaks of men as 'fragments of human beings', as 'dehumanized' and 'estranged' in society, as 'incapable of developing to the full their human potentialities', is not using an idiom peculiar to himself, or even one which only German philosophers used before him. He is speaking as other writers of his day quite innocent of German philosophy, English and French writers, already spoke. Though he often speaks of human nature and the human condition in strange philosophical and German ways, he also speaks of them in other and more familiar ways. But the familar ways are just as ambiguous, just as puzzling, as the others. When he speaks, as we all do, of capacities, frustrations, and illusions peculiar to men, and of their social causes, he is just as elusive and obscure as when he speaks of them in terms borrowed from Hegel; he is just as elusive and obscure as we are. The puzzles that confront us when we try to elucidate how he conceived of man or of alienation and its symptoms and consequences are very like the puzzles we come upon as soon as we try to analyse our own quite familiar ways of speaking about the human condition in modern industrial society. Thus, his account of alienation, obscure though it is, is relevant to our experience. It is more obviously relevant than Hegel's account of it because it is less metaphysical. And yet, if it cuts deeper than the other radical and socialist critiques of industrial society of his day, it does so largely because it owes so much to Hegel.

The first great thinker of the modern age whose description of man's condition in society is in some ways remarkably like Marx's account of alienation was Rousseau. Yet Rousseau rejected the faith in progress shared by so many of his contemporaries. His remedy for the condition he described, though it was not a return to the state of nature or to any earlier social condition, was the setting up of a simpler society, both economically and politically. Thus, his remedy, though it was not exactly regress, was not progress either; at least not in the sense in which progress was then ordinarily understood. He advised mankind to move in a direction different from the one in which he thought they were moving, and yet had little hope that they would take his advice. He was—this preacher of the doctrine that man is naturally good—a pessimist.

His contemporaries who believed in progress did not so much dispute his account of man's condition in society as fail to understand it. Though they saw evils in society, they were not of the kind that came later to be called 'alienation' or 'estrangement'. They were evils which (so they believed) would disappear gradually in the course of time, as knowledge and wealth increased and men learned to use the resources available to them more justly and efficiently to satisfy their wants. But Hegel and Marx, unlike the rationalist philosophers of the eighteenth century whose optimism Rousseau rejected, combined faith in progress with the idea of a human condition like the one deplored by Rousseau. They tried to explain how progress, or the increase of knowledge, power, and wealth, first produced this condition and then afterwards enabled men to surmount it. Their conception of progress was therefore in crucial respects unlike that of the earlier rationalist philosophers. So too was their conception of man as a social being; it was a conception in some ways closer to Rousseau's than to theirs.

The philosophers of the eighteenth century who believed in progress— and I have in mind the English Utilitarians as much as the 'rationalists' on the Continent—conceived of man as an agent conscious of his wants who, because he is rational, can learn from experience and pass on what he learns to succeeding generations. He can contrive means beyond the reach of other animals to satisfy his wants, and in particular can devise new ways of collaborating with others to make a larger use of natural resources. Because he can reflect on his wants and the means of satisfying them, because he is educable in ways peculiar to his species, he continually acquires new wants as a result of what he does to satisfy the old ones. He is progressive therefore in the sense that by his own efforts as he collaborates with others he adds continually to his understanding, his skills, his material resources, and his wants. Provided that his wants do not grow more quickly than his power to satisfy them, his condition improves.

Some of these believers in progress were not much concerned with the quality of human wants, and a few (for example, Bentham) even denied that any are intrinsically superior to others, considered apart from the consequences likely to result from satisfying them. Others did distinguish between lower wants and the higher ones that men acquire as they develop their distinctively human capacities, and they held that progress consists above all in acquiring the higher wants and learning to recognize their superiority. But, in either case, they took it for granted that man tries always to satisfy his wants as far as he can according to the value he attaches to them. He seeks to use his resources efficiently, and when the opportunity offers, combines with others in providing for shared needs. The unhappy man is the man who lacks the resources to satisfy his wants; the happy man is the one who does not lack them. Thus, the great social problem, whose solution promotes happiness the most effectively, is—in a broad sense of the word—'economic': to ensure that supply meets demand and that demand does not grow faster than supply. Or it is partly economic and partly something more, the something more being the requirement to improve as far as possible the quality of human wants. It is, of course, a vast and intricate problem, and grows vaster and more intricate as human understanding increases and both wants and resources multiply. These philosophers of progress, especially the more sophisticated of them, did not believe that progress is smooth and easy, or even that it is inevitable— though they did believe that, having got as far as it had done in their time, it was likely to continue indefinitely—but they did see it as consisting, largely if not entirely, in the increase (and often also the improvement) of human wants and in the growth of the resources, material and cultural, needed to satisfy them.

Hegel and Marx did not so much repudiate this idea of progress as raise questions about man as a social being involved in a course of cultural change which added a new dimension to it, making their idea of progress 'dialectical' in a sense in which the earlier one was not. The rationalist philosophers and the Utilitarians did not inquire how human wants affect and are affected by man's conception of himself, of the social relations in which he stands, and of the world generally. No doubt, they took some interest in these things, but it was peripheral and of little or no consequence for their social and political theory. The problem of the relation of reality to appearance was, for them, confined to the theory of knowledge, considered in abstraction from a social context. It was not, as they saw it, a problem for the social theorist. But it is precisely at the social level that the relation between appearance and reality is *dialectical*. How men conceive of the world depends on how they behave in it, and how they behave in it on how they conceive of it. Their illusions about society and themselves help to make it and them what they are. By their activities they continually transform both social reality and how it appears to them, and in the process acquire illusions which they later discard, passing from one form of illusion to another, as they come closer to seeing themselves and the world as they really are.

No doubt, man, as the rationalists and Utilitarians describe him, has problems and illusions; but they say almost nothing to suggest that he is above all a problem to himself, or that his illusions about the world are intimately bound up with his illusions about himself. The idea of the human *psyche* as largely hidden from itself, as a prey to conflicts it does not understand, as oppressed in a social environment uncontrolled by the beings whose ways of living constitute it, is absent from their theories. Not perhaps completely absent but seldom intruding upon them. The rationalists and Utilitarians do not speak of alienation, even by another name; they do not see social man as both the product and the victim of his own activities, as frustrated or reduced to despair in a cultural world of his own making.

Also, though they admit social conflict and cultural disharmony as facts of life, they fail to see the extent to which they are (or can be) effects of progress, of increasing knowledge, wealth, and power. They were aware that some primitive peoples live in peace and harmony together; and they did not attribute their doing so to their being richer or more powerful, or to their having greater knowledge, than others. They did not even attribute this peace to their better understanding of the social order and greater control over it. Primitive ignorance, as they saw it, was equally compatible with conflict and harmony. And yet they believed, most of them, that the increase of knowledge and of control must lead eventually to social harmony.

So, too, of course, did Hegel and Marx. Hegel, though he rejected perpetual peace, even as an ideal, believed in the coming of the rational state, of a social and political order acceptable to all classes and groups. Marx foretold the coming of a communist society in which men would be equal and free. How far they believed that the coming of the rational state or of the society of the equal and the free was inevitable is open to question, but they certainly implied that it would be attained provided that men's understanding of their environment and their ability to control it continued to increase. And yet, despite this similarity between Hegel and Marx and earlier believers in progress, there is also a great difference between them. Hegel and Marx took larger notice of the disruptive social effects of progress, of the extent to which it brings with it, not only new forms of conflict, but also new forms of error and illusion. Their accounts of these effects, these conflicts and illusions, and especially of the social conditions in which they thrive, differ considerably; but they occupy a large place in both their tales of human progress.

The aspects of Marx's thought that I discuss in this book are the ones in which Hegel's influence is the greatest. Therefore I often compare Marx with Hegel and point to similarities between them, and it may be that to some readers it will seem that I make too much of the similarities and too little of the differences. But, in my opinion, the differences have been exaggerated, and this for two reasons: because Hegel's vocabulary masks the extent to which his ideas about man and society are like Marx's, and because Marx's criticisms of Hegel give the impression that he differs from him more than in fact he does. Though Marx acknowledged his debt to Hegel and often praised him, he rejected his metaphysics in such a way as to create the impression that he had taken certain ideas of Hegel and had applied them to the social sphere as Hegel had not done. He spoke as if his debt to Hegel were a sociologist's or social historian's debt to a metaphysician. But Hegel was as much a social theorist as he was anything else. Indeed, it is arguable that he is at his best as a social and political theorist, and not as an epistemologist or a logician, or even a moral philosopher. Marx has been called a materialist, and sometimes spoke of himself as if he were one. Hegel held that reality is essentially spiritual, which Marx denied. This has been held to be a crucial difference between them. I must confess that it seems to me not to be so, at least in so far as their conceptions of man as a social being and of the course of social change are concerned.

The word *materialist* has been used in several different senses, and it is not always clear in what sense writers about Marx use it when they apply it to him, or in what sense Marx himself uses it. I doubt whether it is possible to elicit from his writings any coherent version of materialism. This does not mean that we can ascribe no definite opinions to him. We can say, for example, that he was not the kind of materialist who holds that mental activities can be reduced to bodily movements and to motions in the brain, or can be treated as mere effects of them. There is virtually nothing in his writings to suggest that he held this view, and a great deal to suggest that he did not. He always speaks of man as a self-conscious, rational, active being who can make choices and can initiate change deliberately. He speaks of man in ways that suggest that he rejected, not only the Hegelian conception of reality as the self-projection or self-revelation of Spirit, but also the Cartesian separation of mind from matter, which implies that everything is made up of elements that are either purely mental or purely physical. But Cartesian dualism is as much rejected by Hegel as by Marx.

Marx also speaks of human behaviour in ways that suggest that he rejected the kind of empiricism, once fashionable among philosophers in Britain, which treats the mind as if it were a flow of sense impressions and their faint copies in memory. Man, as Marx speaks of him, is not only active and purposeful; he is also—in ways to be discussed later—creative and 'self-creative'. Indeed, if he were not all this, he could not be alienated. Though Marx rejected the Hegelian conception of Spirit, his ideas about man and what is involved in knowing (as distinct from mere sensing), in deciding or choosing (as distinct from merely having desires), and in acting in peculiarly human ways, are much more like Hegel's ideas—or, for that matter, Kant's or Rousseau's—than they are like the ideas of Hobbes or Hume or Helvetius.

It is true that Marx sometimes insists, as Hegel does not, that the capacities that distinguish man from other animals are developed in the first place by what men do to satisfy their biological needs, the needs that have to be satisfied if they are to survive and to reproduce their kind. Yet he also admits that the needs they acquire as these capacities develop differ in kind from mere biological needs. They are the needs of self-conscious, purposeful, and social beings, of beings that have beliefs and sentiments which unselfconscious beings could not have. These needs, as Marx describes them, are in some respects strikingly similar to what Hegel in the *Phenomenology of Spirit* calls 'the need for recognition'—a need which he thinks is peculiar to self-conscious rational beings, or at least to beings who acquire reason and self-consciousness in the process of living together.

There is nothing whatever in Hegel's conception of Spirit which precludes his agreeing with Marx that men's distinctively human capacities are developed in the first place by their endeavours to satisfy their biological needs. What is more, this belief is logically quite independent of the doctrine that, among men's social activities, 'material production' (as Marx calls it) is basic in the sense that it has a much greater influence on other activities than they on it, the doctrine sometimes called 'economic determinism'. It has been denied, in my opinion mistakenly, that Marx was an economic determinist. I believe that he was one at times and at other times not; that he quite often took up a position from which he also quite often felt the need to retreat but which he never abandoned decisively because he did not see its implications clearly. Hegel, of course, was never an economic determinist, though he did take larger notice of the economic aspects of life than was usual among political theorists in his day. If economic determinism is a kind of materialism then Marx was, in some moods or contexts, this kind of materialist, whereas Hegel was not.

Marx seems partly to have misunderstood Hegel. Though Hegel spoke of an Infinite Spirit, he never thought of it as something separate from, or temporally prior to, the material world; he thought of the material world as a manifestation or projection of it. He no more denied the reality of the material world than he did that of society and culture. He saw them all as ways in which Spirit reveals itself, and does so necessarily. They are not mere effects or reflections of it, for it exists in and through them. Thus Spirit is inconceivable apart from matter, and man, in whom Spirit is manifest at its higher levels, is, for Hegel as well as for Marx, a creature of flesh and blood, who could not be self-conscious, rational, and social unless he were such a creature. In saying this I do not deny that there are important differences between the philosophies of Hegel and of Marx; I say only that the differences have been misconceived and exaggerated, not least by Marx and by Engels. Or, rather, I suggest that the implications for social theory of the differences have been exaggerated. No doubt, if one man says that reality is the self-development of Spirit and another denies it, and suggests that the assertion is pretentious and empty, there is a real difference between what they say; but the difference is either metaphysical or else between nonsense and sense. In either case, it may be of no great consequence to social theory. To be sure, there are important differences between the social theories of Hegel and Marx: for example, between their conceptions of the state. Yet someone who had no more use for Hegel's notion of an Infinite Spirit than Marx had might still accept his account of the state as a rational, legal, and moral order that forms the minds of its members and gives them freedom.

As I try to explain Marx's conception of man, which seems to me closer to Hegel's than to that of any other of his philosophical precursors, I shall not hesitate to use the word *spiritual*, especially when I speak of wants or needs which he thought were distinctively human; that is to say, peculiar to self-conscious rational beings. I see no reason for avoiding this word merely because Marx was a materialist in some sense in which Hegel was not. After all, that one of Hegel's works which most deeply affected Marx's conception of man bears the word spirit in its title.

To call these wants or needs, as either Hegel or Marx conceived of them, *rational* would be misleading, even though they are wants or needs peculiar to rational beings; for the behaviour they inspire is often irrational. To call them *intellectual* might suggest falsely that purely intellectual activities could satisfy them. To call them *moral* would be as misleading as to call them rational, for the behaviour they inspire is often immoral; though, to be sure, only a being capable of acting morally can be immoral. The wants and needs that I shall call spiritual are those of a passionate and sensitive being who could not be passionate and sensitive in the ways peculiar to his kind unless he were a reasoner, unless he were self-conscious and self-directing, unless he had acquired skills which involve deliberation and calculation and the making of choices.

Marx's ideas about these wants and needs and their social contexts or causes are not the same as Hegel's. I shall take care not to play down these differences, though I shall not, when I try to explain them, contrast Marx's *materialism* with Hegel's *idealism*. Not that I wish to suggest that there is no point to calling Marx a materialist. These two words, materialist and idealist, have been used in a variety of meanings. No doubt, if we had nothing better to do, we could amuse ourselves by showing that Hegel was in some ways a materialist and Marx in some ways an idealist. Nevertheless, taking all the senses in which these two words are used into account, it is probably true that Marx was considerably more a materialist than Hegel was and Hegel considerably more an idealist than was Marx.

Marx, who liked to contrast his idea of the world with that of the author of the *Phenomenology of Spirit*, did not use the word *spiritual* when he spoke of needs or wants which seemed to him peculiarly human. His disciples have been less on their guard; they have, for example, sometimes ventured to speak of the spiritual degradation of the worker, and even of the bourgeois, in bourgeois society. They have then usually had in mind some aspect or other of what Marx called alienation. Sometimes, too, they have spoken of moral degradation. But when they have done this, they have not really wanted to pass a moral judgement on the degraded. The spiritually or morally degraded man, far from being to blame for his condition, may be law-abiding and conventionally respectable; he may not only behave well externally but be well intentioned by the standards of the community he belongs to. He may be a man whose capacities are not yet developed in such a way that he has the wants, attitudes, and beliefs that come with the overcoming of alienation and of the illusions that are marks of it and on which it thrives. What Engels in *Anti-Dühring* calls the 'truly human morality' of the classless society is emphatically not morality as Hobbes or Hume or even Kant conceived of it; it is a morality that makes sense only if we think of man as Marx thought of him, and he thought of him much as Hegel did.

II

Marxism has been influential in three different ways: as a source of ideas for students of society, as a creed to which organized bodies deliberately subscribe, and as a philosophy that helps to determine the values and ends (private and public) of individual men and women. Quite often these three kinds of influence converge, as for example when a professional sociologist or historian belongs to a Marxist party and also has values that are deeply affected by his Marxist beliefs. Nevertheless, these three influences are worth distinguishing, since they often bear unequally on a man (or group of men)—even on a man or group that admits to being Marxist or is generally taken for such.

Marxist theory—if we mean by it Marxist doctrines as they left the hands of Marx and Engels—is now probably less important as an influence on the creeds of parties and other avowedly Marxist organizations than it was some fifty or sixty years ago. This is so (or is likely to be so) because the principles to which Communist parties and their dependent organizations now subscribe are as much Leninist, or even Stalinist, as they are Marxist in the narrower sense of that term; and there are, of course, other ingredients besides. The influence of a particular theory on the policies of a party (or other organization) is in any case difficult to assess, not so much because the party is bound to be selective in its choice of doctrines—

passing over some and laying on others a greater stress than did the author of the theory—as because very different policy decisions can be justified by appeals to the same doctrines. Different practical conclusions are drawn from a doctrine as much because estimates of the situation it is applied to vary as because the doctrine is variously understood. What is more, beliefs and doctrines other than those that belong to the theory influence policy decisions. We do not need to share the naïve scepticism of those who say that in general theory or ideology has little influence on policy, and serves above all to provide justifications for decisions taken on other grounds, to agree that it is easy to exaggerate the extent to which a particular theory or ideology affects the policies of the organized groups that subscribe to it. An official ideology has other functions besides that of being used to guide policy; it is used also to protect official decisions from certain types of criticism, or to help maintain discipline inside the party (or other body) whose orthodoxy it is, or as a label to distinguish that party from others. It could happen—and perhaps does happen quite often —that the influence of a theory on policy decisions actually diminishes as a result of its being adopted as an official creed by some powerful organization. This is the more likely to happen the greater the power of the organization and the more it can suppress criticism of its official decisions.

In countries in which a self-styled 'Marxist' party has a virtual monopoly of power, the influence of Marx's ideas on social studies is apt to be restrictive, and also to bear more upon the language of these studies than on the thinking that goes into them. The need to dress up ideas in the officially approved style does not stifle all independence of mind, but it is inhibiting and debilitating. The ideas of Marx, for all the praise lavished on them, are examined less closely and critically in countries dominated by the Communist Party than in countries not so dominated—or at least than in the intellectually more active and sophisticated of these countries. Thus, where Communists rule, the variety of Marx's ideas and the uses to which they can be put—whether in the form given to them by Marx or suitably amended—are much less appreciated. Even the more avowedly Marxist of social theorists in the West are critical of at least some aspects of Marx's thought, and do not pass over them in silence, while others who are not Marxists and are highly critical of doctrines that 'Marxists' treat as fundamental readily admit that they have learned a great deal from Marx. The Marxism of Marx (and even of Engels) is today a richer source of ideas, a greater stimulus to fresh and ingenious thinking about society and politics, in the West than in the Communist-dominated parts of the world. An impartial observer might well conclude that the more hostile critics of Marxism in the West do greater justice to Marx than do his official interpreters in the Communist countries. They cannot get away with quite such crude misinterpretations of his doctrines, and are bound to admit that in some parts of his writings he himself provides correctives for what is misconceived or too simple in others—even though he does not produce a systematic theory taking proper account of these correctives.

In the West there are few political organizations of any size, except for the Communist parties, whose leaders would describe themselves as Marxists, though there are many whose leaders are influenced considerably by Marx's ideas. Just how far this influence extends is difficult to assess, but not because there is any attempt to hide it. Some doctrines now called Marxist were put forward by others before Marx or else by his contemporaries independently of him, and these non-Marxist versions of the doctrines were sometimes widely accepted in circles in which the writings of Marx were as yet unknown. This is especially true of Latin countries. For example, the doctrine that the state is an instrument of class rule was popular in some intellectual circles and among sections of the working class in France, in Paris and some of the larger towns, for years before the French had heard of Marx. In itself, the doctrine is no more Marxist than it is Proudhonist or Blanquist; and the Paris workers, the most radical in France, were during the period of their greatest revolutionary activity culminating in the disaster of the Commune much more disciples of Proudhon and Blanqui than of Marx. Later, as the prestige of Marxism increased, this doctrine, along with several others of equally mixed origin, came to be thought of as specifically Marxist. Just as, with the growing importance of the English language, many peoples—not excluding even the French—have taken to using English words and phrases to say what they had long been able to say quite adequately in their own languages, so with the spread of Marxism there has been a translation into the Marxist idiom of ideas long familiar in other idioms.

In countries ruled by Communists, the dominant party is, of course, avowedly Marxist, but—as I suggested earlier—the influence of Marx's ideas, as distinct from those of Lenin, Stalin, and other Russian Marxists, is probably fast diminishing. At the same time, ideas which in the West (where they originated) are widely recognized as not being specifically Marxist, because Marx took them over from others or attributed less importance to them than others did, are spoken of in the Soviet Union and other Communist countries as if they originated with Marx. Ideas that are officially approved and are known to have been around for a long time are attributed to him in the same spirit of piety as more recent ideas (and other achievements) are attributed to Lenin, Stalin, or Mao. Just as in Hobbes's commonwealth, all 'salutary' truths are held to proceed from the sovereign or from prophets acknowledged to be true prophets by him. Nevertheless, despite these attributions inspired by piety, the influence of Marx's ideas on the policies and attitudes of political parties calling themselves Marxist has diminished greatly since 1917, when a Marxist party first took control of a large country; and it will probably continue to diminish. These 'Marxist' parties, which are now so powerful in the world, need an orthodoxy to use for a variety of important purposes, and the orthodoxy they have still contains many of Marx's ideas; but they could still use·it for these purposes even if the proportion of these ideas were much smaller than it is. In saying this, I do not in the least imply that ideas, or theories, do not have a great influence on policy; I say only that theories (or selections from them) when they become *orthodox* and remain so for a long time lose much of their influence on policy. Which is not to say that the orthodoxy that includes them loses its political importance; for, as I said earlier, the political importance of orthodoxy consists in much more than its serving as a guide to policy. It serves, for example, the supremely important political function of converting opponents into heretics, and so justifying forms of discipline which would otherwise be found intolerable.

The third influence of Marxism is today easier to detect in the West than in countries ruled by a Communist and self-styled Marxist party. The social philosophies of many Western intellectuals (many but by no means all of them radicals) are to a large extent Marxist; and by social philosophies I mean, in this context, not necessarily elaborate theories but sets of beliefs about society and the human condition which powerfully affect the attitudes of those who hold them to government, to politics, and to social practices and institutions. To the extent that these philosophies are Marxist, the element of early Marxism in them is greater than it used to be, especially if by early Marxism we mean, not doctrines confined to the early writings of Marx, but doctrines whose relative importance to students of Marxism has increased greatly as the early writings have come to be more widely and closely studied. Some elements of later Marxism (or of Marxism that is both late and early) are still prominent in these philosophies—as, for example, the idea of the state as an instrument or condition of class exploitation; while other elements—as, for example, the doctrine that class struggles are more important than other forms of social conflict, or the idea of the proletariat as the essentially revolutionary class—are less prominent than they used to be.

Today, in many intellectual circles that pride themselves on their radicalism, it is above all the idea of 'bourgeois' or 'capitalist' society as a social and psychological burden to the individual, as a system that somehow distorts the values of the people caught up in it, as falsely liberating in a way that no society before it has been, as a kind of fraud that mankind practise unconsciously on themselves; it is this idea, or set of ideas, that is widely attractive, obscure and elusive though it is. It is not only a Marxist idea, for other radicals and socialists of the early nineteenth century also had it; but it is in its Marxist forms, or dressed up in Marxist phraseology, that it is now conspicuous.

It is, of course, an idea that could be accepted even by persons who denied that there was much exploitation of class by class, or of some groups by others, in Western society, or who saw greater evils in it than this exploitation; though in fact most people who accept the idea also believe that there is a great deal of exploitation. Often it is not clear how, in their opinion, these particular afflictions, false consciousness and illusory freedom, are related to exploitation. Often, too, they persist in speaking of class exploitation even though they have something different in mind from what Marx meant by that term: even though what they really deplore is the excessive power of large organizations, or rather of those who run them, and therefore the 'exploitation' or 'manipulation' of all classes by these organizations and their bosses. To be sure, they sometimes argue that the bosses are recruited predominantly from some one class or section of a class, and then take it for granted that 'exploitation' by the bosses, or by the organizations they run, is equivalent to exploitation by the class from which the bosses are recruited. Nevertheless, ordinarily, except when their concern is to fly their Marxist colours, they speak of this exploitation as if it were of all classes by a set of small self-recruiting groups or élites—self-recruiting in practice, even though professing to be otherwise—than of some classes by others.

There are still, of course, owners of property who live off the labour of others, contributing little or nothing in return, and who in that sense are exploiters, though they have less power over others than do many people who sell their labour for a salary, or even a wage. They are not deserving persons whose needs or infirmities or misfortunes entitle them, judged by standards that even a socialist would accept, to receive from society more than they give. It is widely recognized that there is still plenty of exploitation of this kind in the West; and, in the strict Marxist sense, it is exploitation by one class of others. But the 'exploitation' that today impresses people much more, that arouses greater fears and deeper resentments, is of the relatively powerless by the relatively powerful, even though the powerful are paid for the work they do just as the powerless are.

This second sort of exploitation is the more elusive of the two, in the sense that it is more difficult to determine its limits, to decide when power or influence is being used for the benefit of those who use it to the detriment of those subjected to it. Everyone admits that in modern industrial societies, be they capitalist or not, there are vast inequalities of power, and that some of them are inevitable if the advantages of large-scale industry and trade are to be retained. But there is little agreement—indeed, little enough serious thinking—about what kinds are inevitable, what other kinds (though perhaps avoidable) are yet tolerable because of their beneficial consequences, and what kinds ought to be removed because they are altogether harmful or their benefits are too small to compensate for the harm they do—especially the injustices and curtailments of freedom that result from them. Still, confused or elusive though this idea of 'exploitation' is, it is important and is recognized to be so; for already many people take it seriously. They believe that there is far more of this kind of exploitation, far more using people for purposes they do not share or approve or understand, than there ought to be.

I have suggested that it is exceptionally difficult to estimate the influence of Marx's ideas on beliefs about society and the human condition in countries dominated by the Communist Party, precisely because it is dangerous for people to examine these ideas critically. Often they may not know what to make of them, and may find it safer and more comfortable to use Marxist phrases in prescribed ways on appropriate occasions without troubling to inquire, even in the privacy of their own minds, what they mean. The ideas of Marx, along with other ideas from writers whose claim to be Marxists cannot be safely disputed, are used to justify Communist ascendancy and the policies and plans of the rulers. There is little sign of their being used by enemies of the Communists to challenge the social and political order, root and branch.

Yet, in principle, a Marxist critique of, say, Soviet society is possible. The ideas of Marx, suitably adapted, could be used just as effectively to condemn the economy, the social structure, the culture, and the form of government of the Soviet Union as they have been to condemn capitalism, 'bourgeois society', and the 'bourgeois state'. They would then, of course, be used to condemn conditions not foreseen by Marx, just as they are today by Marxists in the West. It is no more difficult to offer a Marxist explanation of how the Soviet Union has come to be as it is than to offer a Marxist explanation of how Western capitalism has developed since Marx died. In my opinion, neither explanation could be completely adequate because Marxism is seriously defective as a theory of social change. But it is not, I think, less well equipped to explain the contradictions of the Soviet economy than those of capitalism or the forms of exploitation and false consciousness prevalent in Soviet society than those to be found in the West. Yet in Communist countries Marx's ideas seem to be used more by factions within the ruling party in their struggles for control over it than by whole-hearted opponents of the type of society, government, and culture that the Communists have brought into being. The deeper the opposition to what the Communists have achieved or tried to achieve, the less it is inspired by Marxism or the less it seeks expression in a Marxist idiom. This, at least, seems to be the case in some of the smaller Slav countries. Disgust with the regime often brings with it distaste for the theory officially approved, even though the theory, restored to the condition in which its founder left it, could be used to condemn the regime.

In the West 'rejection' of the established order, when it takes a Marxist form, is nowadays quite often unconstructive; it is condemnatory without being seriously concerned to change society for the better. Sometimes the rejectors are quietist and resigned; they do not believe that society is changing 'of itself' in desirable ways, and yet despair of their ability to improve it. Sometimes, even, they are cynical in their attitude to it; they speak of it as incurably corrupt and at the same time take advantage of the opportunities this corruption offers to them, on the ground that it would be stupid not to do so. These cynics are exploiters of the system they condemn. As are also the critics of bourgeois society who seek to 'opt out of it', since they can do this only to a limited extent and have perforce to depend in many ways on the society they would like to escape from. They cannot help but live off it and yet their attitude to it is such that they contribute little or nothing to maintaining what they cannot do without.

Often, of course, these consciously Marxist or neo-Marxist rejectors of bourgeois society are not cynical or resigned or hopeless; they believe that there will be, or could be, change for the better and hope to be able to work for it. Yet the hopes are vaguer now. The old faith in the 'revolutionary proletariat', where it has not vanished altogether, is much weaker than it was. There is still talk of 'revolution' as something that the 'contradictions' of capitalism or of 'bourgeois society' will bring about, but there is much more uncertainty as to who the makers of the revolution will be, what forms it will take, and even what the contradictions are that will produce it. Marxism, as it survives now in the West, serves, I suggest, much more to condemn society as it is than to indicate what should be done to transform it or who should undertake the transformation.

My concern is emphatically not with the attempts of Marxists to destroy or transform the bourgeois society they condemn; it is with their reasons for condemning it, and with the social philosophy that lies behind these reasons. It is also with the ideas used in elaborating that philosophy, for I consider, not only how these ideas have in fact been used by Marx and Engels in constructing their theories, but also how they could be used—how far they are suited to such purposes as theirs and how they might be amended to make them better suited.

Marx's ideas can figure prominently in the social philosophy of someone who nevertheless thinks of himself as essentially not a Marxist. As, for example, in the conception of man as a social being of Calvez, whose attitude to Marxism I have already discussed. Calvez is a Jesuit and therefore, presumably, not a Marxist. Yet his book, *La Pensée de Karl Marx*, is admiring and respectful, not just of Marx's social theory in general, but of aspects of it that might be expected not to appeal to a practising

Catholic. Calvez, though he cannot accept Marx's account of religion as a fantasy of alienated man, does not dismiss it as absurd or as altogether wide of the mark. On the contrary, unacceptable though he finds it, he sees implicit in it ideas about the human condition in industrial societies which seem to him profound and largely true.

There are several ways of dealing with Marxism, and I shall not argue that any one of them is the only right way. But I do want to say a little more about Calvez's treatment of Marx's early writings, partly in order to make clear by contrast my own attitude to them, and partly to make a point about the use of philosophy, and especially of such a philosophy as Marx's, which is often overlooked in academic circles, British and American.

Calvez's criticism of Marx is eminently not destructive. He is not concerned to pull apart an edifice which he finds badly constructed and weak; he is concerned rather to make what he can of fragments, to follow suggestions, to discover a grand design behind brief sketches whose connections are uncertain. He is, if you like, excessively constructive; he could be accused of reading more into Marx than is there. His account of what Marx understood by human nature and alienation is elaborate, subtle, and elegant. It is quite impressive to see what becomes of Marxist and Hegelian turns of phrase when a Frenchman and a theologian with a sense of style gets hold of them. There is a high polish put on Marxism, and it shines brightly. How much the more intelligible it becomes for this treatment is another matter.

Calvez's objections to Marxism are quite different from those of its older critics. He does not inquire how useful it is for explanatory purposes. He does not claim for it that the facts support it or complain that they do not. He does not ask what contribution it has made to the social sciences. The burden of his argument against it is that the remedy it offers for the ills it describes is unsatisfying. He finds it in many ways admirable: ingenious, perceptive, imaginative, and rich in ideas. Yet, for all its merits, in the end it will not do, for it does not give man what he needs to enable him to deal adequately with the problems about himself with which he, being the sort of creature he is, is inevitably faced. This objection to Marxism may or may not be justified, but it is not improper or irrelevant. Marxism is, after all, something more than a theory about man and society to be proved or disproved by an appeal to the facts. It may, to some extent, be scientific, but it is something more besides. No one who has studied it and its influence in the world can have doubts about that.

Calvez speaks at times of Marxism almost as if it were a substitute for religion, though one which fails to provide what Christianity gives to those who accept it. He does not see in it merely a faith different from his own which he (being the sort of man he is) cannot accept but which someone else, temperamentally unlike him, might find as acceptable as he (Calvez) finds the Catholic faith, and for reasons in themselves no better or worse than his own. He sees it rather as a philosophy unable to give man what he, by reason of his humanity, needs; a philosophy in which man, given the needs he acquires in developing his distinctively human capacities, cannot find lasting satisfaction. Marx's conception of man is, he thinks, substantially correct. Man is the sort of being that Marx, especially in his early writings, makes him out to be. He is, as Marx says he is, essentially a social being, in the sense that his specifically human needs are developed in him by social intercourse. This is a truth about man more adequately expressed by Marx than by others before him, and a truth which the good Christian or the good Catholic need not and must not reject. Man does have the needs ascribed to him by Marx, but it is precisely because he has them that he cannot be satisfied with such ideals as Marxism sets before him. Marx's conception of man seems to Calvez to be in some ways remarkably close to the Christian and Catholic conception. Much closer, for example, than the conceptions of the rationalist philosophers of the eighteenth century.

It is, so thinks Calvez, much the same conception, *minus* the theology and *plus* the history and sociology. For the Christian conception of man is, of course, unhistorical. It defines a human condition but does not see it as an effect of man's relations with other men and with his natural environment; it sees it rather as an effect of man's relations with God.

I have spoken of a conception of man common to Christianity and to Marxism. To avoid misunderstanding, let me enlarge a little upon what I have said. I have in mind an entirely untheological conception, one which could be adequately defined without reference, explicit or implicit, to God or to other than human purposes. Nobody who accepted it would be committed logically to any belief about God. Therefore, it is not the whole Christian conception of man but only a part of it that Christianity shares with Marxism. If I have understood him aright, Calvez suggests, not that Marx was a Christian without knowing it or that his account of man implies the truth of Christianity, but rather that, if man really is the sort of creature described by Marx, he has needs that Christianity can satisfy and Marxism cannot.

Therefore, in the eyes of Calvez, Marx's rejection of Christianity (and indeed of all religion), misconceived though it is, cuts deeper than its rejection by the rationalists of the century before him. For Marx comes nearer than they do to understanding the needs expressed by some of the most profound of Christian apologists, even though he rejects the religion which, so they think, can alone satisfy these needs. He offers an explanation of the social and human conditions of these needs and predicts their transcendence, their giving way gradually to aspirations that can be satisfied in a worldly order. Marx, therefore, in the eyes of this Jesuit admirer and critic, is, as Voltaire and the Encyclopaedists never were, an enemy within the gates. His being able to see so far into the human condition is evidence of his seriousness, of his imaginative insight into what is involved in being a rational and purposeful creature concerned for its own dignity and worth. For such an enemy Calvez feels great respect and strong sympathy; he is so perceptive, so near being right, and yet so wrong. Calvez tries to argue with Marx on what he believes are Marx's own terms. Marx tried to show how religion arises out of needs peculiar to man, and how it will eventually disappear as his capacities develop and he learns at last to satisfy his needs in a social and natural environment which he understands and controls. Calvez undertakes to show that, given these peculiarly human needs, which Marx understood so much better than did Voltaire and his contemporaries, man can be satisfied only by some such religion as Christianity.

Calvez finds Marxism unacceptable above all for two reasons. Its account of the course of history is illogical in a crucial respect, and its conception of the communist society is a religious idea misapplied. A historical process of the kind imagined by Marx (or Hegel) cannot have a final end, a consummation. It must go on and on unless something happens to stop it. There can be no point along it at which radical transformation ceases because a self-maintaining rational or just order has been attained. If man, by virtue of what is specifically human about his activities, transforms himself as he transforms the social order to which he belongs, he must continue to do this indefinitely. Thus his worldly aspirations must also change continually. There can be no destination, no safe arrival, in this world for men taken generally, no uniquely rational social order in which human potentialities are fully realized. There can only be the worldly goals of individuals and of groups, which change with the social environment as a result of the very activities whose purpose is to achieve them.

Calvez's other reason for finding Marxism unacceptable and delusive is that the idea of the communist society as a remedy for the human condition is a Christian idea translated to a sphere in which it does not apply. It has something in common with the idea of the church triumphant, the community of the redeemed. But the church triumphant is not a worldly organization. The church active here below is the church militant, which, though it is a community of this world different in kind from all others, is not a worldly community made perfect. It is involved in history, which records the activities of men in this world in which they can find God through the ministrations of the church. But the church militant is not a final stage in a historical process, nor yet a community in which mankind come into full possession of their 'human powers'. It is not the human spirit perfected or fulfilled in this world. The church, persisting from age to age, is merely the community through which the individual, if he is found worthy, attains his end, which is union with God. This he may do as well in earlier as in later stages of the church's history; for though the church too changes and develops, as all things worldly must, its capacity to bring men to God does not increase with time.

Thus, for Calvez, there is no movement of the species to a full realization of its powers, though there may be progress in a variety of respects. The historical process leads nowhere in particular; it is the changing world of human endeavour in which individual men strive, successfully or unsuccessfully, to attain their ends. Unless they were involved in it, they could not strive; and they could not live as God intends them to do. The way to salvation is indeed through the world; and this world, man's world, is indeed a world which necessarily changes as a result of man's endeavours inside it. Marx is right when he says that man, because he is self-conscious and rational, as other animals are not, is necessarily involved in a course of social and cultural change, as they are not. Unless he were the sort of being who could be so involved, he would be able to make nothing of religion; he would not have a final end which the church could help him attain. All this the Christian need not, should not, deny. He can admit that the human world, the world of society and culture, the world which is both the context and the result of specifically human activities, is necessarily a changing world, and also that man's living in such a world is a condition of his seeking and attaining his final end. It is a condition, not just in the sense that it is the place where the seeking is done, but in the sense that it is the environment which so educates man that he can become a seeker. Yet the Christian would deny that man's social environment, continually transformed by his activities, becomes eventually such that frustration and alienation disappear. True progress, or movement towards a condition that fully satisfies, is always peculiar to the individual; it is always a pilgrim's progress.

We need not share the faith of Calvez to agree with him that Marx's idea of the communist society is in some respects a Christian idea misapplied. We need not be Christians, either, to accept, in part at least, his other objection to Marxism—an objection which is implicit rather than express. Man, he thinks, is not the kind of being that can be fully satisfied in any social order. Even if we allow that all societies are products of human endeavour to satisfy human needs and spheres in which men develop their specifically human powers and acquire the attributes which put them in their own eyes apart from other creatures, we can still deny that there is any social order in which these powers are fully realized, these attributes perfected, in which men understand themselves and their human world as they really are and are satisfied. We can deny that from Marx's conception of man as an essentially social and self-creative being it follows that in the communist society (or in any other) man finally overcomes the self-estrangement to which, as a self-conscious and rational being, he is peculiarly liable.

On the main point it seems to me that Calvez is right. I see no reason why it should be supposed that there is a wordly condition or social order ideally suited to the essential needs or essential nature of man—if by that is meant a social order such that all men, or all but a few, are satisfied in it. I do not even see why there should be progress towards such an order as men's understanding of themselves and their environment grows. For all I know, it could be that 'primitive' peoples, who lack this understanding (or who would be thought to do so by Marx), are more likely than 'advanced' peoples to be satisfied in their 'human worlds', their worlds of culture, in spite of their having many illusions about them. As I shall try to show later, just as it is not easy to determine what Marx understands by either alienation or false consciousness, so it is not easy to be sure how he conceives of the connection between them. How do we decide that human beings are not alienated? What are their attitudes to themselves and society when they are 'satisfied', when they are 'at home in the world'? What is involved in their developing their potentialities 'fully'? How can they know that they have ceased to be 'falsely' and have become 'truly' conscious? What is the 'truly human morality' of which Engels spoke in a book that Marx read and approved? These are questions that Marx never answered, even though he had suggestive and perceptive things to say about both alienation and false consciousness. I would not share, without many qualifications, Marx's conception of man; but if I did share it, I still would not share his beliefs about the communist society or his hopes of its eventual coming.

Yet Calvez, too, in his turn and speaking as a Christian, goes further than I, for one, can follow him. He speaks as if no man could be fully satisfied with his worldly lot; as if being human involved having needs (even though sometimes unconscious, or half-conscious, needs) that can be satisfied fully only by the Christian religion—or at least by a relationship of man to God of the kind conceived by Christianity. He admits (and to that extent follows Marx) that such needs are produced by the development of distinctively human capacities in social intercourse, and he no doubt would, if challenged, recognize that there have been religions in the world very unlike Christianity. Perhaps he believes that these needs, though they are met (or partly met) by these other religions, while they are still largely unconscious, can be met only by Christianity when they become fully conscious. But if this is what he believes, he does not make clear his reasons for doing so. That men and women have had and do have needs which can only be satisfied by religious beliefs of the Christian type is no doubt true, and Marx's reasons for holding that they will eventually cease to have such needs are far from convincing. But why should we suppose that such needs are shared by all self-conscious rational beings, or even by those of them who reflect deeply on their condition? This suggestion is as arbitrary, as little supported by such evidence as we have, as Marx's belief that the need for religion will disappear when certain kinds of social conditions do so.

Marx and Calvez agree that human beings by their activities in society continually transform their distinctively human needs, which take different forms in the course of social change. If this is so, it is difficult to see why Calvez's suggestion should be any nearer the truth than Marx's. Each in his different way seems to take too narrow a view of the possibilities: Marx in speaking of a capitalist society in which all men are alienated and a communist society in which no man will be so, and Calvez in speaking as if no man could be satisfied in a purely worldly condition pursuing purely worldly goals. To hold that 'worldliness' cannot satisfy is surely to be as dogmatic as to hold that human beings in general, or those of them belonging to certain classes or groups, have been or are dissatisfied (even though sometimes under the illusion of being satisfied) and will be 'truly satisfied' only in a certain type of social order.

I speak at this length of Calvez's book, written by a priest, because it is a striking example of an attitude to Marxism, and even to social theory more generally, which is more common on the European Continent than in the English-speaking countries. Calvez goes about as far as a Catholic can go in accepting Marxism. He is, given his faith, an extraordinarily generous interpreter of a theory which he feels bound to reject. His purpose, above all, is to assess the relevance of Marxism to a being whose concern with the world, even at the level of the seeker after knowledge, is more than merely scientific and more also than merely practical; who cannot help putting about himself, his fellows, and the communities he belongs to questions of a kind that the psychologist and sociologist do not think it their business to answer; and which are not practical questions in the ordinary sense of the word. They are not questions about means to ends already decided upon, or even about what ends are to be preferred to others.

This sort of interest is not confined to the Christian; it is to be found in thinkers who are without religion, as most people understand it. As, for example, in Sartre. His real concern with Marxism has been to decide how much of it is acceptable as a philosophy to live by. He has sought in it what seemed to him lacking in the existentialist philosophy which he constructed for himself when he was younger. Calvez, of course, has not sought in Marxism what he could not find in Catholicism. He is, I take it, a good Catholic who has been moved to inquire why a secular philosophy unacceptable to him has proved attractive to others. His book can be looked upon as an answer to this question: What is it about Marxism that evokes so deep a response in so many of the most intelligent and imaginative men of our time? Calvez has not, so far as I know, put this question to himself in so many words. Yet his book is, I think, impressive above all as an answer to this question. It is an elaborate, well-constructed, and well-written commentary on a number of meagre, obscure, and often unfinished texts which contain some of Marx's most elusive ideas. It is perhaps too elaborate a structure to rest securely on such slender foundations, but that is beside the point I am now making.

Though Sartre has not produced a commentary on Marxism as elegant and as carefully put together as Calvez's book, he has taken what is at bottom the same kind of interest in it. He too has considered its possibilities as a philosophy to live by; though, unlike Calvez, he has hoped to find in it something that he lacked. Neither he nor Calvez has been seriously concerned to question the adequacy of Marxism as a systematic explanation of the human condition in industrial society; to inquire whether, on Marx's assumptions and using his ideas, it is possible to explain satisfactorily the facts, social and psychological, that he tries to explain.

That, presumably, is why they do not trouble to look closely at Marx's assumptions to establish just how clear they are or at his ideas to discover how far he uses them consistently; why they do not seek to reformulate what he says about man and society in such a way that it can be tested by an appeal to the sort of evidence that sociologists or psychologists, or even historians, look for to test their hypotheses. Looking only at those parts of Marxism that excite them, they are concerned primarily to assess it as a way of thinking and feeling about the human condition.

Calvez, for example, seldom puts a question that could be answered by experiment or by an appeal to history or by a survey. For the most part, he either expounds what he believes to be Marx's meaning, or else makes on Marxist doctrines comments which could serve as answers to such questions as these: How far is Marx's image of man an image that man can take to himself? How far is it relevant to what man feels about himself and about his social condition?

This, if you like, involves an appeal to experience, though not to evidence as the scientist understands it. The experience to which Calvez appeals consists of what the intelligent man comes to know about himself as he reflects on life. The appeal is not to external facts methodically observed; to what the psychologist or sociologist or historian records about the behaviour of others. The appeal is rather to what is assumed to be universal in man's experience of himself—even though the vast majority never put it into words, despite its being essentially the experience of a being whose capacities (including reason and will) are developed in social intercourse.

This kind of appeal to experience has long been made by the political and the moral philosopher; and I am so far from questioning his right to make it that I do not see how he can avoid making it. I do not believe that there is nothing to be learnt from systematic reflection about man and society except what can be tested by the sort of appeal to facts, to observation and experiment and the taking of samples, that the social scientist makes. Nor does the only, nor even the most important, contribution that philosophy makes to the study of man consist in the critical examination and elucidation of the assumptions and concepts of the social scientist and the historian. It consists also in the remaking of man's image of himself; in the formulation of new assumptions about human nature, which cannot themselves be tested by an appeal to the facts, though they inspire a whole range of hypotheses that can be so tested.

I would not quarrel therefore with Calvez (or with Sartre) for the way he deals with the aspects of Marxism that have excited him; for confining himself, more or less, to expounding Marx's conception of man as a being who, unlike all others known to us, in some sense makes himself, so that humanity in him is more an achievement than a natural condition; and to showing where this conception departs from what Calvez (or Sartre) invites his readers to believe is really important in man's experience of himself.

Yet in this book I shall not follow their example, or shall do so only to a slight extent. I shall put and try to answer questions of a type that Calvez does not put. I shall look critically at the assumptions that Marx makes about man as a social being, and at the ideas he uses to describe what, in his opinion, is characteristically human about man. I shall be concerned with what the sociologist or political theorist can learn from Marx both positively and negatively: the ideas he does well to take over from him and those which he should rather avoid as empty or as sources of confusion. For Marx, like Rousseau, is both an original thinker and—to put it bluntly—a raiser of false issues, a prolific maker of distinctions where there are no differences, who can yet fail to make at crucial points in his arguments distinctions that need to be made, and a purveyor of nonsense. I believe that his interpreters who fail to recognize the confusion and the nonsense in his thinking (and they are not all Marxists, for some of them take care to warn their readers that they are not) do less than justice to him. By passing off his dross as gold, they risk making the authentic gold pass unnoticed. The more critical of their readers, unpersuaded that dross is gold, will not expect to find gold where they have been told to look for it by guides who cannot distinguish it from dross. Worse even than avowed Marxists as guardians of Marx's reputation as a powerful and original thinker are the worshippers who do not know themselves for such. And there seem to be, among writers about Marxism in the West, at least two of them for every one who calls himself a Marxist. Many a great thinker needs to be protected from his more fervent admirers; but, next after Rousseau, none stands so much in need of this protection as Marx.

In this book I also take the sort of interest that Calvez takes in Marx's philosophy of man, though less than he does. I too try to explain what has made it, and still makes it, so attractive to so many people. I, too, am impressed by it, though not as much as Calvez appears to be. But I agree that it is as well worth study as an ideology, or even as a 'philosophy of life', as it is as a contribution to the social sciences.

CHAPTER II

THE ESSENTIAL NATURE OF MAN (1)

Marxism Compared with Earlier Theories

WRITERS about Marx often claim for him that, unlike many social and political theorists before him, he does not explain or assess social and political institutions by reference to an essential or unchanging human nature. He does not, as Hobbes or some of the Utilitarians do, point to supposedly universal passions or wants of man, and then explain institutions found in all or most societies as established or arising to satisfy them. Still less does he seek to derive from these passions and wants, together with what is assumed to be common to man's situation everywhere, an ideal social order best adapted to satisfy them, or to hold them in check when they are likely to be harmful. On the contrary, Marx holds that men's wants and passions differ from society to society, and from age to age; and holds also that, just as they differ, so too do the claims that men make on one another. There is no unchanging human nature, and no eternal justice.

Marx complains that the classical economists—whom he treats as unconscious champions of the economy they profess to describe dispassionately—take it for granted that men have always been and always will be as they now are. But, says Marx, men now are what the capitalist economy has made them; they were not always so, and we must not assume that they will not change in the future. This complaint against the classical economists may not be justified, or may be so only in part; but it does at least illustrate a point important to Marx: that men's wants and attitudes, and also the claims they make and admit, and their conceptions of the good life (or, in a more contemporary idiom, their images of themselves and of their roles and activities as they would wish them to be) are always changing. Societies differ and societies change, and so too do the men who belong to them. We know nothing of man outside society, and we must not, as some theorists have tried to do, explain what is common to all societies (or what we take to be so) in terms of a pre-social nature of man. We must not postulate a natural man, a man untouched by social influences, and then use him to explain the origins or the functions of social institutions. Man, as we know him, as much in the past as now, has always been a social creature, and we know that his wants and standards and ideas are always changing.

This is the belief attributed to Marx by commentators who like to make much of the difference between him and the major political theorists of the seventeenth and eighteenth centuries. They are not wrong in attributing this belief to him. But, by making too sharp a contrast between him and his predecessors, they make these predecessors appear more simple-minded than they were; and they also—so it seems to me—misinterpret Marx.

Few political theorists of the seventeenth century (not to speak of the eighteenth) actually believed that men had once lived in complete solitude, unaffected by intercourse with one another. They mostly took it for granted that men had always lived in families. That man's nature, as we know it, is a second nature, a nature acquired in society, was an idea familiar to Montaigne—and, no doubt, to other writers who lived long before he did. Familiar too was the idea that men's wants and standards differ considerably from society to society. The philosophers who, in the seventeenth century, spoke of 'a state of nature' and of 'natural man' did not think of themselves as denying what Montaigne and others had said; nor yet as describing a first nature which was man's before he acquired a second nature through social intercourse. Rather, they thought of themselves as describing what is abiding in human nature, what is common to all men (or most men) in all societies, and what everywhere underlies the peculiarities of this or that society. They did not explicitly raise the question whether what they took to be abiding in human nature consisted of wants and passions which men would have if they were outside society altogether. But, when they spoke of natural man, of man in the state of nature, they ordinarily had in mind, not man unaffected by enduring relations with other men, but just primitive man, man without government. They thought of natural man as capable of speech, and therefore of rational intercourse with creatures of his own kind; they thought of him as a begetter and protector of children.

They ordinarily did not use the word *society* in as broad a sense as it came to be used later; they meant by it *civil* or *political* society, just as they meant by natural man, man without government or man without law— in that sense of law which implies that there are authorized interpreters and enforcers of the social rules that men are required to obey. Their purpose was to explain, not all social institutions, but the institutions, political and legal, of what they called civil society. Natural man, as they imagined him, was already social man, in the broad sense of the word *social*, which is the sense that we and Marx are accustomed to use; and if they implied that natural man was unsocial, it was only because they habitually used the word *society* to mean *civil* or *political society*.

Commentators on Locke's *Treatise of Civil Government* have often noticed that what Locke called 'the state of nature' is what we should call a social state. Locke's purpose in writing the *Treatise* was to explain what he took to be the legitimate functions of government, and he thought he could best attain his purpose by considering what motives men might have for setting up government if they were without it. He therefore imagined what their condition would be without government; and that was enough for his limited purpose. He was not concerned to inquire how men might have got into that condition, or to distinguish among their characteristics those they acquired as a result of social intercourse from those they were born with. He thought it enough to attribute to men without government, the wants, passions, and skills they would need in order to conceive of government and desire it, and be able to establish it. What is true of Locke, is true, more or less, of most of the political theorists writing in the seventeenth century, and of many writing in the eighteenth.

An objection to these theorists better founded than that they tried to explain all social institutions by reference to wants, attitudes, and beliefs which they attributed to men as yet untouched by social influences is that they failed to distinguish between the origins and the functions of institutions. They mistakenly believed that the answer to the question *What wants induced men to set up government or to submit to it as it gradually arose?* would also provide them with an answer to the questions *What wants does government now satisfy?* and *What are men's present motives for submitting to it when they submit deliberately and without compulsion, when they consent to it?* Thus, to explain the functions of government or law or property, they thought it necessary to give an account of their origins, and the accounts they gave, owing to their comparative ignorance, were conjectural. Government, as they saw it, maintains conditions enabling men to satisfy certain of their needs. Brought up under government, men take it for granted; they ordinarily obey it from mere habit or because they think it the proper thing to do, without troubling to inquire why it should be so. To bring home to men, apt to take the familiar for granted, just what they owe to government, what could be better than to invite them to imagine their condition without it, and to inquire what they would need to do to remedy the inconveniences of that condition?

To Locke and other thinkers of his age, it seemed reasonable to suppose that the needs which would be unsatisfied if there were no government first moved men to set it up, or at least to acquiesce in it where it arose in some other way. If we suppose that men are rational and conscious of their needs and can change their ways of life the better to satisfy them, must we not conclude that their reason for behaving in the ways which eventually brought government into existence was to satisfy certain needs? And if we imagine a covenant or agreement setting up government, even though there may never have been one, we make clearer both the advantages that men derive from government and the grounds of their obligation to obey it. All this seemed obvious to Locke and to his contemporaries; and so it seemed to them that one answer would do for two questions: *What are the advantages of government on which its claims to obedience rest?* and *What induced men to set it up in the first place, or to acquiesce in its establishment?*

Today it is a commonplace that one answer will not do for both these questions. In Locke's day, and even in the eighteenth century, this was not widely recognized. Or rather it was half recognized: recognized in some contexts but not in others. For example, we sometimes find Rousseau recognizing it, especially when he speculates about the course of social change, as he does in the *Discourse on the Origins of Inequality*; while at other times we find him arguing very much in the manner of Hobbes and Locke. In general, if we take the social and political theorists of the late eighteenth century, we see them sometimes considering a problem in a historical context and sometimes not doing so; sometimes taking account of how institutions transform the needs or wants that give rise to them and sometimes not doing so.

But Marx always took this into account; he was very much aware that the wants that institutions (or conventional modes of behaviour) satisfy are often not the wants out of which they arose. He was aware that institutions create many of the wants to which men point later to explain their origins or to justify them.

This does not mean, of course, that when he set about explaining the origins of government or property or of any other institution that interested him, he did not look to human needs, or to the wants in which they find expression, for an explanation. He looked to the conscious wants, not of men everywhere, but of men so and so situated—broad categories or classes of men defined in terms of their social situation. He did not deny the obvious: that men would never have come to have these wants, if they had not been born different from other animals, if there were not a 'human nature' qualitatively different from mere animal nature; but he insisted that men's actual wants arise always out of the situations in which they are placed, situations which consist, not only of their natural endowments and their physical environments, but of their cultures—of the customs, dispositions, beliefs, and skills passed on to them by their forebears. He took, as Hegel had done, large notice of history. By this I mean, not that he took notice of the mere fact that men had had a long history before the institutions he was concerned to explain arose among them, for that was obvious and nobody was concerned to deny it; I mean that he took notice of their actual condition and how it had arisen. He took notice of the course of social change in which they were involved.

To make my meaning clearer, let me, for a moment, compare Marx with Montesquieu, who has also been called a father of sociology. To Montesquieu it cannot be objected that he explains the social by the pre-social or —to take a similar but not identical objection—that he explains the social by the psychological. Nor is he interested particularly in the origins of government or law or property, taken generally. He is interested rather in how and why forms of government or law or property differ from part to part of the world. He sees them all as products partly of the natural environment and partly of history. Yet he is not concerned, as Marx and Hegel are, with man as a being involved in a course of social and cultural change, in which his wants, ideas, and beliefs are continually transformed; in which they do not just multiply but change in quality, so that man's conceptions of the world and of himself are different at each stage of this course from what they were at the stage before it.

What is true of Montesquieu is even more true of the political theorists who speak of a state of nature and of the classical economists. Because they are concerned, not with how institutions differ from place to place, but with broad types of institution—with political as distinct from patriarchal authority, or with a market-and-money economy as distinct from economies in which money is scarcely used—and with the needs which institutions of that type serve and how they serve them, they imagine a highly abstract situation. But, abstract though it is, it is still social. It is a kind of putting together of conditions, psychological and social, which to the theorist seem relevant, given what it is that he wants to explain. To inquire into the historical origins of these conditions would seem to him irrelevant. Man in the state of nature, as Locke and others see him, is an abstract *social* being taken for granted with no questions asked about how the conditions that define him and his situation arose. So, too, economic man, as the economists imagine him, is an abstract social being, taken for granted. He stands at the beginning of their story, and they endow him with the wants, skills, preferences, and attitudes required to reach their conclusions.

Not that natural man plays quite the same part in the theory of, say, Locke that economic man plays in the theories of the economists. Locke and political thinkers of his school wanted to explain the origins of government and property as well as their functions and the rights and obligations connected with those functions, whereas the economists had a narrower aim, to explain only the functions of a certain type of economy and not its origins or the rights and obligations characteristic of it. Locke's concern, of course, was not to explain how in fact government arose in any particular region, or how different types of government arose in different regions, but to point to certain conditions which (so he thought) must have existed in every region in which in fact it did arise.

An objection often made, by Marxists and others, to theories of the kind that Locke and the classical economists produced is that they are unhistorical. That they are so indeed is obvious, but the point of the objection is not clear. These theorists no doubt believed that their methods were well suited to their purposes, and they may have been right. Or, if they were wrong, it may not have been because their methods were unhistorical.

This complaint seems better founded made against Locke than against the classical economists. He, after all, was describing an imaginary past, which they were not doing. They did no more than make certain assumptions about the wants, dispositions, and resources of men, not at all times and everywhere, but in what they took to be the civilized parts of the world. And yet even Locke and the political theorists who set up arguments on much the same model as his seldom mistook their imaginings for true accounts of past events. They had read their Aristotle and had learnt from him that the *polis* had grown out of the village and the village out of the family. They never supposed that their own peoples had leapt out of a pre-social condition into political society without having had to pass, like the Greeks, through intervening stages. They merely took it for granted that such history as was available to them was irrelevant to their purposes.

The methods of the classical economists were at bottom not unlike those still used by economic theorists today, except that the older theorists were less aware of the limitations of these methods. They too constructed theoretical models, in the sense that they selected from the real world of production and exchange the features which seemed to them of crucial importance, tried to define them precisely, and followed up their implications. Their method was deductive but—so they believed—realistic; they made the assumptions about men's wants and preferences, their capacities and beliefs, and their social conditions, which would, so they thought, throw the most light on the aspects of human behaviour they wanted to explain. To economic theorists today their assumptions may seem too simple or inadequate, and their conclusions too bold, too little qualified. The theories that economists produce nowadays are, no doubt, more refined and less ambitious; the men who produce them are more conscious that they may have failed to take account of important factors, and that conditions are apt to change in unpredictable ways, so that the relative importance of the factors they do take into account also changes unpredictably.

But these objections, well founded though they are, to the theories of the classical economists are not the objections of Marx. He does not accuse Adam Smith and Ricardo of making too crude and too ambitious use of methods, sound enough in themselves, but whose limitations are much greater than they supposed. He does not criticize them for failing *in their own purpose*, for offering an inadequate explanation of the productive system they seek to explain. No doubt, he did find some of their explanations inadequate, judged even on their own terms. But this is the sort of criticism that they too made of each other's explanations. There were, among economists that Marx would call 'bourgeois', harsher critics of Ricardo, as a theorist of the capitalist economy, than Marx was himself. Marx learned far more about the functioning of that economy from the bourgeois economists than, for example, from its early socialist critics.

Marx's objection to the classical economists was rather that they took the social relations, and more particularly the property relations, within which the capitalist economy functioned for granted, without inquiring how they had come to be as they were, and that they failed therefore to take into account some of the social consequences of its functioning as it did. They failed to see that the productive system they sought to explain gave rise to social tensions which must in the end destroy it. They also took for granted the wants, preferences, and attitudes which they attributed to producers and consumers within the economy they studied, without inquiring how far they were the products of social relations which had not always existed and would eventually disappear. Also, since they left these wants and attitudes and the social relations which produced them unquestioned, they in a sense endorsed the capitalist system, presenting it to their readers as essentially rational. They may not have done this deliberately, but they did it all the same, and perhaps the more effectively for not doing it deliberately. They gave the impression that the defects of the system—when they did not merely shut their eyes to them—were inevitable; that they were the price that had to be paid for an economy which, on the whole, ensured that resources were efficiently used to satisfy wants.

These criticisms, which have been taken up and developed since Marx's day by his disciples, are not altogether fair or well directed. Several of the classical economists—as, for example, Adam Smith and Ricardo— did take notice of the defects of the productive system and of some of the conflicts and tensions to which it gave rise. Long before Hegel did so, Adam Smith deplored the fact that the growing division of labour condemned large numbers of people to tedious mechanical work, calling for neither intelligence nor initiative. Ricardo pointed to deep-seated conflicts of interest between different classes, and even suggested that, as a result of them, the capitalist system might come to stagnate. Though the classical economists did not envisage a abolition of private property, they were aware that the system they studied was not static, and that there arose inside it not only new techniques of production but also new forms of organization and new legal devices.

But, we may ask, why should the classical economists, given that their purpose was to explain how a certain type of market economy functioned, inquire into the origins of the property relations characteristic of that economy? Why should they be criticized for not doing what they never set out to do, and what they had no need to do to achieve their purpose?

And if they not only took these property relations for granted but also never questioned their justice, why should that vitiate their account of the capitalist economy, since it does in fact rest on these relations? Economists today, who are no less aware than Marx was that these property relations are not eternal, and who often doubt their justice, still use methods which are in principle the same as those of the classical economists to explain how a market economy in which these relations prevail functions.

To this defence of the classical economists the Marxist might reply that, if they had inquired into the origins of these property relations and had noticed how their emergence was connected historically with the rise of certain forms of production, they might also have noticed that the further development of these forms had social consequences which would in the end destroy these relations. They might still have constructed what are now called 'theoretical models' to explain the functioning of the capitalist economy but they might have been models not of a socially static but of a socially dynamic economy: that is to say, they might have been so constructed as to explain how, given certain social conditions, the development of methods of production and exchange beyond a certain point begins to subvert these conditions. A theoretical model, is, of course, something very different from history; but the study of history is essential to the construction of realistic models, which in their turn provide the historian with fertile suggestions. As a Hegelian or a Marxist might put it, the relation between history and social and political theory is dialectical.

Certainly, the classical economists and the political philosophers, whether contract theorists or Utilitarians, assumed that the type of economy or political system they sought to explain had come to stay. The needs it served were, they thought, the enduring needs of 'civilized' men. Though they did not think of these needs as the needs of natural as contrasted with social man, they did assume that they would not change in the future and were much the same among all civilized peoples. They were either concerned, as for example the economists were, only with civilized peoples, or, as for example the contract theorists, with peoples on the threshold of civilization—with their condition immediately before the emergence of a properly civil society and with the benefits derived from this emergence. They seemed almost to think of civilization as they knew it as a kind of plateau, as a level to be reached, from which there might indeed be a falling back but from which there was no moving forward to something different in kind and superior. They were not interested in the details of the long ascent to this plateau, in the stages of it; which does not mean that they were unaware that the ascent had been long. It means only that it was the reaching of this plateau and what it meant to mankind that concerned them.

Before we attribute this attitude of theirs to their unhistorical methods, or alternatively to their lacking a 'sense of history' (which is what they are often accused of), we might do well to notice what is common to their attitude and to Hegel's, not to speak of other philosophers of history less close to Marx than he was.

Hegel, too, assumed that what he called civil society had come to stay; and civil society, as he described it, is in some ways remarkably like the market economy described by the classical economists. He also assumed that, with the emergence of the modern state (a political order closely bound up with civil society) mankind had reached a social, cultural, and moral level which was the highest of all. This did not mean, for Hegel, that actual states or actual civil societies could not be improved; but it did mean that mankind, or the advanced sections of it, had already grasped the principles on which a rational social and political order could be constructed and that these principles were already to a considerable extent embodied in the established order. The established order could indeed be improved, but the improvement would be in the light of principles already recognized within it, both in its theories and its practices. That is to say, it could be improved by reference to standards which served already to make it the sort of society it was, different from earlier and less 'rational' types. For Hegel, no less than for the classical economists, the Utilitarians, and the contract theorists, the social and political order of Western Europe, with its market economy, its forms of property and of private right, its elaborate and precisely defined structure of public authority, was a plateau of civilization to be reached once and for all.

No doubt, Hegel gave a different account of the social and political order in Western Europe from those given by the contract theorists, economists, and Utilitarians. He had ideas different from theirs about human needs, and these ideas were connected logically with his philosophy of history, his conception of man as a social being whose wants and ideas are transformed by the activities they inspire, and who moves by stages towards a fuller understanding and control of himself and his environment. His explanations and justifications of what Marx was to call 'bourgeois property relations' and the 'bourgeois state' are different in kind from those of, say, Bentham precisely because he has a different idea of human nature and human needs, an idea tied logically to a peculiar conception of history. His reasons for approving of bourgeois property and the bourgeois state are indeed, as one might expect, much more like Marx's reasons for condemning them than they are like Bentham's arguments in their favour.

Hegel and Bentham approve, for different reasons, of the same things; whereas Hegel and Marx approve, for similar reasons, of different things. This ought, perhaps, to move us to scepticism when we are told that the conservatism of 'bourgeois' theorists, their readiness to assume that the social and political order they seek to explain will endure indefinitely, springs from their 'unhistorical' methods and their failure to grasp the 'dialectical' character of man's relations with his environment, and especially his social environment. It would be possible to construct a utilitarian case against bourgeois society, against the forms of property and authority characteristic of it, just as it would be possible to construct a case against it on the basis of Locke's ideas of natural law and natural right. Just as Marx used Hegel's ideas about man and society to condemn what Hegel approved, so one could use Bentham's ideas or Locke's to attack what they defended. Indeed, it not only could be but has been done; as, for example, by William Thompson, Bentham's socialist disciple, and by Thomas Hodgskin, who accepted Locke's account of natural right. The rejection of capitalism was utilitarian or contractualist in Britain (and even in France) long before—with Marx and others—it became Hegelian in Germany.

During the hundred years before Marx began to write, the study of social institutions and activities, or rather speculation about their origins and functions, broadened in scope and gained in depth. It ceased to be concerned almost exclusively with property, government, and law, natural and civil; and it was also less closely tied to practical issues, to attempts to justify or to condemn existing practices. It was broader and also bolder and more conscious of breaking new ground, of putting and seeking to answer new questions. Philosophers, as they were then still called, discussed more freely and imaginatively than ever before the origins of language, of marriage, of religion, of art, of morality, of every type of activity or relation that distinguishes men from other animals. They knew more history, and more also about the civilized peoples of Asia and the primitive tribes of America. It was brought home to them, as never before, how greatly men's wants, beliefs, and values differ from place to place, and how much they change over time. It was also brought home to them that language is a social product as well as a social activity, that men acquire the ideas they use to describe themselves and their environment in the process of acquiring a language, that ideas and words are not related as ends to means—that men do not invent words in order to express their thoughts but learn to think as they learn to use words. Men without language do not have the thoughts they would have if they had language, and merely lack words to communicate their thoughts; they think differently, and are incapable of the kinds of thinking that require the use of words. Finally, it was brought home to them that men, by their activities, create social situations and cultures which transform their needs, together with the passions and beliefs connected with them.

They did not therefore cease to look to men's needs, or to the wants they give rise to, to find the origins of their institutions. For where else could they hope to find them? Social institutions are products of human activity—which is only to say that they arise out of what men do to satisfy their wants, as determined by their appetites, passions, and beliefs, and the situations in which they find themselves. The fact that these institutions, in their turn, affect men's wants does not make them any the less products of activities inspired by the wants. Therefore, if we want to explain the *origins* of particular institutions, we must always look at men's wants, as well as at their situations and beliefs, at the time that the institutions came into being.

But, if we have a different purpose from this, if what we want to explain is no longer the origins of this or that institution but how it is that man comes to be a social being in a way that other animals do not, or how it is that he comes to be involved in a course of social change, then we cannot adopt the same method. We cannot look for our explanation *merely* to the needs or wants of man, or to the passions and beliefs connected with those needs.[1]

Clearly, we cannot look to the needs that man shares with other animals —the needs that are called 'biological', presumably because, unless they are satisfied, the creature that has them dies or grows ill, and the species does not endure. These biological needs do not explain how it is that man *alone* comes to be a social being with a way of life that changes from generation to generation. They are necessary conditions of his being a creature involved in a course of social change; but they are not sufficient conditions.

Marx laid at times considerable stress on man's biological needs. He did this, perhaps, because he objected to what he believed was the too exclusive concern of Hegel and other thinkers with man's moral and intellectual needs—or, as I should prefer to put it, with man's spiritual needs. Reacting against Hegel, and against others too, Marx used language which can mislead. He sometimes spoke as if he believed that the production of what satisfies the biological needs made up the greater part of human life. In fact he believed nothing of the kind. He merely wanted to remind his readers of what he thought philosophers and social theorists had been too apt to forget: that man is an animal and has needs in common with other animals, and that what he does to satisfy them profoundly

[1] In speaking of *needs* and *wants* I have not been concerned to distinguish between them. These two words are sometimes used in the same sense, and sometimes in different senses. The word *want* is the more often used of the two to refer to appetites or desires (or even instincts), and the word *need* to refer to what creatures of appetite and instinct require to keep themselves alive or healthy or to attain or maintain some condition held to be desirable for them. Such creatures can, of course, sometimes lack appetites or instincts in keeping with their needs (as, for example, a man might not be hungry though he required food to keep him alive); or can be moved by appetite or instinct to do what destroys them or does them harm. My concern, however, has been rather with the distinction between the 'natural' and the 'social', as it relates to both needs and wants, than with distinctions between needs and wants.

affects his whole manner of life. But—and this is the point—what he does to satisfy them affects him in ways in which what other animals do to satisfy their needs does not affect them; and it does so precisely because he is, in crucial respects, unlike them. If men and women did not have sexual appetites, and if their offspring did not need care and protection for many years after they were born, there would no such institution as marriage. But other animals also have sexual appetites, and their offspring also, in some cases, need to be cared for and protected for a long time. Yet other animals know nothing of marriage, though some of them are much more attached than others are to their sexual partners.

And yet, if we want to explain how it is that man alone comes to be a social being, we also cannot point to his peculiarly human needs, for they —so Marx tells us—are essentially the needs of a social being. They are needs that have no meaning outside a social environment, and therefore cannot be used to explain how it is that man, alone among animals, has such an environment.

What then must we point to if we want to explain man's social nature and his involvement in a course of social change? Clearly, we must point to his *capacities*. But capacities do not stand to behaviour as the appetites and aversions which spring from—or, perhaps I should say, which indicate—biological needs do; they do not move men to action. Nor are they prior to action in the way that an appetite or aversion is or may be. Capacities are revealed in action and developed by it. Man's basic needs, like those of other animals, are biological; but when, moved by appetite or aversion, he acts in ways that satisfy them, he reveals and develops capacities peculiar to his kind. His action is not solitary; he acts with other human beings, he collaborates and cohabits with them. But then so too do other animals. What is peculiar to man consists in the capacities revealed and developed when he acts with other men to satisfy his needs. It is because he has these capacities that his activities make a social being of him and he becomes involved in a long course of social and cultural change.

No doubt, because men have capacities peculiar to them, they also have needs and wants different in kind from those of other animals. But these peculiarly human needs and wants are effects of the activities in and through which men reveal and develop their capacities. They are effects, in the first place, of what men do to satisfy their biological appetites; though, of course, as these distinctively human wants arise, what men do to satisfy them still further develops their capacities, and creates still further needs and wants, also distinctively human. The social and cultural accretions on the biological multiply indefinitely, so that human life grows more and more complicated and yet never loses touch with its animal origins.

This distinction between biological needs and natural capacities, on the one hand, and the social and cultural, on the other, is implicit in some of Marx's arguments, as it is indeed in those of any social theorist concerned to explain how man is uniquely a being whose capacities are developed through social intercourse. It is a distinction different in kind from that between the pre-social and the social; so that to make it is not by any means to assume that there ever was a time when man was biologically what he is now but was not yet a social being. It is a distinction different in kind from, for example, the one that Rousseau makes in the *Discourse on the Origins of Inequality* between natural and social man. For the state of nature, as he describes it in that *Discourse*, really is—as Locke's state of nature is not—a condition in which there are no social relations between men.

The distinction that I have been discussing, which is implicit rather than explicit in Marx, is logically independent of the doctrine that material pro- duction determines, 'ultimately' or 'in the last resort', the other aspects of social life. This is worth noticing, if only because Marx himself and many of his disciples have failed to notice it. To hold that we cannot explain how living and working together with others of his species affects man in ways in which it does not affect other animals without attributing to him capacities which are peculiar to him and yet not products of social inter- course (though developed by it) is one thing; to hold that there are among his social activities some (namely, those that constitute 'material pro- duction') which determine in general the character of the others, is quite another. Both these assertions might be true; but I see no reason for hold- ing that if the first is true, the second must be so as well. To be sure, Marx does not make this inference, at least not explicitly; for he does not even distinguish between the two assertions. Rather, he seems at times to vacillate between the two, as if he thought them equivalent; and his disciples do likewise.

It is not easy to decide just where to draw the line between material production and the activities supposed to be in some sense determined by it. The mere craftsman is presumably engaged in material production. But what of the artist, the painter or composer, who makes a living by selling what he produces? What of the teacher who is paid to teach, or the writer who lives on his royalties? If we consider services and not goods, how do we decide which are 'material' and which are not? Or must we say that only the production of goods is to count as 'material production'? Or should we, rather, distinguish among services those that are primarily governmental or ideological from those that are not? As, for example, the deliberate making of social rules and ensuring that they are obeyed, the public and official settlement of disputes and imposing of penalties, as *political activities*, from the direction of labour, as an aspect of production? Or, to take another example, training people to conform to social standards and justifying established practices, as ideological activities, from such forms of 'material production' as the imparting of technical skills and the provision of medical services? I do not know whether this has been done, and I can imagine that it would be difficult to do satisfactorily; but it might be worth while seeing how far it could be done.

To be sure, difficult though it often is to draw the line between material production and other activities, there are many kinds of work that most people would be willing to call material production. But these kinds of work are not carried on exclusively in order to satisfy what are called *basic* needs, if by these are meant needs that must be satisfied if men and women are to keep alive and healthy and to reproduce their kind. Clothes are not produced only to keep people warm, nor food only to appease their hunger, nor houses only to provide them with shelter. Nor can we distinguish the clothes, food, and housing produced to satisfy *basic*—or, as they are sometimes called, biological—needs from those produced to satisfy other needs. The clothes that keep a man warm also mark his importance and respectability. We can, no doubt, avoid speaking of *basic* needs and speak of *material* wants instead, meaning thereby the wants satisfied by what we choose to call material production. But, even if we succeeded in making a clear distinction between that kind of production and other social activities, the wants it satisfied would still be the wants of beings who in becoming social also become rational and moral, who have standards, tastes, and preferences deeply affecting their wants, and in their turn deeply affected by activities other than material production—by government and ideology. Many of the wants satisfied by material production could just as properly be called moral or spiritual as material.

I happen to believe that the doctrine, sometimes called or miscalled *economic determinism*, will not bear criticism, and to disagree with defenders of Marx who say that he never subscribed to this doctrine, which was falsely attributed to him by disciples (including perhaps even Engels) and by critics who misunderstood him. This defence is, I think, disingenuous, and in any case is against the weight of the evidence, as I have argued elsewhere.[2] He did assert this doctrine or make statements which imply it, just as he also made statements inconsistent with it. But I am not now concerned to criticize his 'economic determinism', if that is the right word for it. I want merely to point out that he also subscribed to another doctrine, quite different from economic determinism and logically independent of it, though often confused with it; a doctrine which makes much better sense and is therefore worth extricating from the nonsense with which it is too often mixed up. The first beginnings of this doctrine go back as far as Aristotle, but Marx (inspired above all by Hegel) took it up and related it to an account of social change which, obscure though it often is, is also

[2] In *Man and Society* (Longman 1963), Volume II, chapter 5.

imaginative and illuminating. The doctrine asserts that men, as they act together to procure what satisfies their biological needs, develop capacities peculiar to their species and in so doing acquire needs different in kind from those of other animals—the needs of a being that is essentially social and progressive in a way in which they are not.

Social theorists should take care not to confuse two intellectual enterprises which are quite different: the attempt to explain the origins of particular practices or modes of feeling or thinking by reference to men's wants, beliefs, and circumstances at the time that the practices or modes appear, and the attempt to explain what it is about man which makes him uniquely a social being involved in a course of social change—that is to say, in a course of events in which his wants, practices, and beliefs change continually. The first kind of explanation, even when it is largely conjectural, points to particular needs or wants, particular beliefs and circumstances, which may or may not be widespread, and asserts that actions arising from these wants and beliefs and in these circumstances produced these practices or these modes of thinking and feeling. The second kind of explanation proceeds in another way; it does not point to anything temporally prior to the actions producing the effects to be explained, to specific wants and circumstances—even conjectural ones—which moved men to act in specific ways. It points instead to capacities revealed and developed by men's actions whenever they act together, no matter in what circumstances and no matter what their wants may be; to capacities which therefore do not stand to the actions as causes to effects. It asserts that such actions could not have such effects unless they were actions of a certain kind; namely, the kind that both develop these capacities and are exercises of them.

Let us agree, therefore, that it is a mistake to try to explain how it is that man is a social being by pointing to supposedly pre-social needs and situations; but let us also take care not to accuse Locke and others like him of making this mistake, merely because they did not distinguish between these two enterprises and therefore never took the precaution of warning their readers that they were engaged in one of them and not in the other— that they were trying to explain the origins of particular institutions and not what it is about man that makes him uniquely a social being. In their day social theorists had not yet made the distinction I now speak of, and therefore could not take this precaution. Yet we, looking back at what they did, can see that they were engaged in only the first of these enterprises; that they did not raise the question that the second enterprise attempts to answer. They did not even, as so often happens, raise it without seeing clearly what they were doing. We cannot therefore say of them that they confused these two enterprises. In particular, we cannot say it of Locke. It is not Locke who is confused here but rather those of his critics whose objections to him rest on the mistaken assumption that he was trying to explain how it was that man came to be a social being.

Not till the eighteenth century, and especially the second half of it, did social and political theorists seriously engage in the second enterprise. It was then that they set about trying to determine just what it is about man that makes him uniquely a social being involved in a course of history in which what he is and what he conceives himself to be are continually modified by what he does. But, as nearly always happens with pioneers, they did not see clearly the difference between what they were attempting and what, for example, Locke had attempted. They therefore objected to Locke that he had given inadequate answers to questions which in fact he had never put, and they claimed to have improved on his answers. They were confused where he had not been because they were raising, tentatively and obscurely, questions he had never raised and yet were continuing to put the questions he had put. Only gradually did they learn to distinguish the new questions from the old ones, and it was not until they had learnt to do this that it became clear to them that they could not answer the new questions by pointing merely to men's wants and circumstances, whether shared by them with other animals or confined to them alone.

In the eighteenth century, as never before, philosophers—who were in those days also often social theorists—liked to say of man that he is perfectible. He is perfectible as other animals are not. This idea of perfectibility was connected, in their minds, with the idea of progress and indeed was often a modification of it. When they said that man alone is perfectible part of what they meant was that he alone is capable of becoming indefinitely better than he is. But this was by no means the whole of their meaning. Perfectibility, as they spoke of it, was not wholly a moral concept. It contained in it an idea that was morally neutral.

When these philosophers said of man that he alone is perfectible they meant, among other things, that he is educable in a way in which other animals are not, though they too are to some extent learners. No doubt, unless he were educable in this way, he would not be capable of becoming indefinitely better than he is. But then, equally, unless he were educable in this way, he would not be corruptible. Man is uniquely educable in the sense that, when he acts to satisfy his needs, he acquires more than merely practical skills; he acquires a kind of understanding that other animals do not acquire. And because he acquires it, he acquires far greater and more varied practical skills than they do. He acquires the ability to make distinctions and to consider alternatives, to describe and to explain, to teach by precept and not only by example, and to record his discoveries. In acquiring all this, he acquires also those of his wants that are peculiarly human, that differ in kind from mere animal appetites and instincts. He acquires conscious tastes and preferences, and also ideas of excellence and of beauty;

he becomes a maker of moral and aesthetic decisions and judgements. If he could not make distinctions and consider alternatives, he could not be purposeful, as distinct from merely appetitive, and if he were not purposeful, freedom would mean nothing to him. But a creature having purposes and aspiring to freedom also has feelings and desires unknown to other creatures. It differs from them even in these respects because it differs from them in others.

Because man is uniquely educable, mankind are involved in a course of social and cultural change which is essentially a cumulative process. The achievements, material and cultural, of one generation are passed on to the next. Man is the heir of his ancestors in a way peculiar to his species. As Hegel was to put it, man is a 'historical' being. To him alone the past and the future are as important as the present. And this past and future are not each man's separately, beginning with his birth and ending at his death; they are also the past and the future of the communities he belongs to. Every man is involved in mankind in a way that no other animal is involved in its species.

The idea of social and cultural change, even when it assumes a growth in complexity and sophistication, and in technical skills, is logically independent of the idea of *moral* progress. Nevertheless, most of the philosophers who took up the idea and made much of it believed in moral progress. With one important exception, Rousseau. He asserted both that man is perfectible and that he is corrupted by society. Yet even Rousseau is less of an exception than he might at first sight appear, for he contrasted man corrupted by society, not only with man in his innocence untouched by social influences, but also with social man as he might be, or as he might have become, if the course of social and cultural change had been different. Man as he ought to be, for Rousseau as much as for anyone, is a being who can develop his essentially human capacities only by living and working with others of his species.

Clearly, then, it is not those among men's wants that are peculiarly human which bring them to live and work together, for these wants are themselves products of cohabitation and collaboration. They arise in men as they live and work together, and so make of this living and working forms of social intercourse. They are the wants of creatures socially related to one another; that is to say, related to one another as other animals are not, even though they too live together and quite often take action in common. Like other animals men have biological appetites which they cannot satisfy unless they come together. But, because they have capacities that other animals lack, this togetherness, this intercourse in its diverse forms, affects them as it does not affect other animals, and so becomes properly social intercourse.

To all this, two objections could be made: firstly, that other animals besides man are social, and secondly that other animals besides man are educable. These are not, I think, serious objections, but it is best perhaps to consider them for a moment before passing on to other things.

We often, and quite properly, speak of animals as forming a community or society together, and we may then have in mind something more than their spending a great deal of time in one another's company. Wolves form packs and have leaders, and we sometimes speak of this leadership as a social role. Male birds look after their females and their offspring, and the roles of males and females differ. There is admittedly a not unusual sense of the word *social* in which man is only one social animal among others. But there is another sense in which man alone is a social animal. It is the sense that Marx had in mind when he said that man is *essentially* a social being. It is also the sense we use when we speak of the social sciences, for we think of them as essentially sciences of man. There was a time when they were called moral sciences. Today the word *moral* is seldom used in so broad a sense. But we do use the word *social* in a sense which applies only to behaviour that is distinctively *human*, to behaviour of a kind peculiar to a moral being. This sense will, I hope, become clearer when we look more closely at Marx's assertion that man is *essentially* a social being.

Other animals besides man learn something as they take action to satisfy their needs. They acquire skills, and do not do instinctively all that they have to do to satisfy their needs. They not only learn, they also teach; grown animals teach their young to get food or to take cover or to fly. But animals learn only from experience, and not by reflection on experience. No doubt, they *communicate* with one another in some senses of that widely used term, but they do not describe and explain. They acquire merely practical skills. They learn how to do things without learning how things are done. In order to learn how things are done, they would have to learn how to use words (how to think conceptually), and this they do not do.

As a result of acquiring their merely practical skills, they get involved in no process of cultural change. Each generation of animals acquire the same skills as the generation before them—unless, of course, they fall into the hands of men and are specifically trained to serve human purposes. Man alone, as he acquires his practical skills, acquires skills which are more than merely practical. He alone acquires language, or the ability to think conceptually, to describe, to explain, to make theories. That is why, in taking action to satisfy his biological appetites, he acquires needs different in kind from the needs he shares with the other animals. He is educated by his own activities and by intercourse with other men, and it is this education which makes his relations with his fellows in crucial respects different from relations between other animals; which makes them *social* in a sense in which only human relations are so. And it is because he is socially related to others in just this sense that he has his peculiarly human needs.

I have been speaking of ideas that gradually transformed social theory from what it had been in the seventeenth century, in the days of Hobbes and Locke, to what it became in the nineteenth with Hegel and Marx. Or I should say, perhaps more accurately, that I have been speaking of ideas which came to the fore as political theory slowly broadened into social theory. For this broadening of political into social theory involved much more than the application of old methods and ideas to new fields; it involved making new assumptions, using new ideas, putting new questions. In other words, it involved an intellectual revolution, a new way of thinking about man and his social activities. But the men who made this revolution were not aware of the full significance of what they were doing. They did not see clearly how they differed from their predecessors. Unavoidably, in my attempt to explain their ideas, I have made them out to be simpler and less confused than they in fact were. I have made distinctions that the first users of these ideas did not make. For example, I have distinguished between two senses in which the word *perfectible* was used in Rousseau's time, a moral and a non-moral sense. But Rousseau and his contemporaries did not notice the difference between them.

From the beginning, these two ideas of perfectibility were closely connected in the minds of the writers who used them. The believer in a cumulative process of change arising out of capacities peculiar to man nearly always believed also in moral progress, either as something which must happen or as something likely to happen. But, as we now see more clearly than they did, these two beliefs need not go together. We can admit that there is a cumulative process of change, social and cultural, and yet without inconsistency deny that there must be, or even can be, indefinite *progress* in any sense of that word which implies more than just an increase in knowledge, power, and wealth. We can hold, for example, that people's ideas of what is right, good, or admirable change from phase to phase of the process, so that it only makes sense to say that there has been progress or regress during the comparatively short periods when these ideas remain pretty much unchanged. Or else we can hold that, though there are ideas of what is good and right uniquely adapted to enduring needs of social man, though there is what Engels and others have called a 'truly human morality', the increase of knowledge, wealth, and power beyond a certain point produces social conditions making it impossible for men to live by these ideas, to achieve this morality. This, put in different words from mine, was the doctrine of Rousseau. Or we can hold that, though there is a 'truly human morality' which men will achieve eventually, as knowledge, power, and wealth increase among them, they are at some stages of their movement towards it worse off than they were at earlier stages. Marx came at times close to saying this; and in any case it is implicit in his account of alienation, of its origins and its eventual overcoming.

Perfectibility, in the non-moral sense, is one of the two main themes of perhaps the most imaginative and original of Rousseau's essays in social theory, his *Discourse on the Origins of Inequality Among Men*. The other is the corruption of man by society. The first of these themes has been less noticed than the second, and the second has often been misunderstood. It is an early version of a theme repeated in the next century by Hegel and by Marx: man at odds with himself and with society, with the essentially human world in which he acquires his distinctive skills, needs, and feelings and yet is frustrated and dissatisfied. Nothing written by Rousseau has more in it of what later came to be known as Marxism than this *Discourse*, and it is therefore worth our while looking briefly at its general argument.

In it Rousseau speaks only of human activities and of their cumulative effects on the species whose activities they are. As he describes it, the course of social change consists in these activities, in the ways they change —one change leading naturally to another—and in the wants, feelings, and beliefs produced by it and which in turn affect it. In the Hegelian and Marxist idiom, what Rousseau describes is a dialectical process. Living and working together affects men as it does not affect other animals because men are *perfectible*; because they have capacities peculiar to them which ensure that they acquire ideas about themselves and their environment they could not acquire if they lived in isolation. In acquiring them they acquire also needs and passions peculiar to their species, peculiar to moral beings, and which can be satisfied, if at all, only in society. Man in the state of nature, isolated from his fellows and untouched by social intercourse, is much like the other animals. Though he has capacities they lack, he does not exercise them until he is drawn into society with other men. Indeed, he only becomes aware of having them in the process of learning to exercise them; or, in other words, in the process of becoming a social and moral being. In the state of nature, he remains essentially the same from generation to generation; but as soon as he begins to live and to work with fellows, he is caught up in a continual course of change.

Rousseau was not very clear in his mind what these capacities were, and he admitted that his account of the course of social change was conjectural. Nevertheless, we have in this *Discourse* three ideas common to him and to Marx, though Marx, influenced by Hegel, expressed them differently: the idea that the specifically human needs, those that distinguish men from the other animals, are products of men's living and working together, the idea that these needs arise only because men have capacities peculiar to their species developed in them by this togetherness, and the idea that the development of these capacities involves the creature that has them in a course of social and cultural change which is dialectical. We have only to

translate certain passages of the second *Discourse* into a German idiom of
the next century to see how much is common here to Rousseau and to
Marx.

I said a moment ago that Rousseau was not clear in his mind about
man's peculiarly human capacities. His account of them in this *Discourse* is
in some ways obscure and misleading. But about one thing he is clear.
Social man, in whom the distinctively human capacities are developed, is a
maker of choices, a deliberate initiator of change. He is purposeful and
free, as other animals are not; and his being so is involved in his being
perfectible. It is only because he has this capacity of making choices, of
forming purposes and deliberately pursuing them, a capacity which life
and work with others bring out in him, that this life and this work
involve him in a course of change which he does not control, though it
consists only of human activities. If men were not rational and purposeful,
there would be no such course of change, and yet the course, though it is
not fortuitous, though one phase of it leads on to the next, is not rationally
controlled. Here, too, we have an idea common to Rousseau and to Marx,
though Marx was to make much more of it than Rousseau ever did.

Rousseau and Marx were imaginative and perceptive rather than lucid
and rigorous thinkers, and their hold on these ideas was uncertain. Hence
the difficulty of deciding precisely what they meant by them, what conclusions they drew from them, or would have accepted if others had
drawn them. Which is not to deny, of course, that Marx, coming onto the
scene so much later than Rousseau during one of the most fertile periods
in the history of social and political theory in the West, made larger and
more varied use of these ideas than Rousseau did. Rousseau was an
innovator still very much influenced by ways of thinking that Marx discarded. I spoke earlier of two enterprises which it is important to distinguish from one another: the attempt to explain how particular modes of
behaviour and the wants and beliefs connected with them arise out of
wants, beliefs, and conditions temporally prior to them but no less social
than they are, and the attempt to explain what makes man uniquely a social
and 'progressive' being. Rousseau engaged in both these enterprises, but
he did so without seeing clearly that they are different; and this was
another source of confusion in his thinking.

He attempted something that Locke never attempted, and that Marx
dismissed as a useless enterprise; he tried to imagine what men would be
like if they were unaffected by life and work together. One reason why he
did this was that he wanted to explain what is involved in man's being a
social and perfectible creature, and he adopted for his purpose the accepted
method of his day, which was Locke's method. Just as Locke, to explain
the function of political authority in the social life of men, imagined their
condition without it, so Rousseau, to explain how they were affected by

social intercourse, imagined them without it. Man untouched by social intercourse, as Rousseau describes him, is a creature of instincts and appetites, just as the other animals are, and therefore without the ideas of the world and of himself that come with having a language. True, he is not entirely a creature of instinct; he is also, to some extent, a learner. But then so, too, are the other higher animals. But he is as yet incapable of the kinds of learning that come with the acquisition of ideas enabling him to behave, to think, and to feel in ways that are distinctively human. In other words, man, while he is still unsocial, is potentially rather than actually human, if by his humanity we mean the needs and the skills which, once he has acquired them, set him apart, in his own estimation, from all other creatures; which constitute his dignity, and to which he points to justify the claims he makes on his fellows.

If Rousseau's only purpose in describing the state of nature had been to bring out more sharply what is involved in man's being a social and a moral creature, he might have been readier than he was to admit that what he described had never existed—that men and women must always have lived in small groups, with parents looking after their children, if the species were to survive. That being so, they must, since they were per-fectible, have acquired the needs, sentiments, and skills that made social and moral beings of them. But Rousseau had another purpose beyond wanting to explain what it is for man to be social and moral; he wanted also to condemn society, as he actually found it, as the corrupter of man. This he thought he could best do—in my opinion mistakenly—by arguing that man unaffected by social intercourse would be self-sufficient, and therefore harmless to others and to himself. He tried to show that the needs and passions which move men to hurt one another and themselves are produced in them by their ceasing to be self-sufficient, by their be-coming dependent on each other in ways that make them envious, ambitious, and competitive. It was a favourite paradox with him that aggression, whether directed at others or at oneself, is an effect of weak-ness, and weakness an effect of dependence. To drive home his point he felt the need to postulate a 'natural' man who could live without his fellows. This independent being would not, he admitted, develop the capacities that distinguish man, as he actually is, from all other creatures, but at least he would escape the evils that society has brought upon the civilized. Thus it suited Rousseau, the moralist, the denouncer of civilized society, to assert that man had once lived apart from his fellows, independent and unspoilt, and had been better off then than he was now.

At least it suited him in certain moods, and it was rhetorically effective. It was also logically unnecessary as well as unrealistic and likely to mislead his readers, to cause them to misunderstand his philosophy of man and society. As Hegel and Marx (and others) were to show in the next century, there is no need to assume that man once lived apart from his fellow men to explain that he owes what sets him, in his own eyes, apart from and above other creatures to the influence of society upon him. It should have been obvious, even to Rousseau, that a species physically equipped as man is, and whose young come to maturity so slowly, simply could not survive if its members lived quite alone, except for the brief encounters of sexual intercourse. There are many species of animals that do not live alone, and there is evidence in plenty that those that do are not the least aggressive. Rousseau could have learned from Buffon, whom he venerated so greatly, more than enough to make his account of the state of nature seem absurdly unrealistic.

That account is seriously misleading because it suggests that Rousseau condemned society without qualification, when in fact he did nothing of the kind. Man cannot be independent in society; and therefore to contrast his natural independence with his social dependence, while pointing to dependence as a source of corruption, is to suggest that society is necessarily a corrupting influence. But this is not at all what Rousseau believed. On the contrary, he imagined a social and political order in which there would be an equality of dependence accepted by all, a community whose laws and practice would be recognized by everyone as substantially just, and in which therefore everyone would be free in the sense that he wished to belong to the community and wanted it to be as it was. The man who belongs to a community, and whose wants are conditioned by it, is necessarily dependent, in the sense that he cannot satisfy his wants without the help of others. He may be free or he may not be. Whether or not he is depends on whether the community is as he wants it to be, whether its laws and practices conform to his standards of justice, which they will not do (according to Rousseau) unless he takes an equal part with others in deciding what they shall be. There is a world of difference between this equal dependence, understood and willed by the rational and moral beings whom it binds together into a community (a condition that Rousseau calls 'moral freedom'), and the independence of a solitary and unreflective being unable to take stock of its situation, either to accept or reject it. Yet Rousseau contrasts both these conditions, the first as much as the second, with the human condition as he finds it in the Western societies of his own day. They are both, as he describes them, conditions of uncorrupted or (as Hegel or Marx might put it) of unalienated man; conditions of man at peace with himself and his environment, though the first is a condition of wisdom and active goodwill and the second of mere innocence. But it is the first, and not the second, that Rousseau sets up as an example to be followed; and it is of course also the first which in some ways is strikingly similar to the Marxist idea of the communist society.

Having committed himself to a belief never held by Locke, that there probably was a time when men lived in isolation from one another, Rousseau had to explain what eventually brought them together. Since he knew nothing of evolution, as Darwin or Lamarck was to explain it, he endowed pre-social man with all the inherited characteristics of *homo sapiens*, and conceived of him as already, in his isolation, equipped physiologically to become what society was to make of him. Natural man could not speak but already had the brain, jaws, and tongue needed for speech. He had no need of tools but had the brain and the hands needed to use them.

What then brought natural man into society with other men? Rousseau could not say it was his biological needs, for he assumed him to be self-sufficient. Nor could he say that it was his distinctively human needs, for these, he thought, were products of society. He could say only that it was chance. Nature must, from the first, often have proved niggardly, failing to provide men with enough to keep themselves alive; but somewhere, for some reason unknown to us, when this happened, some men, instead of just dying of hunger, got together and by their joint efforts procured for themselves the sufficiency which none of them could have procured for himself alone. In coming together and staying together, they started the process that developed their capacities, and so acquired needs different in kind from those they had had before, the needs of self-conscious social beings making on others and on themselves demands born of 'opinion' and not of mere 'nature'. The needs of 'social' man, unlike those of 'natural' man, are deeply affected by what he thinks of himself and of others, and of what they think of him; they are the needs of a being who, as Rousseau puts it in the *Discourse on Inequality*, derives his sense of what he is from the judgements that others pass on him.

Rousseau's account of the origins of society is wrong-headed in a way that Locke's account of the origins of government is not. Not, of course, because it is conjectural, for Locke's account was so too, but because it attempts to answer a question that he ought not to have put—at least not in the form he put it. Man, already in all essentials as we know him today, was until quite recently without political government. It makes sense to speculate about how he came to acquire it; and if, say, we prefer Aristotle's or Hume's account to Locke's, we can do so and yet admit that the account we prefer is as conjectural as the others. But man, already in all essentials *homo sapiens* (even if we take only his physical equipment into account and not such basic skills as speech), never has lived in isolation, and it was not reasonable, even two hundred years ago, to suppose that he had. Rousseau could have explained, as others did after him, the sense in which man is uniquely social without putting about society the question that Locke put about government.

I have not discussed Rousseau's account of man as a social being to suggest that Marx learnt anything from Rousseau directly, similar though their ideas are in crucial respects. Marx's references to Rousseau are few, and on the whole unflattering and unperceptive. It is to Hegel, the disciple of Aristotle and Kant, and not to Rousseau, that Marx owes an obvious and a large debt; though it could be argued that Hegel owed more to Rousseau than he acknowledged, and more perhaps than he knew. I have discussed Rousseau's account only to help me make some points which seemed to me important before going on to consider in detail Marx's ideas about what is essentially human about man. That he had such ideas, and that they are intimately connected both with his account of a course of social change and his belief that that course is progressive, must be evident to anyone who reads attentively even his later writings, not to speak of the *Economic and Philosophical Manuscripts, The German Ideology*, and other pieces written before he turned his mind to a detailed analysis of the capitalist economy. Marx's conception of human nature is as much central to his social theory as is Hobbes's or Hume's, though it differs in kind from theirs.

CHAPTER III

THE ESSENTIAL NATURE OF MAN (2)

Hegel and Marx Compared

No part of Marx's thought owes as much to Hegel as his conception of man. In the third of his 'Economic and Philosophical Manuscripts' Marx tells us:

The outstanding achievement of Hegel's *Phenomenology* is, first, that Hegel grasps the self-creation of man as a process . . . and that he, therefore, grasps the nature of *labour*, and conceives objective man (true, because real man) as the result of his *own labour*. The real, active orientation of man to himself as a species-being, or the affirmation of himself as a real species-being (i.e. as a human being) is only possible in so far as he really brings forth all his species-powers (which is possible only through the co-operative endeavours of mankind and as an outcome of history).[1]

This is difficult language and calls for closer scrutiny if anything is to be made of it. If I thrust this quotation at the reader before hazarding an opinion as to what Marx understood by such expressions as *self-creation*, it is not in order to bewilder him; it is rather to bring to his notice how large, by Marx's own admission, is his debt to Hegel and especially to Hegel's *Phenomenology of Spirit*. For there is nothing about man upon which Marx insists so much as that he is, in some sense in which other animals are not, 'self-creative', a product of his own activities, his own labour, and also a 'species-being' who realizes his 'species-powers' (the capacities peculiar to his kind) in the course of history by living and working with other men.

Marx also praises Hegel for understanding what it is for man to suffer *alienation*, an understanding that takes us to the root of most social and psychological ills.

The *Phenomenology* [he says] is a concealed, unclear and mystifying criticism, but in so far as it grasps the alienation of man . . . all the elements of criticism are contained in it, and are often presented and worked out in a manner which goes far beyond Hegel's point of view. The sections devoted to the 'unhappy consciousness', the 'honest consciousness', the struggle between the 'noble' and the 'base' consciousness, etc., etc., contain the critical elements (though still in an alienated form) of whole areas such as religion, the state, civil life, etc.[2]

[1] *Karl Marx: Early Writings,* transl. and ed. by T. B. Bottomore (London, 1963), pp. 202–3.
[2] Ibid., p. 202.

Hegel, so Marx tells us, understands what alienation is and how it is related to religion, the state, and other sides of social life; his understanding is vitiated, but he comes close to the root of the matter.

Marx praises Hegel for understanding, better than anyone before him, two essential and closely connected facts about man: that he is 'self-creative' and that he necessarily suffers 'alienation'. Man is the product of his own labour; he becomes properly human as a result of his own activities. He does so in the course of history. Hegel, Marx tells us, 'grasps the self-creation of man as a process'. This process, as Hegel conceives of it, is not the history of any one man; it is the history of mankind.

So, too, the alienation that Hegel speaks of in the *Phenomenology* is a historical phenomenon. It is not something that happens separately to every man during the course of his life; it is what happens to men in communities and groups at certain stages in the course of history. Hegel sees man as a product of history, developing the capacities peculiar to his kind because he is involved in a course of change which he comes gradually to understand.

Yet Hegel's conception of man forms part of a philosophy that Marx rejects. Hegel seems to have believed that nothing, or at least nothing human, is fully intelligible unless it is seen as part of a process whereby Infinite Spirit realizes itself. Reality is the self-realization of the Spirit, the unfolding of its potentialities. Men and their communities are manifestations of Spirit at what Hegel calls the levels of Self-Consciousness and Reason.

Marx objects to Hegel's speaking of Self-Consciousness in the abstract as if it were itself an entity, an Infinite Spirit, and of human activities as if they were ways in which that Spirit expresses itself. The only self-conscious, rational minds known to us are human, and they are essentially embodied minds. All our ideas about spiritual processes are ideas of activities that have their physical as well as their mental aspects. We cannot conceive of mental activities apart from the physical actions in which they are manifest. Mind or Spirit is essentially finite and essentially embodied.

If, then, like Hegel, we persist in speaking of an Infinite Spirit, we are guilty not of error so much as improper speech. The impropriety consists in our speaking of a quality or property of finite things (though there may be an infinite number of such things) as if it were itself an infinite thing. This, I take it, is the point of Marx's protest, in the third of the 'Economic and Philosophical Manuscripts', that 'self-consciousness is . . . a quality of human nature' and 'human nature is not a quality of self-consciousness'.[3] Hegel, he thinks, treats a property of man, his self-consciousness, as if it were not a property but an entity that has properties, an individual, a

---

[3] Ibid., p. 204.

subject or agent; and he treats man as if he were a property of self-consciousness. He turns things the wrong way round.

What Marx says here is only half true. Hegel does indeed speak of self-consciousness, a property of man or of the human mind, as if it were itself a mind, and he also calls it infinite. But he does not treat men (the only self-conscious beings known to us) as if they were properties of self-consciousness, or of an Infinite Spirit. Spirit, as he speaks of it, is not related to finite self-conscious beings as a thing is to its properties; for these finite beings are (according to Hegel) just as much individuals, just as much subjects and agents, as is the Spirit in which they have their being. Spirit is manifest in them, and exists as self-consciousness *only* in being so manifest. The relation between Spirit and finite self-conscious beings, as Hegel speaks of it, is difficult, perhaps impossible, to define; it is perhaps not fully intelligible. It is, I suspect, a running together of several relations, which are intelligible when taken separately but are not so when treated as one relation, in the Hegelian manner. But I must not now discuss what seems to me defective in Hegel's philosophy. My business is with Marx and not with Hegel, and at the moment I want only to point out that Hegel does not speak of men as if they were *properties* of Infinite Mind or Self-Consciousness; he speaks of them as persons, as individuals, as creatures of flesh and blood, just as Marx does and we all do. This is worth noticing; for his idea of man is in crucial ways very like Marx's—a fact we can easily lose sight of if we take Marx's criticism of him too literally.

Hegel says of Spirit that it is self-creative. Marx, though he rejects the idea of an Infinite Spirit as perverse, retains this idea of the self-creative and applies it to man—just as Hegel does—with this difference, that he insists, against Hegel, that it applies only to man and to human communities. He does not so much make new uses of the idea, different from Hegel's, as reject some of Hegel's uses of it.

Spirit, as Hegel conceives of it, is self-creative in the sense that the whole of reality consists only of the activities in and through which it reveals itself. Reality is the process of Spirit's self-revelation; it is a process by stages. Spirit is essentially active; it is what it does. The idea of inactive mind is self-contradictory; and so too is the idea of mind having a nature or character apart from its activities and determining what they are. Mind or Spirit is nothing apart from its activities, and its nature is revealed only in them, and exists only as so revealed. And yet its nature is also formed by them. Gradually it acquires self-knowledge and self-control, because it reveals itself and affirms itself through its own actions, and does so by stages. In the early stages it does not recognize itself in its actions, which therefore appear to it as external to itself; but in the later stages, enlightened by its own actions and by reflection on them, it comes to recognize them for what they are. It recognizes them as its own actions, as revelations of itself; it knows itself in them. Thus, because Spirit is what it does, and its nature is revealed only in the sum of its activities, Hegel calls it self-creative. There is (so it would appear) nothing outside it on which it depends, and there is nothing to it except what it does. It is the system of its activities; it is the process whereby it realizes itself, reveals its potentialities, and comes gradually to know itself for what it is. It is what it does and becomes aware of itself as doing. It is infinite and self-creative; and whatever is finite (including that finite self-conscious being, man) is real only in being involved in its activities.

Though Hegel spoke of an Infinite Spirit revealed in the activities of finite minds, of men and human communities, he never thought of men as passive, or as mere instruments, moved or used by something greater than themselves. The relation of the Infinite to the finite, as Hegel conceives of it, is not external or causal; the finite is not pushed around by the Infinite. On the contrary, the Infinite exists only as revealed in the *activities* of the finite. If the Whole is active, so too are the parts, and the Whole is active only in the actions of the parts; but, whereas the parts limit one another, the Whole is not limited by anything outside it. Infinite Spirit is self-creative; but so, too, in his limited way is man, the self-conscious being in whose activities Spirit is active.

Critics of Hegel have held that his account of ultimate reality is not so much false as unintelligible. Fortunately, it is not my present business to explain why they have done so, or to agree or disagree with them. I suggest only that when we say of a doctrine or a concept that it is unintelligible, we need not mean that there is no sense in it; we may mean only that the doctrine, taken as a whole, is incoherent or self-contradictory and that the concept is misapplied or is a conflation of ideas that need to be kept separate if they are to make sense. This, I suspect, is true of the Hegelian idea of the self-creative. It is a running together of ideas that make no sense in combination but do make sense when used separately on suitable occasions. Several of them are quite often applied to man or to human communities or to social change. The ideas that Hegel uses (and perhaps abuses) in constructing his account of an infinite self-creative Spirit are elaborations upon some quite familiar ways of speaking about the activities of the only self-conscious being known to him and to us, namely man. Or, at least, some of them are. For example, when we speak of a man's character, we speak of something about him revealed in his behaviour and that exists only as so revealed. Yet we also speak of his character being formed by his actions. Clearly, it makes sense to speak of a man, as it does not of a plant or an animal, as making or marring his own character. Man is self-creative in senses in which nothing else known to us is so. This is only part of the truth about him; he is only to some extent self-creative; so that, for example, it makes no sense to speak of him as literally self-created. If we want to avoid nonsense or extravagance, we must take care how we speak of this self-creativeness peculiar to man. But that we can speak of it usefully, and that in doing so we refer to something of the utmost importance about man, is, I think, undeniable.

Marx saw that this Hegelian idea of the self-creative could be usefully applied to man, just as he saw that other Hegelian ideas could be applied to social relations between men or to their social activities. Or, rather, he saw that Hegel's philosophy, especially in *The Phenomenology of Spirit*, was a philosophy of man and society claiming to be that and also something more. He saw it as a mixture of insight and absurdity or, if you like, of realism and fantasy; and he wanted to disengage the realism from the fantasy. It is not so much that he used ideas taken from Hegel for purposes different from Hegel's; it is rather that he criticized Hegel for abusing them, for not confining himself to proper uses of them.

Man, the self-creative being, is, so Marx tells us, a part and a product of nature, even though a part differing in crucial respects from the rest of nature. He is, for all his self-creativeness, a limited being dependent on a natural environment. Even his specifically human activities, those that distinguish him from everything else in nature, are physical as well as mental, and in being mental are also necessarily physical. Marx never speaks of human behaviour as Descartes and other philosophers have done, as if it consisted of two distinct orders of concatenated events, the one mental and the other physical. He never speaks of the mind as if it were something separate from the body, though causally related to it; he always takes it for granted that mental activities are inconceivable apart from the bodily behaviour in which they are manifest. The body is not the peculiar instrument of the mind, a part of the physical world possessed by it or in service to it. What is external to man is as much external to his body as to his mind; and if we can say that he has to learn to understand and control his body, we can say as much of his mind.

In rejecting the Cartesian distinction between mind and body, Marx was merely following where Hegel had led. For Hegel, as much as for Marx, the mind has no identity apart from the body and is not lodged with it as something that could conceivably exist apart from it, and man is an embodied mind active in a natural environment independent of him. Hegel differs from Marx, not in treating mind as something separate from matter, or conceivable apart from it, but in speaking of an Infinite Spirit or Mind. This Infinite Spirit, as Hegel speaks of it, is not separate from nature and the material world, for nature is a projection or manifestation of it, no less than is the course of human history.

Clearly, what is finite and dependent on an environment external to it cannot be self-creative in the same sense as what is infinite. Hegel's Infinite or all-embracing Spirit has presumably nothing external to it. It is as it is because it acts as it acts. There is nothing outside it that limits it. It does not develop its powers, or reveal its nature, by acting upon what is external to it. The material universe is no more its environment than a human body is the environment of the man or woman whose body it is; it is merely an aspect of it.

Marx rejected this conception of an all-embracing Spirit. Just as he thought it absurd to speak of the mind as if it were separate from and causally related to the body, so he thought it absurd to speak of an Infinite Spirit with nothing external to it. The activities of the only self-conscious rational beings known to us are not only as much bodily as they are mental; they are also inconceivable except in an environment external to those beings. Our ways of thinking about self-conscious and rational behaviour presuppose that this is so.

Marx saw this clearly enough. And yet, because he used a vocabulary too much like Hegel's, he never succeeded in explaining in just what sense, within just what limits, man is self-creative. Indeed, he was some-times betrayed by that vocabulary into doing what he accused Hegel of doing, into speaking of a quality or a sum of qualities or a class concept as if it were a thing. He sometimes spoke of humanity, or of man in the abstract, as if it were an actual being, a person, whose essential nature is realized in the activities of particular men; he sometimes spoke of human-ity in relation to particular men much as Hegel spoke of Spirit in relation to particular communities and persons. Also, though he insisted against Hegel that there is no all-embracing Spirit but only finite self-conscious beings active in a physical environment independent of them, he was some-times impelled by an idiom borrowed from Hegel into speaking as if external nature were somehow transformed and 'humanized' as man comes gradually to use it and understand it.

Hegel's philosophy, as no other, was a source of inspiration to Marx, deepening his understanding of both man and society; but the Hegelian vocabulary was a source of confusion and extravagance. He got entangled in it early in life and afterwards never succeeded in extricating himself from it. He learnt much from Hegel, and was right in believing him to be one of the most imaginative and original of social theorists; but unfortunately he did not *unlearn* enough.

Man, the uniquely self-creative animal, is also—as we have seen—unique in another respect; he alone is self-conscious. Or, to speak more carefully than Marx did (for psychology teaches us that there are levels of self-consciousness), man is self-conscious in ways that other animals are not. His self-consciousness and his self-creativeness are, of course, intimately connected.

The animal [says Marx] is one with its life activity. It does not distinguish the activity from itself. It is its *activity*. But man makes his life activity itself an object of his will and consciousness . . . Conscious life activity distinguishes man from the life activity of animals. Only for this reason is he a species-being. Only for this reason is his activity free activity.[4]

To insist in this way on the self-consciousness of man was nothing new among German intellectuals when Marx was a young man; for the influence of the Idealist philosophers was strong upon them. This shift of emphasis to man's *self-consciousness* from the *rationality* so much to the fore in the philosophies of the eighteenth century is significant. The older philosophers, struck by man's use of language, by his ability to think conceptually, had pointed to his unique capacity, when compared with other animals, to assess situations and to take account of the probable consequences of his actions, to adapt means to ends. Man, the thinker and contriver among animals, is uniquely adaptable and educable; he can learn from his own experience and from being taught by others, as no other animal can. Also, because he is adaptable and educable, his needs multiply as those of other animals do not. All this was as much recognized by Hume and the Utilitarians as by Hegel and the Idealists.

What is peculiar to the Idealists is the importance they attach to man's being self-conscious. Of course, self-consciousness—at the level that interests the Idealists—goes along with rationality. Unless man were able to think conceptually he would have no idea of himself as a self in an environment which includes other selves. Nevertheless, it does make a difference to a philosopher's view of man whether, when he compares him with other creatures, he is struck above all by his being rational or by his being self-conscious. The philosopher sharply aware of man's self-consciousness does not think of him so much as a creature who, because he can take stock of his situation and the possibilities open to him, undertakes to satisfy his wants in ways not open to other creatures; he sees him rather as a being who has an image of himself, false or true, and whose wants are profoundly affected by that image. Man, as Hegel and other Idealists see him, differs from the lower animals above all because he is aware of himself as a self-conscious being in regular intercourse with other beings of his own kind. Man is more than a creature whose appetites must be satisfied if he is to be healthy and contented; he is concerned for himself as a person and for others whom he recognizes as being persons like himself. He has a need peculiar to a self-conscious being: a need for self-assertion and recognition, which takes different forms in different circumstances. Man asserts himself, and is not satisfied unless he is recognized by other men for what he asserts himself to be. Man needs self-esteem, and whether or not he can have it depends on the quality of his relations with others *and with himself*.

Marx, in the passage I quoted, speaking of man and what he calls his

4 Ibid., p. 127.

life activities—meaning, presumably, the activities by which man sustains his life—is at pains to make two points: that man is both self-conscious and self-directing, and could not be either unless he were the other as well. Every animal has a life activity—that is to say, must take action to satisfy its wants; but only the animal that is aware of itself in its actions, that learns to think conceptually in the process of acting, necessarily seeks to control its actions, and in so doing to assert itself.

Marx says that man is a *species-being*, and sees a close connection between this property in man and his self-consciousness. Sometimes Marx seems to be saying that man is a species-being because he is self-conscious, and sometimes that he is self-conscious because he is a species-being. It would be a mistake, I think, to inquire which of these two assertions expresses his real belief. I doubt whether he thought of either of these things, self-consciousness and species-being, as being prior to the other; he thought of them, I suspect, as involved in one another, as but two aspects of one process; he saw man becoming self-conscious in the process of becoming a species-being.

What was it that Marx had in mind when he called man a species-being? He appears to have used the term in two senses, of which one at least is clear; for it is the sense in which Feuerbach, from whom he took the term, used it. Feuerbach, in coining the term, did no more than give a name to something that Hegel (and others) had pointed to before him. Man is a species-being in the sense that he is aware of himself as a being of a certain kind; he is conscious of his humanity, of what is common to him with other men.

Though to say of man that he is a species-being is not the same as to say that he is self-conscious, these two qualities in him, as Marx conceives of them, go necessarily together. To be self-conscious, in the sense understood by Marx, man must be able to refer to himself; he must be able to apply the word 'I', or else some proper name, to himself. He must be able to distinguish, in some way that other animals do not, between himself and what is external to him. And this he cannot do unless he can think conceptually.

Psychologists often speak of different levels of consciousness, and even of self-consciousness. They sometimes speak of a dog being self-conscious, and when they do this, they do not speak improperly. A dog may well be self-conscious in some ways in which, say, a starfish is not. In that sense of self-consciousness, a creature may be self-conscious without being able to think conceptually. I say this, not because I want to venture into spheres beyond my competence, but only to guard against misunderstanding. I do not say that whatever is self-conscious, in any usual sense of that term, is also able to think conceptually; I say only that what Hegel and Marx refer to when they speak of self-consciousness implies this ability.

In becoming self-conscious, as Hegel and Marx understand self-consciousness, man becomes aware of himself as a being to whom certain concepts apply, and aware also of other men as beings of his own kind; he becomes aware that there are other selves who are to themselves what he is to himself. Man does not first become self-conscious and then aware of other beings like himself; he becomes self-conscious as he becomes aware of others. He sees himself in others and others in him. These three processes—becoming self-conscious, becoming aware of other selves, and coming to recognize oneself as a being of a certain kind—are inseparable but distinct parts of the same process.

Marx says that 'man is a species-being . . . in the sense that he treats himself as the present, living species, as a universal and consequently free being'.[5] This does not mean literally that man takes himself to be the species he belongs to; it means rather that, in order to behave in the ways characteristic of the species he belongs to, he must recognize himself as belonging to it. A dog behaves like a dog without knowing that it is one; but a man, in order to behave in the ways that distinguish human from other animal behaviour, must know that he is a man. If we define man in terms of the behaviour peculiar to his species, we can say that a man, in order to be a man, must know that he is one; but if we define any other animal in similar terms, we cannot say this of it. Thus, what is peculiar to man is not only that he can know what sort of being he is; it is also peculiar to him that he cannot be that sort of being unless he knows that he is one. 'Man treats himself as the present, living species' means, as I interpret it, that human behaviour involves an attitude of man to himself as a member of a species—an attitude which makes it the kind of behaviour it is. If we take account, not only of Marx's few and rather cryptic references to man as a species-being, but also of how Hegel, who influenced Marx so greatly, conceived of man as a self-conscious being, this seems the most likely interpretation of this particular assertion.

So far I have discussed only one of the senses in which Marx applies the term *species-being* to man. Man, to be properly human, must know that he is man. But Marx also says, in the same context, that 'man is a species-being . . . in the sense that he makes the community . . . his object both practically and theoretically'.[6] What does he understand by man's making 'the community his object, practically and theoretically'? The immediate context does not here afford us much help in interpreting his meaning, and this time we cannot look to Feuerbach to throw light on Marx. But we can offer an interpretation which accords both with what Marx says in other places about man as essentially a social being and with what he says here about man treating himself as 'the present, living species'.

Just as man is aware of himself as a man, as a being of a certain kind, so

<hr>

[5] Ibid., p. 126.   [6] Ibid., p. 126.

he is aware of himself as a member of a community. He acts *as* a member of a community. That is to say, he is not just one of a group who behaves as he does because he belongs to it; for an animal does that. The wolf in the pack behaves differently from the lone wolf, and does so because it is in the pack. But man behaves as he does because he knows that he belongs to a community, because his idea of himself is the idea of a social being. He thinks of himself as a father, a brother, or a son; as a farmer or a tailor; he thinks of himself as socially related to others. No doubt, he sometimes has illusions about these relations; nevertheless, he not only stands in them but is aware that he does so. And he is aware of it not only when he pauses to contemplate himself in relation to others, to reflect upon his social situation, to make general statements about it; he is aware of it also in the practical business of everyday life. He is as much aware of it when he works to gain his living as when he theorizes; and thus, to use Marx's words, 'he makes the community . . . his object both *practically* and *theoretically*'. A community consists of human beings socially related to one another; and so a man who is aware of himself in his relations with others is aware of himself as a member of a community.

The peculiarity of social relations is that whoever is involved in them knows that he is so, though he may be unable to describe them correctly; he is aware of a community and of himself as having a place in it. To have this awareness, he must be self-conscious; and he must also be a species-being in the sense of the term already discussed, he must be conscious of his humanity, of what is common to him and other men. Now, according to Marx, who in this again follows Hegel, it is only in society, only as he grows into social relations with others, that man becomes conscious of his humanity. So that here too we have two things, neither of which can be treated as simply the cause or simply the effect of the other. The child, as it learns to see itself as a person among persons, becomes at the same time self-conscious and conscious of itself in relation to other self-conscious beings. Man cannot be a species-being in one of the senses defined by Marx unless he is also a species-being in the other; he cannot treat himself as the present, living species unless he makes the community his object both practically and theoretically. And he cannot do either of these things unless he is self-conscious, and cannot be self-conscious unless he does them. All this seems to me to follow necessarily, if I have not misinterpreted the two senses in which Marx uses the term a *species-being*.

Marx tells us that it is because man is a species-being that 'his activity is free activity';[7] it is as a species-being that 'he treats himself as the present, living species, as a universal and consequently free being'.[8] To be free, to be able to make choices, to take decisions and act upon them, a creature must be self-conscious; it must be aware of itself in situations in which it

---

[7] Ibid., p. 127.   [8] Ibid., p. 127.

has to take action; it must see itself as an initiator of change. To be so aware of itself, it must know itself as a self that endures, as a self involved successively in many different situations. 'Every self-consciousness,' says Hegel in *The Philosophy of Right*, 'knows itself as universal.'⁹ By this he means that every self-conscious being can distinguish itself from any particular situation in which it finds itself; it not only has wants and takes action to satisfy them but knows that it has them and that it acts. Thus, in this sense of universal, a finite self-conscious being is universal, and is so necessarily. Unless it were so, it could not have a will as distinct from mere desires and aversions. It could not be aware of itself as an enduring agent in diverse situations; it could not see itself as an initiator of change; it could not take decisions; it could not be self-directed and free. The species-being alone, the self-conscious taker of action, is universal and free.

Marx says of man that he is a social being, and sometimes even allows himself to speak of society as producing man. But, at least in his early writings, he takes care to avoid misunderstanding. For example, in the third of the 'Economic and Philosophical Manuscripts', he says 'as society itself produces man as man, so it is produced by him';¹⁰ and a few paragraphs later, 'it is above all necessary to avoid postulating society once again as an abstraction confronting the individual. The individual is the social being'.¹¹

By society producing man Marx means only that the capacities peculiar to man are developed in him by activities that are essentially social. Man learns to think, as only he can do, by acquiring a language, and language is a product of social intercourse; and the behaviour peculiar to man is the behaviour of a being that thinks as only man can do. And so we find Marx saying that 'activity' and 'mind' (meaning, presumably, what is peculiarly human about man's behaviour and mental operations) 'are social in their content as well as in their origin; they are social activity and social mind'.¹² Society consists only of men socially related to one another, of men in social intercourse. If society changes it is only because men come to behave and to feel and think differently; and so it is just as true to say that society is produced by man as to say that it produces him. These two assertions, far from contradicting one another, refer to two complementary processes: to the activities of men socially related to one another and to the effects of these activities on them. Language, for example, which is an effect of social intercourse is also a form of it; and it is a form of intercourse that deeply affects the beings who take part in it.

So far I have been discussing Marx's ideas about man's relations to himself and to other men. But Marx also spoke of man's relations to external nature, to his material environment, and to other animals. Man uses them

⁹ Hegel, *The Philosophy of Right*, transl. by T. M. Knox (Clarendon Press, Oxford, 1942), p. 23.
¹⁰ *Karl Marx: Early Writings* p. 157.   ¹¹ Ibid., p. 158.   ¹² Ibid., p. 157.

to satisfy his needs; and Marx often speaks of him as *objectifying* himself in them. To *objectify oneself* in something external is to consume or fashion or otherwise use it to satisfy a need. This, at least, is one sense in which Marx uses this expression, which sounds odd to English ears. He uses it to refer only to human activities, though other animals also consume and use (and even fashion) what is external to them to satisfy their needs. But these activities do not have the same effects on them as they do on man, and it is the effects peculiar to man (or which he takes for such) that Marx has in mind when he speaks of *objectification*.

Man, in using what is external to him to satisfy his needs, transforms both what he uses and himself. He adapts it to his uses and in so doing develops his powers. In the process of learning to use what is external to him he comes to understand it. And so it becomes an object to him in a double sense: as being there for his use and adapted to that use, and as being an object of his knowledge. Also man, as he develops his powers, becomes his own object in a double sense: as being what his activities make him, and as coming to know himself through them. He cannot know himself until he has produced concepts that he can apply to himself. Thus man objectifies himself through what is external to him; and he does so, not alone, but in society with others.

In this account of Marx's views about man's relation to external nature, I have so far attributed to Marx no opinion which social theorists today would be inclined to reject, though they might prefer to put his meaning in different words. Yet this account of mine might well seem inadequate to some of Marx's interpreters. They might, perhaps, allow that Marx did hold the views I here attribute to him, and then go on to say that these views make up the more obvious and the less original part of his theory about man's relation to external nature.

Calvez, purporting to interpret Marx, says this: 'Nature without man has no meaning [n'a pas de sens], it has no movement, it is chaos, un-differentiated and indifferent matter, and thus ultimately nothing.'[13] And later he adds: 'No doubt Marx admitted a certain absolute priority of nature in relation to man.'[14] Calvez feels no need to reconcile these two statements; he neither explains what it is that Marx recognizes when he admits the absolute priority of nature in relation to man, nor does he see anything inconsistent about Marx's position as he describes it. Thus Calvez gives no real help to the reader of Marx who is puzzled what to make of assertions that seem to him to contradict one another.

I do not deny that Marx had *more* to say about man's relation to nature than I have accounted for. But that *more* is so brief and so obscure that I cannot pretend wholly to understand it. I can say only that it seems to me

[13] Calvez, *La Pensée de Marx* (Paris, Éditions du Seuil, 1956), p. 380.
[14] Ibid., p. 381.

that Marx got himself into a muddle from which he failed to extricate himself because the influence of Hegel was too strong upon him. He learnt from Hegel that man develops his powers by being active in an environment which is transformed by what he does, and comes to know himself and his environment through his activities. He also learnt from Hegel that the concepts that man uses to explain his environment and himself are his own products, and that they change. Man transforms his environment by being active in it, and he also builds up his image of it by using concepts of his own making. At the same time, in transforming his environment, he transforms himself; he develops his powers, acquiring needs, wants, and interests he would not otherwise have. He sees nature from a point of view, and that point of view changes. And so Marx came at times close to saying that nature is a product of man, just as man is a product of nature. He spoke of the relation of man to nature in ways that are echoes of the ways in which Hegel spoke of the relation of Infinite Mind to Nature.

Mind, says Hegel, develops its essence, becomes actually what it is potentially, through its activities in a world which it first takes to be external to itself, and later comes to recognize as its own product. Man— Marx seems at times to be saying—develops his essence, becomes actually what he is potentially, through his activities in a world which begins by being external to him, and which yet, in the end, becomes somehow his world, his product. Man acts on nature, and in so doing becomes human (that is to say, develops the powers peculiar to his kind), and in the process also somehow humanizes nature. He humanizes it by adapting it to his uses and by coming to understand it from his human point of view.

This is what Marx seems to be saying in such passages as these: 'It is only when objective reality everywhere becomes for man in society . . . *human reality* . . . that all objects become for him the objectification of himself. The objects then confirm and realize his individuality, they are his own objects.'[15] Marx here refers to *all* objects, and therefore also to those that man has not fashioned to his use; they are his own, not in the sense that they are his property or are the products of his hands, but in the sense that he has understood them from his point of view. They are objects in the world of his understanding. A little further on, Marx says that 'nature, as it develops in human history . . . as it develops through industry . . . is truly anthropological nature';[16] and the context again suggests that he is speaking, not just of external objects fashioned by human labour, but of the world of which they form part. Again, in the last paragraph of the section from which these two passages are taken,

[15] 'Economic and Philosophic Manuscripts', third MS. in *Karl Marx: Early Writings*, transl. by T. B. Bottomore, p. 161.
[16] Ibid., p. 164.

Marx speaks of 'the essence of man and of nature, man as a natural being and nature as a human reality' becoming 'evident in practical life'.[17]

To some commentators on Marxism such passages as these have seemed profound and exciting. I must confess that to me they seem wrong-headed. The part of nature transformed by what men do is infinitely small compared with the other part, being only the part within reach of their activities. Nature, as a whole, is untouched by them. It is not nature that develops in human history but men's ideas about it. What is the point of saying that '*objective* reality becomes *for* man *human* reality'? What is *objective* reality before it has become *human* reality? If it consists of what man has not yet worked on to adapt it to his uses, we must say that the infinitely larger part of it never becomes human reality. And if it is reality not yet become an object of human consciousness, we must say that in becoming human reality, it is not transformed. In either case, it is absurd to say of it that it is essentially a human reality, for that is to suggest that it is what man makes of it.

No doubt, whatever is an object of consciousness, whatever is sensed or thought about, is sensed or thought about from a point of view; and the point of view of the sensor or thinker changes. All the sensing and thinking we know of is by finite beings, in particular places at particular times. Indeed, our ideas about sensing and thinking apply only to finite beings, and therefore sensing and thinking from a point of view. But even to say this is to imply that there is a world independent of the finite being that senses and thinks, a world in which that being has a place and a time. The idea of an independent or objective world is therefore implicit in the assertion that all experience is from a point of view, and that its content changes when the point of view does so. I here use the term *point of view* in the broad sense to refer to the social and cultural situation as much as to the psychosomatic constitution of the observer and his position in space and time.

Marx, when he insists that man is a natural being, seems to admit this, but he also at other times seems to deny it when he says that nature—having in mind the non-human part of it—by virtue of what man does to use and understand it, somehow becomes human. Man, as he acts in his natural environment and by so doing develops his specifically human powers, at the same time *humanizes* nature.

It is absurd to speak of man 'humanizing' nature merely because he adapts a small part of it to his purposes, and acquires an understanding of it limited by his senses and by the assumptions and concepts he makes and forms in the endeavour to explain it. For man can also explain how that understanding is limited, and why it changes from age to age: he can explain what makes human experience specifically human. He can recog-

[17] Ibid., p. 166.

nize that a creature having senses different from his own and different needs, and yet as capable as he is of making assumptions and forming concepts, would have a different image of the world. This recognition implies that there are here two different images of the same world, and therefore that there is a world independent of both images, and unaffected by either except to the extent that the creatures having the images act upon nature and change a small part of it. So, in the same way, the recognition that man's image of the world changes from age to age implies that there is a world unaffected by this changing image.

But it is not absurd to speak, as Marx does, of man educating his senses in the process of working on nature to satisfy his needs, and of his coming to have an attitude both to what he works on and to his work which is not utilitarian but aesthetic. Marx speaks of a 'sensuous appropriation of the human essence and of human life, of objective man and of human creations, by and for man', and says of this appropriation that it should not be understood 'only in the sense of possession or having'. Indeed, he makes a sharp contrast between this kind of appropriation and the kind which is private property, for he says on the same page that 'private property has made us so stupid and partial that an object is only ours when we have it, when it exists for us as capital or when it is directly eaten, drunk, worn, inhabited . . . utilized in some way'.[18] Then, a little further on, he speaks of

the complete emancipation of all the human qualities and senses . . . because these qualities and senses have become human, from the subjective as well as the objective point of view. . . . Need and enjoyment have thus lost their egoistic character and nature has lost its mere utility by the fact that its utilization has become human utilization.[19]

Thus the objectification of the human essence, both theoretically and practically, is necessary in order to humanize man's senses, and also to create the human senses corresponding to all the wealth of human and natural being.[20]

In these passages, none of them altogether clear, Marx seems to have in mind a kind of possession of himself and of nature by man which is different from using external things and exercising skills merely to satisfy wants, different too from mere understanding or the ability to explain, and different also from mere sensual enjoyment; he seems to have in mind an enjoyment which is at once creative and contemplative, and is therefore a form of self-expression. It is not egoistic because it is not a deliberate use of anything to satisfy one's own wants, it is not a setting apart of it for oneself to the exclusion of others and involves no sense of competing with others. Nature has lost its utility because it is not being used to provide the wherewithal to satisfy a need, and is not therefore a means to an end;

[18] Ibid., p. 159.   [19] Ibid., p. 160.   [20] Ibid., p. 162.

it is involved in the end, or rather in the activity which is both creative and contemplative. The use of it is directly satisfying, and is specifically human because man alone expresses himself through his use of what is external to himself. He alone is capable of 'appropriating his essence', of developing his powers and acquiring self-knowledge through his use of what is external to him. But this knowledge of the self, which is as much aesthetic appreciation as it is understanding in the intellectual sense, involves also the same kind of knowledge of the external world; for man comes to know and appreciate himself only in coming to know and appreciate what is external to him. Therefore, in coming to 'appropriate his essence', to know and appreciate himself for what he is, he comes also to possess nature in the same way. Thus, looked at from this point of view, the 'humanizing of nature', is not literally making nature human, though Marx sometimes speaks as if it were; it is rather man's coming to feel at home in a natural world which he understands intellectually and appreciates aesthetically and in which he is active in ways that satisfy him.

Man the worker, the producer of things to satisfy his wants, as he comes to understand and control his natural environment and himself, acquires the need to express himself and comes to see his activities as forms of self-expression. But the self thus expressed exists only in so far as it is expressed. So man, recognizing his activities as forms of self-expression, sees himself as self-creative. Man *the mere producer*, by his work, which involves acting on a natural environment external to him, develops his powers and educates his senses, and so becomes man the creator, and knows himself for such. The kind of enjoyment of himself and of nature, which Marx calls 'sensuous appropriation', is not passive; it is not sensuous enjoyment. It makes no sense to say of merely sensuous enjoyment that it is an 'appropriation of the human essence' by man, any more than it makes sense to say of a cat enjoying the heat coming from the fire that it is 'appropriating its feline essence'. The appropriation Marx has in mind is active and involves understanding, and yet is clearly more than mere understanding, for Marx calls it sensuous. It must be, at least to some extent, the kind of appropriation involved in aesthetic enjoyment, a kind which is both active and contemplative, self-expressive and appreciative.

Man, in coming to recognize himself as self-creative, attains his majority. He sees that, as a rational, moral, and creative being, he is the product of his own activities, of a long course of social and cultural change which consists only of what he has done and its effects upon himself. He understands himself and his environment, and no longer needs to postulate a creator external to himself. There are no purposes higher than his own in the world, and the world is the sphere in which he expresses himself and realizes his potentialities, in which he comes into his own. His place in the world satisfies him; his aspirations and ideas are in keeping with his powers; he sees that they are so and sees also that they are the achievements of his species, the outcome of man's endeavours through the ages. He is satisfied and secure in a godless world; for his idea of the world is congenial to him. So, speaking metaphorically, we might say that he is man become fully human in a humanized world.

This interpretation of Marx's meaning may seem fanciful even to people who have read his early writings carefully. The passages I have quoted in support of it are not unambiguous, even though I have selected them because they do support it. I may be mistaken, though I think I am not; and in any case, I do not pretend to have given the whole of Marx's meaning. I never find Marx more obscure than when he tries to explain how men get their ideas about the world, how the process of getting them is related to their other activities, and how it affects them. But, clearly, in these early manuscripts, he attaches great importance to what he says about the humanizing of nature, and I have tried to extract from it something which seems to me important and also in keeping with his actual words. *Man appropriates his essence, and nature is humanized.* What sense can we make of these words unless we see both in the appropriation and the humanizing a process at once intellectual and aesthetic? Certainly, no philosopher has insisted more strongly than Hegel on the artist in man, and Marx was never closer to Hegel than when he wrote the 'Economic and Philosophical Manuscripts'.

Man is a producer, a maker, in a sense in which no other animal is. As Marx puts it in an often quoted passage from the first volume of *Capital*: 'Labour is a process going on between man and nature. . . . By thus acting on the external world and changing it, he [man] at the same time changes his own nature. He develops the potentialities that slumber within him, and subjects these inner forces to his own control'.[21] The point is not merely that man the producer develops his potentialities, for other animals, though to a lesser extent, do this. They too gain skill through practice. But man, Marx tells us, 'subjects these inner forces to his own control'. That is to say, he recognizes his powers and skills for what they are and uses them deliberately to achieve his purposes. Man is his own instrument, and because he is his own instrument, he is also his own end. Because he is aware of himself as having skills and because he uses them purposefully, he is in control of himself, his own master. He not only uses his skills, he also deliberately acquires them; he makes himself the sort of person he needs to be to achieve what he wants to achieve. Because he is a maker of things in a sense in which other animals are not, he is also, as they are not, a maker of himself. The special case in which man is a maker or producer, is brought out in a few sentences which follow immediately the ones I have just quoted. 'Many a human architect is put to shame by the skill with

[21] *Capital* (Everyman edn., 1930), i. 169.

which a bee constructs her cell. But what from the very first distinguishes the most incompetent of architects from the best of bees, is that the architect has built a cell in his head before he constructs it in wax.'[22] Just as man can have the image of a cell in his head, so he can have the image of himself. In making his cell, as the bee cannot make it, he asserts himself as a maker, again as the bee cannot. He is the maker who, in making, asserts himself as a maker, at first without knowing it and later consciously.

I have tried to put a few thoughts more simply and clearly than Marx put them, and I hope that I have not attributed to him beliefs that were never his, though I am very much aware that I have not given the whole of his meaning. Marx, deeply influenced by Hegel, failed to make a number of distinctions that need to be made if it is to be clear in just what sense man is self-creative.

Hegel was struck by the extent to which knowledge is active. Merely having sensations is not knowledge. A being that has knowledge must make assumptions and use concepts to build a coherent image of a world out of what is given in sensation. Hegel went so far as to treat knowledge as an entirely creative process. But the creator cannot be any one man, for one man is only one of many and lives in a world common to him with others. So Hegel postulated an Infinite Mind which produces the world it knows, and in producing it and coming gradually to recognize it for its own product becomes actually what it is potentially. This Infinite Mind, at the level of self-consciousness, of conceptual thought and knowledge properly so called, is active in the activities of finite self-conscious beings, of men, and in their cultures and communities. Hegel's conception of reality requires that he should say that Mind produces the world that it knows. Whereas Marx's conception of it requires that he should both treat knowledge as active and also deny that the knower, who is human only and in whose activities no Infinite Mind is revealed, makes the world he knows. Now Marx did, of course, do this: he did treat knowledge as active and did deny that man, the knower, makes the world he knows. But he also sometimes spoke as Hegel did; he sometimes failed to distinguish the knower's image of the world from the world as it is.

I would not quarrel with Marx for not explaining, fully and lucidly, just what knowledge is and how it is acquired. After all, he was primarily a social theorist and not an epistemologist. Indeed, his few scattered statements about knowledge and its relation to man's other activities are so meagre and obscure as hardly to constitute anything deserving the name of theory. Marx's few excursions into epistemology, some of them little more than echoes of Hegel, are brief and uncertain, and nothing coherent can be made of them. I do not say this in criticism of Marx. In my opinion, he

22 Ibid., pp. 169–70.

not only had no theory of knowledge, he also had no need of one to make the points he wanted to make about man the producer and knower and victim of illusions. He had no need to explain just how man builds up his image of the world; he needed only to keep it firmly in mind that to speak of man's changing image of the world implies the existence of a world independent of that image.

Marx, following Hegel, had an important point to make about man in relation to his image of the world. Man's image of himself is bound up with his image of the world, and his specifically human needs and aspirations are affected by these images and in turn affect them. Self-consciousness and world-consciousness go necessarily together. A creature that has merely sensations and responds to them in ways that make for its survival has no idea either of itself as an enduring person or of its environment as a coherent whole. The satisfaction of its desires is the only satisfaction of which it is capable. But a creature that is both self-conscious and world-conscious, that cannot behave in the ways peculiar to its species unless it has some image of itself and of a world in which it is active, must, if it is to be satisfied, be satisfied with these images. Its emotions, its attitudes, its values change with them. The emotional, the moral, and the intellectual sides of its life are intimately connected.

Man's image of the world is an image of both nature and society, and his ways of thinking about nature affect his ways of thinking about society and are also affected by them. All the ideas he uses to describe and to explain what falls within the range of his experience are his own products. Like everything that is human, they too have their history. Of this Marx, the disciple of Hegel, was sharply aware. But nature is not related to man's ideas about it in quite the way that society is. No doubt, Marx was aware of this also, but he did not always take sufficient account of it. He was sometimes too much inclined to speak of man in relation to nature as it only makes sense to speak of him in relation to society, which is a human product as nature is not. In coming to understand society and in learning to control it, man recognizes it as a system of human activities in which he expresses what he is. He rises to a full understanding of what is involved in being human as he learns to understand and control his social environment. The activities that enlarge his understanding of society also enlarge his understanding of nature, but his understanding of society is related to his self-knowledge, and to his aims and the pursuit of them, in ways that his understanding of nature is not. His beliefs about society affect his behaviour in ways that his beliefs about mere nature do not; they affect his image of himself more directly. They are also more quickly changing and less easily defined.

There is an important difference between the ways in which ideas about nature and ideas about society change. As soon as either nature or society is studied systematically, there are two kinds or orders of ideas about it. There are the ideas used in ordinary communication for practical purposes and in everyday discourse about natural events or about human behaviour, and there are the ideas used in explaining these events or this behaviour systematically, in theorizing about them. These ideas overlap and also affect one another. Nevertheless, they are to a considerable extent distinct. The ideas used in everyday communication and discourse form a more or less coherent system, but most users of them have never reflected upon their uses. The people who use them may know nothing of theory, and are often illiterate. But, because these ideas do in fact form a system, and would be useless unless they did, we can say that there is implicit in the use of them an 'image' of the natural world or of society which those who use the ideas share, though they are unable to define it. A man acquires this 'image' as he learns the language of his community. Because he uses it, at this level, mostly for practical purposes, we can call this 'image', whether of the natural world or of society, a *practical image*. It is revealed in how men speak and behave when they go about the ordinary business of life.

Apart from these ordinary uses of ideas, and the 'images' implicit in them, there are other uses of ideas in the construction of theories. These uses are confined to a small number of persons, the ideas are more subject to critical analysis, and there is much more deliberate invention of ideas. There are, alongside the practical images of nature and society, other images that I shall call *theoretical*. The men who have these theoretical images also have the others; they move from thinking about natural events or human behaviour 'philosophically' or 'scientifically' to thinking about them in more ordinary (though not necessarily simpler) ways.

These images, practical and theoretical, affect one another; they change continually, and they differ, not only from society to society and from age to age, but also, quite often, from group to group in the same society, especially if it is large and complex. As we contemplate this diversity and this change, there are two things that we ought to bear in mind when we assess critically some such theory as Marxism that lays so much stress on how men's behaviour affects their ideas and is affected by them. Firstly, practical images of society are apt to differ more widely both from one type of society to another and from group to group in large and complex societies than are practical images of nature. That is to say, the assumptions about society implicit in the social behaviour of different communities or groups are more likely to differ widely than are the assumptions implicit in their ways of speaking about natural events and handling material objects. Secondly, theoretical images, both of nature and of society, differ more from society to society and within complex societies, than do practical images.

For example, our theories about the natural world, our physical and biological sciences, are very different from those of the Greeks, but the ideas we use in thinking and speaking about material objects, plants, and animals for everyday practical purposes differ much less, except to the extent that theory has affected practice. We think and speak of tables and chairs, of flowers and vegetables, of cats and dogs, much as the Greeks did. No doubt, we now have many kinds of material objects (especially tools) unknown to the Greeks, and we have discovered or bred plants and animals they never saw; we need names to apply to the many things known to us but not to them. We also need words to refer to practical skills acquired since their time. But we do not need, for our merely practical purposes, to use general ideas about material objects and their behaviour fundamentally different from theirs.

A man from a technologically primitive community brought suddenly to a modern city soon becomes familiar with the material equipment he finds there, soon learns to use it and to understand those who instruct him in its use. The instructor may even use a kind of pidgin English conceptually much poorer than the native language of the new recruit to industrial civilization. This recruit, if he learns to drive a car, must add a few words to his vocabulary, and acquire some skills perhaps more easily acquired than those of many a craftsman back home; but he need not change his basic ideas about natural phenomena.

But if he is to learn what makes a car work, if he is to understand it as its inventor or designer did, he does need to change his basic ideas; he needs to think of natural phenomena as the scientist does. It is not learning to drive a car that calls for ideas about material objects and their behaviour radically different from those involved in driving a carriage or using a plough; it is learning how a car works. And the scientist or engineer, when he takes the wheel of his car, reverts to a way of thinking about material objects and their behaviour much closer to that of the illiterate carter or ploughman than to the thinking involved in the scientific explanation of natural phenomena or in making inventions and designs which use scientific knowledge.

Man's practical image of society is much more apt to change than his practical image of nature for the simple reason that the social order changes as the natural order does not. The ways in which the Athenian of Aristotle's day needed to think of society merely to sustain effectively his diverse roles in it differ profoundly from the ways in which the modern European needs to think of it to sustain his roles. The Athenian, to be a good father or a good husband or a good citizen by our standards, would need to change his practical image of man and social behaviour far more drastically than he would need to change his practical image of material objects and their behaviour to be able to drive a car or to be a factory worker. No doubt, many, if not most, drivers of cars and factory workers have learned some modern science at school; they have a theoretical image of the natural world in important ways different from Aristotle's. But they do not need to have it merely to acquire the skills involved in being an efficient driver or factory worker.

Perhaps I have taken more time than I need have done to make a few points neglected by Marx; but I think it important to bear these points in mind when we examine critically a theory that lays such heavy emphasis on man's practical activities and their influence on his ways of thinking about himself, his relations with other men, and the natural world.

Marx did not speak of the natural world as Hegel spoke of it, but he did speak of it as he would not have done if he had not been deeply influenced by Hegel. Hegel spoke of it as if it were a projection of Infinite Mind, a manifestation of it, whereas Marx spoke of it as something of which man is, to begin with, only a part but of which he gradually takes possession, 'humanizing' it as he develops his capacities in the process of subduing it to his purposes and coming to understand it. He spoke in his early writings of man's activities in the world and of his coming to understand the world as if they were a kind of infusing of nature with the spirit of man; he spoke of man and nature being involved in a dialectical process which transforms them both, bringing out in man whatever in him is specifically human, and at the same time 'humanizing' nature. Thus, though Marx did not speak of nature in relation to man quite as Hegel spoke of it in relation to the Infinite Mind, he spoke as he would not have done had he not been so much under Hegel's influence. And he spoke absurdly.

What is more, he spoke as he had no need to speak to drive home the two points which to the social theorist are of primary importance: that man develops his peculiarly human powers in the process of collaborating with others to use external nature to satisfy his wants, and that in the same process he acquires images of the world and of himself which deeply affect, and are affected by, his wants. These two points are in themselves perfectly good, and both can be made without reference to a *dialectical* process in which nature is involved with man.

Marx followed Hegel too far. And yet, though he paid handsome tribute to Hegel, he also, in some ways, obscured his debt to him. His social theory owes more to Hegel than he himself allowed; and I speak now of those aspects of the theory that sociologists today treat with the greatest respect. Marx, in rejecting Hegel's conception of reality as Infinite Spirit in process of self-revelation, exaggerated the difference between Hegel's ideas about man and society and his own. I am not suggesting that Marx wanted to obscure his debt to Hegel but merely that, in rejecting the Hegelian conception of the Infinite Mind, he failed to notice the extent to which Hegel, in speaking of that Mind, was also speaking about man and society in ways acceptable to Marx.

Marx complains that Hegel, in the *Phenomenology*, instead of speaking realistically of man (a natural finite being), speaks of Self-Consciousness in the abstract, and describes a process in which a mere abstraction is involved, and therefore describes a formal, vacuous process. This is to suggest that Hegel, when he speaks of Self-Consciousness, is not also speaking of natural, finite beings; and the suggestion is false. Self-Consciousness, as Hegel conceives of it—or, rather, Infinite Spirit at the level of self-consciousness—is active only in the activities of finite self-conscious beings living in communities, and active in a natural environment which is external to them. It may be absurd to speak of Self-Consciousness or of Infinite Spirit in this way, as if men and their activities were manifestations of it; yet the fact remains that Hegel, when he speaks of Infinite Spirit at the level of self-consciousness, is also speaking of men and their activities, and is speaking of them as essentially social. Hegel, no less than Marx, conceives of finite, self-conscious beings developing their powers in a natural environment as they strive to satisfy their wants through activities which are social.

Hegel speaks, as it were, at two levels; he speaks, as Marx does not, of an Infinite Mind which projects a world seemingly external to it but which it later recognizes as its own projection; and he speaks also of finite self-conscious social beings active in an environment external to them, which they come to master and to know, and who thereby develop their powers.

When Hegel speaks at this level, he speaks as Marx does, and this is not the less true because he so often speaks at both levels at the same time. When he speaks of aspects of the Infinite Mind manifest in the activities of finite self-conscious, social beings, he necessarily speaks also of man and society. It is therefore misleading to say, as Marx does, that he describes a formal, vacuous process. It would be much nearer the truth to say that he talks both nonsense and sense, and that the sense he talks is often remarkably like the sense talked by Marx.

I do not say that the essentials of Marxism are all in Hegel; that we have only to get rid of what is perverse in Hegel's *Phenomenology* to be left with a sketch of historical progress which is pretty much the same as Marx's account of the course of social change. I say only that, if we bear in mind that Hegel, when he speaks of Infinite Mind at the level of Self-Consciousness, is also speaking of man and of the course of social and cultural change, we get a better idea of the extent of Marx's debt to him.

Marx has a great deal to say about the production of goods and services and its social and cultural effects, while Hegel has much less. This conspicuous difference between them has been used—not least by Marxists—to make misleading contrasts between their theories. Marx himself claimed to have turned Hegel the right way up. In his preface to the second German edition of *Capital*, he said, 'In Hegel's writings, dialectic stands on its head. You must turn it the right way up again if you want to discover the rational kernel that is hidden away within the wrappings of mystification.'[23]

It is true that, quite often, to get at 'the rational kernel' of what Hegel has to say, the reader must strip away several outer shells of nonsense. But, in this particular instance, it just is not true that to get at what Marx concedes to be sense, the reader has to *invert* what Hegel says. Hegel, when he speaks of nature as a projection of Spirit, may be talking nonsense, but he is not saying the opposite of what Marx says when he asserts that social existence determines consciousness. What Hegel calls Spirit is not what Marx calls consciousness, when he contrasts it with social existence. Social existence and consciousness, as Marx speaks of them, are both, for Hegel, essentially spiritual, for they consist of the activities of self-conscious beings. Hegel nowhere says or implies that consciousness, as Marx conceives of it, determines social existence.

Marx, when he treats material production as if it were somehow *basic* in relation to other social activities, is not speaking of the physical in relation to the mental; for all men's social activities, including material production, are both mental and physical. In rejecting Hegel's conception of Spirit Marx did not *reverse* anything that Hegel said or implied about how material production stands to law, government, morality, or philosophy, or to anything else that Marx might put into the ideological superstructure.

As a matter of fact, Hegel had more to say than most political theorists of his time about economic matters and their social, political, and cultural consequences. Which is not to say that he did not underestimate their importance. Perhaps he did; but if he did, this, I suggest, had nothing to do with his conception of reality. Marx was right in rejecting that conception, but he was not committed to doing so by his assertion that social existence determines consciousness. Whether Hegel, if he had come across this assertion, would have rejected it, I do not know. It is an obscure assertion, and he, ingenious as he was, might well have produced an interpretation of it consistent with his conception of reality. Spirit, as Hegel speaks of it, is manifest in 'practice' just as much as in 'theory'; though practice, as he conceives of it, is not confined merely to production. Yet Hegel does sometimes speak of theory in relation to practice much as Marx was to do; as, for example, in *The Philosophy of Right*, when he says that 'when philosophy paints its grey in grey, then has a shape of life grown old'.[24]

[23] *Capital*, i. 873.
[24] Preface to *The Philosophy of Right*, transl. by T. M. Knox, p. 13.

There is to be found nowhere in the writings of Marx even the most summary refutation of the idealism of Hegel, let alone a clear and concise account of the sense in which he was himself a 'materialist'. But there is to be found something perhaps more valuable: an obscure and incomplete, and yet also suggestive and at times even profound, conception of man as a creative and a social being—a conception which it would be unfair to Marx to call Hegelian, although it owes more to Hegel than to any other precursor of Marx, and more to him than Marx acknowledged.

There is indeed an important and striking difference between Hegel and Marx as social theorists—though it does not consist in Marx's standing Hegel's dialectic up the right way (or for that matter the wrong way). Hegel takes a social and cultural order as a whole and tries to interpret it pointing to features of it which he believes are of the essence of it, marking it off from other orders and 'placing' it in the course of social and cultural evolution, whereas Marx tries to distinguish some sides of social life from others, speaking of them as if they somehow 'determined' the others or as if the others 'reflected' them. He distinguishes between the 'material' and the 'ideological', or between 'social existence' and 'consciousness', or between the 'substructure' and the 'superstructure'—as Hegel never does.

Since the social orders and cultures that Hegel claims to interpret consist of the activities of self-conscious rational beings, the features he points to may well be called 'ideas' in a broad and loose sense of the term; they are needs and attitudes peculiar to such beings and cannot be explained without reference to their ways of thinking about themselves and their environment. Yet these 'ideas' do not stand to social activities (or to social relations) as causes do to effects; rather they are manifest or revealed in them. They are the needs and attitudes, the beliefs and intentions, which make them the sort of activities they are. They are not prior to the activities and do not move men to engage in them; they are inherent in them or constitutive of them. They are as much inherent in what Marx calls 'material intercourse' or 'social existence' as in the activities he calls 'ideological' or refers to as 'consciousness'.

How exactly Marx conceives of the ideological in relation to the material or substructural, or of consciousness in relation to social existence, is far from clear. Sometimes, speaking of the ideological superstructure, he speaks of it as if it consisted of activities and relations different in kind from those that constitute the material substructure, and as if the connection between them were causal. He speaks as if the 'ideological' were somehow ancillary to and supportive of the 'material', serving to maintain and justify it. Ordinarily, he does not deny (though sometimes he comes close to doing so) that the 'ideological' reacts upon the 'material', but he does speak of the interaction between them in ways which suggest that the 'ideological' is, as a causal factor, much the less important of the two. Yet such reasons as he gives to support this assertion are far from convincing.

Marx also speaks at times of the ideological in relation to the material or the substructural, and especially of consciousness in relation to social existence, as if he had in mind a connection which was more than merely causal. For example, he speaks of consciousness 'reflecting' social existence, and even of the ideological reflecting what is basic in relation to it. But just what the connection is, when it is not causal, is never satisfactorily explained. Marx does not even explain what 'consciousness' is. Does it include all forms of specifically human thinking, even the forms inherent in 'material intercourse' or in 'social existence'? If it does, then what is the point of saying that social existence 'determines' consciousness but is not 'determined' by it? Or are we to take 'consciousness' in some narrower sense? Though 'material intercourse' and 'social existence', as Marx speaks of them, may perhaps be identical, 'consciousness' and the 'ideological' are probably not so, for consciousness would seem to be the wider term of the two. Can we say, then, that it is the relation between social existence and consciousness which, as Marx sees it, is not causal or not primarily so, whereas the relation between the ideological and the material is so? Can we say that, for Marx, consciousness is an aspect of social existence, whereas the ideological is separate from the material, consisting of activities different from those that make up 'material intercourse' or 'material production'?

For a variety of reasons—some of which I discuss in later chapters—I doubt whether it is possible to extract from Marx's writings definite answers to such questions as these. Marx piles confusion upon confusion when he speaks of social existence in relation to consciousness, or of material intercourse or production in relation to the ideological. We should therefore not be surprised that he gave so misleading an account of how he differed from Hegel. It was beyond him to define his own position clearly. How then could he have distinguished it adequately from Hegel's?

And yet the differences between them are important. Not only because Marx lays so much more stress than Hegel does on the 'economic factor' but also, and above all, because he is in general so much more concerned to give causal explanations. The Hegelian philosophy of history is at bottom a series of tableaux in which a variety of social and cultural orders are interpreted as stages in a course of change which leads eventually to a fully rational order, for Hegel never makes a serious attempt to explain how out of any one such order another arises. But Marx does do this, at least when he explains in considerable detail how the capitalist system of production emerged and bourgeois society along with it.

CHAPTER IV

ALIENATION (1)

Hegel and Marx Compared

I

THEOLOGIANS, poets, and ordinary men in reflective mood have spoken of man as if he were lost in the world, or as if he were oppressed by it, or have said of him that he is his own enemy, the victim of his own actions. Man at odds with himself and man a stranger in a hostile world are themes as old as poetry and as myth. A human condition which is part of what Hegel and Marx refer to when they speak of alienation has long been familiar to the introspective who see that condition revealed in themselves. St. Augustine and Pascal have spoken of it more finely and more poignantly than Hegel and Marx were capable of doing. So, too, in his less severe, less dignified, more querulous way, has Rousseau. Yet the idea of alienation, as we find it in Hegel and Marx, we do not find in Augustine and Pascal, and we find it in Rousseau only half expressed.

For the idea of alienation is more than just the idea of a human condition—more, at least, if that condition is taken to be a mood or emotion, however intense and persistent, a 'state of the soul', something 'spiritual' in the sense of an attitude to itself and its environment possible only to a self-conscious rational being. Hegel believed that the spiritual condition of alienated man is revealed in several religions, and in none more powerfully than in Judaism and Christianity. He saw these religions not only as symptoms of alienation; he also saw in some of their dogmas and myths the condition of alienated man symbolically expressed. Theology, especially Christian theology, has taken large notice of this condition; and theology, as many social theorists and psychologists would today admit (even the religious sceptics among them) expresses some of man's deepest and most enduring feelings towards himself. The sophisticated believer differs from the sceptic, not in denying that theology does this, but in denying that man's attitude to God is really at bottom *no more* than his attitude to himself and to his personal and social predicament.

One of the earliest social theories in which the idea of alienation takes a large place is Rousseau's. I had almost said that it takes a large but invisible place; for Rousseau has no word for what Hegel refers to as *Entfremdung* or alienation. Nevertheless, he often has the idea of it very much present when he speaks of man in society; for it is an idea, essentially, not just about man or about a spiritual condition, but about man in society, man afflicted by society. If Rousseau had spoken only of a spiritual condition, he would not yet have had the idea of alienation: even though he spoke of it more eloquently, more movingly than Hegel or Marx contrived to do, for he was a great writer, as they were not. But he had an idea of man corrupted by society, and also an idea of society as the unintended and largely misunderstood effect of human activities. He had already the idea of man as the victim of society, of modes of human behaviour, of social practices and received ideas, which he does not know for what they are and is unable to control. Corruption, as Rousseau spoke of it, is more than a moral condition; it is also, and above all, a psychological and social condition. It is not just a disposition to act from evil motives; it is also the sense peculiar to man, to the rational being, that he is the victim of his environment and even of himself—of situations, needs, and even passions, which are essentially social and which he finds oppressive. The idea of alienation, though not the word, is very much present in several of Rousseau's writings, in the *Discourse on Inequality*, in parts of *Émile*, and in some of the letters in *La Nouvelle Héloïse*.

But it was from Hegel, and not from Rousseau, that Marx took the idea. We ought therefore to look at Hegel's use of it before we pass on to look at Marx's. Their ideas of it are in some ways very similar, even though Hegel's idea is closely tied to a conception of ultimate reality that Marx rejected.

We have seen that reality, as Hegel conceived of it, is Spirit in process of self-realization, becoming actually what it is potentially as it externalizes itself as a world which it takes at first to be independent of itself, though it comes eventually to recognize it as its own product. But Spirit does not produce the world in the way that a carpenter produces a table; it does not transform what exists already to make it serve purposes it did not serve before. Nor does Spirit produce the world as God, in some theologies, produces it; it does not create it *ex nihilo*, deciding beforehand what it shall be. The carpenter exists before his table, and intends to make it; and so too God, in these theologies, existed before the world and chose deliberately *that* it should be and *how* it should be. Whereas Spirit, in the philosophy of Hegel, does not exist apart from the world in which it externalizes itself, and it comes to have conscious purposes only in the process of externalizing itself. It is essentially active; it is what it does; it is the world in which it reveals what it essentially is and acquires self-knowledge.

Thus Spirit, in externalizing itself as a world, is at first not aware that it does so; for it rises to self-consciousness only in the process of externalizing itself. It rises to self-consciousness in the self-conscious finite beings in whom, at the level of reason, it is manifest. That is why it at first takes the world to be independent of it. Unless it were self-conscious (which it can be only as manifest in finite self-conscious beings and their communities and cultures), it could not have beliefs about the world; and yet, if its activities, at every stage, were fully conscious, it could not mistake the world, its own product, for something independent of it. But, unless it made this mistake, it could not be alienated; it could not feel itself to be the victim of a world that is a projection of itself not yet recognized for what it is. Thus alienation, as Hegel conceives of it, is possible only because Spirit can be, and indeed in certain of its phases must be, unconscious of some of its own activities and needs. In the Hegelian philosophy alienation is rooted in the unconscious just as surely as neuroses and psychoses are in the psychology of Freud.

Spirit, as it rises to self-consciousness, is manifest in the activities of finite self-conscious beings living in communities; that is to say, in the activities of men living in society with their fellows. It is self-conscious in their consciousness of it, in their ways of looking at the world (which world, of course, includes themselves). It therefore attains full self-knowledge only when *they* come to understand the world as it really is, when *they* acquire a philosophy that explains the world adequately.

Though in the philosophy of Hegel finite self-conscious beings (men) are only a part of the world, they are the privileged part; for it is in them that Spirit attains self-consciousness, and in their knowledge that it comes to know the world as a projection of itself. It is in them, in their activities, that Spirit comes to be fully self-realized. But finite beings have an environment which is independent of them. They really are external to one another in a world of which they are merely parts. Thus, for Hegel as for Marx, men are natural beings in a natural world which existed before they were born, a world in which they emerged.

But men have an environment which is both natural and social, and we can speak of the social part of it as their product. It is not, of course, the product of any one man or group of men, but of large numbers of men over long periods of time. Besides being a product of human activities, it consists of them—of social practices and social relations. Hegel spoke of it as the product of Spirit; it is, according to him, the part of the world in which Spirit is manifest in the activities of finite self-conscious beings, of men. It is the product of human history.

Just as Spirit projects itself as a world without being aware that it does so, though later, as it rises to self-consciousness and self-knowledge, it comes to know that world for a projection of itself, so man by his activities produces a social environment without being aware that he does so, though later, as he rises to an understanding of history and of himself, he comes to recognize that environment as the product of history, of mankind. Thus, man's coming to understand the significance of history is part of the process whereby Spirit attains self-knowledge.

Hegel not only speaks of Spirit as projecting itself as a world which it takes to be independent of it; he also speaks of it as estranged in that world. Again, because he conceives of the world as a projection of Spirit, he speaks of Spirit as estranged from itself. It is not at home in a world which is nevertheless only itself externalized; and is therefore not at home with itself, not reconciled to itself. Now, to be able to feel itself a stranger in the world, to be unreconciled to itself, Spirit must be self-conscious. But Spirit, at the level of self-consciousness, is manifest in the sentiments, beliefs, and activities of finite self-conscious beings—of men. Therefore the self-estrangement of Spirit is manifest in men, in human history.

So too, and for the same reason, is the overcoming of this self-estrangement. Spirit comes to be at home in the world, becomes reconciled to itself, when it attains self-knowledge in the knowledge of it that man has; its recognition of the world as a projection of itself consists in man's recognition that it is so. Its coming to be reconciled to itself consists in man's coming to be reconciled to the world, especially that part of the world which is the product of human history. But the product of history is the evolved human being; it is social man with his potentialities developed; it is the rational and moral being capable of self-direction—of freedom. Man, in coming to be reconciled to the world, comes to be reconciled to himself.

If we reject the Hegelian notion of a self-creative transcendent Spirit, all that remains of his account of estrangement or *alienation*—to use the word which is now the more usual English rendering of *Entfremdung*—pertains to finite self-conscious beings, to men. Alienation then becomes something purely social and human; and this is what it is for Marx.

Earlier, when I was speaking of Marx's conception of human nature, I quoted a passage from the 'Economic and Philosophical Manuscripts' in which Marx pays handsome tribute to Hegel. Marx there praises Hegel for understanding the 'self-creation of man as a process' and for conceiving of 'man . . . as the result of his own labour'. When I quoted this passage I was not yet ready to speak of estrangement or alienation, and I therefore omitted the reference to it. Let me now repair that omission.

Hegel [says Marx] grasps the self-creation of man as a process, objectification as *loss* of the object, as alienation and transcendence of this alienation . . . he therefore grasps the nature of labour, and conceives objective man . . . as the result of his own labour . . . [Man's] affirmation of himself as a real species-being (i.e. as a human being) is only possible in so far as he really brings forth all his species-powers . . . *which can only be done at first in the form of alienation.*[1]

---

[1] *Karl Marx: Early Writings*, pp. 202–3. My italics.

That is to say, Hegel grasps what seems to Marx an important truth: that man develops his powers through activities which involve alienation and the overcoming of it. Man, as he works together with other men, adapts his natural environment to his needs, and in the process of doing so produces a social environment, but he does it without knowing how he has done it. Society, which is a product of human activities, seems to man something external to him, and he feels towards it as towards a thing alien to him which has him in its power. He feels oppressed by it, though it is what he has unconsciously made it, and consists only of human activities, and is the environment in which he develops the capacities peculiar to his kind.

In developing these capacities, man increases his knowledge and self-knowledge, and therefore also his power over himself and his environment, including the social environment which is his own product. In coming to understand society as his own product, he learns to control it; he overcomes the feeling that it is a thing alien to him which has him in its power; he comes to see it as the environment in which he can live as he, with his powers developed, wants to live, in which he can affirm himself, in which he can achieve freedom; he comes to feel at home in it.

II

Though Marx praises Hegel for seeing 'labour as the essence, the self-confirming essence of man', he also complains that 'labour as Hegel understands and recognizes it is abstract and mental labour'.[2] That is to say, Hegel, though he understands that man by his activities develops the powers peculiar to his species and in the process comes to know himself for what he is, takes notice only of some of these activities. Hegel recognizes these activities as social; he understands—no one better—that the ideas men use to explain the world are products of intercourse between them, that the human being becomes self-conscious in becoming conscious of other beings like himself in a world common to him and them, that men are members of one another in the sense that how they think and feel about themselves is intimately related to how they think and feel about others and about the communities they belong to. Hegel understands, as Marx admits, that man is a species-being; and all this is involved in that understanding. To understand that man is a species-being is to understand that he is a social being; that he develops his powers and comes to be aware of himself as a man only in society with others. Marx does not accuse Hegel of forgetting that man's specifically human activities are unintelligible apart from a social and cultural context. Such an accusation would be preposterous, and could only be made by someone who had not read Hegel.

[2] Ibid., p. 203.

Marx's objection to Hegel is that, in his explanation of the course of social and cultural change, he takes account of only some of man's activities to the neglect of others. He takes account only of what Marx calls 'abstract and mental labour'; and that, Marx implies, is to take account of less than enough to explain the course of social change and its effects upon man.

What, exactly, is abstract and mental labour? All specifically human labour involves activities of the kind we call *mental*, for it is disciplined endeavour. And human endeavour, to the extent that it involves thinking, the use of concepts and words, is to that extent abstract. Anyone who, like Hegel, is concerned with what is specifically human about human behaviour cannot help but emphasize that it involves 'abstract' thinking. Since it is the peculiarity of man that he alone among animals is involved through his own actions in a course of social and cultural change which profoundly affects him, that he alone is self-creative, why should not Hegel, who was concerned precisely with this course of change and this self-creativeness, pay large attention to the mental and abstract, the specifically human aspects, of man's labour? Did not Marx himself, in *Capital*, say that 'what from the very first distinguishes the most incompetent architect from the best of bees is that the architect has built a cell in his head before he constructs it in wax . . .'?[3] What, then, is the point of his objection to Hegel? Is not the labour of the architect 'mental and abstract'? Don't the men who with their tools and their hands carry out his design take his verbal instructions? Don't they need to understand his purposes, to think his thoughts, in a way that oxen don't need to understand the ploughman who drives them? Isn't it this understanding that makes the least skilled human labour specifically human?

Marx would not deny it; it is too obvious to be denied, and he himself, as we have seen, sometimes made a point of saying it. His objection to Hegel is rather that he neglected man's practical activities, and was too much concerned with theory divorced from practice, with systematic explanations of the world and man's place in it produced ostensibly for their own sake, to satisfy mere curiosity, and with the effects of these theories on him. He paid too much attention to man the producer of theories, the seeker after truth, and too little to man the producer of the wherewithal to satisfy his material needs; he therefore also paid too little attention to the influence of practice on theory. These criticisms are not wholly unjust, though Marx too often puts them in a misleading way. They are no less and no more just than a criticism that Hegel might have made of Marx, had he lived long enough to read him, that he paid too little attention to the influence of theory on practice.

But I don't want to consider now just to what extent Hegel neglected

---

[3] *Capital*, i. 170.

practice or Marx neglected theory. I don't even want at the moment to attempt what Marx never attempted, to make a clear and useful distinction between practice and theory, between two kinds of human activity which *both* of them involve 'mental and abstract labour', and affect one another in subtle and intricate ways. I want only to compare Hegel's ideas about alienation and its causes with those of Marx. Hegel had, I think, a conception of the course of social and cultural change, and the place of alienation in it, much closer to Marx's than some of Marx's objections to him might lead one to believe. What is more, though Hegel paid less attention than Marx did to what Marxists call 'material production', he certainly did not confine his attention to man's theories about the world, to his attempts —sophisticated or otherwise—to explain his environment or to justify his purposes. He was as much concerned with man's political activities, and with the specifically human need for recognition, as he was with man's ways of thinking about himself and the world. It is, I think, more important to try to determine where Marx agreed with Hegel and where he disagreed than to consider in a general way Marx's not very clear ideas about the relations of theory to practice and his loosely put objections to Hegel's preoccupation with the mental and the abstract.

Hegel, like Marx, conceived of mankind passing from stage to stage in a historical process in which they develop fully their specifically human powers. But Hegel also conceived of them as abandoning one way of thinking and feeling about the world after another, one attitude to life after another, as they come to realize its inadequacy, until at last, enlightened by experience and past failures, they achieve a way of thought, a *Weltanschauung*, which is adequate and satisfying. It is to this aspect of Hegel's philosophy that Marx objects, not because he sees no truth in it, but because he sees it as a part of the truth inflated to look like the whole. There is indeed a movement, intellectual, moral, and aesthetic, from less to more adequate views of the world, from less to more satisfying attitudes to it, but this movement is not autonomous. To understand it, we must look at more than those parts of human life to which Hegel paid the most attention.

In the *Phenomenology* and elsewhere, Hegel sees man subject to wants peculiar to a self-conscious being, and sees him therefore as the possessor of a will. No doubt, he also sees him—this finite being in whose moods, beliefs, and behaviour Infinite Mind, at the level of self-consciousness and reason, is manifest—as a natural being with biological needs which he satisfies by consuming or otherwise using what is external to him. But of these needs, and of what man does to satisfy them, he says little, and passes quickly to what he takes to be the peculiarly human need—the need for recognition.

A self-conscious, rational being is not satisfied in the satisfaction of its biological appetites—the appetites that must be satisfied if it is to keep alive and healthy and have children. To be satisfied it must be *recognized* by other beings of its own kind; it must have its sense of its own worth confirmed by their behaviour to it. Every rational, self-conscious being makes this demand on the others, and the making of it is involved in its rise to self-consciousness. For example, the child does not first become self-conscious and then seek recognition; it seeks recognition as it grows in self-consciousness. It discovers itself—comes to have more coherent, sophisticated, and realistic ideas about itself—in the process of learning how it appears to others, of drawing the implications of their behaviour towards it, and in accepting or rejecting their ideas about it. Thus, to use the language of Marx to express Hegel's meaning, the need for recognition is an essential need of the species-being: the being that is more than a subject of desires and possesses a will, having conscious purposes which mean nothing apart from its ideas of itself as a social being.

Marx never spoke, in so many words, of an essentially human need for recognition, but he did have something very much like it in mind. He did so often, and obviously, in his early writings when he was still greatly influenced by Hegel, but he did so also, though less obviously, in his later writings. Let me give just one example from the first volume of *Capital*, where he says:

> To use an expressive phrase of the ancients: the slave is merely a vocal instrument, distinguished only as vocal from the beast as semi-vocal instrument, and from the inanimate tool as dumb instrument. But he himself is careful to let both beast and tool know that he is of a different order from them, that he is a man. He has the self-satisfaction of convincing himself that he is different by misusing the beast and damaging the tool.[4]

Man has a sense of what is due to him as a human being, as a person, and if he does not get it, is diminished in his own eyes. It matters to him that other men should recognize that he too is a man, a rational and purposeful being, and therefore not to be treated as a mere instrument; it matters to him no less than that his material wants should be satisfied. Marx, especially in his early writings but not only in them, takes almost as large notice as Hegel does of needs of this kind, of the situations in which men fail to satisfy them, and of the effects of this failure.

The idea of progress in the philosophies of both Hegel and Marx is related essentially to this kind of need. Indeed, progress, as they conceive of it, could be defined as man's coming gradually to understand needs of this kind and his learning how to satisfy them. But let me speak more cautiously. This is not the whole of their idea of progress; and in any case is expressed more clearly and developed in greater detail by Hegel than by

---

[4] *Capital*, i. 191, note.

Marx. Indeed, in the philosophy of Marx it is implicit rather than express. Nevertheless, it is bound up logically with certain aspects of that philosophy, and in particular with the idea of alienation and its eventual disappearance in the communist society.

It is said, sometimes, that Marx was a 'moral relativist', or at least that he ought to have been one. Did he not hold that the rules and standards of a society are determined by the interests of the classes that constitute it, and especially by the interests of the dominant class? And again that the class structure is determined by the mode of production? Was he not therefore committed to the opinion that, as the class structure and the interests of classes change, so too do these rules and standards? Did he not deny that there is a morality valid for all men everywhere? And if he did deny it, could he believe consistently in moral progress?

Interpreters of Marx who deny that he believed in this kind of progress do so, presumably, because they think that the belief is inconsistent with his views about the social origins of morality. I shall not consider whether or not it is consistent. I shall argue rather that there is in Marx's philosophy an idea of progress which, even if we deny that it is strictly speaking an idea of moral progress, is nevertheless different from the idea of progress as an increase in mere knowledge or power or material well-being. It is the idea of a movement towards a social order and a culture better suited than any before them to ensure that the essential needs of man, as a self-conscious and rational being, are satisfied. The values and standards of this order are not defined by Marx—or by Engels either, though in *Anti-Dühring*, he calls them the 'truly human morality'. Men will discover them as they come to understand their essential human needs and learn to satisfy them, as they learn to establish 'truly human relations' among themselves. There is thus a course of social and cultural development which is progressive, even though, at every stage of it, men have standards peculiar to that stage.

The standards of each stage are revealed in the behaviour and the attitudes which help to make it the stage it is. For example, where there are masters and slaves, and the slaves are submissive, we have a situation accepted by both masters and slaves. This acceptance is implicit in their behaviour, which is not instinctive or habitual but conventional, or guided by rules. Where social rules are generally obeyed, there are feelings other than fear, motives other than prudence, which move men to obedience. Where slavery flourishes, slaves 'know their place'. They have sentiments, and attitudes 'proper' to their station in life. And yet, so Hegel implies (and Marx too in the passage I quoted from *Capital*), they are also dissatisfied with their place, even though they do not consciously reject it. They are not dissatisfied merely because they don't get enough to eat, or are not as well clothed and provided for as they might be; they are dissatisfied because they are treated like slaves. It is not their biological needs, it is the need for recognition, or (as Marx might put it) the need to affirm themselves, which is not satisfied, even though they do not know it.

If men were not self-conscious beings in need of recognition from one another, there would be no properly social and moral relations among them; and yet these relations may be such that this need and others of the same kind are not satisfied. The rules and attitudes inherent in social relations may be incompatible with the satisfaction of such needs. Indeed, Hegel believed that in the early stages of history, this must be so. Men must learn by an experience which is necessarily painful that they have such needs and how to satisfy them. They must learn to make the demands which adequately express the needs and must create the social conditions and the culture in which the demands are met. Only beings having such needs could be moral; and yet, in the course of history, they first acquire social relations, practices, and values such that the needs are not satisfied, and only later learn to satisfy them by coming to have other relations, practices, and values.

It is implicit in this idea of progress that the self-conscious beings having needs of this kind do not, to begin with, recognize them for what they are. They become aware of them gradually over the course of history as they reflect on the behaviour the needs inspire. Thus there is for mankind, for the species, a process of self-discovery in some respects like the growth of self-knowledge in the individual. Through its dealings with others, the child comes to recognize itself as a person. It makes demands on them, not only for material things, but for attention, affection, and admiration. Some of the demands are met, others are not. The child, in making the demands, asserts itself. From time to time its demands are rejected, and it reflects on the painful experience, and so comes gradually to think of itself as having the right to make some demands and not others. In its own eyes, it becomes one person among others as it acquires ideas about how it is related to them and they to it. It acquires a sense of its own identity in the process of becoming a social and moral being, and becomes such a being by behaving as only a creature needing recognition can behave, and by reflecting on that behaviour. But there are stages in this process of maturation: the child's ideas of itself, of its relations with others, of what it can properly require or expect from them and they from it, change as it grows older, and its later ideas are products of a larger experience and a more developed ability to interpret that experience and to learn from it.

What is true of the individual is true also of mankind. The behaviour inspired by such needs as the need for recognition has effects, social, psychological, and moral, long before the creatures having the needs come to understand them and learn to satisfy them. They may understand the conscious wants or demands that arise from them, and may even be able to satisfy them, and yet not understand the needs nor satisfy them. In the course of history, one type of community after another arises in which the needs are not satisfied, though each type is an effect and an example of behaviour peculiar to beings having such needs. Each type of community has the rules and practices 'characteristic' of it, which are widely accepted while it endures. Yet the unsatisfied, the essentially human, needs (for self-affirmation or recognition) persist. Thus it is that self-conscious beings, that men, can be 'dissatisfied' at one level with the standards they accept at another.

Obviously, if they accept the standards, the 'dissatisfaction' must be unconscious. Their accepting the values of their community implies that they do not seek to destroy or alter established social relations and rules, that they are not revolutionaries or reformers. Yet they are in a condition which, though they do not see it for what it is, is frustrating to them. This sense of frustration seeks an outlet, and can find it only in illusion while they are as yet unable to challenge the conditions that produce it. One such illusion is religion. According to Hegel, men imagine a life other than real life in which they get the recognition denied them in real life; they conceive of a God who recognizes their worth, and to whom they are important for what they are, and a life after death in which they enjoy this recognition. Estranged in this world, they come to believe in another in which they will be at home.

Thus, their sense of estrangement in the social world, which is the world of their own activities in which they develop their capacities, acquire their human needs, and form their purposes, leads at first to illusion. But the unconscious or half-conscious needs which produce the illusions are not satisfied by them, and can be satisfied only in the real world in which men are active and have their being, in which their problems arise and have to be resolved. Illusion is a symptom of impotence; men put up with the shadow only while the substance is out of their reach, while they have not yet fully understood their condition and their needs.

In the Hegelian idiom, self-consciousness is self-transcending; or, as we might put it, self-conscious beings are self-critical and self-correcting. They reflect on their condition and their behaviour, learn to understand them better, and so are able to rise superior to their limitations. The needs peculiar to beings of their kind, which at first they do not recognize for what they are, move them to forms of activity frustrating to them; but in being active they develop their powers and learn gradually to know themselves, a process of learning which necessarily involves their also coming to know the social order and the culture in which they reveal what they are.

Thus men, as self-conscious beings who in being active develop their capacities, are essentially progressive, not just materially and intellectually, but also spiritually and even morally. They move forward, through alienation and the overcoming of it, towards both knowledge and self-knowledge, and therefore towards a more rational control of themselves and of the social and moral order which is the sphere of their activities. Their intellectual progress consists in their increasing understanding of the world and themselves; their spiritual and moral progress in their acquiring standards and attitudes suited to their developed powers and enabling them so to live that such needs as the need for recognition are satisfied. These forms of progress go necessarily together.

This idea of progress is much more obviously Hegelian than it is Marxist; it is much more to the fore and more elaborately presented in the *Phenomenology* and in the *Lectures on the Philosophy of History* than in anything coming from the pen of Marx. Marx had, as it were, a looser hold on it and at times made assertions incompatible with it. Nevertheless, though it is not consistent with every part of his teaching, it is implicit, I suggest, in his account of man as a 'self-creative' and 'self-affirming' being, a 'species-being' who in the course of history suffers alienation and overcomes it. Indeed, I do not see how it could be otherwise: how such a condition as alienation, in its cultural and psychological if not its merely economic aspects, could be explained except by reference to needs peculiar to a self-conscious and rational being, needs of the type of Hegel's need for recognition and Marx's need for self-affirmation.

III

According to Marx, man develops his powers as a self-conscious and rational being in the process of living with his fellow men and co-operating with them to produce the wherewithal to satisfy 'material' wants rooted in biological needs. Marx makes much more of this than Hegel does, though Hegel does not neglect it. Despite this difference between them (which has been exaggerated), it is as much implicit in Marx's account of alienation as in Hegel's, that alienation consists in, or results from, a failure to satisfy, not biological needs, but needs of a different kind: needs that might be called *cultural*, having in mind their social conditions, or *spiritual* in the Hegelian sense that they are peculiar to self-conscious and rational beings. The difference here between Hegel and Marx, as I see it, is not that Marx attaches little importance to needs that are supremely important to Hegel, the needs I have called spiritual; it is that Marx makes a point of insisting, as Hegel does not, that these needs arise out of activities directed in the first place towards satisfying biological needs. Biological needs are prior to spiritual needs and continue to exist when these other needs have arisen. It is in this sense that they and the activities whose purpose is to satisfy them are basic. But, as we shall see in a moment, man's wants as a social being cannot be divided into two categories, of which one is biological and the other cultural or spiritual; for they spring (most of them) from needs of both these kinds.

If we consider biological needs alone, there is nothing about them to explain why man should suffer alienation while other animals having similar needs do not. To be sure, biological needs are not the same in all animals; and man, no doubt, has some which are peculiar to his species, just as the frog or the ant has. The period of physical maturation lasts longer with him than it does with all but a few animals, and nature provides him with less protection against the cold and with less effective weapons. Man must work harder than other animals to keep himself and his offspring alive and healthy, to maintain his species; which is only another way of saying that, in some ways, he is physically less well equipped to survive than they are. I say *in some ways*, for he has a brain which enables him to become a *thinker*, and hands which enable him to fashion and to use tools and therefore to become a *maker*, to an extent impossible to other animals; he is therefore physically equipped to acquire skills different in kind from any they acquire.

Unless he acquired these skills, unless he were physically equipped to acquire them, he could not survive. Nevertheless, these skills, since they involve the use of reason, are different in kind from the skills of other animals, and are acquired in social intercourse. Therefore, true though it is that man, unless he were physically different from other animals (unless, for example, he had the sort of brain and the sort of limbs he does have), could not acquire his peculiarly human skills, and that he must acquire them if his species is to survive, it is also true that he acquires them through social intercourse. Or, rather, his intercourse with others of his species becomes properly social, and therefore different in kind from intercourse between other animals, as he acquires these skills. In acquiring them, he also acquires needs of a different order from those that must be satisfied if the species is to survive; he acquires needs that are not biological, even though they arise from activities that serve in the first place to satisfy biological needs. Biological needs are, therefore, primary in the sense that they come first, and that spiritual needs are born of activities that men engage in in order to satisfy them. But they are not primary in the sense of being more important to those who have them, or even in the sense that what men do to satisfy them has a greater influence on society and culture than what they do to satisfy their spiritual needs.

When I say that spiritual needs (or needs peculiar to self-conscious beings) are as much bound up with Marx's as with Hegel's conceptions of progress and alienation, I do not mean to suggest that Marx distinguished clearly between two different kinds of need. I mean rather that what he says about man as essentially a progressive being who suffers alienation and transcends it is unintelligible unless we attribute to man needs of the kind I have called spiritual; and I mean also that, when we look carefully at what Marx says about man when he speaks of him as a self-creative being subject to alienation, we see that it is above all needs of this kind that he has in mind.

That he failed to distinguish clearly between different kinds of need is, I think, shown by the loose and careless way in which he speaks of 'material wants' and of the 'material production' that satisfies them. Occasionally, he even comes close to speaking of these wants as if they were biological: for example, when he calls 'material production' the 'reproduction of life' in contexts suggesting that this 'reproduction' consists in the making or growing or getting of what preserves the species. But more often he recognizes, either in so many words or implicitly, that the wants supplied by 'material production' are as much social as they are biological, that their satisfaction 'reproduces' not just life but particular forms of social life. For example, when he says: 'Hunger is hunger, but the hunger that is satisfied with cooked meat eaten with fork and knife is a different kind of hunger from the one that devours raw meat with the aid of hands, nails and teeth.'[5] Or, again, when he says, 'Our desires and pleasures spring from society. Because they are of a social nature, they are of a relative nature.'[6]

When Marx says that human desires (or wants) are of a 'relative' nature, he means that they vary from society to society, and also (no doubt) from group to group or person to person, according to its or his place in society. But to say this is not to imply that these wants, 'relative' or changing though they are, do not spring from enduring needs; nor is it to imply that enduring needs are biological only and not also spiritual. The wants rooted in the need for food, sex, and shelter differ from society to society, but so too do the wants (the demands and aspirations) rooted in the need for self-affirmation.

Just as Marx recognizes (not always but often) that the wants satisfied by material production are not mere biological appetites but the wants of a social being, so too he recognizes (or at least implies) that the need for self-affirmation, which he thinks of as an enduring human need, differs in kind from merely biological needs. He says, for example,

> But man is not merely a natural being. He is a being for himself [i.e. he is self-conscious], and therefore a species-being; and as such has to express and authenticate himself in being as well as in thought. Consequently, human objects are not natural objects as they present themselves directly, nor is human sense, as it is immediately and objectively given, human sensibility and human objectivity. Neither objective nature nor subjective nature is directly present in a form adequate to the human being.[7]

[5] K. Marx, *A Contribution to the Critique of Political Economy*, transl. by N. Stone (Chicago, 1904), p. 267.
[6] K. Marx, *Wage Labour and Capital* (F.L.P.H. Moscow edn., 1962), p. 37.
[7] *Karl Marx: Early Writings*, transl. by Bottomore, p. 208.

Man is not merely a natural being, for he is self-conscious and strives to express and authenticate himself; that is to say, to be recognized for what he affirms himself to be. He affirms himself in 'being' as well as in 'thought': that is to say, in his whole way of living and not just in his beliefs about himself. 'Human' objects, as contrasted with 'natural' objects, are objects as they appear to man when he has developed, through social intercourse and through history, his distinctively human capacities; when by his own activities he has educated himself. External nature and his own nature must be what he makes of them in the process of educating himself by his own activities if he is to affirm himself in them to his own satisfaction. Thus man's need to affirm himself, though it is a product of social intercourse and finds expression in changing wants and changing demands in the course of history, is (once it has arisen) just as much an enduring need as are his biological needs, which also find expression in changing wants.

The needs that arise with the emergence of distinctively human qualities and skills are every bit as deep and urgent as are biological needs, and quite often take precedence over them. Unless this were so, men would not despair and kill themselves, as they sometimes do, even when they are sufficiently provided with what they need to keep themselves alive and healthy and to reproduce their kind. They must satisfy their biological needs if their species is to survive, but their spiritual needs they must satisfy to find life worth living. It is the peculiar burden of man that activities and skills necessary to his survival produce in him needs which, if they go unsatisfied, can make survival not worth while.

Thus, to explain how man comes to be alienated, and to explain how he can be a progressive being even though his values change during the course of his progress, we must point, not to his biological needs (even those peculiar to his species), but to needs he would not have unless he were self-conscious and rational. The needs peculiar to a self-conscious being, even though that being does not, to begin with, know them for what they are, are needs of the self—directed to itself as a person or to other selves as persons. For example, the need of the self to affirm or express itself, or the need to be admired or feared or taken account of by others, or the need to be loved. Though a creature can have such a need without knowing that it has it, it cannot have it without being self-conscious and conscious of other selves. Needs peculiar to self-conscious beings are needs of the type that Hegel had in mind when he spoke of the need for recognition.

Though Marx does not speak of man's need for recognition, he does speak, especially in his early writings, of his need to affirm or express or authenticate himself. The difference here between him and Hegel is, I think, little more than verbal. The behaviour that springs from what Hegel calls the need for recognition is pretty much what Marx understands by self-affirmation; it is the endeavour of a self-conscious being, inarticulate though it may be, to realize some idea of itself, an endeavour which is successful only to the extent that others by their behaviour indicate that they accept the idea. Self-affirmation, as Marx conceives of it, is a striving of the self to realize its potentialities; but these potentialities are essentially those of a social being whose idea of itself as it is or aspires to be is an idea of itself in relation to others, and whose sense of its own worth is confirmed by their respect and affection. It is ground common to Hegel and Marx (and for that matter Rousseau) that a man's attitude to himself varies with his attitude to others and their attitude to him. To be secure in his self-respect a man needs the respect of others, and will not respect them unless he can respect himself.

Marx, though he recognizes (often implicitly, but sometimes also explicitly) the crucial importance in the life of man of needs of the kind I have called spiritual, nowhere gives a clear account of them nor explains how exactly they are related to biological needs. Instead, he speaks of what he calls 'material needs' and of the production required to satisfy them, which he calls *material* production. But, clearly, the actual wants supplied by *material* production no more derive from biological than from spiritual needs. If they were merely biological in origin, we should expect them to differ only with the natural environment or with the age or sex or state of health of the persons whose wants they are. But they are the wants of social man, and therefore derive from his spiritual as much as from his biological needs. It is above all for this reason that they differ so much from society to society, from epoch to epoch, and from class to class. A woman who wants clothes to keep her warm and healthy also wants them to help her appear to others and to herself as she would like to appear. She gets her clothes partly to satisfy needs of the kind I have called spiritual. But we cannot predict what kind of clothes she will get if we know only that she gets them to satisfy a need of this kind. It is a need she has whether she is English or Chinese, though the clothes she buys to satisfy it are very different if she is English from what they would be if she were Chinese. They are different also if she is tall and dark from what they would be if she were small and fair. Clearly, the wants supplied by material production not only arise from two different kinds of needs but are also deeply affected by cultural influences which are themselves determined by other things besides these needs.

That is why we can say that the Englishman and the Chinese, or the medieval European and the modern European, are in fundamental respects alike in spite of the differences between their cultures. The likenesses we have in mind are not biological but social and moral. The Englishman and the Chinese, the medieval and the modern European, are alike in having certain needs and attitudes which are essentially those of a social and rational being, for they have no meaning outside a social context. And yet the wants and claims and manners that express them differ considerably from one country to another and one age to another—or, if you prefer, from one culture to another. That is why I have called them spiritual rather than cultural. Man is everywhere the same in respect of needs that are his only as a social being, and yet society changes continually and with it the wants and the attitudes that express these needs. All this we can say, and yet hold, quite consistently, that it is only through a long course of social and cultural change that men come to understand these needs and how to satisfy them.

I have tried to show how much Marx agreed with Hegel, even when he appeared not to do so, and have tried also to bring light into places that he left obscure and to dispel confusions of thought. It is perhaps a pity that Marx never put himself to the trouble of making clear the differences between different kinds of needs. A pity too perhaps that he spoke so readily of *material* needs without explaining the point of calling them so. His was a fertile rather than a tidy mind, and might have been less fertile had it been tidier.

Be that as it may, as we reflect on what Marx said about man as essentially a social being, we learn more than he made clear to his readers, and more perhaps than was clear to himself. We learn that in all societies men have both biological and spiritual needs, and that material production serves no more to satisfy the first kind of need than the second. It satisfies demands that spring from both kinds of need. For both kinds are equally enduring, equally basic, in the life of social man. It is the wants to which these needs give rise—or perhaps, I should say, in which they find expression in this or that society—that are transient because they are affected by manifold cultural influences. But their transience does not entail logically that there can be no progress, no movement towards a social and cultural order in which these needs are better understood and satisfied. 'But Marx', some of his admirers may say, 'must have seen this; it is all too obvious for him not to have seen it.' To which I can only reply: 'Perhaps at times he did see it, or half see it, but he also quite often spoke as he would not have done had he seen it clearly.'

IV

We have seen that Marx, while he praises Hegel for understanding that man is self-creative, 'the result of his own labour', objects to his taking account only of 'abstract and mental labour'. We have seen also that all specifically human activities, not excluding material production, involve conceptual thought, and therefore a considerable element of what can quite properly be called mental and abstract labour. What, then, did Marx have in mind when he made this objection? I have suggested that by 'mental and abstract labour' he probably meant theory as distinct from practice; that is to say, the making of systematic explanations for their own sake or in order to justify or condemn some social condition. If he did mean this, he was much less than just to Hegel, who, as we have seen, took large account of the need for recognition and of the practical activities inspired by it. The *Phenomenology* is not a tale of purely intellectual endeavour; it is also a tale of spiritual and moral progress. If it were not that also, it could not explain what alienation is and how it arises. For alienation does not arise from the kind of imperfect understanding that a more consistent or realistic explanation can correct; it is, as Hegel understands it, a relation of the self-conscious being to itself and its social environment which arises out of unconscious and unsatisfied needs peculiar to such a being. To be sure, the process of coming to recognize these needs and discovering how to satisfy them is a kind of learning. But it is a kind that does not aim at constructing systematic explanations or theories, though it involves a large exercise of reason. On the contrary, it is eminently practical, certainly not less so than the search for more efficient methods of producing wealth. The endeavour to satisfy the need for recognition includes man's political activities, of which Hegel takes large notice, not only in the *Philosophy of Right* and in the *Lectures on the Philosophy of History*, but in the *Phenomenology* as well; and it produces, or deeply affects, many of the wants that 'material production' satisfies.

It is highly misleading to say of the activities discussed by Hegel that they are 'mental and abstract', for some of them are no less practical than is material production. They are not attempts to explain the world or some part of it, or to express feelings about it, but to get satisfaction or power in it. Why then did Marx call these activities, even the practical ones among them, forms of 'mental and abstract labour'? Was this merely an aberration on his part? Or was there some point to his doing so? I suggest that there are several things that Marx may perhaps have had in mind, and which are worth discussing, whether he did or not.

When he contrasted these activities with 'material production', Marx called them all indiscriminately 'ideological'. Though this lack of discrimination can be misleading, there is nevertheless some point to applying this word to these activities. It can be argued that they are *essentially* ideological in a way that material production is not. In this respect, there are three things to be noticed about them. (That Marx noticed the third of them is beyond dispute, but he may also have noticed the other two.)

In the first place, these activities are all, even the most practical of them, even government and politics, pre-eminently verbal. They are all forms of discourse; *essentially* forms of it. They are either attempts to explain the world or some aspect of it, or they express feelings peculiar to articulate beings, or they are demands that such beings alone can make on one another. Even the practical activities inspired by the need for recognition are essentially more than mere attempts to influence the behaviour or feelings of others; they are not like the herding of cattle or the frightening away of an intruder. They involve the making of claims, which only a self-conscious creature capable of discourse could make or recognize, even though the making or the recognition of them is sometimes tacit.

Secondly, these activities are essentially activities of a self-conscious being that has some kind of self-image, however crude and inadequate, and therefore also some image of an external environment, since the two images go necessarily together. They are activities which make no sense apart from the *Weltanschauung* or view of the world of the creature whose activities they are. Whereas material production, which Marx contrasts with them as not being ideological, as not being a form of 'mental and abstract labour', is not an activity *inconceivable* apart from a *Weltanschauung* and a self-image. Other animals besides man engage in material production.

No doubt, human production, as we know it even in the simplest communities, differs greatly from the productive activities of other animals; it is not only incomparably more elaborate and regular, it also involves a good deal of planning. It is an activity of rational beings capable of discourse and it also involves discourse. Instructions are given and taken, technical skills are taught, to a large extent verbally, and there is a vast amount of theory behind production as soon as it gets at all complicated. All this, no doubt, was as obvious to Marx as it is to us. Yet production is an activity conceivable apart from verbal discourse. Indeed, in its simplest forms, it is prior to it. So, at least, Marx thought, for he seems to have believed that mankind acquire the use of ideas above all in the process of learning to work and live together in an ordered way. It is in this process that, according to him, they develop their distinctively human capacities, and conceptual thinking is such a capacity. Working with others to satisfy wants is an activity originally prior to the use of language, even though in all but its simplest forms, it involves the use of it. Whereas the activities that Marx calls ideological are essentially verbal, and they are also intimately connected with the images of itself and the world that every creature capable of using ideas necessarily has.

Thirdly, *and above all*, these activities, these forms of 'mental and abstract labour', involve, as material production does not, 'false consciousness' or illusion. At least Marx thought so, and said so in so many words. To the extent that they survive in altered forms, they will not involve it in the future, when man has fully developed his species-powers; but they do involve it now. They rest on illusion so long as they are activities of alienated man. But material production does not rest on illusion in the same way. It can, of course, indirectly foster illusion when the social relations it gives rise to are frustrating to man, but the thinking actually involved in it is not illusory—or is much less so than the thinking involved in the other social activities of alienated man. The theories stimulated by it and serving to organize, control, and improve it are the most realistic, the least distorted by man's self-image and the needs bound up with it. Or so Marx thought. At times he spoke of science as if it were closely connected with production (even referring to it as a force of production), though he did so without ever explaining just what the connection is. He appears to have believed—sometimes at least—that scientific progress is stimulated above all by production and the technical problems it gives rise to.

I have argued that the need for recognition, though by other names, is almost as much to the fore in Marx's account of man as a social being as it is in Hegel's. In his earlier writings he refers to it directly as the need for self-affirmation; and in his later writings, and more particularly in the first volume of *Capital*, it is presupposed by many of his arguments. I have tried to explain why a philosophy in which the ideas of alienation and the overcoming of it bulk large must assume the existence of some such need or needs. I want now to point to a crucial difference between the social philosophies of Hegel and Marx—a difference which has quite often been misdescribed. Similar though their conceptions are of needs peculiar to a being liable to alienation, their accounts of how these needs arise, of their social origins and effects, differ widely. While Hegel speaks at times—as, for example, in the famous dialectic of the master and the servant in the *Phenomenology*—as if social inequalities arose directly out of the struggle for recognition, the struggle to satisfy a spiritual need, Marx never does so. As he sees it, social inequalities are determined primarily by the character of material production.

It is in the *Phenomenology* that Hegel has most to say about the need for recognition and the activities in which it finds expression. If I may put his argument into my own words, and bring it down to earth by speaking only of men where he speaks in the abstract of Spirit and Consciousness, the gist of it would seem to be this: A man's sense of his own worth is confirmed to him by others when they defer to him. So every man strives to make others submissive to his will. Thus men become enemies. But they are not equally brave or resolute. The more timid among them, rather than risk death, submit to the more resolute; they defer to them without receiving deference from them; they recognize their worth without getting recognition in return. Thus some men become the superiors of others; some become masters and others servants.

From this it would seem to follow that the political community was originally the alliance of the strong, of those whose worth was recognized, against the weak who, failing to get recognition, accepted their inferiority as an enduring condition. The weak, by according recognition without insisting upon it in return, did more than just yield to those more resolute than themselves; they admitted the superiority of others over themselves, they conceded to them a right of command. The strong therefore got more than mere power; they got authority as well.

I have done less than justice to the subtlety of Hegel's account of the lordly and the servile consciousness. That account was not meant to be historical, to explain how authority and differences of social status first arose among men. Hegel's purpose, rather, was to explain a primitive kind of lordship and a primitive kind of submission as manifestations of Spirit. He wanted to reveal what they express, their significance in the lives of the beings related to one another as superiors and inferiors. Since the lordship that Hegel had in mind was primitive, we must suppose that it appeared historically before other more sophisticated forms of authority. But Hegel was not concerned to explain exactly how it arose or how it evolved into later and more developed forms; he was concerned rather to explain the 'essence' of it, what it reveals about the nature of man. It is of the essence of a self-conscious being that it should seek assurance of itself, of its worth, in the attitude to it of other such beings; that it should seek to assert itself in its relations to others and that its idea of itself should depend largely on how it appears to them.

Therefore, we must not think of these seekers after recognition as being literally in a state of nature and of authority then arising among them as some get the better of others in the struggle to achieve recognition. We must not think of the need for recognition as already active in men before they become social beings and as moving them so to behave that they become such beings. Rather, we must think of it and of the conflicts it inspires as necessary conditions of social inequality; for so much is implied by what Hegel says about these conflicts.

Marx explains social inequality differently. He does not deny that conflicts rooted in peculiarly human needs and natural differences of ability and temperament have anything to do with inequality. But he does not point to any such need or to the conflicts it gives rise to, as a primary causal factor. He insists, of course, that men are *essentially* social beings, and recognizes that they stand in social relations with one another because they have abilities and dispositions peculiar to their species developed in them by living and working together. He recognizes, further, that it is because they have these abilities and dispositions that they are self-affirming. Nevertheless, as he sees it, the hierarchical social structure does not arise because men differ in courage, resolution, or intelligence as they seek to affirm themselves. Differences of status arise out of social relations whose character is determined above all by 'material production'; that is to say, by how men procure or produce co-operatively the wherewithal to satisfy their wants.

This is not to deny that the social status of a particular individual depends largely on qualities personal to him or to his ancestors or to whoever else has contributed to his acquiring that status. Even if everyone owed his position in society, high or low, to the degree of his intelligence or courage or enterprise, it would not follow that social hierarchy arose in the first place, and took the form it did take, because men differed in these qualities. For example, to explain how some such organization as an army comes to have the structure peculiar to it, we may point to a variety of social causes rather than to differences of ability among men; and yet to explain how the particular men inside it came by their positions in it, we may take large account of these differences.

We all know (and Marx was not concerned to deny it) that personal abilities, his own or other people's, have a lot to do with determining a man's place in society. They are not the only important factor but they are one factor among others. What Marx denied—though more by implication than expressly—is that the social structure, the way in which society is divided into categories of persons having different roles, rights, and obligations, can be explained to any great extent by differences of ability. These differences do not determine that there shall be a social hierarchy, and are not even a major influence in determining what sort of hierarchy it shall be; though they may have a lot to do with determining the positions of particular individuals within the hierarchy. For example, it is not because some men are more enterprising and ruthless than others that the capitalist mode of production arises. And yet, where it does arise, the enterprising and the ruthless stand a better chance than others of becoming capitalists.

At this point I must qualify what I have said. I have been speaking of what historical materialism implies, of what follows from Marx's generalizations about the course of social change and the place of production in it. Historical materialism plays down the importance of differences in ability and other personal qualities in determining social structure and hierarchy. But this does not mean that Marx's accounts of particular social changes always do so too. Take, for example, his account in the first volume of *Capital* of what he calls 'primitive accumulation'.[8] According to this account, before there could be properly capitalist production, there had to be 'free labour'—that is to say, workers not tied to the soil or otherwise legally bound but free to sell their labour to the highest bidder—and there had also to be rich men who had accumulated resources large enough to hire this labour. This primitive accumulation, Marx tells us, plays much the same part in (bourgeois) political economy as original sin does in theology. In the economists' story, as Marx rehearses it, we have, on the

---

[8] *Capital*, i, chapter 24. Some translators render *ursprüngliche Akkumulation* by 'primary accumulation'.

one side, the chosen few of the industrious, the intelligent, and the thrifty, and on the other, the lazy scoundrels squandering their substance in riotous living. Yet Marx's own account in *Capital* of the process which produced the propertyless worker free to sell his labour and the man rich enough to buy it and put it to profitable use, makes it clear that enterprise and ruthlessness had a great deal to do with it. This process, remember, as Marx describes it, is prior to capitalism and not something made possible by it. Comparing his account of it with the account he foists upon the political economists, we see that the difference lies chiefly in their attributing the emergence of the first capitalists to estimable qualities while he attributes it to qualities less often admired.

Still, Marx did produce, as Hegel did not, a theory of social change which implies that the social structure is determined above all by the mode of production. Precisely what he meant by this and how far he held to it consistently has been much disputed, both by Marxists and critics of Marxism. Yet this difference between Hegel and Marx, whatever it amounts to, does not commit them to radically different conceptions of human nature and alienation. They both assume that men could not be socially related to one another unless they were self-conscious beings in need of recognition from each other; unless they were, in the idiom of Feuerbach, species-beings. Just as it is only as species-beings that men can be socially related, so it is only through these relations, only through social intercourse, that they develop the capacities peculiar to their species. Marx could hold this and yet—in my opinion quite consistently—develop a theory of social change which denies by implication that it is primarily differences in ability and temperament which determine what kinds of relations arise among men. Unless men were intelligent and purposeful as other animals are not, they would not be creatures who seek recognition from one another, or who govern and are governed; and yet government does not arise among them because some of them, as seekers after recognition, are more intelligent or resolute than others. It arises to meet needs and to promote interests determined by the mode of production.

So, too, though it is implicit in what Marx says about alienation, in at least some of its aspects, that only creatures having such needs as the need for recognition could suffer it, he does not explain how they come to suffer it by pointing to behaviour inspired by such needs, any more than by pointing to differences in character and ability. Though men could not suffer alienation unless they had powerful and urgent needs peculiar to their species, the situations in which they suffer it can be explained without reference to such needs; they too can be explained as effects primarily of the mode of production.

In my attempt to show how much there is that is similar in the accounts that Marx and Hegel give of alienation, I have not wanted to impugn the originality of Marx. As we shall see later, when we look more closely at the situations in which, according to Marx, man suffers alienation, and at his account of its symptoms, he had much to say that does not come from Hegel.[9]

My purpose in comparing Marx with Hegel has been to make clearer Marx's own beliefs about man and the human condition. It is easy to give too simple an account of these beliefs, to miss their subtlety. This is a mistake I have myself made in the past, and I have found that one of the best ways of avoiding it is to compare Marx's beliefs with those of the philosopher who undoubtedly had the deepest and most lasting influence on him.

This method has its dangers. Marx is an obscure and difficult writer, and never more so than in his early years when the influence of Hegel on him was strongest. There is always the temptation to make sense of what is obscure in Marx by attributing to him the ideas of Hegel. *The Phenomenology of Spirit* and *The Philosophy of Right*, the two works of Hegel from which we learn most about his conception of man as essentially a social being, are difficult books; if only because, to be able to follow their arguments, we have to get used to unfamiliar concepts. But at least they are systematic treatises. Hegel is methodical and elaborate where Marx is scattered and brief. To make something that fits together out of the fragments on man left to us by Marx we have to look for clues in the philosophy which we know influenced him most—the philosophy of Hegel. This method, I repeat, has its dangers. But what other can we use, if we are not to abandon our enterprise? If we are not to conclude that there is no coherent conception of man to be extracted from Marx's writings: even from the early writings in which, more than in the later ones, he tries to explain what sort of creature man is?

v

In discussing Marx's ideas about man and alienation, I have had much to say about Hegel but almost nothing, so far, about Feuerbach, whose *Essence of Christianity* had so deep an influence on this part of Marx's thought. In the third of his 'Economic and Philosophical Manuscripts', in a section in which he criticizes Hegel's dialectic and his general philosophy, Marx says of Feuerbach that he 'founded genuine materialism and positive science by making the social relationship of "man to man" the basic principle of his theory'.[10] The theory of which Marx is speaking is a theory about man and about religion as a part of man's life. Feuerbach, in explain-

---

[9] Marx, whose judgements were apt to be severe, was unusually generous in his estimate of Hegel; he was probably more familiar with Hegel's writings than with those of any other philosopher, and he sometimes praised them warmly.

[10] *Karl Marx: Early Writings*, p. 197.

ing man and religion, starts from the principle that man is essentially a
social being.

Now, as I have tried to explain, this principle is also Hegelian; it is
implicit in both the *Phenomenology* and the *Philosophy of Right*. Feuerbach
differs from Hegel, not in asserting the principle, but in making it, as
Marx puts it, 'the basic principle of his theory'. In other words, Feuerbach,
unlike Hegel, sees no reason to go behind the principle. He starts from it,
and does not postulate an Infinite Spirit (or anything else) to account for
the world and for man's behaviour in it. He rejects the Hegelian metaphysic. Where Hegel speaks of Self-Consciousness and Reason manifest in
the activities of finite beings, Feuerbach speaks only of men socially
related, what they do, and how they feel and think.

The really important service of Feuerbach to Marx is that he showed
him how much of Hegel's philosophy could be swallowed by a resolute
atheist unable to swallow it whole. Feuerbach, so it seems to me, says
much the same things about man as Hegel says or implies, with this big
difference, that he thinks it enough to say them, while Hegel insists that
there is more to be said, on the ground that the nature of man is fully
intelligible only if he is seen as a finite being in whose social and cultural
activities a universal Spirit is manifest. Feuerbach's conception of man is
contained in Hegel's but is not the whole of it; it is what is left of it when
the Hegelian account of the world as the projection of Spirit is abandoned.
Feuerbach rejected, before Marx did, that part of the Hegelian philosophy
which Marx found unacceptable. In rejecting it, he necessarily did more
than merely reject it. Abandoning the Hegelian conception of reality as the
self-affirmation of Spirit, he had perforce to reformulate Hegel's conception of man as essentially a social being. He had to say in simpler words
what Hegel had wrapped up in metaphysics.

No moderately perceptive reader of Hegel could fail to notice that he,
as much as Feuerbach and Marx after him, saw a man as a being whose
peculiar capacities are developed only in intercourse with his fellows. Yet
Hegel makes this assertion about man in the course of explaining how
Spirit, at the level of Self-Consciousness, Will, and Reason, is manifest
necessarily in communities of finite selves. Many of his deepest, his most
suggestive, utterances about man are, or seem to be, also utterances about
an Infinite, and therefore more-than-human, Spirit, even though they refer
to activities of that Spirit manifest in the behaviour and sentiments of
social man, and existing only as so manifest. If then these utterances about
man are to be separated from what Marx and Feuerbach found unacceptable in the philosophy of Hegel, it cannot be done by the simple process of
endorsing some of Hegel's statements and rejecting others. The operation
is more difficult than that. Hegel's conception of man as essentially a social
being, if it is to be divorced from his conception of Spirit, must be

translated into an idiom not his own. The ideas salvaged from the Hegelian philosophy must be put differently from the way that Hegel put them.

Thus Feuerbach was important to Marx, not only as someone who preceded him in rejecting Hegel's conception of Spirit while retaining some of his most suggestive ideas about man in society, and about the place of religion in the social life of man; he was important to him also as a translator of Hegelian ideas into a different and more acceptable idiom.

Hegel's conception of man as a social being is in fact richer by far than Feuerbach's, as Marx and Engels both recognized. But Hegel does not express himself as simply as Feuerbach does. As, for example, where Feuerbach says: 'Only through his fellows does man become clear to himself and self-conscious; but only when I am clear to myself does the world become clear to me. A man existing absolutely alone would lose himself without any sense of his individuality in the ocean of Nature; he would neither comprehend himself as man nor Nature as Nature.'[11] Or again: 'Only where man communicates with man, only in speech, a social act, awakes reason. . . . Thought originally demands two. It is not until man has reached an advanced stage of culture that he can double himself, so as to play the part of another with himself.'[12]

The idea that man, in his religion, expresses both his sense of what he potentially is, and his feeling that he has not yet become what he has it in him to be, and does so by projecting an ideal image of a Higher Being external to himself; this idea is as much Hegel's as Feuerbach's. But it is not put as boldly, as simply, by Hegel as by Feuerbach, as, for example, when Feuerbach says: 'religion is man's earliest . . . form of self-knowledge. . . . Man first of all sees his nature as if out of himself, before he finds it in himself'.[13] Or again, 'the belief in God is nothing but the belief in human dignity'.[14]

But why, we may ask, does the belief in human dignity take this form of a belief in an external Being, infinitely superior to man? Because, so we are told, man feels that he is not yet what he aspires to be. As Feuerbach puts it: 'In religion man frees himself from the limits of life; he here lets fall what oppresses him, obstructs him, affects him repulsively; God is the self-consciousness of man freed from all discordant elements; man feels himself free, happy, blessed in his religion, because he only here lives the life of genius, and keeps holiday.'[15] Or again, 'all the attributes which make God God, are attributes of the species—attributes which in the individual are limited, but the limits of which are abolished in the essence of the species, and even in its existence, in so far as it has its complete existence only in all men taken together. . . . The history of mankind con-

---

[11] Feuerbach, *The Essence of Christianity*, transl. by Marian Evans (Kegan Paul, London, 1893), p. 32.

[12] Ibid., p. 83.   [13] Ibid., p. 13.   [14] Ibid., p. 105.   [15] Ibid., p. 98.

sists of nothing else than a continuous and progressive conquest of limits . . .'.[16] That religion expresses the aspirations of a frustrated being not yet able to realize its aspirations, and is therefore a myth which both exalts that being and expresses its sense of its own inadequacy: so much is said boldly and simply by Feuerbach. Just as boldly, just as simply, the conclusion is drawn that religion will disappear together with the need for it, as man gains in self-knowledge and self-confidence.

Marx both acknowledged a debt to Feuerbach and compared him unfavourably with Hegel. In a letter to J. B. Schweitzer, he wrote: '. . . compared with Hegel, Feuerbach is extremely poor. All the same he was epoch-making [coming] after Hegel because he laid stress on certain points which were disagreeable to the Christian consciousness but important for the progress of criticism and which Hegel left in semi-mystical obscurity.'[17] Thus Feuerbach's merits, in the eyes of Marx—as indeed in the eyes of many readers of *The Essence of Christianity*—are mostly negative. He adds little of his own to what Hegel had said before him; rather, he extricates some of Hegel's more suggestive ideas about man and religion from the Hegelian metaphysic in which they are immersed. His conception of man is poorer than Hegel's; he takes account of fewer aspects of human life and speaks of them less perceptively. Though he says, again and again, what Hegel more often implies than says—that man is essentially a social being—he takes almost no notice of social conditions, how they arise, how they differ, and how they affect the human beings involved in them. He takes much less notice of them than Hegel does. Speaking of Feuerbach in *The German Ideology*, Marx and Engels say:

because he still . . . conceives of men, not in their given social connection, not under their existing conditions of life, which have made them what they are, he never arrives at really existing active man, but stops at the abstraction 'man', and gets no further than recognizing 'the true, individual, corporeal man' emotionally, i.e. he knows no other 'human relationships' of man to man 'than love and friendship, and even then idealized'.[18]

Though Feuerbach speaks only of man and rejects the Hegelian conception of an all-embracing Spirit, he quite lacks Hegel's sense of history. Only in the most general way does he recognize that man is essentially progressive and social. The ties between men that he takes account of are emotional rather than social and cultural; whereas Hegel, in the *Philosophy of Right*, considers in detail a coherent and highly complicated social and political structure as well as the states of mind of the individuals involved in it, and in the *Phenomenology* offers a subtle, imaginative, and sometimes

---

[16] Ibid., p. 152.

[17] Printed in Marx's *The Poverty of Philosophy* (F.L.P.H. edn., Moscow, n.d.), p. 37.

[18] Marx and Engels, *The German Ideology*, R. Pascal's edn. (International Publishers, New York, 1947), p. 37.

original account of different types of community and culture and of the beliefs and attitudes characteristic of them. The historian, the sociologist, and even the psychologist have incomparably more to learn from Hegel than from Feuerbach.

The Essence of Christianity, seen in historical perspective, is not an impressive book; it is derivative, repetitious, and rhetorical. But those who read it, as Marx did, soon after it was published, found it exciting. They could not find it empty, for it had in it some good ideas taken from Hegel; and yet it was also an act of emancipation from Hegel.

CHAPTER V

ALIENATION (2)

The Condition as Marx Describes it

I

IN the philosophy of Hegel there are two ideas that need to be distinguished because they refer to closely connected things which are easily confounded. These two ideas are *externalization* and *estrangement* or *alienation* (*Entäusserung* and *Entfremdung*). Alienation differs from externalization, though it arises necessarily in the course of it. So, too, in Marx's account of man and society, there are two similar ideas, closely related and yet distinct: *objectification* and *alienation*.

Objectification, as Marx understands it, corresponds, more or less, to Hegel's externalization. Spirit, says Hegel, externalizes itself and in so doing realizes its potentialities; it reveals what it is in the world of its activities. So, too, for Marx, man reveals his nature and realizes himself by objectifying himself.

Externalization, as Hegel conceives of it, is the activity whereby Spirit asserts itself in all its diversity; for it is nothing apart from its works, and comes to know itself for what it is by being active and reflective. Objectification, as Marx conceives of it, is the activity whereby man affirms himself. What man is is revealed in his works; he develops his capacities and comes to know himself for what he is by being active and reflective. He is a species-being: that is to say, a being that develops its distinctive capacities through the activities whereby it comes to know itself as the kind of being it is. Man rises to self-knowledge, and so becomes fully human, by working on nature with other men, to produce what satisfies his wants.

Objectification involves making use of things, and also, and above all, making things for use. To satisfy his wants, man not only consumes or uses what is external to him; he also transforms it to meet his wants, to serve his purposes. Again, in the process of using what is external to him and adapting it to his purposes, he acquires new wants and new purposes; he enlarges his understanding both of what he uses and adapts to his use, and of the activities involved in this use and adaptation. But these activities are his own activities; and so, in enlarging his understanding of them, he comes to understand himself. Therefore, through his actions, he necessarily educates himself; he comes to understand both his environment and himself, both nature and man as a part of nature differing in a fundamental respect from the rest of nature. As he enlarges his understanding, he extends his control of himself and of what is external to him.

My purpose now is to explain Marx's meaning as I understand it, and I therefore use my own words rather than his. But I also want to bring out what seems to me implicit in what he said, though he may not himself have been always aware of it. It is, I think, implicit in Marx's conception of man as essentially self-creative and social, that specifically human activities are the activities of a being whose distinctive skills are more than merely practical. Man cannot come to understand nature and himself as a part of nature, and so acquire knowledge that he can put to practical use, without developing a capacity which is not a practical skill, not a skill in manipulating things for a purpose, but an ability to describe and to explain which involves the use of a language, of a system of ideas in which is implicit a *Weltanschauung* or conception of a coherent scheme of things, a world. Man cannot be self-conscious—cannot, in the Hegelian idiom of Marx, be a being for himself—unless he is also world-conscious, unless he has a *Weltanschauung*. His wants, his purposes, even the most practical of them, are related to his conception of the world. That, indeed, is what makes them specifically human wants and purposes. Birds build nests and beavers build dams without knowing how they do it, without being able to explain what they are doing, and therefore without seeing themselves and what they do in relation to a whole world of things. But men do not build houses or bridges that way. Because they understand what they are doing as other animals do not, they are aware of themselves in what they do and assert themselves in doing it. This, I think, is what Marx implies when, in the third of his 'Economic and Philosophical Manuscripts', he says of Hegel that 'he conceives of labour as the essence of man, the self-confirming essence of man. . . . Labour is man's coming to be for himself . . .'.[1] Marx speaks these words in approval of Hegel, though they come from a passage which, taken as a whole, is critical of him.

This way of speaking about man cannot be reconciled with some of the things that Marx says about how material production is related to 'consciousness', or 'practice' to 'theory'. If we see clearly what this conception of man implies, we have to admit that man is no more *essentially* a practical than he is *essentially* a reflective or contemplative animal. To the extent that his practice differs from that of other animals and is therefore distinctively human, it is the practice of a creature who sees what he does in relation to a world, a coherent scheme of things. It is the practice of a creature who is a maker of explanations, a constructor of conceptual systems, and who could not be practical in just those ways, the ways peculiar to his species, unless he were so. There is no denying, I think, that this is what Marx's

---

[1] *Karl Marx: Early Writings*, transl. by Bottomore, p. 203.

account of man as a self-creative and social being implies, even though he at times seems to lose sight of these implications.

Man the species-being, the self-conscious and world-conscious being, is indeed practical, but his distinctively human skills, even the most practical of them, are peculiar to a being able to construct explanations and theories. When we speak of man in this way, we speak, of course, of man socially related to other men. Objectification is essentially a social process, including both man's operations on nature and the effects of these operations on him. Man exploits nature to meet his needs, and in so doing educates and transforms himself. This exploitation of nature is at the same time a collaboration with his fellows; it is both production and social intercourse. Unless it were both, man could not objectify himself; he could not develop the powers peculiar to his species, and could not come to know himself for what he is—which involves seeing himself in relation to an environment.

Man [says Marx] is directly a natural being. As a natural being . . . he is . . . endowed with natural powers and faculties which exist in him as tendencies and abilities, as drives . . . The objects of his drives exist outside himself as objects independent of him, yet they are objects of his needs . . . indispensable to the exercise and confirmation of his faculties. The fact that man is an embodied, living, real, sentient, objective being with natural powers, means . . . that he can only express his being in real sensuous objects.[2]

This is Marx's way of saying that man can develop his essentially human powers, and come to see himself as a man, only by acting on nature to produce what satisfies his needs. And Marx also says:

The production of life, both of one's own in labour and of fresh life in procreation, now appears as a double relationship: on the one hand as a natural, on the other as a social relationship. By social we understand the cooperation of several individuals, no matter under what conditions, in what manner and to what end. It follows from this that a certain mode of production, or industrial stage, is always combined with a certain mode of cooperation, of social stage.[3]

By the production of one's own life Marx means the production of what is needed to sustain life. This, for human beings, involves living and working together just as much as the having and rearing of children do.

In using and fashioning what is external to them, and in the social intercourse involved in these activities, men develop their powers and acquire a kind of knowledge that is specifically human: the kind which includes the ability to make distinctions, to describe, and to explain. In coming to have this knowledge, they come also to have self-knowledge. Through their work, therefore, they 'objectify' themselves in two senses: they develop their specifically human capacities, acquiring the skills and

---

[2] *Karl Marx: Early Writings*, pp. 206–7.   [3] *The German Ideology*, p. 18.

attitudes that are marks of their humanity; they raise themselves to manhood, and in so doing become objects of knowledge to themselves. They
do not just live, as other animals do; they do not just feel and desire and
behave; they are aware of themselves as persons among other persons of
their own kind, and of the world as a world, as a coherent system. They
could not have the first awareness without the second, or the second
without the first.

Marx often speaks in ways which cannot but seem odd to the reader
unused to his idiom. For example, in the 'Economic and Philosophical
Manuscripts', he says: 'The product of labour is labour which has been
embodied in an object and turned into a physical thing; this product is an
objectification of labour. The performance of work is at the same time its
objectification.'[4]

To the common-sense reader this may seem sheer abuse of language.
Labour is not turned into a physical thing; it does not become its own
product. Men by their labour fashion things external to them to serve
their purposes; and when these things are said to embody their labour, the
word *embody* is used in a metaphorical sense. To say of anything that it
embodies labour is surely to say only that it is a product of labour.

Actually, it is to say a good deal more: for this way of speaking is a
metaphor that expresses attitudes of man towards the products of human
labour which do not consist merely in the belief that they are products
of labour.

We can look at labour and its products in two ways. We can look at
them merely as means to ends. A man makes something useful. His work
is a means to an end, which is some useful thing. And the product of his
labour, the thing he has made, is also a means; it serves whatever purposes
it is used to serve. But we can also look at labour and its products as forms
of self-expression, as involved in personality, as marks of identity. Work
is a form of self-expression in the obvious sense that it is the activity of the
self that makes the greatest demands upon it; it is disciplined or purposeful
activity and not a mere effect of desire or appetite. It is, according to both
Hegel and Marx, the supremely educative activity, the activity which
helps to form the agent as well as the things he acts on. It is through his
work above all that man comes to understand and control himself, that he
acquires his image of himself.

In the *Phenomenology*, in the part of the section on Self-Consciousness,
which treats of Lordship and Servitude (*Herrschaft und Knechtschaft*), Hegel
contrasts the effects of mere desire or appetite with those of labour. Mere
desire or appetite simply consumes or uses external objects, getting
immediate and ephemeral satisfaction thereby. But labour, which is desire
restrained, fashions its object, imposes form on it, and in so doing comes

---

[4] *Karl Marx: Early Writings*, p. 122.

to know it as an enduring and independent thing. In fashioning its object, it is, as Hegel puts it, 'the particularity or the pure being-for-itself of consciousness'. In other words, labour is the disciplined, creative activity through which man attains a sense of his own identity. In externalizing or objectifying himself through his work—or, as we might prefer to put it, in developing his capacities as he adapts what is external to him to his purposes—he becomes aware of himself as an enduring self in a world of enduring things.[5]

Marx not only had ideas about the place of work in the life of man like those expressed by Hegel in this part of the *Phenomenology*; he also, in some ways, made more of the ideas than Hegel did, though he did not do it systematically. They are even more closely connected with man's need to affirm himself, as Marx describes it, than with the need for recognition, as Hegel conceives of it; for this need, according to Hegel, finds expression in conflict just as much as in work. As a self-conscious being who strives to affirm himself, who seeks assurance of what he is, man needs a sense of place in a coherent world, he needs a part or parts to play in an ordered community. It is above all in his work that this need is met, if it is met at all. But, as we shall see in a moment, Marx believed that work may be such as not to meet this need.

If we take the word 'work' in the broad sense to include, not just gainful employment or the getting and making of useful objects or the doing of immediately useful services, but every kind of regular and disciplined activity, we can say that a man's idea of himself and the idea that others have of him depend largely on the work he does. Thus man is essentially a worker, not merely in the sense that he is capable of deliberate and sustained effort, but also because he sees himself as a worker. His worth in his own eyes and in other people's depends on his work, on the deliberate and controlled efforts he makes to achieve something worth achieving, or at least which he thinks is so. Thus work, in the life of man, is not only what has to be done, systematically and daily, to procure what satisfies material wants; it is also what meets (or should meet) what Marx calls the need for 'self-affirmation'.

Though, at this level of generality, Hegel and Marx have similar ideas of the place of work, of controlled, sustained, and worthwhile activity, in the life of man, the similarity ends as soon as we move to a less general, a more concrete, level. On the whole, Hegel believed that men could be satisfied with the work that fell to their lot in existing society. He saw—

---

[5] I have paraphrased Hegel's argument rather than quoted Baillie's translation, which seems to me difficult to follow here. Jean Hyppolite's French rendering makes, I think, better sense of it. See Baillie's translation, p. 238, and Hyppolite's, p. 165. See also Hegel's *Phenomenologie des Geistes* (Felix Meiner Verlag edn., 1952), pp. 148–9. What Hegel says applies rather to mankind or to communities and groups than to men taken individually.

as Adam Smith did—some of the defects of the growing division of labour; he saw that it condemned many people to mechanical and monotonous work. But he never contemplated the abolition of the existing economy and the setting up of another quite different from it to ensure that work was freer, more creative, and more satisfying. Marx's attack on the rigid division of labour owes less to Hegel than to the early socialists and to what he learned about modern industry by extensive reading. And this attack is, of course, as much an attack on the system of property as on the organization or distribution of labour. According to Marx, as long as private property endures, so too will this rigid division of labour.

Now Hegel was an apologist for private property. But he produced arguments in favour of it different in kind from those of Locke and the Utilitarians. Not that he rejected their arguments so much as he added others of his own. He did not deny that property is a useful institution because it enables men to provide for their wants more efficiently; he merely saw other virtues in it. And so Marx, who learnt so much from Hegel, in attacking the institution of property, attacked it on a broader front than he might otherwise have done; he attacked it not only on the utilitarian and economic front but also on what might be called the cultural or even, in the Hegelian sense of the word, the *spiritual* front.

Marx disagreed with Hegel, not so much about the social origins of private property—about which Hegel had not much to say—as about its place in the life of man, its cultural and spiritual significance, the distinctively human needs it helps to bring out and satisfy. In *The Philosophy of Right*, Hegel says that 'the rationale of property is to be found not in the satisfaction of wants but in the supersession of the pure subjectivity of personality. In his property a person exists for the first time as reason.'[6] Hegel is not here denying that the institution of property makes easier the satisfying of wants; he is merely saying that man, if he is to act rationally and purposefully, if he is to be a person, if he is to have a will and not merely desires and appetites, needs to own things. Hegel even says that 'to appropriate means at bottom only to manifest the pre-eminence of my will over the thing and to prove that it is not . . . an end in itself',[7] and goes on to say that 'since property is the means whereby I give my will an embodiment, property must also have the character of being "this" or "mine". This is the important doctrine of the necessity of private property.'[8]

This doctrine, though not perhaps altogether new when *The Philosophy*

---

[6] *The Philosophy of Right*, transl. by T. M. Knox, pp. 235–6.

[7] Ibid., p. 236.

[8] Ibid., p. 236. Cf. Bentham, in the *Theory of Legislation*, p. 111: 'Property is nothing but a basis of expectation; the expectation of deriving certain advantages from a thing which we are said to possess, in consequence of the relation in which we stand towards it.'

of Right was published, is suggestive and important, and there is no trace
of it in the writings of Locke or of the Utilitarians, whose ideas about
property were then the most widely received. It makes sense to argue, as
Hegel does, that it is partly in the process of coming to own things, and
to be recognized as their owners, that human beings learn to behave
rationally and responsibly, to lead an ordered life. It is partly in the process
of learning to distinguish mine from thine that the child comes to recognize itself as a person, as a bearer of rights and duties, as a member of a
community with a place of its own inside it.

But this Hegelian doctrine is at best only a limited defence of private
property. It proves only that private property in some things is desirable;
it does not prove that all things useful to men, or even all things made or
adapted by them for use, ought to be privately owned. For example, it
does not prove that means of production, so extensive that the man who
owns them cannot himself use them but must hire the labour of others to
make a profitable use of them, should be owned privately. As a defence of
the capitalist system of property, it is lamentably inadequate. Indeed, a
socialist could well accept it, and then go on to qualify it in ways that Hegel
did not do. But Hegel accepted the system of property established in his
day, and appears not to have seen that this doctrine of his justified it only
to a limited extent, and could even be used to attack certain aspects of it.

Marx did not accept this Hegelian doctrine, even with large qualifications; he never attempted, as I have suggested a socialist might well do,
to use it to attack capitalist forms of property. In his early writings, he
came close at times to attacking private property *in all its forms*, though
just how literally he meant to be taken is not clear. In one of the 'Economic
and Philosophical Manuscripts', speaking of a type of communism which
he dislikes and calls 'universal envy' and a 'camouflaged form of cupidity',
he says that it 'negates the personality of man in every sphere' and is 'only
the logical expression of private property, which is this negation'.[9] He
says also that 'private property has made us so stupid and partial that an
object is only ours when we have it, when it exists for us as capital or
when it is directly . . . utilized in some way', and that 'the supersession of
private property is, therefore, the complete emancipation of all the human
qualities and senses'.[10] This looks like a wholesale attack on the institution
of private property as undiscriminating as Hegel's defence of it. Did Marx
really look forward to a type of society in which literally nothing is
privately owned, not even such things as clothing, food, furniture, and
houses, things in daily use? Or did he merely want a society in which
people no longer need to assert legal rights to such things, to look to
society—or rather to courts of law and to policemen—to protect them in
the undisturbed possession of them? It is impossible to say.

[9] *Karl Marx: Early Writings*, p. 153.   [10] Ibid., pp. 159–60.

Marx was a young man when he wrote the sentences I have just quoted, and there is nothing quite as sweeping in his later writings. In them, when he spoke of property as something to be abolished for the good of mankind, he had in mind, ordinarily, the private ownership of means of production. Yet even in his later writings, he sometimes failed to discriminate when he might have done so, and he never put himself to the trouble of explaining in what spheres, if any, private ownership is not only harmless but desirable.

Marx's attack on private property was unusually bitter and contemptuous, even among the socialists and communists of his day. He denounced not only the exploitation of man by man, which derived, so he believed, from the private ownership of the means of production; he denounced also the worship of material wealth and its effects, and deference to the rich merely because they are rich. In bourgeois society, as he described it, a man's worth in the eyes of his neighbours, and even his own, depends above all on how rich he is.

My own power is as great as the power of my money. The properties of money are my own . . . I am ugly, but I can buy the most beautiful women for myself. Consequently, I am not ugly, for the effect of ugliness, its power to repel, is annulled by money . . . I am lame, but money provides me with twenty-four legs. Therefore, I am not lame. I am a detestable, dishonourable, unscrupulous and stupid man, but money is honoured and so also is its possessor. Money is the highest good, and so its possessor is good.[11]

This is to exaggerate the importance in bourgeois society of wealth as compared with forms of power and prestige which are often as harmful as wealth and as little connected with estimable qualities in their possessors.

These are not rare sentiments, and Marx, who liked to keep the best literary company, quoted Shakespeare and Goethe to lend weight to them. But they meant more to him than to most people who utter them. They went deep with him and remained with him all his life, as they are apt to do with poor men of great talent who devote their energies to work which brings neither money nor worldly success. In *The Communist Manifesto* he says of the bourgeois that they have 'resolved personal work into exchange value', and have 'reduced the family relation to a mere money relation';[12] and some twenty years later, in the first volume of *Capital*, he speaks of money as the radical leveller that effaces all distinctions—that is to say, all distinctions other than differences in wealth.

Yet Marx was no ascetic. He wanted men to live abundantly. And he also at times saw in labour, or rather in all disciplined and creative effort,

---

[11] Ibid., p. 191.
[12] *The Communist Manifesto* (London, 1948 edn.), p. 128.

a kind of appropriation, which he distinguished from the acquiring of private property and on which he set a high value. Not only the picture that an artist paints, but anything man-made that requires skill and judgement in the making, belongs in one sense to the maker of it, no matter who the legal owner or actual possessor may be. It is not a mere effect of what he has done; it is what he has made, what he has deliberately brought into the world. It is an achievement of his, and he has expressed himself in it. He has put his mark on it, and yet has not done so to the exclusion of others. On the contrary, in putting his mark on it, he has not only affirmed himself and exercised his skills, he has also communicated with others. So, too, in coming to understand something, man takes a kind of possession of it. He may not use it, but he takes it in, brings it into his image of the world, appreciates it. In understanding and appreciating it, he also affirms himself. And this possessing no more excludes others than does the possessing involved in making. This is the kind of possessing that Marx had in mind when he spoke of man humanizing nature, making nature his own, in the same process as he humanizes himself.

The desire for property, the pre-eminent place given to it among legal rights, the severe punishments inflicted on violators of the right, seemed to Marx symbols of man's self-centredness, of his lack of concern for others and therefore for whatever in himself brought him close to others. As he put it in an article on *Bruno Bauer and the Jewish Question*: 'The right of property is, therefore, the right to enjoy one's fortune and to dispose of it as one wills, without regard for other men and independently of society. It is the right of self-interest. It leads every man to see in other men, not the realization, but rather the limitation of his own liberty.'[13] Of the bourgeois conception of liberty he said that it is 'the right to do everything which does not harm others. But liberty as a right of man is not founded upon the relations between man and man, but rather on the separation of man from man. It is the right of such separation. The right of the circumscribed individual, withdrawn into himself.'[14] This attack on bourgeois conceptions of right generally, and on the right to property in particular, goes far beyond an attack on the mere private ownership of the means of production. There could, conceivably, be public ownership of these means, and yet the attitude to private property that Marx condemns still be strong.

The proper attitude to things, the attitude which is proper because it brings human beings together as they develop their capacities, is the attitude of the maker or the knower or the artist. It, too, is a product of work, of disciplined endeavour, physical and mental. It, too, involves a kind of possession (or appropriation), though one different in kind from private ownership as it is understood in bourgeois society, one which involves no

[13] *Karl Marx Early Writings*, p. 25.   [14] Ibid., pp. 24–5.

exercise of rights that exclude others. That there is this other kind of possession, and that it is important, is clear enough. Many a bourgeois would agree with Marx to this extent. What is less clear is how private ownership, as a legal right that excludes others, affects the capacity for the kind of possession that Marx (and not he alone) valued so highly. To what extent and in what ways does it inhibit this capacity by helping to maintain social conditions and attitudes unfavourable to it? Are all forms of it to be condemned on this ground, or only some? And if some only, then which?

Marx's attack on private property is too undiscriminating to enable us to elicit from his writings precise answers to these particular questions. But, apart from this indiscrimate attack on private property in general, there is also an attack on a narrower front: on private property in the means of production. This attack bulks larger in Marx's writings as a whole (as also in those of his disciples), and it is easier to reach precise conclusions about what he thought of it and of its social effects.

II

By his work and through its products man affirms and objectifies himself; he develops his powers and acquires an idea of himself and his place in the scheme of things. No matter what his social condition, he always develops some of his powers and acquires some idea of himself and his place; for that is involved in his becoming self-conscious and purposeful. What he is, what he can do, how he sees himself, are always effects of what he has done and of what has been done by mankind, of his experience and his cultural inheritance. But his ideas of himself and his place may be incoherent and illusory, his aspirations may be confused and unrealizable. Man, in his endeavours to affirm himself, may also frustrate himself. He may seek and not find; he may even seek and not quite know what he is looking for. This unhappy condition is in part an effect of what the person who suffers it has done; for, if he had not developed his powers, he could not suffer it. He could not be incoherent unless he were rational, nor frustrated unless he were purposeful, nor lost unless he were a seeker, nor oppressed unless he aspired to freedom. But this condition is also an effect of his social environment, which is itself the product of what men have done in the past. So the man who suffers alienation is the victim at once of himself and of society.

Speaking of the worker under capitalism Marx says that he is 'related to the product of his labour as to an alien object';[15] and he also says, a little further on:

The alienation of the worker in his product means not only that his labour becomes an object, assumes an external existence, but that it exists independently,

[15] *Karl Marx: Early Writings*, p. 122.

outside himself, and alien to him, and that it stands opposed to him as an autonomous power. The life which he has given to the object sets itself up against him as an alien and hostile force.[16]

In *The German Ideology* Marx says:

The social power, i.e. the multiplied productive force, which arises through the cooperation of different individuals as it is determined by the division of labour, appears to these individuals, since their cooperation is not voluntary but natural, not as their own united power but as an alien force existing outside them, of the origin and end of which they are ignorant, which they thus cannot control . . .[17]

Here again we have statements which, if we are to make sense of them, if we are to see what they purport to tell us about the real world, we must not take literally. A man's labour cannot be outside him, nor can it stand opposed to him as an autonomous power. Nor does the worker, unless he is a Frankenstein, give life to what he makes, and in making it make an enemy. Even the passage from *The German Ideology*, though it can be taken rather more literally, is to some extent obscure and misleading. It is simply not true that men who work together to produce something do not do it voluntarily unless they understand and control their joint efforts. They work together voluntarily provided they are not coerced; and there is no coercion, in any usual sense of that word, merely because those who take part in a complicated system of behaviour do not understand how their parts fit into the system. We must not say, as Marx does, that their co-operation is not voluntary; we must say rather that the system of production was not deliberately established, and is neither understood nor controlled by them. When they neither understand nor control it, it *may* come to seem to them something external to themselves which they have to accept whether they like it or not. They *may* come to find it oppressive and restricting, but they *need* not do so. It is not a sufficient condition of their finding it so that they do not understand and control it.

If we interpret what Marx says in the 'Economic and Philosophical Manuscripts' in the light of what he and Engels say in *The German Ideology*, we can perhaps make sense of it. Marx has in mind, above all, the capitalist economy; and he is not saying that in it the worker's product literally becomes 'an alien object', and that his labour literally 'stands opposed to him as an autonomous power'. Obviously it is not the actual product of a man's labour, the shoe or the shirt he makes or helps to make, which is alien to him, or the actual work he does which opposes him as an autonomous power. It is rather the system in which he is involved; it is bourgeois society or capital as a form of property or the capitalist economy. But an

[16] Ibid., pp. 122–3.   [17] *The German Ideology*, R. Pascal edn., p. 24.

institution or a system of behaviour, though it may be called, not improperly, a product of labour, must be so in a different sense from the sense in which a shoe or a shirt is one.

The capitalist economy can be said to be a product of labour in two different senses, which Marx, without troubling to distinguish between them, seems to have had in mind at one time or another. If we want to explain how the capitalist economy arose, we must look at what men were doing before it arose, at how their behaviour changed and brought it into existence. A mode of production is both a system of behaviour and an effect of earlier behaviour, of what men were doing before it came into being. And of this early behaviour, the most important as a causal factor—at least in Marx's opinion—was production as it used to be. Thus the capitalist economy is a product of past labour. Out of men's activities, especially their productive activities, as they were before capitalism, there arose the capitalist mode of production. This is the first sense in which the capitalist economy is a product of labour.

But this economy, as a system of behaviour, is also, in another sense, a product of labour; and this time a product, not of past, but of present labour. If the worker ceased to work, the capitalist economy would cease to operate; the capitalist would cease to be a capitalist, to get his profits. As Marx puts it in the *Grundrisse*:

The worker, in fact, produces himself within the process [of production], as labour power and as the capital that opposes him, just as, on the other side, the capitalist produces himself as capital, as well as the living labour power that opposes him. Each one reproduces himself in that at the same time he produces his opposite ... The capitalist produces the worker and the worker produces the capitalist ...[18]

This, at least in part, is merely a truism which looks to be more because it is oddly put: it asserts that a system of behaviour survives only as long as the persons involved in it play their appropriate parts. The capitalist economy survives only as long as capitalists continue to behave as capitalists and proletarians as proletarians. Their roles are defined by the system and the system is kept going by their sustaining their roles inside it. Moreover, the roles presuppose one another: there are capitalists only where there are proletarians, and vice versa. But Marx also speaks at times as if the institutions which he says are opposed to labour or alien to it—as, for example, capital—were peculiarly the products of labour, and even of alienated labour, and when he does this, I must confess that I fail to understand him.[19]

[18] D. McLellan, *Marx's Grundrisse* (Macmillan, 1971), p. 105.

[19] In the *Grundrisse* he says: 'All the factors which were opposed to living labour as forces which were alien, external, and which consumed and utilised the living labour power under definite conditions, are now established as its own product and result'. (See D. McLellan, *Marx's Grundrisse*, p. 97.) What does Marx have in mind here? What was the labour that

Of course, it is labour which is productive, especially if labour is understood in the wide sense to include the control of production; and there can be controlled production without capitalism. In the eyes of Marx, the capitalist is *essentially* the appropriator of surplus-value and not the controller of production, for, quite often, he does not control it but hires a manager to do so for him. The workers could, and in the future perhaps will, control it themselves. The capitalist, seen in this light, lives off the proletarian as the proletarian does not live off him. But this does not entail that the relations between owners and workers characteristic of the capitalist system are effects of labour's being the sort of labour it is, and still less of its being alienated.

It is misleading to speak of capital or of the capitalist economy as an effect of labour's being proletarian and alienated, for labour would not be so unless it were part of the economy. It is just as true that labour would not be proletarian unless the economy were capitalist as it is that the capitalist economy would collapse if the proletarian ceased to play his part in it. Still, the worker does, by his work, maintain the economy, and the economy (according to Marx) is such that his work is controlled and his products are used in ways that are frustrating and even damaging to him. This damage, as Marx sees it, consists largely in the worker's attitude to his work and to the system that makes it the kind of work it is. The worker, by his work, maintains a system which is damaging to him, and the system, as it operates, maintains the worker's attitude to his work.

The proletarian worker's attitude to his work arises from its not being the sort of work it must be if he is to find satisfaction in it. He is not his own master at work, he does not decide what he shall do; he does not see his work as a providing for wants, as a useful activity, but only as something that he sells for a wage; and he feels himself to be the victim of a system he neither understands nor controls. His labour, on which his attitude to himself so largely depends, is a commodity.

In a passage I quoted earlier in another connection, Marx says: 'The animal is one with its life activity. It does not distinguish the activity from itself. . . . But man makes his life activity itself an object of his will and consciousness. . . . Only for this reason is his activity free activity.' He then goes on to say: 'Alienated labour reverses the relationship in that man . . . makes his life activity, *his being*, only a means for *his existence*.'[20]

produced these alien and external factors? Presumably not proletarian or alienated labour but labour as it was before it became proletarian or alienated. But, surely, these alien factors resulted not from that labour's being as it was but from other causes: from distributions of power and property which were themselves only in part effects of the division of labour. In the 'Economic and Philosophical Manuscripts', Marx goes even further, saying: 'Thus, through alienated labour the worker creates the relation of another man, who does not work and is outside the work process, to this labour . . . Private property is therefore the product, the necessary result of alienated labour'. (*Karl Marx: Early Writings*, transl. by Bottomore, p. 131.)

[20] *Karl Marx: Early Writings*, p. 127. My italics.

When Marx says that 'man makes his life activity itself an object of his will and consciousness', we must suppose him to mean something more than just that man, in producing the means of his subsistence, is aware that he does so and acts purposefully. For that much is true of him even when labour is alienated. We must suppose him to mean also that man, because he has this awareness, aspires to be a self-directed or free worker. He can be a free worker only because he knows what he is doing and acts purposefully, but he is not always free, for his labour may be alienated. When it is alienated, he lacks freedom and also, so Marx says, makes his life activity, his labour, only 'a means of existence'. Labour, presumably, is always at least that, even when it is free; for no matter how free man is, he must work to produce the wherewithal to keep himself alive and healthy. But, so Marx implies, man's labour, his life activity, which Marx also calls his 'being', must be more than that. It must be an activity in which man develops and uses his capacities in ways that satisfy him, so that he has the sense that he is living as he would wish to live. Marx contrasts man's 'being' with his 'existence', his survival; his 'being' is, or is revealed in, his 'life activity', his conscious and purposeful endeavours. They are the means of his existence, for they keep him alive, but they also give worth and dignity to his life. Or, rather, they can but do not always do so; for it is not enough that they should keep him alive for them to do this as well.

Under capitalism the worker (as Marx sees him), does not look upon his work as a providing for wants but only as something he sells for a wage. He looks upon it as a commodity, and so too does the capitalist. As Marx puts it in the 'Economic and Philosophical Manuscripts': 'Labour does not only create goods; it also produces itself . . . as a commodity.'[21] In the first volume of *Capital*, Marx has the worker say to the capitalist: 'The commodity I have sold you is distinguished from the ordinary mob of commodities by this, that its use creates value, and a greater value than its own.'[22] And Marx says of the worker that he 'does not produce for himself, but for capital. No longer, therefore, does it suffice that he should simply produce. He must produce surplus value. Only that worker is now "productive" who produces surplus value for the capitalist.'[23] Only the worker who enables the capitalist to make a profit is worth employing. Both the capitalist and the worker look upon labour—or, as Marx prefers to put it, 'labour-power'[24]—as something worth using only if it brings a

[21] *Karl Marx: Early Writings*, p. 121.

[22] *Capital*, i. 233.

[23] Ibid. i. 552.

[24] Marx attached great importance to the distinction he made between *labour* and *labour-power*, or the capacity for labour. It is labour-power that the worker sells to the capitalist; it is therefore labour-power that has exchange value. Labour has no value, though the things produced by it have value in proportion to the amount of labour needed to produce them. But when we are discussing Marx's views about man and alienation, this distinction between labour and labour-power is irrelevant, and I therefore ignore it.

profit to the man who buys it. The worker who cannot sell his energy and his skills feels that they are useless, and feels useless himself, no matter how much he and others may be in want of what it takes labour to produce. Where labour is treated as a commodity, it is held to be useful only to the extent that it is marketable.

No doubt, the worker has wants to provide for, his own and his family's, and he sells his labour in order to provide for them. The worker, in a quite obvious sense, is a bread-winner, a provider for wants, and Marx has no wish to deny the obvious. Nevertheless—and this is the point which seems important to Marx—he can sell his labour in order to provide for wants, his own and those of his dependents, without caring whether the products of his labour are useful. No doubt, if he stops to think, it soon occurs to him that unless these products were wanted for some purpose, were useful to someone, there would be no demand for his labour; but what really matters to him is that he should be able to sell that labour. It is not for him to decide how his labour shall be used; it is for the buyer of it to ensure that it is used to produce what satisfies a demand.

When you work to produce what you or your dependents want, or what you are free to barter or to sell (or to give away, if you can afford to be generous), your labour is not a commodity, for there is no purchaser of it to decide how it shall be used. You are your own master, the director of your own labour. Of course, what work you do depends on your resources and skills; and also on wants, your own or other people's. Your opportunities are always limited by your situation—by your resources, your skills, and the usefulness to others of what you produce with those resources and skills. Your being your own master does not entail your being able to provide for your own wants regardless of other people's. You must work in order to live, and you cannot live only on your own products; you must work to produce what others want, and they must work to provide for your wants. You are your own master, not because you are free to work or not to work, or because you are able to produce what satisfies all your wants, but because you are the manager of your own work. You are a deliberate provider for wants; you take decisions about how to use the resources and skills at your disposal to produce what satisfies wants.

But if you have perforce to sell your labour you are not a manager of your work. You decide to go to work to get the wherewithal to provide for wants, but you do not decide how your labour is to be used to provide for wants. You may not even care whether the product of your labour provides for wants; you may care only about getting your wage. This is not to say that you are, as a wage-worker, any more selfish than you would be if you were your own master; you may be willing to make great

sacrifices for your wife and children, and even for your friends and com-
rades. If you were your own master you might be a keen bargainer, and
not at all an altruist; but you would be a provider for wants, and your
attitude to your work would be different. It would be (so Marx implies)
the proper attitude, the attitude in keeping with the real functions of work
in the life of man: for work is essentially a deliberate providing for wants.
It is a rational and disciplined activity calling for a use of both mental and
bodily powers. As Marx puts it in *Capital*: 'The labour process . . . is . . .
purposive activity carried on for the production of use values, for the
fitting of natural substances to human wants.' And he goes on to say on the
same page: 'Of course, the general nature of the labour process is not
altered in any way because the worker engages in it on behalf of the
capitalist instead of on his own behalf.'[25] This is what work essentially is,
but this is not how it looks to the worker under capitalism.

Nor is it how it looks to the man who buys his labour, to the capitalist.
To the capitalist, as much as to the worker, labour is a commodity. No
doubt, the capitalist decides how it shall be used; and he is interested in
the disposal of its products in a way that the worker is not. It matters
to him directly that there should be a demand for them. Nevertheless,
merely as a capitalist, he is not primarily concerned that his product should
satisfy wants; he is concerned above all in getting a good return on his
investment. He is in business, not to provide for wants, but to make a
profit. His products may not even be consumer goods; they may be tools
or components or half-finished goods and his customers may be other
capitalists. As Marx puts it:

Under capitalism, labour power is not sold in order that, by its services or by
its product, it may satisfy the personal wants of the buyer. What he aims at is the
increase of his capital, the production of commodities which contain . . . a portion
of value that cost him nothing and can nevertheless be realized by the sale of
the commodities.[26]

This is Marx's way of saying that the capitalist buys labour in the hope of
producing what can be sold for a higher price than it costs to produce. The
question the capitalist puts to himself is not: How can I use the labour I
buy to provide for wants as effectively as possible? but rather, How can
I use it to make what I can sell at the highest profit? The capitalist does
not hire labour with the same intention as a man who hires a nurse to
look after his sick child; he does not do it even when his firm makes
medicines. 'Fanatically bent upon the expansion of value [the capitalist]
relentlessly drives human beings to production for production's sake.'[27]
The value Marx here speaks of is exchange-value and not use-value. The
capitalist is fanatically bent on increasing his capital, his store of money

and of what can be sold for money. This is what Marx has in mind when he speaks of the 'self-expansion of capital'; it is the use of capital primarily in order to accumulate more capital. And by capital he means money and productive resources privately owned and used with the intention, not of satisfying human wants, but of increasing profits. In the future communist society, there will be a great accumulation of productive resources, and there may even be a high rate of investment—Marx does not say that there will be, nor yet that there will not—but there will be no capital.

Some of Marx's critics, contemplating his portrait of the capitalist, seem to me to make objections which fasten upon a not very important aspect of it. For example, Professor Acton in *The Illusion of the Epoch*, discussing Marx's image of the capitalist in pursuit of profits, makes a criticism which, though it is justified by some of the things that Marx says, misses the real point of his attack upon the capitalist economy as a source of alienation.[28] Marx, says Acton, speaks of the capitalist's pursuit of profits, of money, as a mistaking of the shadow for the substance. Money is worth what it can buy, and to want money for its own sake and not for what it can buy is (according to Marx as interpreted by Acton) to mistake the symbol for the reality. The purpose of work is, or ought to be, to provide for wants, and to work for money rather than for what money can buy is to work to no purpose. To this Acton objects that money is a symbol of success, and to make money for the prestige it brings, and not for what it can buy, is not to chase a shadow, for prestige is real. Marx—so thinks Acton—tends to regard prestige as illusory, which it is not. The pursuit of it in preference to other things may be wrong, but it is not the chasing of a shadow.

Marx did sometimes speak as Acton accuses him of doing, and Acton's point against him is to that extent well taken. Yet Marx also wanted to say something more important about the capitalist than that his pursuit of money (in the shape of profits) is the chasing of a shadow; something which makes perfect sense however real the benefits that the capitalist derives from his profits.

The prestige that comes to the capitalist with his profits is no less real (though less necessary to survival and good health) than the food, clothing, and shelter that the worker acquires by spending his wages. Granted! But we can still make a distinction between two different attitudes to work and business: the attitude of the mere wage-earner or mere maker of profits, who looks upon labour as a commodity, and the attitude of the man who, whether he works in a subordinate capacity or directs the work of others, looks upon labour as a providing for wants.

Industrial capitalism multiplies the number of persons engaged in

[28] H. B. Acton, *The Illusion of the Epoch* (Cohen & West, London, 1955), pp. 230 ff. Actually, this is an excellent book, and I take this example from it only to show how even one of Marx's more perceptive and generous critics can sometimes see less in him than is there to be seen.

production, whether as sellers or as buyers and directors of labour, whose attitude to work is the attitude of the mere wage-earner or the mere maker of profits. What Marx wants to say about this attitude is not that it is morally wrong but that, the more widespread it is, the more men are apt to feel themselves the victims of the productive system in which they are involved. We may think that Marx exaggerates the extent to which this attitude prevails in the capitalist economy, but whether we think so or not, we must concede that this attitude, as Marx conceives of it, has nothing to do with the moral worth of the capitalist's or the wage-earner's motives. Whether the capitalist seeks profits for the sake of prestige or to enable him to indulge the most refined tastes or the most benevolent intentions, and whether the hired worker sells his labour in order to buy food, clothing, and shelter for himself and his family or to get money for drink, labour may still, in the eyes of both of them, be a mere commodity.

III

Marx's attack on industrial capitalism is powerful, and is in many ways convincing. It is also exaggerated, and in some respects misdirected. It exaggerates the extent to which labour is treated merely as a commodity under capitalism, and it attributes to capitalism defects which could just as plausibly be attributed to the scale of production. These defects could perhaps be remedied, at least to some extent, in a controlled economy; and a controlled economy—as we, living a hundred years after Marx, are in a better position than he was to know—need not be *socialist*. At least, not as Marx understood that term: for in a controlled economy there can be considerable profits paid out to people who are not engaged in productive work, and the workers need not control production. What is more, even where there are no profits distributed to non-workers, and the economy is controlled by public authority and the means of production are publicly owned, the workers can still feel helpless in face of the system, and labour be treated as a commodity. No doubt, such a state of affairs would not be socialism, as Marx and most other socialists of his day thought of it, but it is not capitalism either.

Marx insisted that when capitalism came to be abolished, the workers 'collectively' should control production, but he never explained how this control was to be organized. He left that problem for future generations to solve. The workers, presumably, would need to control, not just separate industrial and commercial undertakings, but the vast industrial economy as a whole. How could they do this so as to ensure that the individual worker should no longer feel helpless in the face of a system he was powerless to control? How could they ensure that industrial democracy on a large scale should not be as much of a 'sham' as political democracy was in bourgeois society? Such questions as these did not

concern Marx, and he would perhaps have dismissed as Utopian attempts
to answer them while capitalism survived. Yet his neglect of them did
make it easier for him to attribute to capitalism evils which may well have
other causes. These evils may have arisen along with capitalism, or have
grown worse as capitalism developed, and yet have been due, at least in
part, to causes unconnected with it and likely to survive it. It is a pity that
Marx took so little interest in the effect on labour and on the worker of the
mere scale of production, whether capitalist or not. For though, in his
day, large-scale production was capitalist, he did not believe that it would
remain so always. He did not believe that industrialism and the vastly
extended trade that went with it would disappear with capitalism.

Alienation, according to Marx, arises with production for exchange, and
will not be overcome until the workers collectively take over control of
production. Yet he admitted, at times, not in so many words but implicitly, that it is less production for exchange than the scale of production
and of exchange that produces the attitude to productive work that he
deplores. He says, for example,

> Though urban crafts are based substantially on exchange and the creation of
> exchange values, the main object of production is not . . . exchange value as
> exchange value, but the subsistence of man as an artisan, as a master craftsman,
> and consequently use-value. Production therefore is everywhere subordinate to
> a presupposed consumption, supply to demand, and its expansion is slow.[29]

True, the urban crafts that Marx speaks of here are medieval, and he
would call them pre-capitalist. But production which is capitalist, in which
the workers are not apprentices but are hired men with little hope of ever
becoming masters themselves, can be on a small scale and for a local
market. An employer in a small way hiring a few workers to produce goods
sold locally is just as much a capitalist as the man with ten thousand times
his resources producing goods for sale in half the countries of the world,
and yet his attitude to the workers he hires and to his customers may be
very different—much more like that of the medieval craftsman. His
workers may be skilled men who take pride in their work, and both he
and they may know many of his customers well and have their particular
wants in mind when they work. Yet this small capitalist may be just as
keen on increasing his profits as he would be if he produced goods for half
the world, and his workers just as keen on getting good wages as they
would be if they worked in an immense factory and repeated the same
small operations again and again without caring what they contributed to
the final product. Marx, of course, and quite rightly, looked upon capitalism as a system that encouraged a vast expansion in the scale of production

[29] Karl Marx, *Pre-Capitalist Economic Formations*, transl. by J. Cohen and ed. by E. Hobsbawm (Lawrence & Wishart, London, 1964), p. 118.

and of trade—as far more progressive technologically than any earlier system. But this expansion and this progress are not tied indissolubly to capitalism, and it is important to consider their effects apart from those of capitalism.

Quite often, when Marx speaks of alienation, he points to the fact that the workers do not control the system of production in which they are engaged. He does this not only in *The German Ideology* and the *Grundrisse* but in *Capital* as well. Early and late, it is a recurrent theme in his writings, and early and late, too, he looks forward to the workers taking over control of production. When they do this, they will, he thinks, do more than just take over from the capitalists and their hired managers; for the capitalists and their managers do not control the economy but only particular firms inside it. The capitalist economy, as Marx describes it, is uncontrolled, and the capitalists are in some ways as much at the mercy of the system as the workers are. In the *Grundrisse* Marx writes:

> The social character of activity, and the social form of the product, as well as the share of the individual in production, are here opposed to individuals as something alien and material; this does not consist in the behaviour of some to others but in their subordination to relations that exist independently of them and arise from the collision of independent individuals with one another.[30]

Marx is not to be taken here quite literally. Social activity does consist in the behaviour of some to others, and individuals would not be socially related as they are unless they behaved to one another as they do, the behaviour in question being essentially rational and purposeful. What Marx means, I take it, is that the system has not been deliberately set up by the individuals caught up in it, who do not control it or even, perhaps, understand how it functions as a whole. No doubt, they understand their own roles inside it; they understand what social rules and conventions require of them. But they do not understand how the system as a whole operates. This, presumably, applies to capitalists as much as to workers. I can see no reason why it should not.

What is more, it applies as much to men and women of all classes and conditions of life in pre-capitalist as in capitalist societies. If, then, alienation is worse under capitalism than it is in economically less advanced societies, this cannot be because under capitalism people are less in control of over-all production and exchange and of social conditions generally. It must be for other reasons: as, for example, because economic and social change is more rapid, and because there is more movement from place to place and from some social circles into others. In other words, if there is more alienation under capitalism than in economically less advanced societies, it is above all because economic and social conditions are less static and

---

[30] *Marx's Grundrisse*, transl. by D. McLellan, p. 66.

not because they are less controlled and less understood. Also perhaps, although, along with technical progress, people's understanding of social conditions and their ability to control them increase, their social aspirations grow so fast as to outrun their capacity to achieve them. It may be that, as knowledge and power increase, so too does the feeling among men that they have less of them than they need. Or, perhaps, if their sense of powerlessness is no greater, they resent it more.

No doubt, Marx was aware that men's understanding of their social conditions was increasing under capitalism. Though he accused the bourgeois political economists of bias and of blindness, he also borrowed heavily from them in constructing his own account of the capitalist economy. Yet he did not point to this increase as one among the important causes of at least some aspects of what he called alienation. More surprisingly still, he seems to have taken it for granted that, if the workers took over control of production, this sense of powerlessness in face of the system would disappear. But this is by no means obvious. Control is often imperfect, often only partial. Certainly, in the world today, we cannot say that the governments that undertake to control their countries' economies (not to speak of other aspects of their life) the most completely are the least frustrated in their attempts to achieve their purpose, or indeed have the most coherent and realistic purposes. To be sure, in spite of pretences to the contrary, there is as yet no country whose economy is controlled collectively by the workers; but I see no reason why, if there were, this control should be any more complete or any less frustrating than state control is today.

Marx was too prone to attribute to capitalism what might be attributed to other causes. Still, in his day, large-scale production, rapid social change, and rising expectations were confined to the capitalist part of the world. The earliest factory worker was a proletarian. Taking only a small part in making the finished product, and often not knowing what the part contributes to the whole, he has been more inclined than any hired worker before him to look on his labour as a mere commodity. So, too, it is the industrial capitalist, more than any earlier purchaser of labour, who has bought it, not primarily in order to use it to make what satisfies wants, but to make a profit. Marx was right in holding that industrial capitalism, more than any earlier type of economy, has reduced labour to being a mere commodity. Today there are perhaps other types of economy which do this as much, if not more; but then Marx knew nothing of them.

In the capitalist economy, the work of management, of contrivance, of acquiring knowledge and putting it to practical use is more set apart than ever before from manual work. As Marx puts it:

The divorce of the intellectual powers of the process of production from the manual power, and the transformation of these powers into powers of capital over labour, are completed . . . in large-scale industry based upon machine production. The special skill of each individual machine worker who is thus sucked dry dwindles into an insignificant item as contrasted with the science, the gigantic forces of nature, and with the mass of social labour, which are incorporated into the machine system, and out of which the power of the master is made.[31]

The independent peasant or handicraftsman develops knowledge, insight, and will, even though it be only to a moderate extent . . . Under the manufacturing system, these faculties are needed only by the workshop as a whole.[32]

The knowledge, the intelligence, the enterprise, and the managerial skills devoted to production were never before anywhere near as great, and yet were never before exercised by so small a proportion of those engaged in production.

The condition of the manual worker in an advanced capitalist economy, as Marx depicts it, is pitiful. The factory 'transforms the worker into a cripple, a monster, by forcing him to develop some highly specialized dexterity at the cost of a world of productive impulses and faculties'.[33] Whereas 'in the handicrafts, the worker *uses* a tool, in the factory he *serves* a machine. In the former case, the movements of the instruments of labour proceed from the worker, but in the latter the movements of the worker are subordinated to those of the machine'.[34]

Within the capitalist system all the methods for increasing the social productivity of labour are carried out at the cost of the individual worker . . . they mutilate the worker into a fragment of a human being, *degrade* him to become a mere appurtenance of the machine, make his work such a torment that its essential meaning is destroyed, estrange him from the intellectual potentialities of the labour process in very proportion to the extent to which science is incorporated in it . . .[35]

I must not multiply quotations. My purpose, at the moment, is merely to fit Marx's picture of the degraded, the crippled, the mutilated worker into a general account of what he understood by alienation and what he believed were its causes. The crippling and mutilation he has in mind are not physical; they are moral or—as I prefer to put it in trying to elucidate the doctrines of a man whose conception of human nature owes more to Hegel than to anyone else—*spiritual*. The worker under capitalism is not just *exploited* in the sense of deprived of part of the value of what he produces; he is not just impoverished, poor though he may be; he is *degraded*, and his degradation is part of his alienation.

Marx, when he speaks of the worker under capitalism, says of him that

---

[31] *Capital*, i. 451–2.   [32] Ibid. i. 382.   [33] Ibid. i. 381.
[34] Ibid. i. 451. My italics.   [35] Ibid. i. 713. My italics.

he is exploited, that he is impoverished, and that he is alienated, and he nowhere explains just how these three afflictions differ from one another. But he does define exploitation in such a way that real wages could rise and yet the worker be more exploited. No more is needed for this to happen than for the productivity of labour to rise more rapidly than real wages. In several places Marx speaks of the worker growing poorer as the production of wealth increases. In the 'Economic and Philosophical Manuscripts' he says that 'the misery of the worker increases with the power and volume of his production', and again that 'the worker becomes poorer the more wealth he produces . . . The worker becomes an ever cheaper commodity the more goods he creates. The devaluation of the human world increases in direct relation with the increase in value of the world of things'.[36] It may be that Marx, especially in his earlier writings, did want to say that the worker under capitalism grows poorer absolutely. But in his later writings, and especially in *Capital*, he gives the impression that the impoverishment he has in mind is only relative; as, for example, when he says: 'In proportion as capital accumulates, the condition of the worker, *be his wages high or low*, necessarily grows worse.'[37]

There is perhaps no need to inquire anxiously whether Marx really believed that, as capitalism developed, the worker would grow poorer absolutely. He may have believed it when he was young and the evidence against the belief was still meagre; it is unlikely that he continued to believe it when he was older and the evidence was more abundant. But, be that as it may, this belief has logically nothing to do with the belief that, as capitalism develops, the worker is more and more alienated. His condition could grow worse even though his real wages rose considerably. Marx, after all, did not believe that *only* the worker is alienated; he believed that the capitalist is so as well, and not the less so the greater his profits. Poverty and alienation need not go together. Marx, I think, quite often saw that they need not but did not see it steadily and clearly. Here, as so often elsewhere, he is ambiguous; he alternates between a more subtle and reasonable belief and one that is cruder and less reasonable.

The capitalist economy, as Marx insists again and again, is the most productive yet; the fanatical seeker after profit who 'relentlessly drives human beings to production for production's sake' also creates 'those material conditions . . . which can alone form the real basis of a higher type of society, whose fundamental principle is the full and free development of each individual'.[38] Capitalism, though it allows the worker to be exploited, also produces wealth abundantly; it provides for material wants more copiously than any economy before it. What it does not provide for is the 'full and free development of each individual'. The slave and the

---

[36] *Karl Marx: Early Writings* transl. by Bottomore, pp. 120 and 121.
[37] *Capital*, i. 714. My italics.   [38] *Capital*, i. 651.

serf were, in their time, often more exploited even than the proletarian. Marx sometimes comes close to saying that they were. But he nowhere suggests that they were more alienated than the worker under capitalism. The proletarian is the most alienated, the most wretched of men. In his *Critique of Hegel's Philosophy of Right*, Marx, speaking of the proletariat, says of it that 'its sufferings are universal', that 'the wrong done to it is not a particular wrong but wrong in general', that it suffers 'a total loss of humanity' and 'can only redeem itself by a total redemption of humanity'.39 This is strong, not to say extravagant, language. Marx presumably did not mean that the proletarian is the most inhuman of men; he meant rather that the peculiarly human needs, the ones I have called spiritual, are in him more deeply frustrated than in other men. He suffers by virtue of his humanity more than they do. The wretchedness peculiar to the human condition is revealed in him and to him in its most intense and intolerable form. That is why his class, in redeeming itself, redeems mankind; that is why it is the most revolutionary of classes, the class that comes eventually to will and to achieve the transformation of the whole social order.

Today in the West we see the worker in industry growing more like the bourgeois, or rather we see the differences between these two classes growing smaller as both classes change, so that Marx's idea of the proletarian as the most alienated of men seems to us wide of the mark. Yet he kept hold of this idea all his life. In *Capital*, published over twenty years after he wrote his *Critique of Hegel's Philosophy of Right*, he still spoke of the worker as a cripple and a mere fragment of a man. He had read in the interval many reports of inspectors of factories and other officials in England, and what he learnt from them about the conditions of life and the sentiments of the working class in what was then industrially the most advanced country in the world served only to confirm his belief that the proletarian is the most alienated of men.

Just as the proletarian is the most alienated of men, so capitalism is the economy that brings alienation to its highest pitch. It is the economy in which labour *and* the natural resources to which labour is applied *and* the instruments of labour all become commodities; they all become factors of production, and production, as never before, becomes production for the sake of profit. Factors of production are bought and used to get the best return on them, and are not bought or used when the expected return is too small to justify their purchase or use. That is why in the capitalist economy there can be widespread unemployment and misery, though there are resources and skills and labour enough to provide abundance. The system is such that those with command over labour, the capitalists, are often moved, in order to maintain profits, to restrict production and

39 K. Marx, *A Contribution to the Critique of Hegel's Philosophy of Right*, published in English in Bottomore's edn. of *Karl Marx: Early Writings*, p. 58.

create unemployment and even to destroy what men have produced and still greatly need; it is also such that those who sell their labour are moved to destroy machines for fear that increased productivity should reduce the demand for labour. The peculiarity of the capitalist economy is not that in it more wants go unsatisfied than in more primitive economies; it is rather that it operates in such a way that all who are engaged in production are inclined to treat the factors of production, with labour chief among them, as if they were mere commodities, and so lose sight of the prime function of production, which is the satisfying of human wants. The economy in which labour is incomparably more productive than it has ever been in the past is also the economy in which those who provide labour and those who direct its use are most apt to forget its essential purpose.

IV

I have quoted, perhaps too copiously, from the writings of Marx, and have commented on them. I want now to make a brief summary of the more important of the senses in which Marx spoke of alienation. In doing this, I must make some distinctions that he never made, though they are, of course, implicit in what he said.

Marx, when he speaks of the worker's product being alien to him, sometimes means no more than that someone else appropriates it. More often he has in mind something different from this, though connected with it. He means, not the things produced by the worker which are the property of his employer, but certain consequences of this appropriation. He means, in the first place, labour's being treated as a commodity. It comes to be so treated because the products of some people's labour are appropriated by others. He means, secondly, *capital*, which he sometimes defines, in the fashion of his day, as *stored-up labour*, but also—and more realistically—as a *power of command over labour*. Unless there were men with nothing to sell but their labour, the products of that labour could not be appropriated by others, and the accumulation of capital would not be possible. The worker by his labour enables the appropriator to acquire capital, which is the power to command labour and dispose of its products, and therefore the power to which he, the worker, is subordinate. Thus, as Marx sees it, capital is both a product of labour and a power over it. It is a product alien to the worker in the sense that it is something external to him, to which he is subject, although it would not exist but for his labour. In this sense of alienation, only the worker is affected by it. The capitalist clearly is not, for it is he who has the power to command labour.

But Marx also means by the alienated product of labour something different both from labour as a commodity and from the power to command labour. He means by it the entire productive system, and even the whole social order, considered as an effect of what men have done, an effect which they never intended, do not understand, and cannot control. He means by it a system of behaviour which is historically determined and to which men are required to conform, so that they come to look upon it as something external to themselves. It is this that Marx has in mind when he speaks, as he does in *The German Ideology*, of 'the social power . . . which arises through the cooperation of different individuals', and says of it that it appears to them 'not as their own united power but as an alien force existing outside them, of the origin and end of which they are ignorant, [and] which they thus cannot control'.[40]

In this sense of alienation, the capitalist is as much alienated as the worker. For, though he may direct the labour of the workers he hires, he does not control the productive system. He depends on the market, and must study it and adjust his activities to it, and may be ruined by it, though it is only one aspect of a whole system of behaviour in which he is involved—a system which is as it is, and changes as it does, only by virtue of what he and others do. The system is the context in which the individual acts, which limits his opportunities because it defines the roles open to him, and which forms his mind as he learns to use its symbols and its rules. The social system, thus regarded, is not merely an effect of manual labour; it is an effect of many different kinds of human activity.

The kinds of alienation I have so far distinguished are essentially social phenomena. When Marx speaks of them he calls them forms of alienated labour or alienated products of labour, though, as I have already implied, labour is too narrow a term to convey the full extent of his meaning. These kinds of alienation are more properly effects of activities that include labour than of labour alone. But then the word Marx uses to refer to them is *Arbeit*, which has perhaps a wider meaning in German than *labour* has in English.

Marx speaks not only of alienated labour or the alienation of labour or of products of labour alien to the worker; he speaks also of the alienation of man and especially of the worker. When he does this, he has in mind something of a different order, something which, though it arises in society, is not a social role or a social relation. When we say that labour is a commodity, we speak of the functioning of the economy; we speak of the roles inside it of the worker, the seller of labour, and of the capitalist, the purchaser and director of labour. So, too, when we speak of capital as a product of labour which is also a power of command over it, or when we say of bourgeois society that it is an unintended effect of what men have done in the past, which they neither understand nor control though it defines the social roles open to them, we speak of the functioning of a social system. We do not speak of the human *psyche*, of the feelings and

[40] *The German Ideology*, p. 24.

attitudes of the self towards itself, other selves, and its environment. We could understand what Marx meant by the alienation of labour in its various forms even if we knew nothing of his conception of man as a species-being whose essential need is to affirm himself; whereas we could not without this knowledge understand what he meant by the alienation of man or of the worker. When Marx speaks of alienated man or of the alienated worker he usually has in mind attitudes of man or of the worker to himself or to others or to the economy or social order. He has in mind a psychological condition of a self-conscious being. This kind of alienation, to distinguish it from the other, I shall call spiritual, and the other I shall call social.

There is spiritual alienation when a man feels that his work or his role in society is a burden to him, when it degrades him in his own eyes and other people's. Alienated man has energies or abilities or aspirations that he cannot satisfy. His idea of himself, which depends so much on his work and his social roles, is a burden to him; he is dissatisfied with himself as well as with what he does and his place in society. He is a self-conscious being, a species-being, whose sense of well-being depends on his being active in ways that develop his latent powers, so that he can take pride in what he does and is. The alienated worker, says Marx,

does not fulfil himself in his work but denies himself, has a feeling of misery rather than well-being, does not develop freely his mental and physical energies but is physically exhausted and mentally debased. . . . His work is not voluntary but imposed, forced labour. It is not the satisfaction of a need but only a means for satisfying other needs. . . . Finally, the external character of work for the worker is shown by the fact that . . . in [his] work he does not belong to himself but to another person.[41]

Work is a burden, a source of misery, to the worker, partly because in it he does not find the outlet for his energies which he needs and partly because the feeling that he is the mere instrument of others or of circumstances degrades him in his own eyes. Notice that Marx does not say that work is a burden when its object is to satisfy someone other than the worker; it is a burden when it *belongs* to someone other than him, when he is not his own master at work. Labour is not felt to be oppressive because man must work hard to keep himself and his dependents alive; it is felt to be oppressive only when man is so placed that he cannot get a living by doing the kind of work that would satisfy him.

Man is also alienated spiritually when he feels himself to be the victim of a system he cannot control. This spiritual alienation does not consist in his not being able to control the system, nor yet in his taking it for granted; it consists in his looking upon himself as the *victim* of it, of something

41 *Karl Marx: Early Writings*, p. 125.

beyond his control and external to him, though it is in fact only a system of human behaviour. Man, so Marx implies, never feels this way more acutely than when his livelihood depends, not on his willingness to do useful and congenial work, but on the state of the market. The state of the market, though it is a consequence of what men have done, is not a consequence they have intended. Indeed, they do not see it as a consequence of what they have done, for they were unable to prevent it; they see it as something that happens to them and limits their opportunities in unpredictable and often painful ways. Nobody wants unemployment but it happens—not as a natural calamity but as a product of a system of behaviour beyond the control of the persons whose behaviour it is. Nobody wants work to be monotonous and degrading but it is so because the economy is industrial and capitalist. Both the worker and the capitalist feel themselves to be at the mercy of a masterless economy. Man, the species-being, aspires to be his own master and to affirm himself, and feels that he is an instrument and a victim. He is frustrated, and is degraded in his own eyes.

As he sees himself, so he sees others. As Marx puts it: 'When man confronts himself, he also confronts other men. What is true of man's relationship to his work, to the product of his work and to himself, is true also of his relationship to other men, to their labour, and to the objects of their labour'.[42] The man who cannot respect himself does not respect others; the man who feels himself a victim and an instrument is estranged from other men. They do not matter to him, except as instruments.

Let me end this part of my exposition of Marx's doctrine with a word of warning. I have spoken of social and of spiritual alienation, and have distinguished several forms of both. But Marx nowhere speaks of social and spiritual alienation, and does not make the distinctions I have made. Indeed, he does not always, when he speaks of *alienated labour*, have in mind some form or other of what I have called social alienation, though he does so more often than not; and he does not always, when he speaks of *alienated man* or the *alienated worker*, have in mind some form or other of what I have called spiritual alienation. I have invented these terms and made these distinctions in the hope of disentangling beliefs which, so it seems to me, are implicit in what Marx actually said, though he did not state them clearly and failed to see some of their important implications. I have wanted to make progress in one of the darkest parts of the Marxian forest, and I will not say confidently that I have never lost my way.

[42] Ibid., p. 129.

V

In *The German Ideology* Marx and Engels contrast the situation in which 'each man has a particular, exclusive sphere of activity, which is forced upon him and from which he cannot escape' with 'communist society, where nobody has one exclusive sphere of activity but each can become accomplished in any branch he wishes, [and] society regulates the general production and thus makes it possible for me to do one thing today and another tomorrow, to hunt in the morning, fish in the afternoon, rear cattle in the evening, criticize after dinner, just as I have a mind, without ever becoming hunter, fisherman, shepherd or critic'.[43] They here put forward, as an ideal, not only variety of occupation, but also getting rid of the sharp distinction between work and leisure. In the society of the future, man's condition will be in some respects as it used to be in primitive society before there was a rigid division of labour; he will not be confined to one kind of productive labour but will engage in many kinds, and productive labour—so the passage I have quoted seems to imply—will be no more felt as a burden by the doer of it than will his other activities. Hunting in the morning, fishing in the afternoon, rearing cattle in the evening are just so many activities, like criticizing after dinner, in which a man engages, develops his capacities, and affirms himself. The communist society will, of course, also be different in important respects from primitive society; it will presumably be much more sophisticated and technically much more advanced, and it will also regulate general production, presumably on rational principles and to secure a wide range of opportunities to the individual. It will not be custom-bound, as primitive societies are.

It is worth noticing that the activities mentioned in the well-known passages I have quoted are all, except perhaps 'criticizing after dinner', widespread in primitive societies; and there is even in such societies a good deal of criticism, though perhaps more of neighbours and their doings than of art, science, philosophy, and government. If the authors of *The German Ideology* had spoken not of hunting in the morning but of coal-mining, not of fishing in the afternoon but of ship-building, not of raising cattle in the evening but of working in a factory, the picture they drew would have been not only less attractive but also more obviously unrealistic.

Later, without taking back what he had said before, Marx changed his mind in one important respect. Speaking in the *Grundrisse* of communist society, he says:

Individuals are then in a position to develop freely. It is no longer a question of reducing necessary labour time [that is, the time needed to produce what are considered, given the standard of living, the necessaries of life] in order to

[43] *The German Ideology*, Pascal's translation, p. 22.

create surplus labour, but of reducing the necessary labour of society to a minimum. The counterpart of this reduction is that all members of society can develop their education in the arts, sciences, etc., thanks to the free time and the means available to all.[44]

He says also: 'To economise on labour time means to increase the amount of free time, i.e. time for the complete development of the individual.'[45] And in the third volume of *Capital* he distinguishes between labour, 'the realm of necessity', and 'the realm of freedom' which begins only where labour ceases. Freedom within the realm of necessity can consist only in the workers jointly controlling production; but this control is still not 'the true realm of freedom', which lies beyond it.[46]

The ideal described in *The German Ideology*, though never repudiated, is abandoned. The communist society will also be industrial, and production will be complicated and carefully organized, even though the organizing of it will be done by the workers themselves. There is no more talk of doing one kind of work in the morning, another in the afternoon, and a third in the evening, and the distinction between labour time and free time, or between work and leisure—a distinction which is in any case sharper in industrial and urbanized than in economically simpler societies —is fully recognized. Above all, it is a man's activities in 'the realm of freedom' which are conceded to be the more educative, and the more satisfying. As Marx puts it in the *Grundrisse*, 'the capacity for enjoyment is a condition of enjoyment and therefore its primary means, and this capacity is the development of an individual's talents'.[47] But the individual's talents, so we are told, are developed more in his 'free time' than his 'labour time' activities—even in a communist society.

I do not know whether Marx believed that this was true of all individuals or only of most. After all, the work that has to be done in a highly developed industrial society varies enormously in kind. Some kinds call for great intelligence and initiative, and for a considerable variety of talents, while others call for much less. There will always, in societies of that kind, be a considerable minority of men and women who get deeper satisfaction from their work than from their leisure-time activities. Marx never inquired how production should be organized or how people should be educated so as to ensure that even the less talented have more varied and more satisfying work to do. He condemned the separation of what he called 'mental' from 'manual' labour in the capitalist economy, but he did so without explaining how it was to be overcome after the fall of capitalism. And it is worth noticing that, when he came to distinguish between

---

[44] *Marx's Grundrisse*, ed. by D. McLellan, p. 142.
[45] Ibid., p. 148.
[46] *Capital* (F.L.P.H. edn., Moscow, 1962), iii. 799–800.
[47] *Marx's Grundrisse*, p. 148.

labour time and free time, and conceded that for many people, if not for all, their free-time activities would be educative and satisfying, he never pointed to the workers' control of production as itself an educative and satisfying activity. He did not deny that it would be so; he merely said nothing about it.

Workers' control would, of course, put an end to exploitation, and might ensure that work was less monotonous and was carried on under more comfortable and pleasant conditions. There would no longer be production for production's sake, or in mere pursuit of profit; there would be no more treating labour as a commodity, and the workers would decide how far to reduce their labour time to give themselves more free time. Nevertheless, it was above all to 'the realm of freedom' that Marx, except in his early years, looked for what he called 'the complete development of the individual'. That is to say, this is the sphere of their lives which he believed would provide most people in an industrial society, even though a communist one, with the chance to develop their talents in the ways most satisfying to themselves. Or, at least, this would seem to be what he believed, to judge from the few sentences in which he said enough to give us a clue as to what he really thought about this matter.

Marx believed that capitalist production was progressive in at least two important respects: it enormously increased the productivity of labour, and it also, as smaller enterprises gave way to larger ones, made it easier for society or for the workers eventually to take over control of production. He also at times saw other advantages in it. With capitalism comes large-scale industry, and this industry, even while it is capitalist, is in some ways liberating. Marx claims for it that it 'has torn away the veil which used to hide from human beings their own social process of production, and which used to make enigmas of the various branches of production . . . not only to outsiders but even to initiates'.[48] It also 'gives rise to changes in work . . . [and] to a many-sided mobility of the worker'.[49] And again, even though at the cost of breaking up 'the old family system', it lays 'the new economic foundation for a higher form of the family and of relations between the sexes' by bringing women and young persons and children of both sexes into productive labour outside the home.[50]

Capital may be 'dead labour' which 'like a vampire' keeps 'itself alive by sucking the blood of living labour',[51] capitalist production may have 'sapped the vital energy of the people at the root',[52] and manufacture have transformed 'the worker into a cripple, a monster, by forcing him to develop some highly specialized dexterity at the cost of a world of pro-

[48] *Capital* (Everyman edn.), i. 525.   [49] Ibid. i. 526.
[50] Ibid. i. 529.   [51] Ibid. i. 232.   [52] Ibid. i. 273.

ductive impulses and faculties',[53] but the system does nevertheless shatter illusions and destroy social ties that are inhibiting. It brings man up against his environment, his man-made social environment, in which he expresses what he is, as no system before it. Or, in other words, it brings man up against himself, and forces him to probe deeper into the human condition, to think more boldly, and to act more drastically, than he has ever had to do before.

[53] *Capital,* i. 381.

CHAPTER VI

THE CAUSES OF ALIENATION

IF alienation is to be surmounted or abolished, it is as well to have clear ideas about its causes. But Marx, unfortunately, seemed unable to make up his mind what they were. Sometimes he spoke of alienation as if it arose from private ownership of the means of production, sometimes as if it came with a certain kind of division of labour, and sometimes as if it were a consequence of commodity production or a market economy. In his early writings he said more about the first two of these causes than about the third, but not so much more as to justify our concluding that he decisively changed his mind, giving up some beliefs in favour of others. His accounts of the causes of alienation are brief and confused, and there is no extracting a coherent theory from them. Nevertheless, his arguments, obscure though they are, are worth looking at, for some of them point to important connections between social relations and roles, on the one hand, and beliefs and attitudes, on the other.

I. PRIVATE PROPERTY, THE DIVISION OF LABOUR, AND COMMODITY PRODUCTION

These three alleged causes of alienation—private ownership of the means of production, a certain kind of division of labour, and commodity production—are not mutually exclusive. It is clear that Marx thought them closely connected, though he never explained how precisely they are so. A Marxist concerned to bring order and clarity into this part of the master's doctrine might argue that alienation springs from a kind of division of labour characteristic of a market economy in which there is private ownership of the means of production. Such an argument would square with many things that Marx actually says. There is alienation, he tells us, where labour is treated as a commodity, and it is so treated in a market economy. He also tells us that, where there is alienation, man feels himself up against a system he does not understand and cannot control, though it consists only of human activities, his own included among them. The capitalist economy is an oppressive system of this kind, and is also (by definition) an economy in which the means of production are privately owned by a small part of the community who, to make profitable use of them, must hire labour.

Yet this account of the causes of alienation, though it is in keeping with much that Marx says, is still not *his* account. What is more, it achieves simplicity and coherence by ignoring assertions of his not less interesting than the ones it takes notice of. Rather than fall back immediately on a tidy but selective interpretation of his views, I prefer to consider in some detail the contradictions and contortions of Marx's arguments. For he was wrestling with problems that sociologists and social historians still find baffling.

If we consider what Marx says in the 'Economic and Philosophical Manuscripts', we find him both unwilling to admit that alienation is an effect of private property in the means of production and unable to suggest another cause; we find him contradicting himself, or at least trying to have his cake and eat it. For example, we find him, at the conclusion of a brief and obscure account of how labour comes to be alienated, saying: 'We have, of course, derived the concept of alienated labour from political economy, from an analysis of the movement of private property.'[1] Now this, on the face of it, is to suggest that there cannot be alienated labour except where there is private property; that is to say, as the context makes clear, private ownership of the means of production. Marx's words do not, of course, imply that this kind of property always gives rise to alienated labour, but they do suggest that labour is alienated only where this kind of property exists. For what, we may ask, is it to analyse 'the movement of private property', if not to explain the functioning of an economy in which there is this kind of property? This 'movement' consists, presumably, in the uses to which what is privately owned is put in the economy, and in the effects of the uses on the functioning and development of the economy. And what is 'to derive the concept of alienated labour from this analysis', if it is not to show how labour comes to be alienated in such an economy? And yet, immediately after the assertion I quoted, Marx goes on to say: 'Private property is, therefore, the product, the necessary result, of alienated labour, of the external relation of the worker to nature and to himself'; and again, 'although private property *appears to be* the basis and cause of alienated labour, it is rather a consequence'.[2]

In this early manuscript Marx claims to have done what there is no evidence that he even attempted. At the end of his 'analysis of the movement of private property', he tells us that 'private property appears to be the basis and the cause of alienated labour'. But if, at this point of the argument, this is how it appears, it does so only because his own analysis suggests it. It is the impression that his account of the matter, so far as it is intelligible, creates; and yet, so he assures us at the end of the account, the impression is false. What appears to be the basis and the cause is really an effect. But Marx never explains how this is so; he nowhere in these early manuscripts (nor as far as I know, anywhere else), makes a step

---

[1] *Karl Marx: Early Writings*, p. 131.   [2] Ibid., p. 131. My italics.

towards showing that the private ownership of productive resources is an effect rather than a cause of labour's being alienated.

At this point, in weariness, you may be moved to ask: Do we need to inquire what Marx believed about the causal relations between private property and the alienation of labour? Did he not think of them both as arising out of the division of labour? Does it matter, then, which he thought was the effect and which the cause? Is it not better to consider what he had to say about the division of labour? For, though his 'analysis of the movement of private property' does imply that this type of property is the cause of alienation, it is clear that he himself resisted this implication; that he was looking, even in these early manuscripts, for some other, deeper, cause of alienation, though he failed to make clear what it was. And, surely, this deeper cause, as his later writings suggest, is to be found, if anywhere, in the division of labour?

To these questions (which I have imagined as signs of impatience with my way of dealing with Marx's arguments) I would give two answers. Firstly, like other socialists of his day, Marx expected great things from the abolition of private ownership in the means of production. It would not only lead to equality but would put an end to alienation. But if this type of property is an effect and not the cause of alienation, it is not easy to see how, by getting rid of it, you get rid of alienation. For Marx, as for other socialists, a great deal turns on the system of property; a great deal is achieved by changing it. No doubt, it is possible, in the world as it has now become, that the abolition of private property would cause alienation to disappear, or would make it easier to put an end to it, even though alienation arose in the first place before this type of property. But this, though possible, is by no means obvious; the social theorist cannot take it for granted but must give reasons for believing that it would be so. If he merely takes it for granted, as Marx so often does, he inevitably gives the impression that private property is the cause of whatever he says will disappear when it is abolished.

Secondly, though Marx did indeed point to the division of labour as the cause of alienation, it is not obvious just what kind of division he had in mind. Wherever there is co-operation of any kind (and in all societies, however primitive, there is some), there is some kind of division of labour. While Crusoe was alone on his island, there was no division of labour, though there may have been planned production; but as soon as Man Friday appeared and attached himself to Crusoe, there was a division of labour between the two men. And even if we should want to say that Man Friday was exploited (in some sense of that word), we would have to admit that his labour was not a commodity and was not alienated.

Presumably, then, Marx, when he said that alienation is an effect of the division of labour, did not have every kind of division of labour in mind.

There is a division of labour of some kind in every family and in every tribe, no matter how simple its economy, and Marx never said or implied that in every family and tribe labour is alienated. There will also, presumably, be some kind of division of labour in the communist society of the future, and Marx assures us that there will be no alienation. Clearly, then, when he points to the division of labour as the cause of alienation, he means a certain kind of division. The question then is, *Just what kind?* And this question, as we shall see, is not so easy to answer.

One answer might be: the kind of division that gives rise to private property in the means of production. But this answer is not sufficient; for it does not tell us what the kind is that has this effect, and merely assumes that there is a kind that does have it. And, even if we did establish a correlation between private property in the means of production and a certain kind of division of labour, it would still be an open question which was the cause and which the effect. If further study showed this division of labour to be an effect of private property, we should have to say that the root cause of alienation was this type of property. Marx does sometimes, when he suggests that alienation arises from a certain kind of division of labour, also suggest that this division gives rise to private property, and yet—to the best of my knowledge—he never explains how it does so, he never describes the process. He does no more than assert a connection, and seems to think this enough. Indeed, he does not even make it plain what kind of division of labour it is that produces alienation. He gives some indications, makes some suggestions, but they do not amount to a lucid and adequate account. They are not enough to enable us to point to a type of division of labour clearly distinct from other types, and to say, *this* is the type which (according to Marx) produces alienation and for *these* reasons.

Nevertheless, we must take a look at these indications and see what they amount to. In *The German Ideology* we find this statement: 'Division of labour becomes truly such from the moment when a division of material from mental labour appears.'[3] The point of calling this division of labour *truly such* is that it has certain consequences that Marx and Engels think are important. It separates people from one another in ways that other kinds of division of labour do not. Mental labour consists, presumably, of such activities as directing the labour of others, interpreting and enforcing social rules, administering ceremonies, teaching, making and propagating theories and myths. Such activities go on, to some extent, in all societies, but in some they are not divorced from ordinary manual labour. That is to say, they are carried on by people who also work with their hands. But as soon as some people do most of the 'mental' labour and leave it to others to do the 'manual', or as Marx and Engels here put it, the *material* labour,

---

[3] *The German Ideology*, R. Pascal's translation, p. 20.

the division of labour has consequences it did not have before. Those who do the mental labour are set apart from the others; their status is superior. Society is divided into castes or classes.

In *The German Ideology*, Marx and Engels make it clear that, in their opinion, it is when the division of labour is *truly such* that labour comes to be alienated and the productive system comes to seem oppressive to the persons involved in it. But what they fail to notice is that mental and manual labour can be sharply separate even though there is no private ownership of the means of production and no market economy, no *commodity production*. The converse is also true: there can be this kind of private ownership and a market economy with no separation of mental from manual labour. No doubt, these three things (the separation of mental from manual labour, private property in productive resources, and a market economy) are often found together; as, for example, where there is capitalism. But they need not go together, and in fact quite often do not, though Marx and Engels, at least in *The German Ideology*, take it for granted that they do.

Imagine a simple self-governing community consisting only of farmers and artisans, each of them the owner of his own land or workshop and his own instruments. In this community money is used, and producers sell their own products and buy those of others. There is here private ownership of productive resources and commodity production but no separation of mental from material labour. There is no division of labour that is 'truly such', though there may be an extensive division of it in another and more usual sense of the word. It may be objected that the economy I have just described has never existed in a pure form. That may be so; but equally, the world has yet to see a pure example of a capitalist economy as Marx (or, for that matter, Adam Smith) described it.

Imagine, on the other hand, a highly controlled economy in which all productive resources are 'publicly' owned and consumer goods are allocated to workers in proportion to the work they do and to their 'needs'. In such an economy, there is neither private ownership nor commodity production, as Marx understood these terms, but there could be a more rigid separation of mental from material labour than there ever has been under capitalism.

Marx and Engels speak of the *separation* of mental from material labour. It is not obvious what they have in mind. They could mean a state of affairs inconsistent with equality of opportunity, as we today understand it, or they could mean one consistent with it, though perhaps undesirable on other grounds. In the West in Marx's time it was very difficult for the sons and daughters of manual workers to get the sort of education that would qualify them to do what he called 'mental labour'; today it is considerably easier. But it could be easier still; there could be much greater equality of opportunity than there is now, and yet mental and manual labour be just as separate as they now are. That is to say, a society could be much more egalitarian than our Western societies now are, and yet men and women be even more rigidly confined to the type of work they are qualified to do. Marx and Engels seem to mean, by the separation of mental from material labour, something more than could be abolished merely by establishing what we today call equality of opportunity. In the communist society of the future, as they imagine it, no one will be tied to one occupation and everyone will do both mental and manual labour; and yet technologically this society will be no less, and perhaps much more, advanced than is capitalism.

Though Marx never explained how the division of labour that is 'truly such' is connected with private property and with commodity production, it is clear that he thought the connection close. In *The German Ideology*, he and Engels go so far as to say: 'the division of labour and private property are, moreover, identical expressions: in the one the same thing is affirmed with reference to activity as is affirmed in the other with reference to the product of activity'.[4] This, taken literally, hardly makes sense; but without bothering to inquire whether it makes better sense taken metaphorically, we can see that it does at least imply that a certain kind of division of labour is very closely, perhaps indissolubly, connected with the private ownership of productive resources, with what Marx ordinarily means by 'private property'.

In the third of the 'Economic and Philosophical Manuscripts', Marx says: 'It is precisely in the fact that the division of labour and exchange are manifestations of private property that we find the proof, first that human life needed private property for its realization, and secondly, that it now requires the suppression of private property.'[5] Here again Marx suggests that private property and a certain kind of division of labour (presumably the kind that separates mental from manual labour), go always together, though he does not explain how they are connected. By 'the realization of human life' he means, I take it, what he elsewhere calls the 'development of human capacities' and the 'satisfaction of human needs'. Thus, what he is saying in the sentence I have just quoted is that the division of labour that arises along with private property begins by contributing to a fuller development of human capacities and a fuller satisfaction of needs, and then later stands in their way. Private property must disappear if there is to be a still wider range of activities, or if the individual's opportunity to engage in such activities as society finds room for and his talents put within his reach is to be enlarged, or if more varied wants are to be satisfied. The division of labour that arises with private property both enriches and impoverishes the life of man; it enriches it by

4 *The German Ideology*, p. 22.   5 *Karl Marx: Early Writings*, p. 187.

calling for (or making possible) a wider range of activities, and yet also impoverishes it by shutting the individual off from many activities suited to his talents and by failing to satisfy many of his wants. This is how I interpret this particular argument of Marx's.

It would appear then that the division of labour which produces alienation has three characteristics: it separates mental from manual labour, it goes along with commodity production (that is to say, with production for the market), and it is closely bound up with private ownership of productive resources. Though Marx never explains how these three things are connected, he quite often takes it for granted that they go together, and sometimes even says so in so many words. In taking so much for granted he is, I suggest, mistaken. These three things need not go together. It is easy to imagine an economy in which there is only one of them without the other two. And the mistake is not a small one; it is not of little consequence. For if alienation springs from the separation of mental from manual labour, and there can be this separation even where there is no private property in productive resources and no commodity production, it is not obvious that by abolishing this type of property and this type of production, you get rid of alienation. It may be that you could do it that way, or at least that their abolition would help (though it might not suffice) to bring alienation to an end, but this is something that has to be proved and cannot be taken for granted.

Writers about Marxism sometimes speak as if, in Marx's opinion, man has been alienated in all hitherto existing societies and will cease to be so only in the communist society of the future. It may well be that Marx believed this, or believed it sometimes. It would seem to be implied by his calling religion a fantasy of alienated man; for in all past societies, even the most primitive, there has been some form of religion. Nevertheless, Marx's account (vague though it is) of the causes of alienation implies the contrary: that labour, and therefore man, has not always been alienated in the past. Whether we take the separation of mental from manual labour or private ownership of productive resources or commodity production, or all three together, as the source of alienation, it is clear that there have been societies with little or nothing of any of them. It is a fair inference from what Marx says about the causes of alienation and from what we know of primitive societies that man was a social being long before either he or his labour came to be alienated.

Alienation, though it is a painful condition which man must overcome if he is to be emancipated, if he is to develop his capacities fully and freely, is also a symptom of progress. It arises as the division of labour grows more extensive, as needs and knowledge multiply in societies calling for a wider variety of skills. It is necessary that these needs should multiply—or rather that the wants in which the need for self-affirmation finds expression should require for their satisfaction a deeper understanding of human nature and 'the human world' (or society)—if man is to be 'emancipated', if he is to control the social conditions in which he lives. So long as he accepts these conditions without understanding them, he is not emancipated. But before he can learn to understand and control them, he must feel oppressed by them and revolt against them; he must feel the need to master them. This much, I think, is implicit in Marx's account of the causes of alienation. Alienation is both an effect of progress, of a growing mastery of nature, an ability to use it more effectively to produce what satisfies human wants, and a cause of progress, making more intense and more conscious man's aspiration to control the social conditions in which he lives, the conditions which express what he is and which he must learn to control if he is to live as he wants to live. Alienation, of course, is not in itself liberating, but it is an experience to be passed through on the way to liberation. The human condition, when alienation is overcome, is profoundly different from what it was before man came to be alienated.

Consider, for a moment, the extended family, the clan or tribe, all of whose members are (or are deemed to be) blood relations. There is, in this community, some work that only men do and some that only women do, and some that only children do or only men in their prime or only old men. There is also some work requiring special skills done by a few persons more apt than the others are at acquiring the skills. But, apart from the few with unusual skills, most men, at some period or other of their lives, engage in virtually all the activities reckoned to be man's work, and most women in those reckoned to be woman's work, and there are also kinds of work that both men and women do. Nobody is confined for life to one kind of work, though the kinds of work done in the community are easily numbered, given that the community is small and simple. Nevertheless, within the considerable range of its activities, most men and most women lead a varied life, exercising a considerable range of skills.

In this community neither men nor women look upon themselves as doers of a particular kind of work. If a man from such a community were asked what he was, he might answer, quite simply, that he was a man, or perhaps an old man or a married one, or he might name his clan or ancestry; but he would not name an occupation. If he wanted to boast, he might speak of his exploits in battle or in the hunt, or might name relatives of whom he was proud, but he would not refer to a kind of work setting him apart from and above other men. In this sort of community, there is as yet no separation of low-grade from high-grade work, or of manual from non-manual labour. There may, though there need not, be some private ownership of productive resources and some production for the market. But if there is private property, most men have some, and few (if any) have to make a living by selling their labour to others. In this sort of community there is no alienation but also there is no control of the conditions of life and only a modest development of human capacities. Before there could be a fuller development, there would have to be (according to Marx) a much more extensive division of labour.

A more extensive division brings with it the separation of mental from manual labour and also commodity production; it therefore brings alienation. Or at least this is what, as a matter of history (so Marx thinks), it has brought. The fuller development of human capacities comes with types of social change that bring alienation with them but it also (as we shall see later) makes possible, and indeed requires, that alienation be overcome. But this it can do only if men learn to understand and control their social environment, if they become collectively masters of the communities they belong to.

In *The German Ideology* Marx and Engels say:

The division of labour offers us the first example of how, as long as men remain in *natural* society . . . as long therefore as activity is not voluntarily but *naturally* divided, man's own deed becomes an alien power opposed to him, which enslaves him instead of being controlled by him. For as soon as labour is distributed, each man has a particular exclusive sphere of activity, which is forced upon him and from which he cannot escape. He is a hunter, a fisherman, a shepherd, or a critical critic, and must remain so if he does not want to lose his means of livelihood; while in communist society, where nobody has one exclusive sphere of activity, but each can become accomplished in any branch he wishes, *society regulates the general production* and thus makes it possible for me to do one thing today and another tomorrow.[6]

By a *natural* society Marx and Engels mean, in this context, a social order that men take for granted without controlling or even understanding it. They do not decide that it shall be as it is; they are born into it and accept it much as they do their natural environment, even though, unlike that environment, it consists only of their own activities. Though they do not understand it, in the sense that they cannot explain its operations correctly and do not know how to alter it the better to achieve their purposes, they are familiar with it and are able to sustain their roles inside it.

Now, clearly, if this is what a natural society is, a society can be natural though neither labour nor man is alienated. The extended family or clan that we considered a moment ago is a natural society, though there is no separation of mental from manual labour in it and labour is not a commodity. But then Marx and Engels, in the passage I have just quoted, do not actually say that in every natural society there is alienation; they say rather that where there is the kind of division of labour that gives rise to alienation, it cannot be abolished while society remains natural. Or, more precisely, their words imply, not that there is alienation wherever

6 *The German Ideology*, p. 22. My italics.

men do not understand and control their social environment, but that, where there is alienation, men can bring it to an end only by learning to recognize its social causes and by taking control of society in order to get rid of it.

I have said that Marx in his early writings, though he often took it for granted that the separation of mental from manual labour, private owner-ship of productive resources, and commodity production go together, never made it clear how they are connected. I doubt whether, in his later writings, he came any closer to explaining the connections between them. But he did sometimes recognize, at least indirectly, that they are not always found together. He did so, for example, in the first volume of *Capital*, when he compared capitalism with an older form of production surviving in the India of his day. Let me quote the relevant passage:

> Whereas, in a society where the capitalist method of production prevails, the anarchy of the social division of labour and the despotism of the manufacturing division of labour mutually determine one another, earlier forms of society, in which the separation of industries has spontaneously developed, then crystal-lized, and ultimately been consolidated by the sanction of law, offer, on the one hand, the picture of a purposive and authoritarian organization of social labour, and, on the other hand, that of a system in which the division of labour within the workshop is either non-existent or occurs to a minimal extent.[7]

As an example of one such earlier form of society, Marx points to what he calls 'the small and extremely ancient Indian communities . . . based upon the communal ownership of land . . . and upon a fixed form of the division of labour which is adopted as a cut-and-dried scheme wherever new communities are founded'.[8]

Marx, when he discusses these Indian communities, says nothing about alienation in them; he neither denies nor asserts that it is to be found there. Nor does he speak of the manual worker being 'crippled' in them, or of his being 'mutilated into a fragment of a human being', as he does of the worker in industrial England.[9] It is as clear from what he says in *Capital* as from what he says in his early writings, that alienation attains its highest point in a developed capitalist economy. If then there is alienation in these Indian communities, it is presumably much less serious than it is under capitalism. And yet, in these communities, as Marx describes them, there is a sharp separation of material from mental labour; or, if you prefer, of manual from non-manual work. In each of them, we are told, there is a judge, a book-keeper, a prosecutor of criminals, an overseer of waters, a Brahmin, and other mental workers belonging to a variety of castes and sub-castes. Much the most important of natural resources, the land, is communally owned, and the greater part of what is produced is

---

[7] *Capital* (Everyman edn.), i. 376-7.   [8] Ibid. i. 377.
[9] See *Capital*, i. 351 and 713.

consumed by the producer and his dependents and is not sold or bartered. There is clearly a rigid division of labour, though it is not the kind that arises when production is chiefly for the market; when it is, as Marx often puts it, *commodity production*. Though each man (even more than under capitalism) has what Marx calls a 'peculiar, exclusive sphere of activity from which he cannot escape', private property in the means of production is relatively unimportant and labour is not a commodity.

Comparing these Indian communities, as Marx describes them, with his account of capitalism, we may be moved to ask: Why should there be less alienation in these communities than in a capitalist society? Marx, of course, never put this question. But he did believe that alienation reaches its peak under capitalism, and he made a variety of statements about alienation and its causes, though he never fitted them together into a coherent whole. It is therefore worth while putting the question I have put: Why should alienation be worse under capitalism than in a rigid caste society? What are the relevant differences between the two types of society? Or, rather, what differences should we consider relevant in the light of what Marx tells us about alienation and its causes?

Marx tells us that, in these Indian communities, there is a 'purposive and authoritarian division of labour'. 'The law that regulates the division of labour' is, he says, inviolable, and each craftsman 'works in accordance with traditional custom, but independently and without being subject to any sort of authority, performing in his own workplace, on his own initiative, all the manipulations proper to his speciality'.[10] In other words, the worker, though his occupation is decided by his parentage and he is unable to change it, is his own master at work. He exercises his judgement and makes his own decisions. His work may be manual, or 'material' as distinct from 'mental', but it calls, nevertheless, for some intelligence and some initiative. So the worker, though he has no choice of occupation, is not the instrument of someone else when he is at work. But in capitalist society the worker is such an instrument; he does what he is told. He does not acquire his raw materials and then, in his own time and to the best of his ability, work them up into finished products. Yet he is free to choose his occupation; or, rather, there is no law or custom requiring him to follow one occupation rather than another, or confining him to the occupation of his first choice.

In the chapter of *Capital* in which he describes these Indian communities, Marx also makes a distinction between two kinds of division of labour. Both are to be found in market economies in which productive resources and instruments are privately owned. Marx calls one 'the social division of labour' and the other 'the manufacturing division of labour'. They are not, as he conceives of them, mutually exclusive; both can be

[10] Ibid. i. 378.

found in the same economy. Indeed, in the developed capitalist economy, we do find both, and that is why in that economy alienation reaches its highest point.

Speaking of the social division of labour, Marx says:

... the interconnections [between different occupations] are obscured by their wide spatial distribution and by the great number of separate kinds of labour. But what [he asks] is the nature of the connection between the independent labours of the cattle breeder, the tanner, and the bootmaker? The tie is the existence of their respective products as commodities.[11]

The division of labour he speaks of here is not prescribed by law or custom; it is therefore different from the division that obtains in his Indian communities. As he puts it: 'The social division of labour confronts, one with another, independent producers of commodities who recognize no other authority than that of competition, the coercion exercised upon them by the pressure of their reciprocal interests.'[12]

Though, where this kind of uncontrolled division of labour reigns, men are legally free to enter what occupations they please, the distribution of property, and therefore of opportunity, soon ensures that people who do the menial, monotonous, and ill-paid jobs are in practice confined to them all their working lives. They may move from one such job to another but they can rarely move from jobs of this kind to work that is more absorbing and educative and better rewarded. This social division of labour is one form among others of what Marx and Engels in *The German Ideology* call the division of labour that is 'truly such'. Legally, men are free to do what work they please, but the separation of manual from mental work is in practice almost as sharp as it is in caste societies. It is much easier than in caste society to pass from one kind of manual or one kind of mental work to another, but the line between these two broad categories is almost as difficult to cross. This division of labour arises before the kind that Marx calls 'the manufacturing division of labour', though it tends to produce it and goes on existing along with it. It is the kind peculiar to a free-market economy in which there are no castes and no regulation of labour.

The manufacturing division of labour comes with factory production. Inside the factory there is co-ordination, for every worker does his allotted task. But the task, more often than not, requires little skill and less initiative, and the work of the factory is organized, not by the workers, but by the manager or managers. Thus, the separation of mental from manual labour becomes, in one respect, greater even than before, for there are now many more occupations that call for almost no intelligence and initiative. Where there is factory production, the worker is still further removed from being his own master at work and labour is closer to being a mere commodity. It is then that alienation is at its worst. And, of course,

[11] *Capital*, i. 374.   [12] Ibid. i. 376.

when *Capital* was written, factory production was still confined to capitalist economies in which natural resources and productive instruments were privately owned. Marx had not seen it, as we now do, flourishing in economies which are clearly not capitalist, though it is a matter of dispute whether or not they can properly be called socialist.

In a note at the bottom of one of the pages in which he describes the Indian communities, Marx, quoting from his own *Poverty of Philosophy*, says, 'We may say . . . as a general rule that the less we find authority dominant in the division of labour . . . in society, the more do we find that the division of labour develops in the workshop, and . . . is [there] . . . subjected to the authority of a single individual.'[13] By the division of labour in society, Marx means a system in which in practice (even though neither law nor custom requires it) everyone is confined to one broad type of occupation for the whole of his working life, and by 'the division of labour in the workshop' he means what he elsewhere calls 'the manufacturing division of labour'. He therefore, in this footnote, puts it forward as a general rule that the less men and women are confined *by law or custom* to one kind of work, the more they are under discipline when actually at work. For example, in a capitalist economy, though the worker is legally free to take work where he can find it, he is not his own master at work. In other words, the more there is a free market in labour, the less labour is free. Today this may seem to us a sweeping and false generalization. In the Soviet Union in Stalin's time there was less of a free market in labour than there was, say, in the United States, and yet it is doubtful whether the Russian worker was any more his own master at work than the American. But in fairness to Marx we must remember that he could compare only capitalist with pre-capitalist economies, and that less was known then than is known now about pre-capitalist economies.

Notice that Marx, speaking of these Indian communities, says that labour is organized in them; and notice, too, that he says of the future communist society that it will *regulate general production*. Must we then conclude that these pre-capitalist Indian societies are not what Marx calls *natural* societies? For, as we have seen, a society is *natural*, as he uses that term, when its members do not understand and control it but take it for granted as they do the natural environment. If the 'regulation of general production' presupposes the rational control of society and the overcoming of alienation, why should not the 'organization' of labour do so? Why then should we not say of these Indian communities that they have overcome alienation? Or at least escaped it?

Here again I put a question that Marx never put, though this time it is one that can be answered easily enough. These Indian communities are, indeed, *natural societies*. The 'organization of labour' in them is merely a

[13] *Capital*, i. 377, note.

rigid adherence to custom. Nobody contrived that the productive system should be as it is; it functions as it does, not because men have decided that this is how it should function if they are to achieve what they think desirable, but because they do what is by tradition required of them. Even when they establish, as Marx says they sometimes do, a new community on virgin soil, they do no more than reproduce what is familiar to them. They have castes in the old communities, and so they reproduce them in the new ones; but they do not know how castes arose in the first place nor what their present functions are. They do not understand the social order in which they are involved; they cannot explain it adequately, nor reform it the better to achieve their aims. No doubt, they have theories about it, but these theories are ideologies, forms of false consciousness, fantasies whose origins and functions are no better understood by them than the social practices they purport to explain. Men do not become masters of the societies they belong to merely by recording their customs and reproducing them wherever they go.

Marx says very little about the communist society of the future, but he does say enough to make it clear that it will have a managed economy in a sense in which not even the most custom-bound of pre-industrial societies has one. It will regulate production so as to ensure that men and women are free, that human capacities are fully developed, and human needs fully satisfied. Just what is meant by the full development of human capacities and the full satisfaction of human needs I do not know, and I suspect that most people who use these expressions would be hard put to it to explain what they mean by them. But, be that as it may, it is clear that Marx conceived of the communist society as a community whose members know what social ends they want to achieve and how to achieve them; his conception of it is poles apart from his account of these Indian communities.

I have not discussed at this considerable length Marx's ideas about how the division of labour is connected with alienation, with commodity production, and with the private ownership of productive resources, merely to show how inadequate they are, how many crucial questions they leave unanswered; I have wanted rather to bring out whatever is suggestive and enlightening about them. These ideas may not add up to a coherent explanation, but there is a good deal to be learnt in the process of sorting them out. Marx was sometimes obscure and inconsistent, but he was also perceptive and imaginative.

II. AN IMAGINARY COURSE OF SOCIAL EVOLUTION

It may help us to appreciate better the value of Marx's ideas (obscure though they are) about the causes of alienation, if we imagine four types of society and a course of change from the first to the fourth. The four are all *ideal types*, in Weber's sense of the term, and I am not suggesting that they ever existed exactly as I describe them, and still less that they are successive stages in a necessary or normal course of social evolution. I use them partly to illustrate some of Marx's ideas and arguments, and partly to point to distinctions he failed to make and ought to have made.

The first type of society is the most primitive of all and has no division of labour of the sort that Marx had in mind when he spoke of labour being alienated. There is as yet no clear distinction made between the family and a larger community consisting of families. It is a tribal society of the kind I have already discussed. Both men and women engage in many different kinds of activity, though some activities are confined to men and others to women; and there is plenty of collaboration. Custom regulates what shall be done and how it shall be done, but custom is not codified and, though it may change considerably over long periods of time, no one notices that it does so. No one is self-sufficient, no one is omnicompetent, and everyone leads a varied life. Nobody conceives of the social order being different or better than it is; the roles of the inventor and the reformer are not recognized. Nobody keeps records and nobody constructs theories, though there are myths generally accepted. There is no regular government, but only a resort to elders to settle disputes. There is no private ownership of the means of production, and no public ownership either, for there are no persons with a right to decide on behalf of the community how these means shall be used and no settled ways for the community as a whole to take such decisions; though there are customary rules which limit the right to use natural resources and instruments of production or determine how the products of labour are distributed. Of men in a society of this type, we cannot say that they are *forced* to play their parts in it; they grow easily into them and no organized coercion is needed to ensure that they do what is required of them. Labour is not alienated, nor man either; or, at least, Marx would have to say so, for nothing that he points to as a cause or symptom of alienation is to be found here. And yet, presumably, human capacities are not developed to the full. Marx at least would be committed to saying that they were not, and many of his readers would agree with him. If I hesitate to agree, it is only because I am more at a loss than they are to know what is meant by 'a full development of human capacities'. But I do agree that there are many skills that people acquire in societies of other types that nobody acquires in this one.

In societies of the second type, most men are confined for life to one occupation or to a small number calling for the exercise of closely related skills. There is also a sharp separation of work that brings a high status and other coveted rewards to the doer of it from work that does not, most work of the first kind being what Marx would call mental labour. There is regular government in the sense that there are persons whose recognized occupation is the settling of disputes and the interpretation of rules, whose business is to see to it that obligations of various kinds are carried out. There are also teachers by profession, who either impart information and certain kinds of skills, or who give moral instruction. There are priests and other persons who officiate at ceremonies. Records are kept, and quite elaborate theories are constructed, though they are not 'scientific'. Land and certain other natural resources are communally or publicly owned in the sense that either the people as a whole decide how they shall be used or there are persons with authority to take such decisions on their behalf. Instruments of production are mostly owned, and are used almost exclusively, by their owners. Farmers and their families consume the greater part of what they produce, exchanging the smaller part against the products of the craftsmen; the craftsmen, considerably less numerous than the farmers, consume a smaller part of what they produce and exchange a larger part against the products of the farmers. In this type of society, labour is not a commodity, and most products of labour are not commodities either, except for the small part of them made in order to be exchanged. Marx's Indian communities are societies of this type. They are more consciously conservative, more deliberately respectful of tradition, than societies of the first type; their techniques of production are more elaborate, and they have privileged minorities whose occupations are political and intellectual.

In societies of the third type, there is the kind of division of labour that Marx describes in *Capital* before he goes on to discuss his Indian communities. Men are not confined by law or custom to the occupations of their fathers, though many of them find it expedient to follow in their footsteps. Most men keep to one occupation for their working lives, and if there is movement from one kind of work to another, it is nearly all on one social level; that is to say, it is mostly from one kind of work to another carrying the same social status. Land and other natural resources, as well as instruments of production, are nearly all privately owned, but there is almost no hiring of labour, except for domestic servants in the households of the wealthy. Though a large part of what is produced is consumed directly by those who produce it, there is already a developed market economy, and money is widely used. There are more kinds of work involved in material production than in societies of the second type, and there is much more extensive trade. There are therefore many more transactions between people who are not close neighbours, and the corpus of laws required to regulate these transactions is much larger. There is also a greater need to change the laws deliberately. Thus the work of government is more elaborate. There are more teachers by profession, and more people who spend their lives in making theories. Though the economy is not controlled, there are crude and inadequate theories about it, theories of which governments take some notice, so that, from time to time, they take measures, often ill-judged, in the hope of preventing what the theories condemn as abuses. There are theories, too, about other social activities, and they also have a considerable influence on what governments and private persons do. Lastly, there are theories about natural phenomena; and they are the nearest to being scientific and already have a considerable effect on methods of production, though not nearly as much as in societies of the fourth type. The roles of the inventor and the reformer are still small, but those who govern or teach or make theories are markedly less conservative than in societies of the second type. There are proportionately more of them, and the diversity of opinions among them is greater.

Because abundant records are kept and many and diverse theories are made, there are people around who are aware that society has changed and who believe that it could be different and might be better. Because the kinds of work, among the many that are done, open to any one man are in practice few, and also because theories stimulate ambition and criticism, there are more people in this type of society than in the second type who aspire to what is out of their reach, and who are dissatisfied with the work they do and with their roles in society. Though, taking society as a whole, there are more acquired skills, manual and intellectual, than in societies of the first two types, the development of any one man is apt to be more one-sided. Yet law and religion do not confine a man to one occupation or narrow range of activities as they do in societies of the second type; the individual is supposed to be free to make the best of his life in accordance with his talents. Thus, men's ideas about what might be achieved, given the resources and the skills that are available, are greatly enlarged, while the opportunities open to any particular man are small. What is more, men are more apt to feel themselves at the mercy of mysterious and unpredictable forces. This for two reasons: because the controversies of intellectuals bring it home to them that they belong to a social order they barely understand and do not control, and because the division of labour is already so extensive that they are dependent as never before on strangers, on sources of supply, and on markets remote from them. In other words, for these two reasons, they are more apt to be alienated. Yet labour is still, for the most part, not a commodity, although the economy is already a market economy. More of the products of labour are made to be sold or exchanged, though the sellers are still ordinarily the men who make them. Workers whose work is directed by a superior are either apprentices or else belong to their masters' households.

Societies of the fourth type are capitalist. There is a much more extensive division of labour than in societies of the third type. Manual workers mostly do not own the resources and instruments they use but get a living by selling their labour to those who own them. Many of them work in factories, where each takes only a small part in making the product which is sold. Those who manage the labour of others are remote from them, as never before. Labour is a commodity. The workers leave it to those who hire them to tell them what to do and to decide how they shall do it; they take little pride in their work, which is monotonous and presents no problems calling for intelligence and initiative. They care little or nothing for the fate of their products, which belong not to them but to their employers, who dispose of them to their own best advantage. The variety of mental work done is much greater than ever before but also much more specialized, so that experts are intelligible, within the limits of their competence, only to one another. The natural sciences make rapid progress and their discoveries are used abundantly to improve productive techniques. As Marx puts it in *Capital*: 'Modern industry never regards or treats the extant form of the productive process as definitive. Its technical basis is, therefore, revolutionary; whereas the technical basis of all earlier methods of production was essentially conservative.'[14] Voluminous records are kept, and the historical and social studies develop rapidly. Society changes more and more quickly, and men have this change brought home to them in every aspect of their lives. They come at last to understand that, as their institutions change, so too do they, together with their ways of looking at themselves and at what is external to them. The economy is uncontrolled, and is shaken periodically by crises which get worse as time passes.

In this type of society, if we consider collectively the men and women who belong to it, human capacities are abundantly developed; much more so, certainly, than in societies of our first three types. The diversity of skills and of knowledge is immense. There is extensive and rapid progress, both materially and intellectually. If, however, we consider any man or woman singly, he or she acquires less varied skills than in societies of the first type, and many men and women do work which is duller than most of the work done in societies of the second and third types, where manual workers are mostly craftsmen or farmers. But there is a considerable minority of highly trained persons, whose skills and knowledge are acquired over many years. The exercise of these skills or the use of this knowledge is by no means simple or automatic; so that the work of this minority calls for closer attention, greater initiative, and finer judgement than does, in our second and third types of society, the work not only of craftsmen and farmers but of all but a small handful of brainworkers. Clerks, teachers, and doctors, for example, did not require as great knowledge or even as varied skills in the sixteenth and seventeenth centuries as they do today. It was only men of rare talent, even in those less

---

[14] *Capital* (Everyman edn.), i. 525.

specialized days, who could excel in several ways and exercise more diverse skills than the most gifted of our contemporaries.

It would be difficult to maintain that the rapid growth of the division of labour makes what Marx calls 'mental work' duller than it used to be; it must be on predominantly manual work that it has this effect, but that work is—or still was in Marx's day—the kind done by most people. So that, even if we cannot agree that the greater the division of labour, the duller all work becomes, we can perhaps admit that the more mental work becomes separate from manual work, the duller and the less challenging is manual work. And it is precisely in our fourth type of society that this separation is greatest. It is the manual workers who lead the most restricted lives. Both in their own eyes and in those of the brainworkers, they are the men and women to whom society has least to offer. Yet, because they live in towns and work in factories, because they are much administered and much managed by officials and by employers who deal with them at a distance, impersonally and in large numbers, they must learn to read instructions and to put requests in writing. The slave of the machine who repeats one small operation thousands of times each day must be literate as the Asian peasant or African tribesman who does several different kinds of work calling for considerable initiative and skill need not be.

This fourth type of society changes rapidly, so that people find it difficult to take their social roles for granted. Their needs and expectations change considerably even in the space of twenty years, and do so not only, nor even chiefly, because people grow older. Needs and expectations change much more because the whole pattern of social behaviour changes, so that growing old is no longer, socially and culturally, what it was a generation earlier. There is no easy passing from role to role as youth gives way to middle age and middle age to old age. There is much less reliance on tradition, on a store of wisdom inherited from ancestors. There is also much more moving from place to place in search of work, though work, at least for the manual worker, is in each new place as dull and mechanical as it was before. The manual workers move, not to find work that is more congenial, but merely to find work.

This social order, in which everyone (though no one as much as the manual worker) feels insecure, is more studied and discussed than any before it. There is, therefore, a rapid increase in knowledge (or what passes for knowledge) about society along with much greater social insecurity and a weakening hold of tradition, so that the urge to control society and to change it grows more intense. The scale of production is vastly greater than before; there are often hundreds and even thousands of workers under one management; the planning of production within the larger enterprises is elaborate and looks forward far into the future. The idea of a managed economy comes to seem less fantastic, even to people who dislike the idea. Even the *laissez-faire* economist has an intricate and detailed image of a whole economy in operation, and has ideas about how it should function, and calls upon the government to remove obstacles to its functioning as it should.

Though Marx never described and contrasted these four types of society quite in the way that I have done, I have taken the elements that go to make up my descriptions from his writings, merely choosing my own words in preference to his in the hope of being simpler and more clear. My descriptions are brief sketches, and they neglect important aspects of production, and indeed of social life generally, which Marx discussed often at considerable length. For example, in putting together my description of societies of the second type, though I have drawn heavily on the few pages of the first volume of *Capital* in which Marx speaks of certain Indian communities, I have quite neglected his more frequent and ample comments on medieval Europe. Yet Europe in the Middle Ages was as close to being a society of this type as the India in which these communities survived. But my concern for the moment is not to do justice to Marx's thought, in all its richness, about society in its many forms; it is rather to construct ideal types of society to help bring out certain connections between the division of labour and alienation. I have wanted both to throw light on Marx's ideas and to draw attention to where they seem to me deficient. For example, in societies of the second type, of the type of Marx's Indian communities, there is a rigid and confining division of labour, though land is owned communally and labour is not a commodity; and there is as yet little production for the market. In societies of the third type, there is private property in the means of production and a developed market economy, and still labour is not a commodity. This is worth noticing, seeing that Marx was sometimes at such pains to insist that the root of alienation lies in a rigid and confining division of labour, *and* that there is alienation where labour is treated as a commodity, *and* that labour is so treated wherever there is private ownership of the means of production.

If we contemplate an imaginary course of social change passing from the first of our ideal types through the second and third to the fourth, we notice the range of activities open to the individual (except for a privileged few) getting narrower as the variety of occupations, skills, and knowledge within the community multiplies. Marx says somewhere: 'The worker becomes poorer the more wealth he produces.'[15] The context suggests that, in saying this, he is thinking above all of material wealth. But we could amend his sentence to read: 'Man becomes spiritually poorer, the greater the cultural wealth of his community.' Amended in this way, the

---

[15] *Karl Marx: Early Writings*, p. 121.

sentence gives us part of Marx's meaning when he speaks of the division of labour, and especially of the separation of mental from material labour, as the source of alienation.

Contemplating this course of change, we see that the greater men's understanding and power over nature, the more they are apt to feel themselves the victims of the social order they belong to. We see also that the more rapidly that order changes as a result of their own activities within it, the less secure they feel, the more it seems to them that they are at the mercy of events. Again, the greater men's knowledge and power over nature, the more men there are whose labours are directed by others, and the more all men, including the directors of labour, are exposed to social calamities they are powerless to prevent. If we consider only the privileged few, the intellectuals, the rulers, and the directors of labour, though the work of each of them requires diverse skills and considerable knowledge, each feels that he possesses only a very small part of the skills or knowledge or power possessed between them by the privileged. In short, the greater men's power, taken collectively, the less free and the less secure the individual feels. But, the greater men's power and knowledge, and the more aware they are that the change they do not control is nevertheless an effect of what they and their ancestors have done, the less resigned they are to their fate; they aspire, always more consciously, always more urgently, to determine the conditions of their life. Whatever the spiritual and cultural poverty of the individual, he cannot help but have a sense of the achievements of mankind, he cannot help but feel that life could be rich and free, if only he contrived to make it so, if only he came into his inheritance. Indeed, he could not feel poor unless he felt that potentially he was rich; he could not be frustrated, unless he had a sense of great opportunities close at hand. Alienated man thus becomes eventually and inevitably a revolutionary; he aspires to change the world so that he may become at last what life and reflection have taught him he has it in him to be.

Marx believed that the revolutionary *par excellence* is the proletarian, the most alienated of men. I have already quoted his saying of the workers in industry that 'their sufferings are universal', that the wrong done to them is 'not a particular wrong but wrong in general', and that, because they suffer a 'total loss of humanity' they can only redeem themselves by a 'total redemption of humanity'.[16] The proletarians, the most alienated of men, the worst afflicted by the division of labour and the separation of manual from mental work, the least free and the least secure in an uncontrolled and quickly changing economy subject to periodic crises, are revolutionary in a sense that no class before them ever were. They alone

[16] *The Critique of Hegel's Philosophy of Right* in *Karl Marx: Early Writings*, p. 58.

aspire to destroy one type of society deliberately in order to put another in its place and they alone, when at last their revolt succeeds, put an end to alienation by making men for the first time masters of their social environment. They alone are the redeemers of mankind.

APPENDIX TO CHAPTER VI: ON SURMOUNTING THE DIVISION OF LABOUR

MARX's belief that the division of labour that is 'truly such' (the separation of 'mental' from 'manual' work) can be abolished in a highly industrial society, provided that it ceases to be capitalist, is quite unsupported by argument. Communist society, so it would appear from his meagre account of it, will be just as technically advanced, just as productive as capitalism, and indeed more so; and yet there will be no confining of managerial, administrative, and intellectual work to some people and of manual work to others. Communist society will have something better to offer than what bourgeois liberals understand by equality of opportunity; it will enable everyone to do the kinds of work, engage in the activities, attractive to him. Marx (especially in his early years) took it for granted that, unless this were so, there could be no 'full development of human capacities'. In at least this one respect his idea of the future communist society is like Fourier's idea of the phalanx; the economy will be so managed that everyone inside it will be able to engage in a wide range of activities satisfying to himself and useful to others. But while the phalanx, as Fourier imagines it, consists of some sixteen hundred persons and is technologically simple, Marx's communist society forgoes none of the advantages of modern technology. In the communist society, we are told, 'nobody has one exclusive sphere of activity' but everyone 'can become accomplished in any branch he wishes' because 'society regulates the general production' so as to make it possible for him 'to do one thing today and another tomorrow'.[1] Just how, in an advanced society, production is to be regulated to achieve this result, is never made plain. This, presumably, is a problem to be solved, as so many others, after the revolution; though, as we shall see later, Marx's optimism in this respect was not unshakeable.

Sometimes, though not often, he pointed to developments in capitalist industry which seemed to him promises of better things to come. But he spoke of them only briefly, and never produced a coherent account of how production might change in such a way as to bring the separation of mental from material labour to an end. For example, in *The Poverty of Philosophy* he says: 'What characterizes the division of labour in the automatic workshop is that labour has there lost its specialized character. . . . The need for universality, the tendency towards the integral development of the individual begins to be felt. The automatic workshop wipes out specialists and craft idiocy.'[2] What Marx is saying here, if I have understood him rightly, is that, as labour becomes less skilled (and he assumes that it does so for most workers where there is factory production on a large scale), the need for the all-round development of the workers is more widely and strongly felt. He is not, presumably, saying anything so improbable as that this kind of production does anything to satisfy the need, that the worker at his work in an automatic workshop has greater opportunities to develop a variety of talents than he would have otherwise. The factory

---

[1] *The German Ideology*, R. Pascal's translation, p. 22.
[2] *The Poverty of Philosophy*, (F.L.P.H. edn., Moscow), p. 138.

worker is no specialist or craftsman, and is not required to do work calling for a wide variety of skills; and yet, so Marx suggests, his not being a specialist or craftsman somehow produces in him (or is it perhaps in others?) the feeling that he should be an all-round man. Why this should be so is not explained.

In the first volume of *Capital* Marx makes another point, again in passing on to other things and without developing it. He says there: 'From its very nature, therefore, large-scale industry gives rise to changes in work, to a flux of functions, to a many-sided mobility of the worker. On the other hand, in its capitalist form, it reproduces the old division of labour and the ossified particularisations of that division.'[3] That is to say, large-scale industry offers the worker a wider variety of work; or rather it would do so, if the economy were not capitalist. Large-scale industry, in itself, adds to the variety of life, multiplies the opportunities open to people, but, unfortunately, what this type of industry offers with one hand, capitalism takes away with the other. The conclusion to be drawn, presumably, is that large-scale industry is good and ought to be retained, and that capitalism ought to be abolished.

It matters little that both these points contradict what Marx says in other places; it matters rather more that neither is well taken. Consider the second point first. It is not easy to see why, if large-scale industry tends of itself to offer the worker a wider variety of work, its being capitalist should inhibit this tendency. It may be that capitalism has this effect but it is not obvious that it does. It is not a matter to be taken for granted; there must be reasons given why it should be so. But Marx does not give any. No doubt, in an advanced industrial economy, there are many different kinds of work done; but as we all know now, and as Marx knew better than most people did in his day, the variety of work done in a society can increase greatly and yet the range of occupations within the reach of most persons inside it grow more narrow. What Marx needed to show was that this narrowing of the range was an effect, not of industrialism, but of capitalism; and this he quite failed to do. Indeed, he did not even attempt to do it.

Let us concede that the mobility of labour increases with the scale of industry, for there is evidence that it has done so in the past. Yet the mere fact that workers can move more easily from job to job, and from place to place in search of jobs, does not ensure that the jobs open to them call for a wider range of skills. As Marx himself saw, the worker may move often from factory to factory, from town to town, from one branch of industry to another, and yet find himself doing much the same kind of work everywhere. Nor does the growing scale of industry, even where it increases the proportion of men who do skilled work, help to reduce the separation of managerial, political, and intellectual from manual work. The manual worker who is highly skilled is no more engaged in management or politics or intellectual activity than is the unskilled worker.

In an industrial society efficiency counts for more, perhaps, than it does in pre-industrial societies, and there is a stronger urge to look for talent and to train it; there is a stronger pressure to achieve equality of opportunity. This pressure may well be more inhibited in industrial societies that are capitalist

---

[3] *Capital* (Everyman edn.), i. 526.

than in those that are not. But from equality of opportunity to a full development of human capacities (as Marx understood it) is a far cry.

It is a questionable assertion that Marx makes in *The Poverty of Philosophy* when he says that automation reduces the demand for specialists and skilled workers. In the long run it may increase the demand. But, even if we accept the assertion, it is not clear why this reduced demand should make the need for what Marx calls 'universality', or the broader development of the individual's capacities, more deeply felt. No doubt in industrial society there has been much more talk than in earlier societies of the 'development of human potentialities', of 'self-realization' and 'self-improvement', and so on. But this, surely, is due to other causes much more than to the reduced demand for specialized skills: to the spread of literacy and of formal education, to greater geographical and social mobility, and to the rapidity of social and cultural change, which gives a sharper edge to ambition.

Such expressions as 'the development of human potentialities', 'self-realization', and 'self-improvement', though they are not synonyms, refer to closely similar things; and they are, I suspect, extraordinarily difficult to define. People do not all give the same meanings to them, and many people are uncertain what they mean when they use them. In saying this, I do not deny the importance of such vague ideas as these; they are used to pass judgements that matter greatly to the persons who pass them, and they influence the decisions they make and even public policy. These ideas, in spite of their obscurity or elusiveness, are highly attractive, and were never more so than in advanced industrial societies. They are attractive, I suppose, partly because the range of skills and activities grows quickly wider, and partly because the more rapidly society changes, the less fixed everyone's place inside it and the more widely it is recognized that it is for the individual to make his own place in it. A rapidly changing industrial society is a society of rising expectations, which are as much moral or 'spiritual' as they are material.

In his later years Marx seems to have become less hopeful and more realistic. In the third volume of *Capital*, he says:

the realm of freedom begins only where labour . . . ceases; thus in the very nature of things it lies beyond the sphere of material production. Just as the savage must wrestle with Nature to satisfy his wants . . . so must civilized man, and he must do it in all social formations and under all possible modes of production . . . Freedom in this field can only consist in . . . the associated producers rationally regulating their interchange with Nature, bringing it under their common control, instead of being ruled by it as [by] the blind forces of Nature . . . But it nonetheless still remains a realm of necessity. Beyond it begins the development of human energy which is an end in itself, the true realm of freedom, which however can [flourish] only with this realm of necessity as its basis.[4]

In this passage Marx does not, in so many words, go back on what he said in his earlier writings. He does not go so far as to admit that the separation of mental from material labour can never be abolished, that the division of labour

---

[4] *Capital* (English language edn., Moscow, 1962), iii. 799–800.

that is 'truly such' is a necessary feature of industrial society. But he looks for freedom, which for him is closely connected, if not identical, with a full development of human capacities, not in work but in leisure. Freedom in the sphere of labour means only the control of production by the associated producers, and the realm of freedom begins where labour ceases. There is not a word said here about the control of production ensuring that the producer is not confined to a narrow range of activities, that his work satisfies him more fully because it calls for a wider variety of skills. Nothing about doing away with the division of labour or about labour's becoming 'not only a means of life but life's prime want'—as Marx puts it in the *Critique of the Gotha Programme*. Even in the communist society in its higher phase there will be a realm of necessity contrasted with a realm of freedom. It was not Marx's habit to draw his readers' attention to the fact that he had changed his mind about a matter of cardinal importance in his theory, but it can hardly be denied that he did so in the third volume of *Capital*. He did not, to be sure, go back on the idea that man is uniquely 'self-creative' and has needs which cannot be satisfied until he has learned to control the social order which is his own product and in which he realizes his capacities, any more than he went back on the doctrine that under capitalism the worker is alienated;[5] but he did imply that, even in the communist society, his truly 'creative' activities—those in which he 'affirms himself'—would be separate from the merely 'productive' activities by means of which he satisfies his 'material' wants.

Marx's ideas about the proletariat as the pre-eminently revolutionary class destined to abolish the social conditions that give rise to alienation are, I suggest, less perceptive and less enlightening than his account, obscure though it is, of what alienation is and what it is about man and society that makes it possible. In saying this, I do not mean to imply that alienation is insurmountable, that nothing can be done to alleviate the conditions that produce it or to get rid of the forms of behaviour and attitudes in which it is manifest. It may well be that much could be done, and that the doing of it would require making great changes in the system of production and the social order generally. I mean only that Marx, who had so much that is suggestive to say about alienation, its causes and its symptoms, had very little that is useful to say about how to get rid of it.

[5] In the third volume of *Capital*, p. 86, Marx says: 'the labourer looks at the social nature of his labour, at its combination with the labour of others for a common purpose, as he would at an alien power; the condition of realizing this combination is alien property, whose dissipation would be totally indifferent to him if he were not compelled to economize with it. The situation is quite different in factories owned by the workers themselves, as in Rochdale, for instance'. The Rochdale workers are careful of the productive resources which they own jointly, but even with them, presumably, the 'realm of necessity' and the 'realm of freedom' are separate.

CHAPTER VII

THE REVOLUTIONARY CLASS AND THE REVOLUTIONARY TEMPER

It has been claimed for Marx that he was the most perceptive of the writers who in the nineteenth century put forward theories about revolution. I would not contest this claim. There is more to be learnt about revolution, about the situations in which revolutionaries act and what they do in those situations, from his accounts of events in France from 1848 to 1851, and again at the time of the Commune, than from the accounts of his contemporaries.

But there is also an unrealistic and even a romantic side to his talk about revolution, especially when he discusses it in the abstract. The lack of realism, though not the romanticism, is as much evident in his later as in his earlier writings. The idea of a revolution made in the fullness of time by a class-conscious and organized class that includes the majority (or the near majority) of the people is, surely, quite unrealistic. There has never been any such revolution anywhere in the world. Yet it is this idea, more perhaps than any other, which is set to the credit of Marx when his realism is contrasted favourably with the lack of it among the Blanquists and other revolutionaries of his time.

I want now to do three things: to point to what I find implausible or romantic in Marx's ideas about revolution and to contrast it with what seems to me perceptive and illuminating, to explain the difference (as he sees it) between the proletarians and the bourgeois as revolutionary classes, and to discuss what—for want of a better word—I shall call the 'revolutionary temper', an attitude (or set of attitudes) to society and to social change which in the West was much more evident in the nineteenth than in earlier centuries, and which Marx expressed with peculiar force and even insight. The revolutionary temper is not confined to classes as distinct from other social groups. Thus, what Marx has to say about it does not apply only to societies in which the most important conflicts are between classes.

I. THE REVOLUTIONARY CLASS

Even the less critical of Marx's admirers admit that what he says in his early writings—as, for example, in his *Critique of Hegel's Philosophy of Right*—of the proletariat as the essentially revolutionary class is, much of it, sheer fantasy and rhetoric. He there suggests that it is precisely because the workers are the most alienated of men, the most deprived of 'humanity', that they will make the revolution which, in 'redeeming' their own class, redeems mankind. But how can the most deprived of men—and the deprivation that Marx speaks of is as much cultural and moral as it is material—make that sort of revolution? For the revolution, as he conceives of it, is not a blind revolt; it is made by men who know what they are about. No doubt, it is destructive, but the makers of it know what they want to destroy and why it must be destroyed, and they hold firmly together. They are not mere Luddites giving vent to feelings of anger and frustration; they are men who see that the established order must be destroyed to make way for something better. How, then, can the most alienated, the most 'dehumanized' of men understand what needs to be done, and have the skill and discipline required to do it? Their condition in society, as Marx describes it in his early *Critique*, can hardly prepare them for the role which he predicts will be theirs. They, the most oppressed of men and the most at the mercy of events, who even at work are not their own masters, are to take control of society and eventually to transform it more radically than it has ever before been deliberately transformed.

It is true that Marx, even in his earliest writings, was never a Utopian of the kind that he accused other socialists of being. He never thought of the workers as making before the revolution the blueprint of the new social order to be established after it. Not only the work of reconstruction but the planning of it must be left to the period after the revolution. No doubt, the revolutionary workers, in rejecting the bourgeois order, put forward some principles (though Marx has little to say about them) to justify their rejection of it; they are able to give some reasons for condemning what they condemn. In that sense their rejection is not blind. But these principles, presumably, are general in character. To assert them and to appeal to them in condemning the established order is one thing; to use them as guides in the work of reconstructing society is quite another. For Marx, the task of destruction is sharply separate from the task of reconstruction. Not, of course, in the sense that the principles used to justify destruction are irrelevant when the time comes to reconstruct, but in the sense that revolutionaries must accomplish the first task before they can take the measure of the second.

Thus Marx, even as a young man, was never a Utopian of the kind he himself criticized. Nevertheless, the role he assigns to the revolutionary proletariat, essentially destructive though it is, calls for a high degree of class discipline among them as well as for a considerable understanding of the social order in which they are not only exploited but somehow 'dehumanized'.

In his later writings, Marx, though he still at times speaks of the proletarians as more alienated than any other class in capitalist society, does not say, as he does in the *Critique of Hegel's Philosophy of Right*, that they suffer a 'total loss of humanity'. They are still, in the later writings, 'redeemers of mankind', still so placed socially and culturally that, in liberating their own class, they liberate society as a whole; but they are no longer liberators or redeemers by virtue of their 'total loss of humanity'.

In the early *Critique*, beyond the bare assertion that their sufferings are the worst, Marx makes no attempt to explain why the most alienated and dehumanized of men should be the redeemers of mankind. Did he believe that suffering always brings enlightenment and that therefore the class that suffers most must in the end be the most enlightened? This, surely, is romantic nonsense. The idea of suffering as one source among others of enlightenment is not, of course, nonsense. It is a recurrent theme in literature; but then it is also a recurrent theme that suffering narrows and embitters the mind, and so makes the victims of injustice themselves unjust. In any case, the novelists and dramatists who produce variations on these themes have in mind only individuals, whereas Marx is speaking of a whole class in the community. In their alienated condition, suffering a total loss of humanity, they none the less learn to recognize their condition for what it is, and acquire the discipline and sense of purpose they need to enable them to accomplish the revolution that brings redemption to mankind.

Before looking further at the unrealistic aspects of Marx's doctrine of proletarian revolution, let us see how (in his eyes) that revolution differs from bourgeois revolution. If we look at what he says in pamphlets written after 1848 about the great revolution of 1789–94 and the lesser revolutions of his own time, all of them 'bourgeois' by his reckoning, we see that they are primarily, though not wholly, political; they aim rather at getting power for the bourgeois or for sections of their class than at transforming social institutions. The social revolution, and especially the transformation of the system of property, occurs (not altogether but to a large extent) before the bourgeois become consciously a revolutionary class. Their role, as a revolutionary class, is to complete the social revolution, to put an end to surviving anomalies, and to change the form of government. Of course, the social changes that precede the political revolutions of the bourgeois are not chance events. When social forms change, it is because men and women come to behave differently. The bourgeois social revolution, as much as the political one, is the work of people who have their reasons for doing what they do. But the changes that together make up the social transformation are not seen by those who make them in historical perspective; they may intend each change in turn but not the transformation that results from all the changes together. They do not aspire to make a social revolution.

Again, if we look at Marx's account of particular 'bourgeois' revolutions, we see that he does not think of the revolutionary bourgeois as constituting a united class. Each of these revolutions, as he sees it, is as much a tale of struggle among bourgeois groups as between them and other groups. Class solidarity, if we are to believe Marx (or, rather, if we are to follow up the implications of what he says), is something that the bourgeois have never known.

Lastly, the bourgeois, even when they make their political revolution, do not understand fully the historical significance of what they do. This is not to deny that they act rationally much of the time, if not all of it; that they have interests and pursue them intelligently. At any particular time, they may have a clear idea of what they are trying to achieve, and still have illusions about the social order and their place in it. This is so, not only while as yet they are not conscious revolutionaries, while they make changes that cumulatively transform the social order without being aware of the transformation; it is so even when they come to look upon themselves as revolutionaries. The bourgeois are victims of false consciousness; they are so as much when they are radicals or Jacobins as when they are cautious reformers or conservatives.

With the proletariat it is different. Their task, as a revolutionary class, is to make a social revolution; for though they may not prepare before the revolution the blueprint of a social order to be set up after it, though they are not Utopians, they consciously reject the established social order. They see the need for a radical transformation of society, even though they learn only in the light of experience gained after the revolution how to transform it. But they do know beforehand that in the new society there will be no private ownership of productive resources, that the economy will be managed collectively, and that everyone will have the chance to develop his capacities to the full. That is to say, they are agreed about the problems they will have to solve, even though they must wait until after the revolution to set about solving them.

The proletarians, as they become a revolutionary class, cease to be victims of false consciousness; they come to understand the historical significance of what they do, the course of social change, and the place of their movement in it. They become, what the bourgeois never were, clear-sighted revolutionaries. Though they do not see the future in detail and though they make mistakes, they shed their illusions. They learn from experience; they come to know their limitations, what it is possible for them, as a class, to achieve and what must be left to future generations. They also, in the course of their struggle against their class enemies, become, again as the revolutionary bourgeois never were, a united class. This, presumably, is one reason among others why Marx says of them that they alone are a truly revolutionary class. They are not merely the only revolutionary class in bourgeois society; they are also revolutionary in ways in which not even the bourgeois were revolutionary in the past. They are the most completely, the most consciously, revolutionary of all revolutionary classes. They not only make the last revolution but they make it deliberately and with a clearer sense of what they are doing than any other class.

Not many years after writing his *Critique of Hegel's Philosophy of Right*, Marx put forward, in *The Communist Manifesto* and especially in the pamphlets he wrote about events in France, better reasons for believing that the workers would eventually make a revolution of a kind never made by any class before them, a revolution to liberate mankind. The reasons are better but, in my opinion, still not convincing. The workers, he says, organize to defend themselves against their employers and exploiters, and in so doing acquire a clearer sense of the interests common to them and learn to act effectively in pursuit of them. They acquire discipline and loyalty to their class; they acquire leaders they can trust. No doubt they do; but as much can be said of other classes or groups who combine to define and to pursue common aims. It has still to be shown why the workers should be a uniquely privileged class, why they alone, in combining to define and pursue their interests, should come to understand the social order and how it is changing, should become free of illusion. After all, it is one thing for a group to acquire a clearer sense of what they want from society and to learn how to work together to get it; it is quite another for them to learn how society functions and is changing. The first kind of learning does not lead necessarily to the second.

Sometimes at least Marx was aware of this. He saw that the workers, if they were to become a revolutionary class, would need to acquire beliefs and aims that did not come to them in the mere process of learning to run trade unions to get better pay and conditions of work; they needed a social theory, not just to enable them to make sense of what they learned from experience, but to go beyond it. This theory, presumably, would come to them, not from the organizers and directors of their struggle against the employers, but from intellectuals; from persons like Marx himself able to provide them with ideas and theories placing their efforts and aspirations in a wider context, and thereby changing their direction.

That a class or other social group, to be revolutionary, need some kind of ideology to sustain them and to help direct their efforts is obvious. A great deal of what Marx says about the origins and social functions of theory makes good enough sense. And it was little appreciated in his day. But why should the theories that appeal to the revolutionary workers be any nearer being true, any more free of illusion, than the theories of other revolutionary groups? This is the question that Marx, so it seems to me, never answers. He is merely dogmatic, and resorts to forms of words whose persuasive power comes largely of their being echoes of Holy

Scripture. The most alienated, the most dehumanized of men, in redeeming themselves will redeem mankind. What is this but another way of saying that the last will be first, that the humble will be raised up?

No doubt, the workers' revolution, if ever there is one, will come later than the revolutions that we, following the example of Marx and other nineteenth-century socialists, have learnt to call bourgeois. It will come at a time when history and the social studies are more developed than they were when the bourgeois made their revolutions. We can say, therefore, that if ever the workers do become a revolutionary class, they and their leaders will be able to draw more heavily on history and the social studies generally to explain and justify their aims and activities than 'bourgeois' revolutionaries were able to do in the past. But this we can say also of their opponents, liberal, conservative, and reactionary; they too will have an immensely larger stock of facts and ideas to draw upon. Whenever conditions propitious to revolution arise, both the revolutionaries and their class enemies will be better placed to support their claims by appeals to history and the social sciences. Such good reasons as there are for holding that the proletarians are likely to be more enlightened than any revolutionary class before them are, surely, also good reasons for holding that the bourgeois are likely to be the most enlightened of conservative or reactionary classes. The mere fact that the workers are exploited does not in itself justify the conclusion that they are more likely than their exploiters to see society for what it is. No doubt, the exploited are better placed than their exploiters to understand what it is like to be exploited; but then equally exploiters are better placed than their victims to understand what it is like to exploit others. But why should the exploited be any better placed than their exploiters to understand the social order that makes exploitation possible? They have, to be sure, stronger motives for discovering how to put an end to exploitation, and this discovery may well involve coming to understand how exploitation arises; but then exploiters have stronger motives for discovering how to maintain exploitation when it is challenged, and this too may involve their looking into its origins.

Only if we accept Marx's prediction that capitalist society is doomed can we explain why the workers should shed their illusions about it while the bourgeois remain firmly wedded to theirs. If, as he says, it is the interest of the workers that capitalist society should disappear, while the interest of the bourgeois is that it should endure, and if its disappearance is inevitable, then the workers are more likely than the bourgeois to recognize that it is so. They will not close their eyes to the 'contradictions' that must eventually bring capitalism to an end, but will accept with a good heart this evidence that what they want to happen will happen. But why should we accept Marx's prediction, especially as it refers, not to what may happen whatever men do, but to what they will do? It is a prediction about the course of history, and therefore about how men will behave in the future. Capitalism is not doomed unless the bourgeois and the workers behave in ways that destroy it. Why then should we assume that the bourgeois are less well placed to preserve it than the workers are to destroy it? Or that they have less to gain than the workers have from understanding how it functions? Or, in other words, from understanding what their activities and those of the workers contribute to making it what it is? And if they can acquire this understanding, why should they not decide to change their ways in their own interests?

In Marx's time it was easier than it is now to believe that a large section of a community could form a solid, disciplined, and at the same time revolutionary organization to promote their class or group interests. We have had many revolutions in the world since Marx died, many seizures of power by groups who have set about making great changes rapidly, but we have had nothing like the proletarian revolution he imagined. Small revolutionary groups have played off other groups, sometimes much larger than themselves, against one another and have exploited widely shared grievances and fears, but there has been nowhere a vast and disciplined revolutionary movement whose leaders were united in their aims and whose aims were understood and approved by the mass of their followers. The class-wide discipline and the unity of aim, if they have come at all, have come only after the seizure of power by a revolutionary party. A movement inside a bourgeois society which grew large enough to include virtually the whole of the working class, and in the process became united, disciplined, and class-conscious, would have to act in the open, to be tolerated by the government. If it were tolerated, it would soon be politically formidable, and so concessions would be made to it until it ceased to be revolutionary. The idea of an organized, united, and enlightened revolutionary class is, surely, unrealistic to the point of absurdity. Marx was, I suspect, never as firmly wedded to this idea, even in his later years, as Engels was; but he did at times take it seriously.

I do not deny that Marx had fresh and perceptive ideas about revolutions and the social conditions in which they occur, and even about the workers' part in the revolutions of his own time. He had a sharp eye for the complexities of revolutionary situations, for differences of interest and attitude among groups in conflict or in alliance with one another, for changes of mood and intention among them and of the balance of power between them. As a political observer he had much of the penetration and some of the dry cynicism of Machiavelli, though he could be blinded by prejudice and coarsely abusive. He was afflicted by a German sense of humour. Yet no one in his day wrote with greater insight than he did about the revolutions and revolts that occurred in France between 1789 and 1871. But these revolutions were bourgeois and not proletarian, and the revolts, some of which were proletarian, were not (as Marx himself was at pains to make clear) acts of an organized and class-conscious class. He talked admirable sense about the bourgeois revolutions and proletarian revolts of his own day and the recent past, but not, I venture to suggest, about the proletarian revolution that he imagined for the future.

The bourgeois, so Marx said, had been (and in some parts of the world still were) a revolutionary class. But they were not, and never had been, revolutionary in quite the way he believed the workers would be. At no time, either in France or elsewhere, were the great majority of the bourgeois revolutionary, and those of them who were so (who wanted to make large changes quickly, if necessary by force) were never united in their aims. Marx never claimed that they were. When therefore he called the bourgeois a revolutionary class, he meant that there were revolutionary groups recruited largely from their ranks and enjoying considerable support among them; he did not mean that these groups acted together or even that between them they enjoyed the active support of the majority of their class. He also meant, sometimes, that these groups had aims that were, or were intended to be, for the benefit of the class, or of some considerable part of it. To call a class revolutionary in this sense is realistic, even though it may be difficult to define the limits of the class (to decide what groups belong to it) or to discover how far the revolutionaries are drawn from its ranks or get support from it. But to call a class revolutionary in the sense implied by some of the claims made for the proletariat by Marx (and also by Engels) is not realistic. No doubt, a class could *conceivably* be revolutionary in this sense, but the world has yet to see an example of it. The bourgeois never were so, and the proletarians show no sign of becoming so. Indeed, they show little sign of becoming a revolutionary class even in the less stringent sense in which the bourgeois were so in the past. There have been several revolutions that historians agree to call bourgeois, presumably because most of their leaders belonged by birth or education to some part or other of the bourgeoisie and got their support predominantly from that class. But I can think of no revolution that was proletarian even to that extent, though I can think of several in which the proletariat played a considerable part.

There have, of course, been revolutions which have been called proletarian by the men who made them, by the leaders. In some, the proletariat has taken a significant part, and in others almost no part at all, but in none—not even the October revolution in Russia—have the urban workers or leaders responsible to them (and not merely claiming to speak for them) been in control of events. The October revolution was, I suggest, less a proletarian revolution than the Paris Commune of 1871 was a proletarian revolt. Without the workers' support during the decisive days, the Bolsheviks would never have got power, but from the first power belonged to the Bolsheviks and not to the workers. The October revolution was not, to be sure, the least proletarian of revolutions made in the name of the proletariat; it was more proletarian than, for example, the Chinese or Yugoslav revolutions. To call a revolution made by leaders recruited largely from the middle class and supported mostly by peasants proletarian is surely an abuse of language.

If we reject as mere fantasy Marx's account of the proletarian revolution, we do not need to deny that there are in modern industrial societies deep-seated tensions or 'contradictions' which cannot be resolved except by a radical transformation of society. Nor need we deny that these tensions can give rise to revolutionary situations in which groups resolved to seize power and to use it to transform society radically have the chance to seize it. They may even get most of their support and recruit many of their leaders from the proletariat. If some such group or combination of groups, recruited largely from hired workers and getting more support from them than from other classes, were to seize power and use it to transform society rapidly and radically, it would be no more misleading to call their revolution 'proletarian' than, say, to call the French revolution of February 1848 'bourgeois'. But it would still not be a proletarian revolution of the kind imagined by Marx when he called the proletariat the only truly revolutionary class. And, of course, the radical transformation of society by these groups might do little or nothing to remove the 'contradictions' that produced the revolutionary situation, or might give rise to other 'contradictions' just as painful and disturbing, just as socially divisive, just as productive of alienation.

So, too, if we hold that in the industrial West the workers have seldom been revolutionary, and were more apt to be so in the early days of capitalism than they are now, we need not conclude that they are now a 'contented' class. They may be so or they may not be. Their not being revolutionary is in itself no sign that they are contented, and is consistent with their being very much the opposite. No doubt, their situation in an affluent and literate society differs greatly from that of the poorer classes in the past. There is plentiful evidence that in the past peasants, whether in a condition of serfdom or not, have been discontented and yet not revolutionary; that they have looked upon themselves as oppressed and exploited by the richer classes and by the government, and yet have been resigned to their fate. They were resigned to it because, as they saw it, there was nothing they could do about it. They lived in societies in which the idea that the social order might be deliberately changed and made more just scarcely existed, and least of all among them.

The situation of the workers in the industrial West is, of course, very different. They live in a society in which the idea that big changes can and should be made in the interests of justice is widely accepted, and where the dissatisfied have legal means of putting pressure on the government. Their not being revolutionary is certainly better evidence that industrial workers in the West are not deeply discontented than was the 'docility' of the peasants in the past.[1] Yet it is far from conclusive. There is also evidence pointing the other way—that many workers (for example, in Italy and France) believe that democracy is a sham and that the managerial and professional classes have far more influence on government than their numbers justify. Their 'acceptance' of the system is probably to some extent positive and to some extent negative; they recognize that it has brought them considerable benefits, and they believe that there is little they can do to remedy certain defects from which (in their opinion) they suffer more than the wealthier classes do. They may be wrong in believing this; they may be able to do much more than they think to remedy the defects without resorting to revolutionary action. But if they do believe it, then their 'acceptance' of the system may go along with the conviction that under it they get much less than they are entitled to.

In any case, revolutionary situations could arise in an advanced industrial society even if there were no revolutionary class in it, using the word *class* in the Marxist sense to refer to any group distinguished from others by the kind of property its members own. There would, of course, be revolutionary groups in this society, and they might be drawn more from some classes than from others, but their revolutionary temper might arise much more from conditions peculiar to them as groups than from anything common to them and the classes they were drawn from. Or the society might be classless in the Marxist sense and yet revolutionary situations arise in it. Suppose, for example, it were a society in which the means of production were communally owned, and the officials who managed the economy and the community in general were so much out of touch with the workers as to be looked upon by them as exploiters and oppressors. Might not a revolutionary situation arise then, even though there were no classes?[2]

---

[1] 'Docility' is hardly the word for it. The poor have often in the past broken with a good conscience laws which have seemed to them unjust. Law breaking and resistance to authority have been endemic among social groups that were not, and indeed could not be, revolutionary.

[2] It could perhaps be argued that officials and workers would then constitute two distinct classes, even in the Marxist sense of class. For would not the control of the economy by the officials be tantamount to their collectively owning the means of production, an ownership which would distinguish them as a class from the workers who owned only their labour-power? But this is to use the word ownership in a broader sense than Marx used it. The officials might be appointed from all sections of the community and not just from the families of officials, so that they would not form a caste.

Marx does not make it clear what he understands by ownership, nor how it differs from other forms of control, but he does ordinarily take it for granted that ownership is distinct from public authority. He assumes that the structure of authority in a community is determined

I have begun by looking at the weak side of Marx's ideas about revolution, the side that has attracted—until quite recently—the most attention: the conception of the proletariat as the revolutionary class *par excellence*, the class destined to reach a higher level of consciousness than any class before it[3] and to take over control of society in order to make it classless and communist. This idea of the proletarian revolution made by an organized and enlightened class constituting the majority or at least a large minority of the people has been contrasted with the Blanquist idea of it as made by an élite of revolutionaries who destroy the established order by exploiting the tensions and conflicts inside it, and it has been praised as the more sophisticated and realistic of the two. I concede that it is not simple but I do not see what is so realistic about it.

Unrealistic though Marx's conception of the proletarian revolution may be, there is excellent sense in many of the comments on the great French revolution and above all on the revolutions and proletarian revolts of his own day that he makes in such pamphlets as *The Class Struggles in France*, *The Eighteenth Brumaire of Louis Bonaparte*, and *The Civil War in France*. Even in them there are ill-conceived sentences that have attracted greater notice than they deserve on the mistaken assumption that they put the gist of an argument into a neat formula. Marx's aphorisms—for in this respect he is like Rousseau—are sometimes more of a hindrance than a help to the reader who wants to get at what is really fresh and perceptive in his thought.

largely by the distribution of property inside it. He does, of course, also speak at times of a person's class depending on his place in, or his relation to, production or the productive system. But how exactly are we to understand this? The *rentier* who lives off the interest on his capital and has nothing to do with management can hardly be said to have a place in production, though he is related to it. Since 'production' and 'productive system' are not synonyms, he can perhaps be said to have a place in the productive system, and one different from that of the mere manager or the mere worker. But as much can be said of the managers of a productive enterprise 'owned' by the workers in it, or of the controllers of a productive system or economy, even though they are democratically elected, provided that this management or control is a whole-time occupation distinct from that of ordinary workers. Only if the workers literally manage the enterprises they work in and control the entire economy, only if there is no division of labour between managers and controllers, on the one hand, and ordinary workers, on the other, do they not form distinct classes—if we take Marx at his word when he says that a man's class is determined by his place in the productive system. But did he intend us to take him at his word? As so often, he was equivocal when it was important to be definite.

[3] The thesis that the proletariat will reach a higher level of consciousness than the bourgeoisie is dogmatic; it consists largely of obscure or equivocal assertions, some of which have been puffed up by latter-day Marxists into theories that look impressive until they are looked at closely. In two essays ('Class Consciousness' and 'Reification and the Proletarian Consciousness') in a volume called *History and Class Consciousness*, George Lukacs offers an interpretation of Marx's ideas about class interests, class-consciousness, and the proletarian consciousness which has been much admired. He has indeed shown a rare skill in making unfounded assumptions and confusions of thought seem profound, and in avoiding the simple questions which would show them up for what they are. It would be unjust to accuse Lukacs of shoddy thinking; evasion at that level of dexterity and mystification deserves a better name. But to the student who wants to know how far Marx's ideas can be used to explain the real world, he has little to offer.

In these three essays on contemporary affairs, Marx considers a variety of 'revolutionary situations', describing and assessing the actions of different groups and pointing to the fears and sympathies they arouse. He explains how governments have lost the support of classes and groups that used to support them, how their authority and confidence have been eroded, and in general how conditions have changed in ways that make revolutionary action possible. He explains too how alliances are formed by revolutionary groups and how they are afterwards broken up as the groups come to distrust one another because they have different sympathies and different aims, and how the more conservative groups regain courage and eventually succeed in regaining control. The groups whose alliances and conflicts, whose fears and hopes, whose confusions of thought and aim, he describes, are often—though not always—recruited predominantly from one class or one section of a class, and they look for support or hostility much more from some classes than from others. Marx, when he explains actual revolutionary situations, how they arise and develop, has plenty to say about classes and their interests and attitudes, and much that he says is convincing. Though he does not explain these situations entirely in terms of classes, sections of classes, and their conflicts, he does so to a large extent. Indeed, it is arguable that he exaggerates the importance of class conflicts, that he takes less notice than he should of groups that are not classes, or else mistakenly attributes a class character to them.

And yet, if we follow his explanations in detail, we never find him attributing to any class as large as the bourgeoisie or the proletariat aims or attitudes peculiar to it: that is to say, common to its members and not shared by them with other classes. If there is a class of which he speaks in this way, it is the peasants, especially when, in the *Eighteenth Brumaire*, he explains what made them supporters of Louis Napoleon. But the peasants, as he describes them, were the least class-conscious of classes and the least active politically; they understood the political situation in France less than either the bourgeois or the urban workers did. Though they were not politically organized, they had everywhere in France (according to Marx) much the same hopes and fears. The much more politically conscious and active bourgeoisie and proletariat were also politically more divided. Marx, when he looks at real events and tries to explain them, never attributes solidarity or definite and sustained purposes to any but relatively small groups. It is only when he turns away from real situations and speaks speculatively and in the abstract of society and social classes that he makes large generalizations about class solidarity or about bourgeois or proletarian class-consciousness.

A Marxist might explain this by saying that proletarian solidarity and class-consciousness are to be achieved in the future, and that Marx recognized that they were very far from being so at the time he wrote his pamphlets. This is true enough. But it is also true that there has not been much progress towards greater class-consciousness or greater solidarity among the workers since Marx's day; or else that such progress as there has been has not made the workers a more revolutionary class. They may well have more sophisticated ideas now than they had in Marx's time about society and about their class, and they may still be far from satisfied with their lot. They may still believe, and on better grounds, that they get less than they are entitled to, and that other classes or groups get more. In the West they are certainly better organized now than they were a hundred years ago to push their interests. But they are not any nearer to being revolutionary. Thus, to point out that Marx was aware that the claims he made for the proletariat referred to it as it would be in the future and not as it was in his own day, does not absolve him from the charge that his account of it as the most class-conscious and revolutionary of classes is quite unrealistic.

The importance of what Marx has to say about group conflicts in revolutionary situations does not depend on the groups in question being classes or on their being recruited predominantly from some classes rather than others, or even on their getting most of their support from them. Even if class conflicts—taking the word class as Marx used it—had in fact been less important than they were in his day, there would still be a great deal to learn from his accounts of revolutions and revolts in France and elsewhere, and of the periods of 'reaction' that followed them, about how 'order' breaks down and is later restored and how the breakdown and the restoration affect the behaviour of conservative and radical groups. That is why these accounts are still relevant today when revolutionary situations arise more often from conflicts between national and racial groups than from class conflicts. These national and racial conflicts always have important economic causes as well as causes of other kinds, but that in itself is not enough to make them class conflicts.

Marx's accounts of 'bourgeois' revolutions and of proletarian revolts in bourgeois society (above all, of the Paris Commune) have had much more influence on revolutionaries than his vision of a proletarian revolution to be made in the fullness of time by a highly class-conscious and well-organized working class. In any case, these accounts form the great bulk of his writings about revolution, so that we know far more of what he thought about bourgeois revolutions and the part played by urban workers in them than of what he thought about proletarian revolution. Lenin was inspired, not really by the Marxist vision of a proletarian revolution made when economic and social conditions were ripe for it, but by pamphlets, articles, and addresses written by Marx or Engels, or by the two of them together, on special occasions or appraising particular events.

In these writings they do not preach the doctrine of revolution in the fullness of time. Rather, they encourage the workers (or the groups that claim to speak for them) to take bold action. For example, in the *Address to the Communist League*, written in 1850, they not only revert to the belief, expressed towards the end of *The Communist Manifesto*, that a bourgeois revolution in Germany will be a prelude to proletarian revolution; they also advise the workers and the Communist League what they must do to force the bourgeois revolutionaries to make large concessions to their demands, concessions so large indeed as to lay some of the foundations of socialism in a country which they admit is not yet fully capitalist. They tell them that their battle cry should be *the permanent revolution*. In these occasional writings, Marx and Engels do not forget, from time to time, to remind their readers that the proletariat is still a class in its infancy and has still a long way to go before it attains maturity; and in *The Communist Manifesto* they speak of the proletarian movement as the 'self-conscious, independent movement of the immense majority in the interest of the immense majority', having in mind, presumably, not what it then was but what they believed it would become. Yet, in general, they preach the taking of bold initiatives, the forcing of as many concessions, and the seizure of as much power as circumstances allow rather than the building up over a long period of time of a broad proletarian movement to take over control of society in a remote future.

Later, looking back on their hopes in 1848 and the years immediately following, Engels said that he and Marx had over-estimated the chances of proletarian revolution in the near future. Capitalism would need to develop much further than it had yet done to produce the objective conditions of proletarian revolution. But they had been less mistaken than he supposed, or at least had made mistakes different from the ones he had in mind. Conditions in the West in those years were not less propitious than they were to be later to the seizure of power by a resolute party acting in the name of the proletariat. Such a seizure, had it occurred, would not have been a proletarian revolution, and would not have led to the establishment of a society of equals in which 'the free development of each is the condition for the free development of all'. Yet conditions in the West were as propitious to it in the 1840s as they were in the 1880s or have been at any time since, except perhaps in Germany at the end of the First World War. Not that there was much likelihood in the West of such a seizure of power by extreme radicals, even in the 1840s. In other parts of the world the chances have been greater, and have been taken successfully; as they may yet be in the West.

In any case, such lessons about revolution as the writings of Marx and Engels contain can be useful to small groups, whether or not they claim to speak for the proletariat. Indeed, they quite often have been useful to them, though the proletariat has so far not been much the gainer for it.

II. THE REVOLUTIONARY TEMPER

Apart from practical advice to revolutionaries, there can be found in the writings of Marx—and in those of Engels also, though to a lesser extent—an attitude to society, an attitude of rejection, which is essentially modern, and which I shall call, for want of a better word, the *revolutionary temper*. This attitude is closely bound up with Marx's conception of alienation, and also with his dismissal of what he called Utopianism and his dislike and even contempt for a certain type of radical—as, for example, for Bentham. It is not an attitude peculiar to him, but he did give powerful expression to it; and it is still today—and today perhaps even more than when he was alive—a source of his attraction for persons who might otherwise pay little attention to his beliefs about revolution.

There is, of course, nothing modern about 'rejecting' the established social order just as there is nothing modern about Utopianism. There have always been persons who have wanted to remove themselves from society as they found it, either to live in isolation or to form separate communities of their own. Sometimes, indeed, society has provided for such communities; it has endowed them handsomely in return for their prayers or to enable them to engage in religious practices or in works of charity whose importance has been widely admitted but to which ordinary people have felt no call. There have also been 'dreamers' who have imagined society organized quite differently and much better. Sometimes, they have put forward their dreams as models to be imitated, within the limits of the possible, but more often they have used them to bring out more sharply the defects of human nature and human institutions, without much hope of their amendment. They lived in societies where most people took it for granted either that social conditions do not change or that, if they do, the change is not controlled by men. Sometimes they believed that this change is ordinarily for the worse, or that it is cyclical.

Much more modern than either 'rejection' of society or Utopianism are two closely related beliefs—in progress and in men's ability to change the social order deliberately to bring it closer to their ideals. We can, no doubt, find examples of these beliefs before the eighteenth century but it was then that they became widespread and strong. It was then that the 'improver' of society saw himself rather as trying to make it better than it had ever been than as trying to restore it to an earlier and healthier condition. These two beliefs, in progress and in men's ability deliberately to make large social changes for the better, do not always go together. Montesquieu and Burke held the first and rejected the second. They did not deny that men, provided they confine themselves to making the modest changes which is all that they are capable of making according to plan, can and sometimes do make progress, but they believed that they are doomed to failure and are likely to do great harm if they attempt to change the established order drastically. Thus, presumably, progress, when it does occur, consists (especially for Burke who believed in it more strongly perhaps than Montesquieu did) of countless small steps forward, many of them taken deliberately, and yet, looked at as a whole or over any considerable stretch of time, is always unplanned—except perhaps by God.[4]

Yet these two beliefs have quite often gone together. Believers in progress have often believed in the possibility of large and quick change deliberately made. Sometimes they have been revolutionaries and sometimes not. Bentham was a believer in progress and also a radical reformer, but he was not a revolutionary. At least, it is not usual to call him one, though the word 'revolution' has been used to refer to large and rapid social change, even when it is legal and involves no violence. On the other hand, there have been revolutionaries who, if they have not exactly denied the possibility of large and rapid change deliberately made, have not laid much stress on it; who have looked upon revolution more as an act of destruction and a catharsis than as a planned transformation of society. One such revolutionary was Blanqui, whom Marx admired (or half admired), and another was Georges Sorel, who admired Marx. As I shall argue later, Marx's attitude to revolution was in some respects like Blanqui's; he, too, at times spoke of it as if it were above all an act of liberation from a dead past, a casting off of a burden that is at once social and moral. He also, of course, in other respects, differed greatly from Blanqui; he was, take him altogether, a different kind of revolutionary. But, still, there is the similarity, and it is this aspect of Marx's thought which is connected closely with his conception of alienation and with what I have called the revolutionary temper.

There are different attitudes of 'rejection' or partial 'rejection' of estab-

[4] According to Montesquieu and Burke (and others, too, though they are perhaps the two arch conservatives on the threshold of the modern 'age of progress') there is no enterprise more hazardous than the attempt to transform a social order. Men who aim at making vast and rapid changes get their chance to make the attempt at a time when society is unusually vulnerable: when there are many people who want things to be different without really knowing how they want them to be. The idea of social renovation according to plan is an illusion, and the men who act on the idea delude themselves that they are in control of events when in fact they are not. The consequences of what they do are not what they intended, if indeed they had any clear intentions, and are ordinarily harmful.

If Montesquieu and Burke are right, then revolutions do have a large element of illusion about them. And the verdict of history is, I think, that they do have it. The capacity for self-deception of revolutionaries has been remarkable. But it does not follow that revolutions always do more harm than good. They only do so judged by the standards of conservatives but need not do so judged by standards more widely accepted. And, in any case, they change standards in many respects, though not of course in all. If we take the standards that survive the revolution, that are common to pre- and post-revolutionary society, or that are widely accepted in different kinds of society, it is not obvious that, by reference to them, revolutions always do more harm than good.

lished society just as there are different beliefs about what can be done to
escape from it or to set it right. To bring out more clearly what I want to
say about the revolutionary temper, I must first distinguish between some
of these attitudes and beliefs. Many more (and finer) distinctions than I
shall attempt could be made, but my purpose is merely to point to distinctions that serve a limited purpose: to describe an attitude to revolution
which, though not confined to Marx or found in his writings in its purest
or most extreme form, is at times prominent in them. I want to distinguish
the revolutionary from the rebel and the reformer, and also from the
Utopian who is not a revolutionary and yet believes that his ideal can be
realized. When I speak of 'the rebel', 'the reformer', 'the non-revolution-
ary Utopian', and 'the revolutionary', I speak, of course, of ideal types.
I admit that these terms are not always used in the senses in which I now
propose to use them, and I do not suggest that they ought to be; I merely
use them to help me make some distinctions which are, I hope, worth
making.

There is a kind of rebel, to be found in all ages and among all peoples,
who accepts the standards of the society he belongs to and wants to do
no more than put right what is wrong by reference to them. The wrong
he wants to put right may not be done to him, or not to him alone; it
may be done to a whole group or category of people. Though putting it
right may require making considerable changes, it does not require setting
aside accepted standards, or does so only to a slight extent. It requires
putting an end to practices that do not conform to these standards, and
perhaps also deciding on new practices, new institutions, to ensure that
in the future the old abuses do not return. The sociologist may say that
standards and practices are so closely connected that to introduce new
practices is nearly always, to some extent, to set new standards as well.
Nevertheless, it does make sense to claim for some practices that they are
improvements on others because they conform more fully to principles or
standards which are already generally accepted. This sort of rebel (at least
in his own eyes and often also in the eyes of others) resorts to rebellion
because he despairs of getting justice any other way. He does not see
himself as an innovator; though to the historian who later takes into
account what followed from his actions, he may seem to be one.

There is another kind of rebel about whom Hobsbawm has a good deal
to say in his book, *Primitive Rebels*. This rebel withdraws from society into
a region where he can live more freely. His withdrawal may be from one
or more of several motives. Sometimes he despairs of getting justice in
what he believes to be a corrupt society, or a society dominated by the
rich and the powerful who distort justice to their own ends. Or else the
rebel, though he does not look upon society as oppressive, refuses to pay
the price it extracts from those who receive its benefits. He sees nothing

inherently wrong in having to live as ordinary law-abiding persons do live, but it is not the life for him. Neither of these motives for rebellion—or, rather, for putting oneself out of reach of ordinary society and of those who exercise power and authority in it—entails a condemnation of accepted standards. The man who rebels or withdraws from the first motive condemns, not these standards, but practices that do not conform to them, and the man who does so from the second motive merely 'opts out' of society.

There have been rebels of these kinds in many societies, or on the fringes of society, both in recent times and long ago. The Cossacks were originally for the most part peasants who moved from the more settled and tightly governed parts of the Tsar's dominions into the unsettled and 'lawless' regions beyond. For a time they were raiders and disturbers of the peace, and sometimes even fomentors of rebellion, until eventually they made terms with the Tsar's representatives who recognized their autonomies. Brigands in Corsica and Sicily and other places have stood to the population generally and to the authorities in relations not unlike those of the Cossacks to the Tsars and their officials before they made their peace with them. History records many communities on the confines of a more settled society, or even groups inside it, sometimes in conflict with it and sometimes tolerated by it, whose 'rejection' of society has been free of any desire to transform it. This rejection, whatever its motives, has not been revolutionary.

Different from the rebel is the reformer. He wants to do more than just remedy what are abuses judged by standards widely accepted or in the light of needs widely recognized. He wants to improve on accepted standards or to get needs recognized which are not so already. Often, no doubt, consciously or unconsciously, he plays down the differences between the standards he advocates and those already accepted; for one of the most effective ways of winning people over to wanting what you want is to speak to them as if they wanted it already, or as if they were committed to it by their own principles. The reformer is a deliberate innovator, though it may serve his purposes to disguise the extent to which he is one. He wants to change people's standards and not just their practices. He is also consciously selective in what he rejects; he accepts a great deal of the established order, either because he approves of it or because it seems to him that the time has not yet come for changing it. He is prudent and calculating, not only in choosing his means, but also in choosing his ends. Thus, what makes him a reformer is not just that he refrains from violence; for he may well believe that in certain circumstances violence, or at least illegal resistance to authority, is justified. What makes him a reformer is his rejecting only some features of the established order, his knowing in considerable detail what it is that he wants to change, and his belief that there is so much worth preserving that he must take care how he goes about trying to make the changes he thinks desirable for fear of doing more to damage than to improve the fabric of society. He may be a moderate or a radical reformer, but he is aware that change is costly, psychologically and culturally as well as materially, and he tries to weigh the costs against the benefits.

The Utopian's 'rejection' of established society is more sweeping and whole-hearted. He rejects many of the values which make it the sort of society it is. He wants men and women to be of another mould, to have a different social environment and culture. He constructs a model of society and of human nature as he thinks they should be, and he invites people to take it seriously and to reconstruct reality in its image. His ideal society is, he thinks, adapted to human nature in the sense that it produces the needs and sustains the motives and ideals which enable men to live happily together. What makes him a Utopian is not only his making a model of society as it should be; it is also his belief that society is to be reconstructed not by governments and by legislation so much as by men of goodwill who resolve to change their ways and to set an example for others to follow. He wants these men to form within established society communities quite different from it, communities, not of the elect called to a life beyond the reach of most people and tolerated because society hopes to derive certain benefits from them, but of ordinary folk whose purpose is to prove that the well-being and harmony they have achieved are within everybody's reach. Unlike the reformer, the Utopian has little hope of achieving anything worth while by using such political methods as society provides for reforming itself; he wants ordinary folk to effect their own salvation by changing their way of life in society as it is. He wants them, in one sense, to opt out of society, for he invites them to create for themselves communities which differ radically from it, and in another to stay in it, for their function is to subvert it. As he sees it, society acting through its official representatives cannot be expected to change itself deliberately in the ways he wants it changed, and there is more harm than good likely to come of trying to get control of it by force. The best method is to transform it by a kind of gradual and open subversion. This method, seen from the point of view of the person who adopts it, could perhaps be called 'revolutionary', for there is an abrupt and rapid change in his way of life. Yet society taken as a whole will be changed only gradually. Thus, what makes the Utopian *not* a revolutionary (as I am now using that term) is again not his repudiation of violence—for he may not repudiate it in all circumstances or, even if he does (like Gandhi and his followers) he may not repudiate illegal resistance to authority; it is rather his looking to individuals to achieve gradually by methods of open persuasion and subversion the vision of a good society radically different from society as it is.

The revolutionary is in some respects like the Utopian. He too rejects many of the values typical of society as it is; he too wants men and women to be radically different from what they are, and wants them to live in a quite different environment and culture. Even more than the Utopian he is appalled by the human condition and condemns the social order that produces it. But, unlike the Utopian, he does not believe that that order can be gradually subverted; he believes that it must be destroyed. It must be destroyed, if men are to have a chance to start afresh, to build something better to replace it. Either the groups whose dominance rests on that order will not allow it to be subverted by the methods of the Utopian but will see to it that his experiments fail; or else, if the experiments are tolerated, they will fail nevertheless, for they are made in an unfavourable environment. Sooner or later, the men who make them will be corrupted by that environment. That is to say, either the Utopians and their disciples will lack the power to achieve what they aim at, or their will to achieve it will be undermined. Before there can be any hope of transforming society radically, power must be wrested from the hands of the groups whose interest it is to maintain society as it is, and the social order and culture in which men are corrupted and confused must be destroyed. Revolution is essentially a destructive and cathartic act; it is the act whereby men, in seeking to destroy society as it is, strike hard at the element which makes them what they are. As Marx, following Hegel, reminds us—and the idea was not peculiar to them or even to German philosophers—men have their being, reveal themselves for what they are, in society, which is merely the system of their behaviour. Thus in seeking to destroy it, they repudiate themselves as they are; they seek to escape from their old selves and to renew humanity in themselves. Revolution, seen from this point of view, is an act of collective and deliberate self-liberation or self-purification.

This attitude to revolution, though more prominent in Marx's earlier than in his later writings, is not confined to his youth. It finds expression, not only in the emphasis he lays on the destructive side of revolution and in his criticism of the Utopians, but also in some of the comparisons he makes between the proletariat and the bourgeoisie. Both classes, as he depicts them, are alienated. Yet they are not alienated in the same way or to the same extent. The bourgeois are hypocrites; they do not live up to the principles they profess. Outwardly they honour the bourgeois institution of marriage but in practice they disregard the obligations it imposes on them. So, too, they are dishonest and corrupt judged in the light of their own ideas about the sanctity of contracts and respect for property and for constitutional government. But the workers, as Marx describes them, are not cheats and hypocrites. When they cease to be dupes of bourgeois ideology, when they repudiate bourgeois standards, they do so openly.

They either do not conform to them, or if they do, it is only because they are forced to do so. They do not pay lip-service to ideals which in practice they reject. Yet Marx, for all the contempt he expresses for bourgeois morality, and for all that he says about the workers' rejection of it, describes no proletarian alternative to it; the attitude of the workers to bourgeois ideals and attitudes, as he depicts it, in so far as it is critical, is purely negative. He does not show how they pass beyond what they reject to something different. Painful experience teaches them that they are exploited, that the state serves to maintain this exploitation, which bourgeois morality seeks to justify. Therefore, when they make their revolution, they will put an end to class exploitation, and the state will disappear and so too will bourgeois morality. The workers, in coming to recognize bourgeois society for what it is, know what to destroy but have as yet little idea of what will replace it. Presumably, as they work together to destroy it, they acquire standards of their own which they live up to, or else they could not act effectively, and presumably these standards (or some of them) will survive into the post-revolutionary epoch when the task of reconstruction begins; but Marx does not tell us what they are or how they differ from bourgeois morality.

In his *Critique of Hegel's Philosophy of Right* Marx says that in Germany (and he is thinking of that country as it was in the 1840s) 'every class lacks the logic, insight, courage and clarity which would make it a negative representative of society';[5] that is to say, which would enable it to take the lead effectively in destroying the established order. He then asks, some two pages further on, 'Where is there, then, a real possibility of emancipation in Germany?', and answers, 'A class must be formed . . . which is the dissolution of all classes. . . . There must be formed a sphere of society which claims no traditional status but only a human status . . . and which can only redeem itself by a total redemption of humanity. This dissolution of society . . . is the proletariat.'[6] The idea of the redemption of humanity through the dissolution of established society is not to be found, in quite these words, in Marx's later writings, but it does express an attitude which is more than an aberration of his youth. Indeed, it is not peculiar to him, or even to his century; it has survived into ours.

In *The German Ideology* what is at bottom the same idea reappears in a rather different form:

The alteration of men on a mass scale is necessary, an alteration which can only take place in a practical movement, a revolution; this revolution is necessary, therefore, not only because the ruling class cannot be overthrown in any other way, but also because the class overthrowing it can only in a revolution succeed in ridding itself of all the muck of ages and become fitted to found society anew.[7]

[5] *Karl Marx: Early Writings*, transl. by Bottomore, p. 56.
[6] Ibid., p. 58.   [7] *The German Ideology*, R. Pascal's edn., p. 69.

The class that makes the revolution, the proletariat, purifies itself in making it, and thus acquires the capacity to reconstruct society. It is above all the revolution itself which prepares the class morally for the work of reconstruction; it is the abrupt breaking with the past that is liberating. In Marx's later works, and above all in those of Engels, the emphasis is more on the workers becoming politically mature, on their acquiring class-consciousness in the process of carrying on their long fight against the bourgeois—a process which does not entail, logically, any sudden break with the past or even violent capture of power. In the later writings, if revolution is 'necessary', it is rather because the interests of conflicting classes are irreconcilable than because the workers, the most alienated and then the most disillusioned and clear-sighted of men in bourgeois society, must rid themselves of 'the muck of ages'.

Yet the idea of revolution as an act of cultural and moral emancipation still persists in the later writings of Marx, even though it is there less to the fore. In *The Civil War in France* he says of the working class that

they have no ready-made utopias to introduce *par décret du peuple*. They know that in order to work out their own emancipation, and along with it that higher form to which present society is irresistibly tending by its own economic agencies, they will have to pass through long struggles, through a series of historic processes, transforming circumstances and men. They have no ideals to realize but [have only] to set free the elements of the new society with which old collapsing bourgeois society itself is pregnant.[8]

I do not suppose that Marx means here that when the long revolutionary struggle is safely over, the workers sit back and let the new social order take care of itself; for, after all, they have to organize production inside it and to decide whatever has to be decided collectively. The idea of a society understood and controlled by its members is not renounced in *The Civil War in France*. Yet the revolutionary activity of the workers, even though extended over a long period, is still seen as at once destructive and liberating, as a shaking off of fetters, social, psychological, and moral. And the workers in emancipating themselves still emancipate the whole of mankind; their victory over the bourgeois is not, as the victory of the bourgeois over the feudal nobility was, merely the victory of one class over another; it is also the victory of humanity over itself.

In an often quoted passage from the *Critique of the Gotha Programme*, Marx says that between 'capitalist and communist society lies the period of the revolutionary transformation of the one into the other', which is also a period of 'political transition' in which 'the state can be nothing but the revolutionary dictatorship of the proletariat'.[9] This period comes after the taking over of power by the workers, and is presumably a period of social reconstruction which leads eventually to the emergence of the fully

[8] Marx–Engels, *Selected Works* (F.L.P.H., Moscow, 1950), i. 474.   [9] Ibid. ii. 30.

communist society, but it is also, presumably, a period when the last vestiges of bourgeois morality and bourgeois ideology are eliminated. It is a period when the work of purification continues. At least, many of Marx's disciples have supposed that it is, and their interpretation of him is here probably correct. Bourgeois morals and bourgeois attitudes do not, according to Marx, simply vanish when bourgeois property relations and bourgeois political domination are abolished. 'The muck of ages' has sunk too deep into man's consciousness, and the business of getting rid of it is neither painless nor quick.

Though Marx did on one or two occasions concede that, at least in some countries, capitalism might be abolished peacefully, he was powerfully attracted by the idea that it would have to be destroyed by force. He was disposed to believe this, not only because he held that class interests are irreconcilable and that class conflicts must be fought out to the bitter end, but also because of his hatred and contempt for bourgeois society. His sympathies were always with the revolutionaries who seemed to him to hate it the most fiercely and relentlessly—as, for example, with the Blanquists, even though he thought their ideas about revolution inadequate. He had nothing but contempt for the reformer who seemed to him to accept bourgeois values wholeheartedly, radical though his schemes of reform might be. Take, for example, the insults he heaped on Bentham! Bentham was prolific of schemes of reform, and if a fair sample of them had been put into practice in his day, society would have been greatly and rapidly changed. But he took man as he found him (or thought he found him) and was not concerned that the quality of his life should be changed. He believed in maximizing something which he called happiness; or, alternatively, in helping people to get what they wanted in the order of their own preferences and at the least cost. He was an efficiency expert in a big way. Marx despised him, not for caring about happiness (for Marx was no ascetic and wanted men to live abundantly), but for his shallow bourgeois conception of man. He called him the 'arch-philistine', 'the insipid, pedantic, leather-tongued oracle of the commonplace bourgeois intelligence of the nineteenth century', who 'in his arid and simple way . . . assumed the modern petty bourgeois, and above all the modern English petty bourgeois, to be the normal man'. This 'genius in the way of bourgeois stupidity',[10] simply has no idea of what ails man. He fares worse, this philosophical radical, at the hands of Marx, than even the arch-conservative Burke, the 'famous sophist and sycophant' who said that 'the laws of commerce are the laws of nature, and therefore the laws of God', but who also, in his *Thoughts and Details on Scarcity* had candour enough to admit that 'those who labour . . . feed both the pensioners called the rich and themselves'.[11]

---

[10] *Capital* (Everyman edn.), i. 671 and note.   [11] Ibid. i. 843, note, and 235, note.

Notice, too, that Marx spoke less unkindly of John Stuart Mill, who was by way of being a disciple of Bentham, though rather more cautious as an advocate of reform. For Mill's idea of man was in some ways closer to Marx's than it was to Bentham's; he saw man, to some extent at least, as the victim of society, not so much because its institutions and *mores* stood in the way of his wants being satisfied as efficiently as they might be, but because they prevented his developing his capacities. Mill, of course, was far from being a revolutionary, and the idea of man as diminished and deprived in a social world which he finds alien and oppressive is not at all prominent in his writings. Yet it is not wholly absent from them. Mill did at least deplore the smugness of the spiritually poor who have no inkling of their poverty; and in his eyes it is above all the middle classes, the bourgeois, who are spiritually poor or who are most open to reproach for being so, since they are well-to-do and think of themselves as the educated.

III. REVOLUTIONARY MARXISTS SINCE MARX

Towards the end of his life, in an introduction to a reprint of Marx's *Class Struggles in France*, Engels, referring to Marx's hopes and his own almost half a century earlier, said that history had proved them wrong. Economic development on the Continent at that time 'was not, by a long way, ripe for the elimination of capitalist production'.[12] He went on to say:

The time of surprise attacks, of revolutions carried through by small conscious minorities at the head of unconscious masses, is past. Where it is a question of the complete transformation of the social organization, the masses themselves must also be in it, must themselves already have grasped what is at stake, what they are going in for with body and soul.[13]

Universal suffrage had provided the workers' party with the means of getting in touch with 'the mass of the people', and in the German Reichstag it could speak with authority both to its opponents and to the masses. But in spite of these advantages the party and the class remained, in the opinion of Engels, revolutionary; presumably because their intention, when they got power, was to abolish capitalism, to transform society from the base upwards.

It would be arbitrary to deny that this idea of revolution is Marxist. Engels did not invent it in the late eighties and nineties of the last century when Marx was no longer alive to put him right; there are considerable traces of it in the earlier writings of both the masters. It was accepted by the German Social Democratic Party in the great days when it was the largest, and intellectually the liveliest, socialist and Marxist party in the

---

[12] Marx–Engels, *Selected Works*, i. 115.   [13] Ibid. i. 123.

world, a party not yet shattered by its experiences in the Kaiser's war and in the aftermath of the Bolshevik revolution. Today it is more than half accepted by the Communist parties of Italy and France whose intellectual sterility does not deprive them of the right to call themselves Marxist.

Yet history has proved that Engels was as wrong in 1895 as he had been in 1848 and the years immediately following; it has proved that the time of revolutions carried through by 'small conscious minorities' at the head of 'unconscious masses' is not past. To be sure, the conscious minorities that have made the revolutions have not admitted that the masses they led were 'unconscious'; but in fact they were so at least as much as the masses in 1789 to '94 or in 1848. They were dissatisfied, of course; they had serious grievances, or else the minorities would never have been able to seize power, but they were no nearer to being 'class-conscious' as Marx and Engels understood that term.

These 'small conscious minorities' who have made revolutions among the Slavs and in Asia have as good a right to call themselves Marxists as the German Social Democratic Party had in the past or as the French and Italian Communist parties have today; for they too can find in the writings of Marx and Engels arguments and ideas to justify much of what they have done in the process of getting power, if not also what they have done with it after getting it. But, then, as everyone knows, Marx and Engels had plentiful advice to give about how to get power in the name of the workers and almost none about how to use it for the workers' benefit.

Apart from these two brands of Marxist 'revolutionary' who belong to parties that aim at getting power, there is a third whose concern with parties and with power is less immediate. This brand of revolutionary shares Marx's hatred and contempt for bourgeois society, does not believe that it will reform itself by constitutional means, has lost faith (if he ever had it) in the Communist parties in the West and in the Soviet Union, and sometimes also in other parts of the world. He has even, to some extent, lost faith in the proletariat. His lack of faith in the Communist parties is, of course, no reason for denying his right to call himself a Marxist, though his diminished faith in the proletariat may be so. How can anyone who claims to be a Marxist have serious doubts about the essentially revolutionary character of the workers in bourgeois society? Does he not thereby call in question a doctrine to which Marx and Engels held firmly all their lives?

No doubt he does; and yet this lack of faith in the workers, when we find it in someone who still calls himself a Marxist or acknowledges a large debt to Marx, is seldom unqualified. The doubter justifies it by insisting, even more than Marx did, on the workers' alienation in bourgeois society. Far from denying that the worker is exploited under capitalism, he argues that he is so much alienated in it, so much a victim of false consciousness, that he is incapable of seeing his condition for what it is. The hold of bourgeois ideas and values on the worker, on the victim of the system, has proved to be stronger even than Marx imagined it would be. At bottom, Marx's account of alienation, of its social causes and of the forms it takes, is sound, but the condition is worse than he thought it was, as is proved by what has happened to the workers in the industrial West. This is not to say that they cannot become a revolutionary class, still less that bourgeois society and what it stands for can be destroyed without their turning against it. But it does mean that the task of winning them over to the revolutionary cause is much more difficult than it was once thought to be. Parties and movements that purport to be revolutionary, and that perhaps were so to begin with, are easily corrupted by bourgeois ideas and attitudes. Or, rather, in the West they are liable to this corruption, whereas in economically backward parts of the world, where bourgeois ideas have not taken firm root, they are apt to become authoritarian and to set up conditions that favour other forms of exploitation and false consciousness: forms unforeseen by Marx, though they can be explained easily enough in the light of his theory, of his accounts of exploitation and alienation and their social causes. This type of Marxist admits, no less than the others do, the need to save mankind from bourgeois society, though he is more hard put to it to explain whence the salvation is to come. Sometimes he invests his hopes in groups which he believes are less the victims of bourgeois false consciousness than the ordinary workers are: as, for example, in the Blacks in the United States or other racial minorities elsewhere. And yet, ordinarily, no matter where he expects the initial challenge to come from, he believes (as a Marxist should) that it will not be really effective unless the mass of the workers are won over to support it.

These three types of 'revolutionaries' who persist in calling themselves Marxist differ considerably, both in their ideas of themselves and in their readiness to live up to those ideas. What they profess is not always what they seriously intend. Yet their ideas of themselves have a good deal in common. They are all conspicuously not Utopians, and they see the revolutionary as a liberator, not just of the exploited and oppressed from exploitation and oppression, but of mankind generally from social and cultural conditions frustrating to them and giving rise to false consciousness.

The revolutionary, as they see him, is not so much a planner as a liberator; or, rather, what he plans before the revolution is the revolution, and not the reconstruction of society that is to come after it. Yet he is not a blind agent of destruction. Though he does not claim to predict the future, he does claim to have taken the measure of the present. He claims to know in a general way what ends are to be pursued after the revolution (the abolition of private property, of the division of labour, and of the bureaucratic state) though he does not know how they will be achieved. His appeal is always to the experience of the classes and groups that he seeks to win over. He is not—in the image of himself that he presents to them—the wise man who knows better than they do how they should live. Rather, he is the man who challenges them to recognize their condition for what it is, for what their experience proves it to be. If his message makes sense to them, it is because it spells out the lessons of that experience, and they are at last willing to listen. Thus, at bottom, it is life, it is practice, it is the human condition revealed to them in their own lives when they look critically at it, which teaches them. If they were really satisfied with their condition and with themselves, his message would mean nothing to them. If they listen to it and yet do not reject what it condemns, it is because they are at odds with themselves and are still caught up in a false consciousness.

The revolutionary who claims to be a Marxist does not see himself as appealing either to men's feelings or to abstract principles of justice. He has a theory which purports to explain how they are situated and to dissipate the illusions which prevent their seeing that situation as it is. Their experience is, he thinks, his ally, his advocate with them, for his theory makes sense of it. If, then, they reject the theory, it is because conditions are not yet such as to enable them to look critically at their experience. While his faith in his theory lasts, the revolutionary does not admit that the groups to whom he addresses his message turn a deaf ear to it because they have standards different from his and assess their situation just as realistically as he does, but differently. He sees himself as appealing to them as they really are against themselves as they think they are; to what their own experience, if only they will face it, must teach them against the illusions to which they are still a prey.

In the *Phenomenology*, Hegel, especially in the pages in which he discusses, with the French revolution in mind, what he calls 'absolute freedom and terror', implies that the rejection of an entire social order and of the values that sustain it is essentially a gesture. Not necessarily an empty gesture, not a gesture without effect, but to a large extent either a blind gesture or an extravagant gesture not to be taken at its face value. It is an act whose significance is not fully understood by the man who does it. The revolutionary 'rejects' the established order in the name of principles that no one has yet lived by, and therefore does not know what would be involved in living by them. Compared with the laws and conventions of the established order his principles are highly abstract. His conviction that they commit him to the wholesale rejection of established practices and accepted standards depends largely on his not having yet tried to reconstruct society in the light of them.

Yet Hegel was not in the *Phenomenology* condemning revolution. Rather, he was explaining its place in a course of social and cultural change of which he approved and which he believed was a gradual enlargement of freedom, though with crises and sudden leaps forward in it. Nor was he condemning deliberate innovation on a large scale; he was merely imply-ing that the attitude of the revolutionary rests largely on illusion. Implicit in Hegel's account of progress is the idea that this illusion, at a certain stage in that progress, is not only inevitable but salutary.

Whether or not, or to what extent, the revolutionary attitude rests on illusion, I shall not at present inquire. I have wanted only to distinguish the attitude of the revolutionary from that of the rebel and the reformer, who are also at times ready to use violence or to resort to illegal action. Or, rather, since the word 'revolutionary' is used in different senses, I have wanted to distinguish an attitude, which is modern and which I call the revolutionary temper, from others that are sometimes confused with it. I call it revolutionary partly because it is the temper that Marx ascribes to the proletarians when he speaks of them as the most alienated and the essentially revolutionary class and partly because it is still found today among groups and individuals who think of themselves as revolutionaries and Marxists.

The social theorist, whatever his own sympathies, must recognize the importance of this attitude of rejection in highly self-conscious and rapidly changing societies. In its milder forms, it is often widespread; and the revolutionary is merely the man or woman in whom it is exceptionally strong and persistent. It is worth inquiring how it can happen that men and women come to reject in this way the society and culture they belong to. How is it that essentially social beings come to have aspirations, intense even though vague, which seem to them incompatible with the social order in which they form their minds? Under what social conditions do they acquire such aspirations and the resolve to transform the social order drastically and if need be by force in order to realize them? These are some of the questions that Marx raises when he speaks of man's alienation in society and of the revolution that will put an end to it.

It is often said that the revolutionary knows what he rejects better than what he wants to put in its place. He is accused of being destructive, and this is held to be irrational in him. Perhaps it is so on strictly utilitarian grounds. Why destroy what you have got unless you know what you can put in its place or are likely to get instead of it? To be sure, even the reformer takes some risks; he too knows more about what he wants to abolish than about what he proposes to establish. But, just because his proposals are modest and are adapted with some care to what is long established and familiar, the risks are much smaller, and if things go wrong, it is easier to put them right. It is easier to compare expected benefits with expected and possible losses. But the revolutionary wants to make changes so drastic that the benefits and losses can hardly be assessed beforehand even roughly. He wants society to take a leap in the dark.

This is one way of putting it. There is another. As the revolutionary sees it, men in the society he condemns are victims of the social order and culture in which they live. They learn to recognize their condition, to see it clearly for what it is, in coming to reject the established order and its values. But this they cannot do fully until they have got rid of it. The revolutionary wants mankind, or the part of it that concerns him, to make a fresh start, and yet, as he sees them, men are caught up, not merely in the practices, but also in the ways of thinking and feeling of society as it is. Their first need is to break out of the social and cultural cage that holds them, and this they can do only by breaking the cage. Before they can act constructively, before they can find an effective remedy for their condition, they must act destructively. To someone who has this attitude to society and to the human condition, utilitarian calculations of costs and benefits seem irrelevant.

PART TWO

THE FORMS OF ALIENATED LIFE

CHAPTER VIII

FALSE CONSCIOUSNESS AND THE FORMS
OF ALIENATED LIFE

IN the course of discussing Marx's ideas about alienation and its causes, I have made distinctions he never made. I have not made them just to show how confused he could be; I have made them in the hope that they might help to sort out his ideas and to disentangle what is valuable in them from what is not. I have distinguished the social from the psychological or spiritual aspects of alienation; I have imagined four types of society and a course of change from the first to the fourth in the hope of explaining how there might be progress, not only in technology and science, but also towards social and cultural conditions that satisfy needs peculiar to a self-conscious and 'self-creative' being. I have tried to explain how, at certain stages of this progress, there might be deepening alienation; and I have distinguished what I have called the revolutionary temper from other attitudes of criticism or 'rejection' of established society. I have still to discuss the forms of alienated life.

Labour's being a commodity and the workers' dependence on social processes outside their control (such as capital) are alienation in two of its social aspects; the workers' not being satisfied in their work and their feeling frustrated by, or at the mercy of, these processes are alienation in two of its psychological or even 'spiritual' aspects. But religion, bourgeois morality, and the state are, so Marx says, forms of alienated life. By this he means, I take it, that they are activities that men would not engage in or beliefs they would not hold or values they would not accept unless they were alienated. If labour were not a commodity, if the workers were not dependent on processes beyond their control and did not have needs (even though imperfectly understood by them) which they could not satisfy within the established social order, and if they did not feel oppressed or frustrated within that order, these activities, beliefs, and values would not exist.

Religion, bourgeois morality, and the state are not the only forms of alienated life. Certain kinds of art are so too, and so presumably (at least in some of their aspects) are other kinds of morality besides the bourgeois kind. Yet it is about these three forms that Marx has most to say, especially in his early writings, though by no means only in them. I shall therefore consider only these three forms.

Marx nowhere discusses these 'forms of alienated life' systematically,

though he does, in one way or another, say a good deal about them. And
the same, I think, is true of Engels. Therefore, in my attempt to explain
the significance of calling these things forms of alienated life, I shall take
passages from several of Marx's writings and consider their implications.
And since Engels, both while Marx was alive and after his death, turned
his mind quite often to religion and the state, and put forward views about
them which he believed to be in keeping with those of his friend and
collaborator, I shall not hesitate to refer to his writings also. In any case,
my purpose in this chapter is not to claim that my interpretations of some
of the most elusive of Marx's ideas come closer than others to his real
meaning; rather, it is to look critically at certain beliefs he held or can
reasonably be supposed to have held and to follow up their implications,
distinguishing what is suggestive and illuminating about them from
what is false or empty.

Marx and Engels have more to say about religion, bourgeois morality,
and the state than that they are forms of alienated life. For example, they
quite often (though by no means always) speak of religion as if it were a
kind of class ideology. And the very term they use to refer to bourgeois
morality suggests that it is some kind of class phenomenon. Again, they
call the state an instrument of class rule or class oppression, or else speak
of it in ways which imply that, if there were no classes with irreconcilable
interests, or if some classes were not exploiting or oppressing others, there
would be no need for the state.

These other ideas about religion, bourgeois morality, and the state are
not necessarily inconsistent with the idea of them as forms of alienated
life. Religion's being a fantasy of alienated man does not preclude its
being also a class ideology, nor does the state's being an instrument or a
condition of class rule or oppression prevent its being a kind of activity in
which men would not engage if they were not alienated. But, though these
ideas are not inconsistent, neither Marx nor Engels ever attempted to
produce an account of religion or morality or the state which fits them
together satisfactorily. Writers about Marxism sometimes refer to a
'Marxist theory' of the state, or a Marxist conception of religion or morality. If a theory is an explanation whose parts are put together deliberately
to form a logically coherent whole, and if a conception is a set of clearly
and closely related beliefs, then there is no Marxist theory of the state and
no Marxist conception of either religion or morality. Not even if we take
into account only the ideas of Marx or of Engels, or of both together, and
pay no attention to anything said by their disciples. It is not merely that
critics can point to confusions and omissions in their thinking about these
things; for even the best-constructed, the most carefully thought out, of
sociological explanations of the state or morality or religion is open to this
kind of criticism. It is rather that the thinking of Marx and Engels about

these things consists largely in putting forward disconnected and often ambiguous, though sometimes ingenious, ideas.

There is so much that they leave uncertain, so many obvious questions that they do not put, so many apparent inconsistencies that they make no attempt to dissipate. Take any one of these three things, and consider what we are not told about it! Are all religions, or only some, fantasies of alienated man? If we accept what Marx says about alienation and its social causes, it follows that there have been in the past societies without alienation, or at least without the kind of division of labour which, according to Marx, is the source of alienation. In these societies, presumably, religion was not a fantasy of the alienated. It may have been a fantasy, and the fantasy may have had a social function and social causes, but that function and those causes could have had nothing to do with alienation. So at least it would seem, if we follow up the implications of what Marx says about the causes of alienation. And yet, as we shall see later, several of the few references that Marx and Engels make to primitive religions suggest that man's condition, when these religions flourished, was in some respects like alienation.

If, however, we assume that not all religions, but only some, have their sources in alienation, we get not much guidance from either Marx or Engels as to which they are. They say enough to make it clear that Christianity in its various forms is one of these religions. But are all dogmatic religions fantasies of the alienated? Or only those that promise a life after death? What is it that these religions that flourish where there is alienation have in common? What is the connection between whatever is common to them and the phenomena, social and psychological, that constitute alienation? Hegel, from whom Marx and Engels, like Feuerbach before them, took this conception of religion, looked upon Christianity and Judaism as religions of alienated man, and tried to explain how certain beliefs, hopes, and anxieties of man about himself find expression in these religions. But he did not, as Marx did, point to economic causes of alienation.

The same reasons that preclude all religions being religions of alienated man also preclude their being class ideologies. In primitive societies where the causes of alienation indicated by Marx do not operate there are no classes. Are we to understand that all religions which are fantasies of alienated man are also class ideologies? That a religion may be both the one and the other is clear enough. But if it is the one, must it also be the other? To what extent do alienation and the division of society into classes have the same causes? Both, according to Marx, are connected with the division of labour. But, as we saw in an earlier chapter, there are several kinds of division of labour, and we cannot take it for granted that a kind that produces alienation also produces a society divided into classes.

These are only some of the questions that arise in the mind of the moderately attentive and critical reader as he considers the reflections of Marx
or Engels on religion and its social causes and functions.

So, too, with bourgeois morality, there are several questions that come
readily to mind and to which there is no answer, or no clear answer, in
the pages of Marx or Engels. Does bourgeois morality, as they conceive
of it, consist only of principles and standards peculiar to the bourgeois?
Or does it include at least some that they share with other classes? If it
consists only of what is peculiar to them, it must exclude a great deal that
is in their interest as a class. For the standards and principles of other
classes cannot be a matter of indifference to them. It is their interest,
presumably, that the workers whom they exploit should think and feel as
they themselves do about some things. Quite often Marx and Engels
admit this, at least implicitly; they use arguments which suggest that
bourgeois morality is not confined to the bourgeois but is in large part
shared by them with other classes in what they call 'bourgeois society'.
But they do not always do this; they sometimes speak as if bourgeois
morality were confined to the bourgeois. And, in any case, they never get
as far as distinguishing the part of bourgeois morality confined to the
bourgeois from the part shared by them with other classes. They do not
even, among the values shared by all classes in a bourgeois society, distinguish those which are in the interest of all classes from those which are
more particularly in the bourgeois interest. I shall assume—though there
are passages in *Anti-Dühring* which, taken literally, seem to imply the contrary—that neither Marx nor Engels believed that the entire moral code
accepted by a class constitutes its 'class morality': that is to say, consists of
principles and standards which serve only (or primarily) its class interests as
distinct from the interests of other classes.

What can be meant by calling bourgeois or any other kind of morality
a form of alienated life? Presumably, not all morality is such a form, even
in a society in which there is alienation. There are presumably some standards common to societies in which men are alienated and societies in which
they are not. Marx and Engels do not deny that this is so, and the assumption is reasonable, given that social conditions are in some important
respects similar in all societies. Can we then say that only that part of
morality which is class morality is a form of alienated life? I think not.
As we shall see later, there would seem to be, according to Marx and
Engels, some standards that men would not accept unless they were
alienated, of which it can hardly be said that they serve the interests of any
class in particular. Thus, though it would seem to follow from some of the
things that Marx and Engels say that class morality is a form of alienated
life, the converse is not true. There are aspects of the morality of alienated
man which are not class morality. This must be so, given what Marx and

Engels say, on the one hand, about alienation and its functions and causes and, on the other, about the moral standards of social classes in relation to their class interests.

It must be so; but it does not follow that Marx and Engels recognized that it must be. Some of the standards or ideals that they include in bourgeois morality are not peculiar to the bourgeois and do not serve their interests as against those of other classes. They are merely standards which, in the opinion of Marx or Engels, men would not accept unless they were alienated, and the alienation they have in mind is either peculiar to bourgeois society or much more developed in it than in other societies. By bourgeois morality, the two founders of Marxism (and their disciples after them) would appear to mean, sometimes standards peculiar to the bourgeois but more often either standards that favour bourgeois interests as against those of other classes or standards that men accept because they are alienated in the type of society in which the bourgeois are the dominant class.

There are three ideas about the state prominent in the writings of Marx and Engels: that it is an instrument of class rule, that it is a condition of class exploitation, and that it is a form of alienated life. The last of these ideas is more prominent in the writings of Marx than in those of Engels, and in Marx's early than in his later writings: but it is not confined either to Marx or to his early writings. We can find traces of it in what Engels wrote after Marx's death. Indeed, it is still a considerable element in contemporary Marxist thinking about the state, and is not so only in the form of the crude doctrine that parliamentary democracy is a bourgeois sham.

The first two Marxist ideas of the state are seldom distinguished from one another by writers about Marxism, although they are quite obviously different ideas. To call the state an instrument of class rule is to imply that there is some class or other that controls the machinery of government; it is to imply that the persons who control this machinery are either recruited from this class and are concerned to promote its interests or are responsible to the class or dependent on its favour. But to call the state a condition of class exploitation is not to imply that any one class governs it, either directly or through representatives; it is to imply only that, if there were no state, no class would be in a position to exploit another. Marx and Engels, though they sometimes spoke as if the state's being an instrument of class rule were a defining characteristic of it, quite often admitted, when speaking of some particular state, that no class was in control of it. They were, I suggest, much more wedded to the second than to the first idea of the state; they never, as far as I know, said anything to suggest that the state is not always a condition of class exploitation, that there might be a need for it even if there were no classes.

The state's being a condition of class exploitation does not entail its being also a form of alienated life. It could conceivably be the first without also being the second. No doubt, given the truth of Marx's account of the causes of alienation, we should expect to find alienation wherever we find the state. For the division of labour that produces alienation also gives rise to classes and makes possible the exploitation of some classes by others. But from this it does not follow that the state must be both a condition of class exploitation and a form of alienated life. The fact (if it is a fact) that both alienation and class exploitation are effects of a certain kind of division of labour does not entail that the state is a symptom of alienation, that in the activities which constitute it the alienated condition of human beings is manifest. Nevertheless, Marx had his reasons for speaking of the state in this way. This Marxist idea of the state, though true only in part, is ingenious and perceptive, as I shall try to show when I look at it more closely in a later chapter.

Before I go on, in the chapters following this one, to consider more particularly what Marx and Engels say about religion, bourgeois morality, and the state, I want in this chapter to discuss the idea of alienated life more generally. What is a form of alienated life? How does it differ from a form of life that is not alienated?

I said earlier that a form of alienated life is some kind of activity or system of beliefs or values that men would not engage in or would not hold unless they were alienated. But to say this is not enough, for this is compatible with the forms of alienated life being mere consequences and not also symptoms of alienation. A man who is sick will do things he would not do if he were in good health; he will, for example, do things which he believes will cure him. He may even do them on the advice of his doctor. These actions of his, though consequences of his being ill, are not symptoms or manifestations of his illness. Even when the illness in question is mental, we can distinguish in the behaviour that results from it the part which is a mark or symptom of the illness from the part which is not.

Marx—and this is true also of Engels—when he spoke of religion and bourgeois morality as forms of alienated life thought of them as being more than mere consequences of alienation. He thought of them as symptoms of it, as forms of behaviour and belief that express it, not in the sense that they describe or explain it (for it is a condition which those who suffer from it do not know for what it is) but in the sense that they are marks of it. They are not effects of it which someone who knew their causes could recognize for such; nor are they abortive attempts to remedy it or to deal with problems that arise out of it. They are manifestations of it. That this is true of religion and bourgeois morality, as Marx and Engels conceive of them, is clear enough, but it is also, though less obviously, true of their idea of the state. It, too, is an 'appearance', a 'reflection' of a social and human condition, and not just a consequence of it.

Religion, morality, and the state belong to what Marx calls the ideological superstructure of society. And he says of ideology that it is false consciousness, and also that it is a 'reflection' of activities or conditions to which he gives a variety of names: 'social existence', 'material intercourse', 'the economic substructure', 'the reproduction of life'. Indeed, he says, not just of ideology, not just of false consciousness, that it *reflects* these activities or conditions; he says it sometimes even of consciousness taken generally.

There is no part of Marxist theory more difficult to understand than the part that treats of consciousness in relation to what it reflects. It is not clear what consciousness is (what forms or spheres of human thought and feeling are included in it), nor what it reflects, nor what precisely this reflecting amounts to (what the connection between consciousness and what it reflects is supposed to be). This part of Marxist theory is so obscure and confused that there is no extracting from it a coherent account of how men's ways of thinking are related to other aspects of their life in society. In saying this I do not imply that there is nothing worth extracting from it, that there are no good ideas useful to the student of society buried in it. There are some, and they mostly, as I shall try to show, have to do with alienation and with types of activity and belief said to reflect it. I shall argue that this term 'reflection', difficult though it is to see what it could mean when applied to consciousness (or human thinking taken generally) in relation to 'social existence' or 'material intercourse', does make sense when applied to certain types of illusion (or activities that rest upon illusion) in relation to conditions of the sort that Marxists have in mind when they speak of alienation.

In *The German Ideology*, Marx and Engels, putting forward their views about how men come by their ideas, and comparing their method of explaining these origins with the methods of other German philosophers, say this:

The production of ideas, of conceptions, of consciousness, is at first directly interwoven with the material activity and the material intercourse of men, the language of real life. Conceiving, thinking, the mental intercourse of men, appears at this stage as the direct efflux of their material behaviour. The same applies to mental production as expressed in the language of politics, law, morality, religion, metaphysics of a people. Men are the producers of their conceptions, ideas, etc., real active men as they are conditioned by a definite development of their productive forces . . . Consciousness can never be anything else than conscious existence (*das bewusste Sein*), and the existence is their actual life-process. If in all ideology men and their circumstances appear upside down as in a *camera obscura*, this phenomenon arises just as much out of their historical life-process as the inversion of objects on the retina does from their physical life process . . . We set out from real, active men, and on the basis of their real life-process we demonstrate the development of the ideological reflexes and echoes of the life-process. The phantoms formed in the human brain are also, necessarily, sublimates of their material life-process . . . Morality, religion, metaphysics, all the rest of ideology and their corresponding forms of consciousness, thus no longer retain the semblance of independence. They have no history, no development; but men, developing their material production and their material intercourse, alter along with this, their real existence, their thinking and the products of their thinking.[1]

This long passage (and I have left out parts of the original text) gives us, as concisely as any, the gist of the Marxist conception of how consciousness is related to what it reflects or is determined by. It is far from clear, and when I say that it gives us the gist, I mean only that it brings together into two or three pages a number of ideas that recur again and again in the writings of Marx and Engels. It is a fair sample of a collection of ideas that were never put into good order, and never abandoned. Which is not to say, of course, that Marx and Engels did not also put forward other ideas inconsistent with the ones that make up this collection.

Though this account of the origins of ideas is obscure, we can at least say that it is primarily sociological and not epistemological. Marx and Engels are not here attempting what, for example, Hume attempted in his *Treatise of Human Nature* or Kant in his *Critique of Pure Reason*; they are not trying to explain what is involved in having and using ideas, or how thinking is related to sense experience. They are saying merely that men acquire their ideas in the first place in the process of engaging in material intercourse, or, in other words, in collaborating to produce what they need to satisfy their wants, and more especially the wants that must be satisfied if they are to keep alive and healthy and their species is to endure. For this, I take it, is the point of calling material intercourse 'the life-process'. But this assertion, as far as I can see, is in itself no more and no less in keeping with Kant's account of knowledge and thinking than it is with Hume's. It may be that the reference to 'phantoms formed in the human brain' is a philosophical gesture intended by Marx and Engels to be a rejection of such theories of knowledge as Kant's, but sociologically it is a mere irrelevance. The sociologist who holds that mankind first acquired the capacity to think conceptually in the process of what Marx calls material intercourse is not thereby committed to rejecting Kant's account of what it is to have ideas and to use them.

From the second half of the eighteenth century onwards, the belief that men first acquired language, first learned to use ideas, in the process of working together to satisfy their wants has been widely held among writers interested in the origins of language. Rousseau, the lover of paradox who liked to challenge received opinions, had argued in his *Essay on the Origin of Languages* that the first uses of language had arisen among men to

---

[1] *The German Ideology*, transl. by R. Pascal, pp. 13–15.

enable them to express their feelings towards one another and not to ensure that they could collaborate more effectively. But this thesis, this rejection of what was already becoming a commonplace in 'philosophical' circles, found little support.

Marx and Engels, speaking of the period when men first began to use ideas, to think conceptually, say that at this stage even the language of politics, law, morality, and religion was the 'direct efflux' of material behaviour. But this seems odd. Or at least it makes it difficult to decide what to make of the assertion that the use of ideas is the 'direct efflux' of men's working together to procure or produce what satisfies their wants. On the face of it, this assertion seems to imply that the ideas that arise directly out of this collaboration serve to make it easier and more effective. If the ideas are then used for other purposes, they must surely be adapted to them. How then can they, *in these new uses*, be the 'direct efflux' of 'material intercourse'?

I am not now trying to make verbal points against Marx and Engels but to interpret a difficult part of their theory and to explain where it is confused or defective. I shall assume that, in their opinion, men first acquired and used ideas to enable them to collaborate more effectively in satisfying their wants. I shall call the ideas so acquired and used *the basic language*, and I shall assume that this language serves, not merely to give information, but also to give instructions, to make requests, to make and acknowledge claims, and even to express feelings. That is to say, I shall assume that this language is prescriptive and emotive as well as descriptive. For it is reasonable to assume that it would need to be so for effective use in 'material intercourse', making that intercourse smoother and more efficient. I shall assume further that this basic language is not used to make definitions or to construct general explanations or theories, or in any of the activities that Marx and Engels put into what they call the ideological superstructure. For these other uses would be outside material intercourse.

Marx and Engels speak of 'material intercourse' as if it were somehow basic in relation to other social activities, and I shall assume that part of what they mean by this is that these other activities arise in response to needs which are themselves effects of material intercourse. This, of course, does not preclude these other activities, or some of them, being necessary conditions of further developments of material intercourse. These other activities involve, just as much as material intercourse does, the use of ideas. Indeed, language is of the essence of them, for they are inconceivable without it, whereas there could be primitive forms of co-operative production without the use of language—at least of language of the kind confined in our world to human beings.

I shall suppose that, as these new activities arise, men carry over into them ideas first acquired in material intercourse. But clearly this carrying over cannot leave the ideas quite unchanged. To put ideas to new uses involves changing them, or at least many of them, so that they cease to be the same ideas. There arises therefore a derivative language alongside the basic language, and this language is obviously not related to material intercourse in the same way as the basic language is. It is clearly not the 'direct efflux' of material intercourse. My point is a simple one, and I am not suggesting that Marx and Engels, had it been put to them, would have rejected it. I am saying only that they took no account of it, though it is relevant and has important implications for their theory.

Words taken from the basic language and put to new uses acquire new meanings. The etymologist, in explaining how old words are put to new uses, or are combined to make new words, shows us how men acquire new ideas. If, when old words are put to new uses, or new words are made out of old ones, we say that these new uses *reflect* the old ones, what do we mean by the word *reflect*? Do we mean only *derive from*? If this is all we mean, we say nothing that throws much light on how religion or politics or law or morality or philosophy, or anything else that we do not include in 'material intercourse', is related to that intercourse. Nor does it entitle us to conclude that 'morality, religion, metaphysics, all the rest of ideology . . . no longer retain the semblance of independence' and have 'no history' and 'no development'. No doubt, they continue to be powerfully affected by material intercourse after they have arisen; they do not get loose from it, as a toy balloon does from the child that throws it into the air with no string attached. But, if they too affect material intercourse in their turn (and both Marx and Engels quite often concede that they do), what is the point of saying that they have 'no history', no 'development', and no 'semblance of independence'? To be sure, things that affect one another cannot be independent of one another. What happens to any of them cannot be fully explained without taking into account what happens to the others. But this holds of all the things in question, including 'material intercourse'.

There are, no doubt, degrees of dependence. It can make sense to say of things that affect one another that some affect the others more than they are affected by them. It is not in principle impossible, even in the social studies, to set up criteria enabling us to assess the extent to which interacting phenomena affect one another, to measure their relative dependences; though I am not aware that this has yet been done, and I can see great difficulties in the way of doing it when the phenomena in question make up large and complicated spheres of social life. But I see no reason for holding that, among social activities, those that arise first and from which the others derive, must have a larger influence on the others than the others on them.

When it is said that ideas arise from material intercourse, this can mean

one or other of two things. It can mean that they first arise in this intercourse, and that ideas used in other spheres of social life are derived from
these first ideas, or it can mean that all ideas used outside material intercourse are used in activities which are responses to needs that arise,
directly or indirectly, out of that intercourse. These two are not the only
possible meanings but they are perhaps the most important in this context.
Marx and Engels when they spoke of consciousness as a 'reflection' or
'reflex' of material intercourse or the life-process very probably meant one
or other or both of these two things. They also, no doubt, meant more
than this, but almost certainly they meant at least this much. And this, as
far as it goes, makes good enough sense—though the more indirect the
connection of a need with whatever is said to give rise to it, the more
difficult it is to establish what the connection is and the less enlightening
it is to assert it. If A gives rise to B, and B to C, and C to D, and so on to
N, then, though it follows that, if there were no A there would be no N,
it does not preclude us from saying that N might have been very different
from what it in fact is and yet A have been the same. One thing's 'arising
out' of another, in either of the two senses I have discussed, does not
preclude its being deeply affected by other things besides.

It is misleading to speak of 'reflexes' or 'reflections' in the way that
Marx and Engels do. Not only because there are at least two different
senses in which what is 'derivative' can arise out of what is original or
basic, but also (and above all) because these words suggest some kind
of correspondence or similarity between the derivative and the basic.
They do so especially when they are applied (as Marx applies them) to the
forms of alienated life in relation to the human conditions supposed to give
rise to them. According to him, these forms *reflect* the conditions they
arise from. But if they do, they must do so in a way that consciousness,
taken generally, does not *reflect* material intercourse. The connection
between them and the conditions they *reflect* differs in kind from the connection of consciousness to material intercourse. Or, rather, though they
too arise out of these conditions, as consciousness does out of material
intercourse, there is a further relation between them and these conditions
which there is not between consciousness and material intercourse; and
it is this relation, I suggest, that should be called 'reflection'. For these
forms are not just consequences but are manifestations of what gives rise
to them.

If consciousness, understood as the use of ideas, as conceptual thinking,
is derivative in relation to material intercourse, it is so only in the sense
that the earliest forms of material intercourse preceded it. It is not so in
the sense that material intercourse, once consciousness has arisen, continues to affect it without being affected by it. This Marx admits, often
enough, by implication, though not in the long passage from *The German*

Ideology which I quoted a while ago. In the *Grundrisse*, he says that 'the hunger that is satisfied with cooked meat eaten with fork and knife is a different kind of hunger from the one that devours raw meat with the aid of hands, nails and teeth'.[2] What is it, then, that makes the hunger different, if not the ideas that men have of themselves, their place in society, and what that place requires of them? These ideas deeply affect their wants, even the ones that Marx calls material. When he speaks of material intercourse, the life-process, or the reproduction of life, he quite often (though not always) has in mind not just the production of the wherewithal to meet the bare needs of life, but activities directed to satisfying men's wants as they are at whatever stage of social evolution they have reached. The wants in question, material though they are called, are none the less wants peculiar to beings who think and whose wants depend as much on their ideas about themselves and their environment, especially the social part of it, as on their biological needs.

Men's wants vary with their conceptions of the world, their *Welt-anschauungen*. This indeed is implicit in Marx's idea of man as a social and self-creative being. For if men's ideas did not affect their wants and were mere products of their endeavours to satisfy them, those endeavours would not create new wants. The conception of man as a self-creative being is therefore incompatible with the account that Marx and Engels give in *The German Ideology* of how material intercourse is related to consciousness. If they had said merely that consciousness arose in the first place out of material intercourse and that this intercourse always has a powerful effect on it, they would have said nothing incompatible with this conception. They would then only have repeated what had often been said before them, though in other words. They would have uttered a commonplace. But they said, even though confusedly, a good deal more than this in *The German Ideology*, and they repeated it in a variety of ways in their later writings. To be sure, they also put forward other arguments that contradict what they said in *The German Ideology*, and did so in both their earlier and later writings. But they never, at any stage, produced a coherent account, and one in keeping with their conception of man, of how material intercourse is related to consciousness.

In the long passage I quoted from *The German Ideology*, Marx and Engels, after saying that 'consciousness can never be anything else than conscious existence' and that 'existence' is men's 'actual life-process', then go on to say that in 'all ideology men and their circumstances appear upside down as in a *camera obscura*' and that 'this phenomenon arises just as much out of their historical life-process as the inversion of objects on the retina does from their physical life-process'.[3] As Marx and Engels sometimes—even in *The German Ideology*—use the word 'consciousness' to refer to conceptual

---

[2] *Marx's Grundrisse*, transl. by D. McLellan, p. 25.   [3] *The German Ideology*, p. 14.

thinking in general, the two sentences I have just quoted might seem to imply that all such thinking is illusion and is so necessarily, that our ideas about the world are irretrievably distorted just because consciousness and its object are related as they are. But this, though it is implied by what Marx and Engels actually say, can hardly be what they meant to say. They did not believe that their own account of the relation of consciousness to the life-process was distorted, nor did they think it a uniquely privileged account, the only truth within the reach of mankind.

Though Marx occasionally uses the words 'consciousness' and 'ideology' in the same sense, he does not do so always. Consciousness is the wider term, for it sometimes covers all forms of conceptual thinking, whereas ideology is used nearly always in a narrower sense. Ideology is sometimes called 'false consciousness', which implies that it is only a part of consciousness. What earlier I called the basic language is a form of consciousness but not of false consciousness. Though it is not merely descriptive but prescriptive and emotive as well, its uses are entirely practical. It serves to give information and orders, to make requests, and to express feelings when men act together to produce what satisfies their wants. It is not used to define ideas or to construct theories or to express the feelings men have when they stand back and contemplate or analyse their own activities and the world. I am not suggesting that language has ever anywhere been entirely 'basic', nor yet that Marx thought it had been or was committed to thinking so; I merely use the idea of such a language to help me assess critically Marx's conception of false consciousness and its connection with alienated life. If language were entirely basic, if it were used only for practical purposes, then, though men might quite often be mistaken, they would not have false consciousness, as Marx understood it. They might misdescribe particular things or events, or give inappropriate orders, or make irrelevant requests, but they would not have mistaken ideas about whole aspects of reality, about types of event or activity. False consciousness, as distinct from the making of particular mistakes, arises when thinking is more than merely practical and is also theoretical and contemplative, and especially when it turns to offering general explanations of human behaviour. Though, of course, once false consciousness has arisen, it affects men's practical activities. This I put forward, not necessarily as the truth of the matter, but as an account that helps both to clarify Marx's ideas about ideology and alienated life and to qualify them in ways that make them more coherent and realistic.

False consciousness is mistaken thinking about some aspect of reality, some type of event or activity. But, presumably, not all such mistaken thinking is false consciousness. For science can put forward mistaken hypotheses, often of a very general nature, and adhere to them for a considerable time before it discards them, and Marx, as we know, did not think of science as a form of false consciousness. Science recognizes that its hypotheses and theories are provisional, and has criteria for deciding whether or not they should be discarded for better ones. False consciousness flourishes, presumably, in those spheres of thought which have not yet become 'scientific'.[4] Or, rather, it flourishes among people who have not yet learned to think scientifically about some aspect of reality in which their thinking has ceased to be merely practical.

False consciousness, understood in this way, need not be an effect of alienation. It could arise largely (and indeed always does partly) from intellectual causes: from the fact that men, when they begin to reflect about some aspect of reality and to construct general explanations, lack the ideas and the skills they need to understand clearly what they are doing and to set up criteria enabling them to distinguish truth from error or more adequate from less adequate explanations. From what Marx says in one or two places about primitive religion, it would seem that at least sometimes he came close to recognizing that there could be false consciousness where there was as yet no alienation. He would certainly have been well advised to recognize it, given his own views about the causes of alienation.

It is easy to see how false consciousness could arise, even if men were never in the condition that Marx calls alienation, just as it is easy to see how it could arise even if society were never divided into classes, with some of them exploiting the others. Given the distinction between knowledge and illusion, it is easy to see that the seeker after knowledge, precisely because it takes time for him to understand the nature of his enterprise, is likely to be a victim of illusion. The way to knowledge is through illusion and the overcoming of it. But also, given the fact of alienation, it is not difficult to see how false consciousness can come, as it were, to its service; how alienated man can come to accept illusions about the world which are both symptoms of his condition and compensations for it. So, too, it is not difficult to see how false consciousness can support class interests by providing dominant classes with views of the world and society which justify their dominance and other classes with views which either reconcile them to their condition or sustain them in their efforts to change it. Even if we reject, as I think we must, the suggestion that, if there were no alienation or no oppression of some groups by others, there would be no false consciousness, we can agree that false consciousness is closely related in a variety of ways both with alienation and with class or group oppression.

We should expect the activities that Marx calls 'ideological reflexes' of

---

[4] Neither Marx nor Engels attempts to explain precisely how science differs from other types of systematic explanation. There is no need for me, in developing the arguments of this chapter, to consider in detail what their ideas about science may have been.

material intercourse to have a considerable element of false consciousness about them. We should expect this, whether or not they are forms of alienated life. For they are activities which involve reflective thinking, and therefore the use of more than the basic language. They arise as man seeks to do more than give particular information or control particular actions on particular occasions; they arise as he seeks to explain natural events or human behaviour and its aims in a more general way, as he seeks to define and to control types of behaviour. This is clear enough in the case of religion and metaphysics, which Marx treats as forms of ideology. But it applies also to morality, as soon as it takes the form of definite principles supported by justifying arguments, and to politics, if we understand by it, not any exercise of authority, but the exercise of it in regular ways by persons whose office is to exercise it. Even in material intercourse as yet unaffected by reflective thinking, by attempts at general explanations and justifications, men make claims on one another and respond positively to them, and they also give and receive orders in circumstances in which the right to give them and the obligation to obey them are recognized, even though not defined and justified. Morality and authority of some kind are involved in material intercourse even before it is affected by the more developed forms of thinking which allow of false consciousness. But we must suppose that Marx, when he called morality and politics ideological, had in mind, not the most rudimentary moral rules and forms of authority, but something more sophisticated: that he had in mind types of morality and authority that go along with reflection about how men should live and human communities be organized.

Science, no less than ideology, uses ideas that derive ultimately from what I have called the basic language. And it, too, is a response to needs that arise, directly or indirectly, out of material intercourse. But, presumably, it is not a form of false consciousness, and Marx does not say that it is. On the contrary, both he and Engels speak of it as if it were a type of thinking before whose progress false consciousness or ideology retreats. And yet the victory of science over false consciousness is not, as they see it, the achievement of science alone. For science makes no advances unless social conditions are propitious to its doing so. Men of talent and imagination may produce new ideas but the ideas will not catch on while there are powerful interests that feel threatened by them and no interests that welcome them. Besides, creative thinkers, if they are not to lose heart or to be diverted to some other sphere of activity, need the encouragement that comes of being appreciated by others.

Marx and Engels believed that, in their own time and in the West, social conditions were highly favourable to progress in the natural sciences. Capitalism was, they thought, technically progressive, and the natural sciences, while they helped to make this progress possible, were at the same time stimulated by it. The connection between progress in science and progress in technology seemed to Marx so close that he even, on one or two occasions, included science in what he called 'the forces of production'. In the *Grundrisse*, he calls the progress of science 'one form of the development of human productive forces'[5] and says that 'the accumulation of knowledge and skill, of the general productive power of society's intelligence, is thus absorbed into capital in opposition to labour and appears as the property of capital . . . to the extent that it enters into the productive process'.[6] This treating science as a productive force is hardly consistent with Marx's general pronouncements, in *The German Ideology* and elsewhere, about 'material intercourse' in relation to 'consciousness', but in itself and duly qualified it makes good enough sense. The natural sciences can make (and have made) great advances without being applied to production. Nevertheless, in an age of rapid technical progress it makes sense to say that they (or some of them) are, among other things, 'forces of production'.

Only when they spoke of 'consciousness' (or 'thinking' or 'theory') more or less indiscriminately, taking no notice, or very little, of its different forms and uses, were Marx and Engels tempted to speak of it as a mere 'efflux' or 'reflection' of the 'life-process', or to deny it any autonomous development. They were seldom more careless than when they raised the most difficult of philosophical and sociological issues. Perhaps some instinct taught them that, in these dark regions in which even the most cautious lose their way, it pays to be bold; for the bold at least give the impression that they know what they are about, and it is not easy to prove them wrong. But, carelessly though they spoke of consciousness, they took care not to speak in the same way of natural science. Did they then not include natural science in what they called consciousness? To this question the answer is unfortunately both *Yes* and *No*. It depended on what they were trying to prove at any particular time.

Natural science, for Marx and Engels, is emphatically not false consciousness, even though old theories and hypotheses are discarded for new ones. But social theory, not excluding economics, is so. And yet—so it would seem from what they say of some types of social theory—it is not so always. The claims they make, directly or indirectly, for their own theory make it plain that it is not, in their estimation, an example of false consciousness. Yet they do not claim to be infallible; they recognize that they too may be mistaken, not just about facts, but in some of their general explanations.

They expected their own theories to be improved upon. There had been progress in the social sciences before their time and they expected it to continue after them. They even spoke with considerable respect of some

---

[5] *Marx's Grundrisse*, transl. by D. McLellan, p. 120.   [6] Ibid., p. 134.

of the classical economists, and especially of Adam Smith and Ricardo, though they also accused all bourgeois economists, not excluding them, of having a false conception of the bourgeois social order. Their admiration was not only for the ingenuity and skill of Smith and Ricardo as bourgeois apologists; they conceded that they had themselves learned a good deal from them about the capitalist economy.

In the nineteenth century philosophers and social theorists had not yet raised some of the questions about the methods and limitations of the social studies which today are widely discussed. We must therefore beware of ascribing to Marx and Engels beliefs that they did not hold. To us it may appear that the less obscure of their oracular utterances about consciousness in relation to its object could, if suitably interpreted, apply to the social studies but not to the natural sciences. But we must not jump to the conclusion that they thought so too. Neither Marx nor Engels ever tried to explain systematically how the study of human behaviour differs from the study of the natural world. We can therefore say confidently only this: the claims they make for their own theory imply that the study of society can be scientific in the same sense as the natural sciences were held to be in their day. Like Saint-Simon before them, they believed that the social studies were backward as compared with the natural sciences, and they attributed this backwardness, as he did, largely to the persistence of illusions favouring the interests of powerful classes or groups. Though their ideas about knowledge were never clearly formulated and may have differed considerably from those of Saint-Simon, who borrowed nothing from Hegel, they shared the same faith that 'myth' would eventually give way to 'science' in the study of man as it had done already in the study of nature.

Two beliefs widely (though by no means universally) held by social theorists today would appear to be absent from their thinking: that the explanation of distinctively human types of behaviour differs so much from the explanation of natural phenomena that it cannot be *scientific* in the same sense of the word, though there are criteria for assessing its truth or adequacy; and that this explanation, even if it could be scientific in this sense, would still leave unsatisfied a need for a kind of theorizing about man and society that is evaluative and persuasive.[7] But this kind of theorizing, though not itself scientific, need not be a form of false consciousness; it need not contain beliefs incompatible with the sciences and may indeed lean heavily on them. Today, given the variety of uses to which the word 'ideology' has been put, it might be proper to call such

---

[7] In *Ludwig Feuerbach and the End of Classical German Philosophy*, Engels says of dialectical thinking that it is a 'summation' of the results of the positive sciences, but positive science, as he conceives of it, includes the systematic study of human behaviour. Thus the distinction he makes between dialectical thinking and positive science is not a distinction between the social and the positive (in the sense of natural) sciences.

theorizing 'ideological', but it would not be ideology, as Marx thought of it. Ideology, for him and for Engels too, connotes false consciousness, and so, for them, the progress of science goes along with the decay of ideology.

Nevertheless, in their opinion, it is not the progress of science which alone puts an end to ideology. False consciousness will disappear only when the social conditions (including the interests and attitudes) in which it is rooted are destroyed. And this work of destruction will, they think, be the task of the proletariat. To many of their readers, this last claim, that the workers are destined to destroy the social causes of false consciousness, has seemed no better than a blind act of faith. Still, even if we find this claim for the proletariat extravagant and arbitrary, we may yet be impressed by some of their ideas about alienation and false consciousness.

Marx and Engels spoke of 'theory' in relation to 'practice' as well as of 'consciousness' in relation to 'material intercourse' (or 'social existence'), and their disciples today do so even more freely than they did. It is therefore worth noticing that the first pair of terms, though not unconnected with the second, is yet different, just as it is different from the pair 'ideological superstructure' and 'economic foundation'. It is the fashion among Marxists to use these three pairs of terms carelessly, without stopping to consider how they differ or to what extent they overlap. Are 'material intercourse', the 'life-process', 'social existence', and 'economic foundation' equivalent terms? Sometimes, no doubt, they are and at other times not. It is not easy, looking at how Marx and the Marxists use these terms, to decide how far they refer to the same and how far to different things. That the meanings of the terms do overlap is, of course, obvious, but just how far and in what contexts is not easily determined.

The difficulty with such terms as 'consciousness', 'ideology', and 'theory', though still considerable, is perhaps less. Sometimes, though not often, Marx and Engels speak of consciousness as if they had in mind all forms of distinctively human thinking. On these occasions, clearly, it covers much more than 'ideology' or 'theory'. And even if we exclude from 'consciousness' the forms of thought or discourse carried on in what I have called the basic language, it still remains a term broader than either 'theory' or 'ideology'. Consciousness, limited in only this way, includes more than theory, even in the widest of its usual senses, it includes more than the construction of general explanations and the making of critical assessments of them. It includes, for example, the use in everyday practical discourse of ideas formed in the first place in the attempt to construct general explanations. Such ideas are plentiful in every sophisticated society. Consciousness therefore also includes more than ideology, whether ideology is taken to be merely false consciousness or, more generally, any theory or system of beliefs that gains acceptance because it supports or challenges the established order or some aspect of it.

Theory, if we mean by it the putting forward of general explanations and the critical assessment of them, does not coincide with ideology. For theory includes the natural sciences, which are not forms of false consciousness and do not consist of beliefs accepted because they support or challenge the established order. Besides, 'ideology' or 'the ideological', as Marx and Engels speak of it, includes activities which are not forms of theory, in any usual sense of that term. For example, they call religion ideological, and yet religion is often as much a matter of ritual as of belief. To be sure, the ritual is connected with beliefs which, taken together, provide some kind of explanation of the world or of some aspects of it. Yet the ritual can be valued by persons who do not accept the beliefs or who interpret them in ways peculiar to themselves. Community of religion can be much more a sharing of attitudes and loyalties expressed in ritual than a sharing of beliefs.

The same is true of morality in general and of bourgeois morality in particular. It consists of more than general beliefs, false or true; it consists also of rules or standards used to control or to guide behaviour. We can use rules without knowing how to explain or justify them, even though, where there are important social rules, there are often also widely accepted explanations of them. Of course, to be able to use rules correctly, a man must recognize the situations in which they apply. This involves his having beliefs about his environment, and the beliefs must be largely true, if he is not to misuse the rules. But, clearly, it could not have been these beliefs that Marx had in mind when he called bourgeois morality ideological. He must have been thinking, not of the true beliefs required to use social rules correctly, but of the beliefs serving to explain and justify the rules—beliefs he thought to be false. Yet he used the word 'ideology' to refer also to the rules and not only to justificatory beliefs. The ideological, as he and Engels speak of it, ordinarily covers both theory and practice. Not, of course, all forms of either, but some forms of each.

Marx and Engels never inquired how far the experimental sciences rest on *a priori* assumptions, nor how it comes about that, even in branches of study whose scientific character has long been recognized, these assumptions are from time to time discarded and others substituted for them. But they did speak of the natural sciences, as most people did in their day and still do in ours, as if they were 'value-free'; as if acceptance of their findings (and therefore also of the assumptions they rest on) did not commit the acceptor to any particular beliefs as to what is right or good or desirable. And they believed that the study of society would eventually become 'scientific'.

And yet, despite these beliefs, they refrained from speaking of the social and human studies as they ordinarily spoke of the natural sciences; as if, in becoming scientific, they also became 'value-free'. To be sure, they never argued that human behaviour differs from natural events in ways which prevent the study of it being 'value-free'. Since they never inquired how the study of man differs from the study of nature, they felt no need to argue in this way. But they did take it for granted that their own studies, which they believed to be scientific, committed them to the cause of the proletariat. They did not explain how this was so; they did not even (so it seems to me) face the issues that need to be faced, if such an explanation is to be given. But they did take it for granted that anyone who understood the course of social change as they did—and they claimed that their understanding of it was free of illusion, as bourgeois social theory was not—would share their values.

They did more than merely predict the eventual victory of the proletariat and expect anyone who understood their reasons for doing so to accept them and to join the victorious cause. After all, the victory they predicted might be a long time coming. A man could, quite reasonably, work against it in the hope of putting it off until after he was gone, and in the meantime might do very well for himself. Rather, they expected anyone who shared their conception of man as a social and 'self-creative' being and who accepted their account of the human predicament in capitalist society to see the destruction of capitalism and the coming of socialism as a liberation of mankind.

It makes sense to think of man, as Hegel and Marx do, as essentially social and 'self-creative', and I have tried in earlier chapters to explain the advantages of doing so. But I do not see how it follows from this idea that in the course of social change man moves towards an ever greater understanding and control of himself and his environment; that there is a movement which is liberating in the sense that it leads eventually to a social order in which human practices and values are in keeping with human capacities and needs. As far as I can see, it is quite consistent with this idea that human understanding and productive power, as they increase, should repeatedly create situations and problems which divide men and prevent their achieving a social order satisfying to them. From the idea of man as essentially a self-creative being it follows only that he is continually changed by his own activities, and that this change leads on the whole to greater complexity and sophistication; it does not follow that the course of change is progressive, as either Hegel or Marx understood progress.

Even if we allow that it is (at least from a certain point onwards) progressive, we may still reject the Marxist belief in the proletariat as the prime agent of progress. We may deny that the proletariat's being an exploited class is a good reason for believing that it is any more likely than any other class to acquire a view of society resting upon a true account of this progressive course of change. We may insist that beliefs about society and social change which are free of illusion are no more likely to gain currency in one class than another, and that the reconstruction of society in the light of these beliefs, if ever it is achieved, will be the work of men drawn from all classes. Marx's faith in the proletariat seems to be largely blind.

Yet he had this faith, and his disciples today still have it, or still think it incumbent on them to speak as if they had it. And it is this faith that moves them to speak differently of the theory which they hold to be specifically proletarian from the way in which they speak of the theories they call bourgeois. The relation of theory to practice is, in both cases, said to be 'dialectical'; theory 'reflects' practice and also affects it, for what men do affects their ideas about themselves and the environment in which they act, and these ideas affect their actions. The theory in question is, of course, social theory; it covers both systematic explanations of society and beliefs about it which, though not deliberately put together to explain any aspect of social life, are still not random but form a coherent whole.

But, for reasons never adequately explained, while the dialectical relation of proletarian theory to practice serves to deepen and correct the theory, and to dissipate illusions, this is not the case with bourgeois theory. The bourgeois, apparently, cannot afford to understand society and social change as they really are, for their interests are bound up with the established order remaining essentially as it is, whereas the interests of the proletarians are not tied to it in the same way. On the contrary, it is their interest that this order should disappear and give way to another. They can therefore afford, as the bourgeois cannot, to understand how society is changing. Thus, in the realm of social theory at least, the bourgeois are wedded to illusion in a way that the proletarians are not. And this, so we are told, even though the workers are the most alienated of all the classes of capitalist society!

This theme of the proletariat as a class uniquely privileged in the succession of classes, the sole bearer of truth, and of the bourgeoisie as condemned to illusion, is not convincing. Since Marx's time, others have taken it up and have made more of it than ever he did. Not that they have offered better reasons than his for believing it to be true; but they have inflated it or, perhaps I should say, more respectfully, have orchestrated it. They have elaborated upon it and put it into settings which give it an air of mystery and profundity.

But, whatever we think of this theme, we may still find much that is impressive in Marx's account, not only of religion, but of the bourgeois state and bourgeois morality as forms of alienated life; as activities, beliefs, and values which are both effects of alienation and manifestations of it. We must, of course, modify the account. For 'religion' we must substitute 'dogmatic religions that preach salvation', for 'the bourgeois state' 'the modern state', and for 'bourgeois morality' the 'morality of quickly changing industrial society'. Not that *any* religion or state or form of morality is, taken as a whole, a form of alienated life. But this way of looking at it may throw light on aspects of it or attitudes to it ordinarily neglected. The rude, accusing finger of Marx points in directions in which we do well to look, even if our account of what we see there is not quite his.

The terms 'bourgeois state' and 'bourgeois morality' are not simply misnomers, for the rise of the bourgeoisie and the rise of a certain type of state and a certain type of morality have in fact been closely connected. So, too, the bourgeois have in many ways done better out of the modern state than any other class and have even, perhaps, been more attached than the others to those aspects of the morality of our age that come closest to being symptoms of alienation.

CHAPTER IX

RELIGION

MARX and Engels were not careful thinkers. Often, when they made their pronouncements about religion or morality or law, they spoke as if they had all religion, all morality, or all law in mind. But in fairness to them, we must recognize that neither of them produced anything that could be called even a sketch for a theory of religion, morality, or law. To consider in detail their many references, scattered through their writings, to any one of these aspects of social life, and to sort out the more general from the less general statements, would be a waste of time. The more sensible course—if only because it does not imply that they attempted what they never did attempt—is to look critically at those of their ideas about religion, morality, or law which have attracted the widest notice and to consider how far they are coherent and realistic.

Neither Marx nor Engels tried to explain how religious, moral, or legal ideas and practices actually arise, or even to distinguish between them and other ideas and practices. There is, for example, nothing in their writings analogous to Tyler's account of how men come to conceive of immortality; how, puzzled by their dreams and trying to make sense of them, they come to believe that they have 'souls' or 'spirits' that can leave their bodies when they are asleep, and that these souls survive their bodies; how they then attribute 'souls' to inanimate things and, later still, conceive of them as controlling whole species of things or aspects of reality, and so at last acquire the idea of gods. Except, from time to time, when they repeat uncritically widely held opinions, Marx and Engels have nothing to say about the origins and development of the ideas that belong to 'the ideological superstructure'.

Their concern is primarily with the social functions, and not with the origins or contents, of what they assign to the superstructure—whether it is religion or morality or law or government. What is more, they are interested, not in all of these functions, but only in some.

It would be absurd to criticize them for not doing what they never set out to do—except to the extent that they needed to do it in order to achieve some purpose of their own which they thought important. It is, no doubt, possible to go a long way towards explaining the functions of religion (or morality or law) without going into their origins. But it is not, I suggest, possible to explain adequately the functions of religion, or of some particular form of it, without considering its contents, at least in broad outline. For example, if we want to show that the religions of 'advanced' and 'primitive' peoples have different functions, we can hardly do so without taking into account how the beliefs and ceremonies of 'advanced' religions differ from those of 'primitive' religions. We may not need to go into great detail but we have to point to what we believe are the relevant differences and to explain why they are relevant. And if we point to differences, we can hardly avoid taking notice of similarities and asking ourselves what functions, if any, are common to advanced and primitive religions.

We must not, merely because Marx and Engels confined their sporadic attention to some of the functions of religion or morality to the exclusion of others, be in a hurry to conclude that they were unaware of the others or thought them unimportant. If someone had said to either Marx or Engels that religion or morality (even the morality of bourgeois society) must be more than a symptom of alienation or a class ideology, or more than these two things together, he might well have agreed. We need not believe that either of them was under the illusion that he was putting forward, even in the broadest outline, a comprehensive account of religion or morality. And yet their habit of careless generalization is a source of confusion. If they had taken more notice of the contents of religion or morality, if they had distinguished more between different kinds of principle, belief, and attitude, they could hardly have failed to qualify their assertions in ways which would have made them clearer and more acceptable. They could then have explained more precisely and adequately the functions that interested them particularly: just how and to what extent a religion or a moral code can be a class ideology or a form of alienated life. They might then have made clearer and more enlightening distinctions between types of religion or morality on the one hand, and social functions on the other, and so have been better placed to show how the two are connected.

I

Marx and Engels, in spite of their undiscriminating references to religion in general, were in fact much more interested in 'advanced' than in 'primitive' religions. They were concerned primarily with relatively sophisticated religions, having a large element of theology and ethics about them, and above all with Christianity. These are the religions most easily represented as forms of alienated life, if only because they arise in societies in which there is a 'division of labour properly so called', as Marx puts it. This, according to him, is the division of labour that gives rise to alienation, and whose abolition will eventually put an end to it. Where there is this division, there is what Marx calls 'the production of

ideas'; that is to say, not the emergence of language in 'material intercourse', but the deliberate making of general explanations, the theoretical
as distinct from the merely practical use of ideas. It is, presumably, with
this production of ideas, this emergence of theory, that religion ceases to
be mere fetishism or animism, with no coherent body of doctrines, no
explicit cosmology behind it, and becomes metaphysical or theological
and perhaps also ethical. As the belief in spirits possessing particular
animals or things gives way to the belief in gods who control whole species
or classes of things or events, and these gods are gradually formed into
hierarchies, often with one god supreme among them (who sometimes
emerges at last as the one true God), man's image of the world and of his
place in it grows in coherence and becomes more elaborate. It is, presumably, this image, no longer implicit in particular beliefs and rituals but
explicit in a body of doctrines, which is the distorted reflection of alienated
man's worldly condition. It is a sophisticated image whose coherence
depends largely on its being interpreted and propagated by persons held to
be specially competent to do so, by priests.

Not all sophisticated metaphysical religions are theological. Of those
that are, some are polytheistic or predominantly so. Some do not promise
an 'after-life', or do so only in the form of the doctrine of the trans-
migration of souls. They have no conception of a heavenly kingdom, a
community of the cleansed or the saved, a perfect society out of this world
contrasted with the imperfect worldly society in which men actually live.
Not all metaphysical religions point to the unworthiness or sinfulness of
man, as Christianity does. Thus, though we can say plausibly of all these
religions that they 'reflect' man's social condition, in the sense that they
express symbolically certain attitudes which, in that condition, he has to
himself, to others, and to his environment, social and natural, we cannot
as plausibly say of all of them that they are symptoms of alienation. At
least not unless alienation is given a broader sense than Marx ordinarily
gives it. It is not obvious that all metaphysical religions express man's
sense that he is frustrated by social conditions, and he is not 'at home' in
the world as he sees it, that he is somehow divided within himself.
Christianity and (next after it) Judaism are perhaps the most likely candi-
dates among sophisticated religions for this role of a fantasy of alienated
man. They were the religions that Marx knew most about, and in his day
were still flourishing in the capitalist West.

Hegel who, before either Marx or Feuerbach, put forward this idea
of religion as a symptom of alienation did in fact speak of Christianity and
Judaism as pre-eminently religions of this kind. He thought of all religions
as expressing symbolically man's sense of what he is; as expressing in the
shape of beliefs which are not literally true his image of himself as he is at a
particular stage of his development. In religion man attributes to what is

outside himself qualities that are essentially human, and does so because he does not yet fully understand himself or the world, and especially the social world, in which he develops his human capacities. In that sense, all religion, for Hegel, is a form of self-externalization—a projection of the self and its attributes on to something outside itself, or imagined to be so.

But this, for Hegel, does not entail that religion always expresses man's sense of his own inadequacy or of his being oppressed or limited by his environment, social or natural. The religion of the ancient Greeks, as Hegel describes it, is the religion of a self-confident people who do not feel restricted or abased in their communities. They are not, of course, free in what for Hegel is the highest sense of freedom; for mankind must pass beyond the stage reached by the Greeks for that freedom to be attained. But they are—or so it would seem from Hegel's account of them —contented with their lot, happy in the culture which expresses what they are. If they, or rather mankind, must pass beyond this stage, it is only because man, as a self-conscious and self-creative being, continually by his exertions develops his powers and changes his social condition. Yet the Greeks, according to Hegel's account of them, though they do not know themselves and their world for what they are, are nevertheless a happy people, a people at home in their world as it appears to them.

It is true that Hegel speaks of Spirit, manifest in the history of mankind, as if it were satisfied only when it is fully developed, when all its potentialities are realized. From this it might seem to follow that man, since Spirit is manifest in him, is not satisfied until human potentialities are fully realized. But Hegel's account of the progress of Spirit could be taken to imply only that Spirit, always active in ways that develop its powers, tends always to pass from the condition in which it is to another. It need not mean that Spirit, until its potentialities are fully realized, is always oppressed or frustrated. In any case, whatever the logical implications of Hegel's account of the self-development of Spirit, the fact remains that he did speak of the ancient Greeks as a happy people satisfied with the world as they found it.

In the philosophy of Hegel there are two distinct but related ideas: self-externalization and self-estrangement. Self-externalization is the process whereby self-conscious beings—or as Hegel puts it, Self-Consciousness, which he thinks of as manifest in a plurality of such beings—bring into existence a world, especially a social world, a world of culture, in which their capacities are developed and they seek to realize themselves; and self-estrangement is their sense that they are restricted or oppressed in this world or at odds with themselves in it, even though it is the world of their own activities and the medium in which alone they can be themselves. It would seem then that, while self-estrangement presupposes self-externalization, the converse is not true.

Some interpreters of Hegel and Marx have used the word 'alienation' (or sometimes 'self-alienation') to refer both to self-externalization and self-estrangement, but it is now used mostly in the second of these senses. Though, as a matter of logic, there can be self-externalization without self-estrangement (and indeed must be in Hegel's rational state or Marx's communist society), it is not clear how far either Hegel or Marx believed that the two go necessarily together at earlier stages in the course of progress. That they believed that at these earlier stages there is a large element of fantasy in men's ideas about themselves and the world, is clear enough. Men are not *for* themselves what they are *in* themselves until the rational state or the communist society is in being; it is only then that the scales fall and vision is clear. But just how Hegel or Marx conceived of the connection between fantasy and self-estrangement is by no means clear. Of Hegel especially it would be misleading to say that he held that there is always self-estrangement where there is a large element of fantasy in men's ideas about the world. In his *Lectures on the Philosophy of History*, speaking of the early stages in the course of progress, he suggests, not that men were then self-estranged, but that they had hardly begun to reflect critically about themselves and the world and therefore lacked freedom.

According to Hegel, Christianity is a highly sophisticated religion which expresses, more fully than any other, man's sense of what he is and what he aspires to be. It is also one of the two religions (the other being Judaism) that flourish where self-estrangement reaches its highest point. Thus, for Hegel as for Marx, the human condition is at its worst—or, rather, man's rejection of himself and of the social world in which he affirms himself is most painfully acute—on the eve of his overcoming this self-estrangement, this alienation, and achieving a culture and a social order suited to his developed powers, an order he understands and controls, in which he is in his element and knows that he is so, and is therefore free.

But there is here a crucial difference between Hegel and Marx. Whereas, for Marx, the overcoming of alienation brings with it the decisive rejection of all religion, even the most evolved and sophisticated, for Hegel it does not. Or it would appear not to, for Hegel is equivocal where Marx is definite. Hegel refrains from saying that Christianity is a form of illusion or false consciousness, even though it does not, according to him, express the truth literally. It expresses both man's alienated condition and the overcoming of it, but does so only figuratively. The literal expression of these truths is the achievement of philosophy. But a symbolic or figurative expression, unless it is recognized for what it is, involves illusion. And if it is recognized, then what it says figuratively can be said literally, and the literal statement is the more adequate, the closer to the truth. Philosophy, according to Hegel, achieves a clearer and fuller expression of the human condition than even the highest religion can do. And yet he takes care not to say that philosophy supersedes religion.

Hegel, who had studied theology, took a wider and deeper, as well as a more sympathetic, interest in religion than did either Marx or Engels. He was more perceptive and more discriminating in discussing its forms, though he, too, like many a European of his day, when assessing religions other than his own, was considerably biased by what he knew of his own. If his attitude to Christianity was ambiguous in a way that Marx's was not, this was due in part, no doubt, to his recognizing his debt to it as a philosopher. His conception of history as the progress of Spirit owes a good deal to Christian ideas of Providence, just as his account of how a community is related to its members owes something to the Christian idea of a church.[1] Marx, of course, was aware of his own debt to Hegel, but he was not aware, as Hegel was, of Hegel's debt to Christian theology. It therefore came easily to him, as it did not to Hegel, to be dismissive in his attitude towards Christianity.

Hegel had other reasons besides this one for treating Christianity and Christian theology with respect. He was not an iconoclast or a revolutionary, and had no wish to weaken the hold on people of beliefs and stories which he thought salutary because they reconciled them to their lot. Though he believed that religion reflects the condition—a condition which he held to be as much social as psychological—of those who accept it, he never thought of it as class ideology. He saw it rather as a form of self-expression, communal or individual. As an intellectual writing for intellectuals, he may well have believed that his philosophy, which he held to be literally true, was beyond the reach of most men's understanding.[2] His conception of the philosopher's role in history was different from Marx's. He did not, though he wrote for the educated and intelligent, think of himself as providing any section of society with doctrines they could use to promote their sectional interests more effectively. Whereas Marx addressed his message to a class which he believed to be, despite its lack of book-learning, better able to appreciate it and act upon it than any other class. And that message, he believed, could not be reconciled with a

---

[1] Though Hegel's philosophical debt to Christianity is considerable, his philosophy is at bottom a rejection of Christianity, despite his reluctance to admit it. He may say that Christian doctrines express symbolically anxieties and aspirations which have to be dispelled or realized, if Spirit (or man as the bearer of it) is to achieve self-knowledge and freedom, but logically he is committed to holding that they are not literally true. If his philosophy is true, then these doctrines are not so, for they do not say what he says, though in other words. His philosophy is not really a translation of Christian theology into another idiom, in spite of its considerable debt to that theology.

[2] If he believed this, it is a belief difficult to reconcile with others that he held: as, for example, that understanding oneself and the world as they really are is a condition of attaining freedom, and that in the fully evolved rational state all men are free.

religion that induced the exploited workers to put up with conditions which it was their interest to destroy.

II

In the introduction to his *Critique of Hegel's Philosophy of Right*, Marx calls religion 'the sigh of the oppressed creature, the sentiment of a heartless world, and the soul of soulless conditions' and says that it is 'the opium of the people'.[3] 'The criticism of religion disillusions man so that he will think, act and fashion his reality as a man who has lost his illusions and regained his reason; so that he will revolve about himself as his own true sun. Religion is the illusory sun about which man revolves so long as he does not revolve about himself.'[4] And later on he adds: 'The criticism of religion ends with the doctrine that man is the supreme being for man. It ends, therefore, with the categorical imperative to overthrow all those conditions in which man is an abased, enslaved, abandoned, contemptible being.'[5]

It seems clear that here, at least, Marx is speaking of religion generally and not of any particular type of it. The suggestion here is that religion as such is a mark of oppression and abasement. Unless men felt oppressed and contemptible, they would not resort to religion, which expresses what they feel about themselves and their condition, and also consoles them in it or distracts them from it. To criticize religion is to dispel the illusions in which men seek comfort for their oppressed condition; it is to compel them to see that condition as it is, to face up to it, so that they are moved to put an end to it. Instead of projecting their ideas of themselves as they would wish to be into myths about a life after death in the company of God, they must try to realize these ideas in this world by transforming society and themselves with it.

The immediate task of philosophy, which is in the service of history, is to unmask human self-alienation in its secular form now that it has been unmasked in its sacred form. Thus the criticism of heaven is transformed into the criticism of earth, the criticism of religion into the criticism of law, and the criticism of theology into the criticism of politics.[6]

---

[3] *Karl Marx: Early Writings*, pp. 43–4.   [4] Ibid., p. 44.   [5] Ibid., p. 52.

[6] Ibid., p. 44. Marx makes this same point in the fourth of his *Theses on Feuerbach*, in which again (and perhaps more clearly) he seems to be speaking of all religion. 'Feuerbach', he says, 'starts from the fact of religious self-alienation, the duplication of the world into a religious, imaginary world and a real one. His work consists in the dissolution of the religious world into its secular basis. He overlooks the fact that after this work is completed the chief thing still remains to be done. For the fact that the secular foundation detaches itself from itself and establishes itself in the clouds as an independent realm is really only to be explained by the self-cleavage and self-contradictoriness of this secular basis. The latter must itself, therefore, first be understood in its contradiction, and then revolutionized in practice by the removal of the contradiction.' And yet it might be argued that, even here, Marx is not speaking unequivocally of *all* religion, on the ground that primitive religion, in the form of magic, does not really *duplicate* the world. Did Marx take account of this?

Marx says that the criticism of religion is the unmasking of 'self-alien-ation' in its sacred form, and says it in a context in which he is speaking of religion generally. If we take him at his word, we must attribute to him the belief that *all* religion is a symptom of alienation. But did he really believe this? Did he believe it of primitive as well as of sophisticated religions? Did he believe it, even though in primitive societies the causes of alienation, as he himself describes them, do not operate? For in these societies there is no division of labour 'properly so called', no separation of mental from manual work, and often also no private property in the means of production.

It may be that Marx in the few paragraphs about religion in the intro-duction to his *Critique of Hegel's Philosophy of Right* merely failed to make qualifications which he needed to make to avoid the appearance of contradiction. It may be that, if he had been challenged on this point, he would have conceded that his unqualified generalizations do not in fact apply to primitive religions. But I doubt whether this is so. For, even in this introduction, there is a sentence which suggests that Marx may also have had primitive religions in mind. 'Religion', he says, 'is indeed man's self-consciousness and self-awareness (*Selbstgefühl*) so long as he has not found himself or has lost himself again.'[7] I shall not venture to explain just how *not finding oneself* differs from *losing oneself*, but I take it that Marx is here making a distinction, even though obscurely, between the condition of man when he is not yet sophisticated enough to feel 'lost', when he has not yet tried to describe his condition and to put questions about it, and his condition when he does feel lost precisely because he has such questions and is troubled about himself and his condition. Man not yet sophisticated enough to have lost himself is primitive man. For to be lost, in the sense relevant here, is already a mark of sophistication; it is a sign that man is troubled about his identity, about the sort of being he is. And if he is troubled about himself, he is troubled also about the world in which he seeks an identity. For man, as Marx puts it, 'is not an abstract being, squatting outside the world. Man is the human world, the state, society'.[8]

In the first volume of *Capital* there is a clearer reference to primitive religion:

Those ancient social organizations of production are, as compared with bourgeois society, extremely simple and transparent. But they are founded either on the immature development of man individually, who has not yet severed the umbilical cord that unites him with his fellow men in a primitive tribal com-munity, or upon direct relations of subjection ... This narrowness is reflected in the ancient worship of nature, and in the other elements of the popular religions. The religious reflex of the real world can, in any case, only then finally vanish, when the practical relations of everyday life offer to man none but

_____
[7] Ibid., p. 40.   [8] Ibid., p. 43.

perfectly intelligible and reasonable relations with his fellow men and [with] nature.[9]

It would seem then that primitive man, though not exactly 'alienated' (for the social causes of alienation do not operate in communities of the kind he belongs to) is in a condition analogous to it. His life is narrow and his social condition is one that he learns to accept without understanding or controlling it. As he sees it, he is *fated* to live as he does, for he is not a brute animal but a self-conscious being. He is more than a creature of instinct, appetite, and habit; he is aware that he belongs to a community whose conventions he must respect. He is confined to ways of life not of his own making, which he cannot alter, and about which he has false beliefs. He may not be oppressed, unless he is directly subject to another's will, but he is not free. He is not his own master, for he 'has not yet severed the umbilical cord that unites him with his fellow men'. It is not clear what Marx meant by 'severing the umbilical cord', but he probably had in mind the achievement of some kind of autonomy. In all societies the individual is dependent in many ways on his fellow men, but in some he is allowed a considerable measure of independence, a domain of his own in which he may, within broad limits, do as he pleases. In primitive society, as Marx conceives of it, the individual has no such domain; his whole life is ruled by convention and he lives it closely bound to his community. He never grows out of the family into which he is born, for it is an extended family that includes the entire community. And the community also is not really autonomous, for it is custom-bound. It may be independent of outsiders, but it is not a society whose members control it collectively and adapt its institutions to their purposes and ideals.

In *Anti-Dühring* Engels speaks of religion in almost but not quite the same way as Marx does in *Capital*. 'All religion', he says, 'is nothing but the fantastic reflection in men's minds of those external forces which control their daily life, a reflection in which the terrestrial forces assume the form of supernatural forces. In the beginnings of history it was the forces of Nature which were at first so reflected . . .'[10] And further on he says,

In existing bourgeois society men are dominated by the economic conditions created by themselves, by the means of production which they themselves have produced, as if by an extraneous force. The actual basis of religious reflex action therefore continues to exist, and with it the religious reflex itself . . . It is still true that man proposes and that God (that is, the extraneous force of the capitalist mode of production) disposes. Mere knowledge . . . is not enough to bring social forces under the control of society. What is above all necessary for this is a social act. And when this act has been accomplished, when society, by

[9] *Capital* (Moscow edn., 1954), i. 79–80.
[10] *Anti-Dühring*, transl. by Emile Burns (Lawrence & Wishart, London), p. 346.

taking possession of all means of production and using them on a planned basis, has freed itself and all its members from the bondage in which they are at present held by these means of production which they have themselves produced but which now confront them as an irresistible extraneous force; when therefore man no longer merely proposes but also disposes—only then will the last extraneous force which is still reflected in religion vanish; and with it will also vanish the religious reflection itself, for the simple reason that there will then be nothing left to reflect.[11]

If we compare what Engels says in *Anti-Dühring* about primitive religion with what Marx says in *Capital*, we find that Engels insists more than Marx does on man's sense of being controlled by natural forces. He does not speak, as Marx does, of primitive man not yet having severed the umbilical cord that unites him with his tribe. But from this we must not conclude that, in his opinion, primitive man has a sense only of being dominated by natural forces and not by social forces as well. When Engels describes man's condition in capitalist society, he does so in a way that suggests that it is a condition surviving from the past which becomes under capitalism much worse than it was before. This condition, as he describes it, consists in the feeling men have that they are in the power of forces beyond their control. It arises in them, as it does not in horses or sheep, because they are self-conscious purposeful beings. All animals have to act in a natural environment to satisfy their needs, but man alone is 'confronted' by nature and has the feeling that he is up against it, because he alone seeks deliberately to use nature to achieve his aims. Other animals besides man live together in groups, but man alone 'confronts' the group he belongs to because he alone has conscious purposes which can be favoured or thwarted by social rules and practices.

Whether this condition, whatever form it takes, should be called alienation, or whether that name should be confined to only some forms of it, is perhaps not important. Marx himself, in spite of what he says about the causes of alienation, does sometimes, as we have seen, speak as if there could be alienation where these causes do not operate. A Marxist anxious to preserve the appearance of consistency in the master's doctrine might do so in either of two ways: he might interpret it to mean that these causes (the separation of mental from manual labour and private property) merely aggravate a condition which is older than they are, or he might say that the condition is properly alienation only in these aggravated forms. But the condition, whether or not the Marxist calls it alienation, must be more than merely not understanding and controlling one's environment. For men could conceivably lack this understanding and control, and yet be contented with their lot. They might understand no more than enough to sustain their social roles effectively without understanding how those

---

[11] Ibid., pp. 347–8.

roles fitted together to form a system. If, understanding no more than this, they were contented with their lot, we could hardly say that they were dominated by their social conditions, even if they had false beliefs about them. Not, at least, unless by 'dominated by' we meant only 'unable to understand and control'. But if they were *dominated* merely in this sense they would neither be alienated nor in a condition which, if it were aggravated, would amount to alienation. They might, of course, have a religion with a large element of fantasy to it, but it would not be a fantasy of alienated man.

That religion might sometimes express a happy acceptance of the world, a delight in being alive in it, is an idea lacking in the philosophies of Marx and Engels. Even if we take seriously the implications of Marx's account of the causes of alienation, and therefore insist that, for him, religion is not always a mark of alienation, we have to admit that he always speaks of it as if it were something analogous, as if it expressed a sense of restriction or powerlessness felt to be oppressive, even though not acknowledged to be so. Religion, for Marx (and for Engels, too), is a sign that man is less than he aspires to be, incapable though he may be of putting his aspirations into words. At the root of religion, as they conceive of it, lie anxiety and diffidence and the sense of living in a hostile world; and the hopes it inspires serve above all to allay or to disguise these feelings. In this sense, it is always, even in its primitive forms, an opiate.

If we combine the teaching of Marx with that of Engels while Marx was still alive we reach this conclusion: the world felt to be hostile by primitive man is primarily the world of nature and only secondarily the man-made world, the social world. It is above all natural forces that primitive man feels are dangerous to him and that he seeks in his religious practices to propitiate because he cannot control them. Or else he tries to persuade himself that he can control them by magic, though in fact he cannot. Later, as society grows more complicated, and man's ability to control nature to his own advantage increases, the social world, the human world which he has not yet learned to explain adequately and to control, becomes the heavier burden, the source of deeper anxiety. In this more evolved social order, man's image of himself and his attitudes to himself are more elaborate and sophisticated. He is then a more skilled and a more reflective being, a maker of theories, and his aspirations grow with his skills and his power. He still does not understand his condition for what it is, he is still not *for* himself what he is *in* himself, but his self-awareness has become more discriminating and sensitive. He has become a problem to himself, and feels the need to construct theories to explain the world and his place in it in ways that are reassuring to him. It is then that the metaphysical and dogmatic religions flourish, and then also that man's sense of being estranged from or oppressed by the social world, the human world, is most acute. It is acute precisely because he is more sophisticated, more conscious of his powers and of the obstacles to their exercise, and more demanding. Dissatisfied with the social world which consists of his activities and in which he affirms himself, he is dissatisfied also with himself. He is still not free, but he is closer to having the abilities and the understanding which put freedom within his reach.

In some such way as this, we can overcome, or rather avoid, the contradiction between Marx's unqualified assertions about religion as a symptom of alienation and his account of the social causes of alienation. The manoeuvre is not arbitrary, for though it qualifies these assertions in a way that neither Marx nor Engels qualified them, the qualifications are in the spirit of their philosophy. Primitive man, belonging to a community in which there is no separation of material and mental labour and no private property in the means of production, is not master of himself and his environment in the way that man in communist society will be. He does not, along with his fellows, manage the affairs of his community in the light of values clearly understood and generally accepted, and he does not choose his way of life, does not affirm or express himself in his own individual way. He feels his powerlessness in the face of nature and to some extent also in the face of society; he is, as a self-conscious purposeful being, aware of the limitations of his power, as no mere animal is. In learning to control nature and society, he passes from stage to stage in a course of social change bringing with it forms of division of labour and of property which make him much more painfully aware of his lack of power precisely because he acquires along with them a deeper understanding, more varied skills, and larger aspirations. At every stage of his social and cultural evolution, this self-conscious being aware of his inadequacies (though not always at the same level of awareness) seeks reassurance in fantasies about the world and his place in it, and will not cease to do so until at last he comes to know the world for what it is and learns to 'affirm himself' in it without resort to illusion.

III

The idea of religion as class ideology, more prominent in Engels's writings than in Marx's, is narrower in scope. Though here too they did not put themselves to the trouble of qualifying their generalizations, they said little to justify our attributing to them the belief that religion, in all its forms, is class ideology or something akin to it. There are, I think, better reasons (and I have tried to give some of them) for holding that they thought of religion as *always* a symptom of alienation than that they thought of it as *always* a form of class ideology. Yet this idea was also important to them, and more particularly to Engels.

Clearly, in primitive societies where there are no classes, religion cannot be class ideology. Nevertheless, this aspect of it may be important, and may be so especially in societies in which alienation is at its worst. It is at its worst, according to Marx, where there is a sharp division between manual and mental labour, and also a large accumulation in private hands of the means of production. Alienation is at its worst, therefore, in societies divided into classes, societies in which religion can be class ideology. It is not clear whether Marx and Engels believed that in class societies religion is always, among other things, class ideology, but presumably they would, if asked, have admitted the obvious: that it is always more besides.

In the first volume of *Capital*, Marx passes an ambiguous judgement on Christianity. He says that with its 'cult of abstract man', it is the form of religion best suited to a society in which men treat the products of labour as commodities. Now, according to him, it is above all in capitalist or bourgeois society that labour and its products are treated in this way. But Christianity arose centuries before capitalism. If this 'cult of abstract man' distinguishes Christianity from other religions, and if religious beliefs 'reflect' social conditions (if they express attitudes widely shared by men living in those conditions) how could it happen that Christianity spread all over Europe long before the rise of capitalism? Marx offers us no explanation, though he does, prompted perhaps by an uneasy feeling that so sweeping a judgement on Christianity, left unqualified, is simply not true, go on to say that it applies 'more especially' to Christianity 'in its bourgeois developments, Protestantism, Deism, etc.'.[12]

Engels sometimes speaks of early Christianity as a religion attractive to slaves. But in his article on *Bruno Bauer and Early Christianity*, published in 1882, he says of it that, by rejecting all national religions and addressing itself to all peoples without distinction, it became 'the first possible world religion', and that it expressed the 'universal feeling that men themselves are guilty of the general corruption . . . [and] at the same time provided a form of the universally longed-for internal salvation from the corrupt world'. That is to say, it was a faith suited to becoming a world religion, because it expressed feelings of guilt and hope shared by men of all classes. It was, of course, a religion which spread in a society in which there were great inequalities and much oppression and exploitation, and Engels no doubt believed that the corruption and the guilt were effects of inequality

[12] *Capital* (Moscow edn., 1954), i. 79. Given his beliefs about ideology and its origins and functions, Marx should have said not 'more especially' but 'only'. Putting it the way he does, he gives the impression of carelessness, of not seeing or forgetting what his own account of ideology requires him to say. Did he believe, consistently with that account, that Christianity acquired the cult which made it a religion suited to be a bourgeois ideology only as society became bourgeois? Or did he believe that this cult was part of Christianity long before that, and was later taken over into a class ideology with the rise of the bourgeoisie? Whichever of these two beliefs we attribute to Marx, the implication is still that only some forms of Christianity have been class ideologies.

and exploitation. But this in itself would not make Christianity a class ideology; it would make it at most an ideology suited to a society divided into classes.

It is in his account in *The Peasant War in Germany* of the religious wars of Luther's time that Engels goes furthest in distinguishing between different forms of Christianity as forms of class ideology. This account, since it discusses Christian churches and sects during only the first decades of the sixteenth century, does not, of course, prove that Christianity in all or most of its forms has been class ideology. That is obvious enough. What is perhaps less obvious is that it does not even establish that Christianity in Luther's Germany was primarily class ideology, that its most important function was to sustain and justify different classes (or other social groups) in their conflicts with one another or in their pursuit of their interests. Engels no doubt thought otherwise. He said that 'the so-called religious wars of the sixteenth century involved primarily positive material class interests; those were class wars, too, just as the later internal collisions were in England and France'.[13] This judgement of his follows a criticism he makes of ideologists gullible enough to swallow the illusions that an epoch has about itself. In the sixteenth century men believed themselves to be deeply concerned about religion, and Engels's suggestion is that what they were really concerned about were their material interests. He seems to have taken it for granted that if the religious wars of Luther's time were primarily conflicts in which men engaged in pursuit of their material interests then the primary function of religion at that time was to serve as a cover or to provide excuses for the pursuit of these interests.

But this, surely, is a *non sequitur*! I shall not inquire in just what sense of those terms the interests of the parties to the religious wars were *material* or *class* interests; I shall not, at this stage, argue that Engels was mistaken in calling them so.[14] Even if Engels were correct in his judgement about the religious wars in Germany, it simply would not follow that religion was at that time primarily class ideology. His judgement refers, after all, to religious wars and not to forms of religion. Granted that the parties to these wars, while actually fighting them, were more concerned to push their 'material class' interests than to defend or propagate their versions of the Christian faith, it still has to be shown that the most important function of

[13] *K. Marx and F. Engels on Religion* (F.L.P.H., Moscow, 1957), p. 98.

[14] As a matter of fact, in the sixteenth century, in Germany as in the rest of Europe, religious differences followed class lines only to some extent. No doubt, some classes or social groups were more attracted to one form of Christianity than others were, but the extent of the attraction varied from region to region in Germany as well as from country to country in Europe. Engels, of course, at times admitted this. Again, we should have to expand the notion of 'material interests' to cover a good deal more than 'economic interests' to sustain the argument that the parties to the religious wars were concerned primarily to push their material interests. But I am not here considering what the facts, or even the facts alleged by Engels, prove; I am considering only the implications of what he says about the religious wars.

their faiths was to sustain and justify them in their endeavours to push incompatible class interests. Religion has other important functions besides sustaining the ardour of combatants and helping them to disguise their true motives for fighting each other. Engels may have believed that this was its only important function in Germany in Luther's time, and it is conceivable (though far from obvious) that he was right. But he could not establish his case merely by producing evidence (even if it were good evidence) that the parties to the religious wars engaged in them above all to push their material interests. We cannot assume that the functions of religion which are prominent in one sphere of action, among men fighting for their material interests, are in general its most important functions, even in the country in which the fighting is going on. Any more than we can assume that because lovers, when they quarrel, often appeal to their love to justify the hurtful things they say and do to one another, the prime function of love is to provide this justification. Just as there is more to love than lovers' quarrels, so there is more to life in society than conflict in the pursuit of incompatible interests.

Marx and Engels, when they say of some form of religion that it 'reflects' the class or group interests of its adherents, seem sometimes to imply that it contains beliefs adapted to defending or pushing just those interests. For example, they suggest that certain beliefs or ideas of the Protestants were peculiarly suited to the class interests of the early capitalists. We have already come across Marx's suggestion that Christianity's 'cult of abstract man', especially in its Protestant form, is suited to a society in which the products of labour are treated as commodities, a bourgeois society. Such suggestions as these, even though Marx and Engels do not develop them in detail to show precisely how particular beliefs or ideas are suited to specific class or group interests, have attracted a good deal of attention and controversy since their time.

As a matter of fact, Engels, when he suggests that some class or group adhered to some form of religion because it was its interest to do so, usually does so in a way which does not imply that the religion contained beliefs peculiarly suited to promoting its interests.[15] For example, he suggests in *The Peasant War in Germany* that certain conservative groups who wanted to preserve the existing social and political order therefore adhered to 'the old religion', Catholicism. His words suggest that they remained true to the old faith merely because it was old, and not because it contained beliefs or ideas which in themselves were specially favourable to their interests. Some other religion, with beliefs different from those of the Catholic church, if it had been the old religion, might have suited their purposes just as well. The situation, as seen by Engels, would be better

[15] What I say here of Engels applies also to Marx, to some extent, but Marx has less to say about religion as class ideology than Engels has.

described as one in which these conservative groups had interests in common with the Catholic church than as one in which the Catholic faith served their interests.

Engels and Marx, when they say that a religion *reflects* the class or group interests of its adherents, seem to use this word in at least two different senses: a stricter sense which implies that beliefs belonging to the religion are peculiarly adapted to the interests of its adherents, and a looser sense which implies only that its adherents rally to the religion the better to defend their interests. Religion then serves them as a kind of banner or uniform to show that they stand together, that they are united, but there is no connection between the contents of their faith and the interests common to them. I call the first sense the stricter of the two because the word *reflects*, as it is ordinarily used, suggests that there is some similarity or affinity between reflector and reflected.

Neither Marx nor Engels (and the same is true of their disciples today) distinguishes between these two senses, and quite often the context provides no clue as to which sense he is using. But it is, none the less, worth noticing that there are here two different senses, and that the second and looser sense allows classes (or groups) having widely different interests to use the same religion as a class (or group) ideology, to follow the same ideological flag, to respond to the same slogans. They will not do this, of course, unless their interests are compatible with one another, but this they may be even though they differ widely. And if, in course of time, their interests, from being merely different, become incompatible, and they continue to push their interests under the cover of religion, their religious beliefs are likely to diverge. If the classes all remain attached to the old religion, they may stress different aspects of it as they seek to use it to justify their efforts against one another. Or, alternatively, some of them may adhere to reformed versions of the old religion, or to what they take to be religions different from the old one, though in practice they are likely to have a good deal in common with the old religion (and with one another), since they all flourish in the same society and culture. Nevertheless, the same religion, unaltered or changed only to a slight extent, may, as circumstances change, serve as an ideology first to some classes and then to others, even though class interests change continually and differ greatly from class to class.[16]

---

[16] Engels believed that Christianity in its earliest days was attractive above all to the oppressed or exploited, and especially to slaves, and that only later did it come to serve the interests of the socially dominant classes. Christianity changed considerably both in its doctrines and in church organization during the first centuries of its existence. How were these changes in doctrine and organization related to its becoming the ideology of the oppressors? In becoming their ideology, did it cease to be the ideology of the oppressed? Which changes contributed more to its becoming the ideology of the oppressors, changes in doctrine or changes in church organization? We look in vain for answers to such questions as these in the pages of Engels.

There is much to baffle the reader who looks critically at what Marx and Engels say about Christianity in general or about some particular form of it, when they speak of it as class ideology. Their assertions and arguments provoke questions which they make no attempt to answer. For example, if a religion is to be reckoned the ideology of a class, must it be confined to that class, or at least more widely accepted in it than in other classes? Is this a sufficient condition of its being the ideology of that class, or must it also favour its interests as against theirs, or its interests more than theirs? If a religion shared by all classes helps to maintain a social order in which one class exploits the others, is it the class ideology of only the exploiting class? It might seem so, and yet Marx and Engels do not always speak as if it were so. If a religion confined to an exploited class seems to reconcile it to a social order which makes its exploitation possible, is it the class ideology of that class? Clearly, it is not, if in order to be the ideology of the class, it must not only be widely accepted inside it but also favour its interests. And yet Engels at least, if not Marx also, sometimes speaks as if only the first of these criteria need be satisfied for a religion to be a class ideology.

On the basis of what Engels says about Christianity in its different forms, we could put religions into three categories, according to the ways in which they serve class interests.[17] We could distinguish the religions of dominant classes from those of oppressed and submissive classes, and again both these types of religion from religions of revolutionary classes. The religion of a dominant class, we might say, provides men with additional motives, over and above any they already have, for accepting the social order, for behaving as the social rules require. It does so either by promising rewards and punishments in a life after death, or in some other way. The religion of a submissive class provides men with beliefs enabling them to find compensation in fantasy for their sufferings in the real world.[18] The religion of a revolutionary class justifies claims and attitudes

[17] I speak here of *classes* because Engels ordinarily does so, though what I say applies also to social groups other than classes.

[18] The slaves of the Roman Empire who became Christians were not rebels or revolutionaries. They accepted the social order and looked forward to a blissful union with God in an after life. As seen by Engels, their religion was both a fantasy of alienated man and a class ideology.

In some articles, 'On the Early History of Christianity', published towards the end of his life in *Die Neue Zeit*, Engels compares Christianity when it first began to spread with the working-class socialism of his own day. Like socialism, it was a movement of the oppressed promising salvation from bondage and misery, except that it placed this salvation in a life after death, whereas socialism places it in this world, in a transformed social order. Like socialism, too, it moved irresistibly forward in spite of all efforts to suppress it. And yet, according to Engels, this early and persecuted Christianity differed from the religion that triumphed in the late Roman Empire and in the Middle Ages as 'heaven from earth'! If Engels had lived on into our time, and had witnessed the triumph of 'socialism' over large areas of the globe, he could have pressed his analogy further!

disruptive of the established order. The same religion could, of course, be the ideology of both a dominant and a submissive class, parts of it serving to strengthen men's motives for behaving as they are required to do and other parts 'compensating' them for their sufferings by promises of blessings to come. Medieval Christianity, it might be argued, did both these things. It inclined all classes to accept a social order which favoured some classes at the expense of others, and was to that extent the ideology of the dominant classes; but it also helped to alleviate sufferings which were presumably more acute among the exploited than among their exploiters and was to that extent the ideology of the submissive classes. In saying this I have in mind its orthodox doctrines and attitudes and not its heresies. The religion of a revolutionary class is apt to be heretical, or rather to have a heretical side to it. No doubt, the orthodox and the heretic ordinarily have many beliefs in common, but presumably it is the beliefs peculiar to the heretic which constitute the revolutionary part of his ideology.

As Marx and Engels put it in *The German Ideology*, 'the ideas of the ruling class are in every epoch the ruling ideas'. Thus, a religion's being an ideology of a dominant class does not entail that members of that class alone accept its doctrines and myths and practise its rituals; it entails only that this acceptance and practice serve to maintain the privileges of the class by justifying the social order or by diverting or transforming feelings which might otherwise subvert it. Thus, in principle, a religion could be the ideology of a dominant class, even though sincere adherents to it were rarer in that class than in the others. Engels seems to have believed, not unreasonably, that a dominant class is more apt to be sincerely attached to the religion it professes during the earlier than the later stages of its dominance.[19]

If, however, we say that a religion is the ideology of the class whose interests it favours at the expense of other classes, even though that class is less attached to it than other classes are, are we not led into paradox? Must we then not say that a religion to which a submissive class is strongly attached is the ideology, not of that class, but of the class that benefits from this submissiveness? If a religion is 'the opium of the people', of social underlings who tamely allow themselves to be exploited, is it not the ideology of their exploiters rather than their own? That is, if—as Engels sometimes does—we assume that a religion is the ideology of the class whose interests it favours. Or, if we refuse to call it so on the ground

[19] Presumably, a submissive class is sincerely attached to the religion which is its class ideology. For, if most of its members ceased to be attached to it, it would be a sign that their submissiveness was coming to an end, unless, of course, they were converted to some other religion or ideology which also distracted them from their worldly sufferings without moving them to put an end to them. But in the case of a religion that is the ideology of a revolutionary class, it could easily happen that most members of the class did not understand its doctrines and cared little for it, and that only their leaders were sincerely attached to it. They might have motives for following their leaders other than devotion to a shared religion.

that a class must be strongly attached to an ideology if it is to be reckoned its class ideology, must we not allow that the ideology of a class may favour the interests of another class and be damaging to its own?

I cannot guess how Engels would have answered this question, had it been put to him. As most Marxists do, he ordinarily took it for granted that an ideology widely accepted by a class or group does favour its interests. That an ideology might be less accepted by the class whose interests it favours than by other classes seems not to have occurred to him. An established religion, he believed, supports a social and political order from which the wealthy and the privileged have most to gain. And yet in France at the close of the eighteenth century attachment to the old religion was stronger among the peasants than among the nobles and the rich. The philosophers who attacked religion addressed their books and articles to the dominant and prosperous classes and not to the uneducated and the poor.[20] Engels, no doubt, knew this, but the knowledge did not move him to qualify what he said when he spoke of religion as class ideology.

Though Engels was careless, it is possible to be more discriminating than he was and still to construct on Marxist lines a not unrealistic account of religion as class ideology. I shall venture to construct such an account.

Engels, who made more of this aspect of religion than Marx did ordinarily, when he called a religion the ideology of a class, implied that it favoured the interests of that class. I shall therefore assume that a religion must do at least that much for a class if it is to be called the ideology of that class. Thus, an ideology's being more widely accepted by one class than by others would not in itself be enough to make it that class's ideology. I shall also distinguish, as Engels did not, between two ways in which a religion—or indeed any ideology—can favour the interests of a dominant class or group. It favours them *positively* when it heightens devotion to the established order or otherwise encourages behaviour that sustains it. It favours them *negatively* when it promotes in other classes or groups beliefs and attitudes which prevent their challenging the social order or their acting in ways that disrupt it. This it might do, for example, by inducing them to believe that what happens in this world matters little compared with what may happen in the next.

Religion can, of course, favour the interests of a dominant class or

[20] The philosophers attacked chiefly the Catholic church which supported the monarchy, and they attacked it rather than the monarchy partly because it was safer to do so. If the wealthy bourgeois, who resented the privileges of the nobles, were to get rid of their inferior status (let alone to get political power), the established social and political order maintained by the monarchy would have to be drastically reformed, and the church was the ally of the monarchy. No doubt, the wealthy bourgeois, chafing against privilege, were pleased to see the privileged church attacked. But the attack on the church and on religion was as well received among the nobles, the privileged order, as among the bourgeois. This attack had, of course, its social causes and was more favoured (or resented) by some social groups than by others. But to call it an attack on a class ideology would be absurd.

group both positively and negatively, though it may well be that, more than other ideologies, it favours them negatively rather than positively. Often, it may do little or nothing to attach the exploited and socially inferior to the established order, and yet may so affect them that they are resigned to it as to something which they are powerless to change. In that sense it may quite often be what Marx called it, *the opium of the people*.

And yet its doctrines and myths might sustain the self-respect of believers, their sense of their own worth as rational and moral beings. It might satisfy, at least to some extent, some of the deepest and most persistent needs of a self-conscious 'species-being'. Engels and Marx took little account of this possibility, though they were not committed to neglecting it by their conception of man. If a religion did this for believers, even the exploited among them, we could say that it favoured their interests positively by keeping alive in them feelings which men must have if they are ever to challenge the social order. It would maintain in them the self-esteem without which they could never become effective reformers or revolutionaries. It might keep them quiet for the time being, might make them docile, but it would also preserve in them hopes and sentiments which are conditions of self-assertion. It might hold them back from challenging the dominant classes while they were as yet too weak to make the challenge successfully and yet maintain in them the sense that more was owing to them, as human beings, than they were actually getting. If then, as Engels and Marx did, we believe that this challenge is ultimately in the interest of the exploited, we can say that an ideology which helps to preserve their sense of their own worth, even if for the moment it reconciles them to their lot, favours their class and group interests—while the time is not yet ripe for them to take up the struggle.

Engels would, of course, just as Marx would, deny that man, the species-being, can be satisfied by religion of any kind. Man can be truly satisfied only in this world. The kind of religion which is a fantasy of alienated man, by offering an illusory satisfaction, diverts him from seeking true satisfaction where alone it is to be found. It is also, in the eyes of Marx, a mark of man's abasement. But if this is so, if Marx is right, is it not then absurd to say that the religion of a submissive class favours its interests?

I think not, and for two reasons. Firstly, because it is good Marxist doctrine that the conditions, social and cultural, which make it possible for the exploited to seek satisfaction in this world, may not yet exist; and secondly, because a religion which offers an illusory satisfaction cannot express merely man's sense of his own abasement but must also express his aspirations for himself, his sense of what he might be under better conditions. If he lacked these aspirations and this sense, he would not be attracted by the illusion, and so the illusion helps to preserve him from despair and self-contempt. Therefore, while as yet men cannot recognize that they are alienated, it is better that some of their needs as species-beings should find illusory satisfaction than no satisfaction at all.

If we are Marxists, we will of course insist that religion must eventually disappear if these needs are to be truly satisfied, but we need not deny that in the meantime it can help to preserve in the poor and the wretched the self-respect and the fortitude in adversity which they must not lose altogether if they are ever by their own efforts to find a remedy for their social ills. The slave who is a Christian is, at least in his own eyes, something better than a mere slave; and if his master is also a Christian, he is better than a slave even in his master's eyes.[21] Perhaps Engels, when he called early Christianity the ideology of a servile class, had such thoughts as these in mind. If he had, it is a pity that he did not make more of them in developing his ideas about religion as class ideology.

IV

Until quite recently, the idea of religion as class ideology has received more attention from both Marxists and critics of Marxism than the idea of it as a fantasy of alienated man. Even Marxists would be well advised to admit that these ideas are only part of the truth about religion, which is always more than class ideology and more than a fantasy of the alienated, and is sometimes neither the one nor the other. They would also do well to claim for Marx and Engels that they did no more than draw attention to certain aspects of religion until then neglected by historians and social theorists. Here at least, even for Marxists, modesty is the best policy.

I have not subjected either of these Marxist ideas to searching criticism, for I have been less concerned to point out their limitations than to show how they differ, how they are connected, and what they imply. Few social theorists today would wish to deny that many religions, and perhaps even most religions in societies divided into classes, have been to some extent class ideologies, though they might well reject the greater part of what Engels says about the class character of this or that form of Christianity and might accuse him of exaggerating the extent to which in general

---

[21] This might seem too Hegelian a sentiment to be brought into an account of religion constructed 'on Marxist lines'. But the idea of religion as a fantasy of alienated man was Hegelian before it was Marxist, and it is of the essence of it that religion expresses both man's sense of his abasement and his sense of his dignity as a rational being. Marx, no doubt, liked to emphasize above all the first of these aspects, as for example when he wrote: 'The social principles of Christianity preach cowardice, self-contempt, abasement, submission, dejection, in a word all the qualities of the *canaille*; and the proletariat, not wishing to be treated as *canaille*, needs its courage, its self-feeling, its pride and its sense of independence more than its bread'. (From *The Communism of the Paper Rheinischer Beobachter*, quoted in *K. Marx and F. Engels On Religion*, p. 84). Nevertheless, both aspects are included in the idea, and the idea is perfectly consistent with Marx's account of the social functions of ideology. Religion, even though it is an obstacle to man's achieving what he aspires to when at last it is within his reach, can help to keep those aspirations alive in him while it is still out of his power to realize them.

religion has been class ideology. But I have wanted to look at the implications of certain beliefs about religion rather than to inquire how far history bears them out. In my attempt to elucidate the idea of religion as class ideology, I have therefore paid little attention to what Engels says about particular religions.

The idea of religion as a fantasy of alienated man, though only a part of the truth, seems to go deeper than the idea of it as class ideology. It is closely connected with Marx's conception of man as an essentially progressive being, a 'species-being' who makes his way painfully to a full autonomy in a social order suited to his developed powers. If we knew nothing of this conception of man, which owes so much to Hegel, we could still understand what Marx and Engels had in mind when they spoke of religion as class ideology but their speaking of it as a fantasy of alienated man would mean little or nothing to us.

No believer would admit that religion is merely a fantasy of this kind any more than he would admit that it is merely a class ideology or merely a system of beliefs about the supernatural serving to hold the social order more firmly together. No sociological explanation of religion (though he might allow it a considerable measure of truth) would seem to him to give an adequate account of the place of religion in the life of man. And the sociological explanations of Marx and Engels are only some among the many that sociologists have made. Yet I suspect that, among such explanations, the idea of religion as a fantasy of the alienated comes closer than most to recognizing what religion means to the believer. Not any religion, but the kind of sophisticated religion which appeals to the highly self-conscious believer looking for a faith to live by. Such a believer seeks in religion a view of the world which sustains him morally by promising him communion with a Being incomparably greater than himself. He conceives of this communion as a finding of his essential or true self. If he were to lose his faith, he would, so he thinks, be 'lost to himself' or 'at odds with himself', and also a stranger in an indifferent or hostile world. He would be in a condition not unlike that of alienated man, as Marx describes it. And though he would reject the suggestion that his most cherished beliefs are no more than false consciousness, he might well admit that they cannot be tested empirically and also that they are essentially different from the assumptions about the world on which either science or workaday experience rests.

CHAPTER X

MORALITY, BOURGEOIS AND HUMAN

WRITERS about Marxism sometimes attribute to Marx and Engels the belief that men's interests, determined by the social relations in which they stand, in their turn determine their moral standards. On the face of it, this belief seems wide of the mark. For social beings are moral beings, and their interests and moral standards continually affect one another. Other interpreters of Marx and Engels deny that they held any such 'absurd' belief. For my part, I would say that sometimes they held it and at other times did not; or rather that they occasionally asserted it and more often implied it, and that they also implied the opposite. But I shall not argue in support of what I have just said, for there is no need to attribute this belief to them or to deny that they held it in order to appraise their conception of bourgeois morality.

Marx and Engels have almost nothing to say about how men acquire moral standards or about what kind of standards they are. We do not find them speculating, as for example Hobbes or Hume or Rousseau do, about how men come to conceive of rules whose general observance is, or is supposed to be, in the common interest, or about their motives or reasons for accepting them, or about their ways of using them to control one another's behaviour or to direct their own. They make no attempt to explain what moral judgements are or how moral principles differ from customary and other rules. They do not even distinguish between different types of morality: as, for example, between the moral standards and attitudes of primitive and sophisticated peoples.

No doubt, they recognize (as who does not?) that moral principles and attitudes differ considerably from society to society, and also that in sophisticated societies they are connected with conceptions of man as a free and responsible agent in ways in which they are not in primitive societies. They could hardly have read Hegel without recognizing at least this much. Nevertheless, influenced by Hegel though they were, their ideas about morality, as about religion, were less subtle, less coherent, and less plausible than his.

Marx and Engels have been accused of holding that in societies divided into classes, morality is always class morality. This could be interpreted in either of two senses; that in a class society there are no moral standards common to all classes; or that, besides those common to all classes, there are others peculiar to particular classes. I shall take it that the second interpretation is the correct one, not only because it attributes to Marx and Engels a more reasonable belief, but also because it is in keeping with much that they say.

Their denial that there is an 'eternal and immutable' moral law does not of course commit them to holding that all (or even most) aspects of morality in societies divided into classes are class morality. In *Anti-Dühring* Engels refers to three types of morality in the society of his own day: a Christian morality surviving from the past, a bourgeois morality presently dominant, and a proletarian morality of the future. He admits that these three moralities have much in common but also denies that what is common to them is 'eternally fixed'. He denies that there is an 'eternal, ultimate and forever immutable moral law'. It is not clear just how much he is rejecting in making this denial. Is he denying merely that moral rules are self-evident or *a priori* truths, or is he also denying—what thinkers as different as Hume and Rousseau, have asserted—that there are important social rules indispensable to any society, however it is organized, because human capacities and needs, and also social conditions, are everywhere in important respects the same? I shall take it that he is not denying what Hume and Rousseau asserted. Certainly, he has no need to do so to make the distinction he wants to make between 'class morality' and 'truly human morality'.

Having denied that there is an eternal and immutable moral law, Engels goes on, in the next sentence but one, to say that 'as society has hitherto moved in class antagonisms, morality has always been class morality'. Then, a little further on, he claims that there has, in spite of this, been 'progress in morality', and predicts the eventual coming of a 'truly human morality'.[1] The assertion that 'morality has always been class morality' is presumably not to be taken literally. Engels knew that there were primitive societies without classes, and he did not suppose them to be without morality as well. He probably meant only that, where there are classes and class conflicts, morality has an important element of class morality about it. The 'truly human morality', of which proletarian morality is already the prefiguration, is the morality of the future classless society. It is, presumably, different from the moralities of primitive societies in which classes have not yet appeared, and different, too, from what is common to the moralities of all societies, even though it includes it, or a part of it. It is the morality of mankind when, having developed their capacities to the full in the course of history, they understand and control the social order they belong to.[2]

---

[1] *Anti-Dühring*, transl. by Emile Burns, p. 108.

[2] This notion of a truly human morality is by no means clear. How can we know that human capacities are fully developed? Men can, of course, accumulate factual knowledge about both society and human psychology and can produce more and more sophisticated theories about

My concern now is not with morality in general but with bourgeois morality, as Marx and Engels speak of it and contrast it with the 'human morality' of the future. I shall try to show that bourgeois morality, as they conceive of it, is only to some extent a morality that favours bourgeois class interests. Though it consists of values and sentiments which are either peculiar to bourgeois society or are more marked in it than in earlier societies, these values and sentiments are not confined to the bourgeois as a class and do not always serve to strengthen the social order in which they are dominant. Bourgeois morality, as Marx and his disciples speak of it, includes, or is closely bound up with, forms of cynicism, indifference, and hypocrisy which tend to weaken social ties in any society.

Marx and Engels believed that bourgeois morality and the sentiments and attitudes that go along with it would disappear with the abolition of private property in the means of production and the taking over of the control of production by the workers. Yet they never explained why this should be so, and seem to have merely taken it for granted as if it were so obvious as not to call for explanation. The ills which they attributed to capitalism have been attributed by others to the scale of production or to some of its inevitable consequences. Today these ills are as conspicuous in countries calling themselves socialist as in those which are still called capitalist. To be sure, in these 'socialist' countries the workers do not control production, so that the countries are not socialist, as Marx and Engels (and indeed most socialists in their day) understood that term. But then neither are they capitalist, for they are countries in which private property in the means of production has been abolished. This abolition has not, except to some extent in Yugoslavia, led to anything that deserves to be called workers' control of production, and even in Yugoslavia, this control, to the extent that it exists, is not working-class control of an entire economy but a limited control by the workers of the enterprises in which they work. It still has to be shown that in a vast industrial economy the workers can collectively control production, and that this control, if it were possible, would remedy these ills.

Nevertheless, for all its inadequacies, the critical appraisal of bourgeois morality by Marx and Engels is worth close study. It is sometimes, especially when Marx undertakes it, suggestive and enlightening; it points to aspects of human behaviour and social relations much more prominent in industrial and urbanized societies than in pre-industrial and rural ones. Some of the consequences of commodity production, of the extensive use

them. But why should we believe that this accumulation of fact and sophistication of theory must lead ultimately to their understanding human nature and society in the same way, or at least to their agreeing about how society is to be organized and controlled, and to what ends? To their all having, if not the same values, then at least values such that the differences between them do not lead to conflicts?

of money, and of the growing distance between producer and consumer were described by Marx with remarkable force and subtlety. His attack is on our type of society, and is not the less pointed and telling because he spoke unrealistically of the future. Our society is still in important respects bourgeois. It has, of course, changed considerably, socially as well as economically, since Marx was alive. It is now much less capitalist, as Marx used that term, than it used to be, yet men in high positions in it are still, except in the trade unions, recruited predominantly from the middle classes, many of whose standards and attitudes remain pretty much as they were in Marx's time. Some of these standards are now perhaps just as conspicuous among the privileged and powerful in the countries calling themselves socialist, but that detracts nothing from Marx's condemnation of them.

I

Bourgeois morality, as Marx conceives of it, favours bourgeois-class interests in at least two important ways: it exalts respect for property rights and also respect for contracts assumed to be freely made by the parties to them. Where it prevails, offences against property, even property in means of production not directly used by the owner, are severely punished. So, too, are breaches of contract, even though the persons guilty of them are poor or otherwise socially at a disadvantage. Or, if defaulters are not legally punishable, they are liable to harsh treatment. The poor tenant of a rich landlord, if he fails to pay his rent, is soon ejected. For in bourgeois society, according to this account of it, relations between rich and poor are impersonal to a much greater extent than they were in earlier societies. In all societies the rich, when they make agreements with the poor, impose hard conditions on them. But in pre-capitalist societies in which there is no free market in labour, rich and poor are closer to one another and relations between them are more stable and less impersonal. The exploited, harshly treated though they may be, are in the eyes of their exploiters assets of considerable value. The feudal landlord does not stand to his serfs quite as the capitalist does to his workers. Because his ties with them are more lasting, he is to some extent responsible for their welfare. To be sure, when they have what he thinks is their due, they still have much less than what he requires for himself, but at least he does admit some responsibility for seeing to it that their needs are met. But what matters above all to the rich in bourgeois society is that the poor should respect their property, do the work they are paid to do, and pay their rent when it falls due.

Bourgeois morality puts a high value on the freedom of the individual. Everyone should use such assets as he has—natural talents, acquired skills, and external goods—to his own best advantage. Customary restraints which prevent his doing so should be abolished, so that in the long run even those whose assets are the smallest will gain by the abolition. The individual, in acting rationally to his own advantage, has to work with others or to make agreements with them, and is therefore bound to carry out obligations freely undertaken. He must do his share of the work or must provide whatever he has agreed to provide. These obligations, seen through bourgeois eyes, arise from what the individual undertakes to do in what he believes to be his own best interest. They are the obligations of a rational egoist, unconcerned for the good of others. Or, if he is concerned for the good of others, and is therefore not wholly an egoist, he is concerned only for the good of his family and of a few persons close to him. In bourgeois society, with its immense division of labour, everyone has dealings with many people, is engaged in transactions of many kinds, and is dependent for the satisfaction of his wants on many more people even than he has dealings with. And yet it is, of all societies, the one in which the individual comes closest to being an egoist, to being unconcerned for the welfare of all but a few of the many persons he does business with or depends on.

Like several of the early French socialists, Marx saw in the idea of freedom, as liberals used it in his day, an idea whose prime social function is to justify the egoism of the socially strong. Socially, the man of property's greatest asset is his property, and this idea justifies his using it to his own best advantage regardless of the consequences to others, provided only that he does not do what the law forbids and does what he has contracted to do. The man of property, if he is to make the most profitable use of it, must be able to buy the labour and the skills of others, and it is his interest that there should be a free market in what he wants to buy. Thus, the free use of property by those who have it requires the free sale of labour by those who sell it to get a living. But, clearly, this freedom is much more to the advantage of owners of means of production other than labour than of workers who have only their labour to sell. Their position as bargainers is much stronger. Therefore, the morality which puts so high a value on freedom, on the unrestricted use of one's assets, is a morality which favours owners of property other than labour. It is a class morality.

According to Marx and Engels, this bourgeois conception of freedom is closely connected with the bourgeois attitude to money, which sees in it something more than the measure of exchange values. Money, in bourgeois society, is also the measure of a man's worth. In *The Communist Manifesto* Marx and Engels say: 'The bourgeoisie . . . has left remaining no other nexus between man and man than naked self-interest, than callous "cash payment" . . . It has resolved personal worth into exchange value and, in place of the numberless indefeasible chartered freedoms, has set up that single unconscionable freedom—free trade.'[3] The society in which freedom, conceived as the right to use one's assets to one's own best advantage, is a supreme value is also the society in which the worth of all assets and the ability to put them to profitable use are measured in money. In this society, in which money is the measure of personal worth as well as of exchange value, the rich are treated as if they were worthy merely because they are rich. They think the better of themselves and of each other for being rich, and this attitude of theirs to themselves is endorsed by how others treat them. As Marx puts it in the third of the 'Economic and Philosophical Manuscripts': 'Money is the highest good, and so its possessor is good'.[4]

The capitalist economy is pre-eminently a money economy. In it, as compared with earlier economies, there is a vast division of labour, and there is much greater mobility of both capital and labour. The individual, as a buyer or seller of goods and services, as a maker of contracts, as a taxpayer, as a litigant, even as a receiver of benefits distributed on a large scale, has purely business relations with a wide variety of persons who are not otherwise concerned for him nor he for them. They are, in his eyes, merely persons with whom for his own advantage he has dealings of a particular kind; and he is otherwise as indifferent to them as they are to him.

This aspect of a society in which trade and industry are highly developed, in which money is widely used, and obligations deliberately undertaken take the place of obligations depending on status, had been noticed before the socialists took notice of it. Hegel's account of *civil society* describes a social order in which rational egoists pursue their own interests, unconcerned for the good of others and yet willing to observe the social rules governing their dealings with them. His portrait of civil society is largely a borrowing from Adam Smith's account of the capitalist economy. For Hegel, civil society is only one part of social life, just as the production of wealth is for Adam Smith. Distinct from it is the sphere of the family, whose members are united by ties of affection for one another, and again the sphere of the state, whose citizens are attached to the political community they belong to and to the institutions, manners, and ideals

---

[3] *The Communist Manifesto* (Allen & Unwin, London, 1948 edn.), p. 128.

[4] *Karl Marx: Early Writings*, transl. by Bottomore, p. 191. This idea that, in a society with great inequalities of wealth, money is perversely treated as the measure of personal worth is, of course, an old idea, an idea much older than socialism. It is especially prominent in the writings of Rousseau. But money is only one form of wealth, and moralists have long complained that men are judged by 'external' advantages unrelated to merit, are treated as if they were better or more admirable than others only because they are wealthier, more powerful, or more privileged. The greater the role of money in a society, the greater the likelihood that it will be used as the measure of personal worth; but this does not mean that in societies in which the role of money is small, external advantages unrelated to merit are less apt to be used as measures of personal worth.

which make it the sort of community it is. The separation of these three spheres, or rather the sharper distinctions between them characteristic of modern society, seemed to Hegel a mark of progress and an enrichment of human life.

Marx accepted Hegel's account of civil society, accentuating its darker aspects, but rejected his accounts of the state and the family. He attacked two myths, two 'bourgeois myths', the myth of the state and the myth of the family. He looked upon Hegel's account of the state as the most sophisticated example of bourgeois illusions about it, and took it upon himself to demolish it. I shall leave it to my next chapter to appraise this work of demolition; for Marx has much more to say about the bourgeois state than about the bourgeois family, and what he had to say is more important and perceptive. In this chapter I shall discuss only his attack on the bourgeois myth of the family. But before I do that I want to look more closely at the charge that egoism and indifference are at their worst in bourgeois society.

We have seen that, for Marx, the peculiarity of capitalists is not that they are exploiters, for slave-owners and feudal lords are so as well, not just when occasion offers, but continuously by reason of their social roles. Just as much as the capitalists, they belong to exploiting classes, and the people they exploit are often worse off materially than the proletarians. Nevertheless, again by reason of their social roles, slave-owners and feudal lords are concerned for the welfare of the exploited as capitalists are not. The slave and feudal economies are such that slaves and serfs are not expendable in the way that wage-labourers are, for the prosperity of the master or lord depends on his slaves or serfs being reasonably contented and therefore reasonably well treated by the modest standards traditional in their society. Because the ties of slaves or serfs to their master or lord are more lasting, he is more than their employer or the man for whose benefit they work; he also exercises an over-all authority over them, and that kind of authority carries with it some measure of responsibility for the security and welfare of those subject to it. The slave is in the care of his master, and the serf under the protection of his lord, in a way in which the wage-labourer is not in the care or under the protection of his employer.

The slave-owner or feudal lord often rules a small community which is in many ways self-supporting; he is ordinarily not a producer for the market, or is so only to a slight extent, and is much less dependent than the capitalist on the market for his supply of labour. He is not, as the capitalist (as seen by Marx) is, a ruthless competitor with others of his class. Therefore, exploiter though he necessarily is, and cruel though he may be, he cannot afford to be as irresponsible and indifferent as the capitalist is towards those he exploits. What is more, the slaves or serfs that he exploits are not competitors with one another to anything like the same extent as wage-labourers are. They belong to a small and more or less closed community ruled by a master or lord who need not drive them hard to maintain his status in society and his superiority over them.

Marx sees the capitalist as the most ruthless of exploiters, indifferent to the sufferings he causes or averting his eyes from them; he sees him as heartless rather than cruel. As he puts it in the first volume of *Capital*:

> Capital, that has such good reasons for denying the sufferings of the legions of workers that surround it, is in practice moved as much and as little by the sight of the coming degradation and final depopulation of the human race as by the probable fall of the earth into the sun . . . *Après moi le déluge!* is the watchword of every capitalist and every capitalist nation. Hence capital is reckless of the health or length of life of the labourer, unless under compulsion from society.[5]

The capitalist is, of course, a calculator of cost and benefits, and a more exact and ingenious calculator than the exploiter of earlier societies; for what he measures he measures in money. But he is also a less long-sighted calculator because of the nature of the economy in which he acts and of his relations with the exploited.

That many capitalists, especially in the harsh early days of capitalism, answered to Marx's description of 'the capitalist' cannot be denied. Accused of inhumanity, they quite often resorted to arguments which came down to little more than the plea that they could not afford to be humane, that better treatment of their workers would ruin them. Nevertheless, Marx's account of the capitalist and the man of property is misleading, not so much because it is exaggerated, as for another, and from the point of view of the social theorist, a more important reason. The capitalist market economy does indeed give to the wealthy opportunities of exploitation unknown to earlier societies and, if it is uncontrolled, subjects them to pressures which move them to take the opportunities ruthlessly. But it also makes it possible for them to reduce these pressures on themselves. It provides them, in the form of the modern state, with an instrument they can use to impose upon their class generally, and especially upon employers, obligations which no one of them could afford to undertake if he had to do it alone. The course of social change which produces a type of economy in which both workers and employers of labour are more competitive than ever before also—as Marx himself not only admits but insists—produces a structure of authority more powerful and efficient than any before it. Why, then, should not the capitalists who, according to Marx, control this structure, the state, impose upon themselves restraints which are in their long-term interest as a class, even though they prevent some of their number making as big profits as

---

[5] *Capital*, i. 151.

they might otherwise do? The slave-owner and the feudal lord were concerned for the welfare of their dependents because they saw that they stood to gain in the long run by being so, and not only from motives of humanity. Why should not what was true of them be true also of the capitalist? He, of course, is exposed to the pressures of ruthless competition as they were not, and he cannot act alone in his long-term interest as they could. But it is precisely this competition, so Marx says, which in the long run is fatal to his class. Why, then, if he and others of his class see that it is so, should they not use the state they control to impose on themselves restraints and obligations which are in their interest as a class?[6]

In the passage I just quoted Marx says that capital is reckless of the health of the worker 'unless under compulsion from society'. The compulsion he had in mind was that of the state, which (so he believed) was controlled by the propertied classes. The state might, of course, place restraints upon capitalists merely from fear of what the workers would do if their worst sufferings were not alleviated. But it might also act from other motives: partly from motives of humanity, and even more from motives of enlightened class interest. Exploitation is against the interest of exploiters not only when it drives the exploited to rebellion; it is also against their interest when it reduces the efficiency of the exploited, however docile they may be. While Marx and Engels were alive, there were, in Britain and abroad, laws and regulations protecting workers from the rapacity and recklessness of their employers, and since their time, there have been many more. The growing power of the organized workers, a more enlightened sense of their class interests on the part of the wealthy, and a greater concern for social justice among all classes, have made this possible.[7] These three factors, reinforcing one another, have been at work

---

[6] Marx did, of course, notice that Parliament made laws to put an end to some of the worst excesses of capitalist exploitation, and that these laws were not entirely without effect. Though it was landowners rather than urban capitalists who took the initiative in promoting much of this legislation, it was welcomed by many capitalists. Marx also noticed, especially in the last decades of his life, capitalist attempts to control markets and to keep competition within bounds. Yet the image of the capitalists as a short-sighted class unable to take effective action to avert their ruin as a class, or to make concessions to other classes which might profoundly alter the economy and the social order and yet be tolerable to themselves, seems to have persisted with him to the end.

[7] In the wealthy and 'progressive' West there have been in the present century greater atrocities than there were in the last. Who would venture to say that the Western peoples are *in general* more humane than their ancestors were three or four generations ago? They have developed far more destructive weapons of war and have used them ruthlessly, and they have committed genocide. But I am speaking here, as Marx was, of the attitudes of social classes, and not of belligerent nations or ethnic groups, to one another. The worst atrocity of all, the mass murder of several million Jews, was the action, not of a government acting on behalf of the propertied classes, but of political adventurers who got control of the state by legal means, and then used it for this abominable purpose. But that purpose was theirs, and was not widely shared by any class of the German people. This does not mean, of course, that the Germans of Hitler's time are not to blame for doing so little to prevent their rulers committing this terrible

in bourgeois society, and indeed were so already when the first volume of *Capital* was written.

The charge of *The Communist Manifesto* that capitalism[8] leaves 'no other nexus between man and man than naked self-interest, than callous cash payment' and resolves 'personal worth into exchange value', is no longer made today in quite the form that Marx made it. But there are other charges not unlike it and to some extent inspired by it. Critics of 'bourgeois society', as it is now, still complain that it makes relations between men more 'impersonal' than ever before, so that they judge one another by external standards of success or popularity rather than in terms of what they are in themselves. This complaint is not confined to Marxists, and is not even more prevalent among them than among others, but they too make it, and in making it appeal to the authority of Marx. And the appeal does not rest on misunderstanding. Marx did speak of 'human relations' between human beings in a way that implied that there could be (and indeed were) 'inhuman relations' between them. These 'inhuman relations' are not merely physical nor are they common to humans and animals; they are peculiar to human beings. And just as 'inhuman' relations subsist only between human beings, so too 'impersonal' relations subsist only between persons. Relations can, presumably, be 'inhuman' or 'impersonal' even though they involve no exploitation or cruelty, or even injustice; and there can be such relations in a wealthy community as well as in a poor one.

In bourgeois society, as Marx describes it, men treat each other primarily as means to their own ends, just as they do in Hegel's civil society. This does not mean that they do not recognize one another as rational beings who make claims that ought to be respected; it means only that each of them is concerned primarily for his own welfare, even though he is willing, because he sees that it is to his advantage to do so, to obey rules serving the interests of others as well as his own. In Hegel's civil society (which is only one sphere of social life among others) men come close to treating each other as means only and not also as ends, to neglecting Kant's golden rule. But what, for Hegel, is true only of civil society and not of the family and the state, is true, for Marx, of bourgeois society as a whole—truer of it than of earlier societies, not to speak of the com-

crime, even though their rulers tried to keep what they were doing secret from them, as from the rest of the world. The German people were perhaps more to blame for Hitler's crimes than the Russians were for Stalin's, because they had more to do with his getting power and because in general they were more experienced politically. The atrocities of governments at war or of fanatics who get power in times of crisis are activities different in kind, both in themselves and in their causes, from the exploitation or harsh treatment of some classes by others in normal times. They are also difficult to explain in Marxist terms.

[8] Though Marx and Engels actually say 'the bourgeoisie', it is a system rather than a class that they have in mind.

munist society of the future.[9] Not entirely true, presumably, even of bourgeois society; for we need not suppose that Marx believed that man is ever, in any social conditions, entirely an egoist. He certainly believed that there can be considerable class solidarity in societies divided into classes; and presumably the stronger that solidarity, the more often it gets the better of mere egoism. But he did speak at times as if class solidarity were exceptionally weak in bourgeois society, except among the workers as they learn by experience to hold fast together.

What do people mean who say that human relations are 'inhuman' or 'impersonal'? Sometimes, when they call them 'inhuman', they mean that people are cruel to one another, or heedless of each other's sufferings; but quite often they mean, not this so much, as that they treat one another as instruments in situations in which they ought not to do so. This is often also part of what they mean when they complain that human relations are 'impersonal'. But this is not the whole of their meaning. Often, when they object to this 'impersonality', and even to 'inhumanity', they have in mind dealings which are merely 'official' or 'professional', such that people are concerned with one another only as persons who belong to certain categories. For example, the surgeon who treats his patients merely as cases, and is concerned only to cure them of the ailments in whose cure he specializes, and is otherwise quite indifferent to them. He deals with them professionally and 'impersonally'. But this does not, or need not, mean that he treats them as means only and not also as ends. He may be dedicated to his profession and eager to use his talents for the good of others, and not just to make money and a reputation. He may, indeed, be quite exceptionally conscientious and unself-seeking, and yet his relations with his patients be 'impersonal'. They would not, I suppose, be 'inhuman', though some people, who dislike impersonal efficiency, even where health or life is at stake, might go so far as to call them so.

In a small community in which everyone knows everyone else, it is much less difficult to avoid using people as means only and not also as ends. To be sure, on this or that occasion, someone, preoccupied entirely with his own affairs, may use another person—may, for example, accept some service from him—without at the time being concerned for his good. But on some other occasion he will be concerned for it and go to his help; or be thought ungrateful or unkind if he does not. Whereas in a vast community in which no one can avoid having dealings with many people unknown or barely known to him, everyone quite often makes use of other people, merely taking their services for granted and being otherwise indifferent to them. Some he meets only once or seldom and others only

[9] Logically, this could be true of bourgeois society as compared with both feudal society and the future communist society, even if there were less exploitation in it than in feudal society and a more abundant production of wealth than in communist society.

on occasions when no question arises of his doing anything for them in return. Kant's rule never to treat others as means only and not also as ends can, no doubt, be understood in more than one way. If we take it to mean, *Never make use of others unless you are concerned for their good or can make a return for their services to you*, then, clearly, it must often be broken in the kind of society we live in. We have to make use of many persons to whom we cannot help but be indifferent because no occasion arises for our taking an interest in them and considering their good.

Now, it may well be that people who deplore the 'inhumanity' or 'impersonality' of human relations in our kind of society do not object to the sort of indifferent making use of others that I have described. It may be that they recognize the obvious: that where there is an immense division of labour, no one can help but have many dealings with persons he does not even know. What then do they object to? Presumably, to relations being 'impersonal' when they ought not to be. But, unfortunately, they do not make it clear what they have in mind. They say too little to indicate how we should set about deciding when relations are justifiably impersonal and when they are not. I shall not attempt to make good their omission but shall confine myself to making a few general observations.

In the great industrial societies of the West—not to speak of the rest of the world which has become industrial more recently—the services that the community provides for its members are greater by far than they were a hundred years ago. Let us admit that they are not as fairly distributed as they might be; and that much more could be done than is done for the poor, the sick, the aged, the unemployed, and the otherwise disadvantaged. Nevertheless, though the community could usefully and justly spend more on these services than it does, it already spends a good deal. Many of these services are 'impersonal'. The officials or the professional men and women who dispense them deal in the course of the working day with many 'cases' and are expected to deal with them expeditiously as well as competently. They must not linger too long over any one case, for there are others to be dealt with. Thus, their dealings with most of the people they serve are 'official' or 'professional'; they meet them only in the course of duty. They deal with situations and needs more or less strictly defined and take into account only what is by convention relevant. For, even when criteria of relevance are not laid down in regulations, they must take care, not just to treat like cases alike, but to be seen to do so; or otherwise they may be accused of favouring some and disfavouring others. They are expected to be impartial.

Sometimes, of course, because of the nature of the services they dispense, they are expected to be understanding and compassionate, to enter to some extent into the feelings of the persons they serve. They have to do more than satisfy themselves that these persons fall into some category which entitles them to something; they have also to try to see them as they see themselves and to look at their problems through their eyes. They have to do this, for example, when they are marriage counsellors or psychiatrists, but not when they are surgeons or dentists or dispensers of pensions and other material benefits. And yet, even when the nature of their work calls for compassion, there is usually something professional and detached about their compassion. But is it not desirable that there should be, that they should be able to switch their feelings on and off almost at will? A limited and controlled sympathy for others is often a condition of efficiency at work, even when the work consists of services to the mentally afflicted and the emotionally troubled.

In vast industrial societies there is, apart from the professional dispensing of services on a large scale, also the management of big organizations with thousands of workers in them. In such organizations, the relations of managers with the great majority of their workers are necessarily impersonal. They deal with them as suppliers of labour directed to ends not chosen by the workers, and to that extent treat them as means only and not also as ends. If they also provide for their welfare, they do not, of course, treat them as means; but they may (and often do) treat them 'impersonally' according to the group or category they belong to, as persons to whom a certain description applies. Indeed, usually, in big organizations, the business of directing people's efforts to aims not chosen by them is kept separate from the business of providing for their wants or needs. Therefore, in practice, there are managers whose work is confined to using their workers as means only, and who leave it to others to look after their welfare, to treat them as ends. The workers may often gain by this division of responsibility.

If we compare the industrial societies of the West, the pre-eminently 'bourgeois' societies, with earlier societies, we may be struck by two things: there are far more dealings between persons unknown or indifferent to one another, or whose concern for others is professional and strictly defined; and the claims that people make and their aspirations are more diverse and more apt to change. A man is not expected to follow his father's occupation, and his right to choose the way of life that suits him, to do the work that satisfies him, to be or to try to become the sort of person he wants to be, is more widely recognized—though not precisely defined or understood by everyone in the same way. When he marries or makes friends, he is expected to consult his own feelings and tastes; he has, or claims to have, a larger say in choosing his circles of intimacy. He belongs to a highly 'self-conscious' society in which the social and the psychological aspects of human life are discussed and studied more extensively and more seriously than ever before; in which idiosyncrasy and the need for 'self-expression' are recognized and approved, not only in the narrow circles of the intellectual and the artistic, but also outside them. This cult of the individual, confused though it is, is just as much a characteristic of 'bourgeois society' as is the 'impersonality' of human relations; it too is an effect of a vast division of labour, of greater social mobility, and of the cultural diversity of a fast-changing society aware that it is changing and knowing more than any earlier society about its own past and about societies different from itself. Ought we then not to put this question to ourselves: Could the individual have the opportunities he now claims, realize the aspirations he now has, except in a society in which perforce he has many dealings, and important dealings, with people who are indifferent to him or whose concern for him is cool, professional, and limited, and in that sense 'impersonal'? Or with people who treat him as one of a category and who use him (along with many others) not for his good but to achieve some purpose to which his labours are, in their eyes, only a means?

One of the attractions of Marxism for its votaries, and especially its bourgeois votaries, is its promise that in the communist society these opportunities will be greater than they now are, these aspirations more fully realized, and yet human relations be much less impersonal and much less a using of others as means only. In that society freedom will consist, not in legal rights carefully defined and enjoyed effectively only by the rich, but in opportunities within everyone's reach.

Yet Marx and Engels and their disciples do little more than predict that it will be so. They do not explain how in an industrial society it can be so, how it can be contrived that the opportunities of the individual are enlarged and the need and the wish to treat others merely as means and to deal with them impersonally are abolished or greatly reduced. What will the social order be like in which a 'truly human morality' flourishes? To this question Marx and Engels give no real answer. To be sure, they say that when this morality flourishes, there will be no private ownership of the means of production and no state, and that the workers collectively will control production. But this answer from two writers who never stop to inquire what alternatives there might be in an advanced industrial society to the institutions they condemn, amounts to very little. They do not even attempt in their writings to distinguish between different forms of property or authority or control of production.[10]

---

[10] It might be objected that their theory precludes foretelling how society will be organized in the future, what forms of authority and of control of production there will be in communist society. Why then does it not also preclude foretelling that it will be so organized that certain ills (or what we take for such) will disappear? In any case, though we cannot predict how society will be organized, we can at least consider the possibilities. If we believe that certain institutions in society as we know it produce the ills we object to, we can consider how society should be organized to eliminate those ills. To speculate in this way is not to engage in Utopian thinking. It can help us to decide what we should do, here and now, to remedy our ills; which is worth doing even though we cannot predict how society will change nor how our own values and intentions will be affected by its changing.

II

Marx and Engels speak with contempt of 'the bourgeois family' and of the standards they associate with it. In *The Communist Manifesto* they say: 'the bourgeoisie has torn away from the family its sentimental veil, and has reduced the family relation to a mere money relation'.[11] And they ask: 'On what foundation is the present family, the bourgeois family, based?' They answer: 'On capital, on private gain. In its completely developed form this family exists only among the bourgeoisie. But this state of things finds its complement in the practical absence of the family among proletarians, and in public prostitution'.[12] They say also that 'by the action of modern industry, all family ties among the proletarians are torn asunder, and their children transformed into simple articles of commerce and instruments of labour'.[13]

Judgements not unlike these are repeated in their later writings. In *Socialism, Scientific and Utopian*, Engels claims that with 'the development of industry upon a capitalistic basis . . . cash payment became more and more, in Carlyle's phrase, the sole nexus between man and man. The number of crimes increased from year to year . . . Prostitution increased to an extent never heard of . . . Marriage itself remained, as before, the legally recognized form, the official cloak of prostitution, and moreover was supplemented by rich crops of adultery'.[14] In this same work Engels speaks approvingly of Fourier's 'masterly' criticism of the bourgeois form of the relations between the sexes and the position of women; and he endorses, just as Marx does, Fourier's judgement that a society is to be judged by the way it treats women. Which would seem to imply (a doubtful proposition) that the more willing men are to deal justly with the physically weaker sex, the more disposed they are in general to be just.

When they speak of the 'bourgeois family', Marx and Engels sometimes have in mind the family as it is (or as they imagine it to be) among the middle classes. But quite often they mean by it merely the type of family to be found where trade and industry flourish. They say almost nothing about its structure or origins, but they think of it, presumably, as Hegel does, as small: as closer to what sociologists today call 'the nuclear family' than to 'the extended family' of economically less advanced and less urbanized societies.

In the passage I quoted earlier Engels says that, with the development of capitalist industry, marriage remained as before the 'legally recognized form' of prostitution. By this he means, I take it, that women continued

---

[11] *The Communist Manifesto* (London, 1948 edn.), p. 128.
[12] *The Communist Manifesto*, p. 147.   [13] Ibid., p. 148.
[14] Marx–Engels, *Selected Works*, ii. 110.

to be given in marriage by their families, not to men they loved but to men with whose families their families wanted to be connected, and that marriage put them sexually at the disposal of their husbands. With the coming of capitalism the use of money greatly increased, and so no doubt marrying for money increased also, but this is not to say that marrying for social and material advantage did so as well. Nor does Engels suggest that it did. For all that he says about it, marriage for material advantage may have been just as frequent in 'feudal' (or indeed pre-feudal) as in 'bourgeois' society. He attributes to capitalism only an increase in the kind of prostitution of which marriage is not a legalized form and an increase in adultery.[15]

Sometimes, when they attack the bourgeois family, Marx and Engels object to it only for not being what it is supposed to be, for being in practice very different from what its apologists pretend that it is, but at other times they denounce it as a restrictive institution that will disappear along with capitalism. They do not predict its survival, even in a purified form, in the communist society.

Since Marx was so deeply influenced by Hegel and yet also opposed to him, it is worth while contrasting their ideas about the family. The type of family that Hegel discusses in his *Philosophy of Right* is the type that flourishes where there is 'civil society' and where the economy is broadly similar to the one described by the classical economists. This family, says Hegel, is united by love. When he says this, he does not mean that its members in fact always love one another; he means rather that the claims they make on each other and the obligations they recognize (even though they often fall short of carrying them out) presuppose that there are deep ties of affection between them. We do not understand what the family means to its members, what they look for in it, what they resent not getting from it, if we fail to see that this is so. Hegel, when he says that the family is united by love, is not committed to denying that there are also disruptive sentiments inside it. He is committed only to holding that it is held together by 'love', by bonds of affection and loyalty and perhaps also by forms of behaviour which are thought proper because these bonds are supposed to exist even when in fact they do not.

As Hegel sees it, the family's being united by love is perfectly consistent with its also being based on property, or, as Marx and Engels put it in *The Communist Manifesto*, on 'capital and private gain'. The father of the family provides for his wife and children, as well as for himself, and the independence of the family depends on his 'private gain', on his having

---

[15] It is quite possible that with the growth of towns (an effect of growing industry) there was an increase in the number of women who made a living by selling their bodies for sexual use. But how could Engels know that there was an increase in adultery? That either marital infidelity or unchastity increased with the coming of capitalism?

an income which he and his family can dispose of as they please. He looks after such property as he has for the benefit of himself and his family, and hopes to pass it on to them after his death. The separateness of the family, as a circle of affection and intimacy, rests, for Hegel, on private property and private gain. Hegel is not, to be sure, a Rousseau; his ideal is not a community in which every family man is an independent producer, a farmer who owns his own land and livestock or a craftsman who owns his own workshop and tools. Nor is he a socialist. He does not denounce as unjust an economy in which some men own most of the land and other means of production and others can make a living only by selling their labour for a wage. Yet he does have misgivings about it. The poor, he says, should not have to rely on private charity but the community should make provision for them. Hegel recognizes that where 'civil society' flourishes, the poor are hard put to it to acquire property and are 'more or less deprived of all the advantages of society, of the opportunity of acquiring skill or education of any kind, as well as of the administration of justice, the public health services ... The public authority takes the place of the family where the poor are concerned'.[16] That the poor are victims of society and therefore have claims upon it is acknowledged by Hegel, even though he does not explain in detail how these claims are to be measured and met. They are victims because they cannot acquire the property or the skills and education that would give them dignity and independence as heads of families able to provide for them; or in other words, they are victims of society because they lack sufficient opportunity for private gain.

Part of the objection of Marx and Engels to the 'bourgeois' idea of the family is that it does not correspond with the facts. In capitalist or bourgeois society, the workers own virtually no property, not even their homes. From week to week they live on their wages, and if they lose their jobs they risk being evicted from their homes. To make ends meet, they must too often send their wives and children to work, and must sometimes even drive them to it. So, in practice, family life, as the bourgeois conceive of it, is often beyond the reach of the workers. They lack the security

[16] *Philosophy of Right*, transl. by Knox, p. 149. Though civil society, as Hegel describes it, is a market and capitalist economy, he recognizes that freedom of trade must be controlled 'to diminish the danger of upheavals arising from clashing interests' (*P. of R.*, p. 147), and he approves of 'corporations' in trade, industry, and the professions because they draw men together to promote shared interests and to sustain their weaker associates. He also recognizes that civil society is to some extent subversive of the family, and even says that it 'tears the individual from his family ties [and] estranges the members of the family from one another' (*P. of R.*, p. 148). It is then that his ideas about civil society and the family are closest to those of Marx. But Hegel's conception of the family and its part in the life of man is not altogether clear. Sometimes he speaks of it as if it were older than civil society and even threatened by it, and at other times as if, in the form that interests him in *The Philosophy of Right*, it arose along with civil society. But he does always speak of it as if it were a necessary element in the rational life, and as if it needed private property to sustain it.

that property brings, and are often driven by want to deal harshly with their families.[17]

Want and insecurity are certainly destroyers of family life, and there was plenty of both among wage-labourers in the West while Marx and Engels were alive. Today there is considerably less. Even though the workers do not yet own or control the means of production, they are better paid and have greater security. Materially at least, family life, as Hegel and the bourgeois understood and appreciated it, is more within their reach than it used to be in the hard days of early industrial society. Workers, of course, do not have the 'dynastic' ambitions once so common among the nobles and the wealthier bourgeois; they do not strive to accumulate or consolidate estates to be passed on from generation to generation of their descendants. They aim rather at comfort and security for themselves and their families and at educating their children so that they are better placed to get good jobs. But then, in these days of high taxation, 'dynastic' ambitions are weaker among the rich than they used to be, so that in this respect all classes are more alike. The family—call it 'bourgeois' or not— is today in the West as solid an institution among the workers as among the propertied classes. No doubt, it is 'threatened' now, and perhaps as much so as it was in Marx's day. There are causes at work—though not necessarily the same causes as a hundred years ago—making the reality fall short of the ideal. But there is little reason to believe that these causes, whatever they are, operate more strongly among the poor than the rich.

The observations of Marx and Engels on the family, or the bourgeois family, though markedly hostile, are also perfunctory. They never, as the disciples of Saint-Simon did, preached 'the rehabilitation of the flesh' as against the chastity and marital fidelity favoured by the Christian churches; and they never described, as Fourier did, an ideal community in which men and women practise what has come to be known as 'free love'. But they did take notice of, and on the whole approved, the attacks of the early socialists on the family and the values associated with it. They took it for granted that the family is an obstacle to freedom and happiness which will disappear along with bourgeois society.

It has not disappeared in the countries whose rulers now claim to be disciples of Marx and Engels. Except for a time in Russia after the Bolshevik revolution, this aspect of Marxist teaching has been largely neglec-

[17] In *The Communist Manifesto*, we are told that the family scarcely exists among the proletarians, and that even among the bourgeois it has been shorn of its sentimental veil and reduced to a mere money relation. Who can tell how seriously Marx and Engels took their own words, for they loved to exaggerate? There were plenty of united families among the workers, even in their day. And the care that bourgeois parents took to provide materially for their children and to see them 'well married' is no evidence that bonds of affection were weak in bourgeois families. The family was, no doubt, more idealized in Victorian times than it is now, and the reality often fell far short of the ideal. But was it more idealized then because the bourgeois were better able than they now are to accumulate property and pass it on to their children?

ted by self-styled Marxists in power. In some countries, they have made divorce easier than it used to be, but this, while it has weakened the family in some ways, may have strengthened it in others.[18] It is among Marxists in the West, Marxists not in power, and above all in intellectual rather than in working-class circles, that Marx's strictures on the family are still taken seriously. These Western Marxists might object, not unreasonably, that what has happened in the countries now ruled by self-styled Marxists is not to be used in evidence against Marx. These countries are not socialist, as Marx understood that term, and there is no reason to believe that they are any closer than the capitalist West to achieving what he called communism, the society of the equal and the free. The workers in them do not, except on paper, own the means of production, and they do not in fact control production. The conditions, social and cultural, that would make possible the supersession of family ties by better and more human relations are not to be found in them. But this argument, though sound enough in itself, brings us no nearer to understanding what these more human relations are to be in a society which is still to remain industrial and technically advanced, even when it has ceased to be capitalist and bourgeois.

It is in economically advanced countries in which there is great social mobility that the small family comes into its own, and the extended family, better suited to static (or, rather, to slowly changing) conditions disintegrates. The nuclear family spreads above all with the growth of towns. It was in the West that society first became predominantly urban; and the West is still largely 'capitalist' in spite of great changes since Marx's time in the structure of commerce and industry, in property rights, and even in the distribution of property. The nuclear family first emerged, or first spread widely, in the capitalist and bourgeois West. But today it is spreading also in other parts of the world which, though they are fast becoming industrial and urbanized, can hardly be called either 'capitalist' or 'bourgeois',[19] even though their right to call themselves 'socialist' is questionable.

[18] Of course, 'Marxists', where they have got power, have built up industry in a big way, and this, by encouraging the growth of cities and movement from place to place, has weakened the extended family wherever it was to be found. And their harsh methods—forced labour camps, imprisonments without trial, false accusations of the innocent, invasions of privacy, and ubiquitous spying and delation—have greatly weakened the trust on which all closer social relationships depend.

[19] The term 'bourgeois' is the more loosely used of the two. Nobody in the West or outside it is tempted to call the Soviet Union a capitalist country, but there are hostile critics, by no means confined to the West, who call it bourgeois or who say that it has grown considerably more bourgeois than it used to be. It is not always clear what they mean by this. They mean, perhaps, that men in the professions, and white-collar workers generally, think of themselves as socially superior to manual workers, that they set great store by the external marks of success and are increasingly competitive and envious. 'Bourgeois society', as compared with feudal society, on the one hand, and with the ideal communist society, on the other, is in Marxist

In the West the small family has flourished along with the claim for the individual that he should be allowed to make his own way in life. The man and the woman who marry and set up house together will tolerate much less interference from parents and relations than their ancestors did. Just as the individual claims the right to make the best of his life according to his own ideas of what it should be, so two individuals who decide to live together make the same claim for their joint lives. Yet the small family, made up of individualists who expect so much from life, is subject to considerable strains. Consciously and unconsciously, husband and wife make great demands on each other which they often cannot satisfy; and the same is true of parents and children. Moving more often from place to place looking for work and conditions of life that suit them, they lose old friends and have to make new ones. The less enduring and the less close these other ties, the more they are thrown back on the ties which are supposed to be the most enduring and the closest of all—the family ties.

That the small family imposes great strains on its members is incontestable. It is largely because it does so that divorce is more frequent and less condemned than it used to be. Society must provide means of escape from such close ties when they are felt to be intolerable. And yet it may be that the very conditions which so often make such ties intolerable also create the need for them. The less settled people are geographically and socially and the more impermanent their relations with neighbours and fellow-workers, the greater perhaps their need for ties which remain strong despite their movements from one place to another or from some social circles to others; the greater their need for a small circle of intimacy which moves with them as they move, like the shell of the tortoise. For though in these days of easy travel and easy communications, it is easier than it was to 'keep in touch' with distant friends, the need to be really close to people and important to them still remains.

Fourier, whose attacks on the bourgeois family Marx and Engels approved, wanted people to live in self-sufficing communities of some sixteen hundred souls. Though he did not forbid movement from one community to another, most of his arguments rest on the assumption that the individual will stay in the community he first joins or is born into. The variety he needs in work or leisure or love (and Fourier makes much of the need for variety) will be provided for him within his community. This community (the *phalanx*), as Fourier imagines it, is a kind of extended family whose institutions and ways of life do not change, in spite of the wide variety of activities inside it. Its members are close neighbours to one another. They may change their partners in work or love or play as

---

eyes pre-eminently competitive. Therefore a society that claims to be socialist and is nevertheless competitive, as well as highly conscious of small differences of status, is liable to be called bourgeois by the Marxist disappointed with it.

often as they choose, but their partners still remain fellow-members of the same small intimate community. The ties of children with their parents are less close in the phalanx than in the family as we know it, and this, in the eyes of Fourier, is one of the great advantages of the phalanx; but the children are nevertheless children of the phalanx. They grow up together in a close and stable community in which it is safe to allow them a great deal of freedom. They are not disciplined as children were in France in Fourier's time, but they are cherished and cared for by adults who are close to them. Thus freedom to make and to break even the most intimate of human ties, a freedom that Fourier valued greatly, is to be exercised, not in a vast urbanized industrial society with an immense division of labour, but in a community of close neighbours and friends.

Now it may well be that Marx and Engels thought of the future communist society as a community of friends and neighbours. But they also thought of it as an industrial society more advanced technologically than the capitalist economy of their day. It was to combine the advantages of material progress with the close human ties which this progress, in its capitalist phase, had so largely destroyed. It was to restore these ties at a higher level, a level consistent with aspirations to freedom and self-realization unknown to pre-capitalist societies. But how it was to do this, neither Marx nor Engels explained. The attempt to explain it would no doubt have seemed to them Utopian dreaming. In their philosophy, though to predict is reasonable, to explain how what you predict might be accomplished, how society and production should be organized to achieve it, is unreasonable. A convenient philosophy which allows you to make large promises without making it clear just what you are promising!

III

In *The Holy Family* Marx attacks another aspect of bourgeois society: its attitude to the lawbreaker and to whoever acts wrongly by its standards. He objects not only to the severity of its punishments but also to the quality of its compassion, when it is—or imagines itself to be—compassionate. In the eighth chapter of *The Holy Family*, he examines critically a novel by Eugène Sue, *Les Mystères de Paris*, and also the comments on it of a Left Hegelian writer, Szeliga. In the novel Sue describes, among other characters, a murderer, Chourineur, and a prostitute, Fleur de Marie, who are reformed by a philanthropist called Rudolph. As Sue describes them, they are victims of circumstance. If their social condition and education had been different, Chourineur would not have been a murderer nor Fleur de Marie a woman of the streets. And yet their reformation serves only to make them servile or guilty. Speaking of the reformed murderer, Marx says:

Henceforward all his virtues will be resolved into the virtue of a dog, pure devotion to its master. His independence, his individuality will disappear completely. But as bad painters must label their painting to say what it is supposed to represent, Eugene Sue must put a label in Bulldog Chourineur's mouth, so that he constantly affirms, 'The two words, "You still have heart and honour" [words spoken to him by his "saviour" Rudolph] made a man of me.' Till his last breath Chourineur will find the motives for his actions . . . in that label.[20]

In other words, Chourineur accepts uncritically an image of himself presented to him by his 'moral saviour' and tries to live up to it. He also allows himself to be used as an informer and an *agent provocateur* in Rudolph's crusade against crime and sin.

Fleur de Marie, while still unreformed, has 'vitality, energy, cheerfulness, elasticity of character. . . . She does not appear as a defenceless lamb. . . . She is a girl who can vindicate her rights and put up a fight'.[21] Reformed, she becomes 'a serf of consciousness of sin. In her [former] unhappy situation in life she was able to become a lovable, human individual; in her outward debasement she was conscious that her human essence was her true essence'. But after her reformation 'the filth of modern society . . . becomes her innermost being; continual hypochondriac self-torture because of that filth will be her duty, the task of her life appointed by God himself. Now self-torment will be her good and remorse will be her glory'. Her reformation has deprived her of her capacity to enjoy life, to respect herself, and to stand up for herself. Her 'saviours' have defined her and have imposed on her a definition that diminishes her in her own eyes; they have turned her into a self-punisher, an enemy to herself.

Rudolph, the self-appointed saviour of society's victims, as seen by Marx (though not by Sue), is an evil man. Taking Rudolph's actions as Sue describes them, Marx sees in the would-be saviour the tormentor of those he claims to save, laying a heavy burden of remorse and guilt on them, driving them to be cruel to themselves and to other sinners in the name of virtue. The key to Rudolph's character (though a key denied to his novelist creator) is 'the pure hypocrisy with which he manages to see and make others see in the outbursts of his evil passions outbursts at the passions of the wicked'.[22] Rudolph may find it deplorable that the seducer of a maid-servant driven to crime as a result of her seduction should go unpunished, but he has not a word to say against the social order in which there are masters and servants, and women are the inferiors of men. His ambition is to change the criminal but not the society which makes a criminal of him. Everyone reformed by him is devitalized in the process, made docile towards society and harsh towards himself. The victims of

---

[20] *The Holy Family* (F.L.P.H. transl., Moscow, 1956), p. 220.
[21] Ibid., p. 225.   [22] Ibid., p. 271.

society, whose crimes are acts of self-assertion and rejections of oppressive rules, are morally disarmed; or, rather, their weapons are turned against themselves.

Commenting on Hegel's account of punishment Marx says:

Hegel holds that in punishment the criminal passes sentence on himself[23]. . . . Hegel makes the self-judgement of the criminal no more than an 'idea', a mere speculative interpretation of the current empirical criminal code. He thus leaves . . . punishment as it is.

On the other hand, under human conditions punishment will really be nothing but the sentence passed by the culprit on himself. There will be no attempt to persuade him that violence from without, exerted on him by others, is violence exerted on himself by himself. On the contrary, he will see in other men his natural saviours from the sentence he has passed on himself.[24]

Clearly, the criminal, when he is punished, does not literally pass judgement on himself. But Hegel believed that it is of the essence of punishment that it aims at bringing it home to the offender that he has offended. If he looks upon his punishment as society's act of vengeance on himself, or merely as an evil that he risks calling down upon himself when he breaks the law; if he does not recognize *in foro interno* (if not outwardly as well) that what society metes out to him is what he deserves, then punishment has failed of its essential purpose. It may still be an effective deterrent; but mere deterrence is not punishment, for we can effectively deter an enemy from harming us, though we do not condemn him for wanting to do so. Or we can deter a man from doing good, if it suits us that he should not do it. If society had no rules whose general observance was important to it and evolved no procedures of blame and punishment to ensure that the rules were observed, men would have no sense of right and wrong. They acquire this sense in the process of learning to use social rules, in observing them themselves, invoking them against others, and responding appropriately when the rules are invoked against them. This does not entail—and Hegel was aware that it does not—that anyone who rejects a social rule on the ground that it is immoral is necessarily mistaken in doing so. It means rather that the individual acquires moral principles and dispositions in the first place under the pressure of society, which imposes its rules and attitudes on him while he is still too young to assess them critically. There is, for Hegel, a close and indispensable connection between the sense of obligation that a moral being has and society's blame and punishment of those who break its rules.

The little that Hegel says in *The Philosophy of Right* about the education

---

[23] Ibid., p. 238. I have slightly altered the F.L.P.H. English translation, which renders 'fallt der Verbrecher in der Strafe über sich selbst das Urteil' by 'the criminal must as a punishment pass sentence on himself'.

[24] Ibid., p. 39.

of children implies that they are not made moral simply by having the usefulness (to themselves and others) of important social rules explained to them, so that they willingly observe them. Rather, they are required to observe the rules and are blamed and punished for breaking them long before they are able to see the point of them. This blame and punishment are not mere expedients to get children to observe the rules before they are old enough to understand what they and others stand to gain by their being generally observed. They are essential parts of the process of moral education, creating in children dispositions and sentiments that help to make moral beings of them, even though they are not fully moral until they see the point of the rules and observe them willingly, until reason endorses the sense of obligation which moves them to observance even where there is no risk of detection and punishment.

But Hegel seems to have gone further than this (which is no more than many of his critics would accept); he seems also to have believed that the punishment of *adult offenders by the state*, their public trial and condemnation, educates them, in the sense that it brings out or strengthens in them the sense that they have done wrong. Just how far he believed that criminals do in fact concur with the judgements passed on them by the courts, it is difficult to say. But, presumably, he would not have given the 'philosophical' explanation of punishment which he did give, if he had not believed that they do so quite often. The modern state, in his opinion, comes closer than any community before it to being rationally organized, and the more rational a community, the more likely that its members will have moral standards in keeping with social norms.

Hegel, if he did believe that adult offenders do ordinarily concur with the judgements that 'society' (the courts or public opinion) passes on them, was probably mistaken. The studies of criminologists do not bear him out. Even intelligent criminals who could give a reasonably accurate account of society's attitude to them seldom share that attitude, unless they are law-abiding citizens driven by exceptional circumstances to commit an offence they are unlikely to repeat. Punishment seems rarely to reactivate or reinforce the moral sentiments of habitual offenders or even of first offenders in whom respect for society's rules and standards is not already strong.

In *The Holy Family* Marx neither says nor implies that offenders against 'bourgeois' law and morality have a more 'human' morality of their own to justify their offences. They are victims of social conditions and not martyrs for a higher code. Their disregard for bourgeois rules, legal and moral, is a sign of vitality in them, not of morality. Nor does Marx see in the mere lawbreaker the destroyer of bourgeois society and the liberator of the exploited. The 'revolt' against oppressive conditions which takes the form of crime and immorality is a symptom of social ills and not a remedy for them. Rebellion, if it is to be remedial, must be disciplined and have definite social aims. In the eyes of Marx, there is nothing revolutionary about crime and immorality, even when the standards rejected are those of an oppressive class or of a society in which there is widespread oppression. He does not even suggest that the criminals of bourgeois society are the stuff out of which revolutionaries are made, that they are likely to pass beyond their criminality to a rejection in principle of an oppressive social order. In *The Civil War in France* he notices with approval the absence of crime and prostitution in Paris under the Commune. He does, it is true, blame the Commune for not seizing the assets of the Bank of France and for excessive respect for bourgeois rights of property, but what he blames is the failure of the communal assembly, a public body exercising authority in Paris in the name of the workers and citizens, to take effective action to promote the cause it was fighting for.

Marx, contrasting social conditions in his own day with what he calls 'human' conditions, seems to me to make two doubtful assumptions: that in a society of equals[25] the individual would not find social rules inhibiting, and that there can be effective self-discipline with no strong social discipline, no blaming and punishing by recognized authority, to support it. He makes this second assumption when he says that 'under human conditions punishment will really be nothing but the sentence passed by the culprit on himself'.[26] If Marx were alone in making these assumptions, they might not be worth discussing, for he does not spell them out and there is not much trace of them in his later writings, though he never repudiated them. But other radical critics of bourgeois society, especially anarchists, have made these same assumptions and have done so more conspicuously and fervently. Among anarchists they have the status almost of articles of faith, and there is an anarchist side to the teachings of Marx.[27]

[25] I speak deliberately of a 'society of equals' and not of a classless society. Though Marx took it for granted that in a classless society there would be no great social inequalities, this is simply not true: not if classes are distinguished from one another, as they are by Marx, in terms of whether or not they own certain types of property. The communist society imagined by Marx must be more than a classless society; it must be egalitarian in a stricter sense than that.

[26] *The Holy Family*, p. 239.

[27] This 'anarchist' side is prominent above all in Marx's early writings. Though he never ceased to express his distaste for bourgeois values and to predict the disappearance of the state, his more sustained attacks on the values and on the state as marks of alienation belong to his early years. Neither he nor Engels was much given to taking back what he had said before. There are, of course, with him, as with all prolific writers, shifts of interest and emphasis. For example, in *The German Ideology*, he and Engels take it for granted that in the communist society there will be none of the drudgery which is the lot of the productive worker under capitalism, and they do not distinguish between work and leisure. But in Marx's later writings, this distinction is made, and he speaks of the hours of leisure as hours of freedom and creative activity, recognizing that in any industrial society the work involved in producing the necessaries of life will be monotonous. (Herbert Marcuse in *Soviet Marxism* (Routledge & Kegan Paul, 1958), pp. 234 ff. contrasting Marx's ideas about work with those officially promoted in the Soviet Union, makes perceptive comments on this aspect of Marxism.) And Engels, in

Why should there not be, even in a society of equals, some men and women with wants and passions incompatible with accepted social rules and standards? These rules and standards would, of course, in a society of that kind, be in the common interest; it would be everyone's interest that they should be generally respected. But what reason is there to believe that it is only where there is social inequality, and many social rules and practices that favour the interests of privileged groups at the expense of others, that individuals have 'anti-social' wants and passions so strong that society must resort to punitive measures against them? It is worth noticing that Rousseau, who was the first to preach the doctrine that a developed commercial society corrupts men, producing in them ambitions and passions which move them to break its laws, did not share this belief. He believed, of course, that social inequality is the chief cause of crime and immorality, but from this he did not draw the conclusion that in a society of equals men could rely on each other's goodwill and self-restraint so much that no provision need be made for prosecuting offenders and punishing them, if found guilty.

Rousseau's society of equals is a small community, economically simple and self-sufficing, whose members have much the same tastes and values. We should expect the pressure of opinion in it to be strong and yet acceptable to the individual, given that his aspirations for himself, his family, and the community differ little from those of his neighbours. We should therefore expect offences serious enough for the community to take 'official' notice of them to be few, and we might also expect that offenders should often concur in the judgements passed on them.[28]

an essay *On Authority* directed against the Italian anarchists and first published in 1874, admits the need for authority and even hierarchy in every large organization, socialist or capitalist; though, characteristically, he fails to explain how the forms of authority would differ in capitalist and socialist societies.

That both Marx and Engels had second thoughts about what could be achieved if capitalism were abolished is clear enough, but what exactly these second thoughts amounted to is not easily established.

[28] Rousseau, though he was no anarchist, preached the doctrine, so attractive to anarchists, of man's 'natural' goodness. He held that man's aggressive and harmful passions are produced in him by his social environment, and that the way to change man for the better is to change his environment. Why then the need for the punishment of adults in a just society? Rousseau does not explain. Perhaps he believed that any social order, by making man self-conscious and self-assertive, makes him to some extent ambitious and aggressive, and that therefore even the just society must protect itself against these inevitable effects of social intercourse on the human *psyche*.

It did not occur to Rousseau—any more than to the anarchists of the next century—that it is pointless to speak of man as either naturally good or naturally evil. All the needs and passions he acquires in society, the harmful ones no less than the others, are rooted in wants and instincts that he is born with. It may well be that men are as much congenitally 'anti-social' as 'social'. They acquire in society wants, dispositions, and skills which make social beings of them, and yet society may (as Freud suggested) place restraints on them that they find difficult to bear. Even self-discipline is repressive because it is initially a response to a discipline externally imposed, a partial taking over by the individual of society's repressive role towards him. The self has its revolts against self-discipline as well as against the discipline of society.

Rousseau seems to have expected it. He seems to have expected the con-demned man to acknowledge *in foro interno* the justice of his condem-nation; for this, surely, is the gist of what he meant when he spoke of the lawbreaker being 'forced to be free'. The judgement of his peers would, he thought, bring it home to him that in breaking the law he acted against his own principles. And yet Rousseau believed that, even in conditions of social equality, the community must make provision for the trial and punishment of offenders. Was he mistaken in this belief? Did he fail to notice one of the great advantages of the equality he preached so long and so passionately, to appreciate the full extent of the harmony to be achieved by means of it? I doubt it. I suspect that in this respect at least he was more a realist than the anarchists of the next century.

Marx's conception of the society of equals, even though he nowhere describes it systematically or in detail, is in obvious and crucial respects unlike Rousseau's, which to many radicals today would seem dull and parochial. Marx's communist society is to be highly productive materially and culturally, to give scope to a wide variety of talents, and to provide for a wide variety of wants. In it the individual will be freer than ever before to 'realize his potentialities', to 'express himself' fully, to live as seems good to him. He will live, not in a small, simple, frugal, self-sufficing, unad-venturous community among neighbours with tastes and ambitions like his own, but in a large community with a wide diversity of occupations, tastes, skills, and ideas in it. In a community of that kind, the pressure of 'opinion' on the individual is apt to be smaller than in Rousseau's ideal state, or the 'opinion' that weighs most with him is more often confined to only a section of the community, so that the chances of conflict arising from incompatible ambitions or standards are likely to be greater. Why, then, should there be less need for the community to make provision for the punishment of offenders in Marx's society of equals than in Rousseau's?

That society should aim at reducing the need for punishment, and especially for the punishment of adults, is admirable. And it may well be that an egalitarian society which was also progressive, in the sense that men's understanding of the world and of themselves grew continually, would be better placed to discover effective ways of reducing this need than would a simple, stable, and intellectually unenterprising community of equals of the sort imagined by Rousseau. But to say this is only to state a possibility. It cannot justify our taking it for granted that in a society of equals there would be no need to provide for the trial and punishment of offenders.

It could perhaps be argued that Marx did not take this for granted, or at least not always; that he believed rather that social equality, though in itself not enough to remove the need for punishment, is a condition of society's being seriously concerned to discover how it might be removed or greatly reduced. In the third of his 'Economic and Philosophical Manuscripts', he speaks of communism as 'a fully developed humanism', as 'the true solution of the conflict . . . between freedom and necessity', and as 'the solution of the riddle of history [which] knows itself to be this solution'.[29] This could be interpreted to mean, not that all important social problems are solved with the establishment of equality, but that with its coming men are at last able to study these problems impartially and have the will to solve them.

Even if the official punishment of adult offenders were abolished, it is not easy to see how punishment could be 'nothing but the sentence passed on the culprit by himself'. The self-punisher presumably does more than just take notice of the fact that he has done harm; he also blames himself for having done it. But how, in a society in which nobody blamed anybody but himself, could anyone come to blame even himself? As Marx, in full agreement here with Hegel, acknowledged, how a man thinks or feels about himself depends largely upon how others feel and think about him, and about each other. Reflexive attitudes derive from social attitudes, even when they also to some extent differ from them because everyone's circumstances and temperament are unique. Are we then to suppose that in the society of equals become 'fully human', in the mature communist society, only children will be blamed by others for the harm they do, and that adults will be left to blame themselves? Marx's vision of a society in which the wrongdoer blames himself, and his neighbours console him in his self-inflicted misery, is unconvincing. Indeed, it is not even attractive. True, the wrongdoer will not be exhorted to penitence, as poor Fleur de Marie was, by his 'saviours'; he will not have self-punishment imposed upon him by others. But will he not be a 'serf to consciousness of sin'? Will not the individual, no longer restrained by fear of blame and punishment from others, need to be all the more severe with himself? Marx even suggests that he will need others to 'save' him from the sentence he passes on himself! In society as we know it today the individual is kept in bounds by both self-restraint and restraint by others, by self-blame and fear of blame by others. Is it really desirable that the first of these practices should entirely take the place of the second, even among adults? A moral sense so alert and quick as to make this possible might be more inhibiting even than penalties socially imposed.

[29] *Karl Marx: Early Writings*, p. 155.

CHAPTER XI

THE STATE AS A FORM OF ALIENATED LIFE

MUCH the best known of Marxist assertions about the state is that it is an instrument of class rule which will disappear with the disappearance of classes. But, apart from this doctrine, there are two others which are just as central to Marxist political theory: the doctrine that the state, though not always literally an instrument of class rule, is an effect of the division of society into classes having irreconcilable interests and also a condition of class oppression, and the doctrine that the state rests upon or is sustained by illusions which are symptoms of alienation.

These doctrines are not mutually exclusive: a state could be an instrument of class rule and a condition of class oppression, and could rest on the illusions of alienated men, in the sense that their having such illusions was a condition of the state's functioning effectively. Yet these doctrines, though not mutually exclusive, do not entail one another. Clearly, the third doctrine does not entail, and is not entailed by, either of the other two. There could conceivably be class rule or class oppression, even though nobody had illusory beliefs about the functions of the state. Such beliefs may often make class rule or class oppression easier, by reconciling people to them, but there is no logical necessity in the case.

Where there is class rule, as Marxists understand it, there is necessarily class oppression. But the converse is not true. There can be class oppression where there is no class rule. If class rule meant merely rule by persons who all come from one class, then there could well be class rule without class oppression; for the rulers, though all drawn from the same class, might govern in the interest of all classes. But this is not what Marx and Engels meant by class rule; they conceived of it as rule by one class in its own class interests and to the detriment of other classes. They believed that classes have irreconcilable interests, and that therefore any class ruling in its own interests necessarily sacrifices the interests of other classes to its own. This is so even though there are also interests common to all classes. Thus class rule, for Marx and the Marxists, entails class oppression.

But the converse is not true. For one class to exploit or oppress others, there is no need for it to be actually the ruling class. It is enough that the laws and social institutions should favour this exploitation or oppression, and that the rulers, from whatever class they are drawn, should find it in their interest to maintain these laws and institutions. Their maintaining them would not in itself make them agents of the exploiting class. Marx himself admitted this, at least indirectly. He did not think of the old monarchy in France as the agent of either the nobility or the bourgeoisie; he thought of it rather as maintaining a balance between the two, now favouring one class and now the other. Neither class, under the *ancien régime*, was politically the ruling class, though the king recruited his officials from both classes; but economically and socially they were both, in their different ways, exploiting and oppressive classes. Nor did Marx think of either the first or the second Empire as an example of bourgeois rule. The bourgeois may have ruled France under the first and second republics, but the coming to power of a Bonaparte in both cases marked the end of bourgeois rule. Napoleon I and Napoleon III were supported by a variety of groups drawn from different classes but the government of neither of them was a form of class rule. This follows, not just from the facts as the historian records them, but from Marx's own interpretation of the facts, especially in *The Eighteenth Brumaire of Louis Bonaparte*.

Thus Marx—and the same is true of Engels—though he sometimes called the state an instrument of class rule, was in practice quite ready to admit that a particular regime or government was not dominated by any class. This, on the face of it, is a contradiction, but not, I suggest, an important one. If we look at what Marx says about particular states, we find, as often as not, that he does not speak of them as instruments or organs of class rule. On the other hand, he always speaks as if, where there is a state, there is class oppression; he takes it for granted that oppression or exploitation could not endure for long unless there were a state to maintain the social and legal conditions of it. So, too, though he sometimes admits, at least by implication, that the state, when it first arose, was an effect of class conflict rather than a condition of class oppression, he takes it for granted that it soon becomes such a condition. He implies that, as the state emerges, social conditions change in such a way as to bring about class oppression. Engels, in his *Origins of the Family, Private Property and the State*, implies this even more clearly than Marx does. Therefore, in spite of their sometimes saying with such a show of authority, such an air of having got to the root of the matter, that the state is an organ of class rule, I shall assume that their real position—or perhaps I should say their usual position—is more accurately put in these words: the state is always a condition of class oppression and sometimes also an instrument of class rule. If this is their real or usual position—and I think it is—it has the advantage of being more realistic, or at least less obviously untrue, than the blunt assertion that the state is an instrument of class rule.

In *The German Ideology* Marx and Engels say that the ideas of the class that rules are the ruling ideas of the age. We could amend this to say that the ideas of the socially dominant classes, who may not actually rule but who exploit and oppress, are the ruling ideas of the age. The ideas that Marx and Engels have in mind in saying this are primarily political, legal, and moral ideas; that is to say, ideas men use in controlling and influencing human behaviour, other people's and their own.

To say this is not in itself to imply that the ideas are symptoms of alienation, or even that they rest on illusion, though Marx believed that they are and do. He did not think of the dominant classes as deliberately and cynically inventing and propagating these ideas so as to make it easier for them to exploit the other classes; he thought of the ideas as arising along with the domination, and as being just as sincerely held by the exploiting class as by the others. And he took it for granted that ideas which help to maintain a system that allows of exploitation are to a large extent illusory or rest on illusion; that is to say, they are either false or are acceptable only to people holding false beliefs.

My present concern is with the idea of the state as a form of alienated life and not with Marx's theory of the state, taken as a whole. Though to speak of a theory here is perhaps to use too grand a name. I would rather speak of Marx's ideas about the state than of his theory of it, for he never attempted to fit these ideas together into a whole. It was Engels rather than Marx who produced a theory of the state, in *Anti-Dühring* and in *The Origins of the Family, Private Property and the State*. If this is taken to be the Marxist theory of the state, then it is, surely, the weakest part of Marxism, the most dogmatic, the least well considered. And its weakness cannot be set down merely to the defects of Engels as a thinker. Though the theory is the theory of Engels, the ideas that he tries to fit together into it are as much Marx's as his own, and quite often they do not fit. In his attempt to fit them together, an attempt that fails, he unwittingly draws attention to what is empty or absurd about them; and there is a good deal of it. Marx and Engels seldom talked more nonsense than when they generalized about the state, and Engels lacked Marx's talent for making nonsense seem profound.

Nevertheless, there are at least two of Marx's ideas about the state which are worth close study: the idea of it as a condition of class oppression which is also sometimes an instrument of class rule, and the idea of it as a form of alienated life. There was nothing new in Marx's time about the first of these ideas, though Marx developed it in some fresh and ingenious ways. The second idea comes much closer to being original with him. There are hints of it in Rousseau and even in Hegel, but it finds conscious and elaborate expression for the first time in Marx's early writings. The state always is, and must be, more than either of these things: more than a condition of class oppression, and more than a form of alienated life. It could not be either unless it were much more besides. Yet these two ideas of it are suggestive, and they apply much more obviously to the modern state, the state as it is in developed commercial and industrial societies, than to earlier forms of political authority.

The state could be a condition of class oppression without being also a form of alienated life. It could be either without being the other, and it could be both. Marx believed that it was both. He believed that there is a kind of division of labour, the separation of 'material' from 'mental' work, which produces both alienation and classes having irreconcilable interests, and he believed that the need for the state arises with the emergence of classes. As I hope to show later, there are, if we accept Marx's conception of what is specifically human about man and his account of the social causes of alienation, some good reasons for believing that, when the state is a condition of class oppression, it is likely to be also a form of alienated life. We do not have to be Marxists to admit that the state can be, and often has been, a condition of class oppression (and indeed of other forms of oppression which are just as bad), and also that it can, and often does, sustain and thrive upon widely shared illusions about social institutions and governmental practices. We can admit this even though we reject as hopelessly unrealistic the Marxist belief that the state can be abolished, or will wither away, in advanced industrial societies; that is to say, in societies of the type in which, according to Marx, the economic foundations of 'human emancipation' first emerge.

I

If you want to do justice to what is perceptive and valuable in the reflections of Marx, and even of Engels, on the state, you have to take certain precautions. Otherwise you risk being misunderstood. As everybody knows, the ideas of *state* and *class* are closely connected in the thought of Marx and Engels; they even bring the word *class* into their definitions of the state. It is therefore important to notice that they use these two words, *state* and *class*, in wider and narrower senses. For my present purpose, which is to explain how the state can be a form of alienated life, I need not distinguish all these senses; it is enough that I should distinguish two. Sometimes they use the word *state* to refer to any organized political authority, and sometimes to refer only to certain forms of it, the forms that distinguish what is sometimes called the modern state from earlier forms of government. So, too, they often use the word *class* in a wider sense, which enables them to refer to classes in feudal and even pre-feudal societies, and sometimes in a narrower sense which implies that classes, properly so called, emerged with capitalism.

When, in a general way, in *Anti-Dühring* or in *The Origins of the Family, Private Property and the State*, Engels discusses the rise of the state, he points to a process in which certain activities of the kind we call *political* come gradually to be separate from others and to be recognized as the official business of some persons in the community. These persons are looked upon as acting in a representative capacity, as doing the business of the community, and therefore as holders of public authority. Long before there was this type of authority, there were other older types, paternal and patriarchal but not yet properly political. In the small family, parents who exercise authority over their children do much more besides, and they need not exercise it in prescribed ways, for the exercise to be legitimate. In the extended family, in the clan or tribe, the patriarch, chief, or elder spends more of his time making authoritative decisions, and makes them in a more formal manner, and yet, in the eyes of the persons who feel bound by his decisions, he is as much a relative or companion or fellow-worker as he is a ruler. Clansmen or tribesmen may even make decisions in common, and make them in prescribed ways, without being set apart as makers of such decisions from the rest of the community. But where there is a state, those who exercise authority, who make decisions binding on others, not only do so in prescribed ways; they are also set apart from the rest of the community as its rulers. Their recognized function in the community is to exercise authority, and they owe their status to this exercise.

In this broad sense of the word state, there were states in medieval Europe. But historians, Marxists and others, sometimes speak as if the state, properly so called, arose towards the end of the Middle Ages. Its emergence, they say, gradually put an end to feudalism. When they speak in this way they seem to mean by the state either of two things: a political system in which a supreme ruler directs all other holders of authority how they shall exercise it, or else a system in which a coherent and generally accepted body of rules (a constitution in the wide sense of the word) ensures that subordinate rulers are controlled by their superiors within well-defined limits and that supreme authority is so distributed among its holders that they and their subordinates constitute one body politic. In the Middle Ages authority was distributed between temporal rulers and the church but not in such a way as to make them one body politic; it was also distributed within the temporal sphere between higher and lower magistrates but not in such a way as to ensure that subordinates were effectively controlled by their superiors or were kept in check by well-defined rules prescribing how authority should be exercised.

Marx and Engels sometimes use the word *state* in this narrower sense; they both speak at times as if the state arose with the decay of feudalism. For example, Marx, in an early article on 'The Jewish Question', says: 'The political revolution . . . which made State affairs the affairs of the people, and the political State a matter of general concern, i.e. a real State, necessarily shattered everything—estates, corporations, guilds, privileges—

which expressed the separation of the people from community life'.[1] The
state becomes 'really' a state when these medieval institutions decay or are
destroyed; it then becomes what is often called 'the modern state' or by
Marxists 'the bourgeois state'. It is above all this state that Marx has in
mind when he calls the state 'an illusory form of life' and treats it as a
symptom of alienation. Not that he thinks that men had no illusions about
temporal power in the Middle Ages; it is merely that the illusions he wants
to discuss are illusions which he believes are inherent in the modern or
bourgeois state.

Often Marx and Engels mean by a class any group of persons who differ
from the rest of the community by having rights of property which others
lack or by lacking rights which others have. But they also use the word in
other senses, of which one now particularly concerns us. They sometimes
make a distinction between estates and classes, and when they do this they
use the word *class* in a sense narrower than the one I have just defined. In
this narrower sense, there were no classes in the Middle Ages, though
there were estates. Yet the medieval estates could be distinguished from
one another by their property rights or the lack of them. The medieval
lord had rights of property in the land he held different from the rights of
the serfs tied to that land. Classes, in this narrower sense, emerge with the
modern state.

In *The German Ideology* Marx and Engels say:

> By the mere fact that it is a *class* and no longer an *estate*, the bourgeoisie is
> forced to organize itself no longer locally, but nationally . . . Through the
> emancipation of private property from the community, the State has become a
> separate entity, beside and outside civil society; but it is nothing more than the
> form of organization which the bourgeois necessarily adopt for both internal
> and external purposes.[2]

Some twenty pages later, they say: 'The division between the personal and
the class individual, the accidental nature of the conditions of life for the
individual, appears only with the emergence of class, which is itself a
product of the bourgeoisie'.[3]

How, then, does an estate differ from a class? Or, alternatively, how
does a society divided into estates differ from one divided into classes?
In a society divided into estates, a man's social status is legally recognized
as defining many of his important rights and obligations; his social status
is a legal status. His rights and obligations are those of a serf or a lord,
a free peasant or a burgher; and, more often than not, his social status is
hereditary. He is what his father was. In Europe in the Middle Ages, this
was not true of the priest, but in other societies it has been true even of

---

[1] *Karl Marx: Early Writings*, transl. by Bottomore, p. 28.
[2] *The German Ideology*, transl. by R. Pascal, p. 59.
[3] Ibid., p. 77.

him. In a society divided into estates there is no talk of the rights of man, of rights that people have, regardless of particular occupations or social roles, merely by virtue of being human. Rather there is the idea of a static social order within which, with few exceptions, birth decides what a man's status shall be. Marx and Engels, when they speak of 'the accidental nature of the conditions of life for the individual', have in mind, not the accident of his birth, the status of his parents, but his luck and his exertions during the course of his life. In a society divided into classes, there is—or rather there is supposed to be—great social mobility; it is for the individual by his exertions to make for himself his place in society.

In the Middle Ages, the burghers, the masters of the guilds, were content to establish their supremacy locally in the towns in which they carried on their businesses. They sold most of their goods locally, and could defend their interests adequately by upholding the immunities granted to their towns by charter. The feudal lord ruled over his inferiors without much interference from feudal superiors; he needed to combine with other lords, not so much to maintain his authority over his serfs and other inferiors, as to protect himself from excessive demands made upon him by his feudal superiors. In the Middle Ages there was no widely felt need for powerful central governments because the dominant and exploiting groups were strong enough locally to defend their interests and maintain their ascendancy.

Later, with the expansion of trade and the growth of manufactures, there arose a class of merchants and masters of industry whose interest it was that the guilds and their restrictions should be abolished. As production increased in scale and the producer needed more extensive markets for his goods, it was no longer possible for the men who controlled production and exchange to defend their interests by exercising an authority limited to their own towns. To give them the security indispensable to their greatly extended operations, they needed a government having effective authority over a wide area. They needed not only to be able to make good their rights, to ensure the enforcement of their contracts, over a much wider area; they also needed a more coherent, intelligible, and adaptable system of law. In other words, they needed a centralized and active state, a state strong enough to abolish restrictive customs and to make laws that would be interpreted consistently in all its courts; they needed the modern state, the state that Marxists call *bourgeois*. The feudal lords and the church did not need it, and lost authority and influence with its coming, but the trend of economic change was against them.

The men behind the expansion of trade and industry, eager to take the opportunities created by it, the bourgeois, were a dynamic and enterprising class as no class before them. It was in their interest that old social and economic ties should be dissolved, not only in the towns which were the centres of their own activity, but also in the villages, or the domains of the feudal lords. It was their interest that the serfs should cease to be tied to the soil, that they should be free to find work in the new industries. Marx and Engels do not attribute the liberation of the serfs directly to the bourgeoisie; they point to other causes to explain it. But they see this dissolution of old ties, in both town and country, as serving the interests both of the bourgeois and of the emergent modern state, and they therefore see the bourgeois as supporters of this state in its efforts to extend its authority at the expense of the nobles, the church, and any other groups opposed to it.

Since it was the interest of the bourgeois that old ties should be dissolved, it was also their interest to challenge the idea of a social order in which everyone is born to his place in society. As an enterprising class creating and taking new opportunities, it was their interest to accept and promote new ideas of freedom and equality. As Marx sometimes puts it, it was their interest that the 'personal individual' should replace the 'class individual'; that is to say, that the idea that it is for every man to achieve what he can in society by making the best use of his resources, his natural endowments, and his property, should replace the idea that his opportunities should be determined by the social status of his parents. Hence the doctrine that a man, merely by virtue of being human, has certain basic rights, and that his place in society should depend on his own capacities and efforts, provided that he respects in others what he claims for himself. As the wealth and the influence of the bourgeoisie grow, this doctrine gains wider acceptance; and as it gains acceptance, the modern state, the centralized structure of political authority, grows stronger. For it is to this state that believers in this doctrine look for the reforms and the services which help to put the doctrine into practice. Just as the bourgeois are the most enterprising and efficient of classes in the pursuit of their class interests, so the modern state, the bourgeois state, is the most enterprising and efficient form of government.

Bourgeois society differs from feudal society in another important respect. In it authority and property are distinct and separate. As Marx puts it: 'The old civil society (i.e. feudal society) had a directly political character; that is, the elements of civil life, such as property, the family, and types of occupation had been raised, in the form of lordship, caste and guilds, to elements of political life'.[4] The feudal lord had political authority, had rights of jurisdiction, over the serfs and others living on his land merely because he was the holder of that land, and medieval burghers had similar rights in the chartered towns because they were masters of the guilds. But, so Marx tells us,

---

[4] *Karl Marx: Early Writings*, p. 28, 'On the Jewish Question'.

the political revolution . . . which made the political State . . . a real State necessarily shattered . . . estates, corporations, guilds, privileges . . . The political
revolution therefore abolished the political character of civil society. It dissolved
civil society into its basic elements, on the one hand individuals, and on the
other the material and cultural elements which formed the life experience and
civil situation of these individuals. It set free the political spirit which had, so
to speak, been dissolved, fragmented and lost in the various culs-de-sac of
feudal society; it . . . liberated the political spirit from its connexion with civil
life and made of it the community sphere, the general concern of the people, in
principle independent of these particular elements of civil life.[5]

That is to say, the revolution which made the modern state divorced
political from economic and other social functions. And with this revolution there emerged the idea that the state is a community of persons
whose basic rights and interests must be protected. These rights and
interests were held to belong to the individual, whatever his social position, and the protection of them was therefore, at least in theory, the concern of all who belong to the state.

Now, according to Marx, it is important that the rights of the individual,
merely as such, should be asserted. No doubt, man is essentially a social
being; he develops his peculiarly human powers in assimilating a culture
and learning to sustain social roles, and every culture and all social roles
are particular. Nevertheless, if man is to achieve freedom, if he is ever to
be truly autonomous, he must to some extent dissociate himself from his
parochial culture and social roles; he must assert himself as a mere man, a
member of his species.

The perfected political state is, by its nature, the species-life of man as opposed
to his material life . . . Where the political State has attained to its full development, man leads, not only in thought . . . but in reality . . . a double existence—
celestial and terrestrial. He lives in the political community, where he regards
himself as a communal being, and in civil society where he acts simply as a
private individual, treats other men as means, degrades himself to the role of
mere means, and becomes the plaything of alien powers. Man, in his most
intimate reality, in civil society, is a profane being . . . In the state, on the
contrary, where he is regarded as a species-being, man is the imaginary member
of an imaginary sovereignty, divested of his real individual life, and infused with
an unreal universality.[6]

That is to say, man, in his idea of the state and of himself as a member of it,
sees himself both as a human being distinct from his particular economic
and other social roles and as a citizen, a responsible member of a community of persons like himself; he recognizes himself and others as species-
beings.

[5] Ibid., pp. 28–9 from 'On the Jewish Question'.
[6] Ibid., pp. 13–14.

With the emergence of the state, man leads—so Marx tells us—a double life; and he does so not only in thought but also in reality. For the state, though it is not what it purports to be, does exist; it is a structure of authority which differs in kind from earlier forms of authority. Men, when they engage in distinctively political activities, when they act as rulers or citizens, are active in roles different from their other roles and are conscious of the difference. They distinguish their sentiments and responsibilities as rulers or citizens from their other sentiments and responsibilities; they see themselves as acting in a public capacity. Even the ordinary citizen who holds no kind of public authority does this; he is concerned, he thinks, not just for himself and his dependents but for the community.

Yet Marx also speaks of the citizen 'as an imaginary member of an imaginary sovereignty', and says that he is 'infused with an unreal universality'. In the modern state, man sees himself as a free individual who has rights and obligations not tied to any particular occupation, and also as a responsible member of a community concerned for the good of its members. His idea of himself is different from what it would be in a feudal or caste society; his aspirations are different and are more consciously those of a species-being. What is more, the state, the political community within which he has this idea and these aspirations, really exists; it is not the dream of an after-life but a part of waking life, or real life. And yet it is a part of it that rests on illusion; for the individual cannot live up to this idea of himself, cannot realize these aspirations in the social order in which the state flourishes.

II

The state, as Marx conceives of it, is a form of alienated life in two senses. It would not exist if men were not alienated. Where there is alienation—or rather where it has reached a certain level or takes certain forms—there is a need for the state, for the methods of social control characteristic of it, if social order is to be maintained. The state is thus a symptom or mark of alienation just as it is of exploitation. Where we find the state, where we find order maintained by the methods distinctive of it, we must expect to find alienation just as we must expect to find one part of the community exploited by another. The state is a mark of alienation in much the same sense as, for the medieval political theorist, it is a mark of man's fallen nature. The state, in this medieval view of it, though not a cure for sin, is a kind of remedy for it. It does nothing to eradicate the evil in man but it does protect him from some of its harmful consequences. Man's need of the state as a protection from himself is therefore evidence of his sinfulness. If he were not sinful, he would not need rulers over him to repress and punish him. So, too, according to Marx, if he were not exploited or alienated, he would not need the discipline of the state to keep him obedient to social rules.

But there is another sense in which, in the eyes of Marx, the state is a form of alienated life. It is so, presumably, whatever kind of state it is; though the state he has in mind, when he speaks in this way, is nearly always the modern or, as Marxists often call it, the bourgeois state. Logically the state could be a symptom of alienation and yet alienation not be manifest in the activities which constitute it; just as for the medieval philosopher temporal power could be a remedy for sin and evidence that man is sinful and yet the exercise of that power not be sinful. The practice of medicine is not diseased because there is need for it only where there is disease. But Marx sometimes speaks of the state as he speaks of religion; as if it, too, were somehow a fantasy of alienated man, or at least as if fantasy or illusion were inherent in the behaviour it consists of. He relegates it to what he calls 'the ideological superstructure' of society and says of ideology that it is 'false consciousness'. In *The German Ideology*, he and Engels speak of 'the interest of the community' taking on an 'independent form as the state' and as 'an illusory communal life'; and they say that 'all struggles within the state . . . are merely illusory forms in which the struggles of the different classes are fought out'.[7] The implication is clear; political behaviour is the behaviour of men who are under illusions about what they are doing.

What sort of illusions had Marx and Engels in mind? For a man can be under different kinds of illusions about his own behaviour. He may merely be mistaken about what he is doing. Making his way in the dark, he may believe that he is going into one room when in fact he is going into another. Or he may be mistaken about his motives for acting as he does. He may believe that he is punishing his son because the boy deserves it, whereas his real motive is anger. In that case, if he says that he is punishing his son, he is not mistaken, for what makes his action punishment is that the boy really has done something which justifies his treating him as he does. His illusion is not about the nature of his action but about his motive for doing it. Or he may be mistaken about what causes him to have the motive he does have. He may know that he is angry with his son and not know that he is irritable because he has a bad liver or because he is unhappily married; he may mistakenly attribute his anger to anxiety about his son's future. Or, finally, he may have mistaken opinions about family life and the bringing up of children; he may not understand how the activities that constitute family life and education are related to one another, to other aspects of human life, and to human needs and aspirations.

Marx and Engels were not careful users of words, but the reasonable assumption is that, when they spoke of political activities (and not just

[7] *The German Ideology*, transl. by R. Pascal, p. 23.

political theory) as illusory, they had in mind illusions of the last kind. The judge sentencing a man to two years' imprisonment knows what he is doing just as well as a bricklayer does laying bricks. His work is more complicated and more difficult to describe, but if he is to do it properly, he needs to know what he is doing just as the bricklayer does. He may be more often mistaken about his motives for action than about his actions, but this is true also of the bricklayer. There is no reason to believe that men are more apt to be mistaken about their motives when they exercise authority than when they engage in production or get themselves wives and children, and to explain what Marx meant by calling the state an 'illusory communal life', we need not attribute to him the belief that state officials are more prone than other men to self-deception about their motives.

Illusions of the third kind—that is to say, mistaken beliefs about how we come by our motives—are no more to the purpose here. We seldom stop to inquire how we come to want what we do want, whatever the capacity in which we act, and there is no reason to believe that when we do inquire, we deceive ourselves more often about the origins of our political than of our economic motives. The illusions that constitute false consciousness are not of a kind that can be dissipated by introspection.

The relevant illusions must be illusions of the last of the four kinds I distinguished; they must be mistaken beliefs about types of social behaviour, how they are related to one another or to human needs generally, or to the needs or interests typical of some class or section of the community. The words actually used by Marx and Engels may not always suggest this, but this alone helps to make sense of their relegating, not just theories of the state, but the state itself, to the 'ideological superstructure'. The root of alienation, and therefore of false consciousness, may be in the system of production, but production itself is not ideological, is not a form of false consciousness. Whereas political activity—so we are invited to believe—is ideological; it involves false consciousness in a way that production does not.

The worker and the capitalist are, of course, alienated just as much as the state official is. They too are victims of false consciousness. Marx and Engels leave us in no doubt about this. The proletarians, as they organize to fight for the interests of their class, succeed in the end (as no other class does) in overcoming false consciousness; but they too are to begin with victims of it. So, if we are to make sense of the Marxist account of the state as a form of alienated life, we have to point to a kind of illusion which enables us to do this; which enables us to explain how, in a society in which all men are alienated and victims of false consciousness, political activity is a form of that consciousness, or is imbued with it, in a way that production is not. This we can do only if we suppose that false consciousness consists of illusions of our fourth kind, of mistaken beliefs about types of social behaviour and how they are related to widely shared needs or interests.

We are concerned here, not with ignorance, but with false beliefs about society which have important social effects. In a primitive community men do not know how the social order functions, how different institutions are related to one another and to human needs. They may understand what they are doing and their motives for doing it about as well as most 'civilized' men do, but they are without social theory, realistic or illusory. If they have enduring and elaborate illusions that are widely shared, they have to do with the significance of dreams or the after-life or the power of magic. These illusions have important social effects, but they are not illusions about the social order, about social institutions and their place in the life of the community and of the individual. Or they are so only to some extent and indirectly. In other words, they are religious rather than social illusions.

Illusions widely shared and having important social effects are, presumably, ideological; they are species of false consciousness, whether they take the form of religion or of social theory. But in societies so primitive that there is in them no division of labour 'properly so called', no division of the kind that produces alienation, and no social theory, these illusions, religious fantasies though they are, cannot be fantasies of alienated man. True, Marx sometimes speaks as if all religion were a symptom of alienation, but this can be so only if his own account of the social causes of alienation is false. He cannot have it both ways; he must either qualify his verdict on religion or abandon his account of how alienation arises.

But he need not abandon that account to insist that illusions about society are fantasies of alienated man. False consciousness in the shape of social theory arises in relatively advanced societies in which there is a division of labour 'properly so called'. It arises therefore in societies in which, according to Marx, there is alienation, and it is plausible to argue that its function is to satisfy needs peculiar to the alienated. Alienated man needs to delude himself that he is already what he aspires to be, though social conditions in fact prevent his being so. Indeed, they even prevent his understanding how he could be so. Alienated man is as yet incapable of putting the right questions about his social and personal predicament, of defining his human problems correctly; and his learning to define them correctly is a sign that he is overcoming his alienation. Yet alienated man is already sophisticated man; he is man who has theories about society and his place in it. Or, rather, he belongs to a community in which such theories flourish, and shares to some extent the attitudes they express, though his own grasp of theory may be slight.

Though man was a producer long before he became a citizen, political theory is older than economic theory. It flourished along with ethics among the Greeks, and along with jurisprudence among the Romans, and all three flourished in the Middle Ages; whereas economic theory, except in a rudimentary form, is scarcely to be found before the era of the modern state. Now, according to Marx, it is since the rise of the modern state, that the political side of social life has come to be sharply distinguished from the other sides, with rights of authority clearly separated from rights of property. It is since then also that men have come to think as systematically and elaborately about production and exchange as they had long done about government or morals or law. For even bourgeois political theory is older than bourgeois economic theory or, as Marx more often calls it, 'political economy'. The system of property that bourgeois economists take for granted is a system first explained and justified by political theorists, John Locke chief among them. The bourgeois economist does not offer an economic explanation of how bourgeois relations of property arise, nor does he seek to justify them; he accepts them for what they are, leaving it to others to explain their origins and to argue that they are what they ought to be. As Marx puts it: 'Political economy begins with the fact of private property; it does not explain it'.[8]

Marx had a considerable respect for some of the classical economists, and especially for Adam Smith and Ricardo, and he learned a good deal from them. Their accounts of the working of the capitalist economy seemed to him substantially true. His chief objection to them was that they took bourgeois property relations for granted, and were blind to the cost in human suffering of the economy they studied and to the contradictions inherent in it, contradictions which must eventually destroy it. Their vision of the economy was distorted by their illusions; but the illusions were not of their making. They were borrowed from bourgeois political theory, ethics, and jurisprudence; or rather they were implicit in bourgeois attitudes to man and society which political theorists, moralists, and jurists had tried to express systematically and had sought to justify.

In a passage I quoted earlier, Marx says of man in civil society that he 'acts simply as a private individual, treats other men as means, (and) degrades himself to the role of a mere means'.[9] Later in the same article he says that 'the consummation of the idealism of the State was at the same time the consummation of the materialism of civil society. The bonds which had restrained the egoistic spirit of civil society were removed along with the political yoke'.[10] The civil society he has in mind here is bourgeois society; it consists of the non-political aspects of life in that society. It is in bourgeois society, with the rise of the modern state, that the political aspects of social life become separate from the others as they used not to be, and that a distinctively political consciousness reaches its

[8] *Karl Marx: Early Writings*, p. 120.   [9] Ibid., p. 13.   [10] Ibid., p. 29.

highest point. It is then that the individual leads more obviously than ever before a double life, one as a citizen and the other as a private person. It is then that, in his private life, he is most conspicuously and ruthlessly self-regarding, concerned only for himself and the few persons close to him. To quote Marx once more:

Man as a member of civil society is identified with authentic man, man as distinct from citizen, because he is man in his sensuous, individual and immediate existence, whereas political man is only abstract, artificial man, man as an allegorical, moral person. Thus man as he really is, is seen only in the form of egoistic man, and man in his true nature only in the form of the abstract citizen.[11]

Man as a member of civil society, in his non-political activities, and especially in material production, sees himself as he really is. Or rather he sees his activities for what they are. John Smith may have illusions about the unique individual who is John Smith, but this same John Smith, as the owner of a cotton factory trying to get as good a return as he can on his capital, need have no illusions about his role as a capitalist. His understanding of how the capitalist economy functions may be limited, but he does not need, if he is to be effectively a capitalist, to have false beliefs about what is involved in being one. So, too, John Smith, if he is a wage-worker out to sell his labour as dear as he can, need have no illusions about his role as a worker. The bourgeois economist may have illusions about the capitalist economy, but neither the capitalist nor the worker need have illusions about their roles in production in order to sustain those roles adequately. This is so, no matter how slight their understanding of the productive system as a whole. No doubt, the chances are that they do have false beliefs about the system, and therefore about their roles inside it, but they need not have them in order to behave typically as a capitalist or as a worker.

The politician or civil servant or judge is differently placed. If he is to act effectively in his official capacity, he must not call a spade a spade. If he is a legislator, he must say of the laws he proposes to make that they promote the common good, even though he has no idea of what constitutes that good. He must speak as if the proper function of law were to promote something called the common good, though in bourgeois society its real function is quite different. He may speak sincerely or he may not, but if he is effectively to legislate, he must speak in this way. So, too, the judge, when he is trying a case, speaks of the law as if it were equitable, as if it were, on the whole, for the good of the persons affected by it; he interprets it as he applies it and justifies his interpretation on the ground that the law, so interpreted, makes for justice, which is, he presumes, what the legislator intended. Or, if he dislikes a law which he nevertheless

[11] Ibid., p. 30.

applies because he cannot deny that it is 'good' (i.e. valid) law, though he admits overtly or by implication that it is not just, he does so on the ground that it is in the long run the general interest that the courts should apply all laws whose validity cannot be reasonably denied. But in bourgeois society the laws, as a whole, are not in the general interest. Some may be so but many are not. The judge, in order to act effectively as a judge, must speak of the law as if it were in bourgeois society what in that type of society it cannot be, and must therefore imply that his role as a judge is what it cannot be. He may be cynical or he may not be, but in either case he must say or imply what is false about the law and the judicial office.

The point is not that the legislator and the judge do not know what they are doing while the capitalist and the worker do know. The judge may know his business just as well as the capitalist knows his; he may be just as well aware of what needs to be done if he is to act competently by the standards of his profession. Indeed, his work may be the more difficult of the two, calling for more unusual gifts and for a deeper understanding of human nature. If the capitalist and the judge were asked to give an account of their work and of its place in the life of society, the capitalist's account might well be cruder and more fantastic than the judge's. The point is rather that the judge, to do his work effectively, needs to invoke an ideology which rests on illusion in a way that the capitalist does not. His work is part of the work of the state, and where there is a state there is necessarily a myth of the state. It is a condition of the state's functioning as it does that men, when they are engaged in activities which are the work of the state, or when they discuss them, should have mistaken beliefs about the social significance of what they are doing or discussing. The weakening or challenging of these beliefs is a sign that the need for the state is disappearing.

There is need for the bourgeois or modern state where man already consciously aspires to freedom and yet is not free, where his work and his social roles do not satisfy him, where he is a victim and an instrument; there is a need for the state where the social order is frustrating to the men involved in it. The state maintains this order by repressing behaviour dangerous to it, though the behaviour is itself merely a human reaction to the social order which it endangers. Men behave in ways disruptive of society because society affects them as it does. The state is needed to maintain the social order because that order frustrates man's need to affirm himself and to control the conditions in which he lives. Being able to satisfy this need is freedom; and so the function of the state is to maintain an order that negates freedom.

Yet men speak of the modern state as if its function were to secure freedom by removing human obstacles to it, by protecting essential rights. They seek to justify it on the ground that it limits freedom for the sake of freedom. They speak of it as if it served to prevent men interfering with one another, as if its discipline were salutary because liberating. The modern state proclaims itself, and is proclaimed by its apologists, the champion and protector of the individual. It is supposed to reconcile his rights with the rights of others or—and this is perhaps only another way of saying the same thing—to reconcile his interests with theirs.

This idea of the state as the protector of 'essential' human rights goes along with the idea of equality. The essential rights protected by the state are rights that all men are supposed to have; they are not privileges. The prime business of the state, on this view of it, is not to encourage virtue or wisdom or excellence or anything else given only to the few; nor is it to promote the divine purpose for mankind or to reward merit or to achieve a social order deemed to be good in itself. It is to prevent men from harming one another and to sustain them in their endeavours to acquire the wherewithal to live well according to their own notions of what constitutes a good life. This bourgeois idea of the state is, on the face of it, the most permissive of all, the most liberal, and the most equalitarian.

Speaking of freedom as men conceive of it in the bourgeois state, Marx says that it is 'the right to do everything which does not harm others';[12] but he also says of it that it 'is not founded upon the relations between man and man, but rather upon the separation of man from man'.[13] It is 'the right of the circumscribed individual, withdrawn into himself', and its 'practical application . . . is the right of private property'.[14] This right of property is 'the right to enjoy one's fortune and to dispose of it as one wills . . . and leads every man to see in other men, not the realization, but rather the limitation of his own liberty'.[15] It is the right of property as it is conceived in bourgeois society, where rights of property and rights of authority are sharply distinguished from one another as they used not to be in feudal society. It is the right of property without responsibility.

The feudal landowner was the ruler of a community for whose welfare, judged by the standards of his age, he was held responsible. He was so held precisely because there were rights of jurisdiction bound up with his rights of property. No doubt, Marx, looking back upon the feudal lord across the centuries, sees him as an exploiter and oppressor, but he sees him also as one who had some duties towards the exploited and oppressed because they lived on his land, and under his protection.

In bourgeois society the sharp separation of property and political authority, unknown in a feudal society, changes the appearance of both. A man's property becomes what he may, within very broad limits, do what he likes with; it is primarily a means to his private purposes. He has no duty to others to use it for their benefit; he has merely a duty not to use

---

[12] *Karl Marx: Early Writings*, p. 24.   [13] Ibid., pp. 24–5.
[14] Ibid., p. 25.   [15] Ibid.

it in ways that harm them. Thus the rich man does not hold his property in trust to be used for the benefit of a whole circle of dependents; he disposes of it as he pleases. He may use it to purchase the labour of others without obligation to them other than to pay them the wages he has promised to pay. Hence the capitalist, unlike the feudal lord and the guild-master, is nothing more than the employer of the men and women who work on his property; his only obligation to them is to keep his part of the contract he made with them just as they must keep their part. In bourgeois society, precisely because the owner of property is not responsible to others for his use of it, except in the minimal sense that he must not harm them, it is possible to represent the defence of property as the defence of freedom. And this is precisely what Locke and the other bourgeois theorists did.

Because the capitalist is only the employer of whoever sells his labour to him, the relation between them is contractual, and the contract is deemed to have been freely made between equals. There is an exchange of money against labour, and neither party to the transaction is responsible for the other's welfare or has authority over him. No doubt, the seller of labour is obliged to do for the purchaser what he has contracted to do; but in theory this is as much so when the seller is a solicitor or an architect as when he is a coal-miner or cotton operative. Authority belongs, not to mere owners of property, not to purchasers of labour, any more than to sellers of it, but to public officials who are supposed to exercise it for the protection of all men's rights. The bourgeois conception of the state is the idea of public authority exercised for the benefit of a society of equals who are also free; it is the idea of authority in the hands of a hierarchy of officials who use it impartially to protect individual rights and to enforce contracts freely made.

Those who speak of the state in this way, those who use the bourgeois idea of it, speak as if the capitalist, having no authority over the workers whose labour he buys, has no more power over them than they have over him. They put the buying and selling of labour on a level with all other buying and selling. Purchasers of houses or of horses have ordinarily no more power over sellers than sellers have over them. The contracts made between them are ordinarily contracts between equals. Or, rather, purchasers in general have no advantage over sellers in general.

But this assimilation in bourgeois society of the purchase and sale of labour with the purchase and sale of other things is profoundly misleading, precisely because those who purchase labour ordinarily own the means of production whereas those who sell it ordinarily do not. The capitalist who buys labour has considerable power over the workers who sell their labour to him; and his having no recognized authority over them means only that he has no obligation to use that power for their benefit. *Caveat emptor! Caveat venditor!* The seller must look to his interests just as the purchaser must do. That is the theory. But, in practice, in bourgeois society, when it is labour that is bought and sold, the seller is ordinarily much less well placed than the purchaser to look after his interests.

Again, in the bourgeois state it is assumed that the rules enforced by public authority are in the enduring interest of all who belong to the community. But this they in fact cannot be, while some are rich and many are poor; and this is so, even when the rules are enforced impartially—though in fact they often will not be, for judges and other officials are apt to be biased in favour of the rich against the poor. But even when they are not so biased, the rules they enforce favour the rich without seeming to do so; for many of the rules relate to property, and the enforcement of them is a defence of property unequally distributed. It is therefore a defence of rights unequally distributed; for to own property is merely to have certain kinds of rights. In theory, everyone is entitled to preserve his property and to endeavour to increase it; or, in other words, to maintain these rights and to try to extend them. But, in practice, those who already have property are better placed to acquire property than those who have not; and those who have much property are better placed to preserve it than those who have little. Thus, where there is private property in the means of production, and that property is unequally distributed, the rules defining rights of property inevitably favour those who have much property against those who have little or none.

Just as bourgeois political economists describe the capitalist economy as if it operated to maximize impartially the satisfaction of human wants, so bourgeois political theorists describe the state as if it operated to enforce impartially rules that favour all its members. They speak of the state as securing to all individuals their fundamental rights, their liberty. *Force organized to secure liberty*; this is the bourgeois idea of the state, its public formula, its myth. The myth is not an invention of the political theorists; for they do no more than explain and seek to justify an idea implicit in the behaviour of those who run the bourgeois state. This formula, this myth, embodies an illusion. In a society where freedom is realized, where men can work and live as it really satisfies them to do, there is no need of organized force to secure freedom. In bourgeois society there is a need for the state, for organized force to maintain obedience to social rules, because the rules are in fact incompatible with liberty; because the social order of which these rules are the ligaments frustrates the essential needs of a species-being; because it produces alienated men.

Thus the bourgeois idea of the state rests on illusion, and the illusion is not confined to the political theorist who describes and justifies the state. The idea consists of more than just mistaken beliefs about the state in the mind of whoever studies or observes it. For such beliefs might be corrected and yet the state remain unchanged. It consists of illusions necessary to the functioning of the state; illusions which those who hold public office, whose official actions are actions of the state, must share, or appear to share, if they are to carry out their duties effectively. And the illusions must also be widely shared by those over whom they exercise authority.

In the words of *The German Ideology*:

This crystallization of social activity, the consolidation of what we ourselves produce into an objective power above us, growing out of our control, thwarting our expectations, bringing to naught our calculations, is one of the chief factors in historical development up till now. And out of this very contradiction between the interest of the individual and that of the community the latter takes on an independent form as the State, divorced from the real interests of individual and community, and at the same time as an illusory communal life . . .[16]

The product of men's activity which is out of their control is the social order they belong to; and what is required for the maintenance of that order may run counter to their interests, even their enduring or long-term interests. The point here is not that the interests of some men may be incompatible with those of others; it is rather that the social order may be incompatible with all or most men's interests. This may happen though they do not know it. For they are conditioned by that order and attached to it, and yet are also frustrated in it. They chafe against it, even though they act in ways that maintain it. To justify their actions they appeal to a supposedly common interest, which is not what they take it to be, for it is divorced from their real interests. It is when men are so situated, when they feel the need to preserve a social order that frustrates them, that the state flourishes.

The state, conceived as a form of alienated life, is repressive and oppressive, and yet is also something more. For the myth of the state does express, though inadequately, worldly aspirations that go unexpressed in feudal society. In feudal society there is no talk of essential human rights; and man's sense of his human dignity, of what is owing to such a being as he is, is manifest, if anywhere, in his religious beliefs and does not yet take the form of worldly claims to liberty and equality. In bourgeois society, in the bourgeois idea of the state, it does take this form. No doubt, men do not yet understand the practical implications of these claims; which is only another way of saying that they misunderstand the claims, that they have confused and contradictory ideas about them. To understand a claim adequately is to understand what conditions must hold if it is to be met. Since in fact the claims can be met only in a social order where there is no room for the state, those who look to the state to meet them misunderstand the claims. Their understanding is the understanding of alienated men, and is therefore necessarily distorted; for alienated men have

---

[16] Marx and Engels, *The German Ideology*, ed. by R. Pascal (New York, 1947), pp. 22-3.

needs and aspirations which are frustrated by their own social activities. Since these activities are not merely physical but involve thought and feeling, their needs and aspirations are thwarted and obscured by their own ideas and their own sentiments. This is the sense, or one of the senses, in which men who are alienated are victims of what Marx calls 'false consciousness'.

Given that they have these needs and aspirations, men are in some ways better off in a bourgeois than they would be in a feudal society, and in other ways worse off. Before they can achieve what they aspire to, they must give worldly expression to their aspirations; and this they must do at first by making claims of the kind made in the bourgeois doctrine of the essential rights of man and the bourgeois theory of the state. They give vague and inadequate expression to their aspirations while they are as yet incapable of doing more. Only later do they learn to express them adequately as they painfully discover the social conditions of realizing them. For they discover these conditions, not in the privacy of their own minds, but by engaging in social action and social conflicts. Bitter experience teaches them just what it is they aspire to and how they are to get it. The bourgeois state, whose myth is the distorted worldly expression of man's aspiration to freedom, is also the most powerful organ of repression.

Alienation was never worse than in bourgeois society, nor men ever more the victims of circumstance. The medieval serf, though he lived poorly, was more secure than the wage-worker under capitalism; the medieval burgher, though he could not amass wealth in the way open to the capitalist, was less exposed to total ruin. Manual work was never as dull or precarious as it has come to be for most people in the economy in which labour is freely bought and sold. Inequalities of wealth were never greater or the poor more constrained to accept the terms offered to them by the rich than in the society that proclaims the equality of all men before the law and the rights of man.

Yet this doctrine of equality and human rights, hollow though it appears to whoever sees bourgeois society for what it is, has none the less made for progress in two ways. At least the consistent Marxist must admit that it has, for the illusions that characterize bourgeois society are not random. Nor do they serve only to justify the established order in bourgeois eyes. They also express man's sense that he is a species-being; they express needs that cannot be satisfied in bourgeois society but are none the less needs of a species-being. The doctrine of equality and human rights was progressive in the past because it served to encourage and to justify the attack on feudal institutions, to dissolve social ties which would otherwise have hindered the enormous expansion of wealth and knowledge achieved under capitalism; an expansion which, according to Marx, has established the technical and scientific conditions of human emancipation.

And the doctrine is still progressive in this sense wherever there are survivals of feudalism or of other pre-capitalist social and economic relations.

There is also another sense in which the doctrine is progressive. It expresses, though in a mistaken and ineffectual way, man's aspiration to freedom. He cannot, so Marx tells us, realize this aspiration in bourgeois society; he cannot do it by translating the natural rights he claims into legal rights protected by the bourgeois state. He can realize it only in a different kind of society in which bourgeois ideas about political authority and legal rights have given way to social practices more in keeping with freedom. About these practices Marx has little to say in detail, and so it is impossible to tell just how, in his opinion, they will differ from the exercises of authority and right familiar to us in the modern state. But, whatever these practices turn out to be, they will realize aspirations to equality and freedom which already find expression, even though in an alienated form, in bourgeois society. What is more, the expression they find, even in bourgeois society, cannot be altogether alienated; for it is against the inequalities and restrictions of this society that the proletarians rise in revolt. Even though the task of achieving equality and freedom comes after the revolution, the workers and their leaders must know enough about these ideals before the revolution, while they are still in bourgeois society, to know that they cannot be realized while that society lasts.

III

Marx and Engels are not consistent in their attitudes to either bourgeois ideas or bourgeois institutions. Sometimes they speak of these ideas as if they were altogether illusory, as if their function were merely to make it appear that a political and legal order is in the common interest when in fact it is in the interest only of an exploiting class. But at other times they speak as if the ideas were also in the interest of the exploited, and could be used by them to challenge their exploiters. Ideas of liberty and equality which the bourgeois used in pushing their class interests against the feudal nobility and against the old absolute monarchy might come in time to be used against them by the workers. So, too, an institution like the universal suffrage, invented by the bourgeois in their own class interest while they were looking for allies in their struggle for power, might prove dangerous to them in the long run. So we have in the political thought of both Marx and Engels two different themes. We have, on the one hand, the theme of ideas and practices peculiarly suited to the interests of the bourgeoisie, and which the workers must reject altogether when they take up the struggle against their exploiters; and we have, on the other, the theme of ideas and practices suited to the needs of a revolutionary class, which the workers can take over from the bourgeois and use against them. Ideas and practices adopted by the bourgeois when they put themselves forward as the champions of society as a whole against irresponsible power and a reactionary nobility can become a nuisance to them once they are installed as the dominant class and their position comes to be challenged.

Neither Marx nor Engels gave up either of these themes in favour of the other, not even, as they grew older and wiser, the less in favour of the more plausible of the two. Rather, they turned from the one to the other, as best suited their purpose at the time. And it never occurred to them to combine the two by constructing a theory to explain how ideas of freedom and equality changed gradually as they were used first by one class and then by another, or as they were used first to challenge one social order and then to justify the order that came after it, and later still to challenge that second order. To have produced such a theory, they would have needed to be more discriminating in their accounts of ideas and practices than they in fact were. They would have needed to show how ideas of freedom and equality used to challenge irresponsible authority and class oppression are misconceived by a class which uses them to substitute one form of class oppression for another, and come to be properly understood only when the challenge to class oppression and irresponsible authority is made by a class whose interest it is to put an end to this oppression and to this kind of authority. They would have had to explain what it is to 'misconceive' ideas and how such 'misconceptions' are corrected by experience. But this they never did; or never in sufficient detail to make their meaning plain.

If bourgeois ideas of freedom and equality are merely bourgeois, if they serve bourgeois interests alone, if they have to be discarded altogether by the class that challenges the bourgeois, it is not easy to see why there should be any element of false consciousness about them. Why should merely bourgeois ideas of freedom and equality not be fully realized in bourgeois society, and why should not the bourgeois see clearly that they are realized? Surely, it is only to the extent that the bourgeois have ideas of freedom and equality which are not merely bourgeois, not merely suited to their interests, that they need to delude themselves into believing that in bourgeois society these ideas are realized. The ideas must have implications which the bourgeois cannot afford to see if they are to have the illusions that Marx and Engels say they have about the society they dominate. But if these ideas have these implications, they cannot be merely bourgeois ideas. There are signs that Marx and Engels were at times aware of this, though not sufficiently so to be moved to produce a more subtle, realistic, and clear account of bourgeois political ideas and political practices as forms of false consciousness.

It is above all in *The Eighteenth Brumaire of Louis Bonaparte* that Marx recognizes, at least by implication, that liberty even in bourgeois society is not a merely bourgeois idea. Speaking of the Constitution of 1848 made by the Republicans in France, he says that

[it] constantly refers to future organic laws which are to . . . regulate the enjoyment of these unrestricted liberties in such a manner that they will collide neither with one another nor with the public safety. And later, these organic laws were brought into being by the friends of order and all those liberties regulated in such manner that the bourgeoisie in its enjoyment of them finds itself uninhibited by the equal rights of the other classes . . . this always happens in the interest of public safety, that is, the safety of the bourgeoisie . . . For each paragraph of the Constitution contains its own antithesis . . . namely, liberty in the general phrase, abrogation of liberty in the marginal note.[17]

It is the abrogations of liberty 'in the marginal notes' which are in the interests of the bourgeoisie, and not liberty 'in the general phrase'. Or, alternatively, it is the interest of the bourgeois to proclaim liberty and also to restrict it in certain ways. But, even on this interpretation, it is the restrictions on liberty rather than liberty itself which are exclusively a bourgeois interest.

Further on in this same pamphlet, Marx recognizes that the ideas of liberty and democracy, which the bourgeois proclaim, can be used against them. 'The bourgeoisie', he says, 'had a true insight into the fact that all the weapons it had forged against feudalism turned . . . their points against itself. . . . It understood that all the so-called bourgeois liberties . . . menaced its class rule at its social foundations and its political summit simultaneously, and had therefore become "socialistic".'[18] By the solid foundations Marx means in this context the system of property, and by the political summit the modern state in its parliamentary form. The 'so-called bourgeois liberties' threaten, not only bourgeois control of the state, but also the forms of property on which bourgeois social ascendancy rests. Marx goes on to say: 'The parliamentary regime lives by discussion; how shall it forbid discussion? . . . [It] leaves everything to the decision of majorities; how shall the great majorities outside parliament not want to decide? When you play the fiddle at the top of the state, what else is to be expected but that those down below dance?'[19] Marx then concludes that parliamentary government is a luxury the bourgeois can no longer afford. To keep their social power intact they need another kind of government which reduces their class to what he calls 'political nullity'. The government that Marx has in mind here is the kind of popular autocracy set up by Louis Bonaparte, who made a cipher of parliament and who restricted what Marx calls 'the bourgeois liberties' much more drastically than the Constitution of 1848 had done. This government, since it reduced the bourgeois to 'political nullity', was presumably not an organ or instrument of their class rule, and yet, so we are told, it maintained the social

---

[17] Marx–Engels, *Selected Works*, i. 236.   [18] Ibid. i. 260.   [19] Ibid. i. 261.

order on which their predominance, their superior status, and their ability to exploit rested.

Indeed, if we follow up the implications of what Marx says we must conclude that Louis Bonaparte saved the bourgeois from themselves. For they resisted his attempts to destroy the parliamentary system. They failed to recognize that ideas of freedom, equality, and responsible government, which they had used in the past in their own class interest, could now be used against them. Their attitude to these ideas, and to the practices supposed to implement them, was therefore ambiguous; they wanted both to cling to them and to restrict them in ways acceptable to themselves but not to other classes who would see in these restrictions betrayals of freedom and democracy. Louis Bonaparte, to be sure, was not concerned to save the bourgeois from the consequences of their blindness. He did not, any more than they did, see how the liberties they proclaimed might be dangerous to them. He merely took advantage of the mistakes they made to get power for himself, and in doing so destroyed liberties which they could neither renounce nor use effectively to preserve their social dominance and their class rule.

In *Anti-Dühring* Engels makes what is substantially the same point, though he applies it only to the idea of equality. He says there that, as soon as the burghers of the Middle Ages were transformed into the bourgeois of our era, as soon as this medieval estate became a class of modern society, the proletariat, the 'shadow' of the bourgeoisie, came also into being. Quick upon the heels of the bourgeois demand for equality came the demand for it of the workers. The workers, if we are to believe Engels, took the bourgeois at their word by insisting that 'equality must not be merely apparent, must not apply merely to the sphere of the State, but must also be real, must be extended to the social and economic sphere'.[20] Engels then goes on to say that 'the real content of the proletarian demand for equality is the demand for the abolition of all classes'.[21] The bourgeois, when they pressed for equality, converted a society divided into estates into one divided into classes, whereas the workers, when they press for it, will convert a class society into a society without classes.

Engels might have said that the bourgeois and the workers were using the same word to refer to quite different things. But in the passage I have quoted, he does not say this. On the contrary, he makes a distinction between apparent equality and the real thing; and so implies that the bourgeois and the workers share an idea which the workers take seriously in a way that the bourgeois do not. If equality, as the bourgeois conceive of it, were different from the workers' conception of it, then the bourgeois could establish it fully, even though the workers were left unsatisfied. But, in that case, the equality established by them would be real and not

[20] Engels, *Anti-Dühring*, Emile Burns's translation, p. 120.   [21] Ibid., p. 121.

apparent. Its leaving the workers unsatisfied would not be evidence of its not being really but only apparently established. Engels's argument, in this particular passage, is pointless unless there is an idea of equality shared by two classes; an idea that comes to be used against the class that first proclaimed it and in the process comes to be more fully understood. The bourgeois used the idea in the first place to loosen the hold of feudal restrictions, not only on themselves, but on other classes; it was their interest to use it for this purpose. In that sense the idea was originally theirs, a bourgeois idea. But that purpose once achieved, it soon became evident that the idea had practical implications they had not foreseen and could not afford to admit; that it could be used to attack the social foundations on which their predominance rested just as they had used it to attack feudalism.

The idea of equality that Engels has in mind is presumably abstract. It does not refer to rights or opportunities actually enjoyed in a particular type of society, for it is used to challenge existing legal and customary rights. It is a principle which those who proclaim it justify by pointing to capacities and needs that all men have. The fact that the bourgeois apply it only in the political sphere, and not also in the economic, does not make it a different principle from what it is when the workers apply it, or insist that it should be applied, to the economic sphere as well. Though it is the interest of the bourgeois to apply it only to one sphere, it in fact applies to both. Indeed, Engels goes further than this. When he speaks of 'the withering away of the state', he suggests that applying the principle in the economic sphere causes the political sphere, or at least certain aspects of it, to disappear. He also, of course, as all Marxists do, suggests that political equality is not genuine while there is no equality in the economic sphere; or, in other words, he suggests that the principle cannot be applied to the political sphere alone.

What is it then, if we accept these suggestions, that is illusory about the 'bourgeois' idea of equality? Clearly, it is not the general principle. For the principle, though general, is not vacuous; it can be applied. It can be used effectively to challenge established institutions and to set up others in their place. The bourgeois are victims of illusion, not because they put forward a vacuous principle under the impression that it has practical consequences of the greatest importance, but because they cannot afford to see that it applies much more broadly than they want to apply it, and that it cannot be applied effectively within the narrow limits acceptable to them. They cannot afford to apply the principle consistently because it is against their class interest that it should be so applied, and their false consciousness is revealed, not in their proclaiming the principle, but in their belief that in bourgeois society it is applied consistently.

In the *Eighteenth Brumaire of Louis Bonaparte* Marx argued that it was the class interest of the bourgeois that parliamentary government should be abolished and a popular autocracy set up in its place. He was writing about France, and it may be that he had only the French bourgeois in mind. If he had been asked whether his argument applied equally to the bourgeois in England, he might have denied that it did. And yet the argument comes unexpectedly from the man who in *The Communist Manifesto* had said that the 'executive of the modern state is but a committee for managing the common affairs of the whole bourgeoisie', who repeatedly called the state an organ or instrument of class rule, and who even suggested that parliamentary government is the form best adapted to bourgeois political supremacy. Or, rather, the argument would come unexpectedly to anyone not aware of how little Marx, when he assessed particular situations, allowed himself to be inhibited by his own generalizations and definitions.

If we look closely at Marx's argument, we see that it was not so much parliamentary government as parliamentary democracy that had become dangerous to the bourgeois in France. Under the July monarchy, there had been a restricted franchise, and political power had belonged effectively to the wealthier sections of the middle class. But this had left the poorer sections of the class unrepresented. The February revolution of 1848 which brought down the July monarchy was the work of the radicals among the lesser bourgeoisie as well as of the Paris workers. They demanded and obtained what was then called 'universal suffrage'—or, as we should put it, manhood suffrage. The result was to bring out more sharply than ever before the differences of interest and attitude that separated the groups that Marx called *bourgeois*, as well as the differences that separated these groups from the workers. 'Universal suffrage' also gave the vote to the peasants,[22] a class whose support was essential to Louis Napoleon in his endeavours to get power by playing various groups and parties off against one another. Under the Second Republic the political situation in France soon became very different from what it had been on the eve of the July revolution,

[22] Though Marx spoke of the peasants as a section of the bourgeoisie, he was well aware (as *The Eighteenth Brumaire* proves) that their interests and sentiments differed greatly from those of the bourgeois in the towns. He saw them under the Second Republic as a politically in-experienced and unstable class. Despite their attachment to the land they owned (which is presumably what moved him to speak of them as bourgeois) they were getting, in some parts of France, heavily into debt. Though they mistrusted the radicals in the towns, they also hated their creditors, the 'rich men' to whom so many of them had mortgaged their farms. They were thus, in Marx's eyes, a class that could be 'radicalized' as well as a class whose resentments and fears a political adventurer like Louis Bonaparte could exploit against both the radicals and the wealthier bourgeois.

It is with the spread of Marxist ideas that political writers, especially outside France, have taken to calling the peasants 'bourgeois'. In France in Marx's day the 'bourgeois' were well-to-do town-dwellers or, more generally, groups socially intermediate between the nobles and the manual workers, urban and rural. The term 'the people' was quite often used in a sense that excluded the bourgeois, or the more wealthy of them, as well as the nobles. Calling the peasants 'bourgeois', though useful in some contexts, is misleading in others. It is a pity, perhaps, that an example set by Marx and by others should now be so widely followed.

and it would scarcely have been possible to abolish universal suffrage and to revert to the restricted franchise of the July monarchy. Political conflicts dangerous to bourgeois interests could therefore be brought to an end only by some such methods as Louis Napoleon used to get personal power; only by abolishing parliamentary government altogether by a *coup d'état* ratified by a popular vote, a plebiscite in which the peasants, the bulk of the people, could be relied upon to support the destroyer of the constitution. In France at least, a liberal parliamentary regime had ceased to be useful to the bourgeois because it had become democratic. Popular Caesarism suited them better.

But Marx did not hold consistently to the belief, expressed in *The Eighteenth Brumaire*, that parliamentary democracy is against the class interest of the bourgeois, and Engels went further than he did in rejecting it. Though, as we shall see in a moment, even he did not reject it altogether. Indeed he revived it in a rather different form.

After the fall of the Second Empire, it seemed that in the West the future lay with democracy, or with what we have learned to call liberal democracy. This impression was strengthened by the growing power and wealth of the United States, and by the broadening of the franchise in Britain, first in 1867 and then in 1884. Bourgeois predominance, so it appeared, could survive both 'universal suffrage' and 'free elections', and capitalism fare none the worse for them. Clearly, there was no need to abolish 'the bourgeois liberties', and it was even possible to make some of the worst excesses of capitalism illegal without danger to the propertied classes. Circumstances peculiar to France had enabled Louis Napoleon to establish his personal rule. But in the oldest and largest of the bourgeois democracies, the United States, the constitution was venerated (even though not always obeyed) to the last syllable, and there was no getting power in the streets of Washington by the methods of the Bonapartes. Nevertheless—so Engels tells his readers in 1891, in an introduction he wrote for a reprint of Marx's *Civil War in France*—

it is precisely in America that we best see how there takes place this process of the state power making itself independent of society, whose mere instrument it was originally intended to be . . . We find here two great gangs of political speculators, who alternately take possession of the state power and exploit it, by the most corrupt means and for the most corrupt ends—and the nation is powerless against these two cartels of politicians, who are ostensibly its servants, but in reality dominate and plunder it.[23]

All this happens though there is universal suffrage, and two parties compete for power, and the constitution is respected, at least outwardly.

[23] From Engels's Introduction to the 1891 edition of Marx's *Civil War in France*. See Lewis Feuer's *Marx and Engels: Basic Writings on Politics and Philosophy* (Anchor Books, New York, 1959), pp. 360–1.

What Engels offers us here is an image of a whole people plundered by their rulers, and not of one class exploited by another. Yet this plunder, as Engels describes it, does not exclude class exploitation; it is one more evil added to the evil of class exploitation, though presumably an evil from which the exploiting class suffers as well as the exploited. Nor are the two evils unconnected. Engels does not explain the connection on this occasion, but it is easy to see what it must be, given the Marxist account of the state. If society were not divided into classes, of which some exploit others, there would be no state, and if there were no state, the kind of plunder of a whole people that Engels describes would be impossible. Though the description he gives of the American system implies that the bourgeois are not actually the ruling class—for 'the state power' is said to be 'independent of society' and to exploit it—he is still willing, even in this introduction, to respect the old formula that 'the state is nothing but a machine for the oppression of one class by another . . . in the democratic republic no less than in the monarchy'.[24] Engels was pathetically loyal to the old familiar phrase, even on occasions when it was quite inappropriate. He would have done better to say that the state still protected a system of property enabling some classes to exploit others, even though it had become a democratic republic with rival groups competing for power and using it, when they get it, to plunder all classes.

This image of political plunder superimposed on class exploitation does not, however, give us the whole of Engels's mature thought about liberal democracy. In *The Origins of the Family, Private Property and the State*, first published in 1884, he says that the democratic republic is the 'highest form of the State', the form inevitable in our modern conditions (that is to say, the conditions in the capitalist West in the 1880s), the form 'in which alone the last decisive struggle between proletariat and bourgeoisie can be fought out'. He then goes on to say:

In it wealth exercises its power indirectly, but all the more surely. On the one hand, in the form of the direct corruption of officials . . . on the other, in the form of an alliance between government and Stock Exchange . . . But that a democratic republic is not essential for this fraternal alliance . . . is proved by England and also by the new German Empire, where one cannot tell who was elevated more by universal suffrage, Bismarck or Bleichroder [Bismarck's man of business]. And, lastly, the possessing class rules directly through the medium of universal suffrage. As long as the oppressed class . . . the proletariat, is not yet ready to emancipate itself, it will form the tail of the capitalist class, its extreme left wing. To the extent, however, that this class matures for its self-emancipation, it constitutes . . . its own party and elects its own representatives, and not those of the capitalists. Thus universal suffrage is the gauge of the maturity of the working class. . . . On the day the thermometer of universal suffrage registers boiling point among the workers, both they and the capitalists will know what to do.[25]

We have here a medley of ill-assorted and even contradictory ideas. We are told first that in a democracy the wealthy exercise power the more surely for exercising it indirectly, and then later that the possessing class rule directly 'through the medium of universal suffrage'. Are not the wealthy also the possessing class? If they are (and it is reasonable to suppose that they are), how can they exercise power *indirectly* and yet also rule *directly*? No doubt, some of them could do the first and others the second, but it is unlikely that this is what Engels had in mind. And why should any of them bother to rule directly seeing that power is exercised the more surely for being exercised indirectly? Why should they not all prefer to bribe officials rather than compete for office? How, in this highest form of the state in which the wealthy fight (and lose) the last decisive struggle with the workers, do they also contrive to exercise power *the more surely*? Is there an early period when they exercise it quietly and easily, followed by a later period of conflict when the workers challenge their ascendancy? Are there years when the workers use their votes to give power to the wealthy followed by years when they use them to support parties of their own to attack 'the possessing class' on the political front? But why, while the workers are politically quiescent, give them the vote in the first place? Why not let sleeping dogs lie? Why stimulate their interest in politics by giving them votes which conceivably they could use against the bourgeois?

Engels provides no answers to such questions as these. He was not a careful reasoner, even at his best, and he was far from his best when he wrote *The Origins of the Family, Private Property and the State*. We have here a combination of several Marxist themes: that the state is an instrument of class oppression, that it is a *condition* of this oppression even when it is not literally an instrument of it, that the state is not in fact what those who run it believe that it is or claim it to be, and that the workers nevertheless cannot throw off this oppression except by taking political action. Though Engels fails to explain why the bourgeois cannot maintain their ascendancy without conceding 'universal suffrage', it follows from his description of the democratic state that it is not what its champions say it is. For if their claims for it were true, there would be no oppression of class by class inside it; but this, so Engels says, there assuredly is. Therefore 'the democratic republic' or, as present-day Marxists would call it, 'bourgeois democracy' thrives, not just on ignorance, but on illusion as well. In it both rulers and ruled are afflicted with a false consciousness.

Yet this is not the whole of Engels's verdict on it, any more than it was

[25] Engels, *The Origins of the Family, Private Property and the State*, in Marx–Engels, *Selected Works*, ii. 291.

the whole of Marx's verdict on the Second Republic. For this democracy, which is the scene of the last decisive struggle between the bourgeois and the workers, also creates the conditions in which false consciousness is dissipated. It is the system in which the workers reach political maturity and come at last to recognize that it is the interest of their class to put an end to the capitalist economy, which it must do by first getting political control of society. It is also the system in which the workers achieve and maintain the class solidarity essential to their getting power. The system enables them to develop into a class able and willing to control society, even though it remains a condition of their being oppressed or exploited by the bourgeois. In the bourgeois state the workers gain the experience which moves them in the end to reject the myth of that state, its ideology. And, presumably, this myth wears thin among the bourgeois as well, as their ascendancy comes to be more and more openly challenged. Why else should they resort, as Engels says they do, to competition? How can they buy what would not be for sale if democracy were really what it purported to be, and still keep their faith in the system? Corruption and cynicism go inevitably together. Oppressors retain their illusions about a system which allows oppression only as long as their victims also retain them. For if the victims reject the illusions and attack the system, it can no longer be defended by relatively mild and 'honest' methods in keeping with the illusions; it must be defended by methods which weaken the illusions (if they do not altogether destroy them) among both oppressors and oppressed. The language of illusion, the jargon of democracy, may survive among the cynical who affect to practise democracy, just as the prostitute may speak of love when she means only business; but the illusion is shattered none the less.

Though Marx and Engels often speak as if the state would disappear, presumably for sheer lack of anything to do, with the disappearance of classes, they also say things which make this conclusion seem doubtful. Again and again, they speak of the state making itself 'independent of society', or of its arising in the first place to protect common interests and then becoming an instrument of oppression or exploitation. Its becoming 'independent of society' does not preclude its continuing to be a condition of class exploitation, though it may add another form of oppression to mere class exploitation. The state's being a parasite on society is not the same thing as the propertied classes being parasites on the working class. So, too, the economic conditions which create the common interests that need a state to protect them may also create the property relations that enable one class to exploit another, so that the state acquires a second function in addition to the one it had from the beginning. It helps to maintain the conditions of class exploitation as well as to protect common interests. This second function, so Marx and Engels seem to imply, soon becomes more important in practice than the first, though ideology serves to hide it, or to draw away attention from it, by insisting that the first is the true function.

Even if we accept this account of the state, it still has to be explained why, with the disappearance of classes, the state should disappear. If it arose to protect common interests as well as to maintain the social conditions of class exploitation, why should there not still be a need for it to perform this first function when there is no longer a need for it to perform the second? That the second function in practice takes precedence over the first in a class society, and even prevents its being performed adequately, is no reason for holding that when the second function becomes superfluous, the first does so too. What Marx and Engels say about the origins and the functions of the state does not justify their predicting its disappearance. To justify their prediction they would have to show *either* that the state never has protected any common interests but has only pretended to do so, *or* that social and cultural conditions have changed so much since the state first arose that there is now no need of it to protect these interests. But they do neither of these things. On the contrary, when they discuss the origins of the state (which Engels does more often than Marx) they admit that it arose, at least partly, to protect common interests. What is more, their attack on it as a sham derives most of its force from the suggestion that there are such interests to be protected, which it fails to protect while pretending to do so. It needs to make this pretence to be able to perform effectively its other function of maintaining the conditions of class exploitation.

What are we to understand by the state 'becoming independent of society'? It could mean, perhaps, its ceasing to protect common interests and its promoting the special interests of an exploiting class. Or it could mean the rulers ceasing to be responsible to their subjects generally and their being responsible only to an exploiting class. Marx and Engels may sometimes have had one or other (or both) of these two things in mind when they used this strange formula. But they appear also to have meant by it something different: namely, rulers ceasing to be responsible to any class in society and their coming to have interests of their own to which, if need be, they sacrifice the interests of all classes. It is when this happens that the state is a parasite on society.

But there is an ambiguity at this point in their thinking about the state. They seem to vacillate between two conceptions of it: between the idea of it as necessarily parasitic by definition, and the idea of it as liable to become a parasite. For example, in a letter written in 1890 to Conrad Schmidt, Engels says: 'Society gives rise to certain common functions which it cannot dispense with. The persons selected for these functions form a new branch of the division of labour within society'. This, you might think, refers to the origins of the state and indicates what it is; it arises to carry out certain indispensable functions, and it consists of the persons selected to carry them out, or rather of the structure of relations between them and the rest of the community. But Engels goes on: 'This gives them (that is, the persons selected to carry out these functions) particular interests, distinct too from the interests of those who gave them their office; they make themselves independent of the latter and—the state is in being'.[26] These last sentences suggest that the state proper comes into existence only when the persons whose office it is to carry out these indispensable functions acquire special interests of their own and become independent of the rest of the community—that is, presumably, cease to be responsible to them.

There is nothing peculiarly Marxist about the suggestion that persons appointed to carry out indispensable functions on behalf of a community are apt to become irresponsible and to acquire interests of their own distinct from those of the rest of the community. It is a theme as old as political theory. What is odd and Marxist about the argument of Engels is the suggestion that these persons, if they really were responsible to the community and did carry out their functions properly, would not be exercising political authority; for this is what is implied by his saying that the state comes into being when they become 'independent' and acquire interests peculiar to themselves. This, of course, is only a suggestion; it is not a position that Engels takes up boldly and unequivocally, even in this letter to Conrad Schmidt. And, in any case, it goes against the account he gives in both *Anti-Dühring* and *The Origins of the Family, Private Property and the State* of how the state arises.

The truth is that Marx and Engels make so many and such disparate assertions about the state that they often leave their readers in doubt as to what it is they have in mind when they speak of it. This is especially true of Engels, if only because he has so much more to say about it than Marx has. Sometimes they speak of it as if it consisted in the exercise of a certain type of authority by persons whose recognized function is to exercise it, which is to speak of it as most people do; sometimes they speak of it as if it consisted in the exercise of this type of authority for certain purposes other than those which are officially recognized; and sometimes they suggest that, if it were not exercised for these purposes, it would be very different from what it is—but just how different they do not say. Their references to the state are too often equivocal and evasive or simple-minded.

In an article on *Authority*, first published in an Italian translation in 1874, and no doubt aimed at the anarchists in Italy, Engels writes:

[26] Engels to Conrad Schmidt, London, 27 Oct. 1890—*Selected Correspondence of Marx and Engels*, transl. by Dona Torr (International Publishers, N.Y., 1942), p. 480.

'Everywhere combined action, the complication of processes dependent on each other, displaces independent action by individuals. But whoever mentions combined action speaks of organization; now is it possible to have organization without authority?'[27] He says also that 'wanting to abolish authority in large-scale industry is tantamount to wanting to abolish industry itself, to destroy the power loom in order to return to the spinning wheel'.[28] He then makes this comment:

> When I submitted arguments like these to the most rabid anti-authoritarians, the only answer they were able to give was the following: Yes, that's true, but here it is not a question of authority which we confer on our delegates, but of a commission entrusted! These gentlemen think that when they have changed the names of things they have changed the things themselves. . . . Hence it is absurd to speak of the principle of authority as being absolutely evil and of the principle of autonomy as being absolutely good. Authority and autonomy are relative things, whose spheres vary with the various phases in the development of society.[29]

This makes good enough sense, though it only recognizes a problem without contributing to its solution. It is a problem as important in the political as in the economic sphere. There are, as Engel admits on many occasions, services which a technically and culturally advanced society must provide for itself, services which are not economic, as that word is ordinarily used, but administrative and judicial or—as people with no special motive for avoiding the word say—*political*. The more advanced a society, the more complicated, presumably, these services are, and the greater the need to ensure that the persons who provide them are competent to do so. The problem of reconciling 'authority' with 'autonomy' (or, alternatively, of ensuring that those who exercise authority are responsible to their 'subjects') is every bit as difficult and complicated in the 'political' sphere as in the 'economic'.

Yet Engels, almost perversely, refuses to admit this. For he says in this same article:

> All socialists are agreed that the political state, and with it political authority, will disappear as the result of the coming socialist revolution; that is, the public functions will lose their political character and be transformed into the *simple* administrative functions of watching over the true interests of society. But the anti-authoritarians demand that the authoritarian political state be abolished at one stroke, even before the social conditions that gave birth to it have been destroyed.[30]

For Engels, of course, with his odd use of words, authority ceasing to be political means that it ceases to be used to maintain the conditions of class

---

[27] *On Authority*, by F. Engels, from *Marx and Engels. Basic Writings on Politics and Philosophy*, ed. by Feuer, p. 482.

[28] Ibid., p. 483.   [29] Ibid., p. 484.   [30] Ibid., p. 485. My italics.

exploitation. But why should he assume that the business of looking after common or widely shared interests must be *simple* in a classless society? Why should it not be highly complicated and call for special gifts, training, and experience in those who do it? And if it is complicated and difficult, the problem of ensuring that the persons who do it are responsible to the community, and do not become a privileged group parasitic on it, still remains. Might we not say of Engels what he says of his 'rabid anti-authoritarians': 'This gentleman thinks that when he has changed the name of a thing he has changed the thing itself'?

Might we not say it also of Marx? In his *Critique of the Gotha Programme* he argues that the idea of right, which he takes to be essentially a bourgeois notion, will survive for a time after the workers have taken over control of society. For society will still, economically, morally, and intellectually, bear the marks of the old bourgeois order out of which it arose. Speaking of early communist society before it has outgrown the idea of right altogether, he says:

> This equal right is an unequal right for unequal labour. It recognizes no class differences, because everyone is only a worker like everyone else; but it tacitly recognizes unequal individual endowment . . . It is, therefore, a right of in-equality, in its content, like every right. Right by its very nature can consist only in the application of an equal standard; but unequal individuals (and they would not be different individuals if they were not unequal) are measurable only by an equal standard in so far as they . . . are taken from one definite side only, for instance, in the present case, are regarded only as workers . . .[31]

In this early phase of communist society the principle of distribution, as Lenin was to observe in commenting on this argument of Marx's, is *to everyone according to his contribution*; and this principle still carries with it the idea of right.

At a later stage things are different. As Marx puts it:

> In a higher phase of communist society, after the enslaving subordination of the individual to the division of labour, and therewith also the antithesis be-tween mental and physical labour, has vanished; after labour has become not only a means of life but life's prime want; after the productive forces have also increased with the all-round development of the individual, and all the springs of co-operative wealth flow more abundantly—only then can the narrow horizon of bourgeois right be crossed in its entirety and society inscribe on its banners: 'From each according to his ability, to each according to his needs!'[32]

Notice that sometimes Marx speaks of bourgeois right and sometimes of right quite generally. If he had spoken only of bourgeois right, we might reasonably conclude that some other, in his opinion higher, forms of right would eventually take the place of the bourgeois forms of it. But he

[31] Marx–Engels, *Selected Works*, ii. 22.   [32] Ibid., p. 23.

does not do this; he suggests rather that the very idea of right is somehow bourgeois, or at least that, with the disappearance of the last traces of bourgeois ways of thinking and behaving, society will be able to dispense altogether with the idea of right.

Yet the principle which he attributes to communist society 'in its higher phase' no more allows us to dispense with the idea of right than does the principle 'to everyone according to his contribution'. It too is a distributive principle difficult to apply, and the community which adopts it has the obligation to ensure that it is justly applied. It must devise criteria for assessing needs, and must allow people to claim what they think they need, and must provide methods for deciding on their claims. A highly authoritarian community might, of course, not allow people to make claims and might leave it to officials to ensure that their needs were assessed and satisfied. But Marx's communist society is not authoritarian; and, in any case, an authoritarian society which did not allow people to make claims could adopt the principle, *to everyone according to his contribution*, just as easily as the principle, *to everyone according to his needs*. The notion of *right* is no more and no less tied logically to the first principle than to the second. Nor is it obvious that the business of applying the second principle is simpler than the business of applying the first. Communist society in its higher phase might need to develop highly sophisticated and elaborate procedures to ensure that needs were correctly assessed and adequately and fairly satisfied. Why should we suppose that a fuller (or more all-round) development of the individual and a more abundant production of wealth would of themselves simplify the business of putting into effect the principle, *to each according to his needs*? Surely, we should suppose the contrary: that the more developed and sophisticated men and women are, and the more diversely and abundantly productive society is, the less simple this business of providing adequately for human needs. And the less simple, too, the business of ensuring that each contributes according to his ability.

This is so, not merely because men are lazy and greedy, and so cannot be relied upon to be just, to contribute according to their ability, or to claim only what they need; it is so also, and above all, because abilities and needs have to be assessed authoritatively, if people are to know what is expected of them and what they can expect from others. The more diverse these abilities and needs, the more quickly they change in a 'progressive' society in which methods of production, wants, and aspirations are never for long the same, the more complicated this business of assessment. But Marx distrusted authority, especially when the exercise of it is elaborate and highly organized, and he therefore persuaded himself— or rather half persuaded himself—that there would be little need for it in the communist society. He denounced it and called it 'political', and suggested that men would be able to do without it as soon as they got rid of class exploitation.

There are, of course, excellent reasons for distrusting it, and some of them are to be found in the pages of Marx and Engels. But there are also good reasons for holding that in industrial societies it is indispensable, not only for the sake of order, but also as a condition of achieving freedom and equality. I shall discuss some of these reasons in a later chapter in which I shall be concerned more with general issues and less with the arguments of Marx or Engels.

THE RADICAL'S DILEMMA IN INDUSTRIAL SOCIETY

PREFACE TO PART THREE

IN the first two parts of this book I have been concerned above all with the ideas and arguments of Marx, though to some extent also with those of Engels. In my endeavours to explain their meaning or to point out where their thinking is confused or inadequate, I have made distinctions that they never made and have put and tried to answer questions they never put. Any critical examination of a theory or of a set of beliefs is necessarily an attempt to pass beyond it, and is the more so the more critical it is. I could not explain what seemed to me defective in the arguments of Marx and Engels without raising issues they did not raise.

In this third part I want to discuss questions that moralists and students of society have been trying to formulate and to answer, not only since Marx's time but before it, and I want to discuss them without particular reference to the beliefs of Marx. They are, of course, questions that interested Marx, or are closely related to questions that did interest him. But they are not exclusively 'Marxist' questions, and they are worth considering in a larger context than the mere study of Marxism provides. They are questions about man in society, about his needs and aspirations as a social being, and about the conditions in which these needs and aspirations arise or can be satisfied. They are also questions about the human condition in economically advanced societies which are changing fast and are consciously 'progressive', and the assumption behind the questions is that the conditions giving rise to these needs and aspirations may prevent their being satisfied. My purpose in this part of the book is not to answer these questions but to inquire what sort of questions they are, to consider some of the ambiguities concealed in ordinary ways of putting them, and to suggest how they might be put more clearly or be so formulated that they could be answered.

Marx, though he was a penetrating and suggestive thinker, was also unusually obscure and confusing. Like Rousseau, he understood more than he was able to put clearly into words. But, much more than Rousseau, he has had disciples who have treated his writings as sacred texts, and who have engaged in controversies about them unintelligible to others and perhaps also to themselves. They have not examined his assumptions and arguments critically, and have even resented their being examined in that spirit by others. Rightly so, no doubt, from their point of view, for this kind of examination not only reveals how shoddy and careless Marx could sometimes be but also makes nonsense of some of their favourite controversies. When hitherto unpublished texts see the light of day, they look to them, not for arguments that can throw light on real issues that Marx raised about the human condition and the course of social change, but for quotations they can use to prolong the sterile discussions in which they delight. Today there are Marxist scholars searching the *Grundrisse* for fresh clues as to how Marx conceived of 'social existence' in relation to 'consciousness' or of the 'relations of production' or of 'alienated labour' who have only the scantiest notions of what is at issue. They have read and reread the sacred texts, and are familiar with them, and yet it seems not to occur to them that they cannot achieve their purpose unless they put themselves to the trouble of examining Marx's arguments critically. It is not enough to repeat them or to elaborate upon them in Marx's own idiom; it is necessary to spell out the assumptions on which they rest, to scrutinize the concepts they use, and to see what conclusions follow from them. This is what I have tried to do in the first two parts of the book.

But even this is not enough. For Marx is an oppressive writer, and anyone who has wrestled with his arguments in the hope of understanding them is apt to feel the need to get clear of them, and to consider some of the important issues he raised (or others related to them) apart from his arguments. After all, Marx was only one thinker among others who raised these issues, and his ways of raising them are not necessarily the best. Though Marx, for all his faults, was very much alive as a thinker, there is now—thanks largely to the efforts of his disciples—a dead weight of Marxist theory which is an obstacle to clear thinking about the questions he put or tried to put. Not that the fault lies entirely with his disciples. He could, as the now much admired *Grundrisse* proves, write a great deal and say very little, repeating himself over and over again. Sometimes he was a deep thinker, but at other times he buried deep in words thoughts which turn out to be shallow enough, if not empty, when they are excavated.

Perhaps the greatest advantage to considering questions that Marx and other socialist and anarchist writers put apart from what Marx had to say about them is that it then becomes easier to put them in simple terms without appearing to treat a great thinker disrespectfully. It is above all this advantage that I have sought in this last part of my book. Removed from the shadow of Marxist theory I find that I can see more clearly some perhaps rather obvious things which are too often neglected.

Since the French Revolution two sorts of questions have occupied the minds of moralists and social theorists. The first sort have to do with the individual conceived as a social being who seeks what he may not find in society and who yet would not be the seeker he is if he were not a social being. The first great writer to put questions of this sort—or at least to make much of them—was Rousseau. As the understanding of what man 'owes' to society deepened, so the claims made on society on behalf of the individual increased. No writer before Rousseau went as far as he did in depicting man as essentially a social being whose distinctively human capacities and needs are products of social intercourse. And yet none was more hostile to the established order. Not that he was a revolutionary who advocated its violent overthrow, but he did see it as an unjust order in which the rich exploit the poor and the essential needs of man as a social and moral being are not met.

Questions of the other sort have to do with social groups and categories, with their divergent interests and beliefs, and with conflicts between them. Rousseau did not neglect them, but they came to the fore after his time, during the French Revolution and especially after it, when reflections about the revolution and its causes began to affect social theory. Perhaps the first social thinker to put social groups, their interests and 'ideologies', and conflicts between them, at the centre of his social theory, and in particular of his account of the course of social change, was Saint-Simon.

Hegel was concerned more with questions of the first sort than the second. But, unlike Rousseau, he set his picture of man, whose seeking and finding (or failure to find) are essentially social, in a systematic and elaborate philosophical and historical context, and he affirmed a belief in progress. Marx was concerned with questions of both sorts, though he too, like Rousseau, was less systematic and less skilled at handling abstract ideas than Hegel was. Though he was by no means the only socialist writer of his time to raise both sorts of question, he was, among those who raised them, the boldest, the most imaginative, the most learned, and the most aggressive intellectually. He was not, as Rousseau was, a great writer, but he too was obsessed with the sense of his own rightness and could impose his visions on others.

Historically, these two types of question are connected. They both came to be important at about the same time. It was largely the sense that the individual is frustrated in society as it is, seeking in vain to satisfy needs born of social intercourse but which existing social forms cannot satisfy, which made class and other group conflicts seem to go deeper and to look more irreconcilable than they had done before. The idea of a social and political order that keeps conflicts between individuals within tolerable limits gave way to the idea of group conflicts whose resolution or 'transcendence' requires profound social and political changes.

Yet these two sorts of question need not be connected. Of course, logically, they are separate questions, and nobody has ever supposed otherwise. But it is often taken for granted that they are in fact closely connected because they both arise out of the same social conditions and refer to problems that cannot be solved separately. But this may not be so always. Could there not be forms of society and culture in which the individual is deeply frustrated, in the sense that he acquires needs that he cannot satisfy, even though there are no deep-seated and irreconcilable group or class conflicts? Can we take it for granted, as so many socialist and anarchist thinkers have done, that in removing the social causes of group conflict and exploitation we also remove the social causes of frustration, apathy, and despair? So, too, we can ask: Could there not be societies in which group conflicts were hard fought and keen, and yet individuals were not deeply frustrated?

This second possibility may seem more remote than the first. After all, we can easily imagine a society in which people are unhappy but also so apathetic as to have no stomach for fierce conflicts. But if there are social groups in sharp and sustained conflict with one another, must not their interests differ so greatly that the conflicts will continue until society is radically transformed? And if that is the case, must not the individuals belonging to the groups whose interest it is that society should be transformed be deeply frustrated?

I agree that if we give an affirmative answer to the first of these questions, we should give one also to the second. But need we give an affirmative answer to the first question? Can we take it for granted that wherever there are fierce and sustained conflicts between social groups, the conflicts are always such that they cannot be brought to an end except by a drastic transformation of the established order? I suggest that we ought not to do so. Social groups in keen and sustained conflict with one another need not have widely divergent interests nor widely different ideas about how society should be organized.

I suggest also that when this is the case—when groups in sharp conflict do not have widely divergent interests or ideologies—the conflicts between them may still be a major cause of social change. For the groups engaged in the conflicts have aims and ideals that change continually, so that over a period of time (and not necessarily a long one) big changes can result from their conflicts. We must not take it for granted that the changes that result from conflicts between groups whose interests and ideologies diverge only slightly are smaller than the changes resulting from conflicts between groups whose interests and ideologies diverge widely. Just as we must not take it for granted that between 1780 and 1880 France changed socially and culturally more than Britain did, merely because during that period she had several revolutions and Britain had none.[1]

---

[1] I am not suggesting that revolutionary groups do not make large and rapid social changes. Quite often they do, though they are ordinarily mistaken about their achievements. What results from their activities is often very different from what they intended should result from them (to the extent that they had definite intentions), and they are later tempted to redefine their aims so as to persuade themselves that what they have achieved is what they always wanted. And this is not the only illusion from which they suffer. They are also, after they have seized power, tempted to exaggerate their own contribution to bringing down the regime whose collapse gave them their opportunities. If we take the two most important revolutions of modern times, the French revolution of 1789 and the Russian revolutions of 1917, it would seem that revolutionary groups had little to do with creating the popular distrust of govern-

In this last part of the book I discuss ideas important to radical and socialist thinkers from the latter part of the eighteenth century onwards: such ideas as self-realization, the fuller development of human capacities, moral freedom, equality of opportunity, autonomy at work, the collective control of production and of social activities more generally, exploitation and treating others as ends and not only as means, social conflict, and social harmony. All these ideas are susceptible of a variety of interpretations. Though I compare the ideas of one writer with those of another when it suits my purpose, my concern is not primarily with the beliefs of particular thinkers but with ideas and arguments more generally—with the ideas and arguments used by critics of bourgeois or capitalist society to condemn it, and to suggest alternatives to it. This discussion takes up the next three chapters, and is followed by a final chapter in which I venture upon some general conclusions about the Marxism of Marx and Engels and its influence on theory and practice.

ment and the lack of self-confidence among those who governed which caused the old regime to collapse. No doubt, this distrust and loss of confidence were due in part to ideological causes, to changed beliefs and aspirations, but there is little evidence that these changes were brought about by revolutionary groups—by their propaganda, by their preparing the way, ideologically and politically, for the overthrow of the old regime and their own seizure of power.

CHAPTER XII

SELF-REALIZATION AND FREEDOM

I

MAN, says Marx, should 'revolve about himself as his own true sun'. This absorption of man in himself, or rather in his species, was no new thing when Marx wrote these words; what was new, or at least recent, was putting this forward as a precept. Man his own maker, man the discoverer of himself, who in discovering also creates: the beginnings of such ideas as these go back a long way. But what used to be buried in metaphor, in verbal gestures whose implications were not clear to those who made them, emerged into the light of day as the hold of religion grew weaker.

As has often been noticed since men first began to distinguish one type of religion from another and to inquire into their origins and effects, the more sophisticated religions, and especially the dogmatic ones, are (among other things) answers to a question that man puts to himself as soon as he ceases to take custom and tradition for sufficient guides: *How shall I live?* But to ask how I shall live is to ask also what I shall do with myself or make of myself. If I look for guidance to a God to whose commands I appeal to justify my not doing what others expect or require of me, or to order a part of my life private to me and open only to Him, I set myself up against other men, or apart from them; I claim the right to live as seems good to me, to be, or to strive to become, what I think I ought to be or wish I were.

This claim not only survives the decay of religion but grows stronger; and it has from the beginning, though those who make the claim may not notice it, a non-moral, an aesthetic, side to it. The ideal that a man sets up for himself may not be moral, or may be so only in part; it may, consciously or unconsciously, go against or go beyond commonly received ideas about what is admirable or beautiful or even worth doing and not just morally right or good. The artist who, in 'following his light', abandons or transforms old methods and ideas is just as much deciding what he shall be, what he shall make of himself, as the man who strives to live up to his idea of what God or his conscience requires of him.

Man's claim to be allowed to be himself is an old, old claim; and yet it is a claim of sophisticated man. It is, to begin with, a claim of the educated and the privileged, or rather of a few choice souls among them. The privileged have leisure, and therefore often do not need, when they make this claim, to challenge the social order. They aspire, not to change society, but to come to terms with it, to be allowed to do what they can afford to do, what they can do without invading the rights of others. Or they aspire to do what perhaps cannot be done except at great cost to themselves but is not (or is not by them admitted to be) costly to others.

Yet the claim, though an old one, has only in recent times come to have, for those who make it, democratic and egalitarian implications. In coming to have them, it has also considerably changed in character; it has become bolder and more urgent, and has acquired an air of paradox. For those who make it recognize that the social order, which they want to see transformed, is both outside and inside whoever belongs to it. It is outside him because others belong to it too, and because he must acquire ways of thinking, feeling, and behaving that have evolved independently of him if he is to belong to it; it is inside him because his sense of his own identity, his capacities, his wants, and his aspirations, even those that most distinguish him from others, emerge in him as he acquires a culture, as he grows into a social being. It is outside him because he can feel oppressed by it, and bewildered or lost or worthless inside it, and because he can set himself up against it; it is inside him because he cannot get rid of this sense of oppression or 'find himself' or regain his self-esteem except in a social order which conforms to principles that he makes his own as he becomes a social being and learns what it is to be one. It is outside him because he can strive to change it, to make it as he wishes it to be; it is inside him because in changing it, he also changes himself.

We can, of course, find traces (and more than traces) of these ideas of man as essentially a social being long before the demands for democracy and equality, as we understand them today, arose. Yet these ideas, combined in this way, are modern; they were first brought together by Rousseau, who spoke of democracy and equality as no one before him had done.

It is worth noticing that Rousseau, who was among the first to try to show in any detail how men develop the capacities peculiar to their species through activities which make social and moral beings of them, who recognized that society (at least in its earlier stages) must be the largely unforeseen and unintended product of forms of behaviour which may be voluntary and purposeful but are not consciously directed to social aims, and who urged men to control and transform society to achieve a kind of freedom which he called *moral* and defined as obedience to a law prescribed to oneself, never used such expressions as 'self-realization', 'self-fulfilment', and 'self-improvement'. He never used expressions which since his time have become popular among writers whose ideas about society and freedom are very like those he invented or brought to life again. This is not only because he used different words to say what these expressions are now used to say; it is also because he did not share some of the assumptions and hopes common to writers who use the expressions. He did not want to make some of the claims now made by these writers. He lacked their faith in progress; and though an innovator in some ways, in others he was a seeker for the irrecoverably lost.

'Self-assertion', 'self-expression', 'self-realization', 'self-fulfilment': these words were never, or scarcely ever, used before the nineteenth century; they are all new words compared with others which also mark man's preoccupation with himself, such as 'self-love', 'self-command', 'self-sufficiency', and 'self-assurance'.

These new words, minted and brought into circulation after the French Revolution, are used in several senses and their meanings overlap. And, as if these were not enough of them, others have been added by translators of German books; as for example 'self-development', 'self-affirmation', and even 'self-creativeness'. I shall not consider all these words or distinguish their various senses: I shall merely choose two of them, self-assertion and self-realization, and assign to them meanings that enable me to put a number of questions more clearly than I otherwise could, and I shall try to explain why these questions are difficult to answer or unanswerable. They are questions which have occurred to me as I have tried to understand writers who have used these new words.

What I shall call self-assertion is often called self-expression and some-times even self-affirmation, but whatever the name given to it, it is nearly always the individual (and not the species) who is said to assert or express or affirm himself. But 'self-realization', and other terms close to it in meaning, such as 'self-development', 'self-fulfilment', and 'self-creative-ness', are applied to the species as well as to the individual. Progress, as some writers speak of it, consists in the realization by mankind of human potentialities; it is the species as much as the individual that is self-creative. But I shall be speaking chiefly, if not exclusively, of the self-realization of individuals. It is difficult enough, even in this narrower connection, to make sense of the term; to decide how far it can be used to explain what men do and how they assess their behaviour. And yet to speak of the individual realizing or fulfilling himself does seem to make better sense than to speak of mankind doing so.

Though what I propose to call self-assertion is sometimes called self-expression, these two terms are not synonymous. Often, when we say of someone that he has expressed himself, we mean only that he has com-municated to others some beliefs or feelings of his. Sometimes, such beliefs or feelings 'express' his character, in the sense that they reveal what sort of person he is, even though he may not intend or know that they do so; or they reveal some attitude of his of which he may not be conscious at the time, or indeed at any time. He intends to express his feelings and beliefs, and in doing so, perhaps without intending or being aware of it, expresses himself also in other ways. Artists, since the feelings and beliefs they intentionally express are subtle and idiosyncratic, are often said to express themselves in these other ways.

What I propose to call self-assertion is something different from self-expression in any of these senses. It is the claim that a man makes that others should recognize him for what he thinks he is or aspires to be. In asserting himself, he presents himself to others, even though he does not describe himself. Also, 'self-assertion', as I here use the term, does not imply aggressiveness or lack of consideration for others. It can be aggressive or selfish, but it can also be modest, delicate, and respectful of others. I might have spoken of self-presentation rather than self-assertion, but I have preferred the shorter and the more familiar term.

If we consider what it is that has struck men, ever since they began to speculate about their species, as peculiarly human about human behaviour, we can see that there is an element of self-assertion about it; and we can see too that this element has often been recognized, even though under other names.

One peculiarity of man long admitted is his craving for power and reputation. Even the thinker who, like Hobbes, has argued that men come to want power in the first place the better to provide for their wants, has gone on to say that they soon want it for its own sake. The desire to count with others, to be recognized by them as someone whose wants and opinions matter, is supposed to be peculiar to man as a rational and therefore also self-conscious being. That the desire for power is more than wanting to be well placed to satisfy one's wants generally, and more even than just wanting to control others; that it is also, and above all, a need to impress them, to be exalted in their minds, is too obvious not to have been long noticed and long deplored.

Striving for power is only one, and the most aggressive, form of self-assertion. Another peculiarity of man is that he is provident; he takes account of his future wants and tries to acquire resources to enable him to satisfy them. He puts a high value on security, on being able to rely on keeping the resources he has acquired. The wants he is concerned about are not a random collection that are his merely because they spring from his natural appetites and momentary circumstances; they are related to a way of life that he is conscious of and seeks to maintain. To provide for them is therefore to maintain deliberately a way of life. Man, as a provident being, as a planner, sees himself as an enduring person in a stable environment, as someone with a place in a community. Whether or not he is confined to that place for life, or for only a part of it, and however he comes to be in it, at any particular time, he has a place and knows what it is and wants others to know it. If he is not sure that others recognize his place, he feels the need to make it known to them; and if he does not know their places, feels the need to find out. He may not feel these needs at every casual encounter but he does feel them whenever he is thrown for long into the company of others or has much to do with them. He is insecure until he has 'placed' himself in their minds and has 'placed' them in his, until he and they are 'presented' to one another in their social capacities. The security that consists in a man's being sure that he can provide for his wants, can maintain his way of life, is bound up with the security that consists in his having a recognized place in society; for his wants and his way of life are bound up with that place. All this, though not exactly in these words, has long been noticed, not only and overtly in treatises and essays on man and his behaviour, but also and implicitly in stories and plays and on other occasions when men divert themselves by contemplating the behaviour of their own species.

Yet another peculiarity of man, recognized since the dawn of philosophy, is his being a maker of decisions who knows himself for such, and who could not make them unless he knew that he could. Because he makes decisions, he is ready to answer for what he does; he acknowledges his actions as his own. Even when he disclaims responsibility for an action, there is implicit in the disclaimer the admission that he is the sort of being who is answerable for what he does and who, when he acts deliberately, is free in a sense that other animals are not.

Some philosophers (for example, Hobbes) have defined freedom in such a way that animals other than man can be free, and have put this sense of freedom forward as one important to the political philosopher. But as soon as they have turned to explaining what it is the business of political philosophy to explain—the nature of authority and allegiance, of binding agreements, of laws and other social rules—they have soon passed to using the word in other and more relevant senses. Man's peculiar freedom entails his being answerable for what he does: which he can be even when he is a slave. Only because he is free in this sense can he have authority or be subject to it. Hobbes knew this, really, just as Rousseau and Hegel did, though he perversely defined freedom in a sense irrelevant to his purpose, which was to explain the limits of allegiance.

It is a man's deliberate actions, rather than his unthinking responses to stimuli, which, in his own and other people's opinion, reveal what sort of man he is. These, above all, are the actions that he would have other people understand correctly, or understand in a way favourable to him, not only from fear of punishment or hope of reward, but because he is concerned for his image in their eyes. These, the actions for which he is answerable,[1] are not, as he and others see them, evidence merely of his

---

[1] It is not strictly true that men are answerable only for deliberate actions; but it is true that they are answerable for what they do only because they are capable of deliberate action.

dispositions, as the behaviour of a dog is evidence of its dispositions; they are *gestures*, they have and are intended to have significance, they communicate intentions, beliefs, and attitudes. That deliberate actions have this element of self-assertion to them is implicit in ordinary ways of speaking about them.

Another peculiarity of man, closely connected with the ones already discussed, is that he has rules to guide his own behaviour and to appeal to when he seeks to control the behaviour of others. He is therefore concerned for justice. When he appeals to a rule against another person, he recognizes implicitly that he too would be bound by that rule were he situated as the person is against whom he makes the appeal. The appeal to justice is, directly or indirectly, an appeal to a common interest; it is an appeal to sharers in that interest, and to that extent an appeal to equals. Appealing to rules binding on oneself and others also has, or can have, an element of self-assertion to it, a putting oneself forward as a being capable of obligations and rights, a human being to whom justice is due.

It can be, and indeed has been, argued that these peculiarly human capacities are recognized, not just explicitly by philosophers, but implicitly in ordinary ways of speaking about human behaviour. All distinctively human intercourse rests on the assumption that human beings have these capacities, for what makes the intercourse human is that the beings engaged in it recognize one another as having these capacities. Even the most brutal master does not treat his slave (unless the master or the slave is an idiot) as if the slave lacked them; for implicit in his harsh treatment of the slave is the recognition that he too is a man. The master expects the slave to be intelligently active in his service: to follow instructions, to make decisions, to use foresight, to recognize his own and his master's place in society. The master holds the slave responsible for his actions, and in doing so recognizes, at least implicitly, the slave's right to defend himself, to deny responsibility if he can justify the denial, or otherwise to exculpate or excuse himself. There are, implicit in their ways of dealing with one another, or in their ways of explaining their dealings, principles to which the slave can appeal against his master, even though it is only to his master that he appeals.

Though these characteristics peculiar to man have long been noticed and even discussed in some detail by moralists, jurists, and political writers (as well as by writers without pretensions to philosophy), and though they have this element of self-assertion about them which also has not passed unnoticed, this aspect of them has not been a central theme in treatises about man and society until quite recent times. Man 'expressing' his *self* and not just his beliefs or feelings, man concerned for his identity (for what he appears to himself to be) and requiring or expecting others to take him at his own estimation, is a theme prominent chiefly in the works of nineteenth- and twentieth-century theorists. Related to this theme, and indeed forming part of it, are two other ideas: the first, that a man's happiness, his being satisfied with his way of life, depends on how he appears to himself and to others, on his having a coherent image of himself and being able to live up to it; and the second, that he may belong to a society in which he is unable to acquire such an image or cannot live up to it.

Both these ideas, differently expressed, are to be found in the writings of Rousseau, though his contemporaries did not notice them there. Indeed, the writers who took them up after him often did not acknowledge (and perhaps did not recognize) him as a precursor. Who can blame them? The distance between his French and their German, even when they speak of the same things, is not small. And so these ideas, now so familiar, passed into wider circulation in their later German forms. Man's peculiar need to be accepted by others for what he claims to be, a need born of social intercourse and to be satisfied only through it, though in fact often frustrated by it, a need whose satisfaction is a condition of happiness, of the sense of a life worth living: when today we discuss this need and what has been said about it, we think of Hegel and even of Marx more than of Rousseau.

There is another idea of Rousseau's, one I mentioned earlier, which is closely connected with 'self-assertion': the idea of moral freedom or autonomy. This idea, though less neglected by his contemporaries, has also become familiar to moralists and social theorists in later German versions of it, Kantian, Hegelian, and sometimes even partly Marxist. The idea of freedom as obedience to a law prescribed to oneself is essentially Rousseau's, not only because he made more of it than earlier writers had done and drew larger consequences from it, but because, in the form he gave to it, it differs considerably from the earlier ideas that most resemble it.

Rousseau put forward this idea in two different connections. In one its implications are strongly democratic, and in the other strongly individualist. In the eighth chapter of the first book of *The Social Contract* he defines the sort of freedom he calls moral as 'obedience to the law one has prescribed to oneself'. It differs from natural freedom, which is co-extensive with a man's power (including, presumably, his skill in overcoming or avoiding obstacles in his way) and from civil liberty, which is limited by the general will as expressed in the laws. But in a properly constituted society of equals, the general will embodied in the law coincides, according to Rousseau, with the moral will of the citizen. Provided he has taken part freely and on the same terms as others in making the laws, he has (so Rousseau implies) prescribed them to himself, has freely undertaken to obey them, and is therefore morally free when he obeys them. There are several objections that we need not discuss here to this doctrine; but it does at least entail that obedience to law can be moral freedom only in a community whose members make their own laws and do not choose representatives to make them. Rousseau in developing his argument makes it clear that the citizen, when he acts as a legislator, must exercise his own judgement, must not be intimidated or 'pressured' or deceived, if the laws made by the assembly of citizens are to be expressions of the general will.

In *Émile* Rousseau conceives of freedom (the kind that in *The Social Contract* he calls moral freedom) somewhat differently. He there describes a course of education which ensures that a boy comes to accept a variety of social rules he is bound in conscience to obey; he does so as he learns from experience that their being generally observed is to the advantage both of himself and of others. The boy is not indoctrinated; he is not conditioned or pressured into keeping the rules, and does not keep them merely to earn approval and to avoid disapproval. He is encouraged to consider the rules critically, and learns to use them and to appeal to them as he comes to understand his own and other people's need of them. The rules are needed, not to help people get more pleasure than they otherwise could or to satisfy more of their wants, but to enable them to live and work peacefully together as they pursue their various purposes, of which some are self-regarding and others altruistic. The freedom of Émile, when he is grown up and educated, consists in his being able to form and pursue coherent and realistic aims (whether his alone or shared by him with others) self-restrained by rules that he accepts because he has seen the justice of them. As he learns to recognize their justice, they become for him, not maxims of prudence, but properly moral rules: he feels bound to keep them even to his own hurt, even when he could contrive, to his own lasting advantage, not to keep them.

The process that Rousseau describes is such that the modern sociologist or psychologist might say that Émile 'internalizes' the rules. But Émile does more than just this: for a man can 'internalize' rules, can feel impelled by 'conscience' to keep them, or can feel guilty when he breaks them, even though he has not examined them critically and accepted them on rational grounds. To keep rules because you feel bound to do so and not because you fear the consequences of not doing so, to be 'inner-directed' in David Riesman's sense of the word, to have a highly developed 'super-ego', is not enough to make you morally free.

Self-assertion and the claim to moral freedom do not necessarily go together. There is plenty of self-assertion in all societies, whereas the claim to moral freedom is comparatively recent. Yet the two became prominent in social and political theory at about the same time. The fact of self-assertion (man's concern for how he appears to others and to himself and the actions inspired by that concern), though long noticed, had not been much emphasized, except by moralists who had denounced it as vanity. But, at least since Hegel's time, it has been widely recognized without being condemned. Man, as a social and moral being, cannot help but be self-assertive; his self-assertiveness is involved in his acting effectively as a member of society. It may take harmful forms but need not do so, and in any case is a necessary part of the life of a self-conscious and rational being. Whether or not it takes harmful forms depends largely on how society is organized and how the individual is educated to take his place in it. All these are by now familiar ideas, though everyone who uses them does not understand them in the same way.

Familiar, too, though again variously interpreted, is the idea of moral freedom. This idea, since Rousseau took it over from the Stoics and adapted it to new purposes, has been as much political as moral. The egalitarian democracy described in *The Social Contract* is justified because it makes moral freedom possible, and the course of social and cultural change described by Hegel owes its progressive character to its being a gradual achievement of this kind of freedom. Thus, though self-assertion and moral freedom are by no means the same, nor even always found together (for though the morally free are self-assertive, the self-assertive need not be morally free), these two ideas have grown into prominence together; by which I mean, not only over the same period, but in the same circles.

These ideas have grown important in a society whose members are sharply aware of social differences and social change. In this society there is a great deal of movement from place to place, from occupation to occupation, and even from class to class. A heightened awareness of change and social mobility brings with it a more critical attitude to established rules and practices, an attitude strengthened by the study of history and by the social studies. It is no longer taken for granted, as it was by the Stoics and their medieval successors, that customs and conventions, though they differ considerably from place to place, are adaptations to local circumstances of rational principles everywhere accepted. Even the claim that there are such principles is widely challenged. That there are must be established, not by an appeal to the will of God or by pointing to supposedly self-evident moral truths, but by showing that it is irrational for beings endowed and circumstanced as men are not to accept them for their own guidance and the control of others. And so the idea arises that being morally obliged to observe a rule entails having thought about it and accepted it as being rational. This does not imply that nobody can be justly required to observe such a rule unless he has accepted it on this ground, but it does imply that, if he observes it merely because he has been trained to do so or because others require or expect it of him, his action is not properly or fully moral, and he is not morally free in performing it. A man can, of course, accept on rational grounds a principle requiring him in difficult circumstances to do what is unjustly required of him; and in that case, presumably, he acts morally when he does it. But whether in doing it he is morally free is more open to question. The moralists who speak with approval of moral freedom would perhaps stop short of saying that whenever a man acts morally, he is morally free.

It is easy to see how a heightened awareness of social change might move the moralist and the student of human behaviour to take more notice of the individual's need to assert himself, to maintain his self-esteem by getting others to recognize him for what he claims to be. The more quickly society changes, the more precarious the status of the individual; and the more he is aware of the fact of change, the greater his anxiety about his status. Also, the more he moves from place to place or from occupation to occupation, the more often he finds himself among strangers, and the more urgent therefore his need to establish his identity. He cannot take himself so much for granted because he cannot reckon so much on other people taking him for what he is. So, from noticing the need for self-assertion, often to deplore its consequences, moralists and others passed to speaking of it with sympathy and approval. Here was an essential need of man as a social being which, in society as they found it, was often unsatisfied.

In a society that changes slowly and imperceptibly, men know what is expected of them and what to expect of others; their rights and obligations are definite enough, even though there are no legislatures and courts of law to define them. Though everyone's rights and obligations change considerably during the course of his life, they change predictably. Some are replaced by others as he grows older and does what everyone at his time of life is expected to do, and some are discarded or acquired when he chooses to change his condition where custom leaves him the freedom to choose. But whether or not he is free to choose his condition, the rights and obligations attached to it are known to everyone. His need is above all to maintain his status, whatever it may be; and so his self-assertiveness is essentially conservative. He is concerned that others should recognize him for what he already is, and the modes of address and other gestures that he uses in putting himself forward as the sort of person he claims to be are conventional and familiar. He knows what to do and can rely on others understanding the significance of what he does, even though neither he nor they are able to explain that significance.

II

In a quickly and consciously changing society, ambitions grow and uncertainty increases. The choice of occupations open to a man is wider, he can move more easily from place to place, and is better able to change his status. Therefore his ambitions are, or may be, enlarged. But, just because social change is rapid, the rights and obligations attached to particular occupations and roles are not long the same, and there is less agreement as to what they are. To be sure, in this kind of society, there is plenty of legislation and litigation. Legal rights are more elaborately defined and more effectively protected by the courts. Yet all this is consistent with a man's being socially much more at sea, much less sure of what can reasonably be expected by him and of him. Law settles only some questions, and in any case the law changes frequently, and most people do not know how it changes but must look to experts to tell them. Thus changes of status, and of roles and occupations, whether or not they result from choice, are not only more frequent and varied but are also less often from one definite and familiar social position to another. The same causes that encourage movement from position to position also change the character of the positions.

What is more, in a quickly changing society which is recognized to be such, ambition takes on a new dimension. It does not always take the form of wanting to move from one position to another in an already existing structure; it also quite often aspires to change the structure, to create new occupations, new roles, new ways of life. But this ambition, even when it is deep and urgent, is apt to be vague; those who are moved by it often want for themselves and for others opportunities they cannot realistically describe because they do not know how society would need to be changed in order to provide them.

Where ambition takes these unconventional forms and the need for self-assertion, more widely recognized, is less easily satisfied, there arises at last a new claim, the claim to 'self-realization'. Those who make it think of the individual on whose behalf they make it, not just as asserting his 'identity', but as somehow seeking to discover or achieve it. They speak of the 'self-realizing' individual both as if he wanted to be different from what he is and as if he wanted to 'find himself'—to discover what he is.

Clearly, self-realization and self-assertion are closely related ideas. The man who asserts himself seeks recognition of what he claims to be or to have achieved, and the man who strives to realize himself seeks to become what he aspires to be or to achieve something that proves his worth to himself and to others. To become what he wants to be or to prove himself in some way, he needs to be recognized as a fit aspirant, as a person capable of becoming or achieving what he aspires to, and he may also need opportunities and services that are costly to provide. So he, or others on his behalf, demand this recognition, these opportunities, and these services for him. For him and for others; and so two claims come to be made on society: that it should enlarge the opportunities, the range of effective choices, open to the individual, and that it should provide, as far as possible, equal opportunities to all.

The man who seeks to realize himself wants more than to be recognized as a fit aspirant, more than the opportunities and services he needs to achieve his ambition; he also, when the time comes, wants his achievement acknowledged. He may, as an aspirant, have only vague notions, especially to begin with, of what he wants to be and to do; and these notions, as they gain in precision, may change considerably with time; and yet he not only depends *now* on others for his opportunities, for recognition as a fit aspirant, but will depend on them in the future for assurance that he has succeeded, or at least has failed worthily. Self-realization (whatever it is, and it is by no means easy to describe) involves self-assertion at every stage of it; it involves seeking to be accepted by others—not all others but some—for what one claims to be. Self-realization is never, or hardly ever, a striving for unacknowledged achievement.

Though these two ideas, self-assertion and self-realization, are closely related, they are not always found together. There is, for example, not much trace of the second in the writings of Rousseau, aware though he was that society was changing fast. For he deplored that change. What he wanted was not exactly a return to the past, and yet was not altogether unlike it. His ideal society, while it differs greatly from all primitive societies known to us, is like them in being small and static. He disliked intensely what in his day was already called progress, and believed that men could not be free or equal or happy except in a society that remained, in all essentials, always the same. He took it for granted that this society must be economically simple, and that most people inside it would be content to follow their fathers' occupations and to live much as their parents had done. He was against social conditions that encourage people to move from place to place and from occupation to occupation in the hope of bettering themselves; for such conditions are, he thought, incompatible both with moral freedom and with equality. He was not a conservative, for he disliked society as he found it; and yet he disliked what he saw coming even more than what he saw around him. Though he spoke of moral freedom and not of self-assertion, he did recognize and care deeply for what I have called by that name. He thought it important that men and women should preserve their self-esteem, and saw that they could not do so unless they were accepted by others for what they claimed to be. But the idea of self-realization, as distinct from self-assertion, is scarcely to be found in his writings, even under another name.

Rousseau's disbelief in progress went deep; he not only believed that change was in the wrong direction but that little could be done to set it right. The idea, so prominent in so many philosophies of the nineteenth century, that the lessons of experience are always in the long run salutary, meant nothing to him. He did not see men collectively as necessarily 'transcending their limitations'; he did not see them learning gradually to understand the capacities of their species and the needs that emerge as those capacities develop, until at last they create the conditions, social and cultural, in which these needs can be fully satisfied. He did not, as for example Hegel and Marx did, assume that men in whom these needs are unsatisfied will turn in the end against the conditions that frustrate them, and will do so in ways that are 'creative' because they lead eventually to a deeper understanding of the needs. He did not assume that mankind never set themselves problems they cannot solve.

If we accept self-realization as an ideal, we are not committed logically to belief in moral progress. We can hold that societies that know nothing of this ideal are not inferior to societies that make much of it, and yet also hold that, since we happen to live in a society of the second kind, we should do what we can to help people achieve the ideal. And yet, as a matter of fact, it was believers in progress who were the first to set great store by self-realization as an ideal. They did not welcome every aspect of the changes going on around them but they did believe them to be, on the whole, changes for the better. They wanted more than that those who accepted self-realization as an ideal should be better placed to pursue it; they also thought that men were the better for accepting the ideal. They wanted them to have larger opportunities of choosing how they should live and what they should be, and took it for granted that, given courage and intelligence enough, these opportunities could be enlarged. Unlike Rousseau, they dared to be hopeful; they were not, as he was, Job's comforters to mankind.

In all societies men are self-assertive, though only in some do they aspire to be 'self-creative', to make of themselves what it satisfies them to be. But a man may fail to be accepted for what he claims to be, or may not know what to claim or how to claim it; or he may fail to become what he aspires to be, to prove himself to others and himself, or may fail to set up aims that he can achieve or make progress towards, or may be unable to strive seriously to achieve them, even though he feels that he ought to. He may be frustrated or bewildered, or may lapse into apathy; and, if this happens to him, he is diminished in his own eyes, and perhaps also in the eyes of others. And it is, as we have seen, precisely in the type of society in which men are the most concerned about self-assertion and self-realization, that the risk of such failure is greatest.

Society not only produces in the individual the need to assert and realize himself, and provides him with the means of doing so, and is the witness and confirmer of his success; it is also the medium in which he asserts and realizes himself. It is all these things at once: for he becomes self-assertive and self-realizing in acquiring a culture, and uses social resources, and depends on social acceptance and approval for confirmation of his claims, and his acts of self-assertion and self-realization are essentially forms of social intercourse. He cannot live *for* himself, live the life peculiar to a self-conscious and rational being, without also living *for* others: for that life is largely a life of gestures, of acts whose significance depends on ideas common to the actor and his 'witnesses', as sharers in a culture.

Writers who see more in self-realization than an ideal which arises in a certain type of culture, who look upon its emergence and wider acceptance as marks of progress, often speak as if it were not only the individual but also the species that strives to realize itself. They do not mean to be taken quite literally; they do not imagine mankind aiming at some condition of itself. Rather, they see men acquiring in the course of social and cultural change a deeper and clearer understanding of themselves and the world, and see them transformed in the process. History, as they speak of it, is more than the record of what has been done in the past, though it includes that record; it is a long course of human endeavour in which past achievements, past ways of thinking, feeling, and acting, are carried over into the present and in the process become 'higher' ways.

Assimilating a culture always involves more than appropriating or reproducing what already exists; it also involves changing it. Where there is assimilation, there is also, to some extent at least, innovation as well. Most students of society would agree, not only that the social order changes continually (though the people who belong to it may not notice that it does), but that cultural assimilation is not a passive process, that the present in 'feeding upon' the past becomes different from it. They would agree also that, as soon as men notice the fact of social change (which they often do because it has gathered speed), the change grows faster still. It is not change so much as consciousness of change that is disturbing, and makes men feel threatened or liberated, or both the one and the other.

A sceptic might agree to all this without conceding that the change is moral progress. He might even agree that it brings with it, not only more wealth and power, but a 'deeper' understanding of human nature and the world, and yet deny that the standards and ideals that come later are *higher* than the ones they displace. Whereas the believer in progress (unless by progress he means *only* increase of wealth, power, and knowledge) speaks as if the ideals that come with growth of understanding were not merely different but higher. He either thinks of them as better adapted to needs peculiar to man as a self-conscious, rational, and moral being (needs assumed to be universal even though it takes time for men to recognize them and to learn to satisfy them), or he simply takes it for granted that the ideals are higher because they arise as knowledge and power increase. They are, according to this conception of them, the ideals of a more sophisticated age able to take the measure of what is earlier and simpler than itself. The sophisticated, the 'more developed', can understand the simple, the 'less developed', as the simple cannot understand them. The ideals that come with growing 'maturity' are 'higher' than the ideals of the less 'mature'.

This conception of progress was never more elaborately presented than by Hegel, and is prominent also in the writings (and especially the earlier writings) of Marx. But it is not confined to German philosophers, or even to philosophers. It has taken many forms, some pretentious and recondite, and others more down to earth and apparently more clear. But the clarity is, I suspect, largely an illusion. I have yet to come across an account of progress which explains satisfactorily why the ideals of the sophisticated should be reckoned 'higher' than those of the unsophisticated, or what exactly the distinctively human needs are that men learn to recognize and to satisfy only as their understanding and their powers increase. Even if there are needs peculiar to social and moral beings (as, for example, the need for self-respect and for the respect of others, or the need for an ordered and satisfying way of life), needs that take different forms in different societies and are better understood in some than in others, it is not obvious that to satisfy them in their later, more sophisticated and self-conscious forms is to satisfy them more fully. Nor is it obvious that the better they are understood, the more fully they are satisfied. In a sophisticated society not all men are equally sophisticated. What evidence is there that the more sophisticated, who are more concerned than the others to assess their own capacities and needs, satisfy their needs more fully? Indeed, what evidence is there, that their assessments, subtle though they may be, are correct?

As we watch a child growing up in a more or less stable society, we see it growing in 'maturity'. We see it learning to define the situations in which it acts as adults define them, learning to make the descriptions and assessments which enable it to act effectively according to received standards. It is this learning, much more than the kind of knowledge that the psychologist or the student of society aims at, that counts as growth in maturity. It means something to say of one person as compared with another, if they both belong to the same or similar societies, that one is more mature than the other. It can even mean something to say this of persons who belong to widely different societies, for the societies, despite the differences between them, may be similar in respects which are relevant to the comparison being made. But what does it mean to say of one society as compared with another that its standards are the more mature? Does it mean only that they prevail among peoples who have more of the kind of knowledge that the human sciences aim at? Why, then, if that is all there is to greater maturity, should we say, 'the more mature, the higher'?

There may be reasons why, though biological needs are not less fully satisfied by creatures that do not understand them than by creatures that do, needs peculiar to self-conscious and moral beings are the more fully satisfied the better they are understood. But these reasons, if there are any, are not obvious. The argument: 'the distinctively human needs are the needs of self-conscious beings who have standards and make choices, and therefore the more the human sciences develop, the more fully these needs are satisfied', is not immediately convincing. Neither is the argument: 'only self-conscious beings have standards, and therefore the more sophisticated their theories about themselves, the higher their standards'. The needs of 'primitive' man are no less the needs of a self-conscious and moral being than are those of 'sophisticated' man, and are satisfied by forms of behaviour which involve comparison, assessment, and choice, the use of language and reason. The relevant difference here, presumably, between 'primitive' and 'sophisticated' societies is that, while in the former nobody describes these needs accurately or explains them 'scientifically', in the latter some people do, or at least try to, and their descriptions and explanations influence the others, even when they do not fully understand them. How this ensures that needs in advanced societies are more fully satisfied or higher has still to be explained.

I do not say that no explanation is possible; I say only that I know of none that is satisfactory. But, of course, we need not accept the idea of moral progress to agree that the accumulation of knowledge and power, as it transforms the conditions of life for men, transforms also their needs and ideals and the claims they make on one another. Nor do we have to accept it to agree that the claims to moral freedom and to the opportunity to realize oneself are sophisticated claims which have come to be widely made only in recent times in technologically advanced communities in which the sciences, natural and human, flourish.

No doubt, it is when men come to be aware of social change and can move easily from place to place and from job to job that these claims become popular. It is then that people want to choose their occupations, that they form ambitions which require their living differently from their parents, that they aspire to 'develop their talents'. It is then that equality of opportunity is widely proclaimed and serious attempts are made to achieve it.

Societies in which these conditions hold are intensely competitive, and are as much so when they are not 'capitalist' as when they are. Or at least they have been so up till now; they are today just as competitive where productive resources are 'publicly' as where they are 'privately' owned or controlled.[2] Years before Marx first put pen to paper, critics of capitalism

---

[2] Economists and other social theorists have in recent times had much to say about various forms of ownership and control. But the distinctions they have made have had little influence on arguments at the popular level between champions and critics of 'capitalism'. Just what forms of ownership and control are to be reckoned 'capitalist' or 'socialist'? What kinds of competition do they encourage or curtail? These are questions still largely neglected, even by people who denounce the evils of competition or who extol its advantages.

had argued that in practice it condemned most people to lives of drudgery, even though the variety of occupations inside it was greater than in earlier economies. Since this criticism was first directed against them, capitalist countries have changed greatly, so much so indeed that it can be misleading to call them capitalist.[3] Whether they are now as much open to this criticism as they were in Marx's time has been doubted. What is more (and this is more to the point of my argument), it is doubtful whether they are more open to it than countries which everyone agrees are not capitalist, though not everyone calls them socialist. Today all industrial societies, no matter how they are organized, are (if we compare them with earlier societies) intensely competitive. In all of them, and not least in the ones that pride themselves on being socialist, most of the workers are confined all their working lives to work that is tiring and dull. They may have more leisure now than they had fifty or more years ago, get higher real wages, work in more comfortable and healthier surroundings, and be better provided for in sickness, old age, and unemployment, but their chances of getting work that calls for a variety of skills are not much greater. This is as true of 'socialist' as of 'capitalist' societies. There is little evidence that either competitiveness or confinement to drudgery decreases as an industrial economy becomes more 'socialist'.

In all industrial countries, 'capitalist' and 'socialist', equality of opportunity is proclaimed as an ideal, at least in official circles and in the schools. It may not always be taken seriously but it is affirmed on all suitable occasions; it is part of the authorized creed. Though, in some of these countries, the ideal of service to the community is zealously acclaimed, equality of opportunity is never reduced to no more than equal opportunity of service. It is always admitted that the individual should develop his 'potentialities' also for his own sake, and even that he should be able to choose and achieve a way of life that satisfies him. Wherever equality of opportunity is proclaimed as an ideal, it is spoken of as if it were liberating, and is justified, at least in part, on the ground that people should be able to become what *they* want to be, to achieve what to them seems worth while. It is nowhere justified wholly because it enables the community to make the best use of its members in the pursuit of common ends—not even in the countries where these supposedly 'common' ends are defined by irresponsible rulers. Self-realization, under that name or some other, is an ideal widely accepted, even though the acceptance is often little more than lip-service.

This is not true of moral freedom. Its appeal is much more narrow;

---

[3] For example, to call the American economy of today and the one of a hundred years ago *capitalist* could be seriously misleading if it led one to suppose that the effects of competition or of the distribution of power differ less as between the America of today and the America of the 1870s than they now do as between America and Russia.

which does not mean that it is confined to the Western democracies or even to persons who like to think of themselves as liberals. The socialist or the anarchist who attacks liberalism and calls it a bourgeois sham does not therefore repudiate everything that the liberal understands by freedom, or even the greater part of it. The right of the individual to pursue aims of his own choosing and to live by principles he has accepted because he believes them to be reasonable and just is not repudiated, or belittled, by everyone who attacks liberalism. Quite often the attackers, especially when they are anarchists, claim to take the right more seriously than liberals do, and to be willing to go much further in transforming society to make it possible for people to enjoy it. The fault of the liberal, in the eyes of the anarchist, is not that he cares for this right but that he fails to see (or will not admit) that institutions to which he is still attached prevent its being effectively exercised. Not even Communists repudiate this right, though in the countries they control they take harsh action against anyone who appeals to it in opposing them. They may care little for it in practice, and may insult and humiliate (where they have the power to do so) those who take it seriously; but even they, from time to time, find it expedient to pay tribute to it. Occasionally, they recall Marx's doctrine that, when society is fully communist, the individual will be freer than ever before, even though, to secure this freedom to him, there will be no need of a coercive state or of elaborately defined legal rights enforced by professional courts.

I have been arguing, not that self-assertion and self-realization (or even moral freedom) are peculiar to economically advanced societies in which the sciences, natural and social, and the study of history are well developed, or to societies that are changing fast and are aware that they are doing so, but rather that in these societies they are more discussed and more widely accepted as ideals. In all societies men assert themselves in a variety of ways and suffer when they fail to do so effectively, but only in these 'sophisticated' societies do they take large notice of this aspect of human behaviour. And though self-realization—in the sense of conscious and sustained striving to become what you aspire to be or to achieve what proves your worth—is less widespread than self-assertion, there is no doubt a good deal of it even in relatively simple societies. It may be rare in the smallest and most primitive of all, but we must expect to find a good deal of it wherever a man's status depends on his achievement, on what he chooses to do and succeeds in doing; as, for example, on whom he marries or on what occupation he chooses among several open to him. There is considerable scope for ambition, at least for some people, even in custom-bound and 'static' societies. And where there is scope for ambition, there is scope for self-realization as well; for self-realization and the pursuit of ambition, though they do not exactly coincide, have much in common. And yet, though there is ambition in nearly all societies, it is only in some that the striving to realize one's ambitions (or rather some kinds of ambition) is dignified by such names as 'self-realization' or 'self-fulfilment'. Only recently has the moral right to be ambitious or self-realizing been widely accepted.

Moral freedom has probably meant very little, except to a few people. To take one's principles seriously and to strive valiantly to live by them is not to be morally free, at least not in the sense understood by Rousseau and Kant. For the man of principle may take his principles on trust; he may accept them uncritically as commands of God, or he may receive them in much the same spirit from parents or teachers. Of course, as soon as he learns to use them and has the will to do so, he makes them his own; he no longer observes them because others require it of him but because he requires it of himself. His condition is different from that of the man who observes rules from fear of blame or punishment. But he may still not be morally free in Rousseau's sense of the word, for he may be unable to give good reasons why his principles ought to be observed.[4]

Presumably, moral freedom means nothing to people in primitive custom-bound societies. When the idea of it first arises, it is confined to philosophers and to the small circles influenced by them. In the West the idea begins with the Stoics, and recurs again and again in later philosophies. Not every philosopher who says that there is a law 'higher' than mere civil law or than custom and convention, a law to be preferred to them when they conflict with it, has the idea of moral freedom. Whether he has it or not depends on how he thinks men come to know this law and why he gives it precedence over rules that conflict with it. To reject principles that are commonly received, or not to take them seriously, or to require little of others and oneself, or to be passionately attached to principles of one's own or shared by only a few people: none of these things (nor all of them together) constitutes moral freedom. Not if to be morally free is to be firmly attached to principles critically examined and accepted on rational grounds. All these things—moral scepticism, a lessening of moral seriousness, 'permissiveness', and moral idiosyncrasy—are sometimes desirable and liberating. But they are so far from constituting moral freedom that they are not even good evidence that the people affected by them are on the way to becoming morally free.[5]

---

[4] Being able to give good reasons is not, of course, a condition of being moral, and everyone who becomes moral does so before he becomes morally free (if ever he does become it). The child learns to be moral ('internalizes' rules and becomes its own censor) before it is capable of examining rules critically. The believer in moral freedom is not committed to denying this; though Rousseau, in describing the moral education of Émile, takes too little account of it.

[5] Different from, though related to, the idea of moral freedom is the more popular (or more widely understood) idea of a dedicated life. The man or woman who joins a religious order undertakes special obligations deliberately. But the obligations are special in two senses: they are not widely accepted, and they arise from choosing a way of life held to be in some special

III

It is self-realization rather than moral freedom that is by way of becoming a popular ideal. It consists, as we have seen, in a man's trying to become what he aspires to be, or his trying to achieve something that matters to him because it proves that he is or has become what he wants to be. But a man's ideas about what he wants to be are often vague and variable, and are not the less so, the more gifted and ambitious he is. Notoriously, men have illusions about themselves and want more, much more, than is within their powers. And so some writers have spoken of self-realization (or self-fulfilment) as if it were, or should be, a kind of self-discovery. It is for everyone to find out what he can be, what is within his reach and satisfying to him; it is for everyone to find 'his place in the world', and the sign that he has found it is that he is satisfied in it. He is not apathetic and resigned to his lot but active in ways that give him a sense of well-being or of living to good purpose.

The self-discoverer does not know from the beginning what he will find; he can know it only when he has found it, which he may never do. He tries things out, he reaches in several directions before he finds the one that suits him. And yet his trials and explorations are not random; they depend on his aptitudes, dispositions, and tastes. Nevertheless, self-discovery is always tentative, especially in its early stages.

This idea of 'finding oneself' is odd and obscure. There is nothing odd, of course, about the idea of getting to know oneself, one's capacities and limitations, better than before. Everyone who is at all thoughtful discovers that there are many things out of his reach, not so much for lack of opportunity as for lack of talent. But the idea of a way of life peculiarly suited to one's nature, of a range of activities or a spiritual condition which is the 'fullest' or 'highest' expression of one's self, is odd and romantic. For what suits a man depends as much on his education and experience as on the capacities and dispositions he is born with.

What does it mean to say that a man is unsuited to his way of life? Part of what it means, presumably, is that he lacks the skills, dispositions, and sentiments that would make him satisfied in it. He may lack them for one or more of several different reasons: because he is by nature incapable of acquiring them, or some of them; because he never had the chance to acquire them; because he aspired to other things which he failed to get, and so missed his opportunities or made himself unfit to take them.

Some men are much less adaptable than others, and a few perhaps are so cursed by nature that there is no way of life among those that society

sense out of the ordinary. A man who chooses to get married or to be a farmer undertakes obligations peculiar to his status or occupation, but he does not, in this special sense, dedicate his life. And yet the man who freely joins a religious order may accept its rules and ideas on authority without examining them critically; he may not aspire to moral freedom.

offers (or even could offer if it were reformed within the limits set by available resources, natural and human) that would satisfy them. But it may be that most men, if only they were suitably educated, could be satisfied well enough by several different ways of life. If that is so, then there are, in any one society, several different ways in which a man might 'find himself', several different conditions of himself, social and psychological, each of which would 'realize his potentialities' as 'fully' as any of the others. And if we take many different types of society, then the ways in which he might 'find' or 'realize' or 'fulfil' himself would be far more numerous. The more adaptable a man is, the greater the number of styles of life or of conditions of himself that could satisfy him; and whichever of them is his actual style or condition, he has 'found' or 'realized' himself in it, provided he is satisfied with his lot and is not just resigned to it, provided he is pleased to be what he is and to do what he does.

How, then, can we say of one type of society compared with another that it gives men wider opportunities to 'realize' or 'find' or 'fulfil' themselves? If we take a particular society, or if we compare societies of the same type (or even similar parts of societies that otherwise differ greatly), we can perhaps say of one social arrangement that it is preferable to another because it makes it easier for people to realize themselves. But we can do this only because we take for granted an entire social order and culture, a whole range of institutions, attitudes, ideals, and skills that make a society the type of society it is. If Shakespeare had been alive in the early Middle Ages or had belonged to a much poorer family, he might never have become a great poet. But might he not have 'found' or 'realized' himself in ways just as much to his own and his neighbours' taste, just as 'satisfying' to him and to them, even though he had done nothing worth the notice of posterity?

Rousseau's arguments, though seldom entirely convincing, are often worth close scrutiny, if only because he so often refused to take for granted what seemed obvious to his contemporaries. He never spoke of self-realization, even to reject it, but from what he did say about the human condition we can infer that he cared nothing for part of what is ordinarily understood by it. He would have denounced as harmful, if not absurd, the doctrine that people should be encouraged to develop their powers or talents 'to the full'. To be sure, he wanted the individual to be 'on good terms with himself', to be satisfied with his way of life; and this satisfaction, as he describes it, is not a mere acceptance of one's lot but a deep sense that life is worth living. But he believed that the kind of society in which most men can have this sense gives little scope for the display of talent. His ideal society is simple, modest, and unchanging; there is not much room in it for inventiveness, for experiment, for spiritual and intellectual adventure. And yet, in his eyes, it is not a dull society; for it consists of men and women who keenly enjoy both their work and their leisure. His complaint against the French society of his day was that it condemned most men to frustration, restlessness, or apathy. Though it provided the talented with opportunities to exercise and display their talents, though it encouraged ambition and moved some men to strive hard to better themselves socially or to acquire fame, it was also debilitating; it bored people and weakened their capacity for enjoyment, so that they alternated between apathy and bitterness, between dullness and the frantic pursuit of pleasure or applause.

If we are to believe Rousseau, the mute inglorious Miltons are none the worse for being so, none the less satisfied with their way of life, though the gifts that might have brought fame to them in a different kind of society lie dormant in them or serve modestly to give pleasure to a small circle of neighbours. It matters to everyone that others should think well of him and that he should be able to think well of himself; it matters to the primitive and the illiterate as much as to the literate and the sophisticated. But there is no imperious talent 'which is death to hide', except where society encourages a fierce lust for fame.

To Rousseau the price of talent (or of the achievements or performances that the privileged are disposed to admire) seemed altogether too high. Not because the privileged are exploiters living off the labours of the poor who lack the opportunity to cultivate and display their own talents. Rousseau did indeed think of the privileged as exploiters and of men of talent as their entertainers, parasites feeding on parasites, but it was not the too narrow scope for talent that he deplored. The price that society pays for talent is too high because the striving for superiority that the cultivation of rare gifts entails is socially divisive and a source of misery. Putting an end to exploitation, extending the opportunities of the privileged to everyone, would not suffice to destroy the passions that lead to misery, so long as the cultivation and worship of talent remained as great as before.

The problem that to many radicals today seems the crucial one—how to achieve greater equality in an economically advanced and highly productive society—did not concern Rousseau, who believed that equality can be achieved only in simple societies. The kind of society that calls for a wide variety of skills and that puts a high value on rare skills is complex and sophisticated; it is not a society of equals. Even if it could be contrived that there were no great inequalities of wealth inside it, it could not be contrived that there were no great inequalities of power, influence, and reputation. True equality, salutary because it makes for happiness, puts men on easy and good terms with each other and themselves, and is to be had, according to Rousseau, only in simple societies where men of rare gifts have little chance to prove their superiority to others. Thus, for Rousseau, equality entails mediocrity. Not dullness, not a lowering of vitality or of the capacity to enjoy and to give enjoyment, but mediocrity. Where talent is worshipped, some men look upon themselves as raised on a higher level of humanity; they maintain this sense of superiority in one another, and yet are also fiercely competitive, envious, and uneasy. The man of talent, so much given to vanity and anxiety, is as much as anyone *hors de lui-même*, at odds with himself, a burden to himself. Though he has achieved worldly success, he has not, in the opinion of Rousseau, 'found himself'.

Rousseau was the first, and perhaps the most whole-hearted, enemy of what R. H. Tawney was to call 'the acquisitive society'. The acquisitiveness he condemned was as much the immoderate pursuit of fame and excellence as of power and wealth. To be concerned for your reputation among neighbours who are your equals, to want to serve them even in positions of authority with their consent and for purposes understood and approved by them, to want to be your own master at work and to enjoy a decent independence: all this, according to Rousseau, is good. Man does not live to himself alone. This, for Rousseau as for everyone, meant more than simply the individual's dependence on others for his livelihood, his rendering services to them as well as getting services from them; it meant also that his worth in his own eyes and his sense of living to good purpose depend on their understanding, respect, and approval. Rousseau denied neither the economic nor the moral dependence of the individual on his neighbours; but he wanted, as much in the moral as in the economic sphere, an equality of dependence which was the nearest that an essentially social being could get to independence.

Implicit in Rousseau's mistrust of talent and dislike of the social conditions that give scope to it is a distinction between desire for fame and concern for reputation. The pursuit of fame (and therefore also of the kinds of excellence that bring fame) differs essentially from concern for reputation, because the pursuer looks for recognition and admiration from persons unknown to him and for whom, as individuals, he cares nothing; he wants them to acknowledge his superiority, his being set apart from and above ordinary, unknown persons like themselves. So, too, the man who in a vast community strives for great power wants to affect the lives of large numbers of people of whom he knows nothing, and wants to be raised high above them. The man who strives for great wealth strives for what puts the services of others at his disposal without his needing to serve them in return, for what makes him important to them while they remain unimportant to him. Of course, the rich man needs the services of others, for without their services his riches count for nothing; but he needs particular services rather than particular servants. His servants are expendable, for there are always others with services to sell.

Rousseau was not unappreciative of talent; he admired some of the great writers of the past greatly and was often sensitive and discriminating in his praise of them. Though he was not a man of wide literary sympathies (for he was largely self-taught and many kinds of excellence escaped his notice or left him unmoved), he was a great and imaginative writer. His dislike of rare talent, or rather of immoderate pursuit and exaltation of excellence, was not an effect of narrow sympathies; it sprang from an unusually keen appreciation of the cost, both to society and to the talented, of this pursuit and exaltation. The pursuit of fame, or of forms of excellence that bring fame, can, as much as the pursuit of power and wealth, impoverish the pursuer spiritually; it can move him to sacrifice, not only other people, but himself (or certain sides of himself) to his ruling passion. It is not his talents, not the gifts that he has in larger measure than others have them, that impoverish him; nor is it his choosing an occupation that gives scope to these gifts that harms him. It is his readiness to sacrifice others and himself in the attempt to get for himself, by the exercise of these special gifts, a recognition setting him apart from and high above others. And he seldom gets all the recognition he craves for; often he gets none or else much less than he thinks is due to him. The pursuit of rare excellence, and of the fame it brings, is often a burden and a source of misery to the pursuer.

Rousseau did not deny that the desire for fame encourages excellence, nor yet that the conditions that strengthen this desire give scope to a wide variety of talents. Where these conditions hold, there is an extensive division of labour, and the arts and sciences flourish. Men achieve between them much more than they could do in a simple society. They know much more, have more varied skills, and are much more powerful. Society, taken as a whole, is much richer, not only materially, but also intellectually. A God, indifferent to the happiness of mankind but eager to see what they could do when hard put to it, would wish to see them in conditions that moved them to pursue knowledge, excellence, and fame. He would want them (to use an expression unknown to Rousseau) to develop their capacities to the full. This God, given his tastes, might be well entertained by this richest and most varied of human circuses, but the performers would be miserable.

I have not put Rousseau's meaning in his own words, and I have deliberately exaggerated it. Or, rather, I have followed up some of the implications of what he said, and in doing so have used expressions that came into currency after his time. He had a taste for paradox, and to attribute to him a belief that is paradoxical—that the more fully human capacities are developed, the more difficult it is for human beings to become and to achieve what gives them lasting satisfaction—is not, I hope, unjust. If he never put this belief into words, he came closer to doing so than anyone else as concerned as he was to consider the effects of social conditions on the human *psyche*, and more especially on those beliefs and feelings of the individual which are directed towards himself. And, in any case, this belief, paradoxical though it seems, is worth taking seriously. For why should we assume, as so many believers in progress have done, that whatever 'enriches' mankind, whatever adds to the variety of human occupations, skills, styles of life, and forms of excellence, must in the end make it easier for the individual to find a way of life that satisfies him? Why should we assume it, even if by this satisfaction we mean, not un-alloyed happiness, nor even confidence unmixed with self-doubt and anxiety, but merely the sense that it is good to be alive, to be what one is, to strive for what one strives for, accepting the pains and burdens that are a part of one's lot in life?

IV

From late in the eighteenth century onwards, social theorists and even historians have been much attracted by two ideas: the idea of mankind developing human potentialities more and more fully, and the idea of the individual developing his own powers to the full. Often they have taken to both ideas without inquiring how far, or under what conditions, these two kinds of development assist each other. Sometimes they have been aware, even sharply aware, that they can be incompatible, that conditions making for the fuller development of human powers generally can be frustrating to most men, condemning them to monotonous occupations. That the variety of occupations can increase greatly over the whole of society and yet the choice of occupation open to most people be as narrow as ever and the work they do even duller, was noticed by Adam Smith two hundred years ago, and has been noticed again and again since his time. Yet few of the writers who have noticed it have inquired how society might be organized to ensure that the range of choices open to the individual was wider and his work more varied and interesting.

Some writers, as for example Marx, have confined themselves to stating the problem and to arguing that it cannot be solved while society remains capitalist. Only when the workers take control of society can its resources, material and cultural, be placed at the disposal of all its members, so that they can develop their powers fully. But though Marx tells us that this can be done, and even that it will be done after the collapse of capitalism, he does not tell us how it is to be done. This problem is one that he leaves resolutely to the future. We can find in his writings no clue to an answer to either of these questions: What is involved in a man's developing his powers fully? and, How must society be organized to enable its members to achieve this fullness?

Other writers have imagined a society so organized that its members can lead a 'full' life, can acquire at work and at leisure a variety of skills, and give expression to 'basic' human passions or instincts. Their theories have been attacked for two reasons: because the passions or instincts alleged to be basic are selected and defined so as to enable the theorist to reach the social and political conclusions he wants to reach, and because the theorist fails to explain realistically how such a society might be established. These theories are called Utopian, and serve to bring out more sharply what is held to be wrong with society as it is (by depicting a contrast with it) rather than to provide an alternative.

Still other writers have argued for greater equality of opportunity, and in doing so have ordinarily had in mind making it easier for the gifted children of poor and uneducated parents to get jobs carrying large social rewards (whether in money or in prestige) rather than increasing the range of occupations open to everyone, not just at the threshold of adult life, but during the whole course of it. Yet no writer, so far as I know, has seriously inquired whether increasing the diversity of skills and occupations in society and extending the range of choices open to the individual makes it more likely that people will 'realize themselves'—will form and achieve (or come close to achieving) ambitions that seem to them worth while. Usually, it is just taken for granted that the greater the diversity of skills and occupations in society as a whole and the wider the individual's range of choices among them, the better placed the individual must be to realize himself.

This idea of a fuller development of human powers—whether of the species taken generally or of the individual—is dark and elusive. 'Fuller' means, presumably, closer to being full. What then is the full development of human powers, taken generally? Would it be attained when, somewhere or other and at some time or other, all the skills, tastes, attitudes, and ideas of which men (given the natural endowments of their species) are capable had seen the light of day? Or must all these things be present together at the same time? Or, to put the same questions in different words, must mankind, when this full development is achieved, be doing, thinking, and feeling all that they are capable of, or is it enough that they should have reached the stage in which it can be truly said that at last, either now or in the past, all has been done, thought, and felt that is humanly possible? But what if men acquire the power to alter the capacities they are born with, or these capacities are altered by what they do, even though they never intended it?

This idea of 'the full development of human powers', as soon as we consider it at all closely, begins to look empty or absurd. The attempt to lend precision to it suggests questions that are unanswerable, or are not to be taken seriously, like the questions I have just put. It is obvious that mankind cannot, at any stage in the course of social and cultural change, be doing all that they are capable of. Nor can I see how they could ever know, at any stage, that all human possibilities had at last been realized, now or in the past. And even if they could know it, it might still happen that, at this stage, their powers had greatly declined; for this last period of innovation, though there might be achieved in it some things not achieved earlier, might itself be culturally poor. It might be with mankind, as it is with the artist or thinker who lives on well beyond his prime, adding the last small items to the list of his achievements at a time when he is no longer capable of the finer things accomplished in his maturity and youth.

Shall we say, then, that mankind have developed their powers to the full, not when they have achieved all that they are capable of achieving over the whole course of history, but when they have acquired the widest variety of skills and ways of thinking and feeling that they can have at any one time? But this too is empty talk, for how could anyone know that this condition was realized? Nor do we come nearer to talking sense, if we take into account only skills and ways of thinking and feeling that are held to be admirable, for what men admire differs from period to period and from society to society.

Even if we can say (as, no doubt, we can, given suitable assumptions) that in one society human powers are more developed than in another, we might still reasonably prefer the second society to the first on the ground either that it gives to its members individually a wider choice of occupations or that it gives them a better chance of realizing themselves. For, as we have seen already, we must not take it for granted that the greater the diversity of skills, ideas, tastes, and occupations in a society (that is, the richer it is culturally), the wider the range of choices open to each of its members or the greater his chance of realizing himself. Indeed, we cannot even take it for granted that the wider his range of choices, the better his chance of realizing himself—at least, not if self-realization is taken to mean his becoming or achieving what he finds worth while and satisfying. And yet many people do take this for granted: they are, they say, in favour of widening the choice of skills and occupations open to the individual so as to make it easier for him to realize himself.

Developing powers to the full is almost as elusive a concept applied to the individual as it is applied to the species. A man's developing his powers to the full cannot consist in his acquiring all the skills and dispositions that anyone naturally endowed as he is could acquire if he lived indefinitely. Nobody develops his powers to the full in this sense, and nobody wants to. Nor, really, does anyone want to acquire, during the course of his life, as many as possible of the skills and dispositions that he is capable of acquiring and that social and cultural conditions allow. This second account of what is involved in a man's developing his powers to the full is almost as absurd as the first.

To speak in the abstract of a man's developing his powers to the full, or more fully, makes little sense. If we want to say that he 'realizes himself' as he develops his powers, we must indicate what powers we have in mind. We might point to powers that he needs to develop if he is to become what he aspires to be or to achieve what he thinks worth while. Or, alternatively, we might point to powers which, if he developed them, would make him or his achievements admirable. We have here two different senses of self-realization. A man who realized himself in the first sense might not do so in the second. Milton, if he had been so educated as not to acquire the ambitions he did acquire, or if he had convinced himself that he ought to neglect the rare talents whose cultivation would make him famous, might have realized himself in the first of these senses without doing so in the second. And (who knows?) he might then have been happier, better satisfied with himself and his way of life.

These two senses are, of course, related. Whether or not what a man becomes or does is admirable, he could hardly be said to be realizing himself in becoming or doing it unless he wanted it and thought it worth while. And, even when it is not admirable, he would not (except in rare cases) want it or think it worth while if it were not in keeping with values that he shared with others. Nevertheless, not all aspirations are aspirations to excel. Self-realization, if it consists merely in having aspirations for oneself and seeking to realize them, can be modest.

Rousseau never spoke of self-realization, even under another name. He believed that men, if they were roughly equal and had a considerable measure of independence, would be satisfied with their lot; he attached no particular importance to their forming aspirations for themselves and seeking to realize them. But if he had given thought to self-realization, he would have preferred it to be modest rather than ambitious. Striving for excellence was, he thought, a major cause of unhappiness. But most social theorists have not thought as he did; and some—as, for example, John Stuart Mill—have set great store by this striving. Mill, as much as anyone, is the apostle of 'self-improvement' and of aiming high. He wanted a society that encourages its members to strive hard for excellence, and he assumed that it could do this best if it were culturally diverse and tolerant, and offered the individual a wide range of choices. Yet he accused the England of his day of encouraging mediocrity, though it was more productive, more literate, and more inventive than ever before, and it was becoming easier than it had been to rise socially. His reasons for thinking as he did are not clear. And yet, presumably, he did not attribute this mediocrity to higher production, wider literacy, and increased social mobility, for he believed in progress and these things were all at that time widely accepted as marks of progress. He probably thought them necessary but not sufficient conditions of the greater striving for excellence that he wanted to see. If there was to be less mediocrity and more excellence, men would, he thought, need to be more adventurous and to have greater independence of mind, and also to be more tolerant; but he never explained how it was that in the progressive society of his day they were deficient in these qualities.

Nor did he look at all closely at the excellence that meant so much to him. Notoriously, men's ideas of what is admirable differ from age to age, from society to society, from group to group in society, and even from person to person. What, then, should a man strive for who strives for excellence? Should he aim at (and as far as possible achieve) what he himself finds admirable, no matter how far his ideas differ from other people's? Or should he aim at what is generally admired in the society or the social circles he belongs to? Or at what is admired by the educated? Or by the classes or groups whose opinions carry the greatest weight? It may be that Mill, with his great respect for independence of mind, preferred the first of these alternatives to any of the others; that he wanted men to form their own ambitions without too much respect for the opinions of others, provided that they aimed high (asking a great deal of themselves) and did no harm to others.

If we hold the view that I have attributed to Mill, we may find ourselves committed to consequences that are odd and unconvincing. Let us suppose that Shakespeare, if he had had opportunities he lacked, would have chosen to be a man of action and not an actor and a playwright. Would he not then, if he had been able to do what he wished, have come closer to realizing himself? Would he not have developed his powers more fully? Surely, we should have to say that he would. He would have done so by his own standards. And what standards are more appropriate than a man's own when it is his self-realization that is in question?

Even if we hold (as perhaps many people, if challenged, would) that what a man strives for, if it is to count as striving for excellence, must be admirable, not just by his own standards, but by those of his society or of the educated classes in it, we may still find ourselves committed to conclusions we are reluctant to accept. Let us suppose that in Shakespeare's time, educated Englishmen, though they wrote better poetry and enjoyed it more than Englishmen do now, admired bold men of action more than they did poets; and let us suppose that Shakespeare, if he had had opportunities he did not have, would have achieved what, say, Sir Francis Drake achieved. In that case, by the 'educated' standards of his day (which might well have been his own) he would have come closer to realizing himself than he in fact did. Or, to take another and opposite example, if Francis Bacon, given different incentives and opportunities, could and would have written plays as good as Shakespeare's, he would, by the standards of his day, have achieved less, have developed his powers less fully, than he in fact did. Given the truth of what I have supposed, it is only by substituting our standards for those of Elizabeth's time that we can avoid these conclusions. But our standards, surely, are irrelevant when we are discussing the extent to which Elizabethans realized themselves.

We have opportunities now that our ancestors did not have in the sixteenth century, and we can acquire skills, tastes, and ideas unknown to them. We now develop our powers in ways they could not do, even though they had the powers and lacked only the opportunities. But then in the sixteenth century they had opportunities that we lack, and acquired skills, tastes, and ideas that we no longer acquire. We have, broadly speaking, much the same powers, much the same natural capacities, as they had, though we develop them differently. Why, then, should we say that in our time human powers are more fully developed than in theirs? Or that we are closer than they were to realizing ourselves? Our speaking of these things and making ideals of them, as they did not, is no evidence that we are closer than they were to achieving them.

I do not deny that we can ever have good reason for saying that human powers are more fully developed in one type of society than in another. Of two societies that we compare, one may be much simpler than the other; there may be a much smaller variety of skills, tastes, and ideas in it. In that case *more fully developed* means only *developed in a greater variety of ways*. But I do deny that the more fully developed human powers are, in this sense, the greater the opportunity for individuals to realize themselves.

Nor do I deny that, if we compare two different kinds of society, we can ever say that the opportunity to realize oneself is greater in one than in the other. Notions of excellence and of what is worth while would, of course, differ in the two societies, and so too therefore would men's ambitions, whether they were modest or not. Still, if we had enough information and set up appropriate standards of measurement, we might have grounds for concluding that, on the whole, people had a better chance in one society than the other of forming firm ambitions and achieving them. So, too, it might be possible, even though notions of excellence differed, to show that in one society people were more ambitious, strove harder for excellence, than in the other. It might then turn out that in the less ambitious of the two societies, ambitions were more stable and more often achieved than in the more ambitious. In that case, we might still find people with the preferences of John Stuart Mill putting the second society above the first, even though the rate of failure to realize oneself was greater in it. But to admit that capacities are developed more variously or ambitions achieved more often or excellence pursued more widely and resolutely in one society than another is not to concede that the course of social change, whenever it increases one of these three things (human diversity, self-realization, and the pursuit of excellence) increases the other two as well. It is not to concede that there has been progress in the sense that Humboldt or Mill understood it: that is to say, 'moral' as distinct from 'material' progress—from a mere increase in wealth, scientific knowledge, and power.

Still less is it to concede that the standards of a later age are 'higher' than those of an earlier age because the people who accept them understand themselves, their society, and their culture better. This idea—of which there are many traces in the writings of Marx and his disciples—is to be found again and again, variously presented, in social theories produced from the eighteenth century onwards. It lies at the heart of the modern faith in progress and is pre-Hegelian, though Hegel elaborated upon it more copiously than anyone before him.

It is worth noticing that, though this idea implies that later and more sophisticated achievements are somehow higher than earlier and less sophisticated ones, believers in progress do not ordinarily put philosophers, poets, and artists who come later in the tale of cultural progress higher than those who come earlier, even though, more obviously than the theories of natural scientists, their works express the standards of their age. They do not put Kant above Plato, or Virgil above Homer, or Titian above Giotto, any more than Einstein above Newton. They might perhaps say that the later achievements, even though the gifts required to produce them are not of a higher order, are in themselves higher in so far as they reveal a greater understanding of man and the world. They might claim that in philosophy, history, poetry, and the arts, as in science, there is more than accumulation and growing diversity; there is also an understanding that goes 'deeper'.

Though there are different kinds of understanding involved in these different spheres, greater *depth* in all of them might be taken to mean greater discrimination and comprehensiveness. Later thinkers make finer distinctions and take account of a wider variety of experiences, actual and possible. Though the explanations of philosophers and historians cannot be tested in quite the ways that scientific theories can be, it makes sense to call some more discriminating and comprehensive than others. It means something to speak of progress in understanding, even in spheres where understanding differs essentially from scientific knowledge. Though the business of artists and poets is not to explain but to reveal, we can say of some artists and poets compared with others that they are more sophisticated, meaning thereby, not that their technical skills are greater, but that their understanding of what they speak about or depict or express is more discriminating and wider. Artists and poets too, and not only philosophers, scientists, and historians, 'stand on the shoulders' of those who lived before them, and because they do so, see and feel in some directions 'further' than their predecessors could. And if they stand on other men's shoulders without adding anything to their own stature in comparison with them, the same is true of philosophers and scientists.

There is indeed, in this sense, an enrichment of human experience, a growth of sophistication. But I am not sure that it entitles us to say that the values of later (or culturally more diverse and sophisticated) ages are higher than the values of earlier (or culturally narrower and less sophisticated) ones. For greater diversity and sophistication in the cultural sphere do not entail, any more than greater material wealth does, a general superiority. The old are more sophisticated than the young, but their experiences are not therefore higher in quality nor their purposes more admirable; what they gain in discrimination and many-sidedness they lose in freshness and intensity. Nor are the abilities, sentiments, and aspirations of the sophisticated, whose cultural inheritance is rich, more fully or more adequately human than those of the unsophisticated. Sophistication brings loss as well as gain, and what is lost is just as fully, just as characteristically, *human* as what is gained. Myth is not less fully human than science, nor a Zulu dance than a Russian ballet; for the lower animals are no nearer to making myths than to making science, no nearer to dancing like Zulus than like members of a *corps de ballet*.

To reject the idea of progress as a movement from lower to higher forms of human life—an idea by no means confined to philosophers and those who read their books—is not to reject self-realization as an ideal. This ideal has so far been widely accepted only in a certain type of sophisticated society, for reasons which I have tried to explain. But we happen to live in a society of this type, many of whose practices and ideals are spreading fast over the whole world. In all societies the individual is expected to sustain his roles, to carry out the obligations of his station, adequately, but only in some is his need to prove himself to himself and to others by achieving something held to be admirable or worth while, whether by standards shared by many or a few, or even peculiar to himself,[6] widely recognized and approved.

The ambitious kind of self-realization, the kind admired by John Stuart Mill, the striving to excel, the setting up for oneself of aims difficult to achieve because they make large demands on the self, the proving of one's worth to oneself and others by conspicuous achievement, though closely allied to the desire for fame, is also in important respects different. For

[6] I say even *peculiar to himself*, for though everyone who seeks to prove himself hopes to be accepted by at least some people for what he claims, or aspires to be, his standards may, to begin with, be peculiar to himself, at least to some extent. A thinker or artist, who comes in the end to be widely recognized, is often at first, and sometimes for a long time, unrecognized. People then say of him that in the end he succeeded in 'imposing himself' on his contemporaries or on posterity; he moved them to see the world, or some aspect of it, differently or to look more closely at what they took little notice of before.

fame may be got cheaply, whereas what Mill and others approve is exertion and self-discipline, enterprise, imagination, and firmness of purpose, in the pursuit of aims which a man makes peculiarly his own in the sense that his self-esteem depends largely on his achieving them or on his striving valiantly to do so. In pursuing them, he may hope for recognition from only a few persons. Yet this striving for excellence, even when it is not a pursuit of fame, differs essentially from mere concern for reputation, which may call for little exertion.

People who value this striving for excellence admit that the striver, in setting up his aims, is always deeply influenced by standards which he shares with others, and yet their admiration for him is often the greater the more his standards are peculiar to himself, the more original he is, and the more he succeeds in imposing his standards on others, on being recognized on his own terms. In pursuing his aims, he may (even when he is unsuccessful) do harm to himself or to others; and when the harm to himself is considerable, his pursuit of his aims scarcely deserves to be called self-realization, unless he has foreseen the harm and accepted it as a price to be paid or a risk to be taken. If the harm is to others, then his pursuit of his aims, though it is (looked at from his point of view) a form of self-realization, may be rightly condemned by society. If his aims seem worthless to others (even though not harmful), they will not recognize his pursuit of them, difficult though it may be, as self-realization. They must agree with the striver that what he strives for is excellence before they are willing to concede that his striving is a form of self-realization or self-improvement, or whatever else they choose to call it. But they need not agree beforehand; for he may in the end move them (or some of them) to accept his own estimate of himself and his performance.

To set great store by self-realization, even the form of it that is a striving for excellence, is entirely reasonable; and it is also reasonable to hold that this form of it has come to be much more widely accepted in modern times than it used to be. But, as we have seen, it can happen that the type of society in which this ideal comes to be widely accepted frustrates people in their pursuit of it. Social conditions may encourage them to believe that they ought to aim high and yet make it difficult for them to form firm and realistic aims, and so produce in them the sense that they are aimless and lost. They do not know 'what to do with themselves', and feel inadequate or guilty. Or, though able to form clear and firm ambitions, they may lack the means, material and cultural, to pursue them with much hope of success. Though frustrated ambition may be more immediately and keenly felt and more hotly resented, uncertainty and bewilderment are often more widespread and insidious. Misery and disaffection come as much from hopelessness as from frustrated hopes.

Frustration does not come only of lack of opportunity or lack of resources; it comes also of lack of ability. Who strives for excellence may fall short of attaining it, even though he has had all the advantages that education and social circumstances can provide. Disappointment comes as much from striving too high as from competing with others for what only a few can get. Striving for excellence is always dangerous, whether it is competitive or not, whether it is for what most people value highly or for what is appreciated by only a few. Perhaps Mill understood this, even though he never troubled to point it out. Perhaps he thought such risks worth taking in the service of so high an ideal. If he did, I do not say that he was wrong, though I think it odd that a Utilitarian should think so well of ambitions that put happiness so much at risk.

If, then, we take self-realization or self-improvement, in the sense of striving for excellence, as a thing to be encouraged and provided for— which we may do because, like the younger Mill, we admire it or because we believe that it is an ideal coming to be more and more widely attractive —we must beware of accepting some common but groundless opinions about it. We must not take it for granted that, the more there is of this self-realization, the more likely it is that people will find ways of life that satisfy them. Striving for excellence and happiness, though they are not incompatible, do not run easily in harness together. If happiness is what we want, there are perhaps better ways of getting it than by living strenuously and making large demands on ourselves. Living an active and disciplined life is, no doubt, for most people a condition of happiness, but such a life need not be a pursuit of excellence, and may more often bring happiness when it is not than when it is.

Or if, like Rousseau (and perhaps also Marx, though he does not use these particular terms), we believe both in moral freedom and in everyone's achieving a way of life that satisfies him, we must not assume that these two things go naturally together. It may be possible to have both, but what brings the one need not bring the other. If we want both, we must inquire what conditions enable us to get both. On the face of it, moral freedom would seem to be more closely connected with striving for excellence than with happiness; for, though men could be morally free in a society where there was little striving for excellence, it is unlikely that this striving, as distinct from the pursuit of mere fame or wealth or power, would mean much to them unless they cared about moral freedom.

Even if we do accept moral freedom and self-realization (whether as striving for excellence or in some other form) as ideals, we need not hold, as Hegel and others have done, that they are somehow implicit in the very notions of reason and will, of capacities that are distinctively human. No doubt, only creatures able to reason and to make considered choices could conceive of such ideals and cherish them; and, no doubt too, these particular ideals are sophisticated and have a long history of cultural change behind them. The present arose out of the recent past, and that past in turn out of a more remote one. The historian can show how ideas and ideals, as well as institutions, change and grow in sophistication; and he needs to be something of a philosopher to be able to do it. He can show how ideals we think of as peculiarly our own were clearly present, though in different forms, in earlier times. But all this does not warrant our claiming for our ideals, as compared with earlier ones, that they are more fully human: not even if, like Marx, we deny that they can be realized in society as it is and postpone their realization to the future.

CHAPTER XIII

FREEDOM, EQUALITY, AND PROLETARIAN DEMOCRACY

I

SOCIALISTS and radicals have dreamt of communities in which men and women would be free: that is to say, would be able to choose the occupations and ways of life most congenial to them and would together control production and social conditions generally. Not all of them have shared these ideals: Saint-Simon and his disciples, for example, did not. But many have done so, and among them Marx. Most of them, including Marx, have welcomed the spread of industry and trade, seeing in it a liberating force. Though it makes everyone dependent on an immense number of other people for his well-being, it extends the range of occupations open to him and his opportunities to acquire the skills and the knowledge he needs to lead the kind of life that attracts him. It also provides society with the resources required to educate its members so that they can understand the conditions in which they live and control and improve them. That is to say, though it makes men more elaborately dependent on one another, it also offers them a wider range of choices, and makes it possible for communities and other social groups to be more effectively self-governing. Or, rather, it would do this, if society were organized as it should be. But it also—this spread of industry and trade and of the skills and knowledge that go with it—produces the means and the will to reorganize society. Mankind are on the threshold of a new era, in which both individuals and communities can be more effectively their own masters than ever before. This was the faith of many socialists and radicals in the last century, and it is still the faith of some of them today, though perhaps a faith less firmly held.

The trouble with this faith is that those who have it say too little about how what they believe in is to be achieved. They do not like industrial society as it is, in spite of their hopes for its future. They are among its fiercest critics. Organized as it is, it promises much more than it performs; it proclaims ideals of freedom and popular authority which are out of reach while it remains unchanged. The legal rights that it grants to the individual do not make him effectively free, and the institutions it provides to ensure that those who make decisions on behalf of the community are responsible to the people affected by them fail of their purpose—of their professed purpose. To be sure, laws and governmental institutions would not be what they are unless these ideals—individual freedom and collective self-government—were widely proclaimed and officially recognized, and yet they do not help to achieve the ideals and are even obstacles in the way of their achievement. In the opinion of these critics of industrial society as it now is, it is not so much a question of changing social conditions so that laws and political institutions which now fail of their purpose should become effective, as of changing them so as to make possible the emergence of quite different institutions: of procedures for the making and implementing of rules and policies which really are compatible with freedom and self-government. These new procedures will, they think, be so different from those we now have that they sometimes refer to their emergence as a disappearance of 'the state', and even of 'law' and 'government'. When they do this, they ordinarily do not mean that, in the ideal society as they imagine it, there will be no authoritative making of social rules binding on members of the community and no prescribed ways of applying the rules to individuals or of settling disputes among them; they mean rather that the making and applying of rules, and the settling of disputes, will not be the business of professional holders of public authority but of ordinary members of the community, and that there will be no coercing people to get them to obey rules and decisions made by authority. Or they mean that there will be a much closer approximation to this desirable state of affairs than is possible in society as we know it.

Unfortunately, they say too little about these procedures to make it clear what they might be. It is perhaps easy in the abstract to imagine and to describe in some detail procedures that meet the two conditions laid down: no coercion and no carrying on of public business by 'professionals'—by persons whose recognized whole-time occupation is to carry it on. But it is difficult to imagine an industrial society confining itself to such procedures. In this chapter I shall not try to describe procedures of this kind. Rather, I shall consider the reasons that stand in the way of an industrial society's meeting these anarchist conditions, and I shall look more closely at this idea of personal autonomy or 'self-mastery', which is different from the idea of moral freedom, though in some of its forms closely connected with it.

For the Stoics, who were the first in the West to preach self-mastery as an ideal, it had few social implications; it was a moral or spiritual condition. A slave might achieve self-mastery and yet remain a slave. Though in one sense this Stoic ideal was egalitarian, since everyone could attain it, no matter what his position in society, in another sense it was not; it required no reform of society to reduce inequalities of power and wealth. Nor was it a democratic ideal, for it was, as the Stoics conceived of it, no more likely to be achieved where the mass of citizens had political rights than where they had not. It has affinities with Rousseau's idea of moral freedom, for it consists in living by 'laws of reason' which are accepted as being such. But the differences from Rousseau's idea are also great: in the eyes of the Stoic, the laws are not expressions of a 'general will' and their binding character does not arise from their being made by all for the benefit of all. What is more, a man's ability and will to observe them do not, for the Stoic, depend largely on social conditions. Rousseau's idea of man as essentially a social being liable to corruption by society is no part of the Stoic philosophy.

The champions of democracy in ancient Greece were not much concerned either for self-mastery, as the Stoics understood it, or for the rights and opportunities of the individual, as we conceive of them today, whether we are liberals or socialists or anarchists. No doubt, in the Athens of Pericles, most adult males who were not slaves and who worked for their livings were their own masters at work, but it was not put forward as a principle that everyone should be his own master or else should have a say in running any collective enterprise in which he took part. There was no claim made that the individual should be able to choose his occupation and be given the opportunity to qualify for the occupation of his choice. In a still largely agricultural society in which family ties were strong and there were many slaves, we should hardly expect such claims to be made for the human adult or even the human male adult merely as such. Any more than we should expect it to be recognized that everyone who is domiciled in the community and earns his living inside it should have full citizen rights.

Such attitudes as these are not confined to friends of democracy in ancient Greece or in city states generally. We can find them even among the earliest champions of popular government in the large modern state— the Levellers. No doubt, they wanted to broaden the franchise, and the distinction—so important in the Greek or Italian republics (and even the Swiss cantons)—between natives and resident aliens meant little to them. But their concern was only that men who were already their own masters economically (who were not servants) should have a say in the government of their country. They did not claim for all men (not to speak of women) that they should be their own masters at work or should have a say in running the farms or workshops in which they were employed, any more than they claimed the vote for them all.

Like the Levellers, Rousseau saw a close connection between economic independence and political competence, but he went on to argue that in a properly constituted or just society all men would be both economically independent and politically competent. Freedom of contract between rich and poor, he said, is a sham, because the rich can afford to hold out longer than the poor to get their terms accepted. He wanted a social order and an economy in which men would be roughly equal in bargaining power;

he did not put it in quite these terms but that is substantially what he meant. He did not explain how bargaining power is to be measured, but he took it for granted that men, if they are to be economically independent (that is to say, if they are to be able to reject terms which seem to them unjust), must at least own their means of production, their land, their workshops, and their tools, not collectively but individually. He was passionately an egalitarian, and yet the idea that there could be economic independence, or a rough equality of bargaining power in the sphere of production and trade, without private property, never occurred to him. He was in favour of an extensive public domain to be run collectively by the citizens, but only in order to defray the costs of government. In his ideal community everyone, or rather every head of a family, owns some property and nobody owns so much as to be able to compel others to make unfair bargains to his advantage. Its members have simple tastes and modest ambitions and are therefore uncompetitive. Rousseau was among the first to condemn what Tawney was later to call 'the acquisitive society'.

He believed that the equality he cared for so much would have to be carefully maintained by law, but he never inquired how far the laws required to maintain it might themselves curtail the citizen's independence. He defined a goal or posed a problem without considering in detail how it might be reached or solved. Ordinarily, when it came to giving practical advice, he was apt to be very moderate indeed, judged in the light of his own ideals. Just as, when he advised the Poles how to educate their children for citizenship, he forgot the moral freedom he had so much to say about in *The Social Contract* and in *Émile*, so too, when he intervened in the affairs of his native Geneva, the most that he asked for would, if he had got his way, have fallen far short of making Geneva a democracy. When he acted as a citizen of Geneva, his concern was to go back to the wider oligarchy of an earlier period and not to move forward towards making Geneva a society of equals. He would have thought it unrealistic to attempt to do more. He preached, passionately and eloquently, ideals which he could not bring himself to believe would be realized. The trend of the times, he thought, was against them.

Still, he did preach these ideals, and his sermons found a hearing among men more hopeful than he was. He took it for granted that in a just political community there are neither slaves nor resident aliens excluded from citizenship, and he laid it down that the laws must be made by the citizens collectively. The first of these principles, that no one who is socially included in the community (who makes his home and earns his living in it) should be politically excluded, is neither Greek nor Swiss; it was not in small republics but in the great monarchies that naturalization, or the conversion of resident aliens into full subjects or citizens placed legally on the same footing as the natives, was first made relatively easy. Not that Rousseau was exactly in favour of aliens coming into a country in large numbers to settle in it and acquire citizenship, but his conception of the general will—of what makes laws binding on the persons required to obey them—does entail that, if aliens are allowed in as settlers, they must also be allowed to become citizens.

The doctrine of the sovereignty of the people, as he understood it, seemed to Rousseau the only proper conclusion to draw from what the philosophers had long been saying about consent as the source of political authority. It is as if he were saying to the philosophers: 'You say rightly that this authority belonged to begin with to the people collectively, and that therefore nobody can rightfully exercise any part of it except with their consent. But I say that the reasons for holding that this authority belonged originally to them entail that they can never justly divest themselves of one part of it—the part that consists in the making of laws binding on them all. They must retain this part if the other parts are in fact to be exercised with their consent. Just as it is implicit in man's claim to be free, or rather in the grounds put forward to justify the claim, that there are rights of which he cannot divest himself even voluntarily (for example, by selling himself into slavery), so it is implicit in the claim that political authority belongs originally to the people collectively that there is a part of it, the right to make laws, of which they cannot divest themselves'. Whatever its merits logically, this argument has been widely attractive to radicals, especially in the nineteenth century and after, who for one reason or another have lost faith in representative government. It has appeared in a variety of forms in many different connections. On the face of it, it is not absurd. Just as it makes sense to argue that, though a man can divest himself voluntarily of many of his rights, there are some of which he cannot divest himself because his having them is a necessary condition of his being able to undertake obligations of any kind, so it makes sense to argue that there are political rights which members of a community cannot give up if the conditions that make authority over them legitimate are to be met. Nor is it absurd to hold, with Rousseau, that one of these rights is the right to make laws collectively.

Though Rousseau's principles forbid excluding from citizenship anyone living and working in a community, it is notorious that he himself was no cosmopolitan. He lived most of his life outside his native Geneva, but he was not much in favour of people leaving their own country to settle abroad. His ideal society, though egalitarian, is not welcoming to strangers. Inside it there are no slaves, no persons who are treated merely as instruments and not as persons having ends of their own which others must respect, and there are no metics, no resident aliens whose services are recognized as essential to the community but who are not allowed the rights of citizens. Everyone living in the community, and especially everyone contributing to its well-being by his work,[1] must be a full member of it. Where there is a general will, where political authority is legitimate, there can be no 'second-class citizens' and no 'apartheid'.

Rousseau claimed to see a connection between the equality without which there can be no general will and communal exclusiveness. The connection, of course, was not logical. A community of equals that welcomed strangers wanting to take up residence in their midst and ready to admit them to full citizenship on easy terms would not be acting inconsistently. But Rousseau believed that such behaviour would be unlikely, and he thought it dangerous. In his opinion, men's willingness to treat each other as equals depends largely on their having a strong sense of community, just as this sense is greatly strengthened by their treating each other as equals. Loyalty to the community and equality sustain each other, but the loyalty depends also on men's attachment to the institutions and ways of life of their community. The sense of belonging to a community, which moves a man to treat others whom he recognizes as also belonging to it as equals, or at least as persons having strong claims upon him, carries with it the sense of not belonging to other communities. To feel at home in a community is to feel not at home outside it; and whoever is at home everywhere is really at home nowhere. The rootless man, as Rousseau sees him, lacks strong sympathies, and if he sometimes cares little for social distinctions, this is more from indifference to what others take seriously than from concern for equality.

Equality, in Rousseau's opinion, can be achieved only in small communities. Not only—to mention the most obvious reason—because large communities, to function properly, require elaborate structures of authority that give great power to persons who are virtually irresponsible, but also because it is in small communities that shared loyalties go deep and that men are close enough to their fellow citizens to feel strongly bound to them. Or, rather, it is only in small communities that loyalties shared by everyone, the loyalties that hold the community together, are apt to be stronger than loyalties to particular groups inside it, the loyalties that are, or can be, divisive. Of course, a small community can be deeply divided, especially when there are large inequalities inside it, and sometimes even when there are not. Rousseau would not have denied it. He believed that equality and what might be called fraternity (the ties of sympathy that unite men who recognize one another as belonging to the same group) can be solidly established or deeply rooted only in small communities, and not that they always are so.[2]

---

[1] For Rousseau, as for most writers of his age, 'everyone' meant, in this connection, every adult male. He was no feminist, at least politically.

[2] There is plentiful evidence, since the rise of the modern nation state, that loyalty to a large community can be very strong, that it can transcend narrower loyalties and can flourish even

Rousseau's concern for equality, if we compare it with the egalitarianism of the next century, is conspicuously defective in one respect; he has little to say about the rights of women. Or, rather, he has nothing to say about their political rights or their rights outside the family and the sphere of close personal relationships. In his day no one cared much about these rights. This indifference to the rights of women in intellectual and literary circles in the eighteenth as compared with the nineteenth century is not, I think, a sign that in these circles, in the earlier period, men were more inclined to look upon women as morally and intellectually, or even politically, inferior to themselves. Women have rarely come closer to being treated as equals by men than in some aristocratic and intellectual circles in France in the eighteenth century, and Rousseau moved in these circles, at least for a time. The compliments that he sometimes pays to womankind owe more to what he saw of women in France than in Switzerland, and his indifference to their political and legal rights can hardly be attributed to Swiss or provincial blindness to their undomestic capacities. Rousseau, despite his passion for equality, was indifferent to what later came to be called equality of opportunity, at least in some of its aspects, and it is largely this indifference that explains his attitude to women and to their place in society—an attitude which has far less of masculine condescension in it than is sometimes supposed.

Unlike most of the early socialists and unlike Marx, Rousseau never condemned inequality on the ground that it restricts the range of choices unequally, making it much narrower for the poor than for the rich. I do not say that, if the question had been put to him, he would not have agreed that it is unjust that children of rich parents should have opportunities denied to poor children. But this is a consequence of inequality that he virtually ignored. His ideal society is simple and economically static as well as small, and he took it for granted that in it sons would ordinarily follow the occupations of their fathers. Not that they would be compelled to do so but that ordinarily they would not want to do otherwise. What mattered above all in his eyes was that men, whatever their occupations, should be their own masters and that they should not be constrained by poverty to make unjust agreements to their own hurt. Their freedom, economically, consisted in their being their own masters and in their not having to give way to the superior bargaining power of the rich just as, politically, it consisted in their not having to obey laws imposed on them by others, in their being legislators on equal terms with others. It did not

where there are wide inequalities. There is evidence even that, where it exists, narrower loyalties are not always weakened. Everyone has multiple loyalties; and this is not a fact to be deplored, merely because these loyalties sometimes conflict with one another. It is arguable that both individuals and social groups stand to gain a great deal from these multiple loyalties, just as it is arguable that it is better for a man and those close to him that he should have more than one or two friends.

consist in the opportunity to choose, among the occupations that society finds room for, the one that attracts one most or is best suited to one's talents.

Just as Rousseau took it for granted that, even in the society of equals, men would ordinarily follow their fathers' occupations, so he took it for granted that women would continue to do what had always been considered woman's work, and it never occurred to him that it was a restriction of women's freedom that they should ordinarily have little choice but to become wives and mothers any more than that men were the less free for living in small communities in which every father's son had little choice but to follow in his father's footsteps. Nor did it occur to him, any more than to most people in his day, that women's position in the home, in what he regarded as their natural sphere, might be greatly strengthened by giving them political rights. Given his principles and his conceptions of freedom and equality, it is much more Rousseau's failure to claim these rights for women, than his taking it for granted that they would continue to do 'women's work', that reveals a 'masculine bias' in him, though one shared by both sexes in his time and long afterwards.

If we look at Rousseau's account, in his novel *La Nouvelle Héloïse*, of the domestic economy of his heroine Julie, we see that she is as completely in charge of her section of it, which is the larger and the more important, as her husband is of his. Within the home at least, she is the equal of her husband, and the first among equals. This particular home is a rich one and the efficient running of it, the contriving that everyone in it should be happy, calls for intelligence, tact, insight, and firmness. But even in a modest home, the wife is mistress within her own sphere, which is a large one. The idea that the running of a home is less demanding and calls for lesser abilities than the running of a farm or a workshop, that 'woman's work' is somehow inferior to 'man's work', never occurred to Rousseau. Indeed, it is not an idea that makes sense, except perhaps in an urbanized industrial society, where families are small, education is largely outside the home and in the hands of professionals, and there are labour-saving devices and packaged foods.

Extreme poverty and economic dependence impose heavy burdens on both husband and wife. But in an industrial economy in which the demand for labour fluctuates greatly, this dependence weighs perhaps even more heavily on the husband than on the wife. It is he who, when he loses his job, feels useless, and who, in his destitute condition, is brought up against the outside world; for he is the family's representative in relation to it, in his dealings with officials, creditors, and potential employers. It is he who is then a burden to his wife and not she to him. But Rousseau knew nothing of industrial society. To someone with his views about how society should be organized the equality that really matters, and which has to be maintained deliberately because there are always forces in society that tend to undermine it, is equality between the heads of households. This equality is both economic and political, an equal dependence of neighbour on neighbour and of citizens on the community they belong to: a dependence which is the nearest that man can get to independence while living in society.

It was in the next century, when the West was industrialized, that it came to be widely accepted that a crucial part of a man's freedom consists in his being able to choose his occupation and manner of life. The growth of industry created a labour market on a scale unknown before, and it became a matter of urgent concern to many people that they should be able to sell their labour to the best advantage. That sellers of labour should be equally well placed to do this came therefore to seem important to believers in equality. But some kinds of labour sell at higher prices than others do; and so, if competition between sellers of labour is to be fair, each must, as far as his natural gifts allow, be as well placed as the others to acquire the skills and the knowledge enabling him to sell his labour at the best price. In an industrial society, it was only to be expected that the principle of equality of opportunity should take this 'utilitarian' form.

But this was not the only form it took. In a part of the world in which men moved about in search of work much more than their forefathers had done, and in which sons followed their fathers' occupations much less, it came also to seem important that a man should be able to choose the occupation that suited him best. He might not aim at selling his labour at the highest price; it might matter to him more that his work, and the style of life that went with it, should be congenial to him. He should therefore, as far as natural gifts allowed, be as well placed as others to choose the occupation most likely to satisfy him.

The spread of industry, the greatly extended division of labour, the growth of towns, the unceasing change in productive methods, the proliferation of governmental activities and therefore of transactions between public officials and citizens, have meant that, to equip themselves to make a living and to be able to use the services at their disposal, people have much greater need than they used to have of formal education outside the home. The need for this education has grown so quickly that much the greater part of it has now to be provided at public expense, and almost everyone agrees that it ought to be provided on the same terms to all who need it.

The spread of industry has also affected the family, and therefore the place of women, both inside the family and outside it. Women have become, as never before, not just home-makers but bread-winners. So the claims made for men have come, though less strongly and more tardily, to be made for women as well. These claims made for women—though the people who made them often thought otherwise—were directed more against new forms of exploitation which resulted from the weakening of family ties and the emergence of women out of the sphere which by tradition was theirs (the home and the business carried on inside it or next door to it) than against older forms of 'masculine oppression'. It was above all the spread of industry and the growth of towns that drove women into a 'man's world' in which they were conspicuously the 'weaker' sex. It was not in the home, or in the dairy or workshop that was almost an extension of it, that the economic and social handicaps of women, which prevented their getting equal treatment with men, were striking; it was outside the home in factories, in the mines, and in other large units of production. It is often said that the spread of industry and the weakening, or at least narrowing, of family ties have served to make women more conscious of being socially the weaker sex, and more resentful of their inferiority; it could more truly be said that it is these conditions which have weakened them socially by creating or aggravating the inferiorities they complain of, and that the struggle for women's rights is as much a reaction to this weakening of their position as an attempt to take advantage of opportunities they used not to have. The opportunities that come with industrialization and the growth of towns, with the spread of literacy, and with greater ease of movement, are new for the great majority of men as well as for women. Many of the rights claimed for women in the nineteenth century (and mostly not achieved before the twentieth) were enjoyed by only a small minority of men until quite recently, while others were rights of property and inheritance that meant little except to the well-to-do until the poor grew considerably more affluent.

The growth of industry, the narrowing of family ties, easier movement from place to place, and the greater need for formal schooling of many different kinds, while they produced and strengthened the demand for equality of opportunity also greatly reduced the number of people who were their own masters (or mistresses) at work. Yet this equality, so much acclaimed in modern times, in itself does nothing to mitigate this particular condition, this having to work under the direction of others. It would seem then that the social conditions which produce this demand for equality of opportunity also put economic independence, as Rousseau and his contemporaries understood it, out of most people's reach.

And yet this concern for equality has not just superseded the older concern for independence but has to some extent incorporated it. The demand for equality has taken a variety of forms, and notably three, which it is important to distinguish from one another, though the differences between them often go unnoticed. Sometimes the demand for more equal opportunity takes almost no account of the need for independence: it is then a demand that everyone should have the opportunity to acquire, as far as his native abilities permit, the resources and skills which enable him to compete effectively for the 'rewards' that society has to offer— for wealth, power, and reputation. But the demand also takes two other forms: that everyone should have the opportunity to achieve, as far as his gifts allow, the forms of excellence that he wishes to achieve; and that everyone should be helped impartially to achieve a way of life that satisfies him. A man's being satisfied with his work and manner of life may depend on his being able to excel in some way, but it need not do so; he may be unambitious.

I shall call the first kind of equality, equal opportunity to achieve success, meaning by success the achievement of wealth or power or reputation—of advantages that are easily recognized and are widely held to be desirable. The second kind I shall call equal opportunity to achieve excellence, and the third equal opportunity to achieve happiness.[3]

These three kinds of equality are not often distinguished, and it might be argued that in practice the differences between them do not matter. Is there not one claim behind all three of them: the claim to be able to choose one's occupation and way of life? So why not just speak of equal opportunity to make this choice, and leave it at that? Surely, if a man wants success, as the world understands it, if he wants wealth or power or reputation, will he not, if he gets what he wants, achieve a way of life that satisfies him? And will he not also achieve it, if he strives for excellence and attains it, even though what he strives for means nothing to most people?

True, there is a claim or a principle that lies behind these three kinds of equality. But it is none the less important to distinguish between them, because so much of the criticism levelled at industrial society, as it exists today, is that it encourages the pursuit of success at the expense of the pursuit of excellence or happiness. The distinctions I make, even though seldom made explicit, are often implicit in socialist or anarchist attacks on Western civilization as 'bourgeois' or 'acquisitive' or just simply 'material-istic'. These attacks, though mostly aimed at the West because most of the writers who make them live in the West, could just as plausibly be aimed at the Soviet Union or at some of the countries of Asia and Africa now in process of modernization. The attacks might need to be altered in some respects to reach these different targets, but in essentials they could be the same.

---

[3] It is often said that happiness is rarely achieved when it is pursued deliberately. This is only a half-truth. The deliberate pursuit of pleasure is often self-defeating, and it is a mistake to speak of happiness, as Hobbes and others have done, as the successful pursuit of pleasure or of objects of desire. But this is not what most people understand by happiness; they mean by it rather a way of life that satisfies, such that whoever attains it, seeks to preserve it. It is possible for people to learn from experience what satisfies them, and to endeavour to attain and preserve it.

II

Equality of opportunity to achieve success does not have the same liberal implications as equal opportunity to achieve excellence or happiness. It is easy to imagine an authoritarian society so organized that most people inside it had very little independence, and different occupations carried very unequal rewards, and which yet laid down rules ensuring that there was fair competition for entry into these occupations and for promotion inside them. Irresponsible rulers, in the light of their own ideas of what was socially desirable, might decide what kinds of work to encourage and how they should be rewarded, and might insist also, for the sake of efficiency, that people should be allowed impartially to do the kind of work for which they were best fitted, and should be trained for work in accordance with their natural aptitudes. Equality of opportunity is a principle which first arose, or first became important, in the West in countries which at the time were relatively liberal and in which there was already a considerable demand for democracy, and so there are still many people in the West who think of it as a liberal and democratic principle. It is therefore worth noticing that it can take quite illiberal forms, and can, in these forms, be conscientiously applied in countries that are quite undemocratic.[4]

The pursuit of success and the pursuit of happiness could, under some social and cultural conditions, nearly coincide. Most people could perhaps be so educated as to be competitive in quite conventional ways, and to be so *con amore* or at least without reluctance; they might find the pursuit of worldly success (of social rewards widely valued) congenial to them. They might not be unwilling competitors, yearning to live differently and yet impelled to competition by circumstances they resent and are powerless to remove. But critics who attack what they call 'materialism' or 'the acquisitive society' either deny that this is in fact the case (that the pursuit of success ordinarily brings happiness, even to the successful), or they deplore it to the extent that it is true. A society in which equality is prized

---

[4] It might be argued that in illiberal and undemocratic countries persons in authority, because they are irresponsible, are unusually corrupt and given to favouritism, and that corruption and favouritism undermine equality of opportunity in all its forms. But, even where there is no responsibility to the people, there can be responsibility among holders of authority to one another. The rulers of an 'authoritarian' society can, if they are so minded, take measures that are highly effective against corruption and favouritism. A high degree of intelligent devotion to principles is no less compatible with authoritarian than with democratic government. The truth, perhaps, is that authoritarian governments go more to extremes than democratic governments do: that they reach higher levels of purity and impartiality and also sink to lower depths. This does not mean that in democracies corruption is always kept within modest bounds; it sometimes goes far indeed. But the worst examples of it are to be found in countries that are not democratic. To be sure, some of these countries claim to be democracies, or at least their rulers make this claim for them and ordinary citizens find it expedient to follow their example.

above all because it makes for fairer competition in the pursuit of worldly success is not at all their ideal. They would not like it even if it were a happy society. But they mostly believe that it would not be happy. The pursuit of worldly success is, they think, even where the competition for it is fair, on the whole a source of unhappiness. Where social conditions encourage it, people seek satisfaction where it is not to be found. They seek it in ways which are not to their taste, or which seem to them contemptible or else a turning away from better things. Where worldly success is the aim, the endeavour to achieve it is not its own reward, and may well be distasteful and frustrating, even though the reward is strongly desired.

When a man aims at excellence, it may be of a kind not widely recognized, or perhaps not recognized at all, until he has achieved it and others learn to appreciate what he has done. In that case, as he moves forward towards achieving it, his progress is not the making of a 'career', a movement along a familiar and well-marked way; it is a making of a way that is peculiarly his own. Or, if he does not aspire to excellence, but takes life easily in ways that satisfy him, these ways may still be unconventional. Or his prime concern may be to be as far as possible independent of others, to be his own master. Or, if he works with others, he may want to have a say along with them in directing their joint labours. He may need, if his work is to satisfy him, to be a planner, or at least a maker of decisions about his work, and not just someone who does what someone else tells him to do. He may feel this need strongly, even though his work calls only for modest abilities and efforts, and he recognizes that it does. The claim to independence, to be one's own master at work, or to be able to start new things and take unfrequented paths, differs from the claim to be allowed to prove one's importance or superiority. Nor is it a claim to benefit from the advantages that society offers without contributing anything to it which it values, anything for which there is a demand. The man who cares greatly for his 'independence' does not hold that society owes him a living whatever he may choose to do, however useless his efforts may appear to others; he holds rather that society owes it to him to let him try his hand at new or unconventional things, including new ways of making a living, even at some cost to others (at the cost of his making a smaller contribution to their welfare than he might otherwise make) and at his own risk.

Earlier, in speaking of Rousseau, I suggested that one could, without inconsistency, think it important that people should be satisfied with their way of life and should be economically independent, and yet care nothing for equality of opportunity. Long before other critics of excessive competition and of the acquisitive society, Rousseau condemned the pursuit of worldly success as an obstacle to happiness. For full measure and for the same reason, he also condemned the pursuit of excellence. This indifference to equality of opportunity makes good enough sense in an egalitarian and a champion of personal independence, while society has not yet become industrial, has not yet become a society of the kind in which most people already are living or soon will be. It makes sense, too, on the assumption that the course of social and economic change can be reversed or diverted so as to restore or achieve the social conditions of 'independence', as Rousseau conceived of them. But if we reject this assumption as quite unrealistic and yet think it important that people should strive for excellence or happiness, or should be (as far as possible) their own masters, we do well to press for forms of equality that meant nothing to Rousseau. We do well to press for them, even if we happen to agree with him (as I do not) that the society in which people are most likely to find happiness is economically simple and changes very slowly or not at all.[5] Given that industrialism has come to stay, and with it rapid social change and social mobility, we ought to care deeply for equality of opportunity in some of its forms; we ought to do so even if we dislike 'excessive competition' or 'worldly ambition' or 'the consumer society'. If we share the values of John Stuart Mill or those of Rousseau, or even a combination of the two, we ought to care about equal opportunity to strive for excellence or to seek happiness, or to do both the one and the other.

People who care above all for the pursuit of excellence (or for self-improvement, which is not quite the same thing) often set greater store by the pursuit than by the achievement. For example, John Stuart Mill did so. Though he called himself a Utilitarian, he cared more for self-improvement than for the pursuit of happiness. Perhaps he believed that self-improvement makes for happiness; but if he did, he certainly made no attempt to show how it does so. He offered no good reasons for believing that self-improvers (or, for that matter, pursuers of excellence) are any more likely to be happy than are the lazy and the self-satisfied. Yet he did think it important that men and women should have worthwhile aims and should strive hard to achieve them, even if they should fail in the attempt. He seems to have valued freedom largely because it gives people the opportunity to set up such aims for themselves and to pursue them. What makes him a liberal rather than a radical (as these words are used today), is that he was more concerned to explain and justify this opportunity, and

[5] I see no reason for agreeing with Rousseau. To be sure, some social conditions favour happiness more than others do, but from this it does not follow that there is a social order more favourable than any other to happiness. As Rousseau himself recognized, men's needs and values differ considerably from society to society. Why should we suppose that there is only one social order in which needs and values are consistent with one another, and men have the resources to satisfy and to realize them? Or that this social order is the economically simple society of equals that Rousseau describes?

to discuss what legal rights should be secured to the individual in order that he should have it, than to argue that social conditions needed to be changed drastically to ensure that all sections of the community could exercise the rights effectively.

On the whole, socialists and anarchists have been less attracted than Mill was, and than many liberals have been, to self-improvement and the pursuit of excellence as ideals, and have cared more for the pursuit of happiness. They have also attacked the pursuit of success more sharply; for though some liberals have disliked some of the effects of competition and acquisitiveness, they have also seen great advantages in them. Yet today, in spite of these differences, liberals and the radicals to the left of them agree that both the pursuit of happiness and the pursuit of excellence (and even self-improvement) are good. They agree also that the individual needs a large measure of freedom if he is to pursue them effectively, and that they are best pursued in a democracy. At least, they subscribe to these beliefs, though they do not always behave as if they held them sincerely, and they resent attacks on their sincerity. They are all, in the broad sense, liberals and democrats, though some of the radicals denounce bourgeois democracy, deny that they are liberals, and use the word *liberal* as a term of abuse.[6]

In the early days of liberalism, there were radicals who rejected, not just the parliamentary and other institutions cherished by the liberals, but democracy and the liberal idea of freedom. The disciples of Saint-Simon denied that holders of public authority should be responsible to their subjects for how they exercise it. They wanted a society run by an élite of the enlightened and the competent, answerable to one another for what they do but not to the people. To be sure, they wanted the people to be happy, but they were not concerned that they should have freedom of speech or association, or even a wide range of occupations to choose from. They did not think it important that people should be able to engage in activities not provided for in the plans of the élite for the community. Thus, though they condemned the use of force to maintain order, they were illiberal and authoritarian. No doubt, a community run by such gentle methods as they had in mind would have to be congenial to the great majority of its members, but it would not be democratic or respectful of freedom. Yet the Saint-Simonians were radicals, at least in the sense that they wanted to change the social order drastically so as to improve

---

[6] The political theorist must crave the indulgence of his readers much more than, say, the logician or the natural scientist need do, for he uses a looser vocabulary and cannot—for lack of time or for fear of wearying the reader—take all the precautions needed to avoid misunderstanding. Many an anarchist who despises 'liberalism' and 'bourgeois democracy' values the freedoms that the liberal claims to value and thinks it important that decisions affecting the community should either be taken collectively by its members or by delegates closely responsible to them.

the conditions of life of the poor, and to achieve greater justice and equality.[7]

Today most radicals in the West are champions of freedom and democracy. I speak, of course, of their avowed beliefs, of the ideals they proclaim, and not of their real motives and convictions. Some of them attack the liberals for failing to see what their ideals require, what needs to be done if the great majority of people are really to have the opportunities that the liberals claim for them. While property is distributed and controlled as it is, or the vast 'bureaucratic' state remains in existence, or 'bourgeois' standards are widely accepted, there is not much freedom for most people. According to these radicals, the liberal fails to see that these institutions and standards are obstacles to freedom, and sometimes even defends them as essential to its preservation. Either he is blind or is not a serious champion of the freedom he proclaims. Again, he professes to favour democracy and yet is satisfied with parliamentary government as it exists in the West. He does not see that parliamentary democracy is a sham unless the control of industry is also democratic, and much greater powers are given to smaller communities in which it is easier to contrive that decision-makers are responsible to the people bound by their decisions. In the eyes of his radical accuser, the liberal is either a timid champion of freedom and popular government, or else is more concerned to defend other things which stand in the way of genuine democracy and of freedom (except for a privileged few), though he professes to think otherwise. He is a feeble ally in the struggle for the liberation of the masses, afraid or unable to see social realities for what they are.

Radicals who are revolutionaries attack the liberals for their condemnation of violence and their insistence on legal methods of protest and social change. According to them, the classes that control the state use force and deception to maintain a social and political order which is oppressive, and can do so legally because they make the laws. To excuse, as liberals do, the legal use of force while condemning the illegal use of it as 'violence' is really to betray the ideals in which they claim to believe. In the so-called parliamentary democracies, most people are in fact not free, and government is in fact not responsible to the governed. Therefore the conditions which would make the illegal use of force unnecessary

---

[7] I might be criticized for calling the disciples of Saint-Simon radicals. If they were radicals, have not many fascists been so too? For they, too, have wanted to make (and indeed have made) drastic social reforms which they have justified on the ground that they make for greater social justice and equality. Some fascists have been sincere in their desire to increase justice and equality, at least in some respects. Yet fascists are not ordinarily called radicals, and are thought of as standing to the right and not to the left of liberals. But then it is notoriously difficult to use political labels consistently. Fascists, presumably, are not radicals and belong politically to the Right because they have other goals to which they are willing, if necessary, to sacrifice social justice and equality, and also because they are overtly champions of an authoritarian state ready to use strong methods to maintain its authority.

and unjustified do not exist. But the liberal believes, or affects to believe, that they do exist. He therefore condemns the only methods which could— provided, of course, that they were used by the 'right' people and not by 'fascists' and other exploiters of popular grievances for sinister ends— establish what he says he believes in. If we look at what has happened, again and again, in different parts of the world to idealists who have tried to liberate the masses and to establish popular government by legal and peaceful means, we see that they have always failed of their purpose or been deflected from it. Those who will not learn from experience when the lesson is obvious do not really want to learn, and their devotion to the ideals they profess is suspect.

The line that divides the beliefs of the liberal from those of the radical who attacks liberalism as ineffectual or insincere is, of course, a shifting line. The liberal is today much more an egalitarian and an advocate of state intervention for the benefit of the poor and the socially handicapped than he used to be a hundred years ago. If concern for equality and a readiness to make large reforms at the expense of the rich and the privileged are characteristics of the Left, we can say that in Western countries there has been on the whole a considerable shift leftwards in the last century. This is true, at least, if *Left* and *Right* are defined by reference to attitudes to older forms of inequality conspicuous at the time when these terms first came into general use, and not to newer forms which have grown in importance since then.

The liberals are still as much under attack, and as bitterly and scornfully, by the radicals to the left of them as ever they were. And yet, despite the disputes between them, liberals and radicals still agree in proclaiming two principles: that society owes it to each of its members to enable him, as far as possible, to choose his own way of life, and especially his occupation; and that the greater the authority of any community or organization over its members (that is, the more extensive its claim on their obedience), the stronger in turn their claim to take part in exercising that authority or in choosing those who exercise it. These are, of course, very general principles, and nobody accepts them without qualification; nobody is willing to have them applied always and at any cost. Liberals and radicals disagree, as they always have done, about the extent to which they can be applied, the methods to be used in applying them or in creating the conditions in which they can be applied, and the social costs to be paid. It is these disagreements, since they turn on the concrete and particular, that change continually with changing circumstances, to the confusion of those who take part in them.

Just as the radical accuses the liberal of blindness, insincerity, and half-heartedness on the ground that he tolerates, and even justifies, conditions which are incompatible with the ideals he proclaims, and condemns methods which are often necessary to destroy those conditions, so the liberal in his turn accuses the radical, if not of half-heartedness, then of blindness and equivocation. The institutions denounced by the radical as 'bourgeois shams' and obstacles to freedom and popular government are in fact indispensable means to them in highly developed industrial societies, and the violent or illegal methods to which the radical is too ready to resort weaken sentiments on which freedom and democracy ultimately depend. This is not to condemn resort to violence or illegality under all circumstances, even in a liberal democracy, but it does imply that the attitude of the revolutionary to liberal democracy is an even greater obstacle to the enlargement of freedom and of popular government than the social conditions of which the revolutionary complains; or that it would be so, if it were more widely shared. The liberal too, like his radical critic, can point to the lessons of 'experience' or of 'history', and can argue, no less plausibly than the radical, that whoever refuses to learn from them probably has intentions other than those he proclaims, or will soon come to have them if ever he gets power by the methods he prescribes. He can argue, for example, that, while there have been several instances of force used illegally to destroy illiberal and undemocratic regimes by liberals who have then set up liberal democracies, there has never yet been an example of a liberal democracy forcibly destroyed by radicals who have then set up a more genuinely libertarian and democratic regime.

To some people it may seem that to claim that liberals and radicals differ less in their principles than in their beliefs about the social conditions of realizing them and the methods to be used in creating the conditions, is to belittle the difference between them. I do not think so. The principles are at a high level of generality. This, of course, does not mean that they are empty, but it does mean that there can be wide differences of opinion about how to apply them. I am so far from wanting to play down the differences between liberals and radicals that I believe them to be among the most important political differences dividing people in the West today.

I admit, too, that radicals often attack liberalism in terms which suggest, if we take them literally, that it is the liberal ideal of freedom they object to and not the liberal's beliefs about the conditions and methods needed to realize the idea. For example, they attack liberal concern for 'freedom of speech' or 'freedom of association'. But these attacks are not, I think, directed at the principle that people should be allowed to communicate their beliefs freely or to join organizations to promote shared aims. They are rejections of the 'liberal' claim that the legal rights granted to the citizen by the 'bourgeois' state in fact secure these freedoms to most people, or would be needed to secure them in a truly just society. Or else their purpose is to justify radicals who feel the need to disregard these rights in their efforts to get power or to keep it.

To be sure, when Communists are accused of caring nothing for freedom, the point of the accusation is not that they reject liberal ideas about how freedom is to be secured, and are mistaken in doing so. They are accused of not caring about such things as freedom of speech and freedom of association, except to the extent that to do so helps them to get power. The accusation is often just. We must judge men by their actions; and if we judge the Communists by what they do, there is pretty good evidence that they care little either for freedom now or for the eventual coming of the communist society which is to be freer than any before it. Yet the fact remains that, ideologically, they are committed to freedom. From time to time, in their more candid moments, they admit that in the countries controlled by their party freedom of speech or of association has to be drastically curtailed while the 'social foundations' of equality and freedom are laid and the fight against ruthless class enemies continues. But they never admit that, once these social foundations are laid and the fight ends in victory, it will still be necessary to curtail these freedoms. On the contrary, they claim that they will then be enjoyed fully by everyone, with no need for the legal and judicial apparatus of the bourgeois state.

In their attacks on 'the state' and on 'law', the anarchists are no doubt more whole-hearted and sincere than the Communists are. They can afford to be, since they are nowhere in control and therefore do not yet need to meet the challenge of putting their ideas into practice. Nevertheless, in attacking 'the state', they seldom condemn every kind of formal authority: that is to say, all authority exercised in prescribed ways and held to be binding on whoever belongs to the community or organization in which it is exercised. Just as, in attacking 'law', they seldom deny wholesale the need for the deliberate making of social rules, or for the administering of them by persons authorized to do so, or for the authoritative settlement of disputes. The trouble with them, rather, is that they do not make it clear what they repudiate: what exercises of authority, and how organized, are to count as activities of the 'state', or as the making or enforcement of 'law'. They denounce 'bureaucracy' without explaining what administration would be like if it were not bureaucratic, or how in a modern industrial society it could provide the citizen with the services he has come to expect of it. Or they condemn the 'manipulation of opinion' without explaining what education and the dissemination of news and views would have to be like in order *not* to be 'manipulative'.

This is not to deny that radicals in their attacks on 'bourgeois society' have pointed to specific evils, and even to evils that liberals, given their principles, ought to recognize for such, and which they too often ignore or excuse. Indeed, they have often done so. Their criticisms in detail of

Western society are formidable. But they have failed to explain what they would put in its place. The Marxists among them have been the most eva-sive of all, the most confusing and the most confused, largely because in the countries they dominate they have had to misdescribe their achieve-ments and their aims in order to justify holding on to power.

The liberals, too, have been evasive. They have been reluctant to recog-nize that getting more of the freedom and the democracy they believe in might require drastic changes in the running of the economy and in the organization of government—changes to be made only at a great cost in terms of efficiency, as economists measure it.

III

In primitive societies a man may have varied work to do but he does not think of himself as entitled to choose an occupation or to make a career. He may sometimes work hard and at other times do very little, but his work is rarely 'challenging' in the sense that he seeks to prove his worth to others or to himself by excelling at it. He proves it rather by his courage and skill in war, or his wisdom in counsel, or by gifts of prophecy or magical powers, or in activities which are more ceremonial than produc-tive. In industrial societies the variety of work done is enormously greater, and there is also greater discipline at work, whether imposed by others or by the worker on himself. Some kinds of work call for rare talent, require long training, and carry great prestige. But much work, even skilled work, is monotonous. People may move in search of work more than they do in economically simpler societies, and may even change occupations more often, and yet do work that is monotonous all their working lives. Even a change of occupation may involve little change in the character of the work done, in the skills or initiative it calls for. This is not to say that the work is unpleasant or felt as a burden: if it is well paid, the worker who does it may be pleased to do it, looking upon it as a fair cost to pay for what he gets in return for it.

The worker who does monotonous work may not, for all that Marx says to the contrary, be alienated in his work *merely because it is monotonous*; for he may not work long hours and may have ample opportunity in his leisure hours for more creative activities. As indeed Marx himself admits, at least implicitly, in the third volume of *Capital*, when he says that 'the realm of freedom actually begins only where labour which is determined by necessity . . . ceases' and 'thus in the nature of things . . . lies beyond the sphere of actual material production'.[8] There must, he concedes, be 'labour determined by necessity' in every society, and therefore also in the com-munist society which knows nothing of alienation. It follows that labour

---

[8] *Capital* (Moscow edn., 1962), iii. 799.

which is outside 'the realm of freedom', which is not 'creative' and a form of 'self-affirmation', is not for that reason alone alienated: not if the worker recognizes the necessity of it and does it willingly as a price that has to be paid at all times and everywhere.

Work that calls for rare talents and skills, work that is challenging to the doer of it and is 'creative' and a form of 'self-affirmation', does not for that reason alone cease to be necessary. It, too, deserves to be called *labour*; so that Marx was as much mistaken when, in the third volume of *Capital*, he said that the realm of freedom begins only where labour determined by necessity ceases as when he implied, in *The German Ideology*, that in the communist society all productive work would be included in the realm of freedom. For some people, and they could be a considerable minority, the realms of labour and of freedom coincide or at least overlap. What is more, as Marx would no doubt have admitted, it can be a matter of self-respect even to the worker whose work is monotonous and 'uncreative' that he should do it well.

Did Marx, in his later and wiser years when he conceded that in any highly industrial society a great deal of indispensable work (and perhaps even most of it) is dull, or calls for not much skill or intelligence, still believe that work could be so distributed as to ensure that everyone did a share of the 'creative' as well as of the 'uncreative' and monotonous work? Did he think that this could be done, except at an enormous cost in efficiency? Did he believe that natural differences of ability are not so great as to make this cost excessive? How far, at what cost in efficiency, would he have been willing to go towards establishing a fair distribution of pleasant and unpleasant, or of 'creative' and 'uncreative' work? It is impossible to say, for he gives no clue as to how he would have answered such questions.

In his later as in his earlier writings, Marx held firmly to the belief that the 'labourer looks at ... his labour, at its combination with the labour of others for a common purpose, as he would at an alien power'. The worker does this for as long as he and his companions at work do not themselves manage their joint labours. 'The situation', says Marx, 'is quite different in factories owned by the labourers themselves, as in Rochdale, for instance.'[9] But he does not say that this management by the workers of their joint labours, even though it ensures that the labour does not appear to them as an alien power, is part of 'the realm of freedom' or is creative or a form of self-affirmation. He does not describe it, any more than he explains how under communism the workers' management of the factories or enterprises in which they work will differ from their management of the economy as a whole. And yet, clearly, these activities differ greatly from one another. Though workers' management of a factory may well be

[9] Ibid. iii. 85.

collective, a form of direct democracy, even where there are a few whole-time managers appointed to carry out collective decisions, *how can the management of a vast industrial democracy be so?*

Like Marx after them, the early socialist believers in co-operative production were not much interested in problems of management. Even Fourier, who described in such loving detail the activities of the *phalanx*, his ideal community, had little to say about the actual running of it, about the taking of decisions affecting the community as a whole or any considerable part of it. Saint-Simon and his disciples, who were almost unique in being interested in the direction of a large economy and not of small communities of producers, did not believe in workers' democracy.

These early believers in joint ownership or in co-operative production, or the two together, wanted to relieve drudgery by making it easier for a man or woman to switch from one kind of work to another. This is true above all of Fourier, whose phalanx is designed to give an outlet to the whole range of human passions, to meet all needs, to satisfy all tastes. He wanted to provide, as Marx or Engels might put it, for the 'full development of human powers'. Yet the idea of self-improvement is quite absent from his philosophy. Fourier is the champion of self-indulgence, of present enjoyment, and not of disciplined endeavour or the setting up of aims difficult to achieve and admirable in the achievement. He never speaks, as Marx sometimes does, of the overcoming of obstacles as an 'exercise in liberty', or as 'self-realization' and therefore 'real freedom'.[10] Not that I would make too sharp a distinction here between his conception of work and Marx's. There are, of course, times when Marx, especially the early Marx, speaks of work (when it is not alienated labour) as if it were creative and artistic, as if it were a sustained and disciplined effort on the part of the worker to make or achieve something he values as a mark of his achievement, an effort that develops his powers; and this idea of it appears to fit in easily with his conception of society and culture, of 'the human world', as the product of activities through which mankind develop the capacities distinctive of their species and gradually come to understand and learn to control 'the world' they have produced. But there are times also when Marx, in *The German Ideology* and elsewhere, speaks of work under communism much as Fourier speaks of it in the phalanx.

The idea that work should be pleasant and varied and the idea of it as a disciplined activity in which the worker 'realizes' or 'affirms' himself do not exclude one another; it is possible that work should be both these things at once. Yet conditions which help to make it varied and pleasant may not also help to give it these other characteristics. And it is not easy to see how, in a vast industrial economy, it could be either of these things for most people.

---

[10] McLellan, *Marx's Grundrisse*, p. 124.

The early socialists did not look to their small co-operative communities merely for relief from drudgery or for collective ownership and control; they also look to them to bring men closer together, to overcome the divisiveness and selfishness of capitalist society, to strengthen ties of affection and mutual trust. Some of them, as for example Fourier, disliked the small family because it made its members too much a burden to one another, too demanding in intolerable ways, while at the same time isolating them from outsiders. His phalanx is a kind of artificial great family, large enough to enable its members to make and to break a variety of intimate relationships with one another and yet small enough to sustain a strong sense of community in them all. He wanted to enlarge freedom while also creating strong ties of interest and good feeling among members of the same community.

Marx, at least some of the time, shared these ideals. He condemned capitalism as much because it 'isolates' men from one another as because it makes work a burden to them. It isolates them, not in the sense that it diminishes their dependence on one another or reduces social intercourse between them, but in the sense that it makes them indifferent to one another, except as means to their own ends. And yet he did not, as Fourier did, look to small self-sufficient co-operative communities of producers to foster a sense of community among them. He accepted the advanced industrial society. Did he then believe that workers' management of particular enterprises, on the one hand, and of the entire economy, on the other, together perhaps with freer movement from one type of work to another, would be enough to foster it? But workers' management can take many different forms, especially in a highly complicated and rapidly changing economy. What forms must it take if it is to strengthen the sense of community among men? If it is to make relations between them different in kind, closer, more trustful, and more benevolent, than they are in a 'capitalist' economy, even one with a high standard of living and with powerful trade unions to protect workers' interests?

The sixteen hundred or so members of a Fourierist phalanx all live, work, and play, and find friends and lovers, within the same small community, which satisfies all, or nearly all, their many needs. But the larger the scale of co-operation, and the more limited its purposes, and the more the co-operators have to delegate to agents the business of promoting these purposes, the less the co-operation serves to form close ties of affection and benevolence between them; the less it makes them 'members of one another'. And the more anyone co-operates with different persons in different ways and for different purposes, the less strong his sense of community with the persons he co-operates with for any one of these purposes. His separate pursuit of different interests shared with different persons may make him more tolerant and may develop in him a more discriminating sense of justice, but tolerance and a sense of justice, valuable qualities though they are, especially in large and economically developed societies (capitalist or socialist) with a wide variety of conflicting interests in them, do not necessarily bring with them the close fraternal ties that many of the early socialists—and Marx too in some moods—rated so high.

These socialists may be right in holding that for most people happiness depends as much on forming close ties of affection and community as on being able to choose their occupation or develop their talents, and again, that these 'affective' needs are only partly satisfied in the small family, or are so at too great a cost in terms of frustration and bitterness. But, even if they are right, they pose a problem without indicating how it is to be solved, except at a price that few are willing to pay. Setting up communities of the type of Fourier's phalanx would require giving up the advantages of large-scale industrial production, and few people who are used to these advantages really want to give them up, though they sometimes affect to want it. As for getting the advantages that these small communities are supposed to bring while retaining large-scale production, nobody has yet explained how it is to be done; and least of all Marx and his disciples. It is not enough to say that such production must be 'socialist', or must be managed by the workers 'collectively'.

In the nineteenth century most socialists shared three aims, though they differed in their beliefs about how they could best be attained. They wanted more freedom, greater fraternity, and more democracy, using the last word in a wider than merely political sense. They wanted people to be able to choose kinds of work and styles of life congenial to them, they wanted them to be bound together by closer ties of affection and good-will (which is what I mean here by fraternity), and they wanted them to have a large say in deciding matters of common concern. There were authoritarian socialists—as, for example, the disciples of Saint-Simon—and there were also socialists who wanted the state to take over the owner-ship and control of industry and had little faith in workers' management—as, for example, the Fabians. But most socialists were not then state socialists, and the Marxists were far from alone in their hatred of the 'bureaucratic' state. Not until the last decades of the century were there many socialists who conceded that the modern state, with its immense apparatus of power, had come to stay, and that workers' management, if it were ever achieved, would have to be so under its aegis. Things are, of course, quite different now that there are many political parties in the world calling themselves 'socialist' and either controlling states or com-peting for power inside them.

These three aims, so conceived—freedom, fraternity, and democracy—are not incompatible, though there are difficulties about promoting the three of them together in advanced industrial societies. To ensure that men and women can choose occupations and styles of life congenial to them, they must be taught to appreciate the advantages and disadvantages of the alternatives open to them, and must have the chance to acquire, as far as their natural gifts allow, the skills needed for proficiency in, or enjoyment of, the alternatives they choose. They must also, during their working lives, have reasonable opportunity to move from one job to another or to change their style of life, and to get the training they need to fit themselves for it. They ought not to have to bear indefinitely with the consequences of unfortunate choices made in the past, and in any case their tastes may change. It should also be made easy for them to associate with others who share their aims or their tastes. Lastly, they should be able to break, or at least to loosen, close personal ties which have become a burden to them. Or, rather, society should see to it that they can break or loosen them easily and with as little hurt as possible to others.[11] Fourier believed that all these conditions of freedom could be achieved in the phalanx.

Perhaps they could be achieved also in a developed industrial society, if it were drastically transformed, and could be so without making people highly competitive with one another, or ambitious in the worldly sense. There are socialists who believe that they could be. Could be and must be; for, as they see it, competitiveness and ambition, unless they are mild, put fraternity out of reach. They may, of course, even then, be useful by increasing efficiency in ways from which all classes stand to gain in the long run. Still, the stronger they are, the more they weaken sympathy and benevolence, or the readiness to enter into the feelings of others and to help them without condescension, in which fraternity consists.

Yet these conditions of freedom, though they need not make men excessively competitive and ambitious, may do nothing to bring them closer together. In an industrial society with a vast division of labour, people move around a great deal in search of more congenial jobs and conditions of life, and they ought presumably to be encouraged to do so in the interests of freedom. But this movement, though it enlarges freedom, does not make for closer ties between people or enhance their sense of community. On the contrary, it makes for less close ties. It is perhaps misleading to say that it 'isolates' them from others, or makes them more selfish in their dealings with them. Their dependence on others, their need to do business with them, is in no way diminished by their moving from place to place, by this changing of neighbours and fellow-workers and business associates; and they may be considerate and just in their

---

[11] I do not consider here the belief shared by many people that there are some ties—for example, marriage—into which people should enter only voluntarily and yet should be able to break, if at all, only with great difficulty, even when the ties have become burdensome to all parties. There are, I think, some strong arguments which have nothing to do with religion in support of this belief. But they are arguments for limiting freedom, and are not concerned with the issues I am now discussing, or are so only indirectly.

dealings with them. Their distant and cool relations with most of the people they deal with may be quite to their taste, or at least a price they are willing to pay for other advantages, and above all for freedom. They may want close ties with only a very few persons. But whatever they want, whether they like their condition or not, it is not fraternity as many socialists have imagined and desired it; it is more like what they call (or miscall) the 'self-centredness' or 'isolation' of bourgeois society.

Radicals who have put a high value on fraternity have held equality to be a necessary condition of it. Where there are large differences of wealth, the rich and the poor have little sympathy with one another; they are differently educated and have different styles of life, and these differences keep them 'apart' from one another. The 'apartness' is above all cultural and moral; their values and tastes, their ideas about the world, their motives and intentions in what appear to be similar situations, are so different that rich and poor are foreign to one another. Radicals have often attacked this 'apartness', this lack of community, between rich and poor more sharply even than mere inequality of wealth.

Or so it would seem. They have, of course, condemned the apartness on the ground that it serves to perpetuate the inequality, but this has by no means been their only reason for doing so. They have also valued 'fraternity' for its own sake, and have either preached the brotherhood of all men or of all who belong to the same community. And they have valued equality as a means to fraternity as well as for its own sake.

By equality they have meant more than the abolition of unearned incomes. For there might be no unearned incomes (except for the aged, the sick, and others incapable of productive work) and yet earned incomes be very unequal—as they are, for example, in the Soviet Union. They have meant, if not precisely equal incomes for all regardless of the work they do, or incomes determined solely by needs, at least inequalities kept within narrow bounds. The bounds, according to Rousseau, should be as narrow as is required to ensure that there is a rough equality of bargaining power between people, and that they are not kept apart culturally by differences of education and styles of life. He did not put it in quite these words, but this is substantially what he meant. Other radicals have agreed with him, except that many have believed, as he did not, that this measure of equality could be achieved only by doing away with the private ownership of the means of production.

For most radicals (including Rousseau), equality and popular government are indissolubly linked. Men cannot be equals unless they take part in making the rules and the major decisions of policy of the communities and the more important organizations they belong to, or else choose the persons who make them in such a way that those persons are closely responsible to them for what they do. In Rousseau's small, economically simple, self-sufficient, and sovereign communities of farmers, craftsmen, and small traders, owning their own farms, workshops, and tools, it might be enough that there should be popular government only in the sovereign community. But where there is a highly developed economy and the politically independent community (or state) is large, there must be lesser communities within the larger one and also a variety of organizations taking decisions of great importance both to their own members and to the larger community. In that case, if equality, as the radical conceives of it, is to be achieved, it is not enough that only the larger community should be popularly governed; the lesser ones and the more important organizations must be so too. And it may even be that authority between them should be so divided as *not* to make the larger community sovereign, in the sense understood by Rousseau. According to this view, equality will not endure unless government is popular, for only a popular government will be keen to maintain it, to take adequate measures in time to check developments which, unchecked, must lead to great inequalities. And government cannot be truly popular unless there is a rough equality of wealth, for the rich will always find ways of contriving that authority is used to their advantage and to the disadvantage of the poor.

But what reason is there to believe that equality of wealth and popular government will enhance fraternity, except in small and self-sufficing autonomous communities? Some thinkers—not only Rousseau but socialists as well—have doubted that equality of wealth and popular government can be achieved in economically developed societies whose efficient administration requires elaborate structures of authority, extending over wide territories and with formidable powers concentrated at the top. But, even if we put aside these doubts, why should we suppose that equality and popular government will enhance fraternity in the vast industrial societies of our day?

They may perhaps help to make people more disposed to be tolerant, considerate, and just in their dealings with strangers and with acquaintances to whom they are otherwise indifferent. These attitudes are much to be desired, especially in our type of society, in which everyone has dealings with a large number of people who are not relatives, friends, or neighbours, but on whose services he greatly depends. It is desirable too that people should want justice to be done to groups to which they do not themselves belong and with whom they have few dealings, or none at all. When I say that this is desirable in our type of society, I do not mean that it would not be desirable, if it were possible, in economically simpler societies. I mean rather that it is unreasonable to expect it in these simpler societies, because their resources are much smaller and people know far less about the needs and conditions of life of persons and groups remote from them.

It may be that this tolerance and wide-ranging benevolence and concern for justice are precisely what many people understand by fraternity. But, in that case, what they understand by it is different from what many radical critics of 'bourgeois society' have had in mind. Or at least it is only a part of it; for these radicals have meant by fraternity something altogether warmer and more intimate, more akin to loving-kindness than to these dispassionate attitudes. They have meant something different from what rationalists in the eighteenth century called philanthropy, the goodwill that civilized men ought to feel for all other men, however remote from them socially, culturally, or racially.

Fraternity and philanthropy (or rational benevolence) are not incompatible. But they are different, and the second is no substitute for the first. And it is the second rather than the first that greater equality and more popular government are likely to increase in our type of society: in the industrial and urbanized society in which there is a vast division of labour and everyone depends for his welfare on the services of large numbers of people unknown to him or with whom he has only casual and 'impersonal' dealings. Not that there cannot be a good deal of rational benevolence even where there are considerable inequalities of wealth and the popular element in government is small; but it is this benevolence rather than fraternity which in our type of society is enhanced by equality and popular government.

I do not know how far radicals have exaggerated the need for fraternity, the extent to which most people, to feel secure and happy, need to have close ties with their neighbours and fellow-workers and a strong sense of community with them. Radicals often condemn the small family, as they find it in 'bourgeois society', for being too confining, for imposing excessive strains on its members, and they would prefer a larger sphere of intimacy, of affectionate and trustful relations, to comfort and sustain the individual without confining him. They dislike the partition of the individual's social world into two parts, of which one is small, tight, and frustrating, and the other large, remote, and indifferent, in which he uses others without caring for them, and they do the same with him. But—so it seems to me—they misdescribe this partitioned world, making too much of the disadvantages of each part of it and too little of the advantages. The small family is not as confining as they say it is, and much could be done to make it less so without abolishing it. It has changed greatly in the West in the last hundred years, and gives more freedom than it did to wives and children as compared with husbands and parents, and does so perhaps without weakening the ties of affection and trust between them.[12] Nor is

---

[12] The undoubted rise in the number of divorces and the increase (alleged but not well attested) in revolts against parental authority would not in themselves prove that trust and affection inside the family have grown weaker.

the world outside the family as cold, competitive, and unhelpful as the castigators of 'bourgeois society' make it out to be. Indeed, it is above all the growing concern for social justice outside the family which has made possible the enlargement of freedom inside it.

In any case, the radical critic of capitalist or bourgeois society should ask himself how far the fraternity he cares for so much and which, in his opinion, that society conspicuously lacks, can be attained in *any* advanced industrial society, even if it is socialist and inequalities of income are small and government (or administration) is as near being popular as the scale of its operations permits. He should also ask himself how far freedom as he conceives of it (and his idea of it is much closer to the liberal idea than he is willing to admit) is compatible with fraternity.

IV

Whether a community is large or small, the important decisions of policy inside it are not decisions for experts to take. In a large community, there are, of course, more such decisions taken, and the variety of considerations that are relevant in taking them is apt to be greater. Makers of policy need the advice of more experts, and they also, perhaps, need a longer experience of public business to become good judges of how such business should be done. These are reasons, over and above that of mere size, for preferring representative to direct democracy in large communities. But whole-time elected makers of policy, though they are better placed to learn how to make good use of expert advice, especially when that advice is varied and plentiful, are not therefore experts.

In communities small enough to allow their citizens collectively to make the laws and major decisions of policy, there is still a need for leaders who devote much more of their time to public affairs than the mass of citizens do, who make it their business to look after the doing of the public business, preparing it and guiding the course of it. This must be so unless the community is very small indeed—much smaller, for example, than the democracies of ancient Greece. The leaders take the initiative in defining issues and making proposals; they take much the larger part in debates, and are in closer touch with the experts and with the officials who administer the laws and carry out policy decisions. In a direct democracy no bigger than a big village, the citizens soon divide into an active minority and a much less active majority.

Even though it is formally independent, a community small enough to be a popular democracy must come close to being self-sufficing, if its citizens are to be able to take most of the major decisions of domestic policy without being powerfully influenced by decisions taken outside the community. Their control over their conditions of life might then be smaller than it would be if they were to give up their independence and form a federal union with their neighbours. Yet the citizens acting to-gether might be just as competent, just as well informed and wise in reaching their decisions as elected representatives would be. Their de-cisions would not be decisions for experts to take, though no doubt often better taken after listening to expert advice.

When we pass from communities to mere organizations, and in particu-lar to productive enterprises, the case is different. Their essential purpose is not to look after the welfare of their members but to provide outsiders with specific goods or services. The rulers of a community, since their business is to lay down rules and to define standards that members of the community or some part of them must observe or meet in pursuing their purposes, or else to decide what services the community is to provide them, take decisions different in kind from those taken by the managers of productive and specific-service enterprises. Their business is a different kind of business. That, no doubt, is why we call it government rather than management, whereas we call the persons who run, say, a factory or a bank (or a chain of them) its managers rather than its governors or rulers. The business of managers is both narrower and more a matter for experts than is the business of government; the services or other benefits managers provide are highly specific, and they have to decide how best to provide them with the resources at their disposal. Managers do not, except within narrow limits, have to decide what services or benefits to provide; they do not have to decide between a wide variety of claims for benefits, of which only some can be satisfied. Most important of all in this context, the bene-fits they provide are not primarily for the members of the organizations they control. This is as much so when the organizations are not profit-making as when they are, and as much so when they are public as when they are private.

Why, then, if productive and service enterprises differ so much from communities, should they too be democratic? Why should their members run them, or why should their managers be responsible to the members for how they run them? The case for popular government inside a community is, surely, different from the case for popular management in a factory or bank or army or administrative department. Only in small self-sufficing communities which are also multi-purpose productive enterprises, com-munities of the kind described by some of the Utopians, are government and management scarcely distinguishable, so that popular government is virtually also popular management. But we are now speaking of developed industrial societies.

Many people today, even when they are not socialists, agree that the private owners of an enterprise, or (as is more often the case) the directors nominally responsible to the owners, ought to be fairly strictly controlled in the uses they make of the resources at their disposal. Ordinarily, they favour this control, not because the responsibility of directors and managers to owners is often minimal, but because they believe it to be in the public interest. This control would, presumably, still be necessary in the public interest, even if the enterprise were owned by the workers inside it. Their owning it would not, in itself, bring it any more under 'public ownership and control' than if it were owned by shareholders who took its profits without working in it. Nor would it necessarily ensure that the enterprise was run more for the benefit of the community as a whole.

The claim that members of an autonomous community, if it is to a considerable extent self-sufficing, should collectively own the natural resources and instruments of production inside it, and should be free to use them as they think fit to their own best advantage, is at least plausible, even though also disputable.[13] The same (or rather, a similar) claim made for the workers in a productive enterprise or other such organization is not nearly as plausible. It may be in the public interest that the managers running such organizations should have a considerable autonomy, that they should not be too strictly controlled: but it is not obvious that this is any more so when the managers are the workers themselves or agents responsible to them. The interests of the workers in an organization, productive or not, can run counter to the public interest just as the interests of shareholders can. Even if it were true that the larger a social class, the less its interests (the interests shared by all its members) conflict with the public interest, it would not follow that the interests of small sections of a large class conflict with it less than do the interests of small sections of a smaller class. Nor is it obvious that the interests of separate organizations are less likely to conflict with one another when the organizations are run by their members than when they are not. Socialists and anarchists too often speak as if this were obvious, especially when the members are manual workers.

Socialists who believe that justice requires that the profits of an enterprise (or what remains of them after paying taxes and providing for investment) should be shared among the workers in it need not hold that the workers should run the enterprise. A case still has to be made for their doing so. Besides, many organizations make no profits and do not provide goods or services paid for by the recipients. Some are run by governments, directly or indirectly, while others are privately controlled charitable corporations. Should they too be run democratically by the men and women who work in them? Can they be so, except to a limited extent, if they are to provide efficiently the services which it is their business to provide?

---

[13] It is disputable because natural resources are very unevenly distributed among autonomous communities, so that the naturally poorer ones can be self-sufficient only at the cost of a low standard of living or else, if they rely heavily on foreign trade, may be at a great disadvantage compared with the others.

Of course, efficiency and the prevention of exploitation are not the only relevant considerations, and there are people willing to pay a considerable price in efficiency for other things. It also matters that the worker should be his own master at work, which nowadays he can seldom be on his own but only along with his companions at work. To many radicals this has seemed far and away the best reason for having industrial democracy or, as it is sometimes called, 'self-management'—presumably because it is held to be as desirable outside industry as in it. Self-management, so its champions say, may quite often promote efficiency but is also worth having when it does not. It enhances the workers' sense of their own dignity and weakens their sense of being at the mercy of events beyond their control.

I do not deny that these are great benefits, and may well be worth as much in many workers' eyes as substantial increases in material welfare. I merely inquire how far, and by what means, they are to be attained in advanced industrial societies.

No matter how much the workers run the organizations they work in, the decisions they take are the decisions of managers, and are restricted in many ways. Running a factory or bank, or even a branch of industry or commerce, is essentially different from running or controlling an economy, and the need to control the economy is not—as far as I can see— in any way diminished by putting the enterprises of which it consists under the management of the workers in them. Either the economy is effectively controlled, in which case the managers of enterprises, whether they are capitalists or workers (or their representatives), receive directives from the controllers of the economy; or the economy is not effectively controlled and the sense that the workers have of being at the mercy of events beyond their control is as great as ever. As the early socialists and Marx noticed, the capitalists too are at the mercy of events. Thus, in this respect, nothing is gained by putting the workers in the place of the capitalist, by ensuring that collectively they exercise his functions. On the other hand, if the economy is effectively controlled in the service of ends they understand and approve, their sense of being at the mercy of events is presumably diminished, even though they have no say in running the organizations they work in.

Marx and others have spoken of the workers' controlling 'production', and have presumably had in mind their controlling the economy as a whole and not just particular enterprises within it. But how, exactly, would the workers' control of 'the economy' differ from its control by a democratic state?[14] It could hardly be smaller in scale. Would it be less bureaucratic?

---

[14] Ordinarily, when we speak of 'the economy', we have in mind certain kinds of activity (those we call 'economic', usually without being quite sure where to draw the line between them and non-economic activities) in so far as they take place within the confines of a state,

It is not easy to see why it should be. If it were considerably decentralized, operating at several different levels, and at the same time reasonably efficient, it might need to be very bureaucratic, and the workers might feel about their delegates and agents pretty much as citizens do about their representatives in the 'bourgeois' democracies of the West.

Still, even if radicals have over-estimated the extent to which workers' control of the economy could be less bureaucratic and more genuinely popular than government is in the liberal bourgeois state, it may yet be the case that workers' control of the organizations they work in is both possible and desirable. There is still the claim that it makes them their own masters at work.

No doubt it does, in a sense. But the sense in which people who work together are collectively their own masters at work is different from the sense in which the individual farmer or craftsman or trader is so, and the difference is apt to be the greater, the larger the number of collaborators. When a handful of men and women run a farm or other small business together, their situation—though already significantly different from that of the farmer or craftsman who runs his business without partners—may still be such that the work of management is hardly separate from the work managed. Decisions about what to do and how to do it can even be taken by the workers while they are actually at work, or with only short interruptions in their work. Management is not then sharply separate from ordinary work.

But when the number of workers is large, the business of management, even though the workers do it together, has to be kept separate from the rest of their work. There must be times set apart for it. And if the workers, instead of doing this business themselves, elect representatives (even though from their own number), to do it for them, they have already ceased to be in the literal sense their own masters at work. Their work is in fact directed by others, though they have elected them to do the directing, and need not re-elect them.

In a large organization democratically run, even though some of the running is done by its members collectively, the sense of distance between managers and managed, between 'them' and 'us', is not wholly removed. Relations between them may be closer for being democratic—though not therefore always easier, as the experience of many a trade union proves—but the sense of distance remains. To be sure, the more relations between managers and managed are trustful, the readier the rank and file of the organization are to think and speak of its official policies and decisions as 'ours' rather than 'theirs'. But relations are not always the more trustful

or can be controlled by its government. But Marxists and other radicals look forward to 'the disappearance of the state', and it is not clear how extensive in their eyes the economy controlled by the workers is to be.

for being democratic; and the extent to which they are so may vary considerably from one type of organization, from one sphere of action, to another. If there were good reason to believe that, on the whole, citizens trust their rulers the more (or 'identify' with them the more readily) the more democratic the political system, this would not justify our concluding that the same is true of armies, that soldiers are the more likely to trust their generals, the more an army is democratically organized. Armies, no doubt, differ greatly from political systems, but then so too does industry, even when it operates on a large scale. I do not deny that democracy can, and often does, enhance the sense of community between 'them' and 'us', and that it may do so in industry as well as in politics. I say only that we cannot take it for granted that it will. If it were to do so in industry, that of course would be a great advantage, and one perhaps worth buying at a considerable cost in efficiency.

But this is by no means the only advantage that champions of workers' management have hoped to gain from it. They have complained of the monotony and 'uncreativeness' of labour under capitalism, and have looked to workers' management for a remedy for these ills. For my part, I do not see how it can be a remedy for them, except to a small extent. To be sure, management is, or can be, a 'creative' activity, and as much so (if not more) in large as in small organizations. But it is so, to any considerable extent, only for those who take the initiatives, who make the proposals, or who mobilize opposition to them, who do the talking in whatever bodies take the major decisions. Even where these decisions are taken by the workers or members collectively, most of them (if the organization is large) are mere listeners and voters. Their role is not unimportant, but also it is not exactly 'creative', as the role of a leader may be said to be. And if the workers elect representatives to take the major decisions for them, their role as mere electors, though still important, is even less creative. All or most of the workers in an organization can take a creative part in managing it, only if two conditions hold: if the organization is small and they all take part in making the major decisions.

Work, even in the largest organization, can of course be so organized that a great part of it is done by teams of workers who are left to themselves to get on with the jobs allocated to them. How far this can be done must vary greatly with the character of the work in question. Perhaps, if there were more workers' management in industry, or more management responsible to the workers, work would be more often organized with this end in view; though this is by no means certain. In any case, even managers not responsible to the workers, whether they were appointed by private owners or by some public authority, might find it conducive to efficiency and to good labour relations to encourage autonomous teamwork where it was technically possible. Already, there is a good deal of it in some industries. Even foremen appointed from above often find it expedient in practice to consult the men they work with. Democracy comes easily to collaborators when they are few and leadership calls for no long training or rare skills, especially when the collaborators all belong to the same social class. Actually, it often comes easily enough, under these conditions, even when they do not belong to the same class, as many a person who has served in a small detachment of the armed forces can testify.

Workers seem not always to share the aspirations for their class of the radicals. Often, they seem to care less about managing the businesses they work in than about being well organized to get good wages and conditions of work, and other concessions, from their employers and the government. Radicals sometimes put this down to their being affected by 'bourgeois' ideas or diverted from ambitions they would otherwise have by 'bourgeois' tastes and comforts. But many of the ideas and tastes that critics of bourgeois society call bourgeois are no more bourgeois than proletarian. These critics exaggerate the extent to which workers adopt the habits and standards of more affluent classes. A hundred years ago most middle-class families kept servants and few of their womenfolk went out to work, whereas working-class families kept no servants and many of their womenfolk took work outside the home. Today most middle-class families are in these two respects like working-class families, and yet—to the best of my knowledge—there are no sociologists (not even radical ones) arguing that the bourgeois are being 'proletarianized'. Why should a higher standard of living and more schooling lead to the 'embourgeoisement' of the workers, when doing without servants and women going out to work do not lead to the 'proletarianization' of the middle classes? These two classes may well be more alike in important respects than they used to be. But why speak of these changes as if they involved the cultural assimilation of either of these classes by the other? I suspect that sociologists and political theorists speak of these changes (or of their effects) as *embourgeoisement*, or the cultural assimilation of the working by the middle classes, for no better reason than their occurring in a society they have learnt to call *bourgeois*.

Whatever the cause, the workers in the West seem less concerned to manage the organizations they work in than to defend their interests against those who manage them, whether the organizations are in 'private' or in 'public' hands. They want to be well paid, to have decent working conditions, to be fairly treated by their employers, and to be well organized to press their demands on the management and also on government when it intervenes in industrial disputes. They also want social benefits of various kinds, not only because they are the better for having them, but also because increased security strengthens their hand in their dealings both with employers and with the government. They want to be well placed to make agreements which seem to them just and to their own advantage.

That the work that most people in an industrial society do to earn their livings is dull is a fact that just has to be accepted, as Marx himself recognized in his later years. No doubt, much of the work done in more primitive societies is also dull, or would seem so to men and women brought up in our society. What people find dull varies with their tastes and aspirations. Yet manual work today, if it is as dull as it used to be (and perhaps duller), is also, on the whole, less arduous and much better paid. Office work is dull, too, for the most part, calling for skills easily acquired, and is often repetitive.

I doubt whether workers' management would do much to make manual or routine office work seem less dull to those who do it; which is not to deny that it might be desirable for other reasons. I suspect that most workers in the industrial countries, whether capitalist or not, are more concerned that the economy and the organizations they work in should be efficiently run, so that they can benefit from this efficiency, than that they should take part in running them. They may well doubt whether their taking part in running them would increase their efficiency. Yet experience has taught them that they must be strongly organized, industrially and politically, to ensure that they get a larger share of the wealth created by greater efficiency. On the whole, and not only in the capitalist West, they seem keener to get their share of the benefits that come of this increased efficiency than to take part, either directly or through representatives, in organizing it.

The worker who is most obviously 'creative' is the artist, the poet, or the thinker, who produces what is uniquely his own and is recognized as such by others. Creative, too, is the inventor, who conceives of new instruments and methods, and the reformer, who introduces new social practices or standards. But most men are not 'creative' in this sense, and it is not obvious that they need to be in order to be happy. 'Creative' in a secondary (or different) sense of the word is the craftsman who exercises skill and judgement in producing something well made, and the organizer who does so in directing the work of others. Though there are many people who do creative work of this kind, there are many more who do not. It may well be that most people are capable of this second kind of 'creativeness', though in developed industrial societies few have much scope for it at work. They are not craftsmen and they do not direct the work of others, or not at a level that calls for much skill and judgement. If there were workers' management in the enterprises or organizations they work for, their part in it—though by no means unimportant, any more than the electors' part in a political system—would scarcely deserve to be called creative. If they are to have much scope for creative activities, it must be—as Marx recognized in the third volume of *Capital*, when he contrasted the realm of freedom with the realm of necessary labour—in their leisure hours.

That being so, and if they really want (as no doubt many of them do) opportunity to be 'creative', would they not be well advised to care more about being well paid for the work they do, having a shorter working day and better conditions at work than about workers' management in industry? And do they not in fact care more about these things? There are Marxists who say they do, and who seem to deplore their doing so, and to see in it evidence that they have been corrupted by 'bourgeois values'. But may not these Marxists be mistaken, not in what they say about the workers' attitudes, but in their assessment of them? May not the workers be wiser in this respect than their Marxist (or neo-Marxist) critics and well-wishers?

The healthier and the better educated, and therefore the more active, physically and mentally, people are, the more bored they are likely to be by work that calls for little skill and judgement. One of the 'contradictions' —to use a Marxist expression—of industrial society is that it produces the resources to improve people's health and education greatly and yet requires the doing of a great deal of this kind of work. Yet, clearly, resources ought to be used, even more abundantly than they are today, to improve health and education. At least radicals must think so, if they are true to the libertarian and democratic principles they subscribe to. The fact that so much work is dull does not justify giving an education of poor quality to the children (or adults) who fail to pass the tests qualifying them to do, or to be trained to do, the more absorbing and challenging work. It would not justify it even if—as might well be the case—the cost in terms of efficiency of distributing work so that everyone, irrespective of his natural abilities, did his share both of the dull and the challenging work, should prove altogether excessive. There is more to life than the work a man does to earn his living, and this is the more true, the more productive society is and the shorter the working day. The intelligence and the skills that find no outlet in 'necessary work' may find it in the home, or among friends, or in leisure-time activities, whether in the arts and sciences, or in following public affairs and taking a lively interest in politics.

Whether work that calls for little skill and judgement is felt to be boring by those who do it does not depend only, or even primarily, upon how active in mind and body and how well educated they are; it depends also on how much of it they have to do, under what conditions, and in what company, and above all on what it is the means to, what they get as a result of having done it. Women who go to work in factories, not just to earn money but to escape boredom, do not go there for work that calls for more initiative and intelligence than housework and the care of children do, for it often calls for much less; they go there to find company while their husbands are at work and their children at school. Most people during the course of the day, even the most creative of them, are active in useful ways that tax their intelligence scarcely at all, and yet they do not find these activities dull. In any case, work is creative only part of the time; it is creative, as it were, by fits and starts, and there are long intervals of work that would be dull if it were not preceded and followed by moments of inspiration or stretches of hard thinking or important decisions difficult to take. If the 'creative' worker does not find these intervals dull, it is because he recognizes that they are part of the price to be paid for doing his sort of work. So, too, the 'uncreative' worker may find his work the less dull for recognizing that it is the price he pays for the opportunity to do other things, which have more that is creative and satisfying about them. But to make the best of this opportunity, he must be active physically and mentally, and must be well educated. Just as he must be to carry out his duties and to assert his right as a citizen, or as a member of other associations, even though he is active in them only as a listener and a voter.

I have not argued that the control of production by the workers, by which Marx and other socialists have set so much store, is either impossible or undesirable. I have merely pointed to some of the difficulties in the way of realizing this ideal in developed industrial economies. Marx, so often praised for his realism in contrast with the Utopian dreaming of other socialists, never seriously addressed his mind to the question of how this control should be organized. He did not even distinguish between the control of an entire economy and the control of particular productive enterprises. He did not inquire how this collective workers' control would help to increase the independence of the individual worker or to make him more 'self-directed' or more 'creative' in his work, or in what respects it would serve to make men more equal. I have tried to put some of the relevant and important questions that Marx did not put, to suggest possible answers, or to give reasons why, in the present state of our knowledge, they cannot be answered.

Marx, more than many socialists, has escaped the imputation of lack of realism. The earlier socialists, whom he called Utopian, were simple-minded enough to believe that their schemes might be adopted, and would prove successful if they were. Anarchists have believed either that men of goodwill might 'opt out' of society as it is, or else might transform it gradually without capturing the state and using it to create the social conditions of its own disappearance. But Marx, so it has been claimed for him, was more realistic than the Utopians and the anarchists.

This is surely a misleading claim. He was, as I tried to show in earlier chapters, very much a realist in some ways. His assessments of situations of social conflict and of the advantages and disadvantages of groups and parties engaged in it, were at times extraordinarily perceptive. He understood a great deal about power, its different forms, and how it is lost and won. His judgements on contemporary affairs, bold, fresh, and shrewd, are often admirable. Also, to take another aspect of his thought, obscure and yet valuable, he borrowed more from Hegel which he used to good sociological purpose than any other of Hegel's admirers, and in using it he transformed it. He is the greatest, and in some ways, the most realistic of socialist thinkers.

Yet he too had his fantasies. For example, the fantasy of the proletariat making a revolution and transforming social conditions so as to remove the causes of alienation and make everyone a creative worker in a society of equals, and the fantasy of the disappearance of the state and the abolition of the division of labour in a society that remains highly industrial. Fortunately for his reputation as a hard-headed realist, he never ventured, as the Utopians did, to describe his fantasies in detail. He confined himself to speaking vaguely of 'developing human potentialities to the full' or 'the free development of the individual' or 'social control of production' without explaining what he meant by them or how society would need to be organized in order to achieve them.

To hold, as Marx did, that society needs to be greatly changed if great evils are to be removed, without describing in detail what its changed condition would be like, is not to be unrealistic. To want the workers to have greater opportunities of doing creative work, and to want them to control industry, is not absurd. These are respectable ideals. But whoever subscribes to them ought surely to consider, even though he does so only in a general way and in the abstract, what conditions have to be met for these ideals to be realized. He should point to some of the difficulties, even though he cannot resolve them; put some of the more obvious questions, even though he cannot answer them. He should look some little way into the practical implications of his ideals. To admit to a considerable vagueness and uncertainty, when looking for large remedies to great social evils, whilst aiming at as much precision as circumstances allow, is entirely reasonable. To want more than you can clearly describe or know exactly how to get is, after all, part of the human condition.

But to be in this condition does not justify proclaiming ideals without inquiring at all into what might be involved in achieving them, what society might be like if they were achieved. It is not enough to point to some class or section of society as destined to achieve these ideals, and to confine yourself to explaining how this class or section is to get power. To leave the aim obscure, to put it into the clouds, and to be perceptive and practical only in describing the getting of power, is to invite the ambitious to strive for power without knowing what they will do with it; it is to encourage in them, and especially in their followers, the illusion that they know when in fact they do not. To see great evils in society and to preach that the social order must be radically transformed, and yet to take pride in not being a Utopian, in not venturing to describe what society would be like if it were transformed so as to get rid of these evils, is irresponsible. It is to be, not realistic, but evasive.

CHAPTER XIV

CONFLICT AND HARMONY

I

THE idea of social harmony, of communities whose members do not resort to force to impose their wills on one another, who share the same ideas of justice, settling disputes amicably, and living trustfully and affectionately together, as free men and equals, goes back a long way. It is an old idea taken up in recent times by socialists and anarchists who have elaborated upon it in a variety of ways, and the Marxist conception of the communist society is one version of it among others.

Where there is this harmony, men and women are supposed to be so strongly attached to standards accepted by them all that disputes seldom arise between them, and if they do, are quickly and easily settled by methods that everyone agrees are just. If a settlement goes against a man, he may regret it but he does not feel aggrieved; he believes that justice has been done.

Where there is this harmony, there is no need for 'the organized use of force' (as it is often called) against lawbreakers or to enforce the settlement of disputes. That is to say, there is no need for the 'official' use of force, its use on behalf of the community by persons authorized to use it. But the converse is not true. We cannot say that wherever there is no official use of force, there is social harmony. In some primitive communities there is neither public trial nor official condemnation of offenders, and it is left to their victims or their victims' kinsmen to 'punish' them. There are conventions prescribing how vengeance is to be taken and setting limits to it, but the breach of these conventions is not an offence for the community to deal with officially any more than the breach of any other social rules. In such a community there can be plentiful conflicts and frequent resorts to force, and yet the community not be disrupted: private vengeance within limits prescribed by custom suffices to hold the community together. But this, presumably, falls far short of social harmony, which excludes private vengeance of this sort as much as the official use of force against offenders.

A small and simple community, even if it were not socially harmonious, might know nothing of legislation—might have no procedures for the official defining of social rules or for abolishing old rules and making new ones. So, too, it might make no provision for the official settlement of disputes. It might leave it to the parties to a dispute to choose an arbiter, and the decisions of arbiters and their reasons for taking them might not be recorded or cited as precedents on later occasions. In such a community social rules would, of course, change over time, but there would be no authoritative defining or alteration of them.

A large, economically developed, diversified, and sophisticated community, even if it were socially harmonious, would need to provide for legislation and for the official administration of law. It would need to have agreed methods for declaring the law, for changing it to meet new needs, for publishing it to the citizens, and for settling disputes (or differences of opinion) between them about what the law required on particular occasions. These methods would need to be elaborate, and their efficient operation might call for the services of a large number of public officials—of persons authorized to define, change, and administer the law on behalf of the community. There would, perhaps, if the community were socially harmonious (in the sense defined earlier), be no need to use force against offenders. But, no matter how ready citizens might be to carry out their obligations to each other and to the community, it would still be necessary to make rules for their guidance and to settle authoritatively disputes about obligations and rights; and meeting this need would be a complicated business, calling for abilities and skills requiring special training or experience. There would be a need for 'government', as that word is ordinarily understood, and for a good deal of it. People who say that, if there were no alienation or social corruption, there would be no need for 'government', presumably have in mind only some aspects of it (and perhaps especially the official use of force); or they assume that freedom from alienation or corruption can be achieved only in communities small and simple enough to do without government altogether.

Writers who describe imaginary communities with no official use of force in them, and even no official settlement of disputes, often attribute to their members strong ties of mutual affection and trust and deep feelings of loyalty to the community. They attribute to members of a community different in kind from the family, feelings more often found among close relatives; or, rather, supposed to be proper to them, though not always found among them. The members of a family are, or ought to be, united by love. The ideal is to achieve in a larger community feelings that are ordinarily supposed to be confined to the family or to small circles of friends.[1]

Writers who have imagined these communities united by love (or by feelings akin to it) have also, sometimes, been among the harshest critics

---

[1] Small communities created for special purposes—often religious ones—are also quite often supposed to be united by love, but they are select bodies which do not include everyone living in a particular region or falling within a certain degree of blood relationship. They are dedicated communities.

of the family. In the opinion of Fourier, the family, though supposed to be united by love, in fact is not so; husbands and wives, parents and children affect to have feelings for each other which they do not have, though they may believe (or half believe) that they have them. The family is a nest of hypocrisy, and a source of unacknowledged (and even unrecognized) resentments psychologically damaging to the persons who harbour them and to their victims. According to Fourier, marriage tends to destroy or to distort the feelings supposed to sustain it, and the partners to it are bound together more by interest and by fear of the consequences of separation than by love. Marx's attack on the bourgeois family and bourgeois marriage was more equivocal. Did he believe that capitalism and bourgeois society debase an institution which otherwise might be a good one? Did he believe that in the future communist society most unions between the sexes would be lasting and exclusive, even though not required to be so by the law? It may be that he did, that his verdict on the family and on monogamy was less hostile than Fourier's. Yet both he and Fourier, and several other socialists and anarchists, *seem to have believed* that ideals supposed to be realized in the family, but in fact not realized in it, might be so in a larger community.

I have said purposely 'seem to have believed', for it may well be that the feelings they attribute to people in their ideal communities differ considerably from those usually attributed to a 'united' family. After all, affection, trust, and loyalty take different forms; or, perhaps I should say, we use each of these words to refer to different feelings and attitudes, even though they are similar or often found together. The family, as these critics of 'bourgeois society' have insisted, is (or can be) a conflict-ridden community. Some of the most enduring and bitter hatreds, jealousies, and resentments are generated within it. This need not mean that feelings of love, trust, and loyalty are not also strong inside it, and that they do not serve to hold it together even more than interest and fear do. It would be absurd to conclude, as Fourier seems to do, that disruptive feelings of hatred and jealousy are held in check only by fear and prudence and not by their opposites, by feelings of love and trust and loyalty. Love does not cease to be love, and become a mere pretence, when it cohabits with hatred. Thus the imagined, the ideal, community is both like the family and unlike it: it produces in its members strong cohesive feelings similar to, if not the same as, those that hold the family together but does not, as the family does, produce the disruptive and hurtful feelings.

It might be thought that the ideal community of the early socialists and the anarchists has more in common with the extended family or clan than with the small family of our day. But this is not so. This socialist and anarchist ideal includes a conception of freedom quite foreign to tribal society, a conception which has arisen in precisely the type of society which has produced the small or 'nuclear' family. The clan or tribe is not less ridden by conflicts than is the small family. No doubt, its members trust and feel affection for one another, and are loyal to the community. But their feelings, or rather their ways of expressing them, are highly conventional, and it is difficult to distinguish what they really feel from the sentiments they express because the occasion calls for them. The sincerity, candour, and independence of mind that critics of 'bourgeois society' have so often found lacking in it are perhaps even more lacking in tribal society, and are in any case less recognized as virtues. To be trustworthy, loyal, and honourable—not to betray confidences, to keep your word, to give help when it is properly required of you, not to do or say what brings shame to those who are close to you: these, together with courage, are the virtues most prized among tribesmen. The hypocrisy which is a form of self-deception, and not a deliberate pretence to deceive others, is scarcely recognized by them, any more than is the failure to live up to standards of one's own which may be different from other people's.[2]

The ideals of the Utopians and of Marx are sophisticated, or at least modern, ideals. They owe more to the standards of the bourgeois society that their authors attack, and even to ideas of the family widely accepted in that society, than to the standards and ideas of earlier societies. Fourier's phalanx may be nearer in size to a clan or to a village community than to a small Western family, but the ties between its members, as he conceives of them, are more like the ties that would unite a Western family if some of the claims made for it were true: they are ties of affection and trust that enlarge the individual's capacity for freedom, that sustain him in his efforts to give scope to his tastes and talents, and to find a way of life that satisfies him. Marx says nothing about the size of his communist society but he too conceives of it as a community that both sustains and liberates its members. Inside it men and women are psychologically more secure, more at home in the world of culture which is their own product and the medium in which they 'affirm themselves', and also more free. And what is true of the ideal communities, different though they are, of Fourier and Marx is true also of many others imagined by socialists.

The idea of romantic love has flourished in the same kind of society as the small family. Indeed, this family is quite often seen as the creature of romantic love: it is set up by a man and a woman who come to love one

---

[2] This is not to say that in tribal and other more primitive societies, there are no internal conflicts but only conflicts with others. There is evidence in plenty that in more advanced, more 'sophisticated' societies, internal tensions are not confined to the formally educated classes. That the uneducated classes lack the ideas which the educated use to describe these tensions is no evidence that they are less liable to them. So, too, the absence of these ideas among more primitive peoples does not warrant our concluding that they are free from these ills. But I am now discussing only ideas, contrasting some with others in the hope of explaining them more clearly; I am not inquiring how prevalent the facts are that these ideas refer to.

another and who choose each other as life partners. To be sure, this family and this type of love are also often opposed to one another. In this type of family, parents are often ambitious for their children, and their love for them is often a possessive and a jealous love. They forbid or prevent their children marrying whom they please. Yet the tie between husband and wife, as they see it (or affect to see it), is closer than it is in the extended family. Though, in opposing a son's or a daughter's choice of wife or husband, parents deny the claims of romantic love, they also affirm them in the idea of marriage they subscribe to—whatever they may think of the reality.

Romantic love sets the couple who feel it, in their own eyes, apart from others in 'a world of their own'; it is of its very nature exclusive, just as it is demanding. Yet it is also—until it palls—felt to be liberating; its burdens are all self-imposed or gladly accepted, and so not felt as burdens. The love that unites a family is not romantic love, not even between husband and wife after the first few years of marriage, but it is in some respects like it: it too is demanding, and its burdens—at least as far as the parents are concerned—are self-imposed. When it ceases to be genuine, or when too many contrary feelings have arisen alongside it, its demands are apt to become intolerable. Love which, while it lasts, is a source of strength and therefore liberating, when it decays, leaves the individual caught up in entanglements which he both wants to be rid of and does not know how to shed, or else fears to shed, in case the cost of doing so should prove too high. The ideal communities of the Utopians promise the blessings of love together with escape from the intolerable burdens that come of its decay. They do not promise a life without burdens or an un-strenuous life but a life of burdens willingly accepted, of efforts felt to be worth while. They promise close ties of trust and affection together with freedom: what the small family and liberal society 'promise' between them and so often fail to give.[3]

I would not deny that the ideal of social harmony, in its modern forms, owes something to nostalgia for an older type of community: for the village or one form or other of the small and stable community of neigh-bours. This community, as idealized by those who look back on it, though it is not a family, consists of families often closely related to one another. There is little need of regular administration inside it. Neighbours are not litigious, and most of their disputes are settled by neighbours, especially

---

[3] I would not deny that in tribal and other societies there are strong ties of affection and forms of freedom greatly valued: my point rather is that there are ideas of love and freedom common to liberal 'bourgeois' society and to its Utopian critics which differ from these older ties and forms. There are ideas of personality, of personal relationships, and of their social conditions, peculiar to this society and to its critics. There are even 'cults' of love and freedom peculiar to them; for it is above all this society which has both had ideals *for this world* and recognized its failure to achieve them, and so has laid itself open to criticism in the light of its own ideals.

by older persons respected for their wisdom and impartiality. Even in the West, the village is a recent memory. For a long time, the state and its courts and officials were, in the eyes of the peasants, alien things rather to be avoided than invoked, oppressive rather than helpful; and most people were peasants. The peasant did not go to law and had as little to do as possible with magistrates of any kind. He could not avoid the bailiff or steward of the large estate, and to some extent he looked for help to the priest. But the state and everything pertaining to it were, in his eyes, the business of the upper classes and of the professions that looked after the interests of these classes. The idea of a neighbourly, informal, understanding authority survived among the peasants long after the rise of the modern state. When trade and industry grew, and the towns with them, the peasants who went into the towns to become industrial workers retained this mistrust of the state, seeing it now as the ally of their employers just as they had previously seen it as the ally of the landowners. Not until they formed powerful organizations of their own, the trade unions, and in general acquired the education which enabled them to use the state and its laws and services for their own ends did this distrust of it diminish.

Thus, beneath the level of the state and of the wealthy and educated classes who knew how to use it, there long survived, outside the towns, communities of peasants, who tried to avoid, as far as they could, dealings with the state and to retain their own methods of reaching agreements and settling disputes with their equals, and who therefore, to the extent that they succeeded in this purpose, in keeping out of the clutches of the state, formed 'stateless' societies of their own. And in the towns there were masses of workers who had good reason to look upon the state as the protector of the rich who, with its assistance, could force them to accept hard conditions and unjust bargains. Among both peasants and workers ideas of neighbourliness, equality, and self-help went easily together with suspicion of the state. In the eyes of their socialist and anarchist sympathizers this suspicion was well grounded. They too shared it.

They shared it and went beyond it. For they saw in it, not only an instrument or ally of the rich, but also a source of inequality and injustice, and therefore of conflict. Even in a society of equals, it would necessarily bring with it great inequalities of power, which would lead eventually to the emergence of classes, or at least of social groups having great advantages denied to the rest of the community. The state helps to create social conditions which produce the conflicts it seeks to control. It maintains order, and in maintaining it, resorts to methods which are no doubt indispensable while those conditions endure. But the conditions cannot be removed, for good and all, unless the state ceases to exist. So that, even if the state were used to remove them, it could succeed in this purpose only if, in removing them, it removed itself. The Marxists have held that the state could do this, and would do it if the workers became masters of it. Other believers in the stateless society have been less sanguine, and have not looked to the state for salvation from the state.

The idea of social harmony, at least in its modern forms, is a marriage of two ideas: the idea of the family united by love, and the idea of the community of neighbours who are equals and among whom good relations are maintained without recourse to officials for resolving conflicts or imposing discipline. The two ideas are in fact idealizations; for in the real world both the family and the community of neighbours are torn by conflicts, and the conflicts go just as deep as they do in larger communities. The passions they spring from are just as intense and persistent, and their consequences are just as painful and damaging. If the family and the community of close neighbours do not have to resort to methods of maintaining peace which the champions of the stateless society and of social harmony condemn as sources of inequality, if they can do without rules made and administered by professionals and without 'organized force', this has nothing to do with their being in themselves peaceful; it comes merely of their being small 'face-to-face' communities.

The love (or trustful benevolence) that unites people where social harmony reigns is supposed to be a tolerant love, a love that respects the needs, the preferences, and the tastes of others even where they differ greatly from one's own, a love that is discriminating and just. But these qualities that distinguish this love are in great part the products of life in large communities. I do not mean, of course, that in these communities they are possessed in great measure by most people; I mean rather that it is in such communities, more than in others, that they are recognized as virtues and held up to admiration. It is in societies where everyone has perforce to have dealings with many people to whom he cannot help but be indifferent, to whom he feels that he owes no more than justice and politeness, that the most sophisticated ideas of justice and benevolence arise. It is in them too that it is most obviously a man's interest to be tolerant and respectful of freedom, to concede to others from whom he differs in so many ways what he wants them to concede to him: the right to be different. But these feelings or sentiments, which gain in strength and subtlety in large, varied, and sophisticated societies, affect even the closest and most intimate relationships, which by their nature are the most demanding, so that they are less demanding, or are so in ways that are less restrictive of freedom. It is not because, in economically developed as compared with economically simple societies, conflict is either more or less frequent, more or less intense, that tolerance and respect for freedom grow stronger, or that the need for them is greater; it is because the much greater diversity of conflicts and the greater remoteness from one another of the parties to them call for quite different and more elaborate methods of resolving them.

Tolerance, respect for freedom, and the discriminating sense of justice that goes with them are not, of course, born of indifference any more than they are of close intimacy; they are born, as Hume saw, of the need to extend sympathy far beyond circles of intimacy or close community. They are born, in large part at least, of enlightened self-interest, mistaken though it is to take them for mere forms of it.

II

Critics of capitalist or bourgeois society, whether anarchists, Marxists, or Utopian socialists, have condemned both conflict and competition. Presumably they have not objected to them in all their forms. Sometimes— as, for example, Saint-Simon and Fourier did—they have held that some forms of competition, if not of conflict, are beneficial and have wished to encourage them. But, on the whole, they have not gone far in attempts to distinguish useful from harmful forms of either conflict or competition.

Conflict and competition are not the same thing. The two words are not used indifferently in the same range of meanings, though they are sometimes synonymous. Nor is the difference between them that the first is reckoned harmful, while the second is not: conflict is not harmful competition nor competition conflict that is not harmful. They have both been denounced as harmful and praised as beneficial. Both conflict and competition can be either legal or illegal, and neither need, and both can, involve the use of force. If a race is a competition, so too is a boxing or a wrestling match, and a conflict can be entirely verbal with no party to it laying a hand on another.

I shall not now try to distinguish the various senses in which the two words are used, and to determine how far their meanings overlap. Rather, I shall use the words in senses closely similar to some in which they are ordinarily used and which happen to suit my purpose. When two or more persons are trying to get something that each of them wants, or are trying to get as large a share of it as they can, they can be said to be contestants for it. If none of them claims that it is rightfully his and they contest for it by means whose fairness or legality is not in dispute among them (whatever their private convictions may be), then they are competing for it. The competitors, or some of them, may in fact be acting illegally, or unfairly by reference to standards widely accepted, and their competition may even be criminal, but, provided they do not themselves contest the legality or fairness of each other's activities, they are—I shall say—in competition and not in conflict with one another. If, however, contestants want something, which each of them claims is rightfully his (whether the rights in question are legal or moral), and seeks to get it by getting his right to it recognized, either by the others or by some authority to which he and they are subject, then they are in conflict and not in competition with one another. They are in conflict also, if each seeks to place the others in situations where they desist from further contest, though they do not recognize the superior right of the victor and no authority recognized by them all pronounces in his favour. That is to say, they are in conflict also when they seek to get what they want by compelling others to let them have it.[4]

If we distinguish conflict from competition in this way, it is not obvious that competition is *in general* less harmful or more beneficial than conflict is. Conflict which involves compulsion is immediately harmful to those who get the worst of it, and most societies try to reduce it by a variety of means, of which one of the most important is providing alternative and more tolerable forms of conflict. In the long run, no doubt, even this kind of conflict can be beneficial, but it is in general so dangerous (since the victor in one conflict may be the vanquished in the next) and the harm it does to the defeated is often so great and obvious, that everyone has an interest in reducing the occasions for it. On the whole, it is better that conflicts should be contests for justice carried on by 'legal' means than that they should not be. To be sure, both substantive law and legal methods of seeking justice can be so unjust that the groups who suffer from this injustice are well advised to resort to illegal methods to get the law and these legal methods changed. Still it is, on the whole, their interest that both the law (or other social rules, where there is no law in the strict sense) and legal (or generally approved) methods of seeking justice should be just. That is to say, it is their interest, even when they are justified in resorting to illegal or disapproved methods, to use those methods to ensure that legal or approved methods of seeking justice are just.[5]

Competition may be condemned on either or both of two grounds: because it is unfair and because it has harmful consequences. It is unfair when some of the competitors have advantages over the others which they ought not to have. Unfair competition can easily lead to conflict when

---

[4] The distinction I am making between competition and conflict would need to be further elaborated in the interest of greater precision. In any case, it applies more readily to contests between individuals and groups subject to political authority than to contests between independent political communities.

[5] What I say here needs to be qualified. Not only is it sometimes the interest of victims of injustice to resort to illegal methods of getting justice; it is also at times the interest of the wealthy and privileged sections of a community that, within certain spheres, there should be no legal methods of carrying on conflicts, or that such methods should be ineffectual, so that the rich and the powerful are virtually unrestricted in their attempts to impose their own terms on the poor and the weak. Sometimes, it is the interest of the strong, even when they belong to the same community as the weak and have interests in common with them, that there should be enclaves of anarchy within the legal order, areas of conflict untouched by law or within which illegality goes unpunished, rather than that there should be laws that favour them unjustly. I say nothing here of the bullying of the weak by the strong, when it is not properly conflict but is mere exertion of power to provoke displays of fear or servility gratifying to the powerful.

its unfairness comes to be recognized. But this does not impair the distinction I have made between competition and conflict, for to compete, even though unfairly handicapped and recognizing the unfairness, is one thing, and to engage in conflict in order to get the handicap removed, is another.

Competition, even when it is fair, can have bad effects, psychological and social. It can encourage arrogance in those who gain by it and diffidence and a sense of inferiority in those who lose. Precisely because it is fair and is widely recognized to be so, the belief that those who fail deserve to do so is apt to be strengthened. They may be set down by others, and by themselves, as the least capable of contributing to society or of profiting from what it has to offer; as the ungifted, the naturally poor, the godforsaken, to be pitied and discounted. There are, no doubt, other sentiments of respect and sympathy that run counter to these; but these are sentiments that competition does often encourage even when it is fair. The privileged and the powerful are not necessarily the less arrogant for believing that they have earned their privileges and their power and have not inherited them.

Fair competition can have other bad effects. It can encourage people to form ambitions they cannot achieve or which do not satisfy them when achieved, and can destroy amenities and be wasteful in other ways. Critics of capitalism or of bourgeois society too often attack competition indiscriminately, without pointing to the forms of it which seem to them harmful or unfair, let alone explaining why they should be thought so. Presumably, if competition is to be fair, there must be equality of opportunity: everyone must have as good a chance as anyone else to acquire, as far as his natural gifts allow, the education and other advantages he needs to compete for whatever he wants to get. But the social cost of achieving this equality in developed industrial societies—and it is in these societies above all that it is thought desirable—is enormous. It requires not only a large expenditure of resources aimed at removing the disadvantages of the unprivileged; it requires also elaborate administration. It calls for hierarchy, and therefore for considerable inequalities of power. The attempt to achieve this equality can, and often does, encourage the pursuit of conventional success. But to many socialists and anarchists, competition for success, even when it is fair competition, has seemed a major cause of frustration and unhappiness.

Just as fair competition can be harmful, so unfair competition can have good effects from which the entire community benefits in the long run. It can stimulate inventiveness, the efficient use of resources, and the pursuit of excellence. It has other good effects but these are the ones most often noticed. Critics of capitalism have argued that it is the more likely to have these effects, the fairer it is (or the less people are prevented from taking part in it by the lack of social advantages), and that it cannot be fair while capitalism lasts. I find this argument not altogether convincing, for it takes no account of the effects of scale on competition. Presumably, the fairer the competition (or the fewer the socially disqualified), the more competitors there are; but this increase in numbers may not have the expected good effects. Not because the socially privileged are naturally so much more gifted than the unprivileged that to extend their advantages to the rest of the community adds little to the number of gifted competitors. But rather because, as the scale of competition alters, so too do other things: dispositions, skills, and the kinds of stimulus to which competitors respond. Just as the quality of a literature does not always improve and sometimes deteriorates as population increases and literacy spreads, so it may be with excellence in other spheres. No doubt, it will be much more so in some than in others. But we know so little about the effects, direct and indirect, of the scale on which activities are carried on upon the performance of the persons who engage in them, that we cannot confidently predict that the fairer the competition, the more likely it is to encourage excellence—unless, of course, it can be made fairer without greatly altering its scale and the social conditions in which it takes place.[6]

To discuss the effects, good and bad, of competition, fair and unfair, would take me far out of my way. What is more, the discussion would be largely conjectural, and would consist rather in putting questions and trying to explain their relevance and importance than in giving answers to them. The truth is that both the champions and the critics of competition have been too undiscriminating. They have too often failed to make it clear just what forms of competition they object to or favour, or what bad or good effects they expect from them. Quite often a socialist or anarchist will denounce capitalism on the ground that it is too competitive, and that this competitiveness is a source of conflict and frustration, and then go on to use arguments in favour of equality of opportunity which imply that the scale of competition ought to be increased. Perhaps a case could be made for holding that, if capitalism and the inequalities inherent in it were abolished, harmful forms of competition would, on the whole, be discouraged and beneficial forms of it encouraged. It could perhaps be made while conceding that a wider equality of opportunity would have some bad effects; for these effects might be kept within narrow limits or might be outweighed by the good effects. But the case has yet to be made. It may be that the elements required to make it are already to be found

---

[6] I am supposing, for the moment, that standards of excellence remain sufficiently the same for it to be possible to estimate changes in the quality of performance resulting from increases in the scale of competition. The more these standards change, the more difficult these estimates: and standards change more in some spheres of activity than in others. They also often change as a result of attempts to make competition fairer, to reduce social disadvantages.

scattered in the writings of the critics of bourgeois society. If so, they have still to be fitted together into a comprehensive and convincing argument.

So, too, anarchist critics of our 'conflict-ridden' industrial societies have been too little discriminating in their condemnations of conflict. In discussing its causes, the methods of resolving it, and the conditions that create the need for some methods rather than others, they have failed to make crucial and obvious distinctions. In developed industrial societies, in which conflicts between organized groups are of exceptional import-ance, the parties to these conflicts, even when they do not resort to courts or to official arbitrators, are usually very much aware of their legal rights. They are aware, too, that their opponents, if pressed too far, may take legal action against them. Both the matter and the course of conflicts depend considerably upon the means that society provides for settling them. Conflicts are not confined to societies in which there are legal rights defined and protected by public authority; they occur also in primitive societies which make no provision for the official definition and protection of rights. There is no reason to believe that social harmony is greater (that conflicts are relatively fewer or less fierce) in primitive than in civil-ized societies. Such evidence as we have does not support the conclusion that the methods of settling conflicts that have arisen with political au-thority (with the state) have been effects of a growth in social disharmony. Therefore, critics of the state who look forward to its disappearance, or who speak, as Marx does, of crossing 'the narrow horizon of bourgeois right . . . in its entirety',[7] should explain more clearly what they have in mind. What would social conditions have to be like, in their opinion, so as not to give rise to conflicts that can be settled only by such methods as the state uses? What did Marx mean by 'the crossing of bourgeois right in its entirety'? Did he mean the eventual disappearance of *legal right* as such? Some of the things he says in the *Critique of the Gotha Programme* suggest that this is indeed what he meant. Yet it is hard to believe that he did mean it, for this transcending of bourgeois right is to happen, not in an economic-ally simple society, but one in which 'all the springs of co-operative wealth flow more abundantly'. It is to happen in an advanced industrial society. Is the transcending of bourgeois right to consist then merely in the dis-appearance of forms of legal right which favour some classes against others? But why should this lead to the disappearance of the state? Unless, of course, the state is defined as a political community which protects legal rights that favour some classes against others. That, however, still leaves open the possibility that a political community which protects legal rights but is not a state, might be conflict-ridden and might have to

[7] From the *Critique of the Gotha Programme*, in Marx–Engels, *Selected Works*, Vol. ii (Moscow, 1949).

provide much the same methods as the state now does for the settlement of conflicts.

Not for a moment do I suggest that it is idle to speculate about conditions widely different from those familiar to us. I am so far from believing that this kind of speculation is a form of self-indulgence pleasing only to dreamers but of no use to practical men who want to understand the world and to change it, that my sympathies here are with the Utopians and not with Marx. He rejected their fantasies and took care never to describe in detail the communist society whose coming he nevertheless predicted confidently in his more hopeful moments. I would criticize the Utopians for not being discriminating enough, for not being more perceptive and more precise in their fantasies, for not seeing more clearly what they saw only in imagination. I would *not* say to them: 'These worlds of yours are so different from the world as we know it that we have nothing to learn from them, and are useful only as places we can escape to in imagination.' We also live in a world very different from the Russia described by Tolstoy in his novels, and yet we can learn a great deal from these novels, not only about the Russians in the last century, but about the English in this one. I would say to them rather: 'You should construct your imaginary worlds so that we who visit them in imagination can know our way about them, and see clearly how they differ from the world of our experience.' The Utopian, if he is to deepen our understanding of what we are and what we might be, must, like the novelist or the dramatist, have a clear and a subtle imagination. He must see what he imagines both as a whole and in detail, and must know how to communicate what he sees. The Utopians have too often been careless visionaries, poor in their reasonings and even poorer in their descriptions.

A Utopian fantasy may be 'unrealistic' in either of two quite different ways. Its lack of realism may consist in a putting together of incompatible conditions or traits of character, or in its superficiality or failure to take into account needs or passions likely to be important under the conditions it describes, or in its not noticing likely and important effects of these conditions. It may be unrealistic in the same sort of way as a novel may be so. Or it may be 'unrealistic' in the quite different sense that what it describes is virtually unrealizable, given conditions as they are or are likely to become in the foreseeable future. But of this a Utopian may be well aware. He may admit that what he describes is unrealizable in this sense, and yet claim that his fantasy is instructive, that it is more than make-believe, more than an imaginative 'escape' from reality. If he admits this and his claim is well founded, then to accuse him of lack of realism is pointless.

True, when Marx accused the early socialists (or some of them) of being Utopians, what he had in mind was not exactly that their fantasies were unrealizable in this sense; it was rather that they could not be realized by the methods they advocated. Yet he did not concede that they could be realized by other methods, nor yet that, if they could be, they ought to be. He did not, for example, invite the workers to reorganize society on the model prescribed by Fourier, and confine himself to warning them that Fourier's ideas about how this could be done were unrealistic. Though he did, in his brief references to the communist society of the future, show that he had been considerably influenced by the ideas of the Utopians.

Marx was right. The Utopian socialists did have mistaken ideas about how the social orders they described could be established. Their fantasies were also unrealistic in the second of the senses I distinguished a moment ago. It is unlikely that they could have been realized by any methods that could have been used in social conditions as they then were. This the Utopians failed to see, and Marx did see it. To that extent he was shrewder, more hard-headed than they were.

But there is a more serious charge to be made against the Utopians than the one made by Marx. They were too little realistic in the first and more important of the senses I distinguished. Their accounts of their imaginary societies are too often defective or unplausible or inconsistent. For example, Saint-Simon claimed that in his rationally organized society, the management of the economy would take precedence over the maintenance of order, which was in his day (so he thought) the prime business of government. But he said nothing about the maintenance of order in the rational society to indicate how it would differ from what it was in France in his day. Also, he showed too little sign of understanding that the management of an economy is an enterprise different in kind from the management of a business, and involves taking decisions that businessmen do not have to take—decisions which are as much political as they are economic, even when they have nothing to do directly with the maintenance of order. Yet he ascribed to businessmen, to the 'chefs d'industrie', the leading role in his rational society, presumably on the ground that their experience entitled them to it. The managers of the economy were to manage it for the good of all, and especially for the benefit of the hitherto poorest class, the manual workers. Without being responsible to the workers, they were to enjoy their full confidence, so that authority should be backed only by trust and not, as it always had been in the past, by force.

Owen and Fourier described small co-operative communities and took it for granted that the business of keeping order inside them and settling disputes would be so simple as to require no professional judges and no policemen. They had almost nothing to say about how relations between these communities, or between members of different communities, should be regulated. Owen did not even predict or advocate the disappearance of the state, and seems to have given little thought to the wider political consequences of his social experiments, should they succeed. Proudhon wanted the workers to opt out of the capitalist economy and the state by giving credit to one another, and in general by providing, for their common benefit, any other services they might need after breaking off relations with the capitalists and the state. But he did not explain clearly and in sufficient detail how this could be done.

Since their time there have been other imaginary societies described, of which some of the more interesting have been, not socialist or anarchist, but highly oppressive or manipulative and inegalitarian. Their inventors have intended them to be warnings to mankind and not models to be imitated. But, as far as I know, there has been none which has described comprehensively and in detail how society might be organized to achieve social harmony, as socialists and anarchists have conceived of it: to eliminate harmful forms of competition and conflicts that are now settled by recourse to the services of the bourgeois state. We are still lacking a model with which to compare society as we know it, to help us to decide how far we fall short of attaining social harmony. Such a model need not be acceptable in all its details to be useful; it can help people to clarify both their ideals and their objections to the established order by serving as a target for their criticisms.

III

Connected with this idea of social harmony is the idea of the individual at peace with himself: the healthy mind in the healthy society. This idea of mental peace, of the absence of deep-rooted conflict or tension within the *psyche*, is difficult and sophisticated. I do not mean that in primitive societies, or among the illiterate and unschooled in advanced societies, there is no recognition of (or no words to describe) situations in which a man or woman is torn by contrary passions, or by passion on the one side and what justice or honour or loyalty requires on the other. But these are seen as exceptional or as passing situations, and to recognize examples of them is different from seeing them as lasting conditions in which whole communities or sections of them are caught up. It is different from the idea of men so situated socially and culturally that they feel confined and oppressed by the ways of life of the community they belong to, or cannot live as they aspire to do, or cannot form standards to live by; different from the idea of them as incapable of living as they ought or believe they ought to live, or as incapable of acquiring firm and consistent standards. In primitive societies and among the illiterate, there may well be men and women who suffer from these incapacities, who are 'alienated' in one or other of these ways, but they do not themselves 'recognize' these conditions, unless they have been taught to do so by people coming to them from outside their own community or class.

The writers in the West who first described a condition of the individual who is permanently, and not just in moments of crisis, at odds with himself or morally at sea were philosophers or theologians. They noticed that the condition was much more acute in some men than in others, and they ascribed these differences partly to 'nature' and partly to education. Some men are born more liable to fall into this condition than others are, and some have been so educated as not to acquire the salutary beliefs and dispositions which would enable them to avoid it. These are old ideas which in the West go back at least as far as to the Greeks. Less old and, until the last century, less widely accepted is the idea that this condition arises more from social causes than from faulty education or congenital defects.

Both the Greeks and the Romans imagined a golden age in the past when men were happier and more virtuous than they had since become, and they ascribed to this age some of the characteristics of their own societies as they had been in earlier and simpler times. Thus, the idea of a connection between simpler and more stable social conditions and greater peace of mind is also quite old. It was not born in the eighteenth century in the head of Jean-Jacques Rousseau. And yet Rousseau did much more than revive it. He also transformed it. The idea of man as a rational and moral being formed by society, who can live rationally and morally only in society, and who yet has been 'corrupted' by it so that he cannot live as he aspires to do, but is frustrated and diminished in the very element in which alone he could be adequately himself: this idea—as disturbing as it is obscure—was originally Rousseau's before the Germans got hold of it. There have been many variations upon it since his time.

The individual can be at odds with himself or with society in several different ways. He can accept conventional standards, or at least not reject them, and yet be often moved, by passion or interest, to behaviour not in keeping with them. Or he can form standards of his own at variance with conventional standards, and yet be incapable of living well either by his own or by conventional standards, or by a mixture of the two, because the two conflict and he cannot fix on a compromise which seems reasonable to him: that is to say, cannot decide what he can properly require of himself in a society which falls so far short of his own ideals that he could live up to them only at a cost intolerable to himself or to others for whose welfare he is responsible. Or he cannot acquire firmly held principles, conventional or unconventional, and is therefore morally at sea or apathetic, and yet disturbed and unhappy because he is a prey to feelings of guilt or inadequacy. Or he is a conformist who quickly and easily accepts the standards of whatever circles he moves in but is perplexed and anxious because the standards are incoherent or because he has to move from some circles into others whose standards differ, so that he often finds himself in situations in which accepted moral standards make incompatible claims upon him and he is incapable of deciding between them.

Rousseau, in one or other of his writings, recognized all these possibilities, and others besides, for he was morally and psychologically perceptive even though he was not, as Hobbes was, 'rare at definitions' or good at making clear distinctions. But there are two possibilities of which he, like other moralists of his age, took little account. The first is that a man might be morally at sea and yet not a prey to feelings of guilt or inadequacy. Rousseau took it for granted that social man, if he is to be happy, must have firmly held and coherent principles to guide his conduct. That a man could drift through life morally, or could let morality sit loosely and lightly upon him, and yet be happy, seemed not to occur to him. Perhaps he would have thought it unjust that there should be such men, who do not aspire to virtue and yet carry no burden of guilt, who get the reward without making the effort, living in society without paying the moral tax.

The other possibility of which Rousseau took no account is that men might live comfortably together even though they had different and yet firmly held principles, that they might learn to be tolerant of differences in moral standards as well as in matters of religion, that they might learn to distinguish between standards which they had all to accept if they were to live together peacefully and amicably, and standards, just as firmly held and just as important to those who held them, which could be allowed to differ from group to group and even from person to person. It is his failure to take account of this possibility, in spite of the high value he placed on what he called moral freedom, that most sharply distinguishes Rousseau from the nineteenth-century liberal—from, say, John Stuart Mill.

Most of the socialists and anarchists of the last century, without being conspicuously more liberal than Rousseau had been or more concerned to safeguard moral diversity, were less rigorous and puritanical. In their ideal societies man is not strenuously or self-consciously virtuous, a man of principle, though he is free of guilt and shame and finds it easy to live well. Neither is he apathetic or a drifter. He has keen appetites and strong purposes. His capacity for action and enjoyment is great; he is neither socially ambitious nor resigned to his lot but lives life to the full.

Some of these writers—Fourier above all, and perhaps sometimes Marx as well[8]—thought of the liberation of mankind as a kind of passing beyond morality. Not that man in the ideal community, in the phalanx or in the higher stage of communism—would be always gentle, good-tempered,

---

[8] Though clearly not always, for in *The Holy Family* he sees the offender in the communist society passing sentence on himself.

eager to please his neighbours and to be approved by them; he would be enterprising and bold, intelligent and with a will of his own, and his benevolence would be combined with a keen desire to get the most out of life. To treat others well, he would not need to act from a strong sense of duty, or to be moved by feelings of guilt or shame. But this, presumably, did not entail—except perhaps for Fourier, who went further than the others in rejecting morality—that he would never act on principle, that his every action would be prompted by love or sympathy or prudence or desire, with never a thought given to acting morally. It meant rather that he would never, or hardly ever, be so placed that to act on principle he would need to act 'against his inclinations', to exercise what Kant called a moral will. Most of the time he would act 'spontaneously' without having to make difficult moral choices: he would assess the situations in which he acted sensitively and intelligently and then decide what to do without needing to prove to himself—or to have it proved to him by others—that he ought to do it. If he debated with himself or discussed with others what he should do, his concern and theirs would be to establish the facts of the situation and to consider the consequences of the alternatives open to him and not to raise and resolve matters of principle. Though he would have principles to guide him, he would quickly see, once he had established the facts, what his principles required him to do, without needing to spell them out, even *in foro interno*. And others would see it too, if they agreed about the facts. Deciding what ought to be done, once the facts were clear, would be easy and unselfconscious, even though the actual doing of it might sometimes require courage and energy.

The morality (if that is what it should be called) of the ideal societies imagined by some of the early socialists and anarchists differs from the morality of primitive societies. It is a morality which has passed 'beyond' morality as we now know it, even at its most sophisticated, beyond the need to support social rules with powerful sanctions, whether 'officially' imposed or not, whether external or internal. In primitive societies the individual is not (or is not reckoned to be) conscientious, does not act from a sense of duty in the way he would need to do to be fully moral, as Rousseau or Kant understood that term. He accepts social rules uncritically: which means, I take it, not that he has no idea at all of their being generally useful, nor yet that he is trained to observe them without question as soldiers are to obey military regulations, but that he has never, or hardly ever, given much thought to them, asking himself what purposes they serve and why he should observe them. But he is aware that there are rules, knows how to use them, and recognizes that he will be blamed or punished if he breaks them. He accepts conventional assessments of situations and conventional ideas of what it is proper to do in them. Thus—to the extent that this is a correct account of what he does—his morality is unreflective or even, by the criteria put forward by some Western moralists, not morality in the full sense of the word but a stage preliminary to it out of which it may grow, given suitable conditions, social and cultural.

Primitive man, if he is to behave as convention requires, may not need to be coerced; there may be no established procedures for trying and punishing him when he breaks the rules. It may be enough that he should know that, if he fails to do what the rules require, he will be disliked and avoided and will no longer be able to rely on the assistance of neighbours when he needs it. Though he is not conscientious, he is easily put to shame. But the case with man in the ideal societies where harmony reigns is quite different. Fear of being disliked or despised or of forfeiting assistance is scarcely a motive with him. He is no more easily shamed than he is anxiously conscientious.[9] If he helps others it is because he is actively concerned for their good and not on the principle, *Do as you would be done by*, or from the desire to live up to standards he has set up for himself. He has no image of himself as a man of principle; for to have such an image and to feel guilty at failing to live up to it would seem to him as self-centred as the anxious concern to be acceptable to an omnipotent and omniscient Being, to be one of the chosen.

Again, in the ideal socialist or communist society man is free in a way that he is not in primitive societies. He is sophisticated and aware of diverse possibilities. He is not born to a place in society, to a well-defined set or series of social roles; he does not pass from stage to stage of his life taking up activities that by convention are held proper for that stage. He is enterprising, and lives in the most tolerant of societies. Because he does not feel thwarted or threatened, he is not tenacious of his rights, does not feel the need to protect himself from his neighbours and from the bearers of communal authority, as the liberal of bourgeois imagination does. He is not concerned, as the bourgeois liberal is, with defining and re-defining the claims that he can make on others and others on him, or with constructing elaborate judicial and administrative procedures for testing and making good the claims. Though he is free and enjoys his freedom, or rather enjoys life as he would not do if he were not free, he takes that freedom for granted.

Thus man in the ideal society, just as he has passed beyond morality as the bourgeois moralist has conceived of it, has also passed beyond individualism, as the bourgeois political theorist has conceived of it. This second transcendence does not entail his 'losing himself' in the groups or communities he belongs to, his ceasing to affirm himself in his uniqueness, any more than his transcending bourgeois morality entails his

---

[9] Some Utopians and anarchists—as for example Godwin—have imagined an ideal society of highly conscientious individuals, but many have not.

becoming once again 'conventional' or his ceasing to exercise a fine and discriminating judgement in his dealings with others.[10]

Whatever our assessments of the views of particular thinkers, we can contrast two ideal types of community in which social harmony reigns. In the first, men and women are socially and culturally adventurous and like to strike out on their own; they have strong preferences that differ considerably from those of their neighbours. In the second they are much less adventurous, much more conformist, though just as little intimidated or made to feel small when they choose to be different. In the adventurous community, the individual may be just as gregarious, just as fond of company, as he is in the unadventurous community, though it will no doubt matter to him that he should be able to choose and to vary his company. He may also put a high value on privacy and even, on occasion, on solitude, but this he may do just as much if he is unadventurous. In these two respects, in their love of company and their need for privacy and solitude, the adventurous and unadventurous may be pretty much alike. People who are set in their ways and who have much the same tastes and attitudes are no less disposed to keep each other at a distance by forming exclusive groups than are people whose tastes and attitudes differ considerably and change more easily, though their reasons for wanting to be exclusive, or for seeking privacy or solitude, may not be the same. The lower-middle classes are said to be more 'distant' with one another than manual workers are; but nobody claims that they are more diverse in their tastes and prejudices.

Needing and enjoying company is one thing, needing and enjoying intimacy or close sympathy is another. Some Utopian champions of social harmony have put a very high value on intimacy. In their ideal societies men and women come closer to one another, not in the sense of being more often in company together or of thinking and feeling more alike, but in the sense of entering more deeply into each other's ideas and feelings, of being more sharply and sensitively aware of one another. This closeness of sympathy does not thrive on similarity any more than on dissimilarity. Two fine artists or thinkers, whose visions of the world (or of that part of it which absorbs their interest) differ greatly, may understand one another better, may be in closer sympathy, may learn more from each

---

[10] I must qualify what I have just said. Not all the champions of social harmony share the beliefs I have described. Some have imagined a kind of self-effacement that comes of the individual's identifying himself very strongly with his neighbours or with the groups and communities he belongs to. A man can be an anarchist, condemning the use of force and the administration of justice as it has developed in the modern state, and also believe in this kind of self-effacement—as, for example, Tolstoy did at times. But an anarchist need not be like this. He can predict, as Marx did, the coming of a social order in which the individual's opportunity to affirm himself will be much greater, and yet individualism, in the sense of a concern to provide legal protection for basic rights, will be superseded. We can admit that logically this is a coherent position, even if we hold that, sociologically or psychologically, it is unrealistic.

other, than two mediocrities who imitate the same models, perhaps without being aware that they do so.

The intimacy that deepens understanding and refines sensibility is evident chiefly in two spheres: in relations between 'creative' workers, and in relations of love and friendship, both inside the family and outside it. It comes close to realizing an idea which has meant a great deal to some radical critics of 'bourgeois society': the idea of the individual who 'finds himself' in others or in concerns that he shares with them, who goes beyond self-centredness and isolation, not to lose his distinctiveness, but to enhance it, and who is the more sharply aware of himself for being closely involved with others.[11] These critics want this intimacy to be much less confined than it is in society as we know it; they want society and culture to be such that men are drawn closer together, are more deeply concerned for one another. They want men to be more open, more trusting, more sensitive and understanding in their dealings with one another.

If we consider what has happened to men as society has grown economically less simple and culturally more sophisticated and diverse, it would seem that there has been an increase both of 'isolation' and of 'intimacy'. In primitive societies the individual is less isolated from his neighbours, less protected from intrusion by them by elaborate personal and property rights, and he changes neighbours less often. Socially, and often also geographically, he stays put much more than he does in more advanced societies, especially when they are industrial. But his ties with his closest relatives are less intimate than they are in the small family of our day, and so too perhaps are his friendships. Or, if 'intimacy' is not quite the word I want here, perhaps I should say that in primitive societies the closest ties, despite the affection, trust, and quickness of sympathy that unite the persons tied by them, lack certain qualities that come with greater sophistication of thought and feeling. I have in mind such qualities as discrimination and moral refinement, and the delicacy that is both perceptive and respectful of what it perceives, that hesitates to intrude except where it is welcome: qualities that go along with enhanced self-awareness and a deeper understanding of others.

The sense of 'isolation' that so often afflicts the individual in our kind of society may well come, not so much from the loosening of ties that bind relatives and neighbours together in simpler societies, as from the failure to establish ties of a different kind: ties of friendship and love, even of solidarity and partnership, that meet needs unknown, or less keenly felt,

---

[11] This, of course, is only one side of the medal. We develop our peculiar talents, deepen our understanding of ourselves and others, form our tastes and purposes, and learn to satisfy and pursue them, as much in conflict with others as through sympathy with them. What is more, conflict and sympathy are often closely related, as are love and hatred or envy and admiration. But these are aspects of reality of which Utopians and anarchists have taken much less notice.

in simpler societies. Freedom, privacy, toleration, self-expression, experiment, and adventure, were never more discussed, more valued, more set up as ideals worthy of pursuit, than in the type of society so often accused of 'isolating' men and women from one another, of reducing them all to a flat mediocrity, of making them all alike. This, no doubt, explains in part why this society has been denounced by its accusers as a sham: it has set up ideals which it fails to achieve and yet is reluctant to acknowledge the failure.

The more sophisticated a society, the more concerned it is to define and criticize its ideals and its practices. This not only makes it more aware of the distance between its ideals and its practices but tends also to increase the distance; for constant preoccupation with ideals serves to 'raise' them continually. Therefore the sense of failure, of disappointment, of disillusionment, is the greater and the more painful; and the greater too perhaps is the need to seek compensation in images of an ideal society projected into the future.

These images, if they are to be satisfying, must do more than promise a return to the neighbourliness and intimacy of simpler societies; they must also promise freedom. They must promise both what men have lost (or think they have lost) with the coming of modern society, and what that society was the first to offer but has failed to give. In other words, they must promise an intimacy which is liberating, which is 'life-enhancing' and creative, which gives men larger opportunities of self-expression than they ever had before.

These images are meant to be contrasts with society as it is, and are therefore the more attractive, the more people believe that society is defective in the ways they say it is: that it either 'isolates' the individual by drawing him into relations with others which are shallow, hypocritical, and exploitative or else ties him in bonds which are so confining (as, for example, in the family) that he feels resentment and even hatred where he is supposed to feel love. The isolation has imputed to it several bad effects: it makes whoever suffers from it more self-centred and more willing to use others as mere instruments of his purposes, and also increases his sense of being the 'victim' of the social order to which he belongs. How he appears to others, and therefore also to himself, depends largely on his place in that order, on the roles and activities which it imposes on him or which he can take up inside it, and he does not like his appearance. He stands apart from others, using them (as far as he can) for his own ends, and yet is continually thwarted and discouraged, not so much by enemies and oppressors who wish to hurt him, as by the activities of people indifferent, and perhaps even unknown, to him. He stands apart from others, except for the few who are too close to him—whose closeness, through no fault of theirs or his, is damaging to him and to them. In the narrower and in the wider circle, both inside the family and outside it, he is without the intimacy which is at once sustaining and liberating. In this society, as in all societies, he is dependent on others; but the dependence is a heavy burden because the social ties of which it consists are not ties of trust and affection, or are held to be unjust or are felt to be restrictions on freedom rather than elements of the security which makes freedom possible and desirable.

IV

Socialist and anarchist critics of capitalism or of 'bourgeois society' have pointed to *competition* as a prime cause of the 'egoism' they have deplored, and by egoism they have meant above all the self-centredness of the individual, his indifference to others, and his readiness to use them for his own purposes, to exploit them. They have also pointed to *rivalry* as a cause of egoism. Often, no doubt, they have used these two words, *competition* and *rivalry*, interchangeably to refer to the same thing.

I propose now to use them in different senses to make a distinction not often made, or not sufficiently noticed, by critics of 'the competitive society'. When two or more persons[12] are trying to get the same thing, or as large a share as possible of it, with none of them concerned to prove himself superior to the others, or to be preferred to them (better liked, more esteemed, reckoned more formidable, and so on), I shall say that they are mere competitors. Where there are two or more persons each concerned to prove himself superior to the others, or to be preferred to them, I shall say that they are rivals. Competitors are, of course, often rivals as well. But they need not be, and the element of rivalry is often quite small.

I suggest that it is competition much more than rivalry which is prominent in economically advanced as compared with economically simple societies. And rivalry in advanced societies is as frequent between persons who are collaborators in the same organization or enterprise as between persons who belong to different and competing organizations or enterprises. It is often said that an advanced economy is more competitive than a simple one; presumably because, as the division of labour increases, competition grows more severe. But nobody, to my knowledge, has yet been so ill-advised as to suggest that, the smaller the division of labour or the simpler the society, the less rivalry among men.

It is competition rather than rivalry which is supposed to promote efficiency, and it is also competition which, when it is 'excessive', is supposed to lead to economic anarchy. The more extensive the division of labour—so the argument goes—the wider the choice of jobs. The greater too the competition for jobs among persons who are virtually strangers to

[12] What I say here of persons can apply also to groups.

one another and whose prime concern is to get the jobs and not to prove themselves superior to their competitors. So too, since extended opportunity makes people more ready to move in search of better jobs, there is more competition for things other than jobs—for houses and for services and amenities. The competition is often anonymous, between people who do not even know each other's names, or who would not be interested in one another if they did not happen to be competitors. Competition is often impersonal, whereas rivalry is essentially personal.[13]

Critics of capitalism or of bourgeois society or, more generally, of 'modern' or 'civilized' society, have attacked rivalry as well as competition, but ordinarily without distinguishing between the two or between their effects. Nevertheless, they seem often to have had competition rather than rivalry in mind when they have complained of the individual's isolation in society, or of his readiness to treat others as mere means to his own ends, or of his feeling himself to be the victim of forces beyond his control.

It is true that Rousseau, who was the first to make these complaints, or rather to make much of them, had little to say about competition and a great deal about rivalry, in the senses in which I have been using these terms. He denounced nothing more fiercely than the desire to prove oneself superior to others or to be preferred to them, which he believed—in my opinion mistakenly—to be much stronger in the civilized countries of the West than in other and 'simpler' societies. He saw in this desire one of the sources of men's lack of sympathy for one another and their readiness to use each other for their own purposes. He pointed also to other causes: to the growth of commerce and industry, to the emergence of big towns dominating the economies of vast regions around them, and to the proliferation of middlemen of various kinds: merchants who buy in order to sell what they have bought at a profit, dealers in money (a commodity important only where there is a wide division of labour and extensive commerce), and dealers in law (lawyers, professional judges, and public officials) whose services are needed only because the law is complicated and difficult to apply. These other causes of isolation and exploitation to which Rousseau pointed, though they are not the same thing as competition, grow in importance along with it.

Rousseau and other critics of the society that 'separates men from one another' and makes them 'exploiters' take it too much for granted that indifference to others and readiness to take advantage of their weakness go together. This need not be so—not if the indifference is lack of affection or sympathy or lack of concern for their welfare—as distinct from con-

---

[13] Rivals, indeed, need not even be competitors, except for reputation, esteem, or affection. They may belong to different trades or professions, and each strives to do better in his trade or profession than the others in theirs to prove himself the better man in the eyes of some person or group whose good opinion he wishes to have.

cern for justice. If I have dealings with a man who is a stranger to me, I may care nothing for him personally nor be concerned to help him achieve his purposes, and yet I may think it important to respect his rights, legal and moral, including his right to courteous treatment. In my dealings with him, except for what I owe him in justice and courtesy, I may simply be out to do as well as I can for myself. If, in not caring for him for his own sake and being concerned only to give him his due as I would to anyone else, I am treating him as a means to my own ends, then clearly I can so treat him without exploiting him. Rousseau might perhaps say that in being concerned to deal justly with a man I care for him for his own sake. But this, surely, would be a misleading way of putting it. No doubt, I care for more than just doing as well as I can for myself, for I might achieve that purpose better, if I were unjust. I care also for justice, but there is a difference between my caring for justice and my caring for his own sake for the person I treat justly.[14]

Just as I can be just and indifferent, so I can be unjust and affectionate and caring. I can take advantage of someone's weakness or dependence on me to get more from him than I am entitled to, legally or morally, and yet may also be fond of him and be actively concerned to do him good. I may even be ready to make sacrifices for him which I would not make unless I knew him well and could enter into his feelings and purposes. I can exploit him and yet treat him, not as a means only, but also as an end. Feminists say that men have been (and still are) great exploiters of women, and not least of the women closest to them, whom they love and for whom they make sacrifices they would not make for men. No doubt, love and exploitation can be so defined as to be mutually exclusive, but as we ordinarily speak of them, they are not so. Indeed, they are sometimes so closely connected that it is difficult to tell them apart.

The more we depend on the services of persons unknown or little known to us, the more we need standards governing our transactions with them which they and we respect and which enable us to rely on one another in spite of our remoteness from each other. The society that provides its members with a wide variety of occupations and styles of life and a considerable freedom of choice among them is—or at least so far has been —a society in which the individual has shallow and often ephemeral relations with most people he deals with and has deeper relations with only a few, in the small family into which he is born or which he founds

---

[14] In *Émile*, and also elsewhere, Rousseau uses arguments which imply that men, if they were entirely self-regarding, if they were without genuine affection and concern for others, though they might act justly from motives of prudence, would not care for justice for its own sake. This may well be true, but it does not entail that, whenever one man is concerned to deal justly with another, he cares for that man for his own sake: is fond of him or is concerned for his welfare. Concern for justice may, as Rousseau suggests, be born of benevolence and of prudence, but it can be active independently of them.

with the woman he chooses to marry and the narrow circles of his close friends. In this society the distinction is sharper than in most between the wide circle of acquaintances and even strangers with whom he has dealings, some of them highly important to him, and the small circle of his intimates which is (or is supposed to be) also a select circle, one that he has to a large extent made for himself. This society, as we know it, is a highly competitive society, though it is not always capitalist.[15]

What then do the writers who decry competition and rivalry and their harmful effects want? Do they want the diversity of opportunity that an advanced society can offer without either competition or rivalry, or with much less of them than we now have? This, no doubt, is a reasonable aim. But it is not enough to proclaim it without indicating how it is to be achieved. Or do they merely want to get rid of the harmful effects of competition and rivalry? This, too, is a reasonable aim, if those who have it can explain what the harmful effects are and how we are to get rid of them. Indeed, even if they do no more than describe these effects and explain why they are harmful, with nothing said about how they are to be abolished, this is already a useful undertaking. But to say only that competition is harmful because it isolates people from one another and makes them exploitative, without making it clear what this isolation and exploitation consist in, is not enlightening. We can be indifferent to someone and yet scrupulously just in our dealings with him, and we can care for him deeply and yet be unjust and oppressive. Is indifference harmful, even when it is combined with justice?

A harmful effect often attributed to competition on a large scale is the individual's sense that he is a helpless victim of impersonal forces. But this may be an effect, not directly of competition, even on the largest scale, but of the economic 'anarchy' that results from it when it is uncontrolled. The control of it in a managed economy might not diminish the scale of competition or its intensity, though it would involve doing away with or restricting some forms of it. A managed economy can allow of just as much and as severe competition as an unmanaged economy, even when it greatly reduces the risk of unemployment and gives high wages to workers and generous assistance to the unemployed.

To be sure, this sense of helplessness could arise too in a well-managed economy, especially if it were large and highly centralized. Decisions might be taken rationally and in good time, and yet most people, having nothing to do with them and with little or no understanding of why they

[15] The countries in Eastern Europe that call themselves 'socialist' are just as much *acquisitive* and *competitive* societies as are the 'capitalist' countries of the West, though the acquisitiveness and competition take rather different forms. They are also illiberal societies, but their being so has, I suggest, nothing to do with their being socialist. Indeed, they are the less genuinely socialist for being illiberal—for denying to the individual the freedoms which nearly all socialists (including Marx) have wanted him to have.

were taken, might feel that the conditions in which they lived and worked, the choices open to them, were being decided by others in ways they could not predict. Indeed, in a society with very little competition or rivalry, except perhaps among a small minority of leaders, a society in which jobs were allocated to most people after they had been suitably trained and tested without their being allowed any choice in the matter, the sense of helplessness in the face of unpredictable and impersonal forces might be widespread and painful.

If in primitive communities the individual does not suffer from this sense of helplessness, it is not because he understands society or because he takes part with others in controlling it; it is because the social order and the system of production change very little, and he knows what is expected of him and what is due to him, and can rely on things being in the future much as they have been in the past, and also because he is so often his own master at work, doing it alone or with others who are his equals and cannot impose their wishes on him without consulting him. How he does what he is required or expected to do is determined by customs familiar to him, or is decided by himself, or by himself along with others, or by someone in authority over him who is close to him.

Rivalry which, unlike competition, is as common in 'primitive' as in 'advanced' societies, is also a target for attack by critics of 'the competitive society'. To strive for superiority over others, or to want to be preferred to them, is accounted evil mainly for two reasons: because it provokes ill will towards others (for example, jealousy and envy) as well as other feelings which are reprehensible, if not malevolent, such as the desire to dominate; and because it deflects the individual from his 'proper' course, from seeking to 'realize' himself in ways that are satisfying to him and bring him happiness.

Here again I find myself not so much disagreeing with these criticisms as wondering what to make of them. Who would deny that jealousy and envy are both painful and harmful, especially to the persons who feel them and also, to some extent, to the persons they are directed against? Who would deny that the desire to dominate is so too, often if not always? It can do harm, even when it is satisfied and gives pleasure to the dominator and the dominated, and it can be frustrating and painful to them both. And who would deny that these so often painful and harmful feelings arise largely from striving for superiority?

Yet this striving, which has these bad effects, has good effects also. And the bad effects are not bad without qualification. Jealousy and envy can be overcome, and in overcoming them a man comes to know himself better than he did before. Jealousy, perhaps the most painful of all human feelings, is also the most revealing and the most severely testing. It is felt as a mark of inferiority, and yet the overcoming of it, the learning to control it, is a moral victory. Envy, since it is less violent and more easily disguised, even from the person who feels it, is less disturbing and more insidious. It is more harmful because less often recognized, and because the need to overcome it, to get over the unbearable pain of it, is less strong. The desire to dominate is often closely allied to the desire to guide and protect, just as the desire to be dominated arises often from the need felt by the weak for protection; it can be salutary as well as harmful.

But it is not to these good effects of ill will and of the desire to dominate that I would point; it is rather to the good effects of rivalry, widely recognized though they are. For rivalry, though it can deflect a man from seeking satisfaction where he can find it, though it can make him neglect his talents and tastes in the attempt to outdo others, is also profoundly educative. As sociologists and writers on education so often tell us, the child comes to know itself largely in the process of comparing itself with other children and trying to do as well as or better than they do. It does not compare itself with all and sundry, but with its rivals for parental love and approval, with its class-mates, and eventually, as it approaches maturity, with older children with gifts similar to its own. We learn to walk culturally by trying to keep up with others or to outpace them, and even later, when we strike out on our own, we still compare ourselves with others, though we do it more selectively. Even the great artist or thinker, innovator though he is, compares himself with others and wants to do better than they do and have it recognized that he does. His rare gifts seem hardly to make him less a prey to jealousy and envy than he would be if his gifts were small.

All this is obvious. Even Rousseau, who never tired of attacking vanity and its bad effects, admitted from time to time that it also has good effects; and by vanity he meant above all the need to prove oneself superior to others. Vanity, he believed, does much more harm than good, and many, perhaps most, people would agree with him. It might seem to them that common experience bears Rousseau out. But in fact it does not, for he uses the word 'vanity' in a broader sense than most of us do; he means by it the concern (in all its forms) to impress others. That vanity, understood as he understood it, does more harm than good is by no means certain, though he found it easy to persuade himself that it does by describing its bad effects in great detail and saying very little of its good effects beyond admitting that it has some. The attacks on vanity and rivalry of Rousseau and other champions of social harmony are made on much too broad a front. They should put themselves to the trouble of distinguishing their good from their bad effects. They should do at least this much, even if it is beyond them to explain satisfactorily how the bad effects are to be eliminated and the good preserved.

I do not say this to score a point against them, or to reject their criticisms of our type of society. On the contrary, I believe that the criticisms are often well founded, though they need to be more discriminating. We do proclaim ideals that we fail to achieve, and we do suffer from illusions. There is a sense in which our society is more of a sham than earlier and simpler societies were. This is largely an effect of a heightened self-consciousness. We strive for more, here in this life, than our ancestors strove for, and our worldly aims, since they often go far beyond what is within our reach or familiar to us, are not easily defined. We construct ideals as much to challenge our institutions as to justify them. Since we do not accept society as we find it, do not take it for granted, we need to understand it as we would not need to do, if we merely took it for granted; and we also need ideal standards we can use to guide us in our endeavours to change it. But we have only an uncertain hold on the ideas we use to explain society and on these standards, and we find it difficult to think clearly about society, both as we find it and as we should wish it to be. I am not left unmoved by the strictures of Rousseau and of others on a society as disturbing and disappointing to its members as ours is, but I feel impelled to inquire just what it is they are objecting to, and to look for greater precision than they provide.

From the beginning—and the beginning was with Rousseau—the attack on 'civilized' or 'modern' or 'bourgeois' society has been as much directed at the apologists for it as at the society itself. Rousseau denounced the philosophers for preaching egoism or for excusing it or for trying to prove that all or most of the virtues are refined forms of it. Speculation in the West about the psychological and social origins of morality was more abundant, more ingenious, and more varied from the seventeenth century onwards than it had been at any time since the Greeks, and it laid heavy stress on enlightened self-interest. Hobbes had taught that moral rules are principles whose general observance is in everyone's interest, and that nobody is obliged to observe them unless he can rely on others doing so too. Hobbes qualified this thesis in various ways, and other thinkers qualified it or departed from it more than he did. But it was still very much to the fore among philosophical moralists in the West in Rousseau's time. Indeed, Rousseau himself did not entirely reject it, for there are traces of it in his writings. Rather, his attitude to it was ambiguous: at times he more than half accepted it, while at other times he reacted strongly against it, seeing in love and in attachment to the community and its ways of life sources of morality more important than enlightened self-interest.

Rousseau, the most self-centred of men, reacted strongly against 'the cult of the self' conspicuous among the educated classes of his day and of ours. He did not use this expression, 'the cult of the self', but I use it to refer to the importance attached to such ideals as self-expression and self-realization (though not necessarily under these names) and to the self-absorption of many who accept these ideals. Rousseau's writings, intro-spective and self-centred as they often are, have been in fact a considerable influence in encouraging the cult of the self. Nevertheless, he did denounce it. It is part of what he attacked under the name of egoism. In his ideal society of equals, citizens are public-spirited, warmly attached to the community and even to one another as members of it, but they are not concerned to express or realize themselves or to cultivate their talents.

Rousseau and others who have denounced the egoism of 'civilized' or 'bourgeois' man[16] have had in mind a variety of things: plain *selfishness*, or preferring one's own good to other people's when it is wrong to do so; *indifference to others*, or lack of sympathy and affection for them, or of concern for their good as an end in itself; and *self-centredness* or addiction to self-analysis and self-appraisal or the conscious striving to achieve some idea of oneself as one would wish to be. These are plainly different from one another, and need not go together. A selfish person need not be, and often is not, either indifferent to others or self-centred; and a self-centred person need not be, and often is not, indifferent to others or selfish. Even a person indifferent to others need not be selfish; he can be conscientious and yet lacking in sympathy and affection for others.

Though the accusers of 'civilized' or 'bourgeois' man have convicted him of selfishness as well as of indifference to others and self-centredness, it is the last two of these vices rather than the first which have seemed to them characteristic of him as compared with man in simpler societies. If civilized or bourgeois man is more selfish than the tribesman or villager, it is because social conditions and culture combine to make him indifferent to others and self-centred.

I have already attempted a qualified defence of this indifference, which seems to me inevitable in economically advanced societies. Not only in-evitable but also desirable, to the extent that it contributes to the proper functioning of institutions on which the dispensing of justice, the protec-tion and enlargement of freedom, and the efficient provision of indispen-sable services in vast and highly diversified communities depends. I have argued that the ideas of justice and freedom to which the critics of 'civil-ized' or 'bourgeois' society appeal have been to a great extent products of this society. This, of course, does not mean that we cannot appeal to these ideas to justify far-reaching transformations of the society that produced them. It means only that we must put ourselves to the trouble of distin-guishing between what needs to be changed in it and what must be pre-served if we are to come closer to realizing these ideas. Can we realize

---

[16] I must not give the impression that Rousseau's civilized man is altogether the same as 'bourgeois man', as Marx and other socialists conceived of him. Indeed, there are several different 'models' of both civilized and bourgeois man. But at the moment I am concerned with these models in so far as they are similar.

them except in an advanced economy with an extensive division of labour? Can we have such an economy without a structure of authority and a complicated system of legal rights and obligations? And can we have these things except under conditions such that the individual cannot help but be indifferent to most people he has dealings with? Can we have them except in a society where, in all but narrow circles, justice and good manners count for more than sympathy, affection, and comradeship?[17]

Self-centredness, though it can and often does encourage selfishness and indifference to others where that indifference is harmful, is connected also with the cult of freedom as the opportunity to achieve a satisfying way of life, or to be (or try to become) as one would wish to be. It thrives in the same cultural climate. It is not to be condemned, without more ado, as a kind of narcissism, or as a preoccupation with self that narrows sympathy and weakens goodwill. It can have these effects but need not. Often it is self-critical, and deepens self-knowledge and with it the understanding of others. It can enrich friendship, and lead to a more discriminating and tactful concern for others. It can also be ruthless, as it sometimes is in the man of talent or genius who thinks that his superiority to others entitles him to exploit them, and whose pretensions are so often excused by his admirers. But even the ruthlessly self-centred man of superior talents, thinker or artist or man of action, can enlarge freedom by his example and by teaching others to see further and feel more than they might otherwise do. Rousseau, who hated men's huddling together in towns, said that man's breath is fatal to his neighbours. Is this not as true in the spheres of thought and feeling as it is geographically? Is it not good, at least where freedom and independence of mind are valued (and most Western critics of 'civilized' or 'bourgeois' society have valued them), that men should keep each other somewhat at a distance, selecting a small number of friends from a large number of acquaintances, that intimacy should be a privilege and not a free-for-all?

V

Earlier I suggested that social harmony might be defined as a condition in which people are so strongly attached to shared standards that conflicts seldom arise among them, and when they do can be settled by procedures they all accept as just. I offered this definition because I believed that it explained what radical critics of modern society have had in mind in foretelling or imagining a society with no 'state' inside it, or no 'organized use of force' to maintain order, or no 'oppression'.

[17] There are occasions, of course, when warm and kindly feelings arise quickly between strangers, and also occasions when it is desirable that they should, though in fact they do not. I am not saying that relations should always be cool and remote, except within narrow circles of intimacy, but only that in vast urbanized communities they usually are so, and that there are advantages to their being so.

Consider first social harmony in relation to the state. It is not obvious that the greater this harmony, the less the need for the state—at least not unless the state is defined as an organ of oppression. It is not obvious if the word 'state' is used, as most people use it to refer to a hierarchy of holders of public offices whose authority extends over a given territory, and includes the right to define and to enforce, within limits set by itself, the legal claims and obligations of all persons and bodies active in that territory. It could be that, except in small and economically simple societies, some such hierarchy is actually a condition of people's sharing standards precise enough to meet their many needs and of their being sufficiently attached to them to live together, if not in complete harmony, at least in a condition not far removed from it. In other words, in all but the simplest societies, the state may be a creator or promoter of harmony as well as a means of keeping order in spite of such disharmony as may exist. No doubt, the state can be, and often has been, a promoter of tension and conflict. But this does not touch the point that I am now making, that its function in advanced societies may be as much to promote harmony as to maintain order. This, certainly, was the opinion of Hegel, and he was perhaps right. We could agree with him on this point without being committed to accepting his account of the rational state.

To have this effect, to promote harmony, the state need not actively indoctrinate its citizens, or be in control of education, or lay down principles for the guidance of those who do control it; it may promote it merely by providing methods of defining rights and obligations and of settling disputes such that people who resort to the methods tend to accept certain values. Institutions and values, social practices and the ideas used to explain and to justify them, arise together—as Montesquieu and others taught long before this simple doctrine was caught up in the currents and cross-currents of German philosophy. Which is not to say that they always go easily together, that the ideas are not used to challenge the practices. It is to say only that men would not have the ideas and use them as they do, if they were not familiar with the practices. Our ideas of freedom and justice, to the extent that they differ from earlier ideas, have arisen among us along with the modern state, and in so far as we are agreed about them and can use them to live peacefully and amicably together, this agreement and these uses come of our living together in the modern state. That state is indeed an effect of our learning to live together on a larger scale than ever before, of our having far more elaborate, diverse, and indirect dealings with one another. This is not the less true because it is also a source of conflict.

Logically, there could be a state, in the sense of a large hierarchy of holders of public authority, even though there was no 'organized use of force to maintain order' to compel the unwilling to obey and to punish the disobedient. The officers who constituted the hierarchy could conceivably exercise different kinds of authority carefully defined, could make laws and other decisions affecting the persons under their authority, and yet never resort to force to get their laws obeyed or their decisions carried out. They could be so seldom disobeyed that to create special instruments for dealing with the disobedient would not be worth while. But, though such a state is conceivable, none has yet existed.

The writers who predict or who hope for the disappearance of the state, which they call an instrument of oppression, do not make it clear just what they understand by oppression. Do they mean by it only class oppression? Why, then, should they suppose that, where there is no class oppression, there is no need for an elaborate structure of public authority, or of 'organized force to maintain order'?

Anyone who believes that he has been unjustly required to do what he does not want to do is apt to think of himself as oppressed. He may, of course, be mistaken in believing that the requirement is unjust. If we say— as most people would—that he is not oppressed if what is required of him is in fact just, we still have to allow that he may think he is oppressed, and that the threat of force may be needed to get him to do what is required. People may resent or fear legal oppression (oppression at the hands of established authority) for one or other (or all) of three reasons: because they believe that what is required of them is itself unjust, because they believe that the decision to require it was reached by an unjust method, and because they believe that the persons who reached it cannot be relied upon to be just. The last two of these reasons are especially important when the persons who make the requirements do so by virtue of offices they hold. Though a decision reached by an unjust method can be just, the method would probably not be reckoned unjust unless it were believed that it often resulted in the taking of unjust decisions. If citizens are satisfied that methods of taking decisions are just and have confidence in the impartiality of the persons who take them, they are usually willing, and indeed believe that they ought, to accept some unjust decisions. They accept occasional injustices as a price that must be paid, given human fallibility, for methods and persons that are on the whole just. They distinguish between the merely unjust and the oppressive, and count as oppressive only unjust decisions reached by unjust methods or taken by unjust persons.

I take it that most of the writers who speak of a society without oppression have in mind, not a society in which no official decisions are taken which people are required to obey[18] or in which no such decision is

---

[18] 'Required to obey' in the sense that it is generally recognized that the decisions ought to be accepted because they are officially taken by persons acting within the limits of the authority conferred upon them, even though there is no provision for enforcing their decisions.

ever unjust or thought to be so, but one in which official decisions are taken by methods admitted to be just and by persons relied upon to be impartial by almost everyone, a society in which everyone, whether he holds authority or is merely subject to it, shares the same standards of justice.

This idea of people sharing the same standards calls for closer scrutiny, for it is not as clear as it may seem at first sight. In the most conflict-ridden of communities there are many standards that virtually everyone accepts. Also, it quite often happens that people live peacefully and amicably together even though they hold to different standards. Indeed, in a free and tolerant society they take pride in living on good terms with one another in spite of their differing about matters of principle which they believe to be important. Conflicts between people who belong to the same social group or 'culture' are not necessarily less frequent and bitter than conflicts between people who are socially and culturally different. We cannot say: the more people share the same standards, the more likely they are to be on good terms with one another. The extent to which they need to have the same standards in order to be on good terms must depend upon the range and character of the dealings between them and above all on how far they agree about how to treat persons whose standards differ from their own. In a simple community in which people share much the same standards, there may often be violent disputes because the parties to them are head-strong and there are no methods of settling disputes peacefully which they can be relied upon to accept. When they agree about the facts of a situation they may differ hardly at all about what ought to be done, and yet it may be extraordinarily difficult to get them to agree about the facts as soon as disputes have arisen among them. They may be fiercely quarrel-some, and above all proud and stubborn, and therefore virtually inconcil-able once they have quarrelled openly. Much blood may need to be spilt before they are disposed to make peace.

In a diverse, sophisticated, and swiftly changing society, where there are many different occupations and styles of life, and even types of edu-cation, it is unlikely that disputes will arise only about the facts of situ-ations and not also about the principles that apply to them. There will be differences of opinion about what principles are relevant, and also about which principles should take precedence over others among those agreed to be relevant. In such a society people are aware that differences of prin-ciple arise and lead to disputes that have to be settled. They therefore feel the need for agreed methods of settling such disputes, for principles to be applied when differences of principle arise. They feel the need both for more sophisticated conceptions of justice and for more refined and elabor-ate procedures for applying them to particular cases.

What can two persons do when a dispute involving differences of principle arises between them and they cannot settle it themselves? They can resort to an arbiter they both trust, and agree beforehand to accept his decision, whatever it may be. But this may not in the long run prove satisfactory, especially in a large and complex society. Where parties to disputes choose their own arbiters, disputes involving the same issues may be differently settled. If, however, confidence in justice is to be general and strong, such disputes ought to be settled on much the same terms. Smith and Jones, satisfied with Robinson's settlement of their dispute, may come later to be dissatisfied with it when they see how differently Clarke has settled a similar dispute between Bates and Simpson. Or, later, Smith may come into dispute with Bates, and may want a settlement on the terms decided by Robinson in his first dispute with Jones, while Bates wants a settlement on the terms decided by Clarke in his dispute with Simpson.

No doubt, it seldom happens that two disputes raise exactly the same issues. Still, in a large community in which disputes arise between persons remote from one another, if there is to be confidence that they will be settled impartially and justly, the settling of them must be so organized that like disputes are settled alike. In practice, in such a community, this requires that the settlers of disputes should be professionals learned in the law.[19] This requirement does not, of course, preclude their being elected to their offices, provided they are otherwise suitably qualified. Nor does it preclude the parties to a dispute agreeing between them who is to settle their dispute, so long as the community makes provision for its settlement in the event of their not being able to agree on an arbiter.

Few people today in highly urbanized and industrial societies, 'capitalist' or 'socialist', want the administration of justice to be quite unprofessional. Unprofessional justice is suited only to small and simple communities in which disputes occur only among neighbours. The points at issue in such disputes and the situations in which they arise are widely understood. Whoever settles disputes, whether he is a chief or elder who does so by virtue of his office, or an arbiter chosen by the parties to the dispute, makes his decision under the close scrutiny of the community. Under such conditions, justice can be uniform and recognized to be such, even though the persons who dispense it are not professionals.

Justice can be professional and popular. It can be contrived that those who dispense it are both trained in the law and elected to their offices by the people. Nor need this be a wasteful method, for the legal training

---

[19] By a professional I do not mean just someone who does something *ex officio*, for his doing it may be only a small part of the duties of his office; I mean someone whose recognized business consists chiefly (or largely) in his doing this kind of work. A professional need not always be trained to do his work before he begins to do it, and may acquire his special competence in the course of doing it. Though, when his business is to settle disputes (or to represent the parties to disputes) in complex societies, special training is an immense advantage.

acquired by persons who fail to get elected may be useful to them (and to the community) in other spheres. But why should it be reckoned a great advantage that persons who dispense justice be popularly elected? Their business, even in a democracy, is not to make laws or policies that give expression to 'the will of the people'; their business is to settle disputes impartially and justly. Why should it be thought that their being popularly elected makes it more likely that they will do so?

It is a reasonable maxim that all holders of public offices should be responsible for how they carry out their official duties. From this, however, it does not follow that they should all, even in a democracy, be responsible directly to the people. Other forms of responsibility are possible. Holders of offices, especially when a high degree of professional competence is required of them, can be responsible to their 'profession' or branch of the administration: to some body, elected or appointed, within the profession or branch whose business it is to see that standards are maintained and to take disciplinary action when they are not. Or they can be responsible to some body outside the profession or branch to which complaints against them can be made.

The demand that judges be popularly elected, where it is not justified by mere appeal to the principle that all holders of public authority should be responsible directly to the people, is often inspired by the belief that 'the state' (in the shape of holders of public office, and especially the higher offices) is biased in favour of some classes or social groups against others. That this can be so, and often has been and still is so, is no doubt true. But it is not obvious that it must be so. Nor is it obvious that, when it is so, the popular election of judges is much of a remedy for it.

Radicals often say that in bourgeois countries the legislature, though popularly elected, is strongly biased in favour of the propertied classes.[20] That this has quite often been so cannot, I think, be reasonably denied.

---

[20] Two rather different criticisms of bourgeois democracy are worth noticing. The critic may hold that, even in a bourgeois society, a legislature will be much more concerned to promote widely shared interests, if it is popularly elected than it would be if it were not, but that its intentions are frustrated by an irresponsible bureaucracy subject to pressures from privileged groups. Or he may hold that even a popularly elected legislature is so affected by bourgeois ideology as to be biased in favour of the privileged. Many critics have alternated between these two beliefs, without appearing to notice that they are different.

Critics of liberal democracy sometimes admit that bourgeois courts are often (though by no means always) impartial; that they apply the law, such as it is, to litigants or to offenders without bias, but the courts could, of course, be even more impartial than they are, and the laws be unjust, favouring some classes or groups to the detriment of others. Indeed, it could even happen that the laws, as formulated by the legislature, were not biased but were interpreted by the courts in the light of conventions which were so. This, too, is compatible with the courts not being biased for or against particular litigants or offenders, with their applying the laws and conventions, as they find them, without fear or favour, and in that sense impartially.

Again, the courts may be impartial, and yet the police who arrest and interrogate presumed offenders, and prepare the charges against them, be grossly partial. These are all frequent, and often justified, criticisms of law and law-enforcement in the liberal democracies of the West.

But why has it been so? Has it been because of the social and cultural conditions that have prevailed? Or because *only* legislators and a few other holders of public offices have been popularly elected? The radicals themselves have laid much more stress on the first than on the second of these causes: on social inequalities and their cultural and ideological effects than on the fact that too small a proportion of public offices have been elective. Surely, in this respect, they have been right! Why, given social equality and widely accepted egalitarian principles, should the mere fact that only some offices are filled by popular election, favour some social groups against others? Office-holders who are not elected may perhaps be better placed than they would otherwise be to exploit the public, and may assist one another in doing so. In that case they would constitute a group (or more probably several groups) biased in their own favour. There would then be 'exploitation' of society by the state. But why should there be any bias within the hierarchy of office-holders for some groups outside the hierarchy against others?

There are social and cultural conditions which make it unlikely that holders of public office will exercise their authority justly, even though they are popularly elected; and radical critics of bourgeois democracy have pointed to some of them. That in itself is a considerable service. But it still leaves it uncertain how far, in the interests of justice, holders of public office should be elected by the people. Is it enough that legislators alone should be so, or should holders of other kinds of public authority be so too? Should they be elected at all levels of the hierarchy? Is there a special case for, or against, the popular election of judges? These are all questions left unanswered by most critics of bourgeois democracy, even though some of their criticisms, some of their accusations of gross class bias, are well grounded. Or, if the questions are not left quite unanswered, the brief answers given are not convincing. Because the laws and the courts have been (and often still are) biased in favour of the rich and the powerful where there is social inequality and judges are not elected by the people, it does not follow that in a society of equals judges should be popularly elected. Perhaps they should be, but the case has still to be made.[21]

The case against *non-professional justice* in advanced societies, except in dealing with minor cases, is surely overwhelmingly strong. The case against *popular justice*—if by popular justice is understood the popular election of judges who have been trained in the law—is less strong. Yet there is a case against it which those who favour it should take into account. Even in an egalitarian society whose laws and conventions do not favour

[21] The experience of 'popular justice' in the 'people's democracies' is not strong evidence either way. For these 'democracies' are in fact controlled by a highly disciplined authoritarian party. The idea of popular justice has been perverted to meet the needs of rulers who are irresponsible and yet wish to project an egalitarian and democratic 'image' of themselves and of the societies they may dominate.

some groups unjustly as compared with others, there can be prejudice and passion. Judges who seek re-election might hesitate to take just but unpopular decisions. This disadvantage might be removed by having judges popularly elected and yet irremovable 'during good behaviour', but to resort to this remedy would be to depart seriously from the principle that judges should be responsible to the people. Why bother to have them popularly elected in the first place if they are not to be subject to re-election later? What are the advantages of their being elected as against their being appointed, not necessarily as they are now in most Western countries, but in such a way as to ensure that they are not under pressure from the government and are suitably qualified? According to the critics of 'bourgeois democracy', it is not enough that the laws should be just; the men who administer them must not be unconsciously biased against some groups and in favour of others by a class ideology. This impartiality is to be achieved, so these critics say, not by the proliferation of elections, but by a transformation of society which destroys this ideology at its roots. Why, then, when the transformation is made and the ideology is destroyed, have judges who are popularly elected? Does not popular confidence in the administration of justice depend above all on its being public, cheap, and expeditious, on the high moral and professional standards of courts and judges, and on litigants and accused persons being able to appeal easily and cheaply against decisions they hold to be unjust? What evidence is there that the qualities on which popular confidence in justice chiefly depends are more likely to be found where judges are popularly elected?

I have said nothing to imply that parties to disputes ought not to settle them among themselves, or ought never to resort to unofficial arbiters chosen by themselves, rather than have recourse to 'public justice'. Some Utopians have spoken as if in their ideal societies all disputes would be settled amicably by the parties to them or by resort to private arbitration. Actually, even in the bourgeois world they dislike, many disputes are settled in these ways, and not only among peasants and other unprivileged groups who avoid, as far as they can, expensive and dilatory courts which they believe to be biased in favour of the rich and the expensively educated. How large a proportion of disputes are settled privately in these ways, it is impossible to say; for, apart from the lack of information about disputes that never reach the courts, there is the difficulty of deciding what is to count as a dispute.

This unofficial settling of disputes is, of course, deeply affected by the ideas and methods used in settling disputes officially. The existence of public and impartial courts to which citizens can refer their disputes in the last resort has two important effects: it helps to define and to diffuse standards that can be used in reaching private settlements, and it deters stronger parties from exerting all the pressures they otherwise might exert and encourages weaker parties to resistance.

VI

I have discussed the settling of disputes about rights and obligations under whatever laws (or social rules) there might be. I have said nothing about how disputes as to what the laws themselves should be, might be settled. Nor have I discussed the deliberate breaking of the law, and what society might do to discourage such breaches. I want now to discuss disputes about what the law should be, and then later the treatment of deliberate offenders against the law, especially when the offences are serious, when they are of the sort that are ordinarily called *crimes*—except by social theorists who have special reasons for not giving them that name.

In primitive societies there is virtually no legislation, or nothing that is recognized as such. Social rules do in fact change as they are applied over considerable periods of time in changing circumstances, but they change 'imperceptibly'. Old men looking back over the years may notice that they have changed, but no one seeks to change them or to prevent their changing. In more 'advanced' societies, there is a need felt to change the law deliberately, and there are differences of opinion about how it should be changed and the ends it should serve.

The modern state, as compared with earlier political communities, is copiously legislative, and also very much concerned to regulate its methods of doing its own business. It draws together into a highly organized political whole, not only many smaller and diverse communities, but also a vast number of men and women whose occupations, styles of life, tastes, and values differ greatly. Even where it is not liberal, as liberalism is understood in the West, it often claims to be liberating: to be actively concerned to enlarge the opportunities of its citizens.

Already in the eighteenth century, Western political theorists were turning their minds, on the one hand, to defining rights that all citizens should have, no matter what their occupations and ways of life, and on the other, to a more detailed and critical appraisal of constitutional as distinct from other kinds of law. The rights of the citizen were supposed to define the essential liberties which the community should secure to its members, but they were seen also as the minimal concessions that individuals whose tastes, standards, and ambitions differ must make to one another to be able to live peacefully and amicably together. A man might welcome this diversity, or might merely accept it as a fact of life; but whichever he did, he might conclude that social harmony was best achieved, not by ensuring that people have the same values, but by getting them to agree on the terms on which they could live together in spite of their having different ones. Long before the birth of liberalism, social and political theorists had conceived of men as competitors for the resources required to satisfy their wants, and also as collaborators working together, when occasion served, the better to satisfy them. The function of basic social rules, as they saw it, was to regulate this competition and collaboration. They had long thought of men as having needs that were broadly similar rather than as having standards and beliefs which might be in important respects different. The problem of achieving social harmony in spite of cultural and moral diversity is one that moralists and political theorists in the West began to take seriously only towards the end of the eighteenth century. Indeed, even then, they were rather feeling their way towards recognizing it than facing it squarely.

In a culturally diverse, freedom-loving, and rapidly changing society, it is impossible that people should agree completely about what is desirable and what is right, and yet they must agree to some extent if they are to live peacefully and amicably together. What then must they agree about? They must agree not to impose their own standards on others merely because they are convinced of their rightness, and they must agree about how to reach decisions in matters of common concern, how to settle disputes, and how to deal with breaches of important social rules. The first requirement is merely an extension to the moral sphere of the toleration that Locke advocated in matters of religion, and is met in practice by securing certain rights to the individual. The second requirement is met by establishing appropriate governmental (or decision-making) procedures, including provisions for changing these procedures.

I need not, for my present purpose, indicate, even in broad outline, how these rights and procedures should be defined. For my purpose, at the moment, is merely to insist that, if social harmony is to be achieved in culturally diverse and quickly changing societies, in which moral and other standards differ widely, it can be so only by defining these rights and procedures in considerable detail; or, in other words, by establishing an elaborate system of law which lays down the rights and obligations both of ordinary citizens and of holders of public authority. Where there is such a system, there is also necessarily a state. We cannot, for all that Marx and those who think like him say, have freedom and cultural diversity without the modern state; though we can, of course, as we know only too well, have that state without freedom or cultural diversity—or with very little of either.

We do not have to be philosophers to see the difference between agreeing to something because we believe it is right, and thinking it right to agree to it even though we believe that it falls short of being right. Indeed, we may think it right to agree to it, even though it is not the nearest that we can get in the circumstances to what we think is right. We could, perhaps, by putting pressure on the other parties to the agreement, get

them to concede more to us, but we may not think it right to do so, because it compels them to make larger concessions than they think it
right to make, or because it is in breach of rules of procedure which we
believe are just, or because it weakens mutual trust. This distinction
between agreeing to what is believed to be right and thinking it right to
make concessions to others—a distinction which is highly important
where ideas of right and justice differ considerably (as they do in all
'advanced' and sophisticated societies)—is often neglected, and sometimes
even denied, by critics of Western society who are also champions of social
harmony.

For example, Rousseau, the first and most eloquent of these critics,
argues in the fourth book of *The Social Contract* that the citizen who votes
with the minority in an assembly of upright citizens, an assembly whose
decisions are expressions of the general will, will concede after the event
that he was mistaken in voting as he did. That is to say, in accepting the
decision of the assembly, he accepts what he now believes to have been
the right decision; he does not merely think it right to accept a decision
properly taken even though it is not (in his opinion) the right decision.
He does more than bow to the will of the majority; he makes their beliefs
his own because they are the majority. There is no equivalent to this
morally perverse and logically absurd doctrine in the writings of Marx or
of other critics of bourgeois society who predict the disappearance of the
state and the enlargement of freedom. But they, in their turn, fail to explain
how, where there is no state, social harmony is to be achieved by people
who put a high value on freedom, enterprise, and diversity, and are not to
be satisfied by the stuffy and parochial culture of Rousseau's ideal community; by people who have passed beyond the narrow views and philis-
tine aspirations of bourgeois society.

In a culturally diverse and quickly changing community, there must be
copious legislation and also wide disagreements about law and policy.
This must be so, even if the community is much nearer to being egalitarian
than any industrial society, 'capitalist' or 'socialist', is today. This, of
course, does not mean that, if there is to be social harmony, it matters
less that the laws should be just than that methods of making and administering them should be so. People are concerned that methods of
reaching decisions should be just because they want the decisions to be
just. But it does mean that they attach great importance to these methods
because of the vast amount and the complexity of the business to be
transacted by means of them. Questions of method, political and judicial,
are and ought to be of absorbing interest in such communities. But they
are difficult and complicated questions which can never be finally settled,
since circumstances and therefore needs change continually. To play down
the importance of such questions, or to suggest that they are important

only where there is social inequality and exploitation, is surely absurd.[22]

Except in recent times in the West and in some Westernized countries, the world has known either primitive communities whose methods of taking public decisions and settling disputes have been relatively simple and have been accepted as just (or at least not challenged as unjust) or else more 'advanced' societies in which public business has been largely confined to privileged groups whose decisions the unprivileged and often uncomprehending masses have had to put up with. Only recently have we had 'advanced' societies in which all sections of the population have been politically active, if not directly, then through representatives whose right to speak for them they have recognized. And even in these societies some sections are still much more active, much more adequately represented, than others.

The gradual 'politicization' of the people, far from diminishing the number of political and judicial disputes, has increased them. But it does not follow that social harmony has diminished. It may even have increased; it may be that, in the older liberal democracies, people are more inclined than they used to be to believe that laws and social practices are just or useful, and are more confident that they have the means of establishing or changing them when they are unjust or harmful. In undemocratic societies in which there are great inequalities, the unprivileged who choose not to resort to the courts to settle their disputes with one another but prefer to settle them 'privately', and who dare not resort to them against their superiors, do not therefore live in harmony either with each other or with their superiors. Not at least unless harmony is defined as the absence or scarcity of disputes judicially settled. Even more obviously, the fact that the unprivileged do not claim the right to be consulted politically and do not clamour for reforms of the law is no evidence that they believe that the political system and the laws are substantially just. A great increase in the volume of political and judicial conflict could be a sign of increasing social harmony. It need not be so, but it could be. It could mean that people are resorting more and more to methods of carrying on and resolving conflicts, which used not to be available to them, and which they believe to be substantially just.

[22] Perhaps those who speak of 'the disappearance of the state' have in mind (sometimes at least) not any drastic reduction in the volume or complexity of public business but its 'decentralization' or its being divided into separate and autonomous spheres so related to one another that they do not constitute a single political system—as, for example, according to some historians, the Temporal and Spiritual Powers were related in the Middle Ages, neither of them subordinate to the other and yet having no common superior. The advantages of this arrangement in an industrial society are not obvious.

VII

Nothing has attracted Utopians[23] more than the idea of a society in which there is no crime, or in which there is so little of it, that there is no need to punish criminals. Crime, according to them, is an effect of social conditions which can be removed, and in their ideal communities are removed, so that there is no need to make special provision for dealing with criminals. Marx, in *The Holy Family*, went so far as to suggest that, if social conditions were as they should be, there would be little temptation to commit the offences that bourgeois society treats as crimes, and the offender could be left to punish himself—presumably by blaming himself for what he had done and resolving not to repeat it. How far Marx kept to this belief in later years, I do not know. My concern, at the moment, is not with his beliefs so much as with beliefs of a certain kind.

We should perhaps begin by asking, *What is crime?* Or, rather, what should we take it to be for the purposes of this discussion? Hobbes distinguished crime from sin, the breaking of civil from the breaking of moral law, though of course the two could coincide. But not all breaches of civil law, not even when they are intentional, are treated as crimes; many of them are merely civil offences (torts or breaches of contract), for which the offender is not 'punished', though he may be required to compensate whomever he has injured. If we define a crime as a breach of the law which is punishable, then it follows that, where punishment is abolished, crime is so too. Yet behaviour which is criminal while it is punishable may continue after it has ceased to be punishable. Presumably, by the disappearance of crime Utopians mean something more than the abolition of punishment.

Many actions that are criminal would not be held morally wrong unless the law, as declared by legislatures and administered by courts, forbade them. Indeed, the gap between law and morality is sometimes so great that criminal actions are widely approved, or at least excused. And the converse is also true: actions which are not criminal are strongly condemned as immoral, even though it is widely agreed that it would be a mistake to make crimes of them. Yet these actions which are strongly condemned but are not crimes are not therefore less harmful than crimes are. Moral rules are not necessarily less in the common interest when they do not coincide with the law than when they do. For example, to tell a lie or to break a promise is a punishable offence only under certain circumstances. Sometimes it is held to be a trivial offence and at other times a grave offence; but it is not grave only when it is criminal, and it can be trivial (doing

---

[23] I use this word in a broader sense than Marx did, which allows me to say that he too, at times, was a Utopian. But I do not use it in a pejorative sense, for I believe that the description of ideal societies is an important part of political theory.

little harm and generally held to be excusable) even though it is criminal.

In society as it now is, someone who commits a grave offence which is not criminal is not left to himself to repent of it. He is blamed for it and often suffers greatly at the hands of others for having done it. His action goes unpunished only in the sense that no one whose office is to enforce the law takes official cognizance of it. And if his action is not a civil offence either, nobody who is harmed by it can go to law to get compensation from him for the harm done. Yet, in another sense, he may be greatly *punished*. That is to say, others may act towards him in ways intended to hurt him because they blame his action, and he may know this and be greatly hurt. This kind of punishment, as we all know, is often highly effective, and can be a more powerful deterrent than official punishment.

Often, of course, these two kinds of punishment reinforce each other. The same actions are liable to them both, or an offence that brings one of them upon the offender comes in time to bring the other. An action, as a result of being made a crime, comes eventually to be widely condemned as immoral, or an action which was not criminal is made so because in the meantime it has come to be condemned on moral grounds—as, for example, incitement to racial hatred. But often, too, these two kinds of punishment do not reinforce one another: actions liable to one kind are not also liable to the other. This seems to be so in all societies where the two exist; where there are processes of official punishment developed enough to make the two kinds easily distinguishable.

I know of no systematic study of these forms of punishment which compares their scope and effects, advantages and disadvantages, and so might help to explain how some actions come to be liable to the one form, others to the other, and some to both. I suggested earlier that in many primitive societies there is little or no recourse to public authority, to official arbiters, for the settlement of disputes, not because they are societies of equals (which quite often they are not), but because they are small, and parties to disputes are therefore neighbours in a community of neighbours. Social conventions supported by 'public opinion' are ordinarily enough to keep the peace among them, or to confine displays of violence within tolerable limits. For much the same reason there is little or no recourse to official blame and punishment of offenders, to their trial and condemnation by the community acting collectively or through representatives. The condemnation of offenders by their neighbours, and various forms of ostracism, act as sufficient deterrents. But in more developed and larger communities, just as disputes may arise between persons who are not neighbours, so offences may be committed by persons who are strangers to their victims or are strangers in the place where they commit their offences. And just as the greater complexity of social relations and transactions increases the variety of disputes, so it increases also the variety of offences. There is a need felt for more elaborate procedures to determine what is at issue between disputants or the exact nature of the offence committed and to reach a settlement or impose a punishment according to principles carefully defined and impartially applied. There is a need felt for the community to do officially what neighbours acting unofficially cannot do: for it to take cognizance of disputes and offences which it alone, acting through its representatives, is competent to define and settle or to punish.

Nevertheless, the community takes upon itself only some of the business of settling disputes and punishing offences, and does not even take over completely the part that it makes its own. A man tempted to commit a crime is often deterred from committing it, less by fear of punishment by the courts, than by fear of what his neighbours, or even the general public, would think of him, if he were found guilty. If he could be found guilty and punished without his neighbours knowing about it, he might think the risk worth taking and commit the crime. And yet, if he did commit it, his neighbours might not suspect him of it, let alone believe him to have done it, unless he were brought to trial and convicted.

The larger, the more developed, and the more culturally diverse a community, the greater the chance that actions condemned by some groups inside it are not so by others. Therefore, if persons belonging to the groups that do not condemn the actions are to be deterred from committing them, it will not be by fear of what will be thought of them within those groups; and they may care little for what people outside them think. Also, many of the groups a man belongs to may include few of his neighbours, so that he cares little for what most of his neighbours think of him. Thus, moral and cultural differences can separate neighbour from neighbour as well as one neighbourhood from another. Not completely, of course, but in important respects. The extent to which anyone is affected by the praise or blame of his neighbours will, in these conditions, vary greatly with the sort of behaviour in question. A large and culturally diverse community of this kind does not differ from one that is small and culturally homogeneous in consisting of many small communities, each of them homogeneous, though differing considerably from the others. Moral and cultural diversity pervade its every part.

In the past there have been vast empires made up of many small communities, differing greatly from one another, and yet with much the same standards accepted by everyone inside any one of them.[24] But then these

---

[24] In every community, however small and economically simple, there are different rules and standards for men and women, for adults and children, for people engaged in different occupations. If cultural homogeneity consisted in the same rules and standards applying to everyone in the community, no community would be culturally homogeneous. It consists rather in everyone's accepting, or not challenging, the distribution of roles in the community and not questioning its rules and standards, whether they apply generally or sectionally.

empires have been economically simple, and the communities they consist of have been largely self-sufficing, or there has been not much movement from one to another. These communities have also, in practice, been largely autonomous. Within their own borders they have applied their own laws and customs, and other laws have arisen to regulate their dealings with one another or with the supreme ruler and his officials, or to regulate the transactions between persons belonging to different communities. The cultural diversity within the great cosmopolitan empires of the past, except perhaps in a few of their great towns, differs in crucial respects from what we are familiar with today. Our kind of cultural diversity is not a divergence in beliefs and manners between stable and self-sufficing communities but between highly unstable social groups very much dependent on one another. These groups are always changing. Their beliefs, standards, and practices (those that distinguish them from other groups) are never for long the same, and individuals pass in and out of them continually.

This sort of cultural diversity is, presumably, welcome to people genuinely concerned for freedom, as not only liberals but socialists and anarchists too have conceived of it. And yet, obviously, it presents dangers. There are some rules that even the most libertarian community must require all its members to observe, and others that it must require them to observe according to their occupations and social roles—at least in so far as their carrying them out competently is in the general interest. In a fast-changing industrial society, there must be provision made for the authoritative defining and altering of social rules, and for the settlement of disputes that arise about how the rules apply to particular cases. What then is to be done to people who break these rules or reject these settlements? To people who refuse to do what is required of them by authority? In society as it now is, they are brought to trial and are punished if found guilty.

Most radicals who look forward to the eventual abolition of 'organized force' to maintain order are ready to admit that, while social conditions remain as they are, it not only will not be abolished but ought not to be. The consequences of a premature attempt to abolish it might well be disastrous. Only in the future, if social conditions, standards, and attitudes are greatly and suitably changed, will it be both safe and desirable to put an end to this use of force.

Unfortunately, they say far too little about the conditions, social and cultural, in which this use of force would cease to be necessary. To be sure, they do say that social classes and the exploitation of some classes by others must disappear. But what they fail to take account of is that classes, as we know them today, could disappear, and society still be divided into groups, of which some exploited others. In all societies, people have different rights and obligations, according to their occupations and social roles, and in all but the simplest there are considerable differences of power and influence between them. How do we decide when differences of right and obligation constitute inequalities which entail exploitation and when they do not? Some inequalities are presumably justified as being in the general interest. How do we decide which are in that interest and which are not? Must they be against the general interest, if there is to be exploitation? Under what conditions do unjustifiable inequality and exploitation make people less law-abiding? For, presumably, if it were generally, though mistakenly, believed that inequalities were justified, and if exploitation were not recognized for what it is, people might be very law-abiding, even though they were exploited. These questions are not unanswerable, though they are perhaps difficult to answer. The more the pity, then, that they should have been so much neglected by theorists who needed to answer them to explain how their ideals could be achieved!

In an ideal society in which everyone was disposed to obey important social rules, it could still happen that someone from time to time, through ignorance or blinded by interest or passion, broke such a rule. If it were a rule not authoritatively defined and applied, his friends and neighbours might draw his attention to what he had done, and might persuade him to make amends where that was possible. As we have seen, even in society as it now is, such breaches of moral and conventional rules may be frequent and serious, and yet no need be felt to resort to public authority in dealing with them. The pressure of opinion is held to be enough to keep such breaches within tolerable limits, even though some people are much less sensitive to this pressure than others are. Life goes on, tolerably enough, even though the wicked are liable only to the pressure of opinion, and some of them are cynically indifferent to it.

If the rule broken in our ideal society were one authoritatively defined and applied, the presumed breaker of it might be called upon to appear before some court (or official) whose duty it was to deal with such breaches. If the court were satisfied that he was responsible, it might require him to make amends to whoever was injured by the breach, and might also, if he were held to have been negligent or ill-intentioned, reprimand him for it and require him to pay a fine, in money or in kind. It might even require him to do some work for the benefit of the community.

If he were reprimanded and fined by some body or person acting on behalf of the community, he would, of course, be punished. Now, according to Marx in *The Holy Family*, there would be no such punishment, but only 'self-punishment', in a community in which social ties were 'truly human'. There would then be, not only no trial and punishment by public authority, but no pressure of opinion, no marks of disapproval, from neighbours and acquaintances, at least not towards adult offenders. But though, in the situation I have imagined, there would be official blame and punishment (which not Marx alone but others too have banished from their ideal society), there might still be no use of force against offenders or persons suspected of having committed offences. If they refused to appear for trial or to submit to the sentence passed on them, they might not be arrested or deprived of their liberty in any way. They might merely be deprived of certain benefits while they refused to do what was required of them. Officially condemned and deprived of these benefits, they would probably incur the disapproval of their neighbours. This method of dealing with offenders could be highly effective, though it might sometimes be necessary to resort to force to restrain an offender who became aggressive when the method was applied to him.

Or, alternatively, the courts dealing with offences might not reprimand offenders or impose any fine, in money or kind or labour, upon them, but might merely indicate to them how they should make good, as far as possible, the harm done by their offence. If an offender refused to do what it directed, the court might merely take note of the fact and do nothing more. In that case, it would be left to the offender to decide whether or not to give effect to the decision of the court, with no more pressure upon him than the official recording of his offence and its publication. This method might be a good deal less effective than the withdrawal of benefits from offenders who refused to accept the court's decisions. It would, however, come closer to Marx's ideal of 'self-punishment'; and it would be left entirely to the offender to execute the sentence on himself. The community, or rather the court acting in its name, would then do no more than invite the offender to 'punish' himself and advise him how he should do so.

Or these two methods might be combined, the second method (the one that comes closer to Marx's ideal) being applied to less serious offences, and perhaps even to more serious ones, when they were first offences, and the first method only to serious offences by hardened offenders. But, in an economically developed, culturally diverse, and freedom-loving community, however tolerant and public-spirited its members might be, it would be necessary to resort at least to the second method. It would be necessary to make provision for defining offences, deciding authoritatively whether they had been committed, under what circumstances, and by whom, and indicating what should be done by offenders (or by the community) to make good, as far as possible, the harm done. These are not matters which, in a community of that kind, could be left to neighbours and to 'public opinion'. In many spheres of action, though not in all, it would be for the community, acting officially through its agents, to undertake them. This is so, not so much because no community can rely entirely on the goodwill of its members—for at the moment we are thinking of an ideal community which can rely on it, if not entirely, then to a much greater extent than is now possible—as because in any developed, diversified, and changing society, everyone, no matter how wise and well-intentioned he may be, needs a great deal of official guidance: needs to be told authoritatively what he should do, when he has failed to do it, and how he can make good the harm he has done.

The more a community can rely on the goodwill of its members, and the more it can resort to the second method I described in dealing with offenders, using the first only when the second has failed, the better. To create this goodwill, or rather to strengthen it where it is now weak, would no doubt require large social reforms, as well as reforms in methods of education. But, quite apart from these reforms, even in society as it now is, it might be possible to change methods of dealing with offenders so as to bring them considerably closer than they now are to the methods I have described. The methods we now use seem often to turn offenders 'against society', to make them less willing than they were before to respect its rules and standards; and they are also extraordinarily expensive methods. At a smaller cost and by gentler methods, or at least by methods that rely less on compulsion and imprisonment, we might get better results. Penal reform need not wait on other social reforms to bring considerable benefits to society, though there are limits to what it alone can achieve.

The critics of bourgeois society, or of Western society generally, have pointed to two major causes of 'crime': to the social conditions that incline people to commit it and to the methods of dealing with it that create hardened offenders.[25] If I say that they have pointed to these causes without going far towards explaining what those conditions are or in what ways the methods are harmful, it is not because I wish to belittle their achievement. The thinkers who first raise important questions often do so without putting them clearly, without making the distinctions that need to be made if they are to be put clearly. Later, as the distinctions come to be made, the original, large, vague questions fall apart into a greater number of smaller and more precise ones. To point this out is not to belittle the pioneers.

[25] In this last section I have not discussed the belief that the hardened offender should be treated as a sick person to be cured rather than as a wrongdoer to be punished. This belief did not, I think, appeal to Marx, and it does not appeal to me. By all means let us look for the social conditions that breed crime and try to remove them, and let us try to persuade criminals to change their ways. But why should we treat them as if they were not responsible for what they do? Neither of the two methods I have described treats offenders as if they were sick persons. Quite the contrary. No doubt, offenders can be mentally sick, but it is surely arrogant and dangerous to assume that they are so merely because they do not live up to standards which we think are good. Besides, curing the mentally sick can serve as a cover for cruel and oppressive treatment just as readily as can the punishment of wrongdoers.

CHAPTER XV

CONCLUSIONS

I

I HAVE tried to throw light on some issues obscurely raised by Marx, issues important above all to the social and political theorist, though not only to him, for they also have practical implications. I do not claim for the aspects of Marx's thought discussed in this book that they were more important to him than the others. In the West, especially in academic and intellectual circles, interest in his philosophy has changed direction.

I doubt whether Marx as a social theorist has ever been taken more seriously, or held in greater respect, in English-speaking countries than since the last war. This respect has little to do with the political successes in other parts of the world of movements and parties calling themselves Marxist; or at least not directly. Could any Marxist who took seriously Marx's reasons for condemning capitalism and bourgeois society admire the Soviet Union or the two great 'Marxist' parties of the West, Italian and French, or the China of Chairman Mao? Surely not. He would condemn them, not for venturing to exist under conditions not allowed for by Marx, not for the crime of *lèse-philosophie*, but for being worse than bourgeois in so many ways in which what is bourgeois seems to him bad.

In any case, there is room for doubt as to how far Marx intended to make predictions just as there is about what he predicted. He spoke with energy and conviction, of the future as of the past and the present, but what he wanted to say is not always clear. Philosophy and social theory were never more self-confident than in his day, especially in Germany, and seldom as full of wind. A good deal of air needs to be let out of Marx's assertions, as out of Hegel's, to bring them down to size, to reduce them to statements about the real world which could be true or false. In this book I have been little concerned with Marx's prophecies, and even then only with their contents in so far as they are a help in elucidating his ideas. It seems to me to count for nothing against him that he did not predict what has happened in the world since his time, and to count greatly in his favour that in our efforts to explain what is now happening we still need to use so many ideas taken from him or from thinkers who studied his writings closely.

The greater respect for Marx has been due chiefly to two causes: to scholars turning to aspects of his thought neglected until recently but which seemed to them worth close study, and to so many people besides scholars being impressed by his indictment of bourgeois society. His analysis of the capitalist economy, apart from his description of the condition of the workers, now seems tortuous and old-fashioned, leaning heavily on the ideas and arguments of the classical economists, even though it attacks them for taking the system of property and its social consequences for granted. Economists in the West no longer do take them for granted, and they use ideas unknown to Marx and his contemporaries to explain how the type of economy they study functions, and how it differs from economies which are industrial but not capitalist. In the West today it is the sociologist and even, though to a lesser extent, the political theorist, and not the economist, who look upon the Marxism of Marx as a rich source of ideas, an intellectual quarry not yet exhausted. Just as it is the radical intellectual who finds inspiration in his writings; and, indeed, not only the radical but quite often also the liberal and the conservative, for they too have misgivings about modern industrial society as it has developed in the West. The 'bourgeois society' that Marx and the Marxists attack never had less confidence in itself than it has today.

My concern has been with these ideas and these misgivings. They were not peculiar to Marx and he was not the first to express them but his versions of them are now the most familiar. If I have from time to time compared his versions with those of other writers, it has not been to assess his originality or to deny him credit for what I believe is due to others; it has been rather to help me bring out the strong and the weak points of doctrines that have been and still are widely attractive. I have wanted to do more than examine critically the assumptions and arguments of Marx; I have wanted also to consider more generally certain types of explanation and criticism which happen to have attracted wide notice in their Marxist forms. This is why I have added this third part to the book. Not that the first two parts are confined to examining the ideas of Marx; they too move away quite often from the questions that preoccupied him to broader questions related to them. In this third part I have gone further than I could do in the first two in discussing some of these broader questions and have discussed them in terms different from those of Marx. Yet these questions, too, were born of doubts about the coherence or realism of his ideas, and especially of his conception of man as a self-creative, alienated, and progressive being.

For Marx did not, any more than Hegel did, confine himself to explaining the sense in which man is essentially a social being whose ways of life and ideas are always changing, to showing how human capacities are developed in social intercourse and how men are involved in a course of social and cultural change in which their needs, activities, and beliefs are continually transformed and tend to grow in complexity. He also, as

Hegel did, conceived of this course of change as a movement towards a social order and a culture in which men will see their condition and their needs as they really are, will satisfy their needs fully, and will understand what freedom is and achieve it. He too believed in a kind of progress that would ultimately be 'liberating', and his idea of it, though not the same as Hegel's, was—as I have tried to show—in important respects very like it. Just how firmly he believed in progress is not clear. He may not have believed that the coming of the social order that would liberate mankind was *inevitable*, or he may have believed it confusedly and half-heartedly, or may have been more inclined to believe it when he was young than when he grew older. But there are two beliefs that we can attribute to him with some confidence: that the economically advanced peoples were already in his time brought up against problems which they could solve only by establishing the kind of society and culture that he called communist, and that these peoples were drawing the rest of mankind into their orbit and making them more like themselves. The Western peoples were already at a stage in the course of their development which gave them an unprecedented opportunity to master the social conditions in which they lived and to achieve freedom, and the other peoples would reach it after them. How far Marx believed in a course of change which must eventually have brought men everywhere to this stage, though not everywhere at the same time, is a matter of dispute. It is disputed also whether he believed that they must, having reached it, pass beyond it, by taking the opportunity and achieving communism and freedom. Into these disputes I have not entered, for they seem to me unprofitable. There is more than one answer to each of these questions which could be extracted from the writings of Marx; and in any case the idea of a necessary course of social change culminating in a final achievement of freedom (or of anything else) is unacceptable. Nobody takes this idea seriously any more, not even the disciples of Marx, who merely pay lip-service to it.

I have been concerned above all with Marx's account of this stage and with his reasons for believing that it offered this opportunity to mankind. In my attempts to explain how he conceived of it, I have contrasted his account of it with his accounts of earlier stages, and also his account of it and of less 'advanced' societies with those of other thinkers. My main purpose has been all along in the broad sense philosophical: to assess his ideas, to consider how far they can be used for his purposes. Or else it has been to consider how far other ideas might be used for similar purposes. In other words, my aim has been to consider certain questions, how Marx put and tried to answer them, and how they might be put and answered, rather than to decide whether or not his answers are true. Even when I have discussed his account of how one kind of society developed into another, this has been my main purpose.

It is worth noticing that Marx, when he discusses some actual social change—for example, the emergence of capitalism—points to nothing about it which implies that it was inevitable, that it could not have been otherwise. Only when he speaks of social change in the abstract does he speak of it as if one stage of it led inexorably to the next; and even then not always. His explanations of how things happen in the real world do not bear out this generalization. Any more than they bear out the 'economic determinism' so often attributed to him. He was, I suspect, a believer in 'historic inevitability' in the same vague and occasionally hesitant way in which he was a believer in 'economic determinism'. He inclined to positions which he never defined clearly and which were perhaps loosely connected in his mind with the belief that mankind have been involved in a long course of social change which they have neither understood nor controlled but can now hope eventually to control because it has transformed them in ways which bring this control within reach. But this belief no more implies that the course of change is necessary, that it must pass from stage to stage in a certain order and reach a particular final stage, than it implies that how men collaborate to produce the wherewithal to satisfy their wants determines the general character of the society they belong to.

Marx's claim to have turned Hegel right side up is quite misleading; it proves both that he mistook Hegel's position and was unclear about his own. Hegel never said or implied the opposite of what Marx said; he did not hold that consciousness determines social existence and not the other way about. He implied, rather, that social existence would not be *social* nor social change *dialectical* unless the beings involved in them had *consciousness* in the sense that only men have it—unless they could think conceptually and their ideas and their behaviour continually affected one another. For their behaviour is essentially the behaviour of beings who think conceptually, and it cannot be described without reference to their ways of thinking about themselves and the world.

II

I suggest that one great source of inadequacy and confusion in the thinking of Marx is this: he was much more interested in modern industrial society (which he knew only in its capitalist form) than in societies of other types, and contrasted the other types with it only to bring out more clearly its peculiar features, and yet he indulged in generalizations about the course of social change, or about aspects of social life and how they are related to one another, meant to cover all types of society. A social theorist with preoccupations different from his—one, for example, more interested in comparing 'pre-capitalist' societies with one another— would need to make distinctions between kinds of authority, property, division of labour, family, class, religion, and morality that Marx did not make. But as soon as these distinctions are made, the weakness, not to speak of the absurdity, of some of Marx's general assertions stands out clearly.

There are, I think, at least eleven features of capitalist society of which Marx took large notice. (1) It is a market economy in which nearly all products of labour are produced for exchange and not for consumption by their producers. (2) In it labour is a commodity, and most workers are not their own masters at work, and this profoundly affects their attitude to their work, to society, and to themselves. (3) In the division of labour, the distinction between people who work with their 'hands' and people who work with their 'brains' (directing the labour of others or doing the public business of the community and so on) is more important than ever before. (4) Towns grow in size and come to dominate the countryside not only economically but culturally as well. (5) Social inequalities derive from inequalities of wealth rather than from differences of legally recognized status or from having or lacking political rights or opportunities. (6) The modern state emerges as a highly centralized power which is at once extensive and pervasive, with direct authority over millions of subjects. (7) There arises a social philosophy which assumes that the individual, seen in abstraction from particular social conditions, has basic needs and rights, and explains society and government as providing for these needs and protecting these rights. (8) Men are conscious, as never before, of social and cultural change, and the idea of progress is important to them. (9) The natural sciences develop rapidly, and in their wake the social sciences, so that the hold of old beliefs is loosened. (10) As knowledge increases men aspire to control the conditions of their life but are not able to do so, and so, in this fast-changing capitalist society exposed to severe economic crises, their sense of being the helpless victims, not of the gods or of natural forces beyond their control, but of social forces they have not yet learned to master, is sharpened. (11) In a society in which knowledge and power are increasing, this sense of helplessness gradually gives way to a revolutionary will, to a determination so to transform the social order as to make men masters and not victims of the social conditions in which they live. The class that gives expression to this will is the proletariat. Group and class conflicts having important social consequences are not peculiar to capitalist society, but this kind of revolutionary will is so.

Unfortunately, Marx did not confine himself to contrasting the only type of society he studied closely with the feudal society out of which it arose and in which he was therefore also interested. His comparisons of the modern state with the feudal structure of authority are often fresh and ingenious, but he also made assertions about the state which are clearly not meant to refer only to the modern state but to political authority more generally. For example, when he says that the state is an organ of class oppression, he does not, any more than Engels does, use the word 'state' to refer to types of political authority that arise only under capitalism or use the word 'class' to refer only to classes as they exist in industrial society and not, say, to medieval estates. Political authority is clearly much older than the modern or 'bourgeois' state, and the word 'state' is widely used, by Marx and the Marxists as well as by others, to refer to forms of this authority older than the modern state. Yet Marx was not much concerned to distinguish political authority from other forms of it, or to make it clear which, among the forms of political authority, are peculiar to the state. I do not mean that he does not make explicit distinctions and provide definitions, for a writer can often make his meaning clear without doing that; I mean that he fails to indicate to the reader just what he is saying. Just what is it that is an organ of class oppression and will disappear when society becomes classless?

The division of labour is much older than capitalism, for it exists in some form in every type of society. Under capitalism, of course, it takes forms it does not take in economically less developed societies, or certain forms of it are much accentuated. Marx was imaginative and acute in pointing to some of these forms and to their consequences. But he failed to bring his ideas into good order. For example, he said that the division of labour is the cause of alienation, and he called religion a form of alienated life. As religion is much older than capitalism and flourishes even in primitive societies in which inequalities of wealth or power or status are small, we are left wondering what exactly the division of labour is that gives rise to alienation. Is it the kind peculiar to capitalism? It would seem not, for Marx does not speak of alienation as if it were confined to capitalist societies. We are left wondering, too, whether he believed that all religions are forms of alienated life; for though he appears to be speaking of religion in general when he speaks in this way, he also speaks as if it were not all forms of division of labour but only some that give rise to alienation. If he had taken the trouble to sort out his ideas about the division of labour and about alienation and the forms it takes, he might have produced a clear and consistent account of how they are related; but the fact is that he did not take the trouble.

Sometimes Marx uses the word 'class' in a broader sense which allows him to speak of medieval estates and other even older social groups as classes, and sometimes he uses it in a narrower sense, as, for example, when he contrasts the classes of modern industrial society with the medieval estates. He also makes some enlightening comparisons between medieval estates and modern classes. But he nowhere indicates what, in his opinion, is to count as social inequality. To be sure, he says that it arises from the division of labour. But the division of labour gives rise to many differences which are not inequalities. We get little guidance from Marx as to how we should distinguish social inequalities from social differences which are not inequalities, or even inequalities that are justified from those that are not. Is a classless society one in which there are no social inequalities? Clearly, if we use the word 'class' in the narrower sense, which forbids us to treat estates as classes, there can be great social inequalities in a classless society. But Marx, when he spoke of the classless society, used the word 'class' in a broader sense. Yet, even in this broader sense, the idea of class is tied to the idea of property. People who belong to different classes differ in their rights of property, whether in the means of production or in labour, their own or other people's. But it is easy to imagine a society in which differences in rights of property are small and differences of income, power, and influence are great. A society could be classless in this broader sense of class and yet be far indeed from being a society of equals. The Soviet Union comes close to being a society of this kind. It could, perhaps, be argued that the men who run the Communist Party and the Soviet state jointly own the means of production to the exclusion of the rest of the people. The argument is not implausible, though it turns on treating as a form of property what to most people would seem to be a form of political control or authority. To be sure, it is hard to draw the line between some forms of property and some forms of control or authority. But this is a matter to which Marx and his disciples have devoted little thought. They have not been inclined to make fine distinctions. In Marx's day it seemed less important than it does now to distinguish between forms of authority and forms of property, for in the capitalist West the state was then much less concerned to control the economy than it is now and there were fewer forms of 'public' property, while in other parts of the world there were as yet no industrial societies that were neither capitalist nor socialist—societies which might perhaps be called classless but certainly not egalitarian.

Just as there can be big social inequalities in a classless society,[1] so too there can be extensive exploitation and oppression. Marx does indeed make it unusually clear what he means by exploitation; it is one of the key concepts of his social theory that he actually defines. It is the appropriation of surplus value, and he also explains what he means by surplus value. Yet the concept of exploitation, as he defines it, applies much more readily to a capitalist economy than to any other kind, though it could, no doubt, be adapted to apply to other kinds of economy. For example, if we can say of the men who run the party and the state in the Soviet Union that they jointly own the means of production and therefore form a class apart from the rest of the community, we can also say of them that, as a

[1] Unless, of course, the word *class* is so defined as to make it a necessary truth that a classless society is a society of equals, but it is not so defined by Marx.

class, they appropriate the surplus values created by the other class. To be sure, they do not consume all that they appropriate; they invest some of it and also use it to maintain armies and other public services. But then so too do capitalists in the West, as even the Marxists admit; they invest a part of their profits, and in the parliaments they control tax themselves to provide a variety of public services.

I need not give other examples to support my present argument, which is that Marx, though he does make enlightening comparisons between industrial and pre-industrial societies, does not push his analysis far enough to make it clear just what he understands by some of his most widely repeated and admired generalizations. He is a perceptive and also a muddled thinker; and he is sometimes both the one and the other, if not simultaneously, then in such close succession that the attempt to dis-entangle his thoughts can be richly rewarding. But it is not so always. Some of his most famous utterances, if they are not exactly empty, stand in need of so much interpretation and qualification, if the kernel of truth in them is to be revealed, that the revelation, when it comes, seems a travesty of Marx—except to the reader who has made the painful effort of trying to understand him. 'Surely', says the reader who has not made the effort (perhaps for lack of time) to the reader who has, 'that can't be all that there is to it. Marx was a profound thinker.' Indeed he was, sometimes, but he was not always rigorous and clear, and he could be empty or shal-low. It is his misfortune, perhaps, rather than his fault, that he has so often been admired at his shallowest.

Marx is hard on his readers; he rewards them with his wisdom only after he has punished them with his style and his methods of argument, and he puts them at risk of taking for wisdom what is not so. He is apt to be much undervalued or much over-valued; undervalued by impatient readers who resent being put to so much trouble by an arrogant and un-necessarily difficult writer, and over-valued by readers who like to put a high price on what it has cost them much effort to acquire. If they had got it more easily from another source, they might value it less. A difficult writer, his reputation once made, soon gets himself a cloud of admirers who feel the wiser for repeating profound utterances whose meaning they cannot explain; admirers blessed as it were by the alien touch of genius and mystery.

III

Marx saw a close connection between the emergence of a market economy and the rise of certain forms of political authority and conceptions of right and law. Bourgeois society, with its system of production and exchange in which the individual is seen as a producer and consumer of goods and services whose values are determined by supply and demand, goes along with the modern state and the idea of the citizen as a bearer of rights and obligations impartially protected and enforced. The individual has some rights and obligations, conceived in very general terms and called natural or basic, merely by virtue of being a rational agent who lives and works with other such agents as he seeks to achieve his diverse purposes, and he acquires other and more specific rights and obligations as a result of the choices he makes, by engaging in some among the many occupations and activities open to him or by freely making contracts.

While Marx agreed with Hegel about the salient features of bourgeois society and the modern state, as they appeared to educated people in that society, he went on to argue, as Hegel did not, that this appearance was deceptive. Making the distinction that Hegel made between reality and appearance, between social conditions and practices as they really are and as they tend to appear to the people involved or engaged in them, he claimed to see a wide disparity between the two. For though, like Hegel, he took it for granted (much of the time, if not all of it) that the course of social change was towards a type of society and culture in which appearance and reality would at last coincide, and men would see themselves in their activities as social beings as they really were, he was adamant that this type of society did not yet exist. No doubt, Hegel had not said unequivocally that it did exist, but some of his arguments implied that it was already coming into existence, that it would be an improved version of bourgeois society and the state as they actually were. In the rational society in which reality and appearance coincide, as Hegel imagines it, there is private property and there are social classes, and there is also a structure of public authority, a constitutional state, which carefully defines the rights and obligations of both citizens and holders of authority.

Marx was not hard put to it to show that bourgeois society and the bourgeois state were not what they appeared to be; that is to say, were not what apologists for them said they were. Indeed, Hegel had anticipated some of his criticisms, and though he went much further than Hegel did, he went no further than did other socialists and anarchists of his time. There is much to be said for Marx's attack on society and the state as they were in his day, just as there is much to be said for mounting a similar attack on them as they now are in the West, even though they now differ greatly from what they were in Marx's time, and in ways he did not foresee.

As was already widely noticed in the first half of the last century, one striking feature of industrial societies as compared with earlier ones is that people who belong to them take them (their practices and their standards) much less for granted. Industrial societies change so fast that the fact of change cannot escape notice. Men's social ambitions, their aspirations for this world, are apt to run far ahead of what society can provide, and give rise to demands for freedom, equality, or justice which, though they are often vague, seem to those who make them to require a radical transformation of the social order.

Marx did not condemn these aspirations and demands, for he saw in them a rejection of the established order. If there is to be a revolution, if some class or group of men are to undertake to transform society, they must do more than merely feel frustrated; they must assert principles they can use to condemn what exists and to justify the demands they make. Mere frustration may seek relief in fantasy, especially in fantasies of an after-life, and the energy it generates may not be harnessed to social purposes.

When Marx first turned his mind to social theory, there were two groups of thinkers asserting such principles; there were liberals and there were socialists. Marx attacked them both, the liberals more harshly than the socialists. The liberals, as he saw it, wanted only moderate reforms; they were champions of a social and political order that had already substantially come into being in the more 'advanced' countries of the West. But it was not really for their moderation that he attacked them; for in less 'advanced' countries the changes they called for were by no means small, and this Marx knew. He attacked them rather for falsely claiming that the freedom and justice they proclaimed would be achieved if the changes they asked for were made; he attacked them for believing that their principles could be realized while capitalism survived. But he also attacked them on the ground that their principles were empty, that they were mere bourgeois ideology whose function was to prevent people seeing bourgeois society as it really was. These two reasons would seem to contradict one another, though they could perhaps be qualified in such a way as to resolve the contradiction. The first implies (or can reasonably be interpreted as implying) that freedom and justice, as the liberal conceives of them, could in principle be realized, though not (as the liberal mistakenly supposes) in a capitalist or bourgeois society, while the second implies the opposite, that these liberal ideals are either vacuous or hopelessly unrealistic.

Marx's criticism of the socialists whom he called Utopian is also ambiguous. Did he object *primarily* to their mistakenly believing that their schemes might be put into practice by volunteers whose example would soon be followed by others? It would seem so. For he never tried to show that their schemes were in themselves ill adapted to their purposes, that they could not achieve the freedom or justice or social harmony they aimed at. He criticized the Utopians for being so simple-minded as to believe that the bourgeois would tolerate their schemes if they looked like working, and also for not seeing that, quite apart from the overt opposition to the schemes of bourgeois governments and bourgeois thinkers, social and cultural conditions did not favour their success. Bourgeois society could not be gradually and peacefully transformed by injecting into it social cells of a different order which would then multiply until the organism in which they were lodged had quite changed character. The transformation of bourgeois society could be achieved only on a much larger scale, more drastically, by harsher and perhaps also by more violent methods, and by a large and united social class. And yet Marx also saw in these Utopian fantasies, or in some of them, an indictment of bourgeois society that cut deep, revealing its injustices, the frustrations and suffering inseparable from it, and its hypocrisies. But how could they do this except by appealing to ideals which could not be used to condemn the established order on consistent and realistic grounds unless they could serve also to guide men in the task of social reconstruction? And what better way is there of explaining one's ideals than by trying to describe the conditions of achieving them?

It is not true that in general liberal thinkers have claimed that freedom and justice, as they conceived of them, have been substantially realized in bourgeois society; that is to say, in the advanced industrial countries of their day. Some of them have believed that great changes, social and political, would have to be made if their principles were to be realized. Some, indeed, eventually became socialists as the conviction grew upon them that justice and freedom would be out of most men's reach while capitalism lasted. Their socialism seemed to them to follow logically from their liberal principles as soon as the attempt was made to put those principles into practice in an advanced industrial society. In becoming socialists they did not cease to be liberals, at least not in their own eyes.

If a student of Marxism were asked whether Marx was a liberal, he would not hesitate to say *No*. If he were asked whether Marx cared for freedom, he would say *Yes*, though perhaps less readily. But if he were asked just how Marx's idea of freedom differed from a liberal's idea of it, he might well be at a loss for an answer, at least for a time. In the end he might venture to suggest that while Marx, when he spoke of freedom, may perhaps have had much the same opportunities in mind as the liberal has, he believed, unlike the liberal, that most men cannot have them, or not equally or in the fullest measure possible, while there is private property in the means of production. But many a liberal would be willing to go a long way in curtailing this form of property to ensure that all sections of the community, and not only the privileged, have these opportunities. And if he were accused of misdescribing himself in claiming to be a liberal, he might reasonably reply that what made him a liberal was precisely his thinking it important that people should have these opportunities—and therefore also the legal rights they need if they are to have them effectively in an industrial society.

Our imaginary student of Marxism might then offer another explanation of the difference between the ideas of freedom of Marx and the liberal. He might say that, whereas for the liberal freedom is primarily a matter of having legal rights, for Marx it is primarily a matter of having social opportunities. But this, in itself, would not be a sufficient answer, seeing that the liberal cares about these rights largely because he cares about these opportunities. Nor, presumably, was Marx indifferent to the question of rights; for the opportunities he had in mind could not be secure unless men recognized obligations to and claims upon one another—at least moral obligations and moral claims.

Is the crucial difference, then, between the liberal and Marx, that the liberal asserts and Marx denies that the individual must have *legal* rights if he is to have the opportunities they both agree he should have? This could indeed be a big difference between them, depending upon what is understood by *legal* rights and what institutions are thought necessary to their existence. Marx believed that men would not really be free until the state disappeared, whereas liberals look at the state to enlarge and to secure freedom.

But what did Marx understand by the disappearance of the state? Did he really believe that a developed industrial society could do without legislatures meeting regularly to repeal old laws and make new ones, without administrative departments and courts of law? Did he believe that the common or public business of such a society could be done by the workers in their spare time, or by people who do not make a profession of it? Just what institutions, what practices, did he think would be dispensed with when the state disappeared? In this book I have paid more attention to these questions than students of Marxism ordinarily do. I have argued that they cannot be answered, that Marx says too little to enable his readers to reach definite conclusions. But I have not stopped there. I have gone on to consider what he might have meant by this disappearance, what institutions and practices he might have had in mind, and to inquire how far they are indispensable to any advanced industrial society, capitalist or not. This has been one of my main objects in the third part of the book. Dislike and suspicion of the state are not confined to Marx and his disciples. Indeed, they have soon died out in Marxists wherever they have gained power.

Marx as a denouncer of abuses and illusions that were widely tolerated and shared in his day, and still are so in ours, is sometimes highly effective. His attacks on the 'bourgeois state' and on 'liberal' attitudes are not all empty. Quite often they strike home, both when he denounces practices and when he pours scorn on the arguments used to justify them. But if we try to extract from his attacks on the state and on its liberal apologists criteria to use in deciding which to abolish and which to retain among the manifold activities of the modern state, we soon find that we cannot do it. I do not deny, of course, that there are some political or governmental activities of which we can confidently say that Marx was against them; I deny only that he provides us with principles we can use to decide just what, in his opinion, would disappear with the disappearance of the state, and why he thought it desirable that it should do so. In this sense his attack on the state was undiscriminating. Fortunately for him it was also vague and fragmentary; he never went as far as Lenin was to go in *The State and Revolution*. Slavs rush in where Germans fear to tread.

IV

Bourgeois society, as Marx conceived of it, is in some ways like the older types of society which he called 'natural' and in other ways like the communist society which he hoped would be established sometime after the proletarian revolution.

Man's behaviour in society is essentially the behaviour of a being that thinks conceptually and whose language expresses a view of the world and of himself in it. In that sense it is essentially rational behaviour. But in 'natural' societies, in which custom reigns and social relations and roles are taken for granted, men do not understand or control the social order, though what makes it the order it is, is their behaving as they do, and therefore their having the motives, intentions, and beliefs that move them to behave in that way. They may have explanations of society, how it arose, how it operates, what purposes it serves, but these explanations are largely mythical; they help to make people's roles and obligations more acceptable to them but they do not increase their ability to control society, to adapt it deliberately to their changing purposes, or do so only to a slight extent. They are not the theories of people who aspire to control what they make theories about.

In 'natural' society, since social conventions change slowly and imperceptibly, the individual knows what is expected of him; he is familiar with his social roles. In that sense he is at home in society, even though he does not understand it or control it. He knows what he ought to do, and how to present or explain his behaviour in ways acceptable to others. Also, he is ordinarily either his own master at work, or works for a master who is close to him and whose aims and methods he can understand, or collaborates with equals on a small scale. He may be exploited or ill-treated but there is a sense in which he 'understands' the conditions in which he lives and works. He may not 'understand' them as the historian or the sociologist aspires to do, but he 'knows' what to think about them;

he has little sense of being faced with problems that he cannot even find words for, let alone solve.

Authority sits close to him; he either belongs to some small community that enjoys a considerable autonomy, or the ruler who in fact has the largest authority over him is close at hand. No doubt, long before there was capitalism, there was remote authority exercised over wide territories inhabited by millions of people. But this remote authority, though often oppressive, was also relatively weak; it did not have its agents distributed over the territory in large numbers to control its subjects in many different aspects of their lives, and such agents as it did have it could not control very closely, if only because communications were slow.

Industrial society has changed all this. True, in its capitalist form, as Marx describes it, it is still not understood or controlled. Capitalists do not jointly manage the economy, and are liable to be ruined by crises they cannot foresee and prevent. The bourgeois state, immensely powerful though it is as compared with earlier forms of extensive political authority, rests on illusion. Not only its apologists who produce theories to explain it but the men who run it have mistaken ideas about it. If a 'natural' society were merely one not yet understood and controlled by its members, then bourgeois society, as Marx describes it, might be called 'natural'. And yet Marx does not call it so.

Bourgeois society, misunderstood and uncontrolled though it largely is, differs from the earlier societies that he does call 'natural' because in it people no longer do, and no longer can, take social conditions and social roles for granted. It differs also because they are already putting questions and making claims of a kind that they will not be able to answer or to meet except by learning to control their social environment, and because they have already made some progress in this learning. From what Marx says about the industrial society of his day, it is clear that he believed that in it there had already been progress, not only in the natural sciences and in technology, but also in social practice and social theory. Production was much more efficient, not only because new tools and machines were brought into use, but also because it was better organized by entre-preneurs and managers who aimed at efficiency. Thus, though the economy, taken as a whole, was not rationally controlled, it consisted as never before of productive enterprises that were so, and whose average size was increasing. Production was quite different from what it had been in older societies; it was deliberately progressive, for under the spur of competition it was self-critical and innovatory. To the extent that it was controlled, those who controlled it saw it as their business to ensure, not that customary tasks were well done by conventional standards of good per-formance, but that energy and intelligence were put to the most productive uses.

Marx, though he accused the bourgeois economists of false conscious-ness, recognized that they claimed to be scientists and took this claim of theirs seriously. They aimed at constructing comprehensive and detailed accounts of the functioning of a highly complicated economy, starting from what they believed to be clear and realistic assumptions about men as producers and consumers, and about their interests and resources. What is more, as Marx again recognized, the purposes of the economists in constructing their theories were as much practical as academic; they wanted to influence the making of policy, even when they preached *laissez-faire*. No doubt, the control of general production in the interests of all producers, if and when it is established, will differ greatly from the control of particular productive enterprises in the interests of the capital-ists who own them, and people in a socialist society will have different ideas about production and its proper functions from those of the bour-geois economists. Nevertheless, just as capitalist production, in spite of being 'anarchic', is a long step forward towards a rationally controlled economy, so bourgeois economic theory, ideological though it is, is a long step forward towards a better understanding of economic realities.

Marx spoke less respectfully of bourgeois political than of bourgeois economic theory. Yet he saw it too, together with the type of political authority which it purports to explain and seeks to justify, as a moving away from natural society; it too expresses man's aspiration to under-stand and control his social, his human, environment. It explains the state as a human contrivance for human ends, and in doing so makes claims for the individual of a kind not made before. It asserts his right to order his life as he pleases, provided he respects the same right in others and does them no harm. As Marx puts it in his article on *Bruno Bauer and the Jewish Question*, in its doctrine of the rights of man, it makes of man 'the found-ation and presupposition' of the state. Bourgeois society, on its political as well as on its economic side, is progressive. It is not just a stage through which men pass on the way to communism; it is a stage in which they acquire many of the skills, ideas, and attitudes which will enable them to set up communism when the time comes. Capitalism, says Marx, lays the *material* foundations on which the future society will be built. But we must not be deceived by this word *material*. It lays also some of the cultural foundations, as Marx himself recognized, at least implicitly. Indeed, it could not lay the first without also laying the second. Bourgeois political theory and the bourgeois state both, we are told, rest on illusion. Yet the illusion is essentially different from the myths that sustained older forms of authority; it is the illusion of men who are already beginning to see that their problems are of their own making and can be resolved by their own efforts. The emergence of the bourgeois state and of a highly abstract and yet essentially man-centred or non-religious social and political theory is, in the eyes of Marx, a kind of 'emancipation', and every emancipation, as he puts it (again in the article on *The Jewish Question*), is a 'restoration of the human world . . . to man himself'. That is to say, it brings men closer to understanding and controlling the man-made world (society) in which all their problems arise and can be solved.

Yet bourgeois society and the bourgeois state, progressive though they are, fail to satisfy man's aspiration to control the conditions of his life. They express that aspiration as no earlier society could but their expression of it is confused and ambiguous because their institutions and practices do not allow of its being satisfied. Men will come to understand what freedom is, how it is to be achieved, through their endeavours to achieve it, and not by solving theoretical problems in the privacy of their studies.

In bourgeois society most men are less their own masters at work than they were in older societies. The rational control of production is confined to particular enterprises, and is there exercised, not by the workers jointly, but by the owners and their agents. The economy as a whole is not rationally controlled and is liable to partial breakdowns or crises of increasing severity, from which the workers suffer worst of all. Though there is greater understanding of social processes, it is confined to the socially dominant class and groups adherent to it, and is distorted by the need to preserve and justify their social supremacy. And, in any case, in a dynamic society in which social stability and the appearance of social harmony can no longer be maintained merely by everyone's doing what custom requires, this understanding is not great enough to prevent the crises. In this complicated and fast-changing society, which exalts the rational pursuit of interests, and in which status (as distinct from property) and custom (as distinct from law deliberately made and officially administered) count for so much less, organized authority, though more elaborate, extensive, and professional, and ostensibly more detached and impartial, than ever before, serves in fact to maintain conditions which enable the propertied to exploit the unpropertied classes. Thus Marx's picture of industrial society, as he knew it, though it depicts conditions in which men's understanding and control of 'the human world' are increasing, also depicts them as conditions in which the understanding is vitiated and the control impaired by the determination of an exploiting class to maintain its supremacy.

Since Marx's time this image of bourgeois society and the bourgeois state has been considerably modified, by Marxists and by others; and it has been so largely as a result of developments whose importance Marx was quicker to grasp than were most of his contemporaries: the increasing size of the firm, the divorce of ownership from control, the export of capital to economically backward countries, and a variety of 'restrictive practices'. Everywhere the 'state' makes efforts to control 'the economy', and property rights have been greatly altered and much restricted. In the countries still called 'capitalist', powerful workers' organizations make demands that neither managements nor governments can ignore. How far these changes have made capitalist and bourgeois countries less capitalist and less bourgeois than they were, it is difficult to say. These two words have long been used in several different senses, and the senses have changed with time.

How far can the state go in controlling the economy or in bringing industry and trade into 'public ownership', and the economy still remain capitalist? Does it remain so as long as most enterprises are not managed by some public authority or its agents or jointly by the workers in it, no matter how much the managers are bound by governmental directives and by agreements made with trade unions? Does its being capitalist consist in the fact that a large part of the profits is distributed among shareholders, even though they have no say in managing the concerns that pay the profits or in deciding who is to manage them? Is it the link between formal ownership and control, however tenuous; is it the legal responsibility of managers to shareholders, however unreal, which is the essence of the matter? If the managers of most enterprises were appointed, not by some public authority or by the shareholders or the workers, but by those already holding managerial posts in them—that is to say, if managements were self-recruiting as faculties are at many universities— would the economy still be capitalist? Or would it be so only if the enterprises raised their capital, or some considerable part of it, by getting private citizens to invest in them in return for a share of the profits? These are not questions merely about how a particular word is used, or ought to be. For the word is used to point to features of society and production which those who use it defend or attack. Just what is it that they want to preserve or abolish?

Marx, of course, did not favour state control of production, except perhaps for a time, while 'the dictatorship of the proletariat' lasted; and I say 'perhaps' deliberately for it is not clear what he meant by this dictatorship. After the disappearance of the state, if not already before it, the workers would collectively control production. And Marx took it for granted that when they did so, there would be no more exploitation of some groups by others, that labour or labour-power would cease to be a commodity which the worker sold to others, and that he would therefore no longer be helpless in the grip of social forces he could not control. Now all this could, perhaps, with some ingenuity, be made necessarily true: 'collective control', 'exploitation', and 'labour's being a commodity' could be so defined that it followed logically that, where there was this collective control, there could not be exploitation, nor labour be a commodity, nor the worker helpless in the grip of such forces. Yet, even then, there would still be the problem of how workers' control should be organized to be truly 'collective'.

Marx took care not to describe the socialist economy which he believed (or at least hoped) would come some time after the proletarian revolution. He took pride in not being a Utopian. But, surely, just as he could have explained what he meant by the disappearance of the state without predicting that it would disappear, so he could have explained what he meant by collective control without predicting that it would come? Why, I wonder, should it be more reasonable to predict something without describing it clearly enough to ensure that it is recognizable if it comes than so to describe it without predicting it? To be sure, it is not Utopian; for the Utopian, to deserve the name, must at least describe his ideal, even if he does not predict it. But I do not see that it is any more reasonable for not being Utopian.

Today it is more obvious than it was in Victorian times that an economy can go a long way towards shedding some of the salient features of capitalism, as Marx described them, without coming any nearer to being socialist. Management can be largely self-recruiting and yet considerably restricted by both the government and the organized workers without being responsible to either. There can be public ownership and control of industry and trade with big differences of income and power, differences arising, not just from the need to make the best use of scarce human resources for the benefit of the community, but from the determination of privileged groups to maintain and increase their privileges. There can be this ownership and yet labour still be a commodity, work still be monotonous, and the worker still have no say in directing his work. This public ownership or control has taken many different forms, but if we are to judge it by its effects, it is different from the collective control of production by the workers imagined by Marx, for it has done little to alleviate some of the worst evils of capitalism, as he described them. It may have helped to raise real wages and to shorten working hours, and to that extent have 'emancipated the workers', but it has not given them the sense that they 'control the conditions of their life'.

We must suppose that the collective control of production that Marx had in mind involved something more than the workers in each productive enterprise jointly managing it, for that kind of joint management might leave the economy as a whole just as uncontrolled and just as liable to crises as it was under capitalism as Marx knew it. He had in mind, presumably, control of production on a much larger scale than that, and on more than one level. He believed that, with the spread of industry, a world economy was emerging with every part of it more and more closely dependent on the whole. How could the workers *collectively* control production over the whole world, or indeed over any large part of it? Presumably they would have to do so by choosing delegates to act for them at the higher levels of management: that is to say, by setting up some sort of representative system. How, then, would they ensure that this system was not as much of a sham as bourgeois representative government was, according to Marx? Even if they were much better off materially and better educated than they were in Marx's time, they would still have the problem of organization to solve. But about this problem Marx had nothing to say beyond insisting that it could be solved only by setting up a form of control different from representative government, as bourgeois society knew it. He would not venture an opinion as to how this collective control might be organized so as to put an end to alienation, to labour's being treated as a commodity, to the worker's feeling himself to be the victim of the system. Surely this was excessive caution on his part! Particularly as he could have done it without predicting anything. Unfortunately, he preferred making obscure prophecies to making clear statements about aims worth pursuing even though they may not be fully attained.

This reticence has been defended by Marxists on the ground that if, as Marx says, theory 'reflects' practice, it is unreasonable to speculate about conditions very different from those we have actually experienced, since we lack the ideas we need to describe them adequately. But, in that case, how can we speak, as Marx does, of a future in which problems not yet solved will be solved, or needs or aspirations not yet satisfied will be satisfied? If experience and reflection upon it continually transform our ideas about ourselves and our human world, then the questions we put, the problems we pose, change with time. And even if we see, as we look back on the past, that certain types of question, certain kinds of problem, recur, though in different forms, how can we be sure, or even think it likely, that they will in the future recur in forms which allow of their being finally answered or solved? It is only by reference to human needs, relations, and values, as we understand them, that we can speak intelligibly of men's being equal or unequal, exploiting or exploited, free or not free. How then can we say, with Marx, that in the future, when their needs, relations, and values are differently understood, men will at last be equal and free, and with no exploiters among them?

I have explained in an earlier chapter why I find Marx's few scattered comments about social theory[2] in relation to social practice too obscure

---

[2] I say *social* theory and not theory in all its kinds, for this is the kind of theory of which we can most plausibly say that it reflects practice. To be sure, the natural sciences also develop continually, producing new theories, new assumptions, and new ideas to explain the phenomena they study. They too are affected by changing practice—by the practice of scientists and by social practice more generally. But the practices that affect them are not the phenomena they study. Clearly, the relation of theory to social practice, when the theory is social theory, is in crucial respects different from what it is when the theory is natural science. And though Marx and his disciples, when they speak of theory 'reflecting' social practice, do not always make it clear that it is social theory alone that they have in mind, most of what they say, when it makes sense, does so only of social theory in relation to social practice.

to amount to anything like a coherent account. But I would not deny the obvious: that men's ideas about themselves and their 'human world' (society) are changed continually by experience and reflection upon it. I merely fail to see how this makes it reasonable for Marx to speak of future developments—whether he thinks them highly probable or no more than possible—without explaining what they are. Why should he not tell us much more than he does about the practices and attitudes that would disappear with the disappearance of the state, or about how collective control of production should be organized to avoid some of the worst evils of capitalism?

We cannot solve the problems of future generations for them; we cannot even predict what their problems will be—or we can do so only to some extent. But this does not mean that such social theories as we produce must refer only to the present and the past, that they must not consider the future, that they must not be speculative. Still less does it mean that, when they do consider the future, when they are speculative, they need not be clear. In any case, Marx's own theories do not refer only to the present and the past; they take account of the future and even make what, to the uncritical eye, look like bold predictions, though they turn out, on closer inspection, to be so vague as to be almost empty. It is godlike and impressive to make dark prophecies whose meaning can only be guessed at, whereas to speculate intelligibly about the future is to risk looking foolish when the future comes. But a social theorist should not play safe with the gods; he should take the risks proper to mortals, and take comfort in the thought that to speculate is not to predict and that those who come after him may learn from his mistakes, provided that he makes his meaning clear enough for them to discover what he is mistaken about.

V

I have not been concerned to defend 'bourgeois' society as it was in Marx's time or has since become from the strictures upon it of Marx or his disciples. I have wanted rather to discover what he says about it when he attacks it, what assumptions he makes, and what his reasons are for attacking it. When I have criticized him—and I have done so often—it has been mostly because his arguments have seemed to me logically unsound, or his assumptions unclear or unrealistic, or because he has failed to make important distinctions or qualifications. He is a great thinker, but he is also confused and confusing: his best ideas need to be extricated from the tortuous prose and sometimes even the nonsense in which they are buried. No doubt, Marx is profound, but not always when he seems so to his admirers. I have discussed some of the most difficult and least-well-considered (but not least original and suggestive) aspects of his thought, and have tried to assess their value: to discover how far they contain ideas that can be used to explain social behaviour or to define social standards more adequately. Considered as a social theorist from whom students of society hope to learn, Marx, so it seems to me, has done much good and some harm. He has done good by producing ideas of his own or improved versions of other men's ideas which really are enlightening, or which can be so to anyone willing to take the trouble to sort them out; and he has done harm by encapsulating ideas that are confused or empty in phrases which have gained wide currency and give the people who use them the illusion that they are thinking when in fact they are not.

But Marx has had a great influence, not only on social theory, but on political behaviour; and it is this second influence which is the more important and (to most people) the more interesting, though I have discussed it only a little in this book. To discuss it adequately would require another book as long as this one, if not longer, for no social theorist has had a wider or a more diverse political influence than Marx has. Yet there is a side to that influence that I want to discuss because it is closely connected with two aspects of his thought that I have commented upon several times: his failure to make it clear what standards he is invoking when he condemns bourgeois society, and his ambiguity about the future. To both his admirers and his critics, Marx has seemed to be the great *prophet* among modern social theorists. Did he not prophesy the proletarian revolution and the communist society that was to come after it? But he was equivocal about the proletarian revolution and his pronouncements about the communist society were so non-committal as to be almost vacuous. Just as, in some philosophies, matter without form is the 'something we know not what' in which everything accessible to our knowledge inheres, so in the social theory of Marx the communist society is the something he knows not what to which the whole course of social change tends. Would the proletarian revolution be worth making if the communist society were not to come after it, or at least if the chances of its coming were not thereby greatly increased?

Marx's political influence has been primarily, though by no means exclusively, on the behaviour of leaders who have looked for support to the poorer classes in the community, or else to poor peoples brought into disturbing contact with rich peoples. It is often said that the influence of theory on practice is cruder than the influence of theory on theory, since the finer points of a theory are of little interest to practical men. Whether 'cruder' is the right word here, I do not know; for the influence of theory on practice is even more difficult to assess than the influence of theory on theory. It takes the form of slogans which are not so much crude as of uncertain meaning and are variously interpreted as circumstances change.

Also, the influence on practice of one theorist is so much mixed up with that of others that it is often impossible to decide what comes primarily from him. Just where, in what is called Marxism–Leninism, does Marxism end and Leninism begin? Which doctrines of Lenin are realistic applications of principles taken from Marx to situations unforeseen by Marx, and which are 'betrayals' or 'distortions' of them? This question is not altogether unanswerable: it is possible to point to some among the doctrines of Lenin and to give good reasons for holding that they are true or untrue to Marx's teaching. But it is not possible to go far in doing so, if only because Marx himself is so often obscure or equivocal. In any case, it is not the practical influence of particular doctrines that concerns me now but an attitude to politics that Marx shares with many of his disciples.

The Marxist in politics likes to think of himself as tough, resilient, and realistic, and he finds in the teachings of Marx what he thinks are justifications of these attitudes. He sees himself as a ruthless 'fighter' on behalf of the class or group in whose interests he is fighting. He makes tactical alliances with other classes or groups which he is willing to abandon as soon as he thinks it the interest of the class or group he is fighting for that he should do so. He has learnt from Marx that the good intentions and principles of his opponents and temporary allies are not to be taken seriously, even though the men who profess them may be sincere, for sooner or later objective conditions (which he understands better than they do) will force them to go back on these intentions or to betray these principles. He does not dismiss justice, democracy, and freedom as empty ideas but he knows (or thinks he knows) that, in the social conditions in which he and his opponents and allies have to act, they are ideas that people use to deceive each other and even themselves. He does not take them seriously in a society in which it is unreasonable to do so, since they can be realized only after that society has been destroyed.

There is no denying that this combination of ruthlessness and scepticism has been highly effective in the struggle for power of Marxists in some parts of the world, though not in the parts of it in which 'bourgeois society' has been most highly developed. Wherever in the West conditions have allowed Marxist parties to grow large, these parties have not had much success in the struggle for power. They are no longer in practice revolutionary parties, even though they still occasionally pay lip-service to revolution. They are ineffectual, not because they have ceased to be revolutionary, but primarily for two other reasons: because in the past they have had, on orders from Moscow, to make abrupt changes of policy which have seemed cowardly and cynical even to radicals in the West, and because they have been wedded to slogans which have ceased to be relevant, if ever they were so. Materially the West has become much more prosperous in the last fifty years, but it is not this prosperity which explains the lack of success of Marxist parties in the struggle for power. For the prosperity has not brought contentment with it, nor has it brought Western peoples close to achieving the ideals of freedom and social justice long proclaimed among them. To be sure, some great evils that socialists and liberals condemned fifty years ago are now greatly diminished, but others have grown worse or have come to seem so. The claims that individuals and groups make on one another or on the community in the name of freedom and justice have changed considerably. Or, in other words, their ideas about freedom and justice have changed. But Marxism has contributed little to this change.

This is not surprising, for Marx himself gave little thought to either freedom or justice. He did not inquire how they were to be achieved in a developed industrial society: what opportunities people should have, what claims would need to be made and met, and what social practices adopted, if they were to be achieved. He confined himself largely to denouncing 'bourgeois society' for pretending to achieve them and not doing so, and he put forward some ingenious ideas about 'false consciousness' to explain this deception and self-deception. But to social problems in the concrete, other than problems to do with the carrying on of group conflicts and the getting of power, he never seriously addressed his mind. He was as little interested in these problems as he was in elucidating the ideas men use to state them and the principles they appeal to in their endeavours to solve them.

No doubt, bourgeois society is in many ways a sham. It was so in Marx's day, and is still so in ours. The standards it proclaims are not all consistent with one another, some are empty or ambiguous, and there are many false claims made on its behalf. But how could it be otherwise? It is a highly diversified and quickly changing society, in which expectations continually outrun the resources and skills available to satisfy them. It is also a society whose members cannot take social conditions for granted but are impelled to put questions and to deal with problems which they are hard put to it to state adequately, let alone to answer or to solve satisfactorily. As Marx himself saw, bourgeois society does not differ from earlier forms in having illusions about itself, for they too had their illusions; it differs from them, rather, in being much more aware that it has them without quite knowing what they are. This condition, I suggest, is to a large extent irremediable; it is the price of sophistication. As some illusions are dissipated or die out, others arise, because the questions that men put to themselves about themselves, and about the questions they put, change continually.

We know that our Western societies are 'shams'—or, rather, that there is a great deal of shamming in them, in high places and in low. But we are also faced with problems, as much social as political, on which Marxism throws virtually no light but serves rather to confuse us—problems which, though they may have little to do directly with the getting of power or the winning of victories in 'the class struggle', are of capital importance to anyone who takes seriously the ideals of freedom and justice to which we appeal when we denounce the evils and 'shams' of modern industrial society. I do not mean that writers calling themselves Marxists have thrown no light on these problems; I mean rather that, if they have, it is not by bringing to bear upon them ideas taken from Marx, who had nothing much of his own to say about either freedom or justice. In condemning bourgeois society he quite often appealed to one or other of these two ideas (though he sometimes claimed not to be doing so), and he spoke with contempt of what he called 'bourgeois' conceptions of them, but he did so without explaining what he himself understood by them. Whoever wants to think clearly and realistically about freedom and justice and how they are to be enlarged in modern industrial societies must do so without benefit of Marxism.

It is in the sphere of social conflict and the struggle for power that Marxism has had the largest influence on practice. Though even here the influence has been much greater outside the West than in it. In Western countries all classes in the community have been drawn into politics as only the wealthier classes were in Marx's time, and parties and pressure groups are much bigger than they used to be. This does not mean that the richer and poorer classes are now equally active politically or equally well placed to put pressure on governments but it does mean that the business of politics is very different from what it was a hundred years ago. The workers now have large and stable organizations whose leaders are men of great experience, familiar with the political system in which they operate, and many of them are tough and skilful negotiators. Their business, as they see it, is much more to get concessions for the workers out of employers and governments than to take over control of the economy or of the state. The economy or the political system could conceivably break down in such a way that no peaceful or constitutional solution was possible; there could arise 'revolutionary situations' which would allow resolute men to seize power by violence or illegally. But they would be situations different from the ones in France and Germany that Marx studied when he produced his ideas about revolutions and revolutionary tactics.

Outside the West 'revolutionary situations' have not, to be sure, been quite the same as they were in Germany and France in the middle of the last century. But they have been similar in important respects. In those two countries in Marx's time classes and groups were beginning to engage in politics which had never done so before, so that the character of political activity was changing fast, even for the classes that had been politically active, and parties and pressure groups were nearly all small or ephemeral or obliged to act secretly. Both the dominant groups and the groups that challenged them were politically inexperienced, either because the game of politics was entirely new to them or because it was no longer the game as they had played it until quite recently. But this was true also, and even more so, of Russia in the period ending with the Bolshevik revolution, and of other countries in which native Marxists have gained power by their own efforts and do not owe it to the Russians.

It is in such conditions as these that the condemnation of parliamentary government or liberal democracy or constitutional monarchy, or whatever it is that is emergent and not yet firmly established, as a mere sham is apt to be most effective. Nobody is used to it or knows quite what to expect of it, and nobody is yet attached to it by ties of habit that are difficult to break. All groups are the more distrustful of one another for not yet having learned to do business with each other in the new ways. It is then that the sort of advice that Marx gives in, say, his *Address to the Communist League* is the most likely to pay off; it is then that a resolute group is able to go furthest in playing off other groups against one another, in making temporary alliances profitable to itself in its struggle for power. It has to deal, not with large organizations that have been active for years in the pursuit of more or less well-defined aims, but mostly with small groups, recently formed, bewildered, suspicious, and uncertain of purpose. Whatever is realistic, penetrating, and inspired in the revolutionary teaching of Marx has much more to do with pointing to the opportunities that situations of this kind give to the bold and the resolute than with the slow process of building up a solid democratic workers' movement which is to make a 'proletarian revolution' when 'objective conditions' are 'ripe' for the setting up of 'socialism'.

The really important disputes about policy between Marxists have nearly all been disputes about how parties or groups claiming to speak for the proletariat are to get or retain power or about the conditions that favour their doing so. They have quarrelled about the stage that capitalism has reached in the course of its evolution, how close it is to collapse, and the effect of developments foreseen and unforeseen by Marx on the relative strengths of classes and on the character of class conflicts. They have argued about how 'the party of the proletariat' should be organized, whether or not conditions are ripe for proletarian revolution, how proletarian differs from bourgeois revolution, whether in Russia or elsewhere there can be a 'permanent revolution' which begins by being bourgeois and eventually becomes proletarian. Even these arguments have been, to a large extent, a war of words, a flourishing of slogans, but behind this war there have been genuine disputes, tough and sophisticated, about what should be done to get power or keep it, about what allies to make and for how long.

If, for example, we take *literally* a question much disputed by Russian Marxists, *Was a proletarian revolution possible in Russia in 1917?*, and look to the writings of the principal disputants, we are quickly disappointed. Most of their arguments, and especially those of Lenin, seem to be either irrelevant or superficial. But the question that really mattered to these Marxists, and to none of them more than to Lenin, was not this one but another quite different from it: *Were conditions in Russia such as to allow 'the party of the proletariat' to seize power?* Lenin in particular did not inquire what intentions a party should have, and what its relations to the industrial workers should be, to justify its calling itself 'the party of the proletariat'. Questions about authority and responsibility, about interests and ideals and the extent to which they are shared and known to be shared, questions which are of the essence of the matter when we are considering how far leaders really are the spokesmen of the groups they claim to speak for, interested him scarcely at all. Nor was he much interested in what socialism is and whether conditions in Russia in 1917 were such as to enable a party that seized power and claimed to be socialist to use power to establish socialism. No doubt, the other Russian Marxists were not all as indifferent as he was to these questions, but many of them were. And those who were not indifferent took their arguments less from Marx than from German disciples of Marx whose Marxism was wearing thin precisely because circumstances in Germany, where there was a large 'proletarian party' active in a 'bourgeois state', obliged them to take seriously questions that Lenin could afford to neglect.

There are reasons for believing that, in the world as it now is, revolutionary groups that get power are unlikely to use it to establish either democracy or socialism, even when they profess to be democratic and socialist. They ordinarily get power under conditions which do not allow them to achieve either of these aims, even when they want to do so, which quite often they do not. It would be absurd to condemn them for seizing power under these conditions, for there may be other desirable goals which are within reach. These other goals, if attained, might or might not make it easier eventually to achieve democracy and socialism; but even if they did not, it would not follow that they were not worth striving for. There are forms of oppression and injustice that can be greatly alleviated without putting authority into the hands of the people or making it effectively responsible to them, and without setting up a socialist economy, and conditions may be such that nothing is likely to be done to alleviate them, unless revolutionary groups ready to use tough, undemocratic methods to make drastic social reforms take power. Such groups are not to be condemned outright, without regard to the circumstances, merely because they call themselves democratic and socialist, when in fact they are neither. Just as the Marxist can admit that there is a good deal to be said for liberal democracy, though he calls it a sham, so the liberal democrat can admit that there is much to be said for sham socialism or for sham popular democracy in some parts of the world, even when the shammers call themselves Marxists. Or at least he can admit that, in principle, there could be much to be said for them, that they could be sham socialists and democrats, and call themselves Marxists, and yet achieve many things worth achieving by methods not to be condemned, given the circumstances in which they act.[3]

There is room for disagreement about how much good or evil has been done in the world by men who have wielded power and have claimed to be Marxists. But, surely, it should matter greatly to the critic of bourgeois society and the bourgeois state, who condemns them, as Marx did, for being false to their own principles, or for proclaiming incoherent principles which are products of illusion, that he should distinguish what is genuine from what is sham; that he should try, as far as he can, to clarify his ideas about freedom, justice, and popular authority, and how they are to be achieved in an industrial society. If, however, he sets himself this task, he will find that Marx rather hinders than helps him in his endeavour to accomplish it. Marx's passionate attack on our type of society is, at bottom, a moral condemnation of it and is impressive and moving precisely on that account, but it is an attack which does as much to confuse as to enlighten his readers. He makes them feel that there is a great deal that is wrong with society and the human condition as they are, without making it clear to them just what it is, and above all without providing them with realistic and coherent principles to guide them in their efforts to set it right. And his excuse for this negligence, his claim to be scientific and not Utopian, is shoddy and evasive. It is as if he were pointing with one hand in the direction in which he wanted men to go, and with the other were throwing dust in their eyes.

[3] As a matter of fact, self-styled Marxists who have seized power in countries in which neither democracy nor socialism was possible have done some terrible things which could not be justified by the need to resort to harsh methods to make urgent and drastic reforms. Indeed, they were not even necessary to enable these 'Marxists' to get power or to keep it. They were enormous and quite unnecessary crimes. Such crimes were first committed by 'Marxists' in Russia, especially when Stalin got power but even before that, and the abominable Russian examples have been followed elsewhere. The degeneration of Marxism when it fell among Slavs is not to be counted against Marx, though it is not entirely fortuitous that his doctrines should have been so powerfully attractive to men ready to commit such crimes. Some of his doctrines lend themselves to abuse in the ways in which they have been abused, true though it is that a powerful Marxist case against Stalin and Lenin could be made.

INDEX